Charles and Mary Beard are among the most noted scholars of the American scene. Charles Beard published over thirty books in his lifetime, six of which were in collaboration with his wife. His works have always been controversial, because Beard was never a man to allow traditional views to interfere with his rigorous thinking.

The Rise of American Civilization, a four-volume series of which *The American Spirit* is a part, is perhaps the most well-known work of the Beards. The first three volumes, *The Agricultural Era, The Industrial Era,* and *America in Midpassage,* deal primarily with the various external features of American society—government, politics, economics, and the like. *The American Spirit,* the last volume in the series, is also the most inclusive and comprehensive. It stands by itself as a perceptive analysis of the more intangible aspects of American civilization and it is essential reading for any person who hopes to understand the unique intellectual and moral qualities of America.

CHARLES A. BEARD

and

MARY R. BEARD

THE

AMERICAN

B368
B368

SPIRIT

A STUDY OF THE IDEA OF CIVILIZATION

IN THE UNITED STATES

SCCCC - LIBRARY
4601 Mid Rivers Mall Drive
St. Peters, MO 63376
WITHDRAWN

COLLIER BOOKS
NEW YORK, N.Y.

This Collier Books edition is published by arrangement with The Macmillan Company

Collier Books is a division of The Crowell-Collier Publishing Company

First Collier Books Edition 1962

Copyright, 1942, by The Macmillan Company

All rights reserved—no part of this book may be reproduced in any form without permission in writing from the publisher, except by a reviewer who wishes to quote brief passages in connection with a review written for inclusion in magazine or newspaper.

Hecho en los E.E.U.U.

Printed in the United States of America

Contents

Preface   7

1   The Power of Ideas as World-Views   11

2   Civilization—Center of Interest   19

3   Origins of the Idea of Civilization   63

4   Formulation and Affirmation in the Early Republic   94

5   Amplification in the Popular Upsurge   153

6   In the Sectional Struggle   245

7   The Thrust of Individualism and Pessimism   292

8   Counter-Reformation and Asseveration   336

9   Nature and Incidence of Foreign Criticisms   419

10   World Mission under Arms   477

11   Convergence   502

Bibliography   583

Index   595

20118

Preface

IN THE PREVIOUS VOLUMES of this series—*The Rise of American Civilization*—we dealt mainly, though by no means exclusively, with the outward aspects of civilization in the United States; with expressions in government, politics, economy, institutions, letters, arts, and sciences.

In this volume, an essential complement in rounding out the series, we emphasize the interior aspects of civilization in the United States since 1776. This volume represents an effort to grasp, through an examination of the written and spoken word, the intellectual and moral qualities that Americans have deemed necessary to civilization in the United States.

Out of our studies extending over many years we have reached the conviction that no idea, such as democracy, liberty, or the American way of life, expresses the American spirit so coherently, comprehensively, and systematically as does the idea of civilization. "Spirit" is elusive. But so are all the human imponderables which one seeks to capture and imprison in words. We do not, however, doubt its existence.

In a representation of this Spirit, we must reckon with the intellectual and moral motivation of men and women, as expressed in a wide range of published statements. In our efforts to do this, we have included in our pages studies of books, pamphlets, articles, speeches, orations, newspaper reports, and even fugitive pieces of literature which have not yet been brought into the narrow stream of the written history which celebrates mainly men in high places.

To writers, investigators, and publishers we are under obligations which we take pleasure in acknowledging, although we cannot fully discharge them.

For information relative to the life of Robert Coram, we are indebted, through the courtesy of Grace E. Heilman, Librarian of the Historical Society of Delaware, and to Jeannette Eckman, State Supervisor of the Delaware Writers' Project under the Federal Works Projects Administration.

Joseph L. Wheeler, Librarian of the Enoch Pratt Free Library in Baltimore, and his competent assistants have supplied us with valuable materials, including transcripts of newspaper reports on John Quincy Adams' lecture on civilization delivered in 1840 in Baltimore.

To the authorities of the Yale University Library, Bernhard Knollenberg, and the efficient staff of that institution, we owe heavy debts. Unrestricted access to the stacks permitted us to examine thousands of pamphlets and volumes at a minimum cost of time, and generous loans of books facilitated every step in our inquiry.

We are also under obligations to the authorities and experts of the Library of Congress, the Library of the Johns Hopkins University, the Public Library of New York City, and many libraries, large and small, in other parts of the country.

We are especially indebted to the following publishers for the right to quote from their publications cited in our pages and listed in the Bibliography: Reynal and Hitchcock; Harcourt, Brace and Company; Little, Brown and Company; Charles Scribner's Sons; Harper and Brothers; Doubleday, Doran and Company; Henry Holt and Company; Houghton Mifflin Company; Yale University Press; Lee Furman; McGraw-Hill Book Company; Oxford University Press; E. P. Dutton and Company; G. P. Putnam's Sons; Farrar and Rinehart; J. B. Lippincott; Alfred Knopf; and The Macmillan Company.

Indeed we are under obligation to all the authors, editors, publishers, and printers, old and new, listed in the Bibliography, whose art and enterprise have preserved and made available historic thought about civilization in the United States. This obligation includes debts to private owners of copyrights.

CHARLES A. BEARD
MARY R. BEARD

New Milford, Conn.
Autumn, 1942

The American Spirit

A Study of the Idea of Civilization in the United States

Chapter 1

The Power of Ideas as World-Views

EVERY PERSON, whether primitive or highly civilized, has a conception of himself and the universe in which he lives and works or idles. This is his idea of his world—his world-view. His world-view may be dimly formed, barely recognized, even somewhat surreptitiously held. But a world-view is in the mind of every man and every woman.

Under the guidance and mandates of his world-view, the individual gives meaning to life and frames opinions as to the generalities and details of personal and associational living. With more or less reference to its prescriptions and logic, he acts, he conducts his affairs light and grave. To some world-view all his limited ideas, such as democracy, liberty, authority, are subjected for evaluation.

An individual may deny that he has a world-view. He may say that he has no interest in the world. He may insist that he is an independent, free-swinging person, hedonist or ascetic, choosing his own way of life at his own will; but the denial is itself a world-view—something on the basis of which independence is asserted, whether he is aware of it or not.

Without a world-view, individuals would perforce be too irresponsible for tasks of any kind, even for alms-begging. They would be too feeble-minded to be pleasure-seekers or protesters against pleasure-seeking as folly or sin. Without a world-view, life would be a "gray and lampless waste," intolerable to the human spirit.

In essence and scope, a world-view is an interpretation of all life, of all human history—ever-changing life in ever-changing nature affected by ever-changing life. In form, a world-view is an organization of knowledge, ideas, experience, and desires into the structure of a human drama or epic with an opening, acts and scenes, and intimations of fate, duty, opportunity.

Being an interpretation of all life, of all human history in a setting of nature, a world-view is the view of the "I" which is in every one of us and of the world in which the

"I" operates. As such, it makes answers of some kind to the following primary questions:

Who am I?

What am I? Am I a machine in a fixed mechanism? Or have I some freedom of choice and action in the world of which I am a part?

Where am I—in the world?

What is the intrinsic reality of the world in which I find myself?

What has been going on in the world through time, is going on in my time, is likely to go on tomorrow?

What do I need and desire?

What is the function and destiny of the society in which I am and to which I owe many qualities of my mind and temper?

What are my rights and duties in society—my privileges of self-fulfilment and my obligations of self-sacrifice?

What are the responsibilities of the society in which I live to the world of societies in which this society has its function and destiny?

How are all these questions interrelated in the whole drama or epic of human history to its latest instant merging into the next instant?

These primary questions, though they stand separately in this list, are so interconnected in fact that any answer to one involves answers to all. But since human beings are finite beings and hence not endowed with omniscience, their answers, their world-views, cannot be statements of the whole truth. They are fictions of the whole truth, deemed sufficient unto the day, the occasion, the age, the state of knowledge, the degree of insight and foresight possessed by the person who thinks about his life in the universe and makes replies to his inquiries.

Broadly speaking, there are three sets of world-views— contradictory in nature.

One set includes all the world-views that are pessimistic in their interpretations of life and the world, with varying ethical applications to human conduct. In this group fall all the philosophies which renounce the world as senseless or cruel or filled with suffering for other reasons and offer to individuals the internal peace of forgetfulness or resignation. Such are the negative systems of some Hindu cults and the modified derivative: the system of Arthur Schopenhauer. The ultimate command of pessimism, defeatism, is for withdrawal into Nirvana (No Thing), into quiescence. And the practitioner, while he continues to live physically, can approach the goal of complete negation by giving up the struggle to earn a livelihood or to promote good in the external world; by subsisting on the alms of others in conditions that barely sustain life.

A second set includes those philosophies of life-affirmation and action which hold the mass of humanity in low esteem, are ethicless, and glorify the will-to-power in supermen, at any cost in terms of human suffering. A modern example is in aspects of the world-view expounded by Friedrich Nietzsche, selected and elaborated in support of Hitlerism.

The third set of world-views embraces all the philosophies of optimism, life-affirmation, and activism that proclaim the ethical will to overcome suffering and other evils and make the good or the better prevail in individual behavior and in social arrangements. Within this group come nearly all the great world-views of the Western peoples, especially since the rise of Christianity.

Nothing seems to be more firmly established in history than the fact that great world-views, when imbedded in the convictions of powerful personalities and classes and tenaciously held by a large portion of the people in general, exert a tremendous influence in history, on the fortunes of individuals, on society, on the world. In the history of India is illustrated the force of philosophic negation. In the history of recent Germany, in *Mein Kampf* and the dictatorship of Adolf Hitler, is illustrated the force of ethicless life-affirmation—of the will-to-power. The force of the philosophies of optimism, life-affirmation as ethical will to overcome evils which obstruct the advances of the good life for all, is illustrated in the history of Christianity and the Enlightenment.

The force of the Christian world-view was manifest in the reorganization of life and societies in Europe during and after the disintegration of the Roman Empire. It has been the fashion, no doubt, for some historians to represent the middle ages as a period of total darkness and superstition, to be set off against the brilliance and rationalism of pagan antiquity, and to make Christianity itself the source of the degradation so portrayed.

With the breakup of the Roman Empire there was, beyond question, a steep decline in many forms of intellectual expression. A comparison of early medieval chroniclers with the historians of antiquity, such as Herodotus, Thucydides, Polybius, Livy, and Tacitus, is certainly painful to intelligence. So is a comparison of the art of the catacombs with the art of Phidias, as composition, concept, technique, and magnificence, distressing to the modern imagination. It is likewise true that the lives of many churchmen, high and low, lacked the dignity and humanity of a Socrates, a Seneca, or a Cicero, and that in the course of time clerical speculations often degenerated into the verbose logic-spinning described in Erasmus' *Praise of Folly*.

But the whole thought, life, and work of the middle ages cannot be correctly summed up in such terms. Nor do such terms provide all the criteria necessary to a judgment on the contribution of the epoch to human felicity. While Europe was being torn and decimated by brigandage and brawls, while superstitions ancient and newly acquired were rife, Christian teachers brought to this tumult a new world-view. For the racial and class bigotries of antiquity they substituted universal humanity as the ideal. Despite early tendencies to pessimism and non-resistance, they suffused the idea of equality with a stronger hope of realization than appeared in the universalism of the ancient Stoics.

For a conception of the world as accidents, luck, merciless fates, racial hatreds, and senseless events, often connected with innumerable gods and evil spirits, Christians substituted a conception of the universe as ordered under a Triune God of power, love, and spirit, with humanity united in one brotherhood. The Greek conception of labor as the function of slaves they challenged by proclaiming the worthiness of all labor, by decrying slavery and mitigating its harshness. The good life, praised by Greek philosophers and for the few, was to be made real and for the many by Christianity incarnate in the human relations of the universal fellowship. Thomas Aquinas agreed with Aristotle that the supreme end of every society is the good of its members; but he universalized the good and rooted his conviction in an optimistic world faith pledged to the triumph of the idea. To humanity tormented by endless wars, Christianity offered a sublime vision of peace with justice and mercy prevailing on earth as in heaven. That a passionate force of faith—even to the end of martyrdom—was associated with the course of the Christian idea of the world is surely and abundantly demonstrated in the records of history.

This is not to say that Christian practice always closely conformed to the world-view or that no valid criticisms could be brought against individual churchmen and reverend sisters of every order on grounds of lapses and betrayals. Indeed, in the development of Christianity, even before the Church was rent by the Protestant Revolt, innumerable conflicts arose within the fold of the faithful—struggles against nearly every variety of barbarism, superstition, sensuality, and greed. For this story Catholic literature, old and new, provides materials.

But, when all criticisms are assayed, it remains a fact that Christian thought bridged the gulf, of more than a thousand years, between the dissolution of Rome and the modern age. The Christian world-view and work in harmony with it entered enduringly into the heritage of Western peoples. Even the most outspoken enemies of Christianity could not wholly escape the influence of that world-view as elaborated in systems of logic, ethics, and economy. They did not, could not, start their thinking *de novo,* with a clean slate. During the Renaissance, despite enthusiasm for classical learning and art, humanists did not return to antiquity in theory or practice. While Protestantism severed ties with Roman supremacy and ceremony, it continued to teach essentials of the Christian world-view, carrying them, in the case of some sects, far in the direction of the leveling equality and the social gospel implied in the doctrine of universal mankind.

In the modern age, under another optimistic and ethical world-view, called the Enlightenment, an immense transformation of the Western world was effected. The Enlightenment was hostile to all forms of tyrannical authority in Church and State. By projecting the idea of Progress into a limitless future on earth, by proclaiming the right of the people to govern themselves, enjoy life, liberty, the pursuit of happiness, and general well-being, heirs of the Enlightenment broke the despotism of the old regime and laid out a new course for liberated humanity.

The world-view of the Enlightenment is thus presented in the abbreviature of Arthur Schweitzer in his *Philosophy of Civilization:* "The greatness of the men of the Enlightenment lies in the fact that they set up ideals of the perfection of man, of society, and of humanity, and devote themselves enthusiastically to propagating the same. The force on which they rely for the fulfillment of these is human conviction —the mind of humanity. They demand of the spirit that it should transform men and conditions of life and rely upon its proving stronger than the actual objective world."

Whence did the leaders of the Enlightenment "derive the impulse to set up such high ideals of civilization and the confidence that they would be able to realize them?" Schweitzer asked. "From their view of the world," he replied. "The world-view which is a part of rationalism is both optimistic and ethical. Its optimism consists in this, that a belief is embraced in a general purposiveness, ruling in the world and directed to perfection, in which purposiveness the efforts of men and of humanity toward spiritual and material progress both find sense and meaning, and at the same time become secure of ultimate success. This view of the world is ethical because it regards the ethical as involved in the nature of reason as such, and therefore striven after by man, so that setting aside his egoistic interests he will give up all for the sake of his consuming ideals and will think of the ethical as the decisive standard of measurement in everything. The penetration of the world with humanitarian convictions is for the rationalists an ideal in whose way no consideration is allowed to stand."

This is not to assert that practice in the age of the Enlightenment, any more than in the case of Christianity, always conformed closely to its world-view. The social transformations of the new period were doubtless deep-reaching. The revolutions that shook Western societies, including those of the Americas, occurred in that epoch; and leaders in those upheavals appealed to doctrines of the Enlightenment for justification. But it was also the age of terrible wars, crowned by the desperate adventures of the insatiable Napoleon. For conservative Christians, Catholic and Protestant, in Europe and America, the Reign of Terror was its symbol, the bitter fruit gathered from the tree of the Enlightenment.

Even so, the world-view of that dispensation inspired sacrifices no less unselfish than those made by missionaries and martyrs of the Church Militant. Moreover, that world-view likewise perdured in the midst of many vicissitudes and entered into the conflicts with the Reaction, as the Christian idea had entered into struggles against the conservatives of ancient Rome who refused, until death, to surrender the hope that their old gods and the dominion of the Empire would be restored. Whatever moral judgments may be pronounced upon it, the world-view of the Enlightenment was a powerful force in the course of that history which spanned the years between the modern and the contemporary age.

Up to this point the two world-views—optimistic, ethical Christianity and the Enlightenment—have been treated as if each signified a single system everywhere and at all times in its history. But a caveat must be made. Notwithstanding the unity of conception in the world-view of Christianity, there were diversities in applications in places and times. Early in its development the Church of the faithful was split into Eastern and Western divisions. The Roman Church itself, as creative intelligence stirred fresh ferments, was continually beset by sectaries and interior movements which could be kept within bounds only by displays of resilience and ingenuity at Rome. Furthermore, before the Protestant Revolt, while national states were rising out of feudal chaos, popes, kings, and queens often engaged in harsh contests over prerogatives and perquisites; and, without disowning the general doctrine, the several countries of Catholic Christendom took on particular characteristics. The Gallic Church, for instance, was not exactly like the Church of Spain, Germany, or England. When at length Protestants broke away from Rome, national features were more decidedly marked, with alterations in creed. And, far from being universal, after centuries of propaganda and missionary efforts, Christianity was still confined to a relatively small portion of humanity, if church membership is a test.

A similar diversity in application occurred in the case of the Enlightenment. It too was originally conceived as universal in scope, "good always and everywhere," as a common destiny of mankind. Yet, in concrete manifestations, it took on different forms in the several countries and among the several peoples affected by its influences. It was one thing in the Russia of Catherine the Great, something else in the England of conservative reaction and in the America of the Revolution; and it was another thing in the France of the Bourbons, Voltaire, Marat, and Napoleon. Besides displaying diversities, the Enlightenment, like Christianity, left untouched, or only slightly affected, vast masses of people in Asia and Africa as well as in Europe and the Americas; and also, like the Christian world-view, it encountered opposition everywhere.

When an optimistic, affirmative, activist, ethical world-view, such as Christianity or the Enlightenment, is tenaciously maintained by a large proportion of a population in a given time and place, it imparts a tone, purpose, driving energy, and ethical distinction to the society and the age in which it has that grip on mind, heart, and will. It has power then and there; or, to speak without metaphor, it acts with the force inherent in the convictions of those who cleave to it. It serves as a cohesive agency uniting people in a common consciousness of rights and wrongs, good and evil.

If, however, a given world-view, hitherto dominant in a society, loses its command over thought and will, the cohesive bonds of that society will be loosened. A social collapse may follow unless the world-view is revived by reflective thinking and teaching or is developed into, or supplanted by, another world-view more appropriate to enlarged knowledge and the changed quality of sentiments.

While the Enlightenment and organized Christianity were locked in what seemed to be a deadly combat with each other, during the French Revolution and the general Reaction that quickly followed, creative intelligence was seeking a world-view more in accord with the widening and deepening knowledge of humanity and its history. This quest finally led to the formulation of another comprehensive idea, or world-view—the Idea of Civilization.

Chapter 2

Civilization—Center of Interest

BEFORE THE TWENTIETH CENTURY reached its meridian, the idea of civilization had come into wide, profuse, and miscellaneous use. In the ever-enlarging flood of books, essays, editorials, book reviews, sermons, and speeches from the secular platform, the word was employed as a cabalistic symbol to serve purposes in the minds of writers and speakers. It was brought into the consideration of race and climate, mechanics and hygiene, labor and capital, politics and foreign policies, programs of education, art and letters, and literary criticism. Historians, esthetes, anthropologists, ethnologists, and archaeologists wrote about civilization in times and places far and near, about the decay of its vitality, about the possibilities of revitalizing it in the modern age. Communists, Fascists, and Nazis derided it as "bourgeois," and middle-class orators defended it as the supreme contribution of their class to mankind. Yet miscellaneous, reckless, or bewildering as were the innumerable uses of the word, they generally fell into one of four broad types when they carried any discernible meaning at all.

In many minds the idea of civilization was taken seriously as a world-view, a powerful ultimatum of thought, the highest earthly tribunal for the trial of causes, the crowning sanction for pleas, demands, policies, and actions public and private. So extensively was it used in this sense by innumerable men and women that it seemed to express a deep human need for a new synthesis—an all-embracing formula of life and purpose.

To other thinkers of the age civilization meant the gigantic aggregation of machines, instruments, gadgets, and institutions produced by modern invention—the externals of industry and life. In this sense civilization was often regarded as the foe of culture and individuality or as dangerous to all high values or as disruptive, and thus constituting "the problem" of modern society. In extreme forms it was pictured as a mad Leviathan or Frankenstein monster that was sweeping mankind to destruction.

Again the word civilization was frequently seized upon as

19

a magic symbol to promote special interests—political, economic, religious, literary, or educational.

Was there a cause of any kind to be championed, defended, or criticized before groups, multitudes, or the whole nation?

Was an argument on any subject to be established, as if beyond all dispute, on something more decisive than hope or belief?

Was a common denominator to be found for special and apparently divergent interests, intellectual, moral, political, or economic, that threatened disruption of national unity?

Was any ideal such as liberty, democracy, security, or equality to be grounded in fundamentals?

Were foreign nations to be praised or condemned?

Did the state of the world or any part of it appear to be alarming on account of panics, distresses, strains, civil conflicts, or international wars?

If so, the idea of civilization in some form was almost certain to be brought into the focus of thought, in some fashion and with some ends in view, by writers and speakers undertaking to discuss such questions.

For the fourth type of usage only the term miscellaneous is appropriate. The word civilization figured in "human-interest" stories picked up by cub reporters in the streets, bearing witness to its popularity. A distinguished cartoonist, sensitive like all members of his craft to the spread of ideas among the populace, depicted this one as creeping to the very bridge tables where speech is supposed to be restrained and gaming the preoccupation.

That it had become a household word was indicated in the advertisements of new novels by publishers. In 1941 the jacket extolling *Red Lanterns on St. Michael's* informed the fiction-loving public that this novel "digs down into the philosophy of history which explains the development of human civilization," in the city of Charlestown. On the jacket of another novel, *Lanterns on the Levee,* prospective purchasers were told that behind this volume of recollections of the "gallant, semi-feudal South of fifty years ago" lies "the memory of the most gracious civilization America has produced"—in the Mississippi Delta.

Even into the tribulations of home economics in a world at war, in 1942, the idea of civilization was drawn as serviceable to human purposes. Under a cartoon representing a young wife proudly exhibiting to her husband a rakish hat which she had just bought, the Saturday Evening Post put the following words into the mouth of the irate spouse: "We're fighting the whole Axis; a victory will cost upwards of 300 billions; production is on a seven-day basis; all over the world men are suffering through blood and toil, tears and sweat; civilization itself is in the balance—and you want to know how you look!" When an organization of butlers in New York City announced a war-time code for the elimination of waste in homes, the president of the club explained: "Our employers have gone all-out in support of the fight for civilization and we wish to match them. This is the fight of every stratum of society from the ditch-digger to the industrialist."

But whether couched in laughter and tears, or in grave and cautious language, whether it was the pivotal idea of scientists and scholars talking about sex hormones, cosmic rays, arts, letters, and a changing economy, while celebrating the Fiftieth Anniversary of Chicago University amid "a civilization in transition," or a scheme of thought for deliberations by members of the historical gild in solemn conclaves, the view of the world, of life and its surrounding universe, called the idea of civilization, was unmistakably a center of interest in America as the middle of the twentieth century drew near.

Adjectives almost without number were used to qualify it, bringing it close to the activities of daily life and the fixations of popular purposes. It became "our civilization"; our "industrial civilization"; "democratic civilization"; "material civilization"; "Atlantic" or "Western civilization"; "business civilization"; "Oriental" or "Occidental" civilization; Greek, Roman, Spanish, French, American civilization, and so delimited through the list of attributes applied to peoples and races; "feminine civilization"; "Stoic," "Mohammedan," "Buddhist" or "Christian" civilization; "true civilization"; "monolithic civilization"; "pluralistic civilization." Whether the word was qualified by an adjective or not, had discernible meaning or none, common usage indicated a wide familiarity with it and a warm affection for it, testifying to the fact that this latest world-view had risen to pre-eminence and power in America.

The divergent ways in which the idea of civilization was

employed by persons preoccupied with contemporary questions of life and faith were constantly illustrated by pronouncements made in the name of religion.

To the Reverend Norman Peale, of the Marble Collegiate Reformed Church in New York City, civilization seemed to be a sum of spiritual values. American civilization, he was quoted as saying in 1941, is a religious civilization; the "reason why we love the church is because we get our civilization from it."

In its statement to the public in the same year, the Conference on Science, Philosophy, and Religion, inaugurated under religious auspices, treated civilization also as a summation of values. "The totalitarian way of life," it declared, "is rapidly spreading through the world, to the imminent peril of civilization. . . . Our failure to integrate science, philosophy, and religion, in relation to traditional ethical values and the democratic way of life has been catastrophic for civilization."

Again and again during the Conference, which lasted four days, the idea of civilization was associated in thought with "the dignity and worth of the human personality." And in a statement, officially promulgated, the Conference declared that "no form of government which denies this basic principle can contribute to the preservation of civilization, and indeed no such form of government deserves to be called civilized."

Likewise when leading Protestant, Catholic, and Jewish clergymen and laymen undertook to formulate "a fundamental declaration of religious beliefs held in common by followers of the three faiths," early in 1942, they related their professions of faith to the idea of civilization. "We believe," they agreed, "that recognition of man's dependence on God is essential to the progress of true civilization; that nations, as well as individuals, are bound to acknowledge this, and that education or social theories which would state man's duties, standards and happiness without reference to God are doomed to failure."

On the other hand to the Reverend Harry Emerson Fosdick civilization represented the mechanics of life, an appalling march of inventions and gadgets that threatened the very existence of culture, or the inner spirit, with submergence, if not destruction. Accepting as valid "the convenient terms" of Professor R. M. MacIver of Columbia University, Dr.

Fosdick said in the pulpit in 1936: "Man's life . . . can be divided into two distinguishable though closely interrelated areas, civilization and culture. Civilization is the complex of devices, mechanisms, techniques, and instrumentalities by means of which we live. Culture is the realm of spiritual ends, expressed in art, literature, morals, and religion, for which at our best we live. Civilization is made up of things which we utilize to get something else. Culture is made up of values which we desire for their own sakes." Having made this distinction, Dr. Fosdick declared that "in the mordant phrase of G. Lowes Dickinson, we have been 'contemptuous of ideas but amorous of devices' till now mankind stands, its hands filled with devices, but as bewildered and unhappy as mankind has been in centuries." To what end will mankind use these devices? "To that question civilization does not possess the answer. The answer to that question is never found in a nation's civilization, but in its spiritual culture."

When reflective thinkers in the secular world, moved by the profound disturbances of their age, dealt with what they regarded as menaces to security or to values generally cherished, they gave gravity to their statements by presenting the menaces as perils to civilization. This custom was followed by writers of varied activities and experiences, from public service to scientific research, from law and engineering to the improvement of agriculture. From whatever interest their particular subjects were approached, a common denominator entered into their expositions—the idea of civilization.

Deeply affected by the terrifying license unleashed in the first world war, Raymond B. Fosdick sought the purport and source of the maladies undermining the peace and health of mankind and in 1928 stated the case, as he had worked it out, under the title *The Old Savage in the New Civilization*. Fosdick had long been associated with the public service, municipal and national, and with the vast Rockefeller philanthropies. Urged by his interest in human welfare and by his creative spirit to think intently about society and its pressing problems, he came to the conviction that the supreme issue of his time must be formulated in terms of the old conflict between barbarism and civilization—nothing less. Though by no means oblivious to other features of contemporary society, Fosdick emphasized the mechanical and scientific phase. It was this aspect which, in his opinion, justified the use of the adjective "new." "Civilization," he said, "has, in fact, become a great machine, the wheels of which must be kept turning or the people starve. For millions of human beings it is a vast treadmill, worked by weary feet to grind the corn that makes the bread that gives them strength to walk the treadmill. And with it all has come the speeding up of life, and the spirit of hurry and worry such as our grandfathers with all their lack of conveniences never dreamed of. The human race lives by schedule, according to a stereotyped routine. Our machinery determines where we shall live and how we shall live; we rise, eat, go to work, rest, toil, and sleep again at its bidding. . . . We hurry from birth to death, goaded only to greater haste by our increasingly speedy conveyances, trying to catch up with the machine which we have ourselves created. . . . The sixty Harvard seniors of the class of 1822 would stand aghast at our hectic civilization. Instead of a rural, agricultural, individualist society, they would find a society that is urban, industrialized, and regimented. Instead of an era classical in its tastes and static in its ideas of progress, they would find one that is scientific and mobile."

All about him in his world, Fosdick encountered apprehension. "For a generation our machine civilization had plunged along the track with little misgiving on the part of the passengers as to the safety of the route or the capacity of science as the engineer. And then suddenly the World War flashed the red light of a danger signal across the track, and ever since we have been asking anxious questions of each other, peering around the curves ahead to see what the difficulty might be. We have not stopped the engine, and science is still at the throttle, and the pace is unchecked. But the passengers are uneasy, and apprehension is beginning to spread that the train may not really be under control. Stated in more accurate terms, the question that confronts our generation is whether or not our shifting physical environment has outrun our capacity for adaptation. Is human society being gorged with innovations too great for its powers of assimilation? Are there limits to our ability to absorb alteration and change? . . . It is not the *fact* of change; it is the *rate* of change that constitutes the danger. The overrapid alteration of artificial environment may annihilate mankind no less certainly than the overrapid modification of natural environment wiped out the sabre-toothed tiger and the mastodon."

Despite dangers widely known and feared, science and technology were tearing along at high speed heedless of larger consequences, creating, producing, and using new and powerful devices: "The train will not stop. Rather with every year that goes by, its speed is increasing at a faster and faster rate. The throttle is wide open and our machine civilization is plunging ahead toward an unknown destination. We have scarcely begun the ride. Physics and chemistry have hardly had an opportunity to show us what speed and change really mean. In other words, we are merely at the beginning of progress in the physical sciences. We are entering upon a revolution in our environment far more radical than that through which we have just come. . . . It is probable that the next fifty years will alter the lives of our children far more completely than the last hundred years have altered our own. No, we cannot halt the advance of science. Man has set his hand to this furrow and he will not stop until he comes to its end. Never before has he been seized with so feverish a preoccupation, with such a frenzy of desire." For sporadic scientific advance had been substituted planned, endowed, cooperative advance—the invention of invention.

Concerning this feverish mechanical rush, many assumptions were rife, Fosdick said: "At this point we often make an erroneous assumption. We assume that man's capacity keeps up with his inventions. We assume that, as civilization becomes great, the human stock which is building it also becomes great; that by some alchemy or other there is a rise in individual capacity from generation to generation to match the increasing complexity of our physical environment. We take it for granted that there is some sure inhibition that prevents men from creating machines which they cannot control; and that the very fact that they have created them is proof of their ability to manage them. But this is not a fact. Knowledge may mean power, but it does not necessarily mean capacity. We cannot be dogmatically sure that there has been substantial improvement in the human stock since the days of the Egyptians or the Greeks. . . . Even less sure can we be that this last century which has added so tremendously to our mechanical environment has brought a corresponding improvement in human capacity. In fact, we know it is not true."

Did man, recently up from barbarism, have the brains and character necessary to make humane use of his machines? Fosdick had doubts: "Modern science has revolutionized, not man, but his world. It has made his old ideas infinitely more dangerous. It has taken away his flintlock musket and his firebrand and given him instead machine guns and poison gas. It has brought him into intimate contact with his neighbors, and exposed him to all the irritations that arise from propinquity. . . . To man himself it has brought no change. He remains as he was—a creature of passion, with the old fire ablaze in his eyes, fingering the new implements by which his irritation and self-interest can now be expressed in cataclysmic slaughter. What do we see as we look into the future? Is there sanity enough in the world to handle the weapons which science is so fast creating? Is there intelligence enough to employ them not for destruction but for the building up of an abundant life for mankind? Is there time enough to develop a technique of tolerance and self-control? What use will the old savage make of his new civilization?"

Fosdick's inquiry into the prospects of civilization was soon followed, in 1931, by George A. Dorsey's negotiation of the subject from another point of observation and a different experience. Dorsey's life had been devoted to the study of anthropology and ethnology. He had investigated the conditions of primitive life in many places, visited nearly every part of the earth observing various types of human beings engaged in multiform activities—Europe, South America, China, India, Ceylon, Java, Australia, and South Africa. He had examined particularly the sources of emigration in Italy, Austria, Hungary, Rumania, Serbia, and Bulgaria. Commanding a wealth of materials and writing while the panic of 1929 was running its devastating course, spreading unemployment and misery in every section of the Western world, Dorsey had before his eyes manifestations of almost every kind of distress that mankind could make for itself. Having studied migrations of peoples from places of scarcity in search for places of plenty, he was now witnessing demonstrations of hunger in the midst of abundance, of human incapacity on a colossal scale even in the United States.

Taken in connection with the long chain of tragedies and comedies stretching from primitive times, the depression in the United States—in the land of fabulous riches—became to Dorsey the latest evidence of man's "natural endowment for folly," and gave him reason for affixing a half-humorous title to his bulky volume: *Man's Own Show: Civilization*. With a resentment resembling that of the English writer, Charles Duff, author of *Human Nature*, Dorsey lashed out at the cruelties and enormities inflicted by mankind upon itself. He could not accept history with unreserved optimism. Still he felt compelled to recognize the immense potentialities of civilization for good living despite the terrifying exhibitions of primitive survivals in modern times.

For Dorsey took some account of those aspects of human genius which, conceivably, might in the course of time outweigh man's propensity for folly and cruelty. "Civilization," he said, "is man's historic handiwork; human artifacts, things, ideas, notions, to live with, by and for." It is a great product of man's spirit "created step by step, slowly, laboriously, valiantly. And for his loved ones: wife, children, fellow-men, the family, the tribe, the state, the nation—and some day perhaps may be added, the whole brotherhood of man." Emphasizing in italics the crisis confronted in his day by human nature, he declared *the* main issues to be the *price* paid for the incredibly "great" civilization of his time. Could it be paid? Would civilization prevail? These questons he felt unable to answer. "How serious it is, and especially what its outcome is to be, I do not know, nor can anyone foretell."

Writing while millions were unemployed, under-fed, or half-starved in the United States and soothsayers prophesying prosperity just around the corner, Dorsey was in no temper to predict the triumph of civilization. The potentials of triumph were available in generous volume—in science, invention, the power of mind over materials. These he recognized: "Some day conceivably, our civilization may be higher." If he did not issue a flaming call to hopes, Dorsey dramatized for thousands of American readers the idea of civilization and thus brought more attention to the idea as necessary to the interpretation of history and as a guide to practice.

Another American sounded a tocsin of danger to the whole of civilization—Lothrop Stoddard, Doctor of Philosophy from Harvard University. Believing that popular uprisings, such as had shaken Europe since the crash of the first world war, were threatening to break the very bonds of all social order, he sought explanations of the peril and means of avoiding the calamity so imminent, in his opinion. The results of his searches, united with his judgments, he grouped under a title indicative of his apprehensions and of the worth to be ascribed to the idea of civilization: *The Revolt against Civilization: The Menace of the Under Man,* published in 1922.

In using this title Stoddard defined the term as he understood it: "Civilization is the flowering of the human species. . . . Civilization is complex. It involves the existence of human communities characterized by political and social organization; dominating and utilizing natural forces; adapting themselves to the new man-made environment thereby created; possessing knowledge, refinements, arts, and sciences; and [last, but emphatically not least] composed of individuals capable of sustaining this elaborate complex and handing it on to a capable posterity. . . . In any particular people, civilization will progress just so far as that people has the capacity to further it and the ability to bear the correlative burden which it entails." Civilization "means relative protection from the blind and cruel forces of nature; abolition of the struggle against savage beasts and amelioration of the struggle between men; opportunity for comfort, leisure, and the development of the higher faculties."

But this vast aggregation of things, values, institutions, and practices, ever in process, called civilization, is fragile. History is crowded with the records of civilizations that reached great heights and then lost their capacity to carry on, "falling back to the lower levels of barbarism or even of savagery."

Why was this so? Various theories had been offered in explanation. In this connection, Stoddard referred to *The Law of Civilization and Decay* which had been framed by Brooks Adams, mainly in economic terms and as cycle. Then he summed up: "The ruin of civilizations was variously ascribed to luxury, vice, town life, irreligion, and much more besides. Yet all these theories somehow failed to satisfy." Without asking and answering the question, why and whom they had so failed? Stoddard went on to develop his own explanation: "Within the past two decades . . . the rapid progress of biological knowledge has thrown a flood of light on this vexed question, and has enabled us to frame a theory so in accordance with the known facts that it seems to offer substantially the correct answer."

The "substantially correct answer" Stoddard expounded in chapters headed The Burden of Civilization, The Iron Law of Inequality, The Nemesis of the Inferior, The Lure of the

Primitive, The Ground-Swell of Revolt, The Rebellion of the Under-Man. The War against Chaos, and Neo-Aristocracy. In this exposition the role generally assigned by democratic reformers and mass revolutionists to environment as the civilizing factor was repudiated. Assuming that the prime "cause" of civilization can be ascertained, Stoddard held that it is to be found in superior individuals, in superior races, in heredity as assuring the survival of the élite, in the proportion of individuals capable of creating and bearing civilization. The continuance of civilization, accordingly, depends on the practice of eugenics, on reducing the proportion of the unfit and enlarging the proportion of the fit, on bringing into being a neo-aristocracy able to protect and advance civilization.

Whether this was indeed the "substantially correct answer" is not at this place the point. The crux of the matter is that Stoddard, in his argument, assembled under the idea of civilization what he regarded as the values of the good life and arrayed against them "the revolt" of the "unfit" masses, portending the decline or overthrow of the Western world, including the United States.

Whatever the merits of his conclusions, Stoddard's volume raised a tempest of discussion, critical and favorable. For this storm the times were especially propitious. At the moment the biological, psychological, and moral sources upon which he had drawn for materials were being brought into a nation-wide survey in connection with a concrete issue—the immigration bill introduced in Congress shortly after the publication of his challenging work. Out of the popular furor over the proposed bill and the debates in Congress came the final restrictive Act of 1924. By excluding certain races or nationalities entirely and placing limitations on emigrants of other national origins, this Act incorporated in law certain principles respecting races and élites as bearers of civilization, which had been advocated by eugenists of the Stoddard school as well as by sociologists and economists. Thought about civilization was developing imperatives for the enactment of federal legislation.

No less convinced than Stoddard that adversities lurked in the path of civilization, J. H. Denison, an eminent Protestant clergyman, attributed the troubles to psychological forces, not to the inferiority of races or masses, and suggested other measures calculated to assure the future of civilization. His analysis of the problem and his program of deliverance, he published in his *Emotion as the Basis of Civilization*, in 1928. "The main thesis of this book," Denison explained, "is that every successful civilization has owed its success to an elaborate system by which certain emotions were cultivated; that it has met with disaster when its rulers have neglected or interfered with this system, and that a perfect co-ordination is necessary between the forms of government of the group and the emotions which are developed by its religion and customs." The volume, Professor George Foot Moore observed in a prefatory note to Denison's work, contained "pertinent observations on our own problems and discussion of the feelings and attitudes which in a democracy must replace the fear and awe that dominated civilizations and religions of the patriarchal type."

That something had hampered and was still obstructing the advance of civilization Ezra Parmalee Prentice agreed. That something, however, was not, in his opinion, machines, the inferiority of races or masses, or the lack of correct emotional stimuli: it had been and was hunger, plain hunger. Although a lawyer by profession, Prentice had given laborious years to study and experimentation in the domain of agriculture in many parts of the world, as well as in Massachusetts; and he reached the conclusion that poverty was a basic impediment to civilization. This thesis he unfolded in a vivid narration of mankind's historic struggle for existence—*Hunger and History*—published in 1939. Hunger had been dominant in Dorsey's thought of civilization. It was almost the whole substance of Prentice's thought.

Representing civilization as an advance based on an increasing mastery over the harshness of physical life, Prentice made applications to an interpretation of history: "Hand labor could not produce in sufficient quantity to keep the farmer alive and at the same time supply the many varied activities of a complicated civilization. This is the secret of the 2300 years of what seems to us like stagnation in the useful arts—a stagnation, if we may call it so, which lasted from early history to the beginning of the nineteenth century. . . . It is necessary to recognize the brutal facts of this nature (such as famine and horrible diseases induced by semi-starvation) in order to realize the conditions under which the ancient world lived. It is also necessary to realize that variations in social and political conditions vary in different ratio to the extent to which the hardness of the conditions of physical life can or cannot be alleviated. Poverty in the widest sense is an impediment to the advance of civilization."

It was not merely lone individuals engaged in scrutinizing the tendencies of the times whose thinking revolved around the idea of civilization. In the searchings and exchanges that went on, men and women specializing in various aspects of American life discovered that their lines of thought converged as they sought standards or ideals by which to test inadequacy, progress, or decline in such fields as the arts, sciences, letters, economy, or government. They formed groups for the discussion of specific problems and found these problems merging in one: the nature and course of civilization.

One of the groups, known as the "thirty intellectuals," published in 1922 a symposium entitled *Civilization in the United States,* edited by Harold E. Stearns. Among the contributors to this volume were specialists of distinction in American letters, arts, and sciences, including Lewis Mumford, H. L. Mencken, Zechariah Chafee, Robert Morss Lovett, J. E. Spingarn, Robert H. Lowie, Van Wyck Brooks, Deems Taylor, Walton Hamilton, George Soule, H. W. Van Loon, Elsie Clews Parsons, Katherine Anthony, Frederic C. Howe, Geroid T. Robinson, and Ring Lardner. They approached and criticized civilization in the United States, from their particular vantage points, in terms of politics, law, journalism, scholarship, education, science, philosophy, literature, music, art, the theater, economy, history, advertising, business, engineering, medicine, and sports.

All the primary specialisms of the age in America were brought to a focus on civilization. The volume, as the editor explained, "has been the deliberate and organized outgrowth of the common efforts of like-minded men and women to see the problem of modern American civilization as a whole, and to illuminate by careful criticism the special aspect of that civilization with which the individual is most familiar."

Although the keynote was critical, a constructive purpose was confessed: the advancement or improvement of the civilization subjected to analysis. "We wished to speak the truth about American civilization as we saw it, in order to do our share in making a real civilization possible. . . . American civilization is still in the embryonic stage, with rich and with disastrous possibilities of growth. But the first step in growing up is self-conscious and deliberately critical examination of ourselves, without sentimentality and without fear. We cannot even devise, much less control, the principles which are to guide our future development until that preliminary understanding has come home with telling force to the consciousness of the ordinary man." Judging by the reviews of *Civilization in the United States* and the controversies which followed its publication, America was strongly civilization-conscious.

Five years after the thirty intellectuals had explored the nature and fortune of civilization in the United States, a second group, motivated by the spirit of inquiry common to the times, made another inquest, in 1928, *Whither Mankind: A Panorama of Modern Civilization,* under the editorship of Charles A. Beard in cooperation with Frank E. Hill. This group was not limited to American citizens. To American writers, including H. W. Van Loon, Julius Klein, Howard Lee McBain, C.-E. A. Winslow, George A. Dorsey, James Harvey Robinson, Lewis Mumford, John Dewey, Stuart Chase, Everett Dean Martin, and Carl van Doren, were added Hu Shih, outstanding Chinese scholar and philosopher, later ambassador of China to the United States; Emil Ludwig, German man of letters; and Bertrand Russell, Sidney and Beatrice Webb, and Havelock Ellis of Great Britain. By intention the symposium took in the East and the West, ancient, medieval, and modern societies. Its range of aspects embraced science, business, labor, law and government, war and peace, health, the family, race, religion, the arts, philosophy, recreation, education, and literature.

The Introduction by the editor, sent in draft form to the contributors, outlined the nature of the broad problem to which their thought was to be directed. "All over the world," it opened, "the thinkers and searchers who scan the horizon of the future are attempting to assess the values of civilization and speculating about its destiny." In Europe, in the Orient, in North America, and in South America, "the intellectuals of all nations are trying to peer into the coming day, to discover whether the curve of contemporary civilization now rises majestically toward a distant zenith or in reality has begun to sink toward a nadir near at hand. . . . The very titles of the books have a challenging ring: 'The Decline of the West,' 'Mankind at the Crossroads,' 'The Rising Tide of

Color,' 'The Revolt of the Unfit,' 'The Tragic Sense of Life,' 'The Decline of Europe,' 'War the Law of Life,' and 'The Destiny of a Continent.' " The titles themselves were indeed signs of the age: of spiritual deeps broken up, of efforts to come to grips with the riddle of human history.

"It is not alone the philosophers who display anxiety about the future. The policies of statesmen and the quest of the people in circles high and low for moral values reveal a concern about destiny that works as a dynamic force in the affairs of great nations," the editor said. The fascist revolution in Italy, the communist revolution in Russia, the writhing of Germany under the sting of defeat, the restless stirring of France "wondering about the significance of the ominous calm," Great Britain feverishly searching for markets to keep her industrial wheels turning, the spread of criticism in the United States despite the complacency of the Harding-Coolidge era—all bore witness to the gravity of the central issue presented to the thought of the East and the West.

To economic conflicts in civilization and between civilizations were conjoined racial, national, religious, geographical, and climatic elements. "Beyond America lies Asia. . . . Chinese nationalism cannot find its goal and Japanese economic necessity attain its fruition without disturbing violently one or more of the Western imperial adventurers contending for mastery in the East. These two forces, rather than Gandhi's vain longing for a return to the hand loom and spinning wheel—in defiance of science and machinery—will serve to keep alive indefinitely the interest of the world in the contrast, real and imaginary, between the East and the West."

Would this intellectual and moral concern with the nature and course of civilization—in America and the wide world —pass quickly, like other phantasies and schemes of thought about the universe? In 1927 the editor of *Whither Mankind* seemed certain that it would not: "Anxiety about the values and future of civilization is real. It has crept out of the cloister and appears in the forum and market place. It will not pass; it will endure and increase. Forces as potent as the struggle for existence—economic, racial, and nationalistic—will continue to feed it. . . . Under the machine and science, the love of beauty, the sense of mystery, and the motive of compassion—sources of esthetics, religion, and humanism—are not destroyed. They remain essential parts of our nature. But the conditions under which they must operate, the channels they must take, the potentialities of their action are all changed. These ancient forces will become powerful in the modern age just in the proportion that men and women accept the inevitability of science and the machine, understand the nature of the civilization in which they must work, and turn their faces resolutely to the future."

Incited by *Whither Mankind*, especially by its acceptance of science and machine industry as characteristics, hazards, and promises of civilization, several eminent engineers in New York City decided in 1929 that the time had come in the history of technology for scientists and engineers to investigate the nature and implications of their work in its relations to civilization. Taking the problem posed in *Whither Mankind* as their point of departure and the themes of the papers as indices for their thought, a committee of two, George A. Stetson and W. A. Shoudy, approached the editor of that work with a proposition for a cooperative undertaking, which culminated in 1930 in the publication of the symposium: *Toward Civilization*.

For the enterprise and summation, the original group of engineers selected a distinguished personnel from the professions: Ralph E. Flanders, manager and director of a large machine industry; Robert A. Millikan, physicist; Elmer E. Sperry, inventor and industrialist; C. F. Hirschfield, chief of research for the Detroit Edison Company; Roy V. Wright, managing editor of The Railway Age; Lee de Forest, inventor and pioneer in wireless communication; Dexter S. Kimball, professor of industrial engineering at Cornell University; Thomas D. Campbell, pioneer in large-scale farming; L. W. Wallace, executive secretary of the American Engineering Council; Richard F. Bach, specialist in the arts; Stephen Vorhees and Ralph T. Walker, designers of metropolitan skyscrapers; Lillian Gilbreth, an expert in industrial management; William E. Wickenden, then director of the investigation for the promotion of engineering education and later president of the Case School of Applied Science; Michael Pupin, inventor in the field of telephonic communication; and Harvey N. Davis, president of the Stevens Institute of Technology.

The titles of the papers set for the participants in this new symposium revealed the main lines of their inquiry about civilization: The New Age and the New Man, Science Lights the Torch, The Spirit of Invention in an Industrial Civilization, Power, Transportation, Communication, Modern Industry and Management, Agriculture, Engineering in Government, Art in the Market Place, The Machine and Architecture, Work and Leisure, Education and the New Age, Machine Industry and Idealism, and Spirit and Culture under the Machine.

To the editor was committed the task of describing briefly, in the Introduction, the outstanding features of civilization in the machine age and listing the details in the long bill of indictment brought against machine industrialization by its contemporary critics—the "general indictment" of it "as the foe of all values human and divine." While the several authors varied in their methods of treatment and in the relevance of their thought to the central theme, there was general agreement that scientists and engineers were all enmeshed in the nature and fortunes of civilization, that members of the profession were under obligations to consider ways and means of making civilization prevail over the forces of disruption.

A similar conclusion, namely, that something as comprehensive as civilization was the social contexture in which individuals, professions, and groups of all kinds had to live, work, and make their way, was drawn in a symposium dealing with Negroes in the United States. This opinion, confirmed in the findings of sixteen national organizations, was published as a volume in the American Social Science Series in 1930, under the editorship of Charles S. Johnson of Fisk University, and entitled *The Negro in American Civilization*.

In her Foreword, Mary Van Kleeck, chairman of the executive committee of the National Interracial Conference, stated the problem for the discussion: "What of the status of the Negro in American Civilization?" Then she gave her version of the "limiting factors in American Civilization" as they affected the Negro: "First of all, his is a changing position, set against a background of shifting economic and social conditions. Is he receiving justice, which all Americans would agree is the heritage of their nation? What is justice? . . . Socrates suggested that justice was to be found in the good society. In the process of picturing the good society it was agreed that justice is the final outcome of a wisely functioning scheme of relationships. 'In a state which is ordered with a view to the good of the whole, we should be most likely to find justice, and in the ill-ordered state injustice.'

After long and searching consideration of the essential elements in the good society, this definition was accepted: 'Justice will be admitted to be the having and doing what is a man's own and belongs to him,' or, in other words, 'the power of each individual in the state to do his own work.' "

"The power of the Negro in the United States to do his own work is still hindered at many points," Miss Van Kleeck asserted. "Economic opportunities are limited and restricted. Educational facilities in the sections of the country where the largest number of Negroes live are quite inadequate for either race, and more so for the children of Negroes. Hence conditions are below the standard which should prevail. In a number of states the Negro is deprived of his vote and is unable to help himself to secure an equal measure of justice from the state. Disfranchised citizens cannot share either in the responsibilities or the privileges of citizenship. All these are limiting factors in American civilization. Their limitation is not only upon the doing of justice to the Negro, but also upon the quality of justice in the nation. That this quality of justice in the nation may be achieved through interracial cooperation is a hope for which the findings of social research as revealed in this book give substantial support."

When to the National Council of Women of the United States came the responsibility for forming and conducting an international assembly of organized women, during the Century of Progess International Exposition at Chicago in 1933, its directors selected for the theme of discussion, "Our Common Cause—Civilization," as most appropriate for a world convention at that time. The Council invited a number of American men and women in positions of leadership to join the foreign speakers in the consideration of this subject.

Taking the center of the stage at the opening session to extend an official welcome on behalf of the public, the Honorable Rufus Dawes, President of the Exposition, dwelt upon the importance and significance of the theme. He began his address with a quotation from the Call for the Convention which read: "Technology has created the promise of a world of plenty which for the first time seems to be an attainable goal. . . . Civilization is at a crisis. Unemployment and misery, fear and passion, threaten economic collapse and the dire calamity of war. At the very moment when a Century of Progress celebrates the achievements of science for the comforts of men, the National Council of Women of the United States has summoned this International Congress of forward-looking women to grasp the significance of the present situation and to find the best roads to action in the face of the recognized perils to society and government."

This Call the President of the Exposition endorsed as follows: "The Century of Progress welcomes this Congress, for it is called to discuss the very problem which, in the opinion of its organizers, this exposition would present to thinking men and women of the world, namely, the contrast between technological progress and the imminence of social problems. . . . We, therefore, applaud the wisdom of your organization in opening the discussion of the social and political effects of this marvelous technological process."

The presiding officer of the week's congress, Lena Madesin Phillips, head of the National Council of Women of the United States, opened the regular proceedings by posing this question: "Shall it be Progress?" At once she indicated the spirit in which the question was to be discussed: "If you believe that Providence or Fate determines and that all that a person has to do is to work hard, pay his debts, and vote Republican or Democratic tickets, then you will miss the true meaning of this conference. If you believe that we have always had the poor and slums and inequalities and graft, and therefore always will have them, then you start with a handicap in this Congress. If you believe this to be the climax of civilization, then for you the book is well-nigh closed. If you believe that the Golden Age was that of the Greeks and that, since that period, civilization has gradually declined, you cannot catch the glimpse of that new world of peace and plenty, of security and opportunity for all, which has actuated the movers of this program. But if you can see civilization as a living, growing, changing thing; if you can feel that social justice demands that all should share; if you can discard old beliefs and theories and forms, your fathers' as well as your own, and know that new conditions demand new treatment; if you can be willing to let your works justify your words when you speak of the brotherhood of man; if you can refrain from covering greed and selfishness by the benign cloak of Providence, then you are ready to begin to answer our questions."

Thoughtful responses were made by men outstanding in

American public affairs and by women of recognized leadership in Europe and Asia, in Canada and Latin America as well as in the United States. Among the foreign speakers were women from Germany, Italy, and Austria where the answer to the "crisis in civilization" was then taking the shape of military dictatorships and a totalitarian war on civilization.

For those women the crisis was no academic matter. The air of 1933, even in the United States, was throbbing with the echoes of drum-beating in Europe and Asia and through the week's meetings rang protests against violence as a way of dealing with tragedies of life and history, of solving human problems.

Judge Florence E. Allen, Justice of the Ohio State Supreme Court at the time and soon to be a Circuit Court Justice of the United States, voiced the common hostility to war as the foe of civilization: "When women in this country were enfranchised, it was at the close of the War [in 1918]. . . . The eyes of women the world over, on whatever side they were of that great controversy, were filled with tears, or else we were all of us so blind with resentment and hatred and partisanship and all of the things that are the hideous backwash of war. But now, now that we are quieter and calmer and older, we look back and we see that we did not understand what we were to do with these new-found powers of ours. . . . I take it that . . . we are to talk about the intellectual and spiritual aspects of civilization, and that means that this Congress is to discuss how we can maintain what the race has won and how we can progress, and that means that we have to discuss and we have to decide how we are to rid ourselves forever of the legalized burden of war, and how the right to live, the right of an individual to develop himself and grow just as a plant grows, how that right shall be preserved against all the old fetishes of ancient feudal law. . . . The women in this room can do anything. The women in this room can start the movements that are necessary today to preserve and maintain and advance Our Common Cause, Civilization."

As the report of their general sessions and round-tables, their findings, and their manifesto reveal, the women assembled in Chicago in 1933 from all parts of the world, in association with the men who participated as speakers, accepted the challenges of the opening addresses and bent their minds to the problem of ways and means for advancing civilization, the supreme issue before the Congress. As befitted a great congress held to canvass the subject of civilization, the members reviewed its manifold aspects, from the tillage of the soil to the provision of leisure for the enjoyment of the fine arts, from the conservation of natural resources to the conservation of human life. Never before had such widely representative and concerted efforts been devoted so singly to the theme of civilization; and it was with justification that the National Council of Women of the United States signalized the event by publishing the proceedings under the title of the conference: *Our Common Cause—Civilization.*

In other assemblies, large and small, where citizens gathered to exchange views on the significance and upshot of their labors, they usually gravitated toward the idea of civilization. Whether that subject was set in advance for discussion or not, it came continually into the speeches from the floor as if due to a feeling of necessity. Indeed a dissertation on the idea of civilization in the United States could be written from the reports of American conventions alone during the last quarter of a century.

Through the realm of professional educators, as through the realm of laymen and lay groups, rang the idea of civilization with thrumming resonance. Individual scholars in their studying, thinking, and writing heard the beating of the idea and augmented it in their innumerable varieties of intellectual activity. In the several fields of science and the humanities, gilds of scholars, in committees and large conferences in which the thought, nature, and obligations of their specialties were reviewed, struck the note of civilization with growing insistence. When general assemblies of educators representing all branches of learning were held, either for ceremonial purposes or for the serious consideration of the total obligation resting upon education in the United States, the idea of civilization came into play to give unity, point, and force to the great function of education with which they were charged.

Since civilization was in the actuality of the history which historians studied and taught, it might have been expected that they more than laymen would utilize the idea of civilization for research and publication, thus helping to clarify and illuminate this world-view of history. Indeed the expectation found utterance in their profession as early as 1884 when Andrew D. White, the first president of the American Historical Association, addressed them. "Is it not true," he asked of his gild, "that we, in this Republic, called upon to help build up a new civilization with a political and social history developing before us of which the consequences for good or evil are to rank with those which have flowed from the life of Rome and the British Empire,—is it not true that, for us, the history which, for the use of various European populations, has been written with minute attention to details, must be written in a larger and more philosophic way?" The response, if slow in coming, was at length manifest but no great and comprehensive history of American civilization was written.

In keeping with the matter-of-fact methods of historical research generally pursued in the United States, the process of building up the conception of civilization in history was first carried on in a piecemeal fashion, often by amateurs. Histories of politics, government, industry, painting, music, sculpture, science, architecture, invention, and literature, as phases of civilization, were written, sometimes in the spirit of narrow specialism and sometimes with a vague awareness of their interrelations. Eventually the idea of civilization acquired such authority among professional historians that they began to turn out what they called histories of ancient, medieval, modern, national, regional, and other social orders to which they attached the word civilization.

Taking advantage of elaborate studies already completed and prosecuting researches of his own, Harry Elmer Barnes assumed the difficult task of giving a general epitome of life in the Western world, in his *History of Western Civilization* published in 1935. In his Preface, Barnes stated that he had built his volumes upon "two main convictions. The first is that the history of civilization must be founded upon a broad perspective of time and space that cannot be secured from history alone, but must be grounded in biology, archaeology, anthropology, and sociology as well. The second is that the whole story of human development should be told. Qualifying this, however, is the belief that one must not try to lay exactly the same emphasis on each department or phase of culture in every period of human development. In some epochs the mere struggle for existence has been most important. In others, religion. . . . In another . . . the struggle for wealth and power." Consequently "when treating a particular people in any era," he confessed, "I have attempted to stress especially the most characteristic and illuminating traits of that age and civilization."

While disclaiming any "mission" in the conception and execution of this large historical work, Barnes nevertheless declared: "I do believe that history has no significance except in so far as it enables the reader more intelligently to understand the present and more rationally to work for a better future. History can serve this noble purpose, first by making it clear how we have arrived at our present state of civilization, and second, by helping to lift the weight of the 'dead hand' of error and superstition that has come down from the past. There are few traditional obstructions to clear thinking and sane social action that cannot be wiped away, once these obstacles are candidly examined in their historical origins."

For bringing the history of all the Americas into his broad synopsis of the human experience, Barnes gave three reasons: first, "Any history of Western civilization in contemporary times must take account of the achievements of the Western Hemisphere"; second, "The United States has carried certain cultural and institutional developments— particularly finance capitalism and educational experimentation—much further than any other contemporary area"; third, "Characteristic contemporary developments are much more teachable if they are based upon and illustrated by the American materials with which students in this country are familiar in their everyday life."

Confining himself principally to the contemporary scene in the United States, another historian, John U. Nef of the University of Chicago, declared: "We are faced with the breakdown of established beliefs and traditions concerning religion, conduct, thought, art, and politics." After making his diagnosis of the nation's illness, laying down his postulates, and reviewing remedies, Nef entitled his whole work, published in 1942, *The United States and Civilization*. The disturbances of the age he outlined under the heading: "Civilization at the Crossroads." His postulates he called "Ends of Civilization": humanism, religion, moral philosophy, and art. Having decided that among the origins of present calamities are a decline in the ratio of economic expansion and at the same time too great a preoccupation with "material" things, Nef offered various projects for overcoming difficulties and advancing civilization.

Given his major premise that danger to civilization lay in the neglect of humanistic, religious, moral, and artistic interests, Nef's projects for reform led logically to the promotion of those interests. "Trained authority on moral, intellectual, and artistic questions," he said, ". . . can only be obtained by giving the wisest, the best endowed, the best trained, and the most disinterested philosophers, theologians, writers, and artists a prestige and power of leadership that our American civilization would now make it difficult for such persons to obtain if they existed." For guidance in selecting the superior leaders, Nef proposed to invoke the aid of "the greatest minds of the past."

To provide support for the right kind of instruction Nef evolved a plan under which "the national government would make gifts to endowed universities, colleges, and schools concerned with teaching good moral and intellectual habits and a love of beauty. It would make gifts to churches concerned with the cultivation of faith and good moral conduct. It would create by gifts in various parts of the country a series of establishments devoted to the arts and handicrafts. They would be concerned with music, painting, architecture, and the fashioning of beautiful objects of decoration." Although Nef did not ignore economic utilities in civilization, he insisted that "if civilization is to survive, or if it is to be revived in the future, it is essential that the mind and the spirit should lead, not follow. It is essential that art, and also religion and philosophy, should be independent of material ends."

While professional historians were moving from partial or timid attempts to study civilization into bolder excursions with the idea, professional educators in other departments were beginning to relate their branches of learning to the idea of civilization and its historic reaches. For example, in the case of Thorstein Veblen, classed as an economist, it was his sensitivity to the whole contexture of society in development that gave realism and distinction to his writings. Into his stream of thinking he brought knowledge about the evolution of societies, the course of economic theories and practices, and folkways changing with the development of the arts, crafts, and sciences. And whatever theme he touched, he usually plunged into the dynamism of historic change.

In an essay written in 1906 and later given priority in a series entitled *The Place of Science in Modern Civilization,* Veblen revealed this quality of his insight and imagination. Economic transactions at a given period, he pointed out, occur in society, not in a vacuum, not up in the air. Then he gave his characterization of modern society which was soon to become famous: "Modern civilization is peculiarly matter-of-fact. . . . This characteristic of western civilization comes to a head in modern science, and it finds its highest material expression in the technology of the machine industry." It was obsession with this material expression of civilization to the neglect of other values, in Veblen's judgment, that marked the spirit of the time and might lead to a social breakdown. After Veblen had spoken, no American student of economics who had passed beyond sheer sciolism could fail to associate civilization with economic thought.

Professional philosophers as well as professional historians and economists joined the long train of thinkers who used the idea of civilization as if it stood for a value or reality indispensable in the development of a thesis or the undertaking of an original exploration. In his treatise on *The Social Mind,* issued in 1939, John Elof Boodin, professor of philosophy in the University of California at Los Angeles, referred to it frequently as though it carried a meaning commonly understood. Speaking at one place of Greek antiquity, for instance, he said: "The Greeks, moreover, were haunted by the legend of a great civilization which had preceded theirs—the great Cretan civilization. . . . And Plato in the *Protagoras* points out that contemporary civilization at its worst was vastly superior to that of the cannibals, who had been on exhibition in Athens."

Yet Boodin also employed the term in a more limited and a special sense in his chapter on "The Unit of Civilization," where he treated civilization as subject to progressive modification and promoted most effectively in small community circles. Looking to the future, he foresaw change, or progress: "We must have a deeper appreciation of humanity everywhere, before the greater day can come. The old civilization was concerned with an aristocratic plane and its interests were correspondingly limited. The new civilization must express the fundamentally human plane, not as an ab-

stract universal merely, but in all its complexities, starting
from the concrete associations with their color of tradition,
climate and race, and working out towards the infinite. It
must, as Nietzsche insisted, develop strong, resourceful,
courageous individuals, not slaves of tradition nor of the
herd instinct, but it must develop individuals with community consciousness, joyfully giving of their best to enrich
all."

"The spiritual fruits of civilization," however, Boodin
thought incompatible with the "boasted power-organiza-
tions" of great modern societies, including the United
States. Evidently captivated by the intellectual richness of
ancient Athens, he held that small communities of congenial
spirits offer more ideal conditions for developing higher
types of civilization. Anyway, the idea of civilization seemed,
in Boodin's mind, to stand for the crowning value of human
life and endeavor.

Believing that civilization was in a crisis and that the
philosopher's function was not to keep "civilization's treasures" in an academic cloister, but to help humanity in thinking, Max Otto, at the University of Wisconsin, sent forth a
call for a philosophy that could be used as an instrument
of action in making a better world. "Philosophy has served
men before when their need was similar to the present
need," he wrote in the Journal of Social Philosophy for
July, 1941. "It has been reborn again and again out of just
such crises. Plato designed his Great Community as an older
civilization was falling back before the onslaught of a new
political order. When the medieval world was threatened
with disintegration, Thomas Aquinas built a cathedral of
the mind under whose vaulted ceiling all interests were to
meet in harmony. The social vision of John Locke was written into the militant documents of struggling democracies.
Immanuel Kant, hearing the tramp of the Potsdam grena-
diers, championed the moral integrity of the individual and
the establishment of lasting peace among nations."

Some philosophers had interpreted their function as that
of hiding "the treasures of civilization out of destruction's
reach" while the battle is on, since "suppression" as a "test
of physical might . . . does not belong within the philosopher's province." But Otto was not of that school. "There
are two ways of taking the present world upheaval," he

contended. "We may take it to be the fateful disintegration of civilized life, or we may take it to be a driving search for a better social orientation. Which of these ways is the more realistic one? . . . Well, if it is inherent in philosophic practise to go beyond surface phenomena and not to mistake an aspect of things for the whole reality; if philosophy means disciplined fidelity to the search for fundamental and comprehensive knowledge not merely for its own sake but in the interest of authentic ideals; then the present juncture offers the philosopher an exceptional occasion for social usefulness."

And what was the present conjuncture in July, 1941, which presented to the philosopher an exceptional occasion for social usefulness? Otto became specific: "The vast economic, material body of the world lacks a mind to match it, and is not animated by a commensurate moral spirit. This backwardness is the tragic inadequacy of our time. It is the basic problem which the agencies of aspiration and intelligence have to solve. It is the problem which, more than any other, calls upon philosophy for new vision and creativeness."

In setting forth his own vision and his conception of creativeness, Otto expressed the opinion that "the revolt of the masses," to use the idiom, must be taken into account with "sympathetic understanding." No dignity was attached to the profession of philosophy, he said, if "philosophy must be regarded as a wholly intellectual occupation, and the philosopher cannot take the field for anything less spiritual than an idealism for which a man is to live and work on an empty stomach, secure in nothing but his poverty, rewarded only by an illusion of spiritual triumph over those who rob him of the material essentials of manhood." If philosophy was to "counteract the spread of cynical disbelief in mankind, in political government, in truth, good will, moral integrity," where was it to begin?

It was not to begin, Otto averred, by taking the position assumed by that "distinguished American poet, Archibald MacLeish," who "in criticisms of his countrymen for their emphasis upon physical comfort, has eloquently voiced an ideal which is popular among philosophers who are anxious to protect philosophy from material contamination." Not merely, as proclaimed by MacLeish and men of his inclination, "in the hard and stony passes of the human spirit—the strict Thermopylaes of time where even if a man is killed he cannot die" is the real issue "to be fought." No, Otto declared, "the real issue is to be fought in the hard and stony passes of existing conditions where if a man is killed he is dead as a door nail and no one cares a damn." In this real world of labor and struggle, the new philosophy that is to serve civilization must find its forum and battle-ground, Otto insisted.

Writing in 1941 on a large subject which he called *The Destiny of Western Man,* published the following year, W. T. Stace, a Doctor of Letters from Dublin University and former member of the British civil service, teaching at Princeton University, devoted about one-third of his book to considerations placed under the head of "Civilization." His main purpose, he confessed, was "to prove, by rational argument, the truth of the Christian ethics," and to discredit the Germans in whose consciousness only has the Nietzschean philosophy, which he narrowed to his own purposes, "taken a vital hold."

It was in relevance to this operation that he deemed the idea of civilization necessary to the business of demonstration. The first line of Stace's first chapter ran: "Civilization is organized goodness." On his eighth page he said: "I shall have to discuss in this book the heritage of our civilization. . . . I do not know how to define the term, but whatever else it means it at least implies an attempt to live in a *better* way than did our uncivilized ancestors." Yet he seemed to think that even the Germans had some civilization, for on the next page he referred to "the totalitarian type of civilization."

In his final chapter, Stace restricted the issue to a choice between Nietzsche and Christ. As to this preference, "It is the Christian principle of life which provides the fundamental feeling basis not only of our civilization but of all human society. It is the foundation of pre-Christian societies, of non-Christian societies, of societies which have never heard of Christianity. This may sound paradoxical, but it is not. For the Christian principle, which is sympathy, was not invented or discovered by Christianity. . . . What Christianity did was to give to sympathy its proper place in life, to thrust it into the foreground as the ruling principle of life. Hence there is no paradox in the assertion that the Christian principle of sympathy is in fact the basis of all society, whether the society be nominally Christian or not."

Specialists in academic circles who came together in committees or conferences and tried to offset the centrifugal tendencies of specialization by fixing upon some common center of their several interests, often found it in the idea of civilization. An example is afforded by the work of the Commission on the Social Studies in the Schools, created by the American Historical Association in 1929. The Commission, composed of representatives from history, politics, sociology, and professional education, early in the proceedings, directed its attention to the character of American society in which, and for the benefit of which, instruction in the humanities was designed. After a scrutiny of that subject the Commission adopted the following formula, incorporated in *A Charter for the Social Studies*: "The people of this country are engaged in no mere political experiment, as often imagined, but are attempting to build a civilization in a new natural setting, along original lines, with science and machinery as the great instrumentalities of work." Within this frame of reference the Commission pursued its inquiries and developed recommendations.

When a group of scholars, representing many branches of learning, entered into collaboration in connection with the centenary celebration of New York University, they embodied the results of their labors in a symposium entitled *Trends of Civilization*, issued under the sponsorship of Charles G. Shaw, professor of philosophy at that institution. In his introductory comments on the theme, Shaw declared that man had always been interested in civilization. But, unlike many contemporaries who used the term without fear and without research, Shaw undertook to define it: "By civilization we mean the improvement or perfection of man's outer condition; it concerns man's relation to nature and his fellow man. It is a state of affairs, and is both physical and social. . . . Man is naturally social and is thus apt for civilization. . . . The arts and sciences, governments and industries, ideals and institutions that man has elaborated may not have elevated him above savagery, such savagery as was witnessed in the World War, but it is the tendency to elaborate just such things that constitutes civilization. . . . Furthermore, when we are inclined to doubt that the result of civilization has meant human betterment, we cannot overlook the fact that such betterment has been the purpose of civilization."

Taking up the relation of ideas to deeds, Shaw asked the question: "What are we profited when we have a set of terms: nature, humanity, culture, civilization?" This was his answer: "The translation from fact to idea, from human deeds to human words, can never be literal. However it is not impossible for us to identify the meaning of the idea in question. In the case of both culture and civilization, we find the point of departure, if not the norm, in the contrasted idea of nature. . . . When we refer to nature as the contrary of civilization, we do not have in mind the exterior order of things which surrounds man. Man at once humanizes the world by perceiving it; he makes it something like himself by means of his human arts and sciences. But this philosophical and scientific conception of the world, which yields a kind of intellectual cosmos, is not the natural order which concerns civilization. Here the situation is dynamic, not intellectual. It is a living state of affairs, in which nature acts upon man, and man reacts upon nature. Hence it is not the forms of the world—space and time—which appeal to man and engage his attention, but the forces of the world—matter and motion—which challenge his will and are involved in the problem of human civilization. What nature has done for man has been observed already in the evolution of the human species from the Peking man to the man of the present. But this has nothing to do with civilization. *Civilization is man's own work*."

Concentration on the idea of civilization appeared the following year, 1933, at the University of Cincinnati, in a symposium organized under the direction of George A. Hedger and given the title *Introduction to Western Civilization,* a historical view of the subject. Hedger himself seemed to regard civilization, whatever it was precisely, as something already constructed and he called for a more intensive study of the processes by which it had been built. "The quest for a more intelligent interpretation of experience in the world about us," he said, "involves two major considerations. The first is knowledge of the nature of man himself. The second is a knowledge of the nature of man's social environment—that is to say of his culture or civilization. In neither case can one confine himself to observations and study of the existing world. It is necessary to venture far into the past. . . . It reveals us to ourselves and illuminates our relations to the life and thought about us. . . . Man is . . . a social animal. . . . Once man is started on the path that winds down to the present, it becomes necessary to examine the slow, painful process by which he lifted himself from a remote, bestial existence to that *high place which we designate as civilization*." If culture and civilization were thus used interchangeably, at all events civilization was as central as culture in Hedger's thought applied to history.

At a conclave of specialists—psychologists, sociologists, anthropologists, ethnologists, and historians—held under the auspices of the American Historical Association during its sessions of 1939–40 in the national capital, the subject of the correct way of interpreting and writing history was discussed and the idea of culture was advocated as the right indicator. The leading papers presented were collected and published under the editorship of Catherine F. Ware in a volume called *The Cultural Approach to History*.

Although in these papers read at the conference the idea of culture, in its proper static sense as representing a fixed pattern of behavior, was generally adopted, several participants in the symposium also employed the word civilization. Sometimes they seemed to make it synonymous with culture and at other times they indicated that it meant something else; but they made no attempt to define civilization when they used the word.

As a matter of fact most of the papers had little or no relation to history, and the idea of "a cultural approach to history" almost amounted to a denial of history and civilization alike—both of which necessarily connote elements of dynamics and uniqueness in personalities, events, and places. As a whole the symposium was inconclusive in thought, but it served to call the attention of historians once more to matters besides wars and politics and thus reflected and stimulated interest in civilization.

When educators in general were dismayed by the dissolving tendencies of specialization, by the desiccation, pessimism, and futility of academic minutiae pursued as ends in themselves, and sought a center, or principle, for the organization of research and training, they frequently made the idea of civilization the intellectual standpoint from which to attack the elective system. In many leading colleges "orientation courses" in civilization were established with the object of unifying and imparting a meaning to the study of the humanities and to applications of the natural sciences. Where the idea of civilization was not specifically introduced for purposes of orientation, a combination course on science, art, letters, ethics, and esthetics was sometimes attempted in a kindred quest for unity and meaning in educational effort.

In the course of time the intensification and spread of interest in the idea of civilization affected thought about the curricula of historical instruction in universities and colleges. Evidences of this awakening appeared in 1937 at Harvard University when that institution established the degree of Doctor of Philosophy in "the History of American Civilization." Commenting on this innovation in higher learning, the editor of The Saturday Review remarked that Harvard had "in mind primarily the man who wants to study American life in terms of American thought, art, history, and social institutions without wasting his time in work irrelevant to his purpose but hitherto required for the doctorate."

The new arrangement at Harvard made three fields of study a requirement for all candidates for that degree: the economic history of the United States, the history of literature in the United States, and the history of political theory in the United States. It allowed candidates to select three additional fields from the following list: "the history of religion and theology in the United States, the history of philosophy in the United States, the history of science, the history of the fine arts, the history of religion and theology, the history of philosophy, the history of political theory, the history of European literature (especially English)," and other subjects useful in the preparation of theses.

Joining in the struggle against the anarchy of specialism running riot, college presidents rallied to the idea of civilization as an instant help in time of need. Indeed if they were to do anything more than preside over intellectual disorder, they were bound by their office to search for some unifying principle of education.

While the alarms created by the march of totalitarianism

in Europe were spreading in the United States, the president of Princeton University, Harold W. Dodds, speaking at Andover in 1937, placed his reliance on certain processes of civilization to preserve democracy in the United States: "Our civilization is precarious but it contains one new and hopeful element, the ideal of democracy, which requires that those who have the benefit of education fuse their civilization with the mass." And in 1942 Princeton announced a new program of studies in American civilization.

In opening the autumn session of the Stevens Institute of Technology in 1941, the president, Harvey N. Davis, gave publicity to the launching of a new, unifying course in the humanities. This course, he said, "will focus, during the first term, on three specific periods which have influenced the development of contemporary civilization"—Greek, medieval, and modern times. "The second term," he continued, "dealing with modern civilization, will confine itself as strictly as possible to one of the most significant tendencies of the period—the rise, development, and rule of the middle class." By the study of civilization, presumably, engineers were to be the better equipped for the discharge of their functions in American society.

At the University of Chicago, in the spring of 1942, a special course called "Study of Civilization" was organized under an executive committee composed of President Robert M. Hutchins, Robert Redfield, professor of anthropology, Frank H. Knight, professor of social science, and John U. Nef, professor of economic history. The program of studies was divided into three sections: philosophical, historical and cultural, and methodological. The members of the group, according to their announcement, "plan to study the manner in which historically customs and beliefs have been formed in societies—primitive and civilized. Through this study they will attempt to clarify some of the broad problems of human living. They plan to study the interrelations between the various social sciences and humanities, especially the interrelations between economics and moral and political philosophy, in such ways as to bring out the significance of research and education along these lines for the problems of the individual and of society. They hope to help graduate students who participate in their work, to acquire a broad cultural foundation in the great works of thought and art that have come down from the past and to consider the relevance of these works to modern problems of learning and conduct."

That the idea of civilization was firmly established in the popular as well as the academic mind by 1942 was demonstrated by the profuse use of the word in the public addresses of statesmen, politicians, publicists, and radio speakers. Few if any of the major issues, crises, and conflicts of the twentieth century were canvassed without copious references to the nature, virtues, fortunes, and catastrophes of civilization. Such references occurred in connection with everything that seriously concerned the interests and prospects of American politicians—imperialism or adherence to the older tradition; nationalism or internationalism; domestic unrest or the stakes of "great" diplomacy; the legal position of women or labor legislation; the Square Deal, the New Freedom, the New Deal; making the world safe for democracy by war or non-intervention in foreign quarrels. In public discussions of all these matters, and more, appeared arguments and assertions involving concepts of civilization.

In almost every form of political discourse, from presidential messages and radio broadcasts to double-shotted editorials in rural weeklies, civilization was represented as favored and promoted by the "right" policies or vitiated by the "wrong" policies. With endless repetition appeals were made to that majestic word civilization as to an ultimate court for the adjudication of human causes. In a giant parade of the wise in civilization, Presidents, Senators, and Representatives joined mayors, assemblymen, and village politicians, men and women, without discrimination of sex, color, or previous condition of servitude.

Near the close of the nineteenth century, Great Britain was warring with the Boers in South Africa and the United States was suppressing a revolt of the natives in the Philippines. In both countries ideologues were telling the world that the Anglo-Saxons were called by God to spread civilization among peoples sitting in darkness. It was in this age that Mark Twain delivered his analysis of civilization, enumerated what he esteemed as its virtues, and burst out in wrath against the claim that imperialism was spreading civilization among benighted peoples. At the moment Tory vaudeville artists in Britain were entertaining music hall crowds with jingo songs and quips, and Republican politicians in the United States, frightened by the rising tide of revolt at home under the banner of Bryan democracy, were diverting the public by the excitement of war and the lure of doing good to the Filipinos as soon as they were thoroughly conquered. Mark Twain was in London at the time and on January 27, 1900, he wrote to his friend, J. H. Twichell, in Hartford, Connecticut, what he thought about the new rhetoric of war. He expressed the opinion that the defeat and fall of Britain in the Boer war "would be an irremediable disaster for the mangy human race," but he was full of anger at the appeals made to the sanction of civilization by war parties there and in America.

For the purpose of making it plain to Twichell that he had a definite idea of what he was talking about when he spoke of civilization, Mark Twain gave a list of its qualities as he discerned them: "Happiness, food, shelter, clothing, wholesale labor, modest and rational ambitions, honesty, kindliness, hospitality, love of freedom and limitless courage to fight for it, composure and fortitude in time of disaster, patience in time of hardship and privation, absence of noise and brag in time of victory, contentment with a humble and peaceful life void of insane excitements—if there is a higher and better form of civilization than this, I am not aware of it and do not know where to look for it."

Then Twain pronounced his judgment on the British and the Americans for their use of the word civilization: "I suppose we have the habit of imagining that a lot of artistic, intellectual, and other artificialities must be added, or it isn't complete. . . . My idea of our civilization is that it is a shabby poor thing and full of cruelties, vanities, arrogancies, meanness, and hypocrisies. As for the word, I hate the sound of it, for it conveys a lie; and as for the thing itself, I wish it was in hell, where it belongs."

In spite of his fury, however, Mark Twain realized that neither the idea nor the thing could be so easily disposed of, for he immediately added: *"Provided* we could get something better in the place of it. But that is not possible, perhaps. Poor as it is, it is better than *real* savagery, therefore we must stand by it, extend it, and (in public) praise it."

The next outbreak of war on the American calendar was the entrance of the United States into the first world conflict in 1917. Frenchmen described that war as a war for civiliza-

WITHDRAWN
SCCGC LIBRARY
4601 Mid Rivers Mall Drive
St. Peters, MO 63376

tion and on monuments erected to soldiers who had fallen in combat they carved the words: "Died for civilization." After the long and frightful struggle had come to an end for a season, when the British struck their "Victory Medal," they officially styled the war, as if for all time: "The Great War for Civilization." Speaking for the United States, President Wilson at first proclaimed it a war for democracy and to end wars. At length he described it as a war to underwrite civilization. In 1919 during a continental tour which he undertook with the object of committing the country definitively to the League of Nations, he declared that America could not carry alone the burden of civilization. Speaking to the citizens of Tacoma in this vein he exclaimed: "You have got to guarantee and underwrite civilization, or you have ruined the United States!" Beyond that view, political imagination could scarcely soar.

In explaining and defending the domestic policies known collectively as the New Deal or the foreign policies which he pursued, President Franklin D. Roosevelt referred great decisions to the mandates of civilization. Speaking in 1937 of measures pertaining to social welfare adopted by Congress under his leadership, unemployment in particular, he asserted that "the inherent right to work is one of the elemental privileges of a free people. Continued failure to achieve that right and privilege by anyone who wants to work and needs work is a challenge to our civilization and to our security." In his message of August 21, 1941, informing Congress that he had recently held a conference with the British Premier, Winston Churchill, and that they had agreed upon an eight-point charter for the world, President Roosevelt avowed that their "declaration of principles at this time presents a goal which is worth while for our type of civilization to seek."

Not to be outdone in higher wisdom by their leaders and orators, political parties as organized bodies often officially justified their faith and works by allusions to the idea of civilization. In an hour of deep division in 1940, for example, the Democratic party reflected its internal conflict by incorporating in its platform two items related to the subject. One, forced upon President Roosevelt by an opposition on the floor, declared: "We will not participate in foreign wars, and we will not send our Army, naval or air forces to fight in foreign lands outside of the Americas, except in case of attack. . . . The direction and aim of our foreign policy

WITHDRAWN

has been, and will continue to be, the security and defense of our own land and the maintenance of its peace." The other item, written under presidential direction, asserted: "It is America's destiny, in these days of rampant despotism, to be the guardian of the world heritage of liberty and to hold aloft and aflame the torch of Western civilization."

In moments of high tension, columnists professionally occupied with the instruction of statesmen, politicians, and citizens in correct ways of conducting public affairs, put forward the idea of civilization in vindicating their pronouncements, in offering a guarantee of finality. When in 1942 an English gentleman sent Dorothy Thompson a gold sovereign, coined in Queen Victoria's reign, as a token of appreciation for her many services to Great Britain, Miss Thompson found warrant for that service in "a greatness in Britain" and in the excellence of Victorian civilization. "The Victorian Age," she declared, in acknowledging the gift publicly, was "more than a British epoch." It was a "world epoch." And civilization in that epoch she defined as equilibrium: "That world seemed eternal. Civilization, it appeared, had reached its pinnacle. An equilibrium had been established in which it seemed that freedom had been forever brought in gentle discipline to order, and order made tolerable by freedom."

Frequently, when Walter Lippmann felt the need of an imperium loftier than his own, he braced his instructions to the public with some inexorable demand or force of civilization. In his columnar message to the American people on December 1, 1941, he had occasion to tell members of Congress exactly what their duties were under the Constitution, and he then informed leaders of the Republican party that, since Congress had approved the foreign policies proposed by President Roosevelt, they were bound to support those policies henceforward. In conclusion he intimated that Congress need not worry about its prerogatives, that it did not amount to much anyway, and that the public must look to civilization rather than Congress for the preservation of popular institutions. "If the problems of our times are solved successfully," he asserted, "parliamentary government will survive because our civilization has survived."

In the swelling volume of contemporary literature, serious and casual, in which the idea of civilization figured, confu-

sion arose over peculiar treatments given to the idea of civilization and the idea of culture—two idea-formulations with different roots in etymology and history. To the starting of this confusion Americans contributed their full quota. And the intellectual turmoil they created was turned into a pandemonium by an inflow of uncritical European writings and translations.

The American contribution to the general misunderstanding took the form of a careless use of both words in which they were frequently made identical in meaning. The nature of the American misapprehension was revealed in books, pamphlets, and articles without number. It was also illustrated in library classifications. Anyone who desired to get a comprehensive view of the confusion confounded merely had to examine a card catalogue of any great American library under the respective heads: Civilization and Culture. No additional documentation was necessary on the point.

Bewilderment was added to perplexity when Oswald Spengler's *Der Untergang des Abendlandes* was translated into English under the title, *The Decline of the West*, and published in New York City in 1926. In sum and substance and total upshot, Spengler's massive pile of pretentious erudition was an elegy on the death of *Kultur* in the vile uprush of *Zivilisation*, and a paean to the man of blood and war.

The author of this tour de force, which reverberated in two hemispheres, had not been a professional student of history or society. His former work had been done in mathematics; at all events he had been an upper-class master or professor of mathematics in a *Gymnasium* at Hamburg from 1908 to 1911, before he withdrew from the academic world to embark on the career of a publicist.

In July, 1918, while the world war was raging, the first volume of Spengler's German edition appeared. The second volume came out in 1922 while his native land, Germany, was in the agony of defeat and humiliation; but, in origin at least, the giant tract was not merely a war book. "The complete manuscript," he said, "the outcome of three years' work, was ready when the Great War broke out" in 1914 and had simply been revised, or polished, in the intervening years before publication.

Although Spengler spoke of his treatise as "a philosophy of history," the forms of his thought were not historical or humanistic but mainly biological, morphological, and ana-

logical. Indeed it was reported that he had proposed to call it "Outlines of a Morphology of History," which would have been appropriate, but accepted from his publisher the more provocative title as better suited to the temper of Germans and the Western world at the hour of publication. In any case, the explanatory subtitle in German was *"Umrisse einer Morphologie der Weltgeschichte"* which was translated in a misleading fashion for the English edition as "Form and Actuality."

Regardless of its truth, significance, or value, Spengler's huge collection of abstractions, metaphors, and concrete illustrations drove deep into American thought the idea that civilization is merely the late stage of social development which follows and marks the death of culture. "Every Culture," he declared with oracular assurance, "has *its own* civilization. In this work, for the first time the two words, hitherto used to express an indefinite, more or less ethical, distinction, are used in a *periodic sense*, to express a strict and necessary *organic succession*. The Civilization is the inevitable *destiny* of the Culture, and in this principle we obtain the viewpoint from which the deepest and gravest problems of historical morphology become capable of solution. Civilizations are the most external and artificial states of which a species of developed humanity is capable. They are a conclusion, the thing-become succeeding the thing-becoming, death following life, rigidity following expansion, intellectual age and the stone-built, petrifying world-city following mother-earth and the spiritual childhood of Doric and Gothic."

Further on he said: "In every Culture the quantum of work grows bigger and bigger till at the beginning of every Civilization we find an intensity of economic life, of which the tensions are even excessive and dangerous, and which it is impossible to maintain for a long period. In the end a rigid, permanent-set condition is reached, a strange hotch-potch of refined-intellectual and crude-primitive factors . . . unless, of course, the crust is being disintegrated from below by the pressure of a young Culture."

For intellectuals, American and foreign, fond of grandiose theories, yet undisciplined by an intensive study of history as actuality or as thought, Spengler's disposal of civilization by the use of the cyclical theory provided a sensational topic for table talk, reviews, and other displays of wisdom. His use of spring, summer, autumn, and winter as "spiritual epochs" in the careers of nations seemed to minds charmed by metaphors a demonstration in natural law; and it was taken seriously and applied repeatedly to many purposes by imitative writers.

Spring, Spengler solemnly averred, is marked by "rural-initiative. Great creations of the newly awakened dream-heavy Soul. Super-personal unity and fulness. Summer. Ripening Consciousness. Earliest urban and critical stirrings. Autumn, Intelligence of the City. Zenith of strict intellectual creativeness. Winter. Dawn of Megalopolitan Civilization. Extinction of spiritual creative force. Life itself becomes problematical. Ethical-practical tendencies of an irreligious and unmetaphysical cosmopolitanism." Considered as a "culture epoch," civilization is characterized by "existence without inner form. Megalopolitan art as a commonplace; luxury, sport, nerve-excitement: rapidly-changing fashions in art." As a "political epoch," civilization is characterized by Domination of Money (Democracy), then Caesarism, and finally "primitive human conditions slowly thrust up into the highly civilized mode of living."

Whatever meaning the arbitrary and fanciful divisions into epochs may have carried in the author's brain, Spengler's judgment of history certainly conveyed to American readers the notion that "Western civilization" was doomed and that another Caesar, the conquering man of blood and iron, would bring it to an end. It furnished substance for heated conversations and assertions among critics of American society, among young people depressed by the post-war feeling that they were a "lost generation" or suspicious of the idea of progress as merely the latest historic mirage.

The promiscuity of thought into which Spengler's provocation was plunged was increased by another German work, *Verfall und Wiederaufbau der Kultur,* written in 1923 and published the same year in an English translation as *The Decay and the Restoration of Civilization*. The author of this volume, Albert Schweitzer, educated at the University of Strassburg, Doctor of Theology, Doctor of Philosophy, and Doctor of Medicine, asked: "What is civilization?" And his reply was: "The attempts to distinguish between civilization as what the Germans call 'Kultur' and civilization as mere material progress aim at making the world familiar with the idea of an unethical form of civilization side by side with the ethical, and at clothing the former with a word of historical meaning. But nothing in the history of the word 'civilization' justifies such attempts. The word, as commonly used hitherto, means the same as the German word 'Kultur,' viz., the development of man to a state of higher organization and a higher moral standard. . . . The establishment of a difference between them is justified neither philologically nor historically."

But another learned German writer, Ernst Robert Curtius of Heidelberg University, in his *Die Französische Kultur*, published in 1932 in English as *The Civilization of France*, despite the interchange of the two titles, made a clearcut distinction in the text of his treatise between culture and civilization. "*Kultur* and Civilization," he wrote, "are wholly different in aim. To sum up: on the German as well as the French side, both these words and conceptions were set in opposition to each other. In both countries this was admitted." This statement Curtius supported by one of the keenest analyses of French civilization to be found in any language.

The proposition that there is a positive conflict between *Kultur* and *Zivilisation*, Thomas Mann had sustained with great fervor and eloquence in a war tract written in September, 1914, and published the following year in his *Friedrich und die grosse Koalition*. Mann declared that the two ideas were not only antithetical throughout, but also that the antagonism constituted one of the many forms of opposition between spirit and nature—*Geist* and *Natur*. Culture, he proceeded, does or can embrace determination of mind, taste, adventuresomeness, orgiastic cults, St. Vitus' dances, bloody deeds, colorful horrors, and more besides. "Civilization, however, is reason, enlightenment, softness, morality, skepticism, dissolution—spirit. Yes, the spirit is civil, is bourgeois; it is the sworn enemy of driving force, passion; it is antidemonic, antiheroic; and if one says that it is also against genius, this is absurd in appearance only."

In keeping with this exposition Mann concluded his essay with the assertion that the Germans were far less in love with the word civilization than their Western neighbors—always preferred the word and idea *Kultur*. Why did they feel this way? Because the word *Kultur* "has a pure human content; whereas we feel in the other word *Zivilisation* a political sense and thrust which is not attractive to us; . . . because

WITHDRAWN
SCCCC—LIBRARY
4601 Mid Rivers Mall Drive
St. Peters, MO 63376

this most intrinsically introspective people, this people of metaphysics, pedagogy, and music, is not a political people, but a people oriented toward morality.

"Thus in political progress, it has shown itself less interested in, and less impressed by, democracy, parliamentary government, or indeed republicanism than other peoples; . . . the Germans are unrevolutionary in an exemplary fashion, are the one really unrevolutionary people." Other nations adopt civilization, civilian patterns of morality. But the Germans have a dislike for the pacifist ideals of civilization; the idea of civilization is too shallow for their deep and irrational souls; in German militarism, conservatism, and morality there is a quality that utterly rejects civilianism as the highest goal for humanity.

By pointing out the civilian, political, and democratic corollaries inseparable from the idea of civilization, Mann made unmistakable the basic opposition of the two ideas—Civilization and Culture. Any uncertainties that may have remained were cleared up for readers of the German language by Norbert Elias in *Über den Prozess der Zivilisation* in 1939. Elias showed, in an excursus on this subject, that the degree of opposition between the two ideas had fluctuated in time, according to the predilections of writers and with reference to the internal and external affairs of France, Germany, and England.

In origins, Elias demonstrated, the opposition had been sharp, as sharp as the differences between the rigid class structure of feudal Germany and the more mobile interconnections maintained by the French aristocracy and the bourgeoisie. Subsequently, however, the sharpness of this antagonism was softened by some German writers, and even by a more general usage in Germany. For example, the German liberal, G. F. Kolb, writing in 1843, took into his concept of culture the idea of progress that had hitherto been banned in Germany, and brought his idea of *Kultur* near to the idea of civilization. During the late nineteenth century, after Germany had become strong in Europe and had embarked on imperialism, the antagonism between the two ideas was temporarily moderated in German usage.

But conservative German writers never accepted this rapprochement and, however close it appeared to be at times, it was never complete. Indeed, given the class structure in Germany, the political quietism of the German bourgeois, and

Germany's growing struggle for power in the world against France and England, the two ideas could not have been amalgamated and made identical in any case. "The history of the German pair of conceptions 'Zivilisation' and 'Kultur,'" Elias concluded, "is geared in the closest possible manner into the relations between England, France, and Germany." German liberals tried to crowd into the idea of culture the social, political, and rational inferences of civilization and failed. The domestic and foreign affairs of Germany defeated them. To this defeat the history of the two ideas bore indisputable witness.

If Americans had adhered strictly to the etymology of the two words, they could have escaped the intellectual anarchy in which they floundered when they used them, for the records were definite and available for both as etymology. Culture stemmed from the Latin word *cultus* which among early Romans meant tillage of the soil, care of and attention to the soil—the thought and act of farming. Doubtless in early times the propitiation of and reverence for the gods of agriculture facilitated a transfer to religion or cult.

Whether *cultus* was treated in its orginal or realistic sense or in relation to religious rites, it involved the care of soil, flocks, and crops, and care for the gods. Children, members of the family, and neighbors also needed and received care and attention. In time, *cultus* came to mean attention to the human body as well as soil and crops, to education, modes of life, refinement, ornaments, decoration, and splendor even if meretricious (from *meretrix*, a prostitute). Culture also became associated with display by rulers and their courtiers.

While *civis*, the root of the word civilization, signified the life, rights, duties, and moderation of citizenship—a care for public affairs—*cultus* carried different implications. Culture as tillage of the soil was private; as adornment, cultivation, or elegance, it was also private or could be, although as religious rite in private or family interest it could be more communal. At all events in its origins it had nothing to do with the State, democracy, or the progress of society.

In the English language, culture appeared about three hundred years before civilization. Early in the fifteenth century it was used in a double sense: as husbandry and as worship. In the course of time it acquired other connotations. By the close of the nineteenth century, for instance, it had come to mean also "the training, development, and refinement of mind, tastes, and manners." Matthew Arnold, who wrote recklessly of both culture and civilization, defined the former as "the acquainting ourselves with the best that has been known and said in the world." While discriminative French thinkers from the end of the eighteenth century were careful to maintain the distinction between civilization and culture, English and American writers were prone to use them interchangeably and thus to encourage mental confusion.

With such turbulence swirling around the pivotal term civilization, the question was raised whether the American people knew the meaning of that imperious word at all. In 1941 the question was put to the public by Virginia Gildersleeve, dean of Barnard College and president of the International Federation of University Women, during an address dealing with the proper training for defense and containing an appeal to the Government of the United States for aid in directing that training. As quoted in the press, Dean Gildersleeve said: "We expect our citizens to rally to defend Western civilization, but alas, we have not given them any chance to learn what Western civilization is."

Was her generalization too sweeping? Or was it highly suitable that, in the welter of talking and writing about civilization, Western or any other kind, American citizens, including educators, should seek the meaning of the word used so freely, so commonly, often with such ardor, as a symbol of authority and power, as a magic thing under the enchantment of which they were all to live, work, learn, vote and, if the President of the United States or the National Congress decreed, die?

Chapter 3

Origins of the Idea of Civilization

THE KEYWORD civilization is a newcomer in the long history of thought. Who first committed it to paper? Doubtless this question never will be answered; at least it cannot be answered now. Where was it first used? No conclusion on the matter has yet been reached, although surmises and guesses have been made. For what needs of the human spirit was it created? What did it mean in its origins and early usage?

Whenever and wherever the word civilization may have first come into use, it certainly found its way into print in England and France between the middle and the close of the eighteenth century. Which country gave it that distinction is not known; but it was circulating in English writing and speech before 1772, as Boswell indicated in his diary under the date of March 23, that year. Boswell thought so highly of the word that he tried to persuade Samuel Johnson to insert it in the new edition of his *Dictionary*, then in process of preparation. But, governed perhaps by the lexicographer's customary conservatism, the adamant old Tory, Dr. Johnson, was callous to Boswell's plea. "He would not admit *civilization*," Boswell noted, "but only *civility*. With great deference to him, I thought *civilization*, from *to civilize*, better in the sense opposed to *barbarity*, than *civility*." As a formula of the upper class tradition, which he loved to serve, "civility" was more satisfactory to Dr. Johnson than the new word.

The word rejected by Johnson in 1772 was incorporated three years later by a non-conformist clergyman, John Ash, in his *New and Complete Dictionary of the English Language*, published in 1775. Ash declared that he had included all the words he "could find or remember" and evidently in the course of his searching and recalling he had picked up the word civilization. By entering it in his list, he started it on its long journey through English dictionaries.

Lexicographers in France, if the word enjoyed the same degree of circulation there, were equally conservative. According to a good authority, Lucien Febvre, it was not in any of the dictionaries that may have been consulted by Montesquieu, Voltaire, Turgot, or their contemporaries. In compiling their great *Encyclopaedia*, the French philosophers under the leadership of Diderot, ignored its existence as a subject for an article, although they may have had some acquaintance with it. Not until more than twenty years after Ash had adopted it in England did the French Academy put its seal upon the word by including it in the revision of the *Dictionnaire* issued in 1798. Before the century closed, however, this stamp of respectability had been given in France to the word and the idea of civilization.

The scanty records of the dictionaries still leave obscure the precise origins of the idea in France, England, and the United States.

But in the case of France scholars have made researches and have discovered important materials bearing on the word and on the circumstances in which the idea of civilization began its career and attained intellectual and moral force. By a curious coincidence two thoroughgoing studies of the subject appeared in the same year, 1930, one by a French scholar and the other by a German scholar. The first was Lucien Febvre's report on the history of the word for a symposium on *Civilisation—le Mot et l'Idée*. The second was J. Moras' *Ursprung und Entwicklung des Begriffs Zivilisation in Frankreich* (1756–1830) published in the Hamburger Studien zu Volkstum und Kultur der Romanen. These two volumes were followed in 1939 by a third work which gave to the idea of civilization a broad social and historical setting: *Über den Prozess der Zivilisation* by Norbert Elias, the first volume of his *Wandlungen des Verhaltens in den weltlichen Oberschichten des Abendlandes*. In this treatise, Elias brought to light the social and psychological origins of the idea of civilization amid the changing relations of the secular classes in the Western world, examined its relations to the German idea of *Kultur*, and gave it a definite position in the revolutionary movements and international conflicts of the modern age.

From these three researches into the origins of the idea of civilization in France three fundamental conclusions emerged: (1) the word civilization appeared in French writings between 1750 and 1760; (2) the word spread rapidly and widely after 1770—following the outbreak of the conflict between Great Britain and her American colonies; (3) despite some affiliations with the old word civility, the idea of civilization had in the very beginning of its construction the highly dynamic and political sense that was to be associated with it continuously and intimately through the coming centuries.

The first appearance of the word *civilisation* which Febvre was able to report was in *L'Antiquité devoilée par ses usages* —a work by an engineer, M. Boulanger, published in 1766, seven years after the death of the author. In the passage cited by Febvre, Boulanger spoke of a savage people becoming civilized and of civilization as a continuous process. The year after the publication of this work, l'Abbé Badeau wrote: "Landed property is a very important step toward the most perfect civilization."

Though significant for its coming history, the uses of the word civilization by Boulanger and Badeau seem to be rather casual. At all events, if Elias is correct in his historical findings, the idea did not spring into swift and head-stirring circulation at once, in that decade of the eighteenth century in France. Before it struck fire, two terrific socio-political upheavals occurred: in 1773 Americans of Boston threw British tea into their harbor, giving a signal for the American Revolution; in 1774 on the death of Louis XV, a struggle for power in the French court was precipitated which eventuated in the French Revolution. The idea of civilization had apparently made no impression upon Raynal by 1770 when he published the first volume of his philosophical and political history of the Indies. At least he did not use the word a single time in its pages. But four years later, in writing his second volume, he used the word frequently, as if it had become for him a commanding and indispensable term. By this time Diderot had adopted it. In 1774 Holbach declared that nothing put more obstacles in the way of public felicity, the progress of the human reason, and the complete civilization of men than the continual wars into which thoughtless rulers allowed themselves to be drawn. In 1776 Démeunier, in a work on the customs and habits of different peoples, spoke confidently on the *progrès de la civilisation,* therewith recognizing the dynamic character of the idea.

While French usage of the word civilization has been the subject of intensive research by scholars, its history in the English language has been little heeded. Although Adam Ferguson printed the word in his *Essay on the History of Civil Society,* published in 1767, the Oxford English Dictionary, in treating civilization as a social process, reports nothing earlier in English writings than Boswell's note on the term in 1772; all additional references are to later publications. Febvre indulged in some speculations over priority of use: was it French or English? But he gave no definite reply; nor could he. In the present state of knowledge all that can be said with assurance is that the word came into English writing near the middle of the eighteenth century and that it received in England no such general amplification as in France before the end of that century.

No exhaustive searches into the first uses of the word civilization in the English colonies and the United States have yet been made, but it certainly was in the American vocabulary early in the Revolution. When the captive General Burgoyne complained to the American officer, General Gates, about the treatment accorded to British officers and soldiers interned in Massachusetts after the surrender at Saratoga, he accused the inhabitants of lacking "the hospitality or indeed the common civilization to assist us." Presumably Burgoyne was speaking a language which Gates could understand. Certainly leaders of thought and writers on the American side of that war, such as Jefferson, Mercy Warren, and John Adams, were familiar with the idea and brought it into their thinking about history, society, and government. Later in the eighteenth century the word was employed by writers, prominent and obscure, with references to numerous aspects of life, opportunity, policy, and destiny in the United States.

As to the meaning of the word in the minds of those who created it and disseminated it, its etymology gives clear instructions. The word was Latin in sources. It stemmed from the noun *civis,* a citizen, male or female, a fellow-countryman, a native or inhabitant of a country. Out of the same stem came *civilis,* belonging to citizens, relating to public life, civil as opposed to military, civil as opposed to criminal, citizenlike, that is, gracious, affable, and courteous. Out of this stem came also *civiliter,* signifying in a public-spirited manner as becomes a citizen, fair play, constitutional methods of government.

In the course of time, either in the middle ages or near the opening of the modern age, lawyers devised the Latin word *civilizare* and applied it to the act of turning a criminal process into a civil process. From this verb was derived, by the opening of the eighteenth century, a noun, *civilization,* which meant "a law, act of justice, or judgment, which renders a criminal process civil." From some source, possibly the law, the English verb *to civilize* had been taken over for general purposes, at least as early as 1601, and employed as meaning to bring to civility, to make civil, to tame, to bring out of a state of rudeness and barbarism, to instruct in the arts of life, to enlighten, refine, and polish. "The Gospel," declared an English writer in 1641, "Christianizes men and then civilizes them." It may have been from this general usage of the verb *to civilize*, rather than from the legal source, that the word civilization, as a social process, came into circulation near the middle of the eighteenth century.

Whatever relation the social word civilization bore to the legal term civilization, its dynamic character, inherent in the verbal formative *-izare* was confirmed by its early treatment in French literature. In the case of Boulanger, cited first by Febvre, the word was employed as if its content was generally understood in that sense; he emphasized the fact that the act of civilization is to be regarded as continuous, without end. When Badeau declared landed property to be a step toward the most perfect civilization, he evidently had in mind civilization as development, as marked by steps or stages, with a goal in the future. Its dynamic connotation was preserved by those who used the term with etymological precision.

But this precision was not always retained. The word came to be used in a static sense by four kinds of persons and for different reasons. Thinkers faithful to the idea of civilization as a social process legitimately spoke of "stages" in civilization with full recognition of the fact that there was in reality no such thing as a stage in civilization, save in the sense of "a period of development, a degree of progress, a step in a process," each dynamic. To speak of stage in this sense was merely an act of thought necessary to dealing with a social process, an eternal flow of generations, ideas, interests, and agencies. This was, then, merely an act of thought which represented a stage in civilization as an imaginary pause— a figment of the imagination convenient for treating the subject of civilization. In this use of the word, properly understood, the dynamic meaning was preserved.

Other thinkers, however, who recognized the dynamic nature of civilization, for one reason or another dropped into the habit of speaking of "stages" or "ages" in civilization as if its history consisted of "layers" or "periods" in which the process of change stopped or a given routine prevailed absolutely.

Often they gave to these stages or ages specific names, such as barbaric society, savage society, matriarchal society, patriarchal society, and industrial society; or they gave to each age a particular character, such as the stone age, the bronze age, the iron age, the dark age, the power age, the bourgeois age, or the capitalistic age, as if there had actually been breaks in the social process or as if none of the old had perdured into the new. What such thinkers actually did was to attach to the age or period in question a single characteristic as if a phase had been the whole and even a pause in the process. Although legitimate when due cautions and qualifications were employed, as a rule this practice introduced grave misconceptions into the idea of civilization.

The dynamic meaning of the idea in the correct sense was wholly or partly rejected in favor of a static sense by conservatives and radicals. Some conservatives used the word to describe the society in which they lived and which they wished to preserve against changes deemed undesirable by themselves; as perfect or as nearly perfect as it could be, given human nature. For them the idea of civilization became an instrument with which to combat the dynamism of civilization as reality. Some radicals, on the other hand, accepted the idea of changes, stages, or periods in the previous development of society, applied the idea of civilization to one or more stages, but proposed to close the historic process finally by a spring into some kind of utopia or fixed order, Fourierist or Marxist. But such conservative and such radical conceptions of civilization were in flat opposition to the original etymological conception of the word; and what is more: to the historic fact of eternal change in society which changes in generations, ideas, interests, and agencies.

Since the word civilization began to come into wide circulation in France while the Enlightenment was in full flower, it has often been assumed that it was identical with the worldview of the Enlightenment. But this is an unwarranted assumption. Leaders of the Enlightenment did not use the word at all for a long time. And some of them never used it, as far as is known today. If the idea of the Enlightenment, its philosophy, was in some respects in harmony with the idea of civilization, in other and important respects the two world-views diverged. Indeed when the idea of civilization was fully formulated in

France in its etymological purity, it was so opposed to several basic doctrines of the Enlightenment that it signified a breach with the Enlightenment and, for operating purposes, supplanted that world-view in the minds of persons deeply conscious of the intrinsic nature of civilization.

The point of this breach with the Enlightenment cannot be too strongly emphasized, for many writers have blurred both the Enlightenment and Civilization by making them one and the same. They have ignored the newness of the word civilization and have put it into certain writings of French philosophes who had not put it there themselves, who had given no evidence that they were acquainted with the word and the idea at the time of their writing.

The practice of carrying the word civilization backward in time beyond its origins and inserting it into the pages of writers who had not used it, as alleged, is well illustrated in H. T. Buckle's commentaries on Voltaire's historical theories in his *History of Civilization in England*, published in 1857. Buckle quoted in translation the following passage from Voltaire: "I want to know what were the steps by which men passed from barbarism to civilization." Actually what Voltaire said in his French tongue was that he wanted *de voir par quels degrés on est parvenu de la rusticité barbare de ces temps à la politesse du notre*.

A similar practice in the loose translation of French words was followed by J. B. Bury in his treatment of Voltaire and Rousseau in his *The Idea of Progress*. Speaking of Voltaire's historical writings scattered through the years from 1745 to 1769, Bury said: "Voltaire's work amounts to a complete survey of the civilization of the world from the earliest times to his own. If Montesquieu founded social science, Voltaire created the history of civilization."

The central piece of Voltaire's historical writing was his *Essay on the Manners and Mind of Nations . . . from Charlemagne to the death of Louis XIII*, the title of which suggested to other writers the idea of civilization. But the French title of his essay was *Essai sur les moeurs*, not Essay on Civilization, and the word *moeurs* means manners, morals, habits. It was a term to which the world culture may be more suitably attached than the word civilization. Moreover, an examination of Voltaire's original texts on history discloses the fact that he was not thinking of civilization, if that word had come to his attention at all, while he was composing his

Essai between 1745 and 1756. Neither in spirit nor in contents did his historical work correspond to the idea of civilization, even though Bury declares that it "amounts to a complete survey of civilization from the earliest times to his own."

In reality, Voltaire's work on history was devoid of the unity, consistency, and interpretative character that would have marked a history of civilization written in accord with its dynamic, progressive, optimistic meaning. Voltaire had no philosophy of history whatsoever. Bury conceded this when he said: "Voltaire believed that events were determined by chance where they were not guided by reason."

Voltaire's historical thinking was more impressionistic than systematic. His interests, it is true, were far wider than the old staples of history—intrigues in courts, diplomacy, wars, and contests for personal power. His versatile mind was attracted to manners, customs, arts, sciences, and letters; and, in a disconnected fashion, he often dealt with those subjects. But he did not "create" the history of civilization or so entitle his work. His expressions of optimism respecting the progress of science, industry, and humane customs were moderate and never inspired by the confidence out of which the idea of civilization sprang and developed in significance.

In a kindred manner Bury missed the newness and significance of the word civilization and entangled it in the Enlightenment by associating Rousseau with it, in discussing the question: "Was Civilization a Mistake?" As in the case of Voltaire, he made Rousseau appear to be speaking in terms of civilization when in fact he had not used that word at all. Commenting on two discourses or essays written in 1750 and 1754, Bury stated that "the view common to these two discourses [is] that social development has been a gigantic mistake, that the farther man has traveled from a primitive simple state the more unhappy has his lot become, that civilization is radically vicious."

Referring immediately to Rousseau's first essay, *Discours sur cette question: La Rétablissement des Sciences et des Arts a-t-il Contribué a Épurer les Moeurs?* Bury remarked: "In his first *Discourse* he begins by appreciating the specious splendour of modern enlightenment, the voyages of man's intellect among the stars, and then goes on to asseyer that in the first place men have lost, through their civilisation, the original liberty for which they were born, and that arts and sciences, flinging garlands of flowers on the iron chains which bind them, make them love their slavery; and secondly that there is a real depravity beneath the fair semblance and 'our souls are corrupted as our sciences and arts advance to perfection.'"

Yet a careful reading of the *Discours* discovers no use of the word civilization by Rousseau. If Febvre's researches are conclusive, the word was not in print at the time the volume was written; and anyway, the idea ran counter to Rousseau's views of society. Certainly the word is not in the passage paraphrased by Bury. The words which Bury translated as civilization are *les peuples policés*, that is, peoples polished or urbanized. What Rousseau actually said was that peoples lose their liberty through becoming refined or urbanized. He was praising the tough fiber, the rude integrity, the independent martial virtues of the countryman as contrasted with the character of the cityman.

Rousseau's championship of the countryman and his virtues was as ancient as Greek and Roman thought about human nature in society and anticipated a long line of modern social thinking. In expressing a care for the mass of people below the level of *politesse* and urbanity, Rouesseau was dwelling upon the needs and rights of unprivileged orders whose claims were to form in future years and centuries a necessary element in all comprehensive thought about civilization. Both Voltaire and Rousseau contributed to the critical methods that bore fruit in the idea of civilization: Voltaire by the support he gave, if moderate, to the idea of progress; Rousseau by reckoning with the people in general.

Although several writers associated with the Enlightenment did use the word civilization after it came into circulation, all of them who adopted it, save Condorcet, used it formally. None, except Condorcet, explored its significance or gave it a formulation in an interpretation of humanity's history and potentialities. In truth, most of the philosophes of the Enlightenment, notwithstanding various affinities in spirit with the idea of civilization, were hostile to one or more of its basic, vital connotations.

Standing out vividly in the history of the two world-views—Enlightenment and Civilization—are two pertinent facts: *first,* the idea of civilization was not formulated into a comprehensive world-view as an interpretation of humanity's history in the physical universe until all the great philosophes of the

Enlightenment, with the exception of two or three, were dead; *second,* its formulation did not come until two revolutions— one in America, the other in France—were shaking the Western world to its foundations. Saint-Pierre died in 1743, Montesquieu in 1755, Voltaire and Rousseau in 1778, Diderot in 1784, Mably in 1785. Only one of the philosophes, Condorcet, lived to take an active part in the French Revolution and to see the theories of the Enlightenment tested in the fiery furnace of hard practice. And it was Condorcet who first developed the idea of civilization into the world-view of history-interpretation, after 1793—using in the process many ideas of the Enlightenment, discarding others, adopting principles which it had rejected, displaying creative power of thought, giving breadth and force to the idea of civilization.

An effort to comprehend the nature of the idea of civilization as a world-view, with special reference to French realities, makes it necessary, therefore, to study Condorcet, his circle of reflective thinkers—French, English, and American —and the circumstances connected with the formulation of this idea which he completed just before his tragic ending in 1794. The setting, the companions, the demiurgic intellectual and political activities of the times, as well as Condorcet the man and thinker, all come into the operation of discovering the meaning in the idea of civilization in France as a world-view, a theory of interpretation of history.

The scion of a noble family, born in 1743, the year of Abbé Saint-Pierre's death, Condorcet, after some education under Jesuit auspices, took up his residence in Paris in 1762, achieved honors as a mathematician, and became a colleague of the men then at work in the Enlightenment—Voltaire, Diderot, Turgot, and Quesnay, for example. In 1786 he married Sophie de Grouchy, daughter of the Marquis de Grouchy, a young woman of talents, high spirits, and zealous interest in the intellectual current then running in a swollen stream.

The home of the Condorcets, as described by J. Salwyn Schapiro in his *Condorcet and the Rise of Liberalism,* was a center at which leading personalities of the time gathered to discuss the momentous issues of the age. To their home came not only compatriots but also English and American thinkers of the first order. Adam Smith was a guest of the household and Madame Condorcet translated his *Theory of Moral Senti-*

ments into French. Still more significant for the formulation of the idea of civilization, two idealists of the American Revolution became intimates of the circle. The first was Thomas Jefferson who succeeded Franklin as the American minister to France in 1785. The second was Thomas Paine who spent most of the time between 1789 and 1802 in France. Madame Condorcet translated many of Paine's speeches into French, and Condorcet worked closely with him in evolving revolutionary tactics and drafting constitutional plans for France after the political storm broke there in 1789. In addition, Condorcet, as much as any of his French contemporaries, if not more, appreciated the importance of the American Revolution for the history of the world, and made it a point to study with great care documents which were issued during and after that Revolution, especially those reflecting its democratic aspects. It was here that he diverged in fundamental respects from the majority of the philosophes who had fostered the Enlightenment. Great leaders among them despised democracy, the mass of the people, notwithstanding all their prating about "humanity."

As Schapiro says, "for the masses, *la canaille,* the philosophes had the most withering scorn and the utmost contempt. According to Voltaire they were cattle and all that they required were a yoke, a goad, and fodder. The communistic Mably was no less severe in his hatred of democracy than was the bourgeois Voltaire. . . . D'Holbach hated the masses as 'an imbecile populace who, having no intelligence and no common sense, is always ready to be the instrument and the accomplice of turbulent demagogues who wish to trouble society.' " Although Condorcet cherished no such hatreds, even in the early stages of his development, he too had feared democracy and advocated property limitations on the right to vote.

From the humanity about which they talked and wrote endlessly the philosophes also excluded women. Their attitude toward women, as Shapiro documents it, "was, on the whole, conventional. They shared in the popular view that woman was naturally inferior to man. The most revolutionary of the philosophes, Rousseau, had the most traditional view of women. Rousseau restricted women to position of wife and mother, whose education and activity were to be severely limited. Diderot wrote a severe condemnation of women, as an inferior sex, who were constantly conspiring to maintain their domination over men."

Whatever reservations Condorcet had entertained on the subject of democracy, when he came to the final act of presenting his world-view he criticized historians for leaving the people out of account and took the position that "history should concern itself chiefly with the condition of the masses of mankind." In that treatise he espoused the doctrine of popular sovereignty in government, while recognizing the need for political machinery to refine and mature the pressure of public opinion on government.

In his attitude toward women, Condorcet differed from the French philosophes. He maintained that women in general were naturally equal in mental power to men in general but that the character of their education and discouragements by conventional men and women acted as repressive forces on women. In his vision of the future, woman was to have full freedom in developing her powers, enjoy the same social and economic rights as man, and as an *être sensible* possess and exercise full citizenship.

Although his doctrines pertaining to women flowed logically from his major premise on human rights, they were no doubt influenced in part by his personal experiences with women. His wife had been his constant companion, hostess to the visitors at their home, and a critical thinker in the intellectual activities of their circle and in the course of the French Revolution. To that association Condorcet added two lofty tests of woman's character and moral power. When he was proscribed by the Terrorists, it was Madame Vernet who risked her life for him by giving him a secret refuge in her house; and it was a woman, Madame Condorcet, who supported him, herself, and their daughter during this hour of trial "by painting miniatures and selling lingerie."

With tense brevity Schapiro tells the story: "When Condorcet received news of the execution of the Girondins he became concerned, not about himself, but his benefactress, who was violating the law in harboring a refugee. If he was discovered in her house she, as well as he, would be dragged to the guillotine. Condorcet told Madame Vernet that he would leave her pension. But that brave and generous woman refused to hear of it. 'The Convention has the power to put you outside the law (*hors de loi*), but it has not the power to put you outside of humanity. You will remain' she told him. . . . He made efforts to escape from his retreat, which were, however, foiled by Madame Vernet who kept a watchful eye on her guest. . . . He wanted to leave the pension because of the danger to *her;* and she refused to let him do so because of the danger to *him.* One day Condorcet managed to elude his watchful benefactress and escaped her house in disguise"—to his tragic doom. But in the meantime, dissuaded by his wife from merely completing a memoir justifying his part in the Revolution, he had finished at Madame Vernet's home the manuscript of his work which, as Schapiro says, was to "justify mankind itself" and ground the idea of civilization for all time in an interpretation of history.

The manuscript which Condorcet left behind him was a historical sketch of intellectual progress called *Esquisse d'un Tableau Historique des Progrès de l'Esprit Humain.* Although this book, published in 1795, contained in its title the word Progress and modern writers have treated it under the head of Progress, it was not just that world-view as formulated in the Enlightenment. It was in truth a theory of history that constituted a revolution in thought about the nature, origin, and course of all human societies through the immensity of the past, projected into the eternity of the future. Its import is unmistakable when it is placed between interpretations of history prior to the opening of the eighteenth century and interpretations of history generally prevailing among writers of history in our own times. It was as revolutionary in its consequences as the idea that the kind of history taught in the schools and read by politicians, statesmen, and citizens has a determinative effect upon the actions and destinies of nations.

What Condorcet really did in this revolutionary act of thought was to fuse two relatively new ideas with the idea of civilization. One which he used was the idea of progress, formulated early in the eighteenth century as an optimistic interpretation of human powers and destiny and a projection of progress into the indefinite future. The second was a theory of interpretation or philosophy of history which had been formulated near the middle of the eighteenth century.

This is not the place to enter into a thousand-page exposition of the rise and progress of history interpretations in Western thought—a recondite subject which some of the keenest minds of the past two hundred years have studied, speculated upon, and written about. But five general propositions will hint at the high significance of Condorcet's performance. (1) Between the rise of Christianity and the opening of the seventeenth century, history was extensively treated as if it had been merely chapters of more or less unrelated accidents and mechanisms in which God interfered at times and in places at His own pleasure and for His own ends in executing His great design. (2) Late in the seventeenth century Bishop Bossuet in France laid history on the foundations of universality, but retained the idea of divine interventions at divine pleasure. (3) Near the middle of the eighteenth century Montesquieu made the beginning of a social history by showing that various laws, customs, institutions—parts of the social ensemble—are not accidental but have necessary interrelationships synchronously. (4) A few years later Turgot, rejecting the old theory that history moves in circles and indeed all theories of history combining accidents, incidents, and divine interventions, declared that "All the ages are linked together in a succession of causes and effects which bind the [present] state of the world to all the states that have gone before." (5) Condorcet united the conceptions of Montesquieu and Turgot with the idea of progress, treated the history of the ages as a necessary succession of stages or orders, with progress or creative energies at work in this development, all bound in a tendency to accumulate for mankind immense advantages, constituting in effect the grand progress of civilization.

If to those who knew nothing about the intellectual history of mankind this contribution by Condorcet seemed remote and speculative, anyone who stopped to inquire under what fragments of views he himself was actually making practical decisions of the gravest import could realize that Condorcet had given mankind a body of thought and fact— a world-view—not to be lightly rejected. More than this. As Condorcet's theory of history seeped into academies, history books, scholars' studies, essays on history, arguments and contentions based on alleged historical proof, and a hundred other forms of writing, it helped to alter the mental and moral outlook of multitudes who never had heard of his name and would have disowned him if they had known the sources of their thinking. Are we bound to a treadmill that ever goes around and around through the ages? Do we stand still doing the same things and getting nowhere? Do we slide downward into degradation and evil? Is everything just No-Thing?

Or is there progress in human good and ground for faith in improvement? Condorcet was as great and as important for the history of civilization as are these questions and the answers which men and women make in ordering their individual and collective actions.

The divisions of the *Sketch* indicate the nature of Condorcet's argument: men united into hordes; pastoral state and transition; progress to the alphabet; Greece; progress in sciences; decline of learning to the Crusades; printing; throwing off the yoke of authority; from Descartes to the French Republic; future progress. The historical part traced the progress of humanity, through nine epochs, to the degree of civilization that had been reached in 1793, especially in France, England, and America.

Besides using the word civilization frequently in his pages, with definite meaning, Condorcet employed it to cover a long process in history to which his chapters on the past were devoted. Although he occasionally referred to civilization as a state of things, his conception of the term embraced its original, intrinsic, and dynamic significance. To Condorcet, civilization at any place or time was merely a stage or degree in the endless process of human development toward more sublime achievements.

Without attempting to explain just how humanity crossed the great divide between barbarism and civilization, Condorcet opened with a survey of social beginnings: "The first state of civilization observable in the human species is that of a society of men, few in number, subsisting by means of hunting and fishing, unacquainted with every art but the imperfect one of fabricating in an uncouth manner their arms and some household utensils, and of constructing or digging for themselves a habitation; yet already in possession of a language for the communication of their wants and a small number of moral ideas, from which are deduced their common rules of conduct, living in families, conforming themselves to the general customs that serve instead of laws, and having even a rude form of government. In this state it is apparent that the uncertainty and difficulty of procuring subsistence, and the unavoidable alternative of extreme fatigue or an absolute repose, leave not to man the leisure in which, by resigning himself to meditation, he might enrich his mind with new contributions. The means of satisfying his wants are even too dependent upon chance and the seasons, useful to excite an industry, the progressive improvement of which might be transmitted to his progeny; and accordingly the attention of each is confined to the improvement of his individual skill and address."

Progress in civilization was, therefore, necessarily slow but, despite many vicissitudes, it continued until civilization represented by the degree attained in his own time was reached. "It is between this degree of civilization and that in which we still find the savage tribes, that we must place every people whose whole history has been handed down to us, and who, sometimes making new advancements, sometimes plunging themselves into ignorance, sometimes floating between the two alternatives, or stopping at a certain limit, sometimes totally disappearing from the earth under the sword of conquerors, mixing with those conquerors, or living in slavery; lastly sometimes receiving knowledge from a more enlightened people, to transmit it to other nations . . . form an unbroken chain of connections between the earliest periods of history and the age in which we live, between the first people known to us, and the present nations of Europe." Such was Condorcet's panorama of peoples in varying stages of "civilization" from barbarism to his own era.

To Condorcet it seemed that the great achievements in the process of civilization had been brought about by the advancement of knowledge, the invention of the alphabet, Greek thought, the invention of printing, and the scientific revolution effected in the century preceding the French Revolution.

Condorcet's limitation of progress to "the improvement of intelligence," John Morley long afterward pronounced "the most fatal of the errors" in the *Sketch*, in that it measured "only the contributions made by nations and eras to what we know; leaving out of sight their failures and successes in the elevation of moral standards and ideals, in the purification of human passions. . . . One seeks in vain in Condorcet's sketch for any account of the natural history of western morals, or for any sign of consciousness on his part that the difference in ethical discipline and feeling between the most ferocious of primitive tribes and the most enlightened eighteenth-century Frenchmen, was the result of an evolution that needed historical explanation, quite as much as the astrolatry of one age and the astronomy of another. . . . The grave and lofty feeling, for example, which inspired the last words of the *Tableau* [his *Sketch*]—whence came it?"

Moreover Condorcet transferred to Christianity his hatred for ecclesiastics and theology, ignoring the humanizing and civilizing influences of its ethical teachings on the passions and distempers of human beings. His scornful treatment of religion was not only one-sided; it belied the scientific spirit which he exalted and, as Morley said of it, it was utterly damaging to the completeness of his *Sketch*.

By his neglect of moral forces in history and his scorn for the Christian religion, Condorcet failed to press his formulation to the full limits of the content imperative to the idea of civilization. In concentrating on the progress of knowledge, he departed radically from the spirit of the idea as his friend Thomas Jefferson had conceived it years before the *Sketch* was written, vitiated his thesis for many thoughtful readers, and made it insufficient, if not wholly unacceptable, in this respect, to a large body of Americans who formulated, affirmed, and applied the idea of civilization.

But Condorcet was deeply concerned with the application of knowledge to human welfare—surely a problem in all places and times—far more than many a critic who deplored his neglect of morals and religion. Hitherto, he lamented, historians had busied themselves with the minority who lived on the labor of others and had overlooked the mass of impoverished and oppressed workers in country and town. Committed by his ultimate revolutionary convictions to the humanity-ethos, to the idea of equality among all men and women, Condorcet insisted that in the coming years the whole body of people would be brought into the tasks and rewards of civilization.

In history the fact of progress is established, he contended. Knowledge of this fact when applied enables humanity to shape the direction of civilization and to accelerate it. "The movement," as Bury compressed Condorcet's philosophy, "may vary in velocity, but it will never be retrograde so long as the earth occupies its present place in the cosmic system and the general laws of this system do not produce some catastrophe or change which would deprive the human race of the faculties and resources which it has hitherto possessed. There will be no relapse into barbarism. The guarantees against this danger are the discovery of true methods in the physical sciences, their application to the needs of men, the lines of communication which have been established among them, the great number of those who study them, and finally the art of printing."

From his theory of history already made, Condorcet deduced a guarantee that in the coming years the advance of civilization would be assured, stimulated, and widened by conscious, reasoned, and planned promotion. Calamities deep and dark might intervene. Yet the strength of civilization would not fail; would, in fact, effect greater gains in the future. "We shall find in the experience of the past, in the observation of the progress which the sciences, which civilization, have made to the present, in the analysis of the march of the human spirit and of development in the human faculties, the strongest motives for believing that nature has set no limits to our hopes."

Sensitive to the dilemma of human misery persisting side by side with civilization, Condorcet sought to come to grips with it. He fully understood that the political revolution, making men equal in voting power and before the law, had not resolved it, had not introduced the social equality which civilization required. He acknowledged the existing inequality in wealth, inequality of persons possessing wealth and persons depending merely upon their labor for subsistence, inequality in education, inequality in health.

But, rejecting the arguments of contemporary communists, he sought other ways than theirs out of the dilemma, without attempting to go into details. Some inequalities could be smoothed away, he thought, by a system of life insurance, by popular education, and by improvements in medical science; and in the course of time the progress of knowledge and science would make the civilized way of life flourish without recourse to violence. He was not utopian in the sense of expecting an immediate or distant closure of the struggle toward perfection. He regarded the evolution of civilization as having no finite limits.

True to the cosmopolitan spirit of his age in France, Condorcet looked forward to a removal of disparities in civilization throughout the world, realizing the ideal of equality among all branches of mankind. In the civilizing process, spreading everywhere, the backward peoples of the earth would be brought up to the level of civilization existing in

England, France, and the United States and the staggered line of mankind's march made straighter. Indeed, by the very nature of his historical interpretation, he was committed to this hope. All human beings, he maintained, possessed the faculty of reasoning and could acquire knowledge. No race was excluded from humanity. Through civilization wars among nations would cease; and civilization, however strongly marked by national peculiarities, would become universal.

In Condorcet's *Sketch* the idea of civilization was given its first systematic relation to a theory of history. And before the eighteenth century came to a close, the idea of civilization had acquired such an influence in Western thinking that reflective participants in the turbulent events of the age, whether revolutionary or counter-revolutionary in partianship, often felt under compunction to try men and causes by its standards. As time passed it became increasingly difficult to discuss the ideas and interests pitted against one another in the forum of opinion without reckoning with the idea of civilization.

Even conservatives could be pleased with and utilize the word when it was defined simply as "the state of being civilized." What conservative could think of the social order which he defended or desired as only half or partly civilized? What patriot, content with the degree of civilization attained in his own country, could avoid looking upon its civilization as completed or practically completed?

Moreover, conservatives, finding themselves losing ground in the contest during the period of the French Revolution, could see good tactics in taking over the idea so potent in the campaigns of radicals and in rendering it innocuous or turning it to account in their cause. At all events, before the end of the century that high priest of the conservative Reaction, Edmund Burke, appropriated the word civilization, made it static, and declared himself the champion of civilization against the vulgar, brutal, and swinish multitude engaged in making the Revolution in France. And Burke's example was followed, if sometimes cautiously, by many writers occupied in defending historical conservatism in France, England, and the United States against the progressive spirit of civilization as it was affirmed by Condorcet, Thomas Jefferson, and Thomas Paine.

But conservatives were seldom, if ever, perfectly happy

with the word civilization. Nor were they able to monopolize it or neutralize it entirely by restricting its meaning to some order of society which they deemed so high as to be about perfect. Even when they added the adjective "true" to it and spoke of "true civilization," they acknowledged its troublesome nature. The kinetics of the idea eluded their grasp and persisted, gaining force as the idea was developed and applied; as changes, apparently remorseless, continued in unfolding history, shattering historical conservatism and altering "the static orders" which they fain would have defended to the last ditch.

For a long time circumstances in France were especially propitious for the study, application, and documentation of the idea of civilization. From 1789 to 1850 France was in a highly convulsionary condition. The first revolution was followed, it is true, by a restoration of the Bourbon monarchy. But in 1830 the Bourbon regime was overthrown and a "liberal" Orleanist monarchy substituted, that is, a bourgeois government with Louis Philippe as the titular head and François Guizot serving him as minister or prime minister. Driven underground for the moment, republicanism broke out again in 1848 and abolished that monarchy, only to culminate in the empire of the third Napoleon. Even so, the revolution of 1848, strongly marked by socialist agitations, went far beyond mere politics. Its agitations, long in preparation, affected every feature of society—economic, scientific, literary, and philosophic.

Such, in bare outline, were the circumstances in France which favored a continuous concern with the idea of civilization, its use in discussions of revolutionary events visible to the eye, and efforts to apply it in the interests of dynamism or stablization. The very names of French thinkers who assumed intellectual leadership in this period suggest the versatility and vigor of French thought about the interpretation of history— such names as Madame de Staël, Guizot, Taine, Michelet, Saint-Simon, Fourier, Louis Blanc, and Victor Cousin.

During this period, in which French thought displayed high tension and creative tendencies, if sometimes mere sentimentality, British thought in respect of the idea of civilization was singularly sterile. Great leaders of the Enlightenment, such as Voltaire, Diderot, Lafayette, Madame Roland, and Montesquieu, had derived inspiration from British political theory, had praised the liberty enjoyed by British subjects, had caught revolutionary fervor from the example of British resistance to royal absolutisms; for the British middle class had put a king to death in 1649 and dethroned another in 1688.

But after 1793 Great Britain became the representative and organizer of the counter-revolutionary movement in Europe. The British government, with profuse brutality, suppressed democratic agitations at home and, with dogged pertinacity, formed against France coalitions or working agreements with the most despotic and tyrannical governments on the Continent—Russia, Prussia, and Austria. Following the final defeat of Napoleon in 1815, the British governing classes, the privileged orders, opposed democratic agitations with all the weapons of intelligence and physical force at their command; with fierce intolerance. There were protestants, no doubt, notably Byron, Shelley, and Robert Owen; but the British aristocracy, as the bulwark of the Tory reaction, was little interested in promoting civilization. It was more interested in stopping the processes of civilization which threatened its Throne and Altar, its privileges and plunder.

Thought in America was influenced by repercussions from European events, directly and indirectly. Through the years of revolutionary agitations in France and reactions in England, American sympathies were strongly on the side of French reformism, at least until the Reign of Terror. To be sure, in important quarters, Tories who remained in the United States after the winning of independence kept preference for English conservatism warm and in this propensity were joined by many Federalists with whom they were usually associated in politics. But Tories and Federalists gradually lost power and by 1820 they were little more than a fretful and quarrelsome minority.

As J. Franklin Jameson rightly interpreted it in a compact little volume, *The American Revolution Considered as a Social Movement*, the upheaval in America had rocked society from center to circumference. It was followed by a repudiation of privileged orders and by an insurgent democratic movement which culminated in the triumph of Jefferson in 1800. After the die was cast even leading conservatives united with democrats in developing a new order of human relations on this continent; and in vital respects this new order presented a sharp contradiction to the old regime in Europe, against which the revolutionary energies of France were likewise directed.

Each popular uprising in Paris was greeted with enthusiasm by democrats in the United States. If a few American students from New England went to conservative Germany to secure university training, holding aloof from Oxford and Cambridge, many Americans visited France and thousands of Americans got an education in French ideas, theories, and sentiments through reading French authors. Varieties of evidence point to the conclusion that the development of the idea of civilization in the United States was deeply and persistently influenced by French thought or, speaking more strictly by the historical record, the influences were reciprocal.

In several ways the American spirit was prepared for an interchange of opinions on the subject of civilization. Patriots in the new nation claimed to have uprooted privileged orders, established self-government, and started popular movements on the course to the fulfilment of equalitarian logic. And it was around this general theme in another setting that political debate and agitation revolved in France, with the idea of civilization coming into greater prominence and power as the discussion proceeded amid the turbulence of French experience.

In the twistings and turnings of the struggle between the Revolution and the Reaction in France for dominion over the French mind, the idea of civilization gained in degree of sovereignty. As Lochore documents the case in his *History of the Idea of Civilization in France,* the idea seems to have escaped few of the prominent thinkers and writers active in that country during the first half of the new century. It was conspicuous in the analysis and interpretation of every primary theme of public and private life, from criminology, democracy, family, and feminism, to history, politics, and science. Schools of religious and secular thought appeared unable to carry on their work without attacking, defending, or at least discussing the idea of civilization in its bearings upon their special interests. Among the leading expositions of the idea the following had particular relevance to American affairs and found large receptivity in the United States: civilization with bourgeois individualism as upshot; and civilization with reformism or socialism as upshot.

The first type of exposition was developed in its classic form by François Guizot, savant, statesman, and orator. Guizot was the son of Protestant parents belonging to the middle class. His father perished on the scaffold during the Reign of Terror and young Guizot received his early education in Switzerland to which his mother fled with him. Owing to his adoption of moderate views as he became an adult, he was able to return to Paris in 1805 under Napoleon's regime, study law, and then take up literary pursuits. After achieving a reputation by his translation of Gibbon's *The Decline and Fall of the Roman Empire,* he won an appointment at the Sorbonne as lecturer in modern history.

During the conflicts that followed the downfall of Napoleon and the restoration of the Bourbons, Guizot steered a middle course. He warned Louis XVIII that only the pursuit of a liberal, or compromise, policy could assure the continuance of the monarchy. Although still a young man Guizot had become convinced that the hope for peace and progress lay in a steady course between the absolutism of the old order and the Jacobinism of the Revolution. He rejected, alike, the militarism of Napoleon, the despotism of the Bourbons, the extreme fervor of democracy, and all communistic systems. He proposed, in short, a moderate program of political theory and practice.

Many immediate influences contributed to the formation of Guizot's character and opinions. His early studies were carried on under the supervision of his mother who, at great personal solicitude and sacrifice, guarded and educated her children left fatherless by the Revolution. Later, in Paris, he became acquainted with members of the Academy; and at various salons, including that of Madame d'Houdetot, he took part in discussions of philosophy, literature, history, art, sciences, old times, new times, and foreign countries.

Through his marriage to Pauline Meulan, he came into closer contact with aristocratic families. She was herself a writer of some distinction, with important literary connections. But she was not a defender of the old regime. If Guizot remembered bitterly the Terror which had guillotined his father, his wife was able to think of the Revolution as a whole, in a more objective way. A student of Locke, Condillac, and Helvétius, she had acquired an intimacy with revolutionary thought and was inclined to liberty of opinion. Although the cruelty of the revolutionary outbreak was repugnant to her, the bigotry and cruelty of the monarchists were also alien to her nature. It was said of her later that she combined the refinements of the old regime with the "frank, open, and somewhat unconventional habits of the Revolution." After planning to write on the history of France and the Revolution in England, she urged Guizot to take up the projects and promised to do the drudgery for him. In such circumstances he began the work that ended in his *Histoire de la Civilisation en Europe* and his *Histoire de la Civilisation en France*.

In various writings and lectures, including his treatise on the origins of representative government, Guizot openly revealed his underlying purpose. It was to combat revolutionary excesses: "to separate revolutionary excitement and phantasies from the advances of justice and liberty reconcilable to the eternal laws of social order," and to elicit interest, especially among the rising generation, in those phases of European and French history which had a direct bearing on the advancement of civilization in France. The people had just emerged from the furious struggle against old France in which the good had often been condemned with the evil. They were indifferent to, if not full of anger toward, their heritage from previous ages. The time had come, he proclaimed, to clear away the ruins, to substitute thought and equity for hostility, to exalt the principles of liberty instead of the arms of the Revolution, to vanquish ignorance, prejudices, and inveterate antipathies which stood in the way of concentrating talents on the tasks of civilization.

With this large objective in mind, Guizot studied the great problems of social organization in the name of which parties and classes had exchanged heavy blows in the centuries past: the sovereignty of the people and the power of kings; monarchy and republicanism; aristocracy and democracy; unity and division of powers. Patiently he traced the efforts of the French people to make order out of chaos, the recurring struggles of royalty, nobility, clergy, citizens, and masses through the different phases of their destiny—the glorious but incomplete development of French civilization, of which the Revolution had been but a chapter preliminary to inspiring tasks now ahead.

In his *Histoire de la Civilisation en Europe*, which later, in translation, had an immense vogue in the United States, Guizot expounded his conception of the work he had undertaken. He opened with the debate over the question whether civilization is a good or an evil. One party had derided it as teeming with mischief for mankind; a second party had praised it as the means by which humanity would attain the highest dignity and excellence. Coupled with this inquiry was another: Is there a civilization of the whole human race, a course for all humanity to run, a destiny for it to accomplish, a growing heritage to be transmitted from age to age, with nations contributing to the riches of their successors— a common stock carried on until the end of all things?

Having raised these questions, Guizot confidently replied to them: "For my part, I feel assured that human nature has such a destiny; that a general civilization pervades the human race; that at every epoch it augments; and that there is, consequently, a universal history of civilization to be written. Nor have I any hesitation in asserting that this history is the most noble, the most interesting of any, and that it comprehends every other."

Civilization, Guizot insisted, was among the facts of history. "It is so general that its nature can scarcely be seized; so complicated that it can scarcely be unravelled; so hidden as to be scarcely discernible . . . but its existence, its worthiness to be described and to be recounted is not less certain and manifest." Civilization is "the great fact in which all others merge; in which they all end, in which they are all condensed, in which all others find their importance." If you should take all other facts—institutions, commerce, wars, and details of government—if you would form some idea of them as a whole, see their bearings on one another, appreciate their value, pass a judgment on them, what would you want to know? "Why, what they have done to forward the progress of civilization . . . what influence they have exercised in aiding its advance." Even the evil nature of events is to be partly overlooked if they have contributed to this progress in civilization.

Coming to the content of the idea, Guizot defined civilization as embracing all the wealth of the people, all features of its life, all the powers of its existence, and as presenting two aspects. "Two elements, then, seem to be comprised in the great fact which we call civilization": the progress of society and the progress of individuals; or the melioration of the social system and the expansion of the mind and faculties of man.

Running parallel or intermingled in history are changes in the individual and changes in his exterior relations. Is either element alone sufficient to constitute civilization? Here Guizot confronted the fundamental problem in civilization: Is it reforms in systems or in the internal spirit of individuals that advance civilization? And he resolved that conflict by summoning the contestants as witnesses. When any great exterior reform in society is proposed, its adversaries declare that it will not improve the mental and moral state of the people, but its friends assert that it will lead to the progress of intelligence and morals. When advocates of interior or intellectual and moral reforms plead their cause, they declare that it will also lead to the melioration of systems—better social conditions and the more equitable distribution of life's blessings. The two are in fact forever inseparable in the thought and practice of mankind.

Hence, Guizot concluded, "it is the intuitive belief of mankind that these two elements of civilization are intimately connected; that they reciprocally produce each other." The expansion of intelligence redounds to the advantage of society, and the great advances in social improvement, in turn, are of service to individuals. Moral reformers seek to bend their reforms to the advantage of others, and to institutionalize them.

But when Guizot began to select the materials for his history of civilization he chose to write on "the exterior events of the visible and social world," while merely expressing a wish that it were possible for him to write the history of the interior world also—the intellectual and moral advance of individuals. In fact he did not cover even the "visible world" —all the arts, applied sciences, and meliorative forces made objective in institutions. He confined himself mainly to the rise and development of political and ecclesiastical institutions. He represented the State principally as the guardian of order and property, as property was then conceived, and left to individuals the promotion of civilization as represented by other phases of life. In actual performance Guizot anticipated the social philosophy of William Graham Sumner who, in

1872, two years before Guizot's death, took up at Yale University the elaboration of the doctrine that, if government keeps order, protects property, restricts its functions within narrow limits, the initiative and energy of individuals will carry forward and advance civilization.

While Guizot's written history lacked comprehensiveness in substance, it affirmed the dynamic nature of the idea, a faith in history as progress, development, advancement. The very word civilization, he said, "awakens, when it is pronounced, the idea of a people which is in motion, not to change its place but to change its state, a people whose condition is expanding and improving. The idea of progress, development, seems to me to be the fundamental idea contained in the word *civilisation.*"

By improvement Guizot meant not merely "the improvement of social relations and public well-being," but also the development of individual life, "faculties, sentiments, and ideas." He expanded this definition: Christianity, appealing to the sentiments and aspirations of the people, did not at first attack the evils of the Roman State; yet in time the spirit which it awakened did find expression in higher forms of social welfare. Through fifteen centuries the civilization of Europe had been slowly and continuously unfolding and "the vista of an immense career" loomed on the horizon. This thesis Guizot proffered as fact, not as a metaphysical explanation of the universe in the fashion of German philosophers; and the very method of treatment made his work all the more attractive to the pragmatic temper in the United States.

For this and other reasons, Guizot's histories of civilization, in English translations, acquired an extensive circulation in America to the end of the nineteenth century and beyond. Successive reprints in cheap form proved its enduring interest. In a letter to Jared Sparks, president of Harvard College, in 1851, Henry C. Carey, the economist, declared that "Guizot's 'History of Civilization' is used in half the colleges of the country." Carey complained that it was, unfortunately, "a mere mass of facts communicated in the most unphilosophical manner," and that Guizot's first chapter "exposed his entire inability to define the thing of which he wrote, proving that it was with him a mere word, not a distinct idea." And in complaining, Carey gave vent to the opinion that Americans should be emancipated from bondage to European writers, especially when they proffered theories of democracy current in Rome and Paris. Nevertheless, Harvard made Guizot a Doctor of Laws the very next year and his histories long maintained their popularity.

While Guizot was proclaiming his doctrines and later exemplifying them as head of the French government under the bourgeois monarch, Louis-Phillipe, other French writers were explaining and applying the idea of civilization, often extending it to embrace socialism of some type. Among writers of this bent who were influential in the United States were Saint-Simon, Michelet, Considérant, Sismondi, and Fourier.

All agreed that the idea of civilization had positive social content; that the bourgeois police-state, preserving order and protecting property, was not enough; that human misery could not be overcome by such a system of government; that the logic of the Revolution, with its premise of equality, brought the whole body of the people into purview; that the advance of civilization required drastic alterations in property relations, in the prevailing modes of producing and distributing wealth. But whether the process of civilization would be long in time and ever-creative or soon brought to a triumph in a kind of utopian order was an issue on which they greatly differed.

Fourier visualized "the perfect society as the final state in a process of historical change whose principal epochs after the fall from Eden are savagery, patriarchy, barbarism, civilization, guarantyism, simple association, and finally complete association of harmony." The term civilization, used in a special sense, he applied to the period in which he found himself—the society which he contemned as "unorganized, irrational, the prey of caprice, force, and fraud."

In a special sense it was also used by Parke Godwin, the American reformer, under the title *Constructive and Pacific Democracy*, in 1843, an Americanized edition of the *Manifesto* on Fourierism, prepared by Victor Considérant, Fourier's disciple. Attacking the negativism of political democracy and the creed of laissez faire, Godwin declared: "Your democratic civilization, which began in aristocratic feudalism —the progress of which has emancipated the working-classes from direct and personal servitude only—will end in a monied aristocracy that leads to a collective and indirect servitude just as oppressive as that from which we have so lately been relieved." Godwin prefaced his edition of the *Manifesto* with a quotation from W. H. Channing confessing a belief that "our present low state of civilization" will not last forever and "in Christianity and in the powers and principles of human nature, we have the promise of something holier and happier than now exists."

While Fourier treated history as a series of stages culminating in the existing civilization full of evils and proposed to move on into a utopia of associationism, his older contemporary, the Comte de Saint-Simon, likewise a socialist, subscribed to a view of civilization more akin to that held by Condorcet. Indeed Saint-Simon accepted Condorcet as his master in many respects while dissenting in others. In his interpretation of history Condorcet had attributed progress largely to the development of knowledge and the rational faculties. Like so many among the philosophers of the French revolutionary era who were battling against the authoritarianism of Church and State, he had derogated the role of religion in human affairs and disposed of the middle ages as a wretched barrier in the way of civilization. But Saint-Simon viewed Christianity as a humanizing force in history and it so appeared in his interpretation of history as a progressive movement. Moreover he recognized the fact that all great phases of civilization in development are intimately related and must be considered in any comprehensive system of thought about civilization. Thus, for Saint-Simon, the middle ages, instead of being merely the miserable epoch of barbarism so often depicted by hostile writers, actually signalized advance in the progress of humanity toward "the golden age" which "is not behind us, but in front of us."

On this interpretation of history Saint-Simon based his "law" of historical development—the alternation of periods of organization or construction with periods of criticism or revolution. In this scheme, as he framed it, the middle ages had been constructive. They were followed by an era of criticism and revolution. Now a new period of organizing work had opened. In the new period the sciences would be positively applied to the improvement of social conditions, in the humane spirit; and scientists, as organizers and managers, would assume a constructive role akin to that of the clergy in the middle ages.

Their first task would be to ameliorate the lot of the working classes, that is, the great majority of the people, and their method of accomplishing this end would be socialistic. When the new age of construction arrives, the revolutionary or critical ideas of democracy, liberty, and equality must be cast off as inapplicable to the formation and operation of a scientific and managerial order of economy and society. In support of his program, Saint-Simon invoked the spirit of "the new Christianity."

Besides proclaiming the approach of an industrial society under scientific management, thus substituting a positive conclusion for Condorcet's endless progress, Saint-Simon—now following Condorcet's line—searched for methods of bringing peace to Europe. In this connection he had his American experience to guide him. He had taken part in the American War of Independence and was proud that he had been a soldier under George Washington. The Americans had formed a federation of states and pointed the way, he thought, to an organization of the European states. So looking upon war as a deadly foe of civilization, as nearly all the exponents of the idea had done, Saint-Simon proposed a union in Europe to suppress it. Under his plan each European state would have its own legislature and a general congress would control common affairs. In this way the energies of the nations would be released from war and directed to the production of goods, scientifically managed, making possible an extension of the area of civilization.

Despite variations in emphasis and careless usages, the idea of civilization in France, treated as a composite made by fusing the conceptions of Condorcet, Guizot, and other thinkers in that line, enclosed in its comprehensive worldview an interpretation of history as a progressive conflict between civilizing and barbarizing influences, actions, and instruments; the advocacy of a general equality of human beings in rights to life, liberty, and the pursuit of happiness; all manifestations of the true, the beautiful, the useful, and the good; the employment of the sciences, arts, letters, mechanical inventions, and all other fruits of the creative spirit for the advantage of mankind; a diversity in the achievements of civilization among peoples and nations; the establishment of international peace; and unending progress in the advancement of commodious and humane living. If some French commentators on the idea, such as Saint-Simon and Fourier, thought that civilization would eventually be closed in a final order, in a utopia, nearly all anticipated the continuance of the process of civilization in the ages to come.

From this survey emerges the conclusion that the origin and general formulation of the idea of civilization synchronized in Europe with the rise of unrest in the American colonies, the revolution against Great Britain, the establishment of the Republic, and efforts of Americans to strengthen and enrich the independent society which they had brought into being. French and British thinkers developed the idea with reference to the history, spirit, and controversies of their respective nations. In the United States intellectual leaders examined it, made their own formulation, and applied it to the special circumstances of this country, in the conviction that the conditions of social life, the spirit of the people, the abundance of resources, and remoteness from what Jefferson called the eternal wars of Europe gave unique features to civilization in America and afforded magnificent opportunities to advance it swiftly on this continent.

Chapter 4

Formulation and Affirmation in the Early Republic

AFTER THE YOKE of the British government had been cast off and the Republic safely launched, reflective thinkers in the United States meditated upon their heritage, the place of the recent revolutionary act in the long drama of mankind, and its significance for the future on this continent. They sought to lift the veil on the destiny of the new nation that had been brought into being. They bent their minds to charting a course for the realization in practice, public and private, of the humane principles to which Americans were committed in great official documents—republican ideals, self-government for the people, rights to life, liberty and the pursuit of happiness, and administration for the general welfare. This realization, they thoroughly understood, meant widening the break with feudal and barbaric laws, customs, and institutions, surviving from old times and places, and avoiding the perils of tyranny, insolent riches, and enervation. Such was, in broad outlines, their world-view; and the new idea of civilization, which fitted it exactly, was given concrete applications and firmly fixed in American thought before the revolutionary generation passed from the scene.

To the development of the idea in various relations Americans of many communities turned their power of thought—in the South, in the Middle States, and in New England. Among the eminent exponents of civilization were members of the old colonial stock and new immigrants. In the intellectual operation representatives of nearly every class in American society participated—"the rich and well born," the humble in origin, and the middling rank of birth, comfort, and influence. Their occupational interests ranged from law, medicine, and education through planting and independent farming, pamphleteering and letters, to public service, state and national. Some of them had the best formal education that America could afford, at William and Mary, Harvard, and Yale. Others were self-educated, by self-discipline as readers and students and in the informal university known as the struggle for existence. Some brought to the task experiences gained as disputants in contests over liberty with Great Britain, in the Revolution, at council tables, in high public positions at home and as ministers to other governments, as observant travelers in Europe, as actors in political scenes on the continent of Europe.

Learning and a knowledge of many languages, living and dead, as well as experience, were marshaled in the process of developing the idea of civilization in its applications to the new nation. The classics were utilized, legal treatises were examined, the Bible was consulted, the literature relative to the struggle for liberty in Great Britain was reviewed. Ancient and modern history was searched for precedents and principles. The sciences, "natural and moral," were put into requisition. Studies of social beginnings among the American Indians yielded instructions on primordial human nature and life in a "natural" order. It is scarcely too much to say that the full strength of contemporary intelligence and knowledge was enlisted in the enterprise of vitalizing the idea of civilization with reference to American conditions and purposes.

Concerned above all with the practical consequences implicit in the idea of civilization, these reflective thinkers wrote no systematic works on the idea as an abstraction. Instead, they made use of it in treatises on history and political science; in pamphlets and addresses dealing with the opening to men and women of new opportunities in keeping with the principles of 1776; and in letters and papers setting forth opinions on the nature of the human drama to which the rise and growth of the United States contributed creative and thrilling acts. With increasing frequency the idea of civilization was put to service as a controlling conception for the better ordering of policies and actions in the general welfare. Before the period of the early Republic closed, the new and revolutionary idea had been widely adopted as an American world-view of destiny, opportunity, and responsibility in the United States.

Of the nine Americans in the early republican era from whose works illustrations and affirmations respecting civilization are chosen, four—Thomas Jefferson, John Adams, Mercy Warren, and John Quincy Adams—anchored it in long history, as giving meaning to history and to that phase represented in the United States as destiny and opportunity and obligation. Two—Robert Coram and Thomas Paine—

were especially concerned with immediate applications to pressing issues, particularly the issue of human misery. Two —Thomas Paine and Joel Barlow—were popularizers of the idea and disseminated it among a multitude of readers in America and Europe. One—Joel Barlow—while instructing his own generation, was a prophet also and sought to poetize, in the form of an epic narrative, the outlook for civilization in America. One—John Quincy Adams—took the issue of civilization to the country in popular lectures, after having sought to enlist Congress and the people in a grand national program for the advancement of sciences, arts, and letters and for the use of the public lands and resources to effect a "progressive improvement, physical, moral, political, in the condition of the whole people of this Union."

Before he went to France and met Condorcet personally, Thomas Jefferson, the ideologist of the American Revolution, had somehow discovered the idea of civilization and used the term in the ethical sense demanded by its very etymology, in a work which, by an extraordinary concatenation of circumstances, was first printed in France. Unlike Condorcet who had neglected moral forces in his *Sketch*, although he was himself inspired by them, Jefferson included them in his interpretation of history; he accepted the ethical teachings of Christianity as necessary to the good life, individual and social. In fact Jefferson's range of interest covered the principal aspects of civilization—politics, economy, ethics, esthetics, the arts and sciences in their practical applications, and progressive improvement by the exercise of creative intelligence. In a letter written after he had retired from the public service, he showed that he understood the idea of civilization as a world-view, as an interpretation of history "from the infancy of creation to the present day," to quote his own words. And with amazing precision he enumerated and described those features of American society which differentiated it fundamentally from every society in the Old World.

The work in which Jefferson early employed the word civilization was his *Notes on Virginia*. This volume was prepared from memoranda which he had collected from time to time for his own guidance in public and private affairs. It was drafted in 1781–82 in response to a letter from M. de Marbois of the French legation in the United States, mainly to provide detailed information on America for use in France and partly to offset French aspersions to the effect that everything degenerated in the New World. A copy of Jefferson's edition which he had printed privately in Paris was shortly afterward published in French; an English edition appeared in London in 1787 and a German edition in 1789.

In his *Notes* Jefferson said: "It is civilization alone which replaces women in the enjoyment of their natural equality. That first teaches us to subdue the selfish passions, and to respect those rights in others which we value in ourselves." Although he did not, like Condorcet, accord full civic equality to women, Jefferson, in these brief sentences, made it clear that he relied on civilization as the great moral force for conquering anti-social passions and for realizing the human values inherent in the rights proclaimed by the Declaration of Independence, to the logic of which women afterward appealed with effect in their struggle for equal citizenship.

Three necessary connotations of the idea of civilization—the worth of the human being, the capacity of human nature for self-government and improvement, and the promise in humanity emancipated from a feudal order—Jefferson embodied in a statement distinguishing conservative European doctrines from those upheld by himself and his party. "The doctrines of Europe were," as he phrased the case, "that men in numerous associations cannot be restrained within the limits of order and justice, but by forces physical and moral, wielded over them by authorities independent of their will. Hence their organization of kings, hereditary nobles, and priests. Still further to constrain the brute force of the people, they deem it necessary to keep them down by hard labor, poverty, and ignorance, and to take from them as from bees, so much of their earnings, as that unremitting labor shall be necessary to obtain a sufficient surplus barely to sustain a scanty and miserable life. And these earnings they apply to maintain their privileged orders in splendor and idleness, to fascinate the eyes of the people, and excite in them an humble adoration and submission, as to an order of superior beings. Although few among us had gone all these lengths of opinion, yet many had advanced, some more, some less, on the way."

Speaking for himself and his party of the people, Jefferson then drew the distinction: "We believed . . . that man was a rational animal, endowed by nature with rights, and with an innate sense of justice; and that he could be restrained from wrong and protected in right, by moderate powers, confided to persons of his own choice and held to their duties by dependence on his own will. We believed that the complicated organization of kings, nobles, and priests was not the wisest or best to effect the happiness of associated man; that wisdom and virtue were not hereditary; that the trappings of such a machinery consumed by their expense those earnings of industry they were meant to protect, and by the inequalities they produced exposed liberty to suffrance. We believed that men, enjoying in ease and security the full fruits of their own industry, enlisted by all their interests on the side of law and order, habituated to think for themselves, and to follow reason as their guide, would be more easily and safely governed, than minds nourished in error, and vitiated and debased, as in Europe, by ignorance, indigence, and oppression."

The superiority of the lot of the common people in America over their condition in Europe, Jefferson held, was a feature of the American society long destined, if not forever, to give it qualities of its own. Like Abigail Adams and other Americans who had made observations in the two worlds, Jefferson was deeply moved by the contrast. "Ignorance, superstition, poverty, and oppression of body and mind, in every form," he wrote to George Wythe from Paris in 1786, "are so firmly settled on the mass of the people that their redemption from them can never be hoped. If all the sovereigns of Europe were to set themselves to work to emancipate the minds of their subjects from their present ignorance and prejudices, and that as zealously as they now endeavor to the contrary, a thousand years would not place them on that high ground on which our common people are now setting out." If, later, the revolution in France seemed to promise the emancipation which Jefferson wished to happen, the violence and wars which succeeded the first stages of the uprising dampened his hopes for an early enlightenment of the masses and their elevation to a position of respect and well-being in society.

Yet Jefferson placed a firm reliance on that feature of civilization which Condorcet also stressed, namely, the capacity of mankind for progress. In a letter to John Adams, written in 1813, he gently chided him for even hinting that their generation could not expect to improve on the principles, practices, and institutions of their ancestors: "One of the questions, you know, on which our parties took different sides, was on the improvability of the human mind in science, in ethics, in government, etc. Those who advocated the reformation of institutions, *pari passu* with the progress of science, maintained that no definite limits could be assigned to that progress. . . . You possess, yourself, too much science, not to see how much is still ahead of you, unexplained and unexplored."

Thus called upon the carpet by Jefferson, Adams lightened his burden of misgivings and replied by renewing a declaration of faith in "progressive improvement" in the arts and sciences and in "the advancement of civilization," which he had published as far back as 1787.

In fact all of Jefferson's intellectual and moral interests were in accord with the idea of civilization as it was being enlarged toward its fulness. His love of music, his concern for the practical and fine arts, his attachment to the ethical teachings of Jesus, his implacable resolve during the eight years of his presidency to keep the United States out of the wars raging in Europe, his advocacy of a national university, his contributions to the advancement of education in Virginia, his unflagging zeal for the promotion of the natural sciences, his keen awareness of the tragic consequences of slavery, the very library which he assembled, incomparable among the private collections of the time, combined with his trust in human nature and its potentialities for good—all indicated that his world-view was essentially expressed in the idea of civilization.

That all these interests at some time came under the idea of civilization in his mind, Jefferson indicated in a response which he made to William Ludlow who had evidently laid before him a plan of social reform in 1824. In this letter, written two years before his death, Jefferson expressed the belief that civilization was the great destiny of mankind. He acknowledged the conjectural nature of the evidence but committed himself to the conception.

"The idea," he said, "which you present of the progress of society from its rudest state to that it has now attained, seems conformable to what may be probably conjectured. Indeed, we have under our eyes tolerable proofs of it. Let a philosophic observer commence a journey from the savages of the Rocky Mountains, eastwardly towards our sea-coast. These he would observe in the earliest stages of association living under no law but that of nature, subsisting and covering themselves with the flesh and skins of wild beasts. He would next find those on our frontiers in the pastoral state, raising domestic animals to supply the defects of hunting. Then succeed our semi-barbarous citizens, the pioneers of the advance of civilization, and so in his progress he would meet the gradual shades of improving man until he would reach his, as yet, most improved state in our seaport towns. This, in fact, is equivalent to a survey, in time, of the progress of man from the infancy of creation to the present day. I am eighty-one years of age, born where I now live, in the first range of mountains in the interior of our country. And I have observed this march of civilization advancing from the seacoast, passing over us like a cloud of light, increasing our knowledge and improving our condition, insomuch as that we are at this time more advanced in civilization here than the seaports were when I was a boy. And where this progress will stop no one can say. Barbarism has, in the meantime, been receding before the steady step of amelioration; and will, in time, I trust, disappear from the earth."

Jefferson's idea of civilization was more than a general interpretation of mankind's history in a linear development. He believed that civilization could be, and was being, diffused among aboriginal peoples through contacts with those more advanced. Replying in 1812 to an inquiry from John Adams respecting American Indians, he spoke of his experiences with Indians in Virginia and said that the Cherokees "consisting now of about 2,000 warriors, and the Creeks of about 3,000 are far advanced in civilization. They have good cabins, enclosed fields, large herds of cattle and hogs, spin and weave their own clothes of cotton, have smiths and other of the most necessary tradesmen, write and read, are on the increase in numbers. . . . Some other tribes are advancing in the same line. On those who have made any progress, English seductions will have no effect. But the backward will yield, and be thrown further back. Those will relapse into barbarism and misery."

Ten years later, when Jedediah Morse invited Jefferson to join a great national society "for the civilization and improvement of the Indian tribes," he expressed sympathy with the object, while declining to serve. The purpose, he assured Morse, "is one which I have ever had much at heart, and have never omitted an occasion of promoting while I have been in situations to do it with effect, and nothing, even now, in the calm of age and retirement, would excite in me a more lively interest than an approvable plan of raising that respectable and unfortunate people from the state of physical and moral abjection to which they have been reduced by circumstances foreign to them."

The depth of Jefferson's feelings relative to the civilization of the Indians was evident in many official actions and addresses while he was in a position to do something about it. Indeed he made such a point of it that the Virginia legislature, in its farewell message to him on February 7, 1809, placed his Indian policies among his memorable services to his country. After listing his notable actions in the sphere of domestic policy, the legislature declared: "These are points in your administration which the historian will not fail to seize, to expand, and teach posterity to dwell upon with delight. Nor will he forget our peace with the civilized world, preserved through a season of uncommon difficulty and trial; the good will cultivated with the unfortunate aborigines of our country, and the civilization extended among them."

Troubled by what he felt to be demoralizing relations between masters and slaves and pondering the feasibility of colonizing freed Negroes in Africa, the original home of the race, Jefferson was consoled by the thought that such colonization might be the means of spreading civilization in the dark continent. "Going from a country possessing all the useful arts," he wrote in a letter of January 21, 1811, "they [emancipated Negroes] might be the means of transplanting them among the inhabitants of Africa, and would thus carry back to the country of their origin, the seeds of civilization which might render their sojournment and sufferings here a blessing in the end to that country."

Sharing in general Jefferson's revolutionary ideals, Thomas Paine also concurred with him in his interpretation of history as a civilizing process. But Paine worked out the idea of civilization more specifically in many directions and applied it with a higher degree of insistence in his consideration of social welfare. This he did with particular care in two tracts which became famous in Western thought: *Rights of Man*, published in 1791, and *Agrarian Justice*, issued six years later in 1797. The *Rights of Man* acquired special importance in attracting attention to the idea of civilization from two facts: the dedication of the first part to George Washington and the second to M. de La Fayette, great leaders of the revolutionary age; and the enormous circulation which the manifesto immediately attained and held over a long period of time. It literally made millions familiar with the idea of civilization, in the Old World and the New. Unquestionably, Paine was the greatest popularizer of the idea that the revolutionary age produced.

Paine's *Rights of Man,* written in reply to Edmund Burke's attack on the French Revolution, rested in general upon the theory that all men possess natural rights; that society originated in a social compact among freemen; that society and civilization underlie all governments; that the despotism of governments and privileged orders had intruded upon the pristine liberties; and that it was the function of revolution to assert the rights of man, overthrow all forms of tyranny, and promote civilization. Composed during the early stages of the French Revolution, it was also characterized by that optimism which contemplated the triumph of liberty and civilization, even in Europe, age-old home of oppression and servitude.

This optimistic view Paine expressed at the close of the part dedicated to President Washington: "It is not difficult to perceive, from the enlightened state of mankind, that the hereditary governments are verging to their decline, and that revolutions on the broad basis of national sovereignty, and government by representation, are making their way in Europe; it would be an act of wisdom to anticipate their approach, and produce revolutions by reason and accommodation, rather than commit them to the issue of convulsions. From what we now see, nothing of reform in the political world ought to be held improbable. It is an age of revolutions, in which everything may be looked for. The intrigue of courts, by which the system of war is kept up, may provoke a confederation to abolish it: and an European congress to patronize the progress of free government, and promote the civilization of nations with each other is an event nearer in probability, than once were the revolutions and alliances of France and America."

In his introduction to the second part of the *Rights of Man,* dedicated to La Fayette, Paine depicted America as taking the lead in revolution and civilization. He opened with a reference to the axiom of Archimedes: "Had we a place to stand upon, we might raise the world." Then he applied it:

"The revolution in America presented in politics what was only theory in mechanics." The tyranny and antiquity of habit were so deeply rooted in the Old World "that no beginning could be made in Asia, Africa or Europe, to reform the political condition of man. Freedom had been hunted round the globe: reason was considered as rebellion; and the slavery of fear had made men afraid to think."

But the revolution in America had given despotism everywhere a shock, Paine declared. This revolution had been more than a mere separation from England; it had been accompanied by "a revolution in the principles and practice of government." The spell of despotism once broken was continuing to dissolve. "Government founded on a *moral theory, on a system of universal peace, on the indefeasible, hereditary rights of man,* is now revolving from west to east by a stronger impulse than the government of the sword revolved from east to west. It interests not particular individuals but nations in its progress, and promises a new era to the human race."

The peculiar features of life in America had prepared the way for this revolutionary leadership: "As America was the only spot in the political world where the principles of universal reformation could begin, so also was it the best in the natural world. An assemblage of circumstances conspired, not only to give birth, but to add gigantic maturity to its principles. The scene which that country presents to the eye of the spectator, has something in it which generates and enlarges great ideas. Nature appears to him in magnitude. The mighty objects he beholds, act upon his mind by enlarging it, and he partakes of the greatness he contemplates. Its first settlers were emigrants from different European nations, and of diversified professions of religion, retiring from the governmental persecutions of the old world, and meeting in the new, not as enemies, but as brothers. The wants which necessarily accompany the cultivation of a wilderness, produced among them a state of society, which countries long harassed by the quarrels and intrigues of governments, had neglected to cherish. In such a situation man becomes what he ought to be. He sees his species, not with the inhuman idea of a natural enemy, but as kindred." If the governments of Asia, Africa, and Europe had begun on a principle similar to that of America or had not been corrupted "very early," they would have been in "a far superior position to what they are."

The revolution precipitated in the peculiar conditions of American life would be followed, it was natural to expect, by other revolutions, Paine supposed. "The amazing and still increasing expenses with which old governments are conducted, the numerous wars they engage in or provoke, the embarrassments they throw in the way of universal civilization and commerce, and the oppression and usurpation acted at home, have wearied out the patience, and exhausted the property of the world. In such a situation, and with such examples already existing, revolutions are to be looked for. . . . If universal peace, harmony, civilization and commerce are ever to be the happy lot of man, it cannot be accomplished but by a revolution in the present system of governments."

But a consideration of government in this revolutionary movement is not enough: "Almost everything appertaining to the circumstances of a nation has been absorbed and confounded under the general and mysterious word *government*. . . . It may therefore be of use in this day of revolutions, to discriminate between those things which are the effect of government, and those which are not. This will best be done by taking a review of society and civilization, and the consequences resulting therefrom, as things distinct from what are called governments."

So Paine started the second part of his *Rights of Man* with an essay entitled "Of Society and Civilization," and he gave all the subsequent pages to an examination of that subject, with government represented as an aspect of society and civilization, not the whole affair of life.

"A great part of that order which reigns among mankind is not the effect of government," he said. "It had its origin in the principles of society, and the natural constitution of man. It existed prior to government, and would exist if the formality of government was abolished. The mutual dependence and reciprocal interest which man has in man, and all the parts of a civilized community upon each other, create that great chain of connection which holds it together. . . . No one man is capable, without the aid of society, of supplying his own wants; and those wants acting upon every individual, impel the whole of them into society, as naturally as gravitation acts to a centre. But she [nature] has gone further. She has not only forced man into society by a diversity of wants, which the reciprocal aid of each other can supply, but she has implanted in him a system of social affections, which, though not necessary to his existence, are essential to his happiness. There is no period in life when this love for society ceases. It begins and ends with our being. . . . Government is no further necessary than to supply the few cases to which society and civilization are not conveniently competent."

Faithful to the interpretation of history generally followed by the natural rights school and to doctrines proclaimed in the Declaration of Independence, Paine did not discriminate between the small society, as it had existed in primitive times, and the highly advanced society, represented by contemporary nations in which government had become a powerful instrument of consolidation and maintenance. Like other members of the school, Paine regarded government as a kind of despotic intrusion upon the idyllic bliss of "original society."

In a large measure, therefore, he was romantic about social origins, but, if he minimized government, he was true to the idea of civilization in making government only a part of civilized life: "It is to the great and fundamental principles of society and civilization—to the common usage universally consented to, and mutually and reciprocally maintained—to the unceasing circulation of interest, which passing through its innumerable channels, invigorates the whole mass of civilized man—it is to these things, infinitely more than any thing which even the best instituted government can perform, that the safety and prosperity of the individual and of the whole depends. The more perfect civilization is, the less occasion has it for government."

Having entrenched welfare and progress in society and civilization, Paine explored the origins of old governments, the idea of republic and democracy, the theory of constitutional government as representation built on democracy, and creative efforts expressed in new constitutions. Great gains had been made for mankind, he granted, but the dark blot of misery had not been erased. "Customary language has classed the condition of man under the two descriptions of civilized and uncivilized life. To the one it has ascribed felicity and affluence; to the other, hardship and want. It is nevertheless true . . . that a great portion of mankind, in what are called civilized countries, are in a state of poverty and wretchedness, far below the condition of an Indian. I speak not of one country, but of all. It is so in England, it is so all over Europe."

What is the explanation? "It lies not in any natural defect

in the principles of civilization, but in preventing those principles having an universal operation; the consequence of which is, a perpetual system of war and expense that drains the country and defeats the general felicity of which civilization is capable. All the European governments (France now excepted) are constructed, not on the principle of universal civilization, but on the reverse of it. . . . The inhabitants of every country, under the civilization of laws, easily associate together; but governments being in an uncivilized state, and almost continually at war, they pervert the abundance which civilized life produces, to carry on the uncivilized part to a greater extent. By thus engrafting the barbarism of government upon the internal civilization of a country, it draws from the latter, and more especially from the poor, a great portion of those earnings which should be applied to their subsistence and comfort. . . . What has served to continue this evil, is the pecuniary advantage, which all the governments of Europe have found in keeping up this state of uncivilization. It affords to them pretences for power and revenue, for which there would be neither occasion nor apology, if the circle of civilization were rendered complete."

Yet, while disparaging government, especially of a despotic nature, Paine insisted that it be taken into account in efforts to overcome misery and degradation in society: "Whatever the form or constitution of government may be, it ought to have no other object than the general happiness. When, instead of this, it operates to create and increase wretchedness in any of the parts of society, it is on a wrong system and reformation is necessary."

Brooding on ways and means of improving the condition of Europe, where he was then carrying on his democratic agitations, he advocated a concert of European powers to prevent war there, the diversion of military and naval expenditures to civil uses, popular education, old age pensions, and public workshops for the unemployed. Reformed and redirected, government might thus, he thought, become an instrument of civilization rather than an obstacle to its advance.

In the second part of his *Rights of Man* Paine had said that "government is no further necessary than to supply the few cases to which society and civilization are not conveniently competent; and instances are not wanting to show that every thing which government can usefully add thereto, has been performed by the common consent of society, without government." He proposed, it is true, various correctives of inequality by government action, but his emphasis in that tract was on civilization as a condition or process apart from government, often at war with it. On the other hand, in his *Agrarian Justice,* published in 1797, Paine displayed less certainty that progress in civilization, unaided by government action, would inevitably raise the level of general welfare.

Civilization itself might be challenged: "Whether that state that is proudly, perhaps erroneously, called civilization, has most promoted or most injured the general happiness of man, is a question that may be strongly contested. On the one side the spectator is dazzled by splendid appearances; on the other, he is shocked by extremes of wretchedness; both of which it has erected. The most affluent and the most miserable of the human race are to be found in the countries that are called civilized. . . . The life of an Indian is a continual holiday, compared with the poor of Europe; and, on the other hand it appears to be abject when compared to the rich. Civilization, therefore, or that which is so-called, has operated two ways: to make one part of society more affluent, and the other more wretched, than would have been the lot of either in a natural state."

Unquestionably the condition of people in the primitive order of society was idealized by Paine. Indeed it was a part of romantic tactics in that revolutionary age to condemn hateful features of the living present by setting up some lost utopia. Yet there was no doubt about the sufferings of nameless masses in the most highly civilized societies.

Anyway, for good or ill, Paine knew very well there could be no return to the state of nature. "It is always possible," he said, "to go from the natural to the civilized state, but it is never possible to go from the civilized to the natural state." The abundance of land required for primitive economy was no longer available. "When . . . a country becomes populous by the additional aids of cultivation, art, and science, there is a necessity of preserving things in that state; because without it there cannot be sustenance for more, perhaps, than a tenth part of the inhabitants. . . . Cultivation is at least one of the greatest natural improvements ever made by human invention. It has given to created earth a tenfold value." Since a return to primitive freedom is out of the question, what is to be done, if human happiness and welfare are considerations of civilization? How is the contradiction to be resolved?

These questions Paine answered by proposing government action in the interest of civilization. He proceeded on this line from an axiomatic base: "The first principle of civilization ought to have been, and still ought to be, that the condition of every person born into the world, after a state of civilization commences, ought not to be worse than if he had been born before that period." From this it followed that "To preserve the benefits of what is called civilized life, and to remedy at the same time the evil which it has produced, ought to be considered as one of the first objects of reformed legislation."

The problem thus presented, Paine reasoned, springs out of the private ownership of the earth and its resources, whereas it is the value of the improvements only which should belong as individual property to the proprietor. As if recognizing the force of individual enterprise in making improvements and advancing the arts of agriculture, he did not propose the common ownership of land. Instead, he advocated a ground-rent tax levied against proprietors to raise a fund from which to make a fixed sum available to every person arriving at the age of twenty-one, "as a compensation in part, for the loss of his or her natural inheritance," and to pay an annuity to every person fifty years old or more. This was not "equal justice"; it was what Paine called "agrarian justice."

Despite diversity in his treatment of the matter, Paine's idea of civilization contained definite elements: the process of civilization is inexorable in a settled and complex society; it includes the progress of the sciences and the arts, especially those of practical application; it is in conflict with poverty and the evils of poverty; the very idea itself calls for correction or softening of those evils; and government, as an instrument of civilization, must be employed to assure a more equitable distribution of the benefits of civilization.

If often placed by political historians at the opposite pole from Jefferson, from whom indeed he was long estranged, John Adams was in accord with Jefferson on the proposition that mankind had made progress and was capable of making more progress in civilized ways of life. Experienced in practical action and temperamentally cautious, often gloomy, Adams was familiar with objections to the theory of progress. But in studying government, as a co-maker of a new government, he went into the history of government and came to the belief that, with the advancement of civilization and humanity, difficulties in the path of success for the American experiment could be overborne; that there was hope even for European progress. This conclusion he documented in 1786 when, as Minister of the United States in London, he wrote his *Defence of the Constitutions of the United States*.

That his belief was grounded in fundamentals Adams made impressively clear in the Preface to that treatise on political institutions: "The arts and sciences, in general, during the three or four last centuries, have had a regular course of progressive improvement. The inventions in mechanic arts, the discoveries in natural philosophy, navigation, and commerce, and the advancement of civilization and humanity, have occasioned changes in the condition of the world, and the human character, which would have astonished the most refined nations of antiquity." This past, at least, seemed secure to Adams.

In that year he thought that the process of civilization was transforming the Old World and might continue to do so without invoking the agency of violence. "A continuation of similar exertions is every day rendering Europe more and more like one community, or single family. The checks and balances of republican governments have been in some degree adopted at the courts of princes. By the erection of various tribunals, to register the laws, and exercise the judicial power—by endulging the petitions and remonstrances of subjects, until by habit they are regarded as rights—a control has been established over ministers of state, and the royal councils, which, in some degree, approaches the spirit of republics. Property is generally secure, and personal liberty seldom invaded. The press has great influence, even where it is not expressly tolerated; and the public opinion must be respected by a minister, or his place becomes insecure. Commerce begins to thrive; and if religious toleration were established, personal liberty a little more protected, by giving an absolute right to demand a public trial in a certain reasonable time, and the states [Estates] were invested with a few more privileges, or rather restored to some that have been taken away, these governments would be brought to as great a degree of perfection, they would approach as near to the character of governments of laws and not of men, as their nature will probably admit of." In other words, the rulers of Europe might, within the limits of their capacities, move into a higher state of civilization by making concessions to the new spirit.

Europe, Adams thought, might learn from American experience in the construction of governments: "If men are now sufficiently enlightened to disabuse themselves of artifice, imposture, hypocrisy, and superstition, they will consider this event as an era in history. Although the detail of the formation of the American governments is at present little known or regarded either in Europe or America, it may hereafter become an object of curiosity," that is, of concern.

Adams was conscious of the resistance which the privileged orders of Europe might offer to the advancement of civilization as an upward movement of humanity. But his hope for European regeneration was strong and he was surprised that already the science of free government had made so little progress there. "In so general a refinement, or more properly a reformation of manners and improvement in science, is it not unaccountable," he asked, "that the knowledge of the principles and construction of free governments, in which the happiness of life, and even the further progress of improvement in education and society, in knowledge and virtue, are so deeply interested, should have remained at full stand for two or three thousand years?" Yet he remembered that Americans, unlike Europeans, were "unembarrassed by attachments to noble families, hereditary lines and successions, or any considerations of royal blood."

To the science of free government, Americans had made a cardinal contribution without the aid of the elaborate mysteries, theories, and genuflections of Europe. "It will never be pretended that any persons employed in that service [of setting up constitutional governments] had interviews with the gods, or were in any degree under the inspiration of heaven, more than those at work upon ships or houses, or laboring in merchandise or agriculture; it will forever be acknowledged that these governments were contrived merely by the use of reason and the senses, as Copley painted Chatham; West, Wolf; and Trumbull, Warren and Montgomery; as Dwight, Barlow, Trumbull, and Humphries composed their verse, and Belknap and Ramsay, history; as Godfrey invented his quadrant, and Rittenhouse his planetarium; as Boylston practised inoculation, and Franklin electricity; as Paine exposed the mistakes of Raynal, and Jefferson those of Buffon, so unphilosophically borrowed from the despicable dreams of De

Man. Neither the people, nor their conventions, committees, or sub-committees, considered legislation in any other light than as ordinary arts and sciences, only more important."

The business of government in the United States was thus allied by Adams to the practical arts and sciences that entered into the advancement of civilization. In framing their new constitutions, he explained, the American people consulted the great architects skilled in that art and examined the buildings they had erected, the ruins or partial ruins of all, and sought to adopt the advantages and reject the inconveniences of all. "The people were universally too enlightened to be imposed upon by artifice; and their leaders, or more properly followers, were men of too much honor to attempt it. Thirteen governments thus founded on the natural authority of the people alone, without a pretence of miracle or mystery, and which are destined to spread over the northern part of that whole quarter of the globe, are a great point gained in favor of the rights of mankind. The experiment is made, and has completely succeeded; it can no longer be called in question, whether authority in magistrates and obedience of citizens can be grounded on reason, morality, and the Christian religion. . . . The institutions now made in America will not wholly wear out for thousands of years. . . . After having known the history of Europe, and of England in particular, it would be the height of folly to go back to the institutions of Woden and Thor."

Although in numerous writings Adams voiced doubts about the power of human nature to maintain civilized ways of life idefinitely, he constantly vouched for the tenacity of social propensities in human beings. Upon these propensities he relied in fortifying his expectations for humanity. That the social bond could never be broken he tersely asserted in his *Discourses on Davila,* published in 1791 while he was Vice President of the United States: "Men, in their primitive conditions, however savage, were undoubtedly gregarious; and they continue to be social, not only in every stage of civilization, but in every possible situation in which they can be placed."

It was, therefore, with good reason that Jefferson, after their reconciliation in their later years, twitted Adams about his alleged departure from his early faith in mankind. Like Jefferson, he had hailed the progress of the arts and sciences, recorded with satisfaction the advancement of civilization, accepted a social view of human nature, and declared his faith in the future of the United States, as clearly differentiated in constitution from Europe and resolutely set on an independent course, which "ought to be our rule." In this respect the author of the Declaration of Independence and the author of *Defence of the Constitutions of the United States* were in agreement.

Confirmation of their agreement is in the written record. The intensity of Adams' belief in civilization did undoubtedly fluctuate with his experiences and moods. In a letter to Jefferson on June 28, 1813, he sighed: "I am weary of contemplating nations from the lowest and most beastly degradations of human life to the highest refinement of civilization. I am weary of Philosophers, Theologians, Politicians, and Historians. They are an immense mass of absurdities, vices, and lies. Montesquieu had sense enough to say in jest, that all our knowledge might be comprehended in twelve pages in duodecimo, and I believe him in earnest." It all seemed to be the old contest between good and evil over again: "This logos of Plato seems to resemble, if it was not the prototype of, the *Ratio and its Progress* of Manilius, the astrologer; of the *Progress of the Mind* of Condorcet, and the *Age of Reason* of Tom Payne." Then in a spirit of raillery, Adams exclaimed: "I could make a system too."

But in another letter to Jefferson, written on the same day, Adams responded to the latter's banterings about his disbelief in progress, and reasserted the convictions of his earlier years: "I might have flattered myself that my sentiments were sufficiently known to have protected me against suspicions of narrow thoughts, contracted sentiments, bigoted, enthusiastic, or superstitious principles, civil, political, philosophical, or ecclesiastical. The first sentence of the preface to my defence of the constitution[s], volume 1st, printed in 1787, is in these words: 'The arts and sciences, in general, during the three or four last centuries, have had a regular course of *progressive* improvement. The inventions in mechanic arts, the discoveries in natural philosophy, navigation, and commerce, and the advancement of civilization and humanity, have occasioned changes in the condition of the world and the human character, which would have astonished the most refined nations of antiquity,' etc. I will quote no farther; but request you to read again that whole page, and then say whether the writer of it could be suspected of recommending to youth 'to look backward instead of forward' for instruction and improvement."

Political misfortunes had overtaken Adams. Partisan foes had embittered his years with stringent criticisms of his motives and principles. The terror of the French Revolution and the greater terror of the Napoleonic wars had intervened. But Adams assured the doubting Thomas at Monticello that he still adhered to the avowal of 1787.

Occupying a clear position in the controversy that divided Jefferson and John Adams in their middle years, Mercy Warren, a severe critic of Adams' alleged monarchical tendencies, a stanch believer, as she avowed, in "democratic principles," placed squarely in the great drama of civilization the revolutionary act in which they were all participants. Many circumstances conspired with her character and talents to deepen and quicken her thought about the idea of civilization in relation to American history. She was the sister of James Otis, a pioneer in resistance to Great Britain's policies, and the wife of General James Warren, an officer in the revolutionary war and a member of the democratic wing in politics. Associated through friendship and sympathy with major leaders in the Revolution, one of the earliest herself to proclaim independence as the need and logic of events, a shrewd observer of trends, a student of history and classical literature, an active pamphleteer in the intellectual defense of the American cause, Mercy Warren, later called "the penwoman of the Revolution," brought an informed and versatile mind to bear on the nature and course of civilization in the United States.

To leave a record of the age, to set forth the spirit and events of the independence movement, and to perpetuate the principles which it proclaimed and represented, Mercy Warren wrote a *History of the American Revolution* in three volumes. In this *History* she used the idea of civilization with reference to certain situations and problems in a manner that indicated a keen appreciation of its connotations. Civilization, she discerned, had entered into the making of American history, as of all history.

Colonial beginnings, she said, were laid in civilization: "America was now a fair field for a transcript of all the virtues and vices that have illumined or darkened, disgraced and reigned triumphant in their turn over all the other quarters of the habitable globe. The progress of every thing had there been remarkably rapid, from the first settlement of the country. Learning was cultivated, knowledge disseminated, politeness and morals improved, and valor and patriotism cherished, in proportion to the rapidity of her population. This extraordinary cultivation of arts and manners may be accounted for, from the stage of society and improvement in which the first planters of America were educated before they left their native clime. The first emigrations to North America were not composed of a strolling banditti of rude nations, like the first people of most other colonies in the history of the world. The early settlers in the newly discovered continent were as far advanced in civilization, policy, and manners; in their ideas of government, the nature of compacts, and the bands of civil union, as any of their neighbors at that period among the most polished nations of Europe."

To Mercy Warren civilization was a process, for she spoke of "the degrees of civilization," but it was not an inexorable process advancing surely toward the goal of higher perfection. When, for instance, she linked civilization with patriotism, she warned the American men and women of her time against the perils of an over-refinement that enervates and destroys. "Valor," she said, "is an instinct that appears even among savages, as a dictate of nature planted for self-defense; but patriotism on the diffusive principles of general benevolence, is the child of society. This virtue with the fair accomplishments of science, gradually grows and increases with civilization, until refinement is wrought to a height that poisons and corrupts the mind."

Though she realized that civilization was in history, in history already made and in the course of making, Mrs. Warren recalled the dissolution of older republics through greed for riches, lust for power, and decay of moral stamina. And in this cautious temper, while acclaiming the Revolution and the Republic, she dwelt upon those virtues and practices which she deemed necessary to the endurance and advancement of civilization in the United States.

The distinction between American society and the societies of Europe, drawn by Jefferson and Adams, Mercy Warren also made basic to her treatment of the Revolution. "Americans," she declared, were "born under no feudal tenure, nurtured in the bosom of mediocrity, educated in the schools of freedom." They had "never been used to look up to any lord of the soil, as having a right by prescription, habit, or hereditary claim, to the property of their flocks, their herds, and their pastures." The democratic principles which they accepted were "the result of equality of condition." Americans must be constant in the nourishment of those principles; otherwise "a superfluity of wealth, and a train of domestic slaves" would "naturally banish a sense of general liberty, and nourish the seeds of that kind of dependence that usually terminates in aristocracy." The experiment of liberty, she urged them to remember, had often been tried and failed. But she counted on the vitality of the revolutionary principles for the outlawing of servility, the extension of equality, and the conquest of poverty.

In the uncompiled symposium on the idea of civilization in the United States, the medical profession and the middle region were represented in part by the writings of Benjamin Rush of Philadelphia, for a brief period a Surgeon General in the revolutionary war. Though conscientious in the discharge of his duties as a physician, Rush had larger social interests and framed programs for the improvement of American life through various agencies, including public education. In 1796 he issued a pamphlet on the subject: *A Plan for the Establishment of Public Schools and the Diffusion of Knowledge in Pennsylvania,* one among numerous projects of the kind promulgated in the early days of the Republic. His argument for the proposal Rush sought to strengthen by an appeal to the idea of civilization. "Learning in all countries," he said, "promotes civilization, and the pleasures of society and conversation."

In various letters and papers, Rush pictured the social order in America and the prospects for its development. Referring to the frontier regions of his state, he described three types of setttlers: the poor family inhabiting a log cabin and living a hard life; the family a grade higher but still far from perfection in habits and efficiency; and finally the family with fertile land, good buildings, a commodious dwelling, diversified crops, a fine garden, and a bountiful table, supporting schools and churches, benevolent and public spirited. "It is in the third species of settlers," Rush declared, "that we behold civilization perfected. It is to the third species only that it is proper to apply the term of farmers." And he was happy to add, if with some exaggeration, that two-thirds of the farmers of Pennsylvania had arrived at what he called the perfection of civilization.

Most farmers, Rush thought, started at or near the bottom, passed through the second or intermediate stage, and arrived at the condition of civilized living. It was this general, though by no means universal, experience of farmers in the United States that presented to Rush and his contemporaries such a contrast to the martyrdom of the masses toiling on the land in Europe or driven from it by the avaricious landlordism of England. Whether the farmers described by Rush as having the lowest standards of living were in reality far above the average serfs still bound to the soil in France and in countries beyond the Rhine, it is undeniable that American cultivators of the earth had freedom of movement and extraordinary chances to improve their standard of living. That made a fundamental difference between the two worlds.

Without referring specifically to civilization in America in this instance, Rush in fact gave an analysis of its features in a letter to an English friend, written in 1790, the year after the federal Constitution had gone into effect. Beginning at the top of the social ladder, he indicated that certain conditions were unfavorable to three types of possible immigrants: "Men of independent fortune who can exist only in company, and who can converse only upon public amusements" should not come to the United States. "Literary men, who have no professional pursuits, will often languish in America, from the want of society." America at the moment offered "little encouragement to the professors of most of the fine arts. Painting and sculpture flourish chiefly in wealthy and luxurious countries." But "teachers of music have been more fortunate."

For what types of immigrants did America offer immediate opportunities? Rush furnished a list, beginning with farmers. For cultivators of the earth, America is "the first asylum of the world." Though capital was needed, America had room also for "mechanics and manufacturers," or craftsmen, of every type. "Every art connected with cultivating the earth—building ships, and feeding and clothing the body, will meet with encouragement in the country." For laborers, even indentured servants, the avenue to security and the benefits of civilization was open. They were not precluded from forming "respectable connections in marriage." Indentured servants, after earning their liberty, like all other free citizens, enjoyed the right of holding public office; no stigma rested upon them. "Gentlemen of the learned professions"—teachers, lawyers, physicians, and clergymen—were doing well in the United States. Schoolmasters in reading, writing, grammar and numbers had opportunities in America, including the prospect of rising into the learned professions.

The general conditions in the United States, Rush explained, were favorable to such types of immigrants. "Our citizens," he said, possessed the "versatility of genius." There was room enough "for every human talent and virtue to expand and flourish." There was freedom for all religious denominations; three Roman Catholics then held seats in Congress. All offices, except the presidency, were open to the foreign-born who became citizens, and naturalization was easy. Domestic concord was encouraged by the system of government: evils could be removed by frequent elections, so that the people "will seldom appeal to the less certain remedies of mobs or arms." The pressure of the population on "the means of subsistence," a source of wars, was not a problem in the United States and this fact alone would "probably" reduce the temptation to carry on war.

Thought about civilization in the United States was running far deeper into the structure of American society than Benjamin Rush intimated in his letter of 1790 and it was pressed further by persons undistinguished by notice in later histories and biographies. The very next year after Rush described, with easy optimism, the happy state of the American people as a whole, Robert Coram of Delaware, of the middle region, published a tract of 107 pages in which he dealt with the subject of civilization and made what seems to have been the first extended exposition of the conflict between civilization and misery in the comparatively fortunate United States.

Coram called his little volume *Political Inquiries: to Which Is Added a Plan for the General Establishment of Schools Throughout the United States.* On the title page he designated himself modestly as "The Author of some late pieces in the Delaware Gazette," if over the signature of "Brutus." Judging by the letter and spirit of the argument which he now published, Coram belonged to the left wing of the American Revolution—the wing not content with the state of things prevailing after victory and the adoption of the Constitution.

When a child about three years old Coram was brought by his parents from England to Charleston, South Carolina, where his father established himself in business in 1765. After the American Revolution broke out the elder Coram turned loyalist and left Charleston, in 1778; but the boy, then about sixteen or seventeen years of age, enlisted in the South Carolina navy and went to France with a stormy petrel of democratic politics, Commodore Alexander Gillon.

As Gillon was delayed in getting a frigate from French agents, young Coram, on a recommendation from Benjamin Franklin, minister of the United States in Paris, volunteered to serve with John Paul Jones as a midshipman. While in charge of the men fighting on the mizzentop of the *Bon Homme Richard*, he played a courageous part in the sanguinary and memorable battle with the *Serapis*. Having won a citation from Jones for "gallant behavior" in this action, Coram rejoined Gillon and was with him on board the *South Carolina* when the ship was captured by the British in 1782.

Discharged from a British prison ship at the close of the war, Coram, some time afterward, went to Delaware, married, and established a home in that state. He kept a school, acted as a librarian for the Wilmington Library Company, edited and published the Delaware Gazette, and became associated with leaders of the incipient anti-federalist party that was in time to carry Thomas Jefferson into the White House. Elected a member of the Delaware constitutional convention in 1792, Coram took a special interest in the framing of Article VIII, Section 12, which instructed the legislature to provide for "establishing schools and promoting arts and sciences." Death cut him short at about the age of thirty-five —five years after he had issued his tractate on universal education for the American people.

In his Introduction, Coram stated the problem yet to be faced under avowed principles of the Republic: "Whoever surveys the history of nations with a philosophic eye, will find that the civilized man in every stage of his civilization, and under almost every form of government, has always been a very miserable being. When we consider the very splendid advantages, which the citizen seems to possess; the grand scheme of christianity; the knowledge of sciences and of arts;

the experience of all ages and nations, recorded in his libraries for a guide, how mortifying must it be to him, to reflect,
that with all his boasted science and philosophy, he had made
but a retrograde advance to happiness."

From a wide variety of sources, Coram cited authoritative
accounts of the poverty, suffering, degradation, and crimes in
European societies, of barbaric legislation against the propertyless, and the barbaric punishments meted out to the poor
and unfortunate masses of mankind. By comparing life even
among American Indians, with which he evidently had some
familiarity, he put "civilized" men to shame.

Having posed the problem, Coram located its source in
the European conception of human nature: "Europeans have
been taught to believe that mankind have something of the
Devil ingrafted in their nature, that they are naturally ferocious, vicious, revengeful, and as void of reason as brutes,
&c, &c. Hence their sanguinary laws, which string a man to a
gibbet, for the value of twenty pence. They first frame a
hypothesis, by which they prove men to be wolves, and then
treat them as if they really were such."

Making use of facts drawn from the observation of primitive people in America, Coram assailed the hard hypothesis
on which the European view rested: "It is serious truth,
whatever may have been advanced by European writers to
the contrary, that the aborigines of the American continent,
have fewer vices, are less subject to diseases, and are a happier people, than the subjects of any government in the
Eastern world."

In his search for the clue to the contradiction between
civilization and misery, Coram explored the origins and ends
of government and the origin of private property. With reference to primeval government, he confessed that the subject
was clouded in obscurity; but held "as to the origin of Modern Governments, they seem chiefly to have been founded by
conquest." If origins were obscure, the professed end was
clear: "The end of government, we are told, is public good;
by which is to be understood, the happiness of the community."

Taking this at face value, a gross inconsistency had occurred: "The great body of the people in Europe are unhappy, not to say miserable; there needs no other argument,
to prove that all the European governments have been
founded upon wrong principles; since the means used have

not produced the end intended." As an illustration, he cited a passage from Abbé Raynal describing the wretchedness of the French peasant: "Whether tenant or subject, he is doubly a slave; if he has a few acres, his lord comes and gathers where he has not sown; if he has but a yoke of oxen, or a pair of horses, he must employ them in the public service; if he has nothing but his person, the prince takes him for a soldier. Everywhere he meets with masters, and always with oppression."

From government, Coram turned to the origin and nature of property: "In the comparative view of the civilized man and the savage, the most striking contrast is the division of property. To the one, it is the source of all his happiness: to the other, the fountain of all his misery. By the holy writ we are informed, that God gave to man dominion over the earth, the living creatures, and the herbs; human laws have, however, limited this jurisdiction to certain orders or classes of men; the rest are to feed upon air if they can, or fly to another world for subsistence. This parcelling out to individuals, what was intended for the general stock of society, leads me to inquire farther into the nature and origin of property. I am not quite so visionary, as to expect that the members of any civilized community will listen to an equal division of lands: had that been the object of this work, the author had infallibly lost his labor. But a substitute [education], and perhaps the only one, is highly practicable."

In the course of his inquiry into the subject of property Coram had occasion to examine the doctrines of William Blackstone in that branch of jurisprudence. The famous author of the commentaries on the laws of England was the outstanding philosopher of the conservative reaction in Great Britain and many of his highly fanciful legal constructs, conceived in the imagery of the Tory class, with which he was in sympathy, had general currency among conservatives in the United States. Blackstone's dicta were taken seriously by lawyers as a rule and enabled them, later, with the aid of feminists, to befuddle the public for generations to come. Had he desired to do so, Coram could scarcely have avoided discussing the issue.

With a moderation ironical in temper he remarked: "Doctor Blackstone seems to have been extremely cautious how he ventured upon his inquiry into the origin of property, as if fearful of some defect in his title. . . . He obliquely censures the conduct of the generality of mankind, who, he says, will not give themselves the trouble to consider the original and foundation of the right of property. But when he reflects upon the probable consequences of a rational investigation of this subject, he flies his ground. 'These inquiries,' says he, 'it must be owned would be useless, and even troublesome in common life. It is well, if the mass of mankind will obey the laws when made, without scrutinizing too nicely the reasons of making them.' . . . That is, in plain English, lawyers may know the obligations of society; but the people not."

After an extensive analysis of Blackstone's argument respecting the way in which the dominion of man over the earth, celebrated in the Book of Genesis, became divided into such uneven portions among the children of man—an analysis marked by knowledge and ingenuity—Coram concluded: "Had Dr. Blackstone been disposed to give his readers a true account of the origin of landed property in Europe he might have said, exclusive property in lands originated with government; but most of the governments that we have any knowledge of, were founded by conquest: property therefore in its origin, seems to have been arbitrary. He might then have expatiated upon the difficulty and inconvenience of attempting any innovations upon the established rules of property. This would have sufficiently answered his purpose, and saved him much sophistry and absurdity, and not a little impiety: for it is surely blasphemy to say, that there is a necessity of abrogating the divine law contained in the text of Genesis, to make room for human laws, which starve and degrade one half of mankind, to pamper and intoxicate the rest. 'But after all,' continues the Doctor, 'there are some few things, which must still unavoidably remain in common: such (among others) are the elements of light, air and water.' Thank you for nothing, Doctor. It is very generous, indeed, to allow us the common right to the elements of light, air and water, or even the blood which flows in our veins."

Here, Coram thought, lay the tragedy of civilization: "It is a melancholy reflection that in almost all ages and countries, men have been cruelly butchered, for crimes occasioned by the laws; and which they never would have committed, had they not been deprived of their natural means of subsistence. But the governors of mankind seem never to have made any allowance for poverty; but like the stupid physician who prescribed bleeding for every disorder, they seem ever to have been distinguished by an insatiable thirst for human blood. The altars of a merciful God, have been washed to their foundation, from the veins of miserable men; and the double-edged sword of Justice, with all its formality and parade, seems calculated to cut off equally the innocent and guilty. Between religion and law, man has had literally no rest for the sole of his foot. In the dark ages of Gothic barbarity, ignorance was some excuse for the framing of absurd systems; but in the age in which Dr. Blackstone lived, he should have known better; he should have known that the unequal distribution of property was the parent of almost all the disorders of government; nay, he did know it, for he had read Beccaria. . . . There is no necessity for concealing this important truth; but much benefit may be expected from its promulgation—It offers a foundation whereon to erect a system which, like the sun in the universe, will transmit light, life, and harmony to all under its influence—I mean—*a system of equal education.*"

After searching for the best mode of alleviating the miseries of mankind "without disturbing the established rules of property," Coram decided that education was the most effective. In this connection he contrasted education among the Indians with the practices followed by the white inhabitants of the United States. The Indians, he said, off by themselves, provided a direct and efficient training in the arts of obtaining a livelihood and of living in their communities. Among the whites, on the other hand, the conditions of education were disgraceful and degrading: "The country schools, through most of the United States, whether we consider the buildings, the teachers, or the regulations, are in every respect completely despicable, wretched and contemptible. The buildings are in general sorry hovels, neither wind-tight nor water-tight. . . . The teachers are generally foreigners, shamefully deficient in every qualification necessary to convey instruction to youth, and not seldom addicted to gross vices."

For the metaphysical speculations of American scholastics Coram entertained a contempt akin to that of Erasmus for the "logicians and sophisters" of his time. "Mankind," Coram protested, "ever inclined to the marvelous, run astray in search of a phantom, an ignis fatuus, while they neglect those simple and palpable truths, which could only conduct them to that happiness, they are so eagerly in search of. How many volumes have been wrote upon predestination, free will, liberty and necessity; topics which are not properly the objects of the human understanding, and of which after we have wrote a thousand volumes, we are not a whit wiser than when we began: while the economy of society is but little understood, and the first and simplest principles of legislation entirely neglected."

This intellectual concern with phantoms, in Coram's opinion, led to a disregard for visible follies in society: "Nothing is more obvious than that every person in a civilized society, should contribute towards the support of government. How stupid then is the economy of that society conducted, which keeps one half of the citizens in a state of abject poverty, saddling the other half with the whole weight of government, and the maintenance of all the poor beside! Every citizen ought to contribute, to the support of government, but all obligations should be within the limits of possibility; a man, at least, should be able to pay a tax, before he is compelled to do it as a duty. But the pauper, who cannot procure even the vilest food to spin out a miserable existence, may indeed burthen, but can never support the government. The English, whose absurdities we are at all times proud to imitate, in this respect seem justly to have deserved the keen satire of Dr. Swift, who says, the sage professors of Laputa were employed in extracting sun beams out of cucumbers, calcining ice into gun powder, and making fire malleable. The policy of the English government appears to have been to make the mass of people poor, and then to persecute them for their poverty, as their vagrant acts abundantly testify; those acts . . . are a manifest abuse of civilization—they are impolitic, barbarous, inhuman and unjust, and would disgrace even a society of satyrs."

Coram also deplored the indifference which left the masses of the people in Europe ignorant and benumbed: "Among the great body of the people in polished Europe, among the laboring poor, how rare is it to find a man possessed of any thing equal to the general knowledge of an ingenious savage? The European artist [artisan] is expert in the particular article of his trade or art. Thus a pin-maker is dextrous at making pins; but in every thing else he is as grossly stupid; his understanding is as benumbed and torpid as it is possible for any intellectual faculty to be." The English have universities for the sons of wealthy subjects, but "the body of the people are ignorant." France is crowded with "fat, lazy, lubberly ecclesiastics" but the nation is "a rude and ignorant rabble, utterly incapable of profiting by the golden opportunity which now offers [in the early stages of the revolution]. . . . Humanity is wounded by the outrages of the mob in France; but what better can be expected from *ignorance*, the natural parent of all enormity?"

In the United States also, Coram found conditions highly objectionable. "Here provisions are made for colleges and academies, where people of property educate their sons, while for the poorer rank of people no provisions are made, even for instruction in reading and writing." To support his contention, Coram quoted Noah Webster: "The constitutions are republican, and the laws of education are monarchical." This divergence between theory and practice he attributed to the fact that "most of the American legislatures are composed of lawyers and merchants. What is the reason? Because the farmer has no opportunity of getting his son instructed, without sending him to a college; the expense of which, is more than the profits of his farm. An equal representation is absolutely necessary to the preservation of liberty." The rich farmer may get himself into the legislature; "yet if through a deficiency in his education, he is unable to speak with propriety, he may see the dearest interest of his country basely bartered away. . . . Education therefore to be generally useful, should be brought to every man's door."

The private colleges and academies were failing in their public obligations. They were not training all citizens for their common responsibilities: "Education should not be left to the caprice, or negligence of parents, to chance, or confined to the children of wealthy citizens: it is a shame, a scandal to civilized society, that part only of the citizens should be sent to colleges and universities to learn to cheat the rest of their liberties."

Having stated his objections to contemporary educational facilities and methods in the United States, Coram addressed himself to the problem of the reconstruction necessary to attain the posited ends; namely, an education which would fit people to acquire the means of subsistence and assume their public obligations as citizens of the American Republic. By way of preliminary, he agreed with Noah Webster that the laws should provide for "such a distribution of lands, and principles of descent and alienation, as shall give every citizen the power of acquiring what his industry merits."

Furthermore good citizenship must have an economic and labor underwriting: "Society . . . should furnish the people with means of subsistence, and those means should be an inherent quality in the nature of the government, universal, permanent, and uniform. . . . The means I allude to, are the means of acquiring knowledge; as it is by the knowledge of some art or science that man is to provide for subsistence in civil society."

Coram's constructive proposals recognized the work-ethos as basic to good citizenship and dealt with the elementary preparation of the people for work in the arts and professions necessary to earning security: "Education then ought to be secured by government to every class of citizens, to every child in the state. The citizens should be instructed in sciences by public schools; and in arts, by laws enacted for that purpose, by which parents and others, having authority over children, should be compelled to bind them out, to certain trades or professions, that they may be enabled to support themselves with becoming independency, when they shall arrive to years of maturity." The object of the public schools should be "to teach the rudiments of the English language, writing, book-keeping, mathematics, natural history, mechanics and husbandry."

The second stage in education should be the training of mind and hand practically, through a properly regulated apprenticeship of a new type under the direction of "persons professing mechanical or other branches"; and this apprenticeship should be regulated by appropriate legislation "without having recourse to the common or statute law of England." The circumstances in America permit a different procedure: "I think a more humane and liberal policy might be established. . . . Indeed it is high time to check that blind adherence to trans-atlantic policy, which has so generally prevailed."

The type of education thus described should be equal for the children of the people. Although all persons are not mathematically equal, the doctrine of equality, if scorned "by some very grave personages," is widely accepted in America, and an equality of mental powers, as well as rights, does generally prevail among the children of the people. "The inhabitants of the United States are more upon an equality in stature, and powers of body and mind, than the subjects of any government in Europe. And of the United

States, the states of New-England, whose governments by charter verged nearest to democracies, enjoy the most perfect equality. Those who live ashore, are all legislators and politicians; and those who follow the sea, are all captains and owners."

The kind of public education to be provided for the people should also be equal throughout the union: "I know no reason why the country should not have as good schools as the sea port towns, unless indeed the policy of this country is always to be directed, as it has been, by merchants. I am no enemy to any class of men; but he that runs may read." States should be divided into districts of convenient size, substantial brick school houses built within easy reach of the children, and well paid and competent teachers assured to each district.

"No modes of faith, systems of manners, or foreign or dead languages should be taught in those schools." No medals or premiums should be offered to excite emulation among the children. Such competition turns boys who were bosom friends into fierce contentious rivals and, by introducing jealousy and envy among the girls, would "put to flight all the tender, modest, amiable virtues," leaving nothing "but malignant passion in their stead."

By these reforms, Coram trusted, civilization would be advanced and misery vanquished. With all the people trained in the sciences and arts of earning a livelihood and in meeting the obligations of citizenship, firm foundations would be laid for the development of American society on its revolutionary lines.

His argument closed with an exordium: "And now, my fellow citizens, having thus, tho' in an indigested manner, shewn you the great cause of all the evils attendant on an abuse of Civilization; it remains with you to apply the remedy. Let it not be said, when we shall be no more, that the descendants of an Eastern nation, landed in this Western world, attacked the defenceless natives, and 'divorced them in anguish from the bosom of their country,' only to establish narrow and inequitable policies, such as the governments of our forefathers were. But let us, since so much evil has been done, endeavour that some good may come of it—Let us keep nature in view, and form our policy rather by the fitness of things, than by a blind adherence to contemptible precedents from arbitrary and corrupt governments. Let us begin by perfecting the system of education, as the proper foundation whereon to erect a temple to liberty, and to establish a wise, equitable and durable policy; that our country may become *indeed* an asylum to the distressed of every clime—the abode of liberty, peace, virtue and happiness—a land on which the Deity may deign to look down with approbation—and whose government may last till time shall be no more!"

Of all the Americans who, inspired by the idea of civilization, gave meaning to universal history and to the function of the United States in it, none represented such a peculiar combination of interests, training, and experiences as Joel Barlow, graduate of Yale College. None employed the idea with a fuller understanding of its nature or its significance for the dramatic scenes of the Revolution and the republican adventure.

If Barlow was chiefly remembered in later years as the fervent patriot who wrote *The Columbiad*, he was in fact no chauvinist, no mere provincial unfamiliar with European civilization. Of his active and varied life, at least seventeen years were spent in the Old World; and as a climax to his European adventures death overtook him in Poland where, at the age of fifty-eight, on a mission from President Madison, he was seeking an audience with Napoleon in behalf of the commercial interests of the United States. A few days after the defeat of Bonaparte at Beresina, Barlow died in a village near Cracow, and in the earth of Poland, not of his native land, his narrow home was made.

Born in Connecticut, the son of Samuel and Esther Hull Barlow, a prosperous farming couple, young Barlow, after spending two months at Dartmouth College, entered Yale, in 1774, just as the American revolt against British dominion was exploding into violence. During his undergraduate days, in the summer vacation of 1776, he made an excursion into war with action in the campaign on Long Island. While still a young man he studied philosophy at Yale, prepared himself for the law and was admitted to the bar, took part in editing the American Mercury, served as a chaplain in a Massachusetts brigade, and tried his hand in business. Amid these experiences his fertile and fermenting mind was plotting and executing literary ventures. He was one of the Hartford Wits who, in 1787, delivered a satirical blast against the popular party, then being ridiculed as democrats—the party threatening the conservative wing of the revolutionary front.

In 1788 Barlow went to Europe as the representative of an American land company which quickly collapsed in fraudulent transactions and left him to make his way alone. Soon he was caught in the movement of thought and agitation that culminated in the explosion of the French Revolution. Shedding his New England conservatism, Barlow devoted himself to study, writing, propaganda, and financial speculations in England and France until 1805 when, urged by his wife "to go home and be respectable," he established himself in Washington. There he spent six years in undiminished literary, scientific, and business activities.

While living in Europe, Barlow took part in revolutionary enterprises, wrote a trenchant political document called *Advice to the Privileged Orders of Europe,* invested money in French consols, composed poetry, translated into English Warville's *New Travels in the United States,* urged President Washington to prevent war between England and France, translated Volney's *Ruins,* completed his long epic, *The Columbiad,* and devised an American institution "for research and instruction in the arts and sciences," outlined in his *Prospectus of a National Institution to be Established in the United States,* published in 1805, the date of his return to his native land. During those educative years, the incipient New England Federalist became transformed into an American democrat, fiercely loyal to America as a country of unique qualities and promises, while treasuring, despite his qualms, a faith in the possibilities of democracy in the Old World torn by upheavals within.

In the course of his wanderings and searchings, Barlow acquired a comprehensive world-view. As early as 1787 he arrived at the belief that the process of civilization was irresistibly enfolded in enormous movements of history. In an oration delivered at Hartford on July 4th of that year he discussed the opposing qualities of the revolutions in other countries and in the United States, with special reference to civilization. In Europe, he said, "the faculties of human reason and the rights of human nature have been the sport of chance and the prey of ambition. And when indignation has burst the bands of slavery, to the destruction of one tyrant, it was only to impose the manacles of another. This arose from the imperfections of that early stage of society, which necessarily occasioned the foundation of empires on the eastern continent to be laid in ignorance, and which induced a total inability of foreseeing the improvements of civilization, or of adapting the government to a state of social refinement."

On the other hand the prospects for civilization in America were peculiar and gratifying: "I shall but repeat a common observation when I remark that on the Western continent the scene was entirely different, and a new task totally unknown to the legislators of other nations was imposed on the fathers of the American empire. Here was a people thinly scattered over an extensive territory, lords of the soil on which they trod, commanding a prodigious length of coast and an equal breadth of frontier—a people habituated to liberty, possessing a mild and benevolent religion, and highly advanced in science and civilization. To conduct such a people in a revolution, the address must be made to reason, as well as to the passions. And to reason . . . the solemn address was made." It was a people so happily placed in the world, with such abundant resources and "enlightened," that made the revolution in America and here emancipated the process of civilization from the barbarism, ignorance, ambition, and tyranny that blocked its course in Europe.

Five years later with the French Revolution then well advanced on its way, Barlow, in his *Advice to the Privileged Orders in Europe,* contrasted the barbaric foundations of governments, ruling classes, and society in the Old World with the prospects of mankind in America. The tyrannies of Europe were all aristocratical tyrannies. There wars were waged not by the people or for popular causes but by despots for their own ends. The feudal system, the military system, the ecclesiastical system, and the administration of justice were at bottom conspiracies against humanity. In the ecclesiastical policy was constantly maintained "a uniform, cold-blooded hostility against the social harmonies of life." Improvements and reforms might be made in the one or another phase of the European system but, stemming from its barbaric origins and dominated by privileged orders, it seemed to be beyond reconstruction in the interests of humanity. As compared to civilization in Europe, America presented new creative urges in its economy, its liberty, its equality, its popular government, in everything that gave encouragement to mere human beings, the underprivileged.

Heartened by the French Revolution seven years after his

attack on the privileged orders of Europe, Barlow modified and elaborated his opinions respecting the Old World, in an address "To His Fellow Citizens of the United States" dated at Paris, in December 1799—a document concerned mainly with political measures. In this pamphlet, he rooted civilization in the primordial wants and needs of mankind; "The art of governing a nation is the art of substituting a moral to a physical force. . . . Hence great societies may be moved, millions of persons protected, industry and virtue universally encouraged, idleness and violence completely restrained, without lifting the hand of one man upon another. . . . Our mutual wants and aids are the elements of our civilization; they have already civilized individuals to a great degree, convinced them of their relative dependence, and taught them the art, as well as the convenience, of living together in peace."

Whether owing to a change in his convictions or a desire of improving relations between France and the United States, or under the spell of French cosmopolitanism, Barlow now contemplated, indeed predicted, the extension of the civilizing process to the relations between states hitherto and at the moment immersed in wholesale war. Our mutual wants and aids, he said, "have made some progress too in civilizing states; and their energy must be infallible in carrying on the work of harmony and happiness; till nations shall stand in the same relation to each other as families do at present in the best regulated community. The *civilization of states* is the great object to be aimed at in the present stage of the progress of human affairs. . . . Many persons imagine that states or nations can never be civilized more than they are at present; that among them the savage principle, or *the right of the strongest*, will always be resorted to.

"But why should we despair . . . ? The mutual dependence of men is universal, and it is perpetual. . . . There is no reason why civilization, after having softened the temper of individuals, and harmonized the component parts of state, as acting among themselves, should forever stop short at that point, and leave the state a savage without, while it is social and peaceful within. . . . Our hopes of progressive civilization are well founded. . . . It seems then that the tendency of civilization is to diminish the number of nations."

While he admitted that the conduct of states in ancient and modern times did not harmonize with his principles of peace, Barlow thought that the representative and democratic federalism of the United States might be applied to the states of Europe, "if the powers of government in every associated state were in the hands of the people." If the privileged orders could be overthrown and the interior social structure of each state reconstituted on American principles, a confederation of states might be extended throughout Europe "and be as lasting as was imagined by the fervid benevolence of St. Pierre." Thus Barlow's assurance came down to a hope resting upon an "if"—if the system of privileged orders could be supplanted by democracy on the American model.

Although holding out to his fellow citizens the prospect that the civilization of states might be made the next deliberate step in progress, if it was not inevitable, Barlow was careful to remind Americans that their own civilization was not complete, that they had to be on guard against the foes of civilization within as well as without. He made it plain to them that there could be no such federation of states as he proposed unless the civilizing process was maintained within each state; unless by their interior civilization they became sufficiently alike to make federation possible and workable.

One section in his address of 1799 Barlow devoted to "the means of securing interior liberty in the United States." Here he made a plea for "the science of political perspective," under which "the approaching changes in our situation should be distinctly noticed, and their consequences profoundly meditated. Our nation is young in respect to the date of its independence, the habits of thinking incident to this condition, and the trial we have had of our political institutions." The occupation of the rest of the unoccupied territory impended; relations with Spanish, French, and English colonies in the neighborhood would call for wisdom in negotiation so that amity would prevail. "The events are easy to foresee; they must be provided for; and it depends on you from this moment to say whether they shall redound to our advantage, and to the extensive benefit of ages and nations; or whether they shall bring destruction to our hopes, and overturn the fairest fabric of human policy that the world has hitherto seen."

In counseling his fellow citizens on matters of "interior liberty," Barlow prescribed the following points of policy. The federal government should be kept out of debt and its expenditures held within moderate limits. The government should be transferred as soon as possible to the proposed capital on the Potomac; it would have been better for national unity if it had been fixed eighty or a hundred miles up that river. Care should be given to the improvement of roads and water communication, to facilitate transportation, intercourse, travel, and the flow of mails, adding to the assimilation of manners and inspiring confidence and friendship among the people of all regions. "A universal attention to the education of youth, and a republican direction given to the elementary articles of public instruction, are among the most essential means of preserving liberty," sustaining representative government, teaching the people their duties and rights. Ignorance "is everywhere . . . an infallible instrument of despotism." The frontier territories must be managed under a wise policy that will draw them gently into the general unity through intercourse, commerce, migration, education, and manners. Since "a military establishment of any magnitude is extremely incompatible" with political liberty, "universal attention" must be given to "the arming and disciplining of the militia." If a large professional army were maintained, "it would soon be found impossible to keep us out of unnecessary wars . . . a calamity to be avoided in all possible cases by all rational means."

Another section of Barlow's address to his fellow citizens dealt with "the means of vindicating our commercial liberty," that is, with foreign policy in this relation. Pondering on the future, he indulged in the dream that privateering in war would be abolished, that the rights of neutrals in time of war would be defined and fully preserved, and that the seas would be free for neutral goods. "There ought to be no contraband of war liable to seizure," he said. "Your object is to remain at peace with all mankind, and to maintain a perfect neutrality whenever the Powers of Europe are at war. You ought therefore to publish a solemn declaration of this intention, and likewise a clear definition and declaration of the rights of neutrality which you mean to enjoy." The example set by America would spread: "Your efforts might finally point out to Europe the great desideratum of good men, the means of establishing perpetual peace. You would prove beyond contradiction, that an *unarmed neutrality* is better than an armed one."

Lest he be set down as an unpractical visionary, expecting an immediate Elysium, Barlow made it patent that he was looking far ahead: "My great anxiety to serve the cause of liberty, and accelerate the progress of civilization has alone induced me to address you these letters. I can have little hope whatever that my arguments will produce any immediate effect in exciting your attention to theories so abstracted from the great passions of the day. But principles remain, when the books that first contained them are forgotten; and I have so much confidence in those I here advance as to believe they will descend to some future friend of humanity, who will find a more fortunate moment for their reception, and place them before the world in a clearer point of light. The prospect of thus contributing to a distant good has made me write with pleasure; and it ought to engage you to read with patience."

Returning to an aspiration of his youth, that of writing a philosophic epic on America, first sketched in his *Vision of Columbus*, Barlow reworked, expanded, and labored over the early poem and published the results in two sumptuous volumes, *The Columbiad*, at Philadelphia, in 1807. In this "epic," Hesper, the genius of the Western world, appears before Columbus sick and in prison, broken and defeated, and reveals, as in a dream prophecy, the contribution of Columbus and the America he discovered to the civilization of the world. In an effort at colorful pageantry, Barlow dramatized the feudal ages, intrepid mariners going forth on their voyages of discovery, the migration of peoples to the New World in colonization, the storm and stress of the American Revolution. His story, or play, closed with a hymn to "the future glories of America."

Barlow's audacious Homeric effort has been censured by professional critics as a poetic failure, as an "unfortunate" excursion into letters by an ebullient patriot, as lacking in taste, skill, and power. To use the language of one, it "has been transfixed with jests—all of them variations on Hawthorne's laughter at 'its ponderosity of leaden verse.'" By another critic the poem is dismissed as a mere "geographical, historical, political, and philosophical disquisition." It has been admitted that *The Columbiad* contains "passages of grandeur" and that, amid "its forced sublimity and its declamatory and gaudy rhetoric," there are lines "really fine and free in both conception and execution." But beyond such concessions, literary criticism, whatever that may be, has been unwilling to go.

Considered as poetry, *The Columbiad* can hardly be called a work of art. Considered as a treatise in geography, history, politics, and philosophy, however, it holds an important place in the history of the idea of civilization in America. And it attracted attention in Europe as well as the United States.

When the Massachusetts scholar, George Ticknor, visited Lord Byron in 1815, the master English poet of the revolution in Europe talked "a great deal about America; wanted to know what was the state of our literature, how many universities we had, and whether we looked upon Barlow as our Homer." Ticknor did not report his reply to Byron's questions respecting the Homeric qualities of *The Columbiad*. Perhaps Barlow's work offended the good Federalist from New England, as much as its sentiments pleased Jeffersonian Republicans.

Whether Barlow himself fancied that he had written masterful poetry or was modest about his genius, he certainly intended *The Columbiad* to be a philosophic narratvie bearing on the history of civilization and on the characteristics of civilization in America. He made the point specific in his Preface: "In the poem here presented to the public, the objects, as in other works of the kind, are two: the fictitious object of the action and the real object of the poem. The first of these is to sooth and satisfy the desponding mind of Columbus; to show him that his labors, though ill rewarded by his contemporaries, had not been performed in vain; that he had opened the way to the most extensive career of civilization and public happiness; and that he would one day be recognized as the author of the greatest benefits to the human race. This object is steadily kept in view; and the actions, images and sentiments are so disposed as probably to attain the end. But the real object of the poem embraces a larger scope: it is to inculcate the love of rational liberty, and to discountenance the deleterious passion for violence and war; to show that on the basis of the republican principle all good morals, as well as good government and hopes of permanent peace must be founded; and to convince the student in political science that the theoretical question of the future advancement of human society, till states as well as individuals arrive at universal civilization, is held in dispute and still unsettled, only because we have had too little experience of organized liberty in the government of nations to have well considered its effects.

"I cannot expect that every reader, nor even every republican reader, will join me in opinions with respect to the future progress of society and the civilization of states; but there are two sentiments in which I think all men will agree: that the event is desirable, and that to believe it practicable is one step towards rendering it so. . . .

"My object is altogether of a moral and political nature. I wish to encourage and strengthen, in the rising generation, a sense of the importance of republican institutions; as being the great foundation of public and private happiness, the necessary aliment of future and permanent meliorations in the condition of human nature.

"This is the moment in America to give such a direction to poetry, painting and the other fine arts, that true and useful ideas of glory may be implanted in the minds of men here, to take place of the false and destructive ones that have degraded the species in other countries; impressions which have become so wrought into their most sacred institutions, that it is there thought impious to detect them and dangerous to root them out, though acknowledged to be false. Wo be to the republican principle and to all the institutions it supports, when the pernicious doctrine of the holiness of error shall creep into the creed of our schools and distort the intellect of our citizens. . . .

"To my country, therefore, with every sentiment of veneration and affection, I dedicate my labors."

If *The Columbiad* could be curtly brushed aside as a literary product, the independent sentiments expressed were celebrated by a German poet of undoubted power and enduring fame, Goethe, a contemporary of Barlow, who had with keen perception watched the revolutionary storms of the age. In a few lines written in 1827, Goethe, like Barlow, exulted in America's escape from the historical fixations of old Europe into a freer life:

> Amerika, du hast es besser
> Als unser Kontinent, der [*or,* das] alte,
> Du hast keine verfallenen Schlösser
> Und keine Basalte.

> Dich stört nicht im Innern
> Zu lebendiger Zeit
> Unnützes Erinnern
> Und vergeblicher Streit.

Benutzt die Gegenwart mit Glück!
Und wenn nun eure Kinder dichten,
Bewahre sie ein gut' Geschick
Vor Ritter-, Räuber- und Gespenstergeschichten.

When Goethe wrote these lines he was probably under the influence of impressions gathered from reading the book on American travels recently published by Prince Bernhard of Saxe-Weimar. He had also, it seems, read a German work on American geology and mineralogy in which the striking unity of American physical geography was contrasted with European geology broken and torn by volcanic upheavals that had left basaltic wreckage in their wake. At all events no translation of his poem into verse, or indeed prose, could possibly convey its whole meaning and spirit, but the general meaning of his substantive words is clear and the lines may be freely rendered as follows: "America, thou hast it better than our old Continent. Thou hast no ruined castles, no such geologic chaos. No useless memories of old history and futile strife vex thy inner spirit in this living hour. Mayst thou use thy present time with good fortune! And now when thy children write, may a good fate protect them against knight-, robber-, and ghost-stories."

A younger contemporary of Goethe but also indisputably great in his own field, philosophy, Georg Wilhelm Friedrich Hegel, likewise declared that America had an important role to play in universal history yet to be made. Without attempting to deal extensively with the United States and what he called "the dreams to which it may give rise," he said in his *Philosophy of History* that America is "the land of the future where, in the ages that lie before us, the burden of the World's History shall reveal itself. . . . It is the land of desire for all those who are weary of the historical lumber-room of old Europe. Napoleon is reported to have said '*Cette vieille Europe m'ennuie.*' " What had so far taken place in the New World, Hegel maintained, was "only an echo of the Old World," but still America was "the land of the future."

By no means endorsing the whole view of Barlow, Thomas Smith Grimké of Charleston, in the South, set forth a similar conception of civilization in America shortly after *The*

Columbiad appeared. He did this in an Oration delivered in St. Philip's Church on the Fourth of July, 1809. Young Grimké belonged to a prominent family. His father, Judge Grimké, stood high in the legal profession. His sisters, Sarah and Angelina, were in after years to free their slaves and go North to participate as eloquent crusaders in the anti-slavery cause. Urged by his father, Grimké surrendered his plan to enter the Episcopal ministry, joined the legal profession, and rose to eminence at the bar.

But his great interest was in the future of his country. He was a stalwart defender of the Union, in a state which was eventually to launch the secession movement, and an advocate of temperance, educational reform, and peaceable relations between the United States and other nations. With respect to education, by means of which young Americans were to be trained for their duties as citizens, he held that it "must partake deeply and extensively of the vital spirit of American institutions"; that it should include manual training, science, modern history, and literature; that provision should be made for the higher education of women; and that, while the spirit of religion must be fostered, improvement in the material condition must be promoted in the interests of the good life for all.

In Grimké's vision of America, union was "the vital principle of our permanence and happiness." Disunion would make divided states faithless and suspicious in time of peace, bitter and destructive enemies in time of war: "Vain would be the testimony of speculation, and equally vain the combined experience of four thousand years, could we not trace their application to ourselves; and discover in our domestic and foreign relations arguments for our union, which the sophist cannot answer, and the skeptic dare not doubt." The union contributed to "the rapid progress of public prosperity." It represented "the principle of renovation," of revolution in contrast to despotism, made the legislative power the delegated will of the people and civil authority the representative force of all, the "real government of the people." Against a background of long and destructive history in Europe, Grimké pictured "our government" as "the only just medium between despotism, where the rights of nature vanish in the slavery of the subject, and pure democracy, in which the subordination of the citizen is lost in the licentiousness of the man." Such, in the long history of nations, was the renovation effected by independence and union in America, as Grimké interpreted the human experience.

With renovation, Grimké united "the principle of improvement." Both attain "the height of perfection only in a republic like ours." Although foreign and domestic policies must vary with the conditions of the country, this maxim of progress is binding upon statesmen. "Whilst agriculture, manufactures, and commerce shall be the main pillars of American greatness, the spirit of improvement will govern the policy of our national legislature."

To the spirit of union, renovation, and improvement, he added "the influence of the social principle" in strengthening the bonds of American society. The social principle lies deep in the nature of mankind: "In examining the operation of this universal cause, we may trace it distinctly in its emanations from the parent to his family, from the individual to his neighbors, and thence to the wider circle of his friends and acquaintances. We may perceive it successively varying and enlarging, as it interweaves the several ranks of Society, unites the diversified classes of the town with the more uniform inhabitants of the country, and combines the influence of individuals and families, of cities and provinces, in forming the complex, but harmonious system of society. . . . We may follow the principle of association from each state to its neighbors, and from them to the union at large. And as the prospect expands, we shall behold the ties of nature and friendship, the calls of duty and interest, the rights of man, and the privileges of the citizen, uniting to form the sacred and mysterious bond of our union."

Union, renovation, improvement, and the widening social nexus—these are forces operating in America. Circumstances also have conspired with labors to give uniqueness to America: "He, who casts his eye over our happy land, must perceive that we form a little political world in ourselves: that our country seems, as was said of Laconia, to be but the patrimony of a band of brothers: that we appear to be another favored race, sent out by Heaven, from the storms and miseries of Europe, to dwell in this land of promise."

All these principles cherished in "this land of promise, under the favor of Heaven," Grimké found illustrated in "the rapid progress of our country, since we became a confederate republic." And he unrolled the scroll of his diagram for the future: "If we begin with our own State, we shall behold our political and civil institutions continually improving; religion and knowledge more widely diffused; civilization extending in the country, and refinement in the city; discordant parts successively assuming the uniformity of the whole, and confusion gradually subsiding into order. Travel through each of our sister States, and you may observe with pleasure and surprise the operation of similar principles. These will be seen, however, to vary with the nature of the country, the genius of the people, and the spirit of the Constitution.

"Then conceive yourselves elevated to an eminence, whence the eye may embrace the wide circuit of our happy land. Think what it was when we first became a nation; consider its present state, and mark the gradual advancement of prosperity and power. See the forest retiring, and the village expanding into the populous town: see this in turn swelling into the magnificence and greatness of the city. . . . Behold the genius of enterprise collecting his bands of adventurers, and leading them to the western wilds. Behold! the mountains open to afford them a passage; the dark wave of the desert rolls back at their approach; the gloomy spirit of solitude retires before them, and the grateful wanderer builds the verdant altar to agriculture and peace. Then behold! the forest bends beneath his strokes, the orchard smiles on the hill, the harvest waves in the valley, and the song of the reaper is heard in the silence of the wilderness."

But this America is a part of the world, and cannot be insulated from it: "In vain might we build ramparts of foreign prohibition, like the walls of Jericho, they would fall of their own accord. America then, must be connected with other nations, and must be influenced by them." But not for evil: the dangers of foreign intrigues and divisions at home are ever present. "The policy therefore of our young and flourishing country, is to preserve our interests as distinct as possible from those of other nations."

In union, however, is the guarantee that American security will be preserved. While the confederacy lasts, "other governments may perplex but cannot confound us; they may injure our interests, but not our liberties; they may exasperate us mutually as citizens, but never can arm us against each other as enemies." Where is the freedom of the citizen and his happiness the basis of the constitution, the rights of man revered, the victim of foreign persecution afforded a haven—

a country so various in its resources? "It is in America." What prayer can an American utter? That the American Republic may be "the center of universal knowledge, universal happiness, and universal freedom."

Bound by overlapping years of life to the generation of the Revolution and the generation of the popular upsurge, John Quincy Adams, son of John and Abigail Adams, occupied an exceptional position in the history of thought about civilization in the United States. Spurned by the old Federalists who hated him for going over to Jefferson on grounds of foreign policy, swept out of the presidency by the democratic uprising under Andrew Jackson whom he regarded as a barbarian, feeling himself deserted by his God, nevertheless Adams held fast to a vision of his country and its destiny which he had formed under the stimulus of great leaders in the early Republic, especially George Washington, the first president, and his father, the second president.

Until the dramatic day when his last sleep came upon him at his post of duty in the House of Representatives, John Quincy Adams kept that vision before him in the hours and moments of his full strength. Although his constituents in the Plymouth district stood steadfastly by him, the most powerful figures during his later years were against him. "He found the chief part of the gentlemen of Boston and its vicinity," said his biographer Morse, "the leading lawyers, the rich merchants, the successful manufacturers, not only opposed to him, but entertaining towards him sentiments of personal dislike and even vindictiveness." Defenders of slavery, North and South, near the end of his career, developed a resentment against him that became speechless only after the limits of vituperation had been reached. Still the "old man eloquent" hewed to his line. Only at the judgment seat of history, long afterward, did he receive vindications that were denied to him in life.

In considering both theory and practice, Adams kept the idea and the substance of civilization in mind. A student of the classics ancient and modern, of history old and new, versed in the thought of contemporary Europe through reading and long residence abroad while in the service of his country, he developed a strong sense for history and an alertness for the currents of opinion in his own time. Toward the close of his life, in the autumn of 1840, he put into a small compass his interpretation of history in an address delivered in Boston, New York, Brooklyn, and Baltimore. The clue to his thinking was revealed in the title: "The Progress of Society from the Hunter State to that of Civilization."

Popular interest in the man and the theme was demonstrated by the large and enthusiastic audiences that greeted Adams in the four cities and by the space given to his lecture in the columns of the newspapers. "An immense concourse of people" assembled to hear him in Baltimore, of whom "a large proportion was ladies," and "hundreds went away disappointed, on finding the interior of the spacious building so thoroughly filled as to allow of no further ingress."

The outline of Adams' lecture on the progress of society from its beginnings to civilization and the general nature of his thought on the subject were fully reported in the Baltimore papers, especially in The Sun. He opened by laying down a fundamental proposition embraced in the idea of civilization as it had already been formulated, namely, that man is a social being capable of and given to progress. "Man, of all animals," said the lecturer, "is social. Beasts, and birds, and fishes are gregarious. They live in herds and flocks and schools; but there is no progression beyond their original condition. Even the beaver, the bee and the ant, that, in their communities, seem to be actuated by a motive of common interest, act only by an unprogressive instinct. No social principle unites them; no mutual accumulation of property and intelligence, advances their condition. But man, gifted with an immortal spirit in union with his material body, is a being of progression."

After affirming this social principle, Adams then at great length traced the evolution of mankind successively through the hunter state, the pastoral state, the condition of the tiller of the soil, and finally the civilized state, in which the husbandman and the townsman both fill their appropriate stations. Civilization "is a consequence of agriculture and the arts to which it leads. Art leads to science, and invention to discovery—while navigation and ship-building, in extended branches, are the great results." But civilization is not a static thing: "Man's life is now one of action and meditation, and these lead to the progressive improvement of himself and others, of his country and his kind. Self-love and social intercourse are preserved in their beauty and utility. . . . This world is but a great firmament of moral and intellectual light, which should serve to point us toward eternal glory in the life to come."

Having sketched the rise of civilization out of primitive conditions, Adams concluded his lecture without attempting to trace its course in the modern age, to the regret of some among his auditors in Baltimore, at least of the writer who represented The Sun. "Our only disappointment," the reporter commented, "was at finding the hour so soon expired, and the lecture closed just at the point where an interest was most excited. We looked forward to the moment when Mr. Adams should dismiss the three preceding states in the progress of society, and analyze, with his keen discrimination, the elements of civilization as they now exist. Particularly did we look for such an exposition of the true social principle, as one with his age, experience, and great observation could give."

Such an exposition, the reporter explained, would have had a bearing on immediate social controversies in America: "The various movements in different quarters, within the last twenty or thirty years, to develop more fully the social principle in society . . . have almost invariably run into Utopian extremes. True individuality has been lost in extra-social organizations. The happy medium between selfishness and true social feelings, has not yet been attained in the 'civilized' state. It would have been applying most admirably the excellent and sage remarks of the address, had the lecturer, in his lucid style, enlarged upon the cultivation of the social principle as alone designed to elevate mankind into the higher state of civilization, towards which they are at this day rapidly ascending."

John Quincy Adams' conception of civilization was more than theoretical. It comprised all those elements of content included by great systematists of the idea: the social nature of human beings, arts, sciences, all branches of economy, inventions, government, Christian ethics, education, and letters—all dedicated to the progress of mankind in society. And with reference to several of these elements, Adams, by intensive study, accumulated special knowledge for his own guidance as a social being and a public servant.

Few, if any, public men of his day knew or cared more about natural science and its potentials for civilization than Adams did. His *Report on Weights and Measures*, literally prepared with his own hand while he was Secretary of State, gave evidences of a scientific mind mastering an amazing number of details. Fifty years later the mathematician, Charles Davies, member of a committee appointed by the University Convocation of New York to inquire into the proposed act of Congress respecting the adoption of a metric system for the United States, declared that Adams "examined the whole subject with the minuteness and accuracy of mathematical science—with the keen sagacity of statesmanship, and the profound wisdom of philosophy. To that report nothing can be added and from it nothing should be taken away. Hence the committee have published it in full, that the public, and especially the teachers of the country, may understand the entire subject in all its phases and relations." Nearly a hundred years afterward the chairman of the Royal Society of Canada, chosen to consider a phase of the subject, pronounced Adams' report "still a classic."

In his seventy-sixth year, in 1843, notwithstanding the infirmities of age, Adams made a toilsome journey to Cincinnati to deliver an oration at the laying of the cornerstone for the astronomical observatory to be built there. This he did for the advancement of science in the service of humanity. Writing before he made the trip, he said: "My task is to turn this transient gust of enthusiasm for the science of astronomy at Cincinnati into a permanent and persevering national pursuit, which may extend the bounds of human knowledge, and to make my country instrumental in elevating the character and improving the condition of man upon earth. The hand of God himself has furnished me this opportunity to do good."

Safe again in his home, Adams once more entered his dream in his records: "It is not much in itself. It is nothing in the estimation of the world. In my motives and hopes it is considerable. The people of this country do not sufficiently estimate the importance of patronizing and promoting science as a principle of political action; and the slave oligarchy systematically struggle to suppress all public patronage or countenance to the progress of the mind. . . . This invitation had a gloss of showy representation about it that wrought more on the public mind than many volumes of dissertation or argument. I hoped to draw a lively and active attention to it among the people, and to put in motion a propelling power of intellect which will no longer stagnate into rottenness. I endulge dreams of future improvement to result from this proclamation of popular homage to the advancement of science."

The American Union, the great principles to which it was consecrated, and correct policies for public action, John Quincy Adams believed, were in full accordance with the humanistic doctrines expressed in the idea of civilization. The Declaration of Independence he venerated as "a leading event in the progress of gospel dispensation," and maintained that "its principles lead directly to the abolition of slavery and of war, and that it is the duty of every free American to contribute to the utmost extent of his power to the practical establishment of those principles."

The fortunate position of the American people upon this continent endowed with immense natural resources, Adams held, favored the realization of those principles: "The public lands are the richest inheritance ever bestowed by a bountiful Creator upon any national community. . . . Ages upon ages of continual progressive improvement, physical, moral, political, in the condition of the whole people of this Union, were stored up in the possession and disposal of these lands. . . . I had long entertained and cherished the hope that these public lands were among the chosen instruments of Almighty power, . . . of improving the condition of man, by establishing the practical, self-evident truth of the natural equality and brotherhood of all mankind, as the foundation of all human government, and by banishing slavery and war from the earth."

Long before John Quincy Adams became the sixth president of the United States he had directed his thought to the problem of administering the nation's magnificent endowment of natural resources for the advancement of civilization in the United States. As Senator, diplomat, Secretary of State, President, and, at the end, as a member of the House of Representatives, he studied this problem, this opportunity, this possible achievement.

In the policy which he deemed alone worthy, the Federal Government was to hold and honorably manage the material treasures of the public domain in the interest of the whole people, developing canals and railways, giving employment to labor, banishing fear, slavery, and war, promoting the arts and sciences, making the good life prevail. To accomplish this purpose it was necessary to have constructive legislation by Congress and to establish a system of public administration competent in every branch, freed from the savage scramble for the "spoils of office," and dedicated to the public welfare. Otherwise, John Quincy Adams said, the American Union would cast away its natural heritage and live "from hand to mouth."

In command of documentary evidence, Brooks Adams in 1919 put the following construction upon his grandfather's ideals: "Never since the world was made, had any community been so favored as was the American by the gift of Providence of what was practically, for them, an unlimited store of wealth, which, for many generations, would raise them above the pressure of any competition which would be likely to engender war. The only serious problem for them to solve, therefore, was how to develop this gift on a collective, and not on a competitive or selfish basis. Dominant private interests as a motor would be fatal. Mr. [John Quincy] Adams believed when he entered the presidency that this task might be done by an honest executive, relatively easily, were he supported by an intelligent and educated civil service. . . . Were a single capitalistic or speculative class to get control, the interest of the whole must be sacrificed to the few and ancient injustice must prevail. For the type of government which Mr. Adams contemplated had necessarily to be one capable of conducting a complex organism on scientific principles."

Placed in this perspective, the comprehensive scheme of thought for the future of the United States, incorporated in John Quincy Adams' first message to Congress—one of the few illuminating documents of the kind since Washington's state papers—assumes a special significance for the idea of civilization in America. In that manifesto to the nation, he arrayed government on the side of civilization: "The great object of the institution of civil government is the improvement of the condition of those who are parties to the social compact and no government, in whatever form constituted, can accomplish the lawful ends of the institution but in proportion as it improves the condition of those over whom it is established."

Applying the broad principle to concrete practice, Adams declared that "roads and canals, by multiplying and facilitating the communications and intercourse between distant regions and multitudes of men, are among the most important means of improvements." But he did not stop there; he went on to assert that "moral, political, intellectual improvement are duties assigned by the Author of Our Existence to social no less than to individual man. For the fulfillment of those duties governments are invested with power, and to the attainment of the end—the progressive improvement of the condition of the governed—the exercise of delegated powers is a duty as sacred and indispensable as the usurpation of powers not granted is criminal and odious."

After these affirmations came more details. "Among the first, perhaps the very first, instrument for the improvement of the condition of men is knowledge, and to the acquisition of much of the knowledge adapted to the wants, the comforts, and enjoyments of human life public institutions and seminaries of learning are essential." So Adams renewed Washington's proposal for the establishment of a national university, which had also been commended by Jefferson and Madison. But that was not enough. He demanded "the improvements of those parts of knowledge which lie beyond the reach of individual acquisition," and called upon Congress to consider exercising its powers under the Constitution through the enactment of legislation "promoting the improvement of agriculture, commerce, and manufactures, the cultivation and encouragement of the mechanic and of the elegant arts, the advancement of literature, and the progress of the sciences, ornamental and profound."

If the powers belonged to Congress, "to refrain from exercising them for the benefit of the people themselves would be to hide in the earth the talent committed to our charge—would be treachery to the most sacred of trusts. The spirit of improvement is abroad upon the earth. . . . While dwelling with pleasing satisfaction upon the superior excellence of our political institutions, let us not be unmindful that liberty is power; that the nation blessed with the largest portion of liberty must in proportion to its numbers be the most powerful nation upon earth, and that the tenure of power by man is, in the moral purposes of his Creator, upon condition that it shall be exercised to the ends of beneficence, to improve the condition of himself and his fellow men. . . . Were we to slumber in indolence or fold up our arms and proclaim to the world that we are palsied by the will of our constituents, would it not be to cast away the bounties of Providence and doom ourselves to perpetual inferiority?" Already states were building canals and founding institutions of learning. The

Federal Government must act boldly also for the benefit of the Union as a whole.

But Adams' grand conceptions were deemed trite, amusing, irrelevant or intellectual posturing by his opponents and he was defeated as a candidate for re-election. The natural resources of the nation which he would have dedicated to the improvement of the condition of the people were handed over to exploitation by private interests. "The thirst of a tiger for blood," he cried, "is the fittest emblem of the rapacity with which the members of all the new states fly at the public lands. The constituents upon whom they depend are all settlers, or tame and careless spectators of the pillage. They are themselves enormous speculators and landjobbers. It were a vain attempt to resist them here."

After John Quincy Adams was driven from the White House, the Government of the United States, established for promoting the general welfare and providing common defense, fell into the hands of a political party committed to the narrowest possible interpretation of its powers and to the defense of slavery at all costs. To such a low point did the idea of the National Government sink that John C. Calhoun could oppose accepting James Smithson's gift to the United States for the establishment of an institution to increase and diffuse knowledge among men, and allege, in support of his position, that Congress had no power under the Constitution to accept such an endowment. Had it not been for the heroic efforts of John Quincy Adams, while he was a member of the House of Representatives, the Smithsonian Institution might not have been founded.

In these circumstances the final years of John Quincy Adams' life were filled with grief. He watched the extraordinary treasury of natural resources, which he wished to have administered efficiently for the common good, dissipated among private interests. He witnessed politicians, nominally acting as public servants, actually engaged in grabbing and gambling in public lands. Against his grand idea of a national civilization he found opposed and apparently triumphant Calhoun's conception of civilization as restricted to communities called sovereign and independent states, and as lending countenance to human slavery besides. In his moments of depression he had doubts whether the Union could long survive the forces of disintegration.

Yet in other moments Adams had reveries of slavery extirpated—even by the sword. As early as 1820 he confided to his *Diary* the thought that in a coming civil war slavery would be expelled from the whole continent, adding: "And calamitous and desolating as this course of events in its progress must be, so glorious would be its final issue that, as God shall judge me, I dare not say that it is not to be desired." As events moved toward this crisis, he publicly delivered his prophecy on the floor of the House of Representatives in April, 1842.

Within twenty years, history-as-fact had vindicated John Quincy Adams on the slavery issue and impeached John C. Calhoun. What another century would do to vindicate him also as against the despoilers of the public domain was evident to his descendants. If in his last days of despondency John Quincy Adams felt that his life in the public service had been a failure, that harsh judgment on his career could be attributed perhaps to the fact that his faith was not as strong as his vision was large and luminous.

In the great affirmations made by writers who placed the seal of their approbation on the idea of civilization in the United States, during the early years of the Republic, four general Propositions stood out clear as noonday. There were variations in the precise language of these statements. There were differences in the relative stress laid upon them. The illustrations adduced to support them varied in character and concreteness. But the Propositions were made essentials of the idea. They gave meaning and veridicality to it. They filled the amplitude of its reach with intellectual constructs which, it was believed, could be authenticated out of common human experiences, verified by reference to established facts of history. More than this, these four Propositions gave a high degree of certitude to the faith that civilization would not perish in the United States; that destiny was in its favor; that the American people had powers competent to grapple with their opportunity; that despite lapses and deficiencies they would measure up to the obligations imposed upon them by civilization.

I. First among the Propositions was that the idea of civilization involved nothing less than a complete theory of human history from the beginning to the latest hour and carried positive intimations as to the future of mankind. In this theory of history, naturally, European experiences bulked large, for the American population had come to America mainly from European countries. But in this theory of history, universal in scope, two facts were set forth with confidence: (1) There had been progress in the sciences, arts, skills, and knowledge available for the steady conquest of the physical world, and the conditions for continuous progress were especially favorable on the American continent; (2) Ever associated with this progress, indeed an essential of it, was the social principle —primordial in the structure and evolution of society—which was to be given greater range for action in the United States where the people were more emancipated from the despotic prescriptions and the accompanying servilities of Europe.

2. Correlative to this theory of history was the second Proposition: that America, though an offshoot from Europe, was no mere duplication of European ideas, institutions, and practices. People had crossed the sea from Europe to the New World; they had brought with them arts, skills, ideas, habits, and institutions useful for the practice of individual and social living, together with many follies and superstitions. But in the transfer from the Old World, huge aggregations of servitudes, servilities, barbaric laws, and historic cruelties had been left behind. And whatever the nature of the remaining and continuous ties with Europe, the offshoot, the American branch of the European family, could never in fact return to the fold, any more than a branch to a tree trunk; could never take over the whole European heritage; could never be the same as European civilization or any national manifestation of it in the British Isles or on the Continent. For good or ill, this divergence was fated and American writers on civilization in the early Republic rejoiced in this fate.

3. Given these two Propositions rooted in historical realities, the third Proposition inexorably followed: In the nature of things, civilization in the United States, being fundamentally different from civilization in Europe, must continue to differ, for history is irreversible. In giving validity to this third Proposition, the writers of the early Republic relied upon four types of fact:

1) The first was the fact of time. The American society was founded and developed in the full light of the modern age. The origins of its founding, unlike those of European societies, were not lost in pre-historic darkness, in mythological time, in the dim twilight of barbarism, pagan gods, super-

stitions, ignorance, and fears. There could be no question either that, as to time, American society was founded and developed in the age when science, arts, crafts, and critical thought made tremendous strides and wrought political and intellectual revolutions in England and on the continent of Europe.

2) The second type of fact which gave validity to the proposition respecting uniqueness was related to population. The American population consisted of immigrants from many European nationalities. They were in the main self-selected immigrants drawn from the middling and working orders of Europe, not from the orders of princes, lords and ladies, knights, and ecclesiastics. In this population was a large body of dissenters, Protestant and Catholic, who had fled from persecution, oppression, and poverty in the Old World. In the New World, from whatever race or nationality they had sprung, immigrants and settlers were not as hostile to one another as they had been on the other continent; here they were all Americans, as Crévecoeur called them.

3) The third type of fact adduced to support the proposition respecting uniqueness pertained to the geographical theater in which American civilization occurred. This theater was separated from Europe by three thousand miles of water. It was vast in area. It was richly endowed with arable land and other resources. Just how vast was the area or how rich the endowment was not yet fully realized; nor how the land under American jurisdiction would expand; but enough was known to have a transforming effect upon the minds of the immigrants who lived and worked on American soil. Still more important, the extent of virgin soil and resources permitted a large population of Americans to escape from the thraldom of scarcity which tied the divided peoples of Europe to a low level of subsistence and restricted the benefits of civilization mainly to privileged orders. There was ease, comparative at least, of movement through the states of the Union and for the improvement of the individual's lot there was an ample zone of experimental liberty.

4) The fourth type of fact regarded as validating the proposition respecting uniqueness related to social conditions. Despite slavery and poverty, which were constantly deplored, a great equality of condition existed in the United States. No privileged orders ruling by prescription and divine right were established by law to govern, instruct, indoctrinate, and tax

the whole body of the American people. Not only that. Great national documents, including the Declaration of Independence and the Constitution, gave moral justification to the resolve that general welfare must prevail. They provided pledges that the American spirit, to which they gave written expression, would extend equality and raise the level of social well-being —the supreme test of a high civilization.

4. Springing out of the theory of history in which was civilization, out of the time element in American origins and development, and out of the facts of uniqueness, or variation in other forms, was the fourth Proposition: that the people of the United States had both a boundless opportunity and an unlimited obligation to elevate their civilization and equalize the distribution of its benefits by individual, associated, civic, and political determinations and activities. And as a corollary: they had the faith, the optimistic philosophy, the will, and the power to accomplish this work. In the United States great numbers of the population were emancipated from the class rigidities of Britain and Europe. The nation was remote from the wars of Europe; possessed the resources and the skills; could efface poverty, slavery, misery, and the barbaric laws and customs inherited from the long past in other lands. It could develop a home for humanity—provide an asylum for the oppressed of Europe who were prepared in spirit to share in this tremendous enterprise; could by example excite the imagination of Europeans in their countries and inspire them to burst the bonds that chained them, rise against their oppressors, and institute just and beneficent governments where they were. American writers were aware that the revolt of the masses in Europe might be as terrible as the oppressions which had been long endured. They had doubts and fears about outcomes of such a revolt. Nevertheless in their belief in human potentialities they looked forward eagerly, if not steadily, to a universal, perhaps wavering, progress in civilization through the will of other peoples, also, in their places and times.

Having waged a successful revolution, having seen the American people escape the historic reaction of a military dictatorship when George Washington spurned the scepter, having labored for the institution and preservation of popular governments, the Americans who affirmed the idea of civilization in the United States in the early years of the Republic were not closet philosophers—not intellectual dreamers mooning over theoretical Gardens of Eden. Behind their Propositions was power of accomplishment. The heritage which they transmitted to the succeeding generation was more than a body of paper doctrines or dogmas. They bequeathed the substance, the instrumentalities, and the spirit for a grander civilization in the United States.

Chapter 5

Amplification in the Popular Upsurge

As THE SECOND generation of Americans assumed control of the Republic, they took over the idea of civilization, amplified it, that is, enlarged its representative significance, and applied it with cumulative force to thought about America as destiny, opportunity, and responsibility amid the changing circumstances of the age. References to it increased in number not only in discourses, treatises, essays, and correspondence, but also in the multiplying pages of popular publications. It was more fully explored for content and meaning. It was more often employed in discussions of great public issues. It appeared more frequently as a vision of potentialities and obligations, individual and social; as a sanction for policies pointed in the direction indicated by its goal; as a symbol of permanence and change under which elementary values were to be preserved and alterations in subsidiary theories and practices were to be progressively effected in bringing the real into ever closer harmony with the ideal.

As a form of thought and an instrument of action, the idea of civilization was used in relation to the personalities and events of the period. The new age witnessed the upswing of democracy, including the sharing of women in the aspirations and activities of the democratic movement, rapid developments in science, invention, industry, the arts, education, journalism, the westward advance of the people, and other types of practical and intellectual activity.

Partly induced by changes called external, certainly affiliated with them, partly representing the exfoliation of inherited ideas, and partly springing from the exercise of creative intelligence, broad movements of thought marked the spirit of the age. These movements represented a consideration of the nature of democracy and the American people; a search for wider economic policies appropriate to the realities and possibilities of American life and the logic of the democratic ideal; a growing desire to accept the uniqueness of American society and the development of an American philosophy of life; an evaluation of progress in America; a discussion of the

153

attitude to be taken by churches as organizations and by the clergy toward this democracy, liberalism, progress, and civilization; a quest for a construct of written history to provide anchorage, authority, and guidance for civilization in the United States; and efforts, through the expanding press, to make the idea of civilization an archetype of concentration for a larger proportion of the people.

The characteristics of the age, inseparable in fact, were not, and could not be, wholly separated in the discourses and literature of the time. Thought about any feature was usually penetrated by thought about others. Consideration of civilization in general was commonly associated with attention to particular aspects of civilization, such as the upswing of democracy and repercussions in antagonisms to slavery; progress in inventions and the rising factory system; the organization of industrial workers to improve the conditions of their labor by collective bargaining; education for an enlarging and polyglot population being widely enfranchised; exercise of the freedoms guaranteed by the federal and state Constitutions—free speech, free press, right of assembly, right of petition; modifications of law and refinements of practice pertinent to family and sex relations; the disposition of the public lands; economic policies suited to the expansion of American society across the continent by business as well as by agricultural enterprise. In discussing such topics, writers who dealt with them in terms of civilization usually cut across more than one boundary, in necessary recognition of their interrelationships.

Consequently in any systematic treatment of the idea of civilization during this long period of American history, topical divisions into parts can be for convenience only; the divisions cannot be absolute if they correspond to the facts in the case. And, owing to the immense bulk of literature bearing on the subject, only writings deemed representative and illustrative can be surveyed in a single volume.

The reciprocal influences of democracy and civilization, for example, were explored in a great document on the United States—Count Alexis de Tocqueville's report on his extensive and intensive studies in this country at the beginning of the popular upsurge, *De la Démocratie en Amérique*. Tocqueville's preparation for his researches in the United

States, George Wilson Pierson has described with scholarly care and sensitive appreciation in his *Tocqueville and Beaumont in America*. That intelligent French observer of character and events in America had attended lectures on civilization given in Paris by Guizot, the first great writer who treated the subject of civilization as a theory of history exemplified in the actual history of Europe and France. After referring to other preparatory experiences of those exceptional students of American society, Pierson says: "More important still to the development of their thought, however, they were together attending a stimulating course of lectures given by one of the greatest of the *Doctrinaires* . . . Professor Guizot . . . now, back again in his chair . . . was confining himself strictly to his subject, the early civilization of Europe and of the French, and was outlining the development of the people with such consummate ability and apparent precision as to draw large and enthusiastic audiences. But his lectures were none the less suggestive, Tocqueville and Beaumont found. Particularly interesting were the Professor's insistence on the *enchaînement* of events, and his theory that history was governed by certain inexorable laws. The young men listened with avidity and took many notes. But there was one idea that was too big to be put on paper. Guizot believed in progress, in the gradual, inevitable forward march of society through the slow growth and rise to power of the Middle Class. In the course of its advance, Guizot pointed out, the 'Third Estate' had humbled feudal lords and aristocracy, levelled class distinctions and churchly privilege; now it was attacking the monarchy. . . . That meant, reasoned Tocqueville, that all inequalities would disappear, that the nations were being swept toward a more equal distribution of rights and privileges, as on an irresistible tide; in short, that the tendency of the age was toward democracy." For Tocqueville, the young aristocrat, this was strong medicine, but it helped to fit him for his survey of civilization in the United States.

When Tocqueville arrived on American soil in the spring of 1831, ostensibly to study prisons in the United States but in fact to study "in detail and as scientifically as possible" the mechanism and inner energies (*ressorts*) "of that vast American society," he had in mind the luminous idea of civilization. Repeatedly during his long journeys, his observations, and his conversations with Americans, the idea helped to shape his inquiries and enliven his thought. He used it again and again in his letters and in his notes. In those papers and in the final text of his work on *Democracy in America*, he frequently referred to civilization as a summation of values, a synthesis of social forces, a standard of measurement, or a term of description. Whether he was observing conditions of life in seaboard cities or on the frontier, whether he was dealing with some particular detail or trying to see things in a large perspective, he found the idea helpful in making interpretations or providing general settings or formulating authoritative conclusions.

Tocqueville had been in New York City only a few days when he inquired in a letter to a friend in France: "To what cause do you attribute the prosperity of this nation? Is it to political institutions or to material and industrial causes? What degree of civilization do you suppose this people has reached, and precisely what forms does this civilization take?" Later, during their visit in Boston, his companion Beaumont compared society there with society in New York City, bearing civilization in mind: "There are in society others besides business men. They are interested here in the fine arts and literature; there is a class of persons engaged in neither trade nor industry and whose pastime is to live with all the *agréments* (satisfactions or pleasures) provided by an advanced civilization."

During a journey into the interior of New York, Tocqueville was struck by the signs of achievement he discovered there and set down in his notes: "If the country is new, one sees at each step that it is an old people which has come to inhabit it. When by a fearful trail through a kind of wilderness you have succeeded in reaching a dwelling, you are astonished to meet with a civilization more advanced than in any of our villages."

While he was in the forest regions of the Great Lakes he was astonished by the uniformity of civilization in the New World. He had been under the impression, he said, that he would find in America, as in Europe, centuries of difference between civilization in some parts and in others, and would discover American people in various stages of civilization from "the wilderness savage" to "the opulent city patrician." But, accepting the testimony of his own eyes, he felt bound to record: "Everywhere extreme civilization and nature abandoned to herself find themselves together and as it were face to face. . . . The plane of a uniform civilization has passed over it [American society]. . . . The portion of the territories longest and most completely settled has reached a high degree of civilization. . . . Those who inhabit these isolated places [on the frontier] have arrived there since yesterday; they have come with the customs, the ideas, the needs of civilization. They yield only to savagery that which the imperious necessity of things exacts from them." Excited by the speed of the process, Tocqueville declared that he and Beaumont had found civilization advancing like "a forest fire (*incendie*) through the wilderness."

In writing the argument and text of his *Democracy in America* from his notes, memories, and documents, as Tocqueville came to deal with crucial issues in the United States he sometimes looked upon them as challenges to civilization or as involving the fortunes of civilization on a grand scale. Reflecting upon the practical turn of American science and its probable influence on American character, he said: "Because the civilization of ancient Rome perished in consequence of the invasion of the Barbarians, we are perhaps too apt to think that civilization cannot perish in any other manner. . . . It is a fallacy then to flatter ourselves with the reflection that the Barbarians are still far from us; for if there be some nations which allow civilization to be torn from their grasp, there are others who trample it themselves under their feet."

Near the end of his first volume, Tocqueville confronted the gravest of all the political questions that were being debated in the age of nullification in America, namely, the dangers of national disruption. Appreciating the magnitude of the peril, he made a thoughtful examination of the centrifugal and the centripetal forces at work in American society and an ingenious calculation of probabilities as to outcome, without claiming insight enough to penetrate the veil. Having estimated the pull of forces, however, he concluded that "the civilization of the North appears to be the common standard, to which the whole nation will one day be assimilated."

After he had completed his great treatise and approached the application of his findings on America and his opinions about the United States to the disturbances produced by the march of democracy in his native land, Tocqueville, in a moving Introduction, at one point treated the alignment of forces in France as if drawn for and against civilization:

"There are virtuous and peaceful individuals whose pure morality, quiet habits, opulence, and talents fit them to be the leaders of the surrounding population. Their love of country is sincere, and they are ready to make the greatest sacrifices for its welfare. But civilization often finds them among its opponents; they confound its abuses with its benefits, and the idea of evil is inseparable in their minds from that of novelty. Near these I find others, whose object is to materialize mankind, to hit upon what is expedient without heeding what is just, to acquire knowledge without faith, and prosperity apart from virtue; claiming to be the champions of modern civilization, they place themselves arrogantly at its head, usurping a place which is abandoned to them, and of which they are wholly unworthy."

A line-by-line study of the materials assembled by Pierson, combined with an examination of the matters which engaged Tocqueville's interest in America, warrants the conclusion that the conception which covered his intellectual inquiry was no less comprehensive than the idea of civilization; that democracy was, for him, a phase of civilization. This impression is confirmed by a minute study of the plan and text of Tocqueville's treatise on *Democracy in America*. Even in those chapters which deal particularly with political institutions he ranged far beyond constitutions, laws, and the immediate practice of politics to consider the relations of economics, social conditions, manners, morals, education, and religious opinions to the nature and functioning of government in all principles and details.

Any lingering doubts as to the breadth of Tocqueville's interest appear to be removed by a scrutiny of the chapters in the second part of his survey. There he inquired into the philosophic methods of Americans, the principal sources of belief, aptitudes for general ideas, religion, pantheism, faith in the perfectibility of man, addiction to practical rather than theoretical science, taste for science, literature, and art and their cultivation, study of the classics, some sources of poetry, the drama, characteristics of historians, parliamentary eloquence, love of equality, individualism, influence of associations in civil life, the newspapers, restraints on individuals, desire for general well-being, care for worldly comforts, the honorable nature of all callings, preference for industrial employments, probability of a manufacturing aristocracy, softening of manners with equalization of social conditions, easy and simple intercourse, influence of democracy on economy, wages, and the family, women and the relations between the sexes, customs, morals, armies and warfare, and the effect of democratic ideas and feelings on politics.

In some respects Tocqueville's procedure comported with the spirit of Guizot's teachings. Without making systematic the distinction which Guizot drew between the "exterior" and the "interior" of civilization, Tocqueville brought both into his calculations as he observed various aspects of American civilization. In his first volume, after a chapter on the "Exterior Form of North America," he described the outward, or institutional, characteristics of political affairs and the social conditions and leading traits of the people which gave shape to and sustained the democratic republic. The remainder of the great work, devoted to the influences of democracy, was almost entirely filled with discussions of the "interior" features of civilization in the United States—with the nature of the American intellect, feelings, and manners, the qualities and directions of minds and sentiments.

As if working in the tradition which Condorcet had set, Tocqueville also turned his trenchant mind upon that half of society which had received little attention in the histories written by his instructor, Guizot: namely, women. Surprised, indeed startled, to find American women so free in conduct and spirit, so buoyant in conversation and yet so much cooler to seductive blandishments than the French women whom he had known or known about, the young French aristocrat gave an increasing amount of consideration to the role of women in the American democracy—"mistresses of their own action," as he called them. He had long talks about this matter with the democratic American, of French and English descent, Joel Poinsett, who explained women's self-government as due, in part, to the absence of idle aristocratic men whose main interest was in philandering.

Tocqueville's patient, curious, and remarkably objective study of American women—of their self-confidence and security, their courage in ill fortune, their character and education, their social equality with men, the domestic happiness which they effected, their philanthropic activities, and their innate and acquired refinements despite limitations still imposed upon them by custom and law—convinced him that American women played a constituent function in the Republic. Finally he declared: "If I were asked, now that I am drawing to the close of this work, in which I have spoken of so many important things done by the Americans, to what the singular prosperity and growing strength of that people ought mainly to be attributed, I should reply, To the superiority of their women."

Nothwithstanding the large place assigned to democracy in his pages, Tocqueville might have appropriately called his treatise *De la Civilisation en Amérique*. As Pierson indicates, the author had in his mind no rigidly limited definition of democracy and used the term in many senses. Moreover Tocqueville was for a time uncertain as to the precise nature of his inquiry and synthesis and as to the exact title to be given to the completed work. With respect to his final decision on the point, it is pertinent to note that he chose the formula *De la Démocratie en Amérique*, that is, *Of Democracy in America*, not *Democracy in America*, as his title has been rendered in English translations and thus given a descriptive positivism which did not harmonize with the text itself.

With keen insight John Stuart Mill, a friend of Tocqueville, comprehended the temper and constituency of this famous treatise. "The value of his [Tocqueville's] work is less in the conclusions drawn than in the mode of arriving at them," Mill commented. "He has applied, to the greatest question in the art and science of government those principles, and the methods of philosophizing, to which mankind are indebted for all the advances made by modern times in other branches of the study of nature. It is not risking too much to affirm of these volumes, that they contain the first analytical inquiry into the influence of Democracy. For the first time, that phenomenon is treated of as something which, being a reality in nature, and no mere mathematical or metaphysical abstraction, manifests itself by innumerable properties, not by some one only; and must be looked at in many aspects before it can be made the subject even of that modest and conjectural judgment which is alone attainable respecting a fact at once so great and so new."

In spirit and execution, Tocqueville's work—essentially sociological and psychological—placed democracy in the great stream of history for which Condorcet had formulated his theory making civilization the motif. Tocqueville's "specific creed," as Pierson calls it, was that "the progressive elimination of privilege and inequality had been the unperceived but fundamental law of the past, as it would continue to be the great gravitational principle of the future, for at least another century to come." If Tocqueville contemplated this "law" with some quandaries as to its beneficial nature, he was convinced of its reality.

But entirely apart from all debate over the controlling formulas of Tocqueville's philosophy, or world-view, the substance of his work stands as written. In fact, though he wrote for the French, he gave to Americans a realistic description and interpretation of their civilization in its manifold relations to democracy during the opening stages of the political upheaval under Andrew Jackson's banner.

Tocqueville's treatise on democracy, although it contained historical intimations, did not go far into history. On the other hand, formulators of the idea of civilization in the early republican period, while they had grounded it in a theory of history and recognized the "law" of equalization, had been chary about using the word democracy in that connection, if they adverted to it at all. They had not, as a rule, committed themselves openly to democracy. Indeed the very word had been so suspect that even Jefferson had seldom mentioned it; never, apparently, in any state paper or public address.

By 1830, however, members of Jefferson's Republican party were proudly calling themselves Democrats and the word was gaining respectability in other circles. The time was ripe for some sympathizer with democracy to give it more meaning and higher credentials within an interpretation of history. This intellectual enterprise was undertaken by George Bancroft who discharged it by identifying "the progress of the people," that is, the advance of democracy, with "the progress of civilization," and by binding the civilization of his age to long history.

Born and reared in Massachusetts, educated at Harvard, trained for technical scholarship in Germany, Bancroft by heritage belonged to the Federalist tradition. But he broke from it. While yet a young man, on that fateful July 4th, 1826, when John Adams and Thomas Jefferson lay dying, Bancroft, in a public address, placed himself without reservation on the side of democracy. Instead of praising the aristocratic doctrines of Adams, he celebrated the principles of Jefferson: "With the people the power resides, both theoretically and practically. The government is a democracy, a determined, uncompromising democracy; administered immediately by the people, or by the people's responsible agents." To this address Bancroft later referred as "a radical, democratic, levelling, unrighteous oration."

Besides publicly acclaiming democracy, Bancroft offered himself as a candidate for the state legislature on the local Democratic ticket and, according to the Boston Atlas, sank down into the abyss: "The 'Workingmen,' as they style themselves, better known, however, in that city as the 'idle men,' who adjourn from the halls of infidelity and atheism, from the dram shops and the dram cellars, to their various places of meeting, to devise some scheme by which they may live on the earnings of industrious men—are loud in the praise of their new leader and co-worker, Mr. Bancroft."

Undaunted by criticisms, Bancroft continued to maintain that democracy "is the party of progress and reform . . . enfranchises the human mind . . . struggles for equal political rights . . . puts the plow into the hands of the owner . . . respects humanity, and struggles for universal education and universal suffrage. . . . Democracy is practical Christianity." Writing to John Quincy Adams, he said: "It was Hamilton, it was the financial aristocracy of that day, which bore down your father. . . . There is fast rising in New England, a moral Democracy, in harmony with Christianity, in harmony with sound philosophy, in harmony with the progress of civilization."

In two addresses to scholars Bancroft explained his philosophy of history as the struggle of and for civilization, assured increasing gains through the progress of the people, by the very nature of God and His universe. The first oration, delivered at Williamstown College in August, 1835, dealt with "The Office of the People in Art, Government, and Religion"; the second, on "The Progress of Mankind," was delivered before the New York Historical Society in 1854.

In the first address Bancroft declared: "It is not by vast armies, by immense natural resources, by accumulations of treasure, that the greatest results in modern civilization have been accomplished. . . . The exact measure of the progress of civilization is the degree in which the intelligence of the common mind has prevailed over wealth and brute force; in other words, the measure of the progress of civilization is the progress of the people. Every great object, connected with the benevolent exertions of the day, has reference to the culture

of those powers which are alone the common inheritance....
The defense of public liberty in our own halls of legislation
penetrates the plains of Poland, is echoed along the mountains of Greece, and pierces the darkest night of eastern
despotism. The universality of the intellectual and moral
powers, and the necessity of their development for the progress of the race, proclaim the great doctrine of the natural
right of every human being to moral and intellectual culture."

Bancroft's second oration encompassed "the necessity, the
reality, and the promise of the progress of mankind." Speaking on this occasion to the members of the New York Historical Society, he dwelt on the historian's duties and on
history as the unfolding of civilization. "It is because God is
visible in History that its office is the noblest except that of the
poet. The poet is at once the interpreter and favorite of
Heaven. . . . But history, as she reclines in the lap of eternity, sees the mind of humanity itself engaged in formative
efforts, constructing sciences, promulgating laws, organizing
commonwealths, and displaying its energies in the visible
movement of its intelligence. Of all pursuits that require
analysis history, therefore, stands first. It is equal to philosophy; for as certainly as the actual bodies forth the ideal, so
does history contain philosophy. It is grander than the natural
sciences; for its study is man, the last work of creation, and
the most perfect in its relations with the Infinite."

In the history of mankind "the course of civilization flows
on like a mighty river through a boundless valley, calling to
the streams from every side to swell its current, which is always growing wider, and deeper, and clearer, as it rolls along.
Let us trust ourselves upon its bosom without fear; nay,
rather with confidence and joy. Since the progress of the race
appears to be the great purpose of Providence, it becomes us
all to venerate the future. We must be ready to sacrifice ourselves for our successors, as they in turn must live for their
posterity. . . . You brothers, who are joined together for the
study of history, receive the lighted torch of civilization from
the departing half-century, and hand it along to the next. In
fulfilling this glorious office, remember that the principles of
justice and sound philosophy are but the inspirations of common sense, and belong of right to all mankind. Carry them
forth, therefore, to the whole people; for so only can society
build itself up on the imperishable groundwork of universal
freedom."

But in the stream of human history, in which the course of civilization flows inexorably under God's providence, the conflict between the real and the ideal ever rages under the impetus of party aspirations. "In public life, by the side of the actual state of the world, there exists the ideal state toward which it should tend. . . . The course of human destiny is ever a rope of three strands. One party may found itself on things as they are, and strive for their unaltered perpetuity; this is conservatism, always appearing wherever established interests exist, and never capable of unmingled success, because finite things are ceaselessly in motion. Another may be based on theoretic principles, and struggle unrelentingly to conform society to the absolute law of Truth and Justice; and this, though it kindle the purest enthusiasm, can likewise never perfectly succeed, because the materials of which society is composed partake of imperfection, and to extirpate all that is imperfect would lead to the destruction of society itself."

Between the party of conservatism and the party of revolution, "there may be a third, which seeks to reconcile the two, but which yet can never thrive by itself since it depends for its activity on the clashing between the fact and the higher law. Without all the three, the fates could not spin their thread. . . . Society always has within itself the elements of conservatism, of absolute right, and of reform. . . . The statesman, whose heart has been purified by the love of his kind, and whose purpose solemnized by faith in the immutability of justice, seeks to apply every principle which former ages or his own may have mastered, and to make every advancement that the culture of his time will sustain. In a word, he will never omit an opportunity to lift his country out of the inferior sphere of its actual condition into the higher and better sphere that is nearer to ideal perfection. The merits of great men are to be tested by this criterion. I speak of the judgment of the race, not of the opinion of classes."

Confident that civilization was dynamic, ever advancing with the progress of the people, through the struggles of parties, Bancroft was equally sure that mankind at large, not privileged classes, furnished the spirit of this triumphal procession: "There is a *spirit in man*: not in the privileged few. . . . It is the attribute of the race. The spirit, which is the guide to truth, is the gracious gift to each member of the human family. Reason exists within every breast." Moral affections are planted everywhere. Sentiments of truth, justice, and beauty, gifts of mind and heart, powers of thought, creativeness, and benevolence, are universally diffused. No class or set of classes monopolizes them. All men and women, despite differences in attainments, partake of the genius of mankind. "The Indian mother, on the borders of Hudson's Bay, decorates her manufactures with ingenious devices and lovely colors, prompted by the same instinct which guided the pencil and mixed the colors of Raphael. . . . The power which leads to the production of beautiful forms, or to the perception of them in the works which God has made, is an attribute of Humanity."

In every manifestation of civilization, Bancroft declared, a relation with the spirit, thought, and efforts of common humanity is to be observed. Is it a question of the arts? "In Athens, the arts were carried to perfection, when 'the fierce democracie' was in the ascendant; the temple of Minerva and the works of Phidias were planned and perfected to please the common people. When Greece yielded to tyrants, her genius for excellence in art expired; or rather, the purity of taste expired; because the artist then endeavored to gratify a patron, and therefore, humored his caprice; while before he had endeavored to delight the race."

In the middle ages, art flourished after religion had opened an asylum for the people: "There the serf and the beggar could kneel; there the pilgrim and the laborer were shrived; and the children of misfortune not less than the prosperous were welcomed to the house of prayer." Then "the souls of Giotto, and Perugino, and Raphael, moved by an infinite sympathy with the crowd, kindled into divine conceptions of beautiful forms. Appealing to the sentiment of devotion in the common mind, they dipped their pencils in living colors, to decorate the altar where man adored." But when the wealthy nobility became patrons, the arts declined into chaotic and merely sensuous forms: "Painting, no longer vivified by a fellow-feeling with the multitude, losts its greatness in the attempt to adapt itself to personal humors."

Is it a question of art criticism, of placing valuations on works of art? The people have a decisive influence in this matter also: "The sentiment of beauty, as it exists in the human mind, is the criterion in works of art, inspires the conceptions of genius, and exercises a final judgment on its productions. For who are the best judges in matters of taste?

Do you think the cultivated individual? Undoubtedly not; but the collective mind. The public is wiser than the wisest critic."

In the history of democracy and the arts there is a lesson for those who would promote the arts in the United States: "If with us the arts are destined to a brilliant career, the inspiration must spring from the vigor of the people. Genius will not create to flatter patrons or decorate saloons [salons]. It yearns for larger influences; it feeds on wider sympathies; and its perfect display can never exist, except in an appeal to the general sentiment for the beautiful."

In letters, as well as in the arts, the influence of the people is felt: "Demosthenes of old formed himself to the perfection of eloquence by means of addresses to the crowd. The great comic poet of Greece, emphatically the poet of the vulgar mob, is distinguished above all others for the incomparable graces of his diction. . . . At the revival of letters a distinguishing feature of the rising literature was the employment of the dialect of the vulgar. Dante used the language of the populace and won immortality; Wickliffe, Luther, and at a later day Descartes, each employed his mother tongue, and carried truth directly to all who were familiar with its accents. Every beneficent revolution in letters has the character of popularity; every great reform among authors has sprung from the power of the people in its influence on the development and activity of mind. The same influence continues unimpaired."

The same law of popular power holds good in the civilization of politics: "In like manner the best government rests on the people and not on the few, on persons and not on property, on the free development of public opinion and not on authority." Gifts of mind are bestowed upon every member of the race: "Lands, estates, the produce of mines, the prolific abundance of the seas, may be usurped by a privileged class. Avarice, assuming the form of ambitious power, may grasp realm after realm, subdue continents, compass the earth in its schemes of aggrandizement, and sigh after other worlds; but mind eludes the power of appropriation; it exists only in its own individuality; it is a property which cannot be confiscated and cannot be torn away; it laughs at chains; it bursts from imprisonment; it defies monopoly. A government of equal rights must, therefore, rest upon mind; not wealth, not brute force, the sum of the moral intelligence of the community should rule the State. Prescription can no more assume to be a valid plea for political injustice; society studies to eradicate established abuses, and to bring social institutions and laws into harmony with moral right; not dismayed by the natural and necessary imperfections of all human effort, and not giving away to despair, because every hope does not at once ripen into fruit."

The very bonds of society are the bonds knit by the people; the individual is fleeting, temporary, vacillating; the community of people has endurance, patience, continuity, collective wisdom. "Individuals are but shadows, too often engrossed in the pursuit of shadows; the race is immortal: individuals are of limited sagacity; the common mind is infinite in its experience: individuals are languid and blind; the many are ever wakeful: individuals are corrupt; the race has been redeemed: individuals are time-serving; the masses are fearless: individuals may be false; the masses are ingenuous and sincere: individuals may claim the divine sanction of truth for the deceitful conceptions of their own fancies; the Spirit of God breathes through the combined intelligence of the people. Truth is not to be ascertained by the impulses of an individual; it emerges from the contradictions of personal opinions; it raises itself in majestic serenity above the strife of parties and the conflict of sects; it acknowledges neither the solitary mind, nor the separate faction as its oracle; but owns as its only faithful interpreter the dictates of pure reason itself, proclaimed by the general voice of mankind. The decrees of the universal conscience are the nearest approach to the presence of God in the soul of man. . . . It is hard for the pride of cultivated philosophy to put its ear to the ground, and listen reverently to the voice of lowly humanity; yet the people collectively are wiser than the most gifted individual, for all his wisdom constitutes but a part of theirs."

Passing from the arts, government, and the strength of collective wisdom to religion, Bancroft also associated that aspect of civilization with the strength of the people. When Christianity first made its way into Rome, he reminded his audience, it was not the rich, the cultivated, the powerful who first opened their hearts and minds to the new faith. It was the humble, the slave, the plebeian. Was the mission of Paul "to the emperor and his minions? to the empress and her flatterers? to servile senators? to wealthy favorites? Paul preserves for us the names of the first converts: the Roman Mary and Junia; Julia and Nerea; and the beloved brethren;

all plebeian names, unknown to history. . . . Had Christianity been received at court, it would have been stifled or corrupted by the prodigal vices of the age; it lived in the hearts of the common people; it sheltered itself against oppression in the catacombs and among tombs; it made misfortune its convert, and sorrow its companion, and labor its stay. It rested on a rock, for it rested on the people; it was gifted with immortality, for it struck root in the hearts of the million."

In the advance of civilization, ever stimulated by the spirit and progress of the people, Bancroft believed, ancient ills yet lingering would be banished from the earth. Strides were being taken toward the extinction of human servitude. Labor was moving forward with civilization. It was gaining in freedom and dignity. Even more—"the auspicious revolution in its conditions has begun."

At length, out of the travail of the ages, out of civilization as the progress of the people, Bancroft exulted, would come the ideal organization of society, the victory of humanity: "This will be the last triumph; partly because the science of government enters into the sphere of personal interests, and meets resistance from private selfishness; and partly because society, before it can be constituted aright, must turn its eye upon itself, observe the laws of its own existence, and arrive at the consciousness of its capacities and relations. The system of political economy may solve the question of the commercial intercourse of nations, by demonstrating that they are all naturally fellow-workers and friends; but its abandonment of labor to the unmitigated effects of personal competition can never be accepted as the rule for the dealings of man with man. The love for others and for the race is as much a part of human nature as the love of self; it is a common instinct that man is responsible for man. . . . No practicable system of social equality has been brought forward, or it should, and it would have been adopted; it does not follow that none can be devised, for there is no necessary opposition between handcraft and intelligence; and the masses themselves will gain in the knowledge of their rights, courage to assert them, and self-respect to take nothing less. The good time is coming, when humanity will recognize all members of its family as alike entitled to its care; when the heartless jargon of over-production in the midst of want will end in a better science of distribution; when man will dwell with man as with his brother; when political institutions will rest on the basis of equality and freedom."

In universal history unfolding through the centuries, Bancroft said in his peroration, America, though indebted to other countries and times for priceless values, had played a magnificent role in civilization conceived as the progress of the people, had set worthy examples to mankind, and confronted still greater opportunities for more splendid achievement: "Our free institutions have reversed the false and ignoble distinctions between men; and refusing to gratify the pride of caste, have acknowledged the common mind to be the true material for a commonwealth. Every thing has hitherto been done for the happy few. . . . The world can advance only through the culture of the moral and intellectual powers of the people. To accomplish this end by means of the people themselves, is the highest purpose of government. . . . The duty of America is to secure the culture and the happiness of the masses by their reliance on themselves. The absence of the prejudices of the old world leaves us here the opportunity of consulting independent truth; and man is left to supply the instinct of freedom to every social relation and public interest. . . . We have made Humanity our law-giver and our oracle; and, therefore, the nation receives, vivifies, and applies principles, which in Europe the wisest receive with distrust. Freedom of mind and of conscience, freedom of the seas, freedom of industry, equality of franchises, each great truth is firmly grasped, comprehended, and enforced."

To Federalists and Whigs of the old school in America and spokesmen of privileged orders in Europe, Bancroft's philosophy of history as democratic civilization doubtless seemed to be pure romance. Once, when he encountered Leopold von Ranke, the historian of the conservative reaction in Europe, he was informed by this "master of history" that his history of the United States was "the best book ever written from the democratic point of view." He might have retorted that Ranke's history was the best from the reactionary point of view, but Bancroft contented himself with saying in a letter to a friend: "I deny the charge; if there is democracy in history it is not subjective, but objective as they say here, and so has necessarily its place in history and gives its color as it should."

As a matter of fact, however, Bancroft's historical writings had fallen far short of conformity to his philosophy of history as democratic civilization and became more conservative in tone as he finished the last volumes. In the Introduction to his first volume, published in 1834, he described the country as having almost reached the acme of perfection in that year of Andrew Jackson's reign. If there was a degradation of labor against which he protested in his various orations, he failed to take note of it in this memorandum on history. If the fair scene of liberty, progress, and enlightenment, in which "every man may enjoy the fruits of his own industry," was marred by chattel slavery, Bancroft apparently overlooked it here. If the America described as the land of milk and honey was Democratic, it was not exactly democratic. If his eulogy so pleased the managers of the Democratic party that President Van Buren could appoint Bancroft head of the Custom House in Boston, his history was no history of democracy or of civilization, though both terms figured in his pages.

Like Tocqueville and Bancroft, philosophic in his interests, Ralph Waldo Emerson was attracted by the idea of civilization then gathering momentum. More inclined than they to a definition of terms, however, he undertook an analysis of the idea itself. But he also considered it in relation to the upswing of democracy and made concrete applications of the idea to issues involved in that form of insurgency.

How early Emerson adopted the idea it is impossible to discover with exactness, but it is certain that he had appropriated it for his thinking before he reached the climax of his powers. In an essay on *Politics*, set in a world-view and published in a series issued in 1844, he declared: "We think our civilization near its meridian, but we are yet only at the cockcrowing and the morning star." The clue to its advance, Emerson thought, at that moment, lay in moral force and genius, or creative intelligence: "In our barbarous society the influence of character is in its infancy. As a political power, as the rightful lord who is to tumble all rulers from their chairs, its presence is hardly yet suspected. Malthus and Ricardo quite omit it; the Annual Register is silent; in the Conversations' Lexicon, it is not set down; the President's Message, the Queen's Speech, have not mentioned it; and yet it is never nothing. Every thought, which genius and piety throw into the world, alters the world. The gladiators in the lists of power feel, through all their frocks of force and simulation, the presence of worth."

Somewhat later, certainly near the outbreak of the civil war, Emerson deemed the idea deserving of his extended study and he published the results in an essay on "Civilization," subsequently included in his volume on *Society and Solitude*. In his opening sentence he gave a tentative definition in the simplest possible imagery: "A certain degree of progress from the rudest state in which man is found,—a dweller in caves, or on trees, like an ape,—a cannibal, and eater of pounded snails, worms, and offal,—a certain degree of progress from this extreme is called Civilization." Here the conceptions—contrast, progress, and degree—reappear.

But, Emerson said, "it is a vague complex name, of many degrees. Nobody has attempted a definition. Mr. Guizot, writing a book on the subject, does not. It implies the evolution of a highly organized man, brought to supreme delicacy of sentiment, as in practical power, religion, liberty, sense of honor, and taste. In the hesitation to define what it is we usually suggest it by negations. A nation that has no clothing, no iron, no alphabet, no marriage, no arts of peace, no abstract thought, we call barbarous. And after many arts are invented or imported, as among the Turks and Moorish nations, it is often a little complaisant to call them civilized."

Although he complained that Guizot had left the idea vague, Emerson devised no comprehensive definition either. Like Guizot, he recognized the fact that the subject involved "interior" and "exterior" aspects—matters of the human spirit and matters of visible practice; but he did not organize his essay under these two heads. Instead, he dealt with several characteristics of civilization in his discursive way.

In considering those "feats of liberty and wit" properly interwoven with civilization, he listed certain items. He was sure that "the effect of a framed or stone house is immense on the tranquillity, power, and refinement of the builder. A man in a cave or in a camp, a nomad, will die with no more estate than the wolf or the horse leaves. . . . Invention and art are born, manners and social beauty and delight. 'Tis wonderful how soon a piano gets into a log-hut on the frontier. . . . Another step in civility is the change from war, hunting, and pasturage to agriculture. . . . Another success is the post-office, with its educating energy augmented by cheapness . . . ; so that the power of a wafer or a drop of wax or gluten to guard a letter, as it flies over sea, over land, and comes to its address . . . , I look upon as a fine meter of civilization." Among the other "meters" Emerson named "the division of labor, the multiplication of the arts of peace," and "the skilful combinations of civil government" which, "though they usually follow natural leadings, as the lines of race, language, religion, and territory," restrain strong passions and promote harmony in society.

Conquest of nature's elements was in Emerson's mind both a manifestation and a lever of civilization: "The farmer had much ill-temper, laziness, and shirking to endure from his hand-sawyers, until one day he bethought him to put his saw-mill on the edge of a waterfall; and the river never tires of turning his wheel: the river is good-natured, and never hints an objection." Electricity carries messages. The very tides drive the rolling mill. "That is the way we are strong, by borrowing the might of the elements. The forces of steam, gravity, galvanism, light, magnet, wind, fire, serve us day by day, and cost us nothing. Our astronomy is full of examples of calling in the aid of these magnificent helpers."

Indeed, to Emerson, despite his transcendentalism and preoccupation with the over-soul, the new scientific knowledge and its application to the practical arts in the service of mankind were among the marvelous achievements of modern civilization. They awakened his awe and fired his imagination: "The ship, in its latest complete equipment, is an abridgment and compend of a nation's arts: the ship steered by compass and chart,—longitude reckoned by lunar observation and by chronometer,—driven by steam; and in wildest sea-mountains, at vast distances from home,

> 'The pulses of her iron heart
> Go beating through the storm.'

No use can lessen the wonder of this control, by so weak a creature, of forces so prodigious. I remember I watched, in crossing the sea, the beautiful skill whereby the engine in its constant working was made to produce two hundred gallons of fresh water out of salt water every hour,—thereby supplying all the ship's want."

Among his external items Emerson included climate, yet without exaggerating its influences: "Climate has much to do with this melioration. The highest civility has never loved the hot zones. Wherever snow falls, there is usually civil freedom. Where the banana grows, the animal system is indolent and pampered at the cost of higher qualities: the man is sensual and cruel. But this scale is not invariable. High degrees of moral sentiment control the unfavorable influences of climate; and some of our grandest examples of men and of races come from the equatorial regions,—as the Genius of Egypt, of India, and of Arabia."

Other external items Emerson considered and listed as not decisive. Towns piled on towns, states on states, and wealth on wealth, the quartz mountains of California dumped down in New York, constellations of cities, steam power, gas lights, and rubber shoes—these, he said, do not furnish real tests of civilization. The real tests are in the daily life of people and families, in their self-direction, their associations, in their qualities and virtues, not in quantities of things. In "the cubic values America has . . . a better certificate of civilization than great cities and enormous wealth. In strictness, the vital refinements are the moral and intellectual steps." In the presence of humane values, "it is frivolous" to insist on mere inventions as a criterion of judgment respecting the degree of civilization in the United States.

The diffusion of knowledge was for Emerson, as it had been for other exponents of the idea, a sign of civilization—a force in it that worked for equality and the dissolution of special privilege. It overruns "all the old barriers of caste," and, by "the cheap press," brings "the university to every poor man's door in the newsboy's basket. Scraps of science, of thought, of poetry, are in the coarsest sheet, so that in every house we hesitate to burn a newspaper until we have looked it through." Even contradictory manifestations of life are drawn into the process of civilization: "The very prison compelled to maintain itself and yield a revenue, and, better still, made a reform school, and a manufactory of honest men out of rogues . . . all these are examples of that tendency to combine antagonisms and utilize evil, which is the index of high civilization."

The "right position of women in the State" Emerson made another "index" of civilization as Jefferson had done, but with a theory of that position more in harmony with the democratic era: "Poverty and industry with a healthy mind read very easily the laws of humanity, and love them; place the sexes in right relations of mutual respect, and a severe morality gives that essential charm to women which educates all that is delicate, poetic, and self-sacrificing, breeds courtesy and learning, conversation and wit, in her rough mate; so that I have thought a sufficient measure of civilization is the influence of good women."

An elemental force of civilization he declared to be the development of the moral sense, as giving direction to genius and talent: "There can be no high civility without a deep morality, though it may not always call itself by that name, but sometimes the point of honor, as in the institution of chivalry; or patriotism, as in the Spartan and Roman republics; or the enthusiasm of some religious sect which imputes its virtue to its dogma; or the cabalism, or *esprit de corps,* of a masonic or other association of friends. The evolution of a highly destined society must be moral. . . . It must be catholic in aims. . . . Civilization depends on morality. Everything good in man leans on what is higher. This rule holds in small as in great."

Without great humane objectives cherished by the mind and heart, neither favorable climate nor the conquest of nature nor the acquisition of things could make civilization: "As our handiworks borrow the elements, so all our social and political action leans on principles. To accomplish any thing excellent, the will must work for catholic and universal ends. A puny creature walled in on every side, as Daniel wrote—

> 'Unless above himself he can
> Erect himself, how poor a thing is man!'

but when his will leans on a principle, when he is the vehicle of ideas, he borrows their omnipotence. Gibraltar may be strong, but ideas are impregnable, and bestow on the hero their invincibility."

Such were Emerson's tests of civilization. What then were his tests of barbarism? "Where knowledge cannot be diffused without perils of mob-law and statute-law,—where speech is not free,—where the post-office is violated, mailbags opened, and letters tampered with,—where public debts and private debts outside of the State are repudiated,—where liberty is attacked in the primary institution of social life,—where the position of the white woman is injuriously affected by the outlawry of the black woman,—where the arts, such as they have, are all imported, having no indigenous life,—where the laborer is not secured in the earnings of his own hands,—where suffrage is not free or equal,—that country is, in all these respects, not civil, but barbarous; and no advantages of soil, climate, or coast can resist these suicidal mischiefs." By these direct injunctions Emerson made plain to his country-men that America, in his view, had not attained a perfect civilization, to be praised without qualifications.

It is evident from an examination of Emerson's essay on civilization that, while he did not, with Bancroft, identify civilization with democracy, he associated with the idea many elements of democracy: all the people, equality, universal suffrage, diffusion of knowledge throughout society, applica-tion of the arts and sciences to the universalization of com-modious living, the cultivation of the social spirit, the refine-ment of man and woman in society, and the development of individuality.

Again and again, in other writings, he expressed his sym-pathy with democracy, considered as policy and ethical aspi-ration. In his essay on *Politics* he declared: "Of the two great parties which, at this hour, almost share the nation between them, I should say, that, one has the best cause, and the other the best men. The philosopher, the poet, or the religious man will, of course, wish to cast his vote with the democrat, for free trade, for wide suffrage, for the abolition of legal cruelties in the penal code, and for facilitating in every manner the ac-cess of the young and the poor to the sources of wealth and power."

Yet, in this very declaration, it is obvious that Emerson did not make American civilization synonymous with democ-racy. Nor turning from theory to practice did Emerson pay deference to the Democratic party as embodying, even ap-proximately, the broad philosophy of democracy. He spoke with unrelieved disgust of the "hordes of ignorant and de-ceivable natives and armies of foreign voters who fill Pennsyl-vania, New York, and New Orleans and . . . those unscrupu-lous editors and orators who have assumed to lead these masses. . . . Democracy becomes a government of bullies tempered by editors. . . . The Democratic party is the party of the Poor marshalled against the Rich. . . . But they are always officered by a few self-seeking deserters from the Rich or Whig party. . . . These leaders are Whigs and associate with Whigs, that is, they are the dining, drinking and dancing and investing, class, and by no means the digging and hoeing class." To the Whigs he ascribed wealth and cultivation; but he characterized them as timid, "merely defensive of property," aspiring to no real good, proposing no generous policy, befriending neither the poor nor the immigrant nor the Indian. "From neither party, when in power, has the world any benefit to expect in science, art, or humanity, at all commensurate with the resources of the nation."

Having in mind the ideal of civilization, sensitive to the civilizing work yet to be done in America, Emerson could find no party or cause that measured up to his standards. He thought that "the American Revolution was political merely"; whereas the French Revolution of 1848 had "a feature new to history, that of Socialism." To many specific reforms, he lent the power of his voice and pen, but to none of the imposing plans presented by the utopians could he give his full allegiance as answering the problem that perplexed him. In the objectives of Fourier, Owen, Alcott, and Channing for renovating institutions and destroying drudgery, he admitted a hint of benefits for humanity. Still he believed that none of their designs would accomplish the ends sought: "Not in the way these men think, in none of their ways."

An advocate of liberty, fearing the despotism of the State, expecting no miracles from the mere uproars of democracy, he sought a method of advancing civilization in America that "combines union with isolation," that is, the cohering and humanizing force of society with the responsibility and creative energy of the individual. In this process, democracy would count: "In a Democracy every movement has a deep-seated cause. . . . It is necessary that you should know the people's facts. If you have no place for them, the people absolutely have no place for you. . . . The constitution of things is on the people's side, and that is a reason not liable to a fallacy." This affirmation was in line with the idea of civilization, but Emerson did not believe with Bancroft that what was called democracy automatically worked for the advancement of civilization.

Whatever inadequacies democracy displayed in America, Emerson welcomed, however, its divergence from the practices of Europe governed by hierarchies of power. He believed that civilization in the United States was, and should be, executing a program of its own. He had traveled widely enough in Europe and was familiar enough with European history to be informed respecting innumerable facets of its life, economy, theories, and customs. And the American contrasts that impressed Tocqueville impressed Emerson. The best of them, as he estimated values, he gladly accepted, without undue pride, as parts of the American heritage. While considerably affected by German transcendentalism, he taught that Americans should work creatively with all their abilities, at all aspects of civilization, sedulously avoiding meretricious imitations. In 1837 he exclaimed: "Our day of dependence, our long apprenticeship to the learning of other lands, draws to a close. The millions, that around us are rushing into life, cannot always be fed on the sere remains of foreign harvests. Events, actions, arise, that must be sung, that will sing themselves."

In declaring American independence anew, Emerson indulged in no reckless boasting, in none of the quarrels over the merits of American civilization that released the vituperative fervor of many contemporaries on both sides of the Atlantic Ocean. For him many things in American destiny were fixed by the history of the American people on this continent, as indeed they also seemed fixed for Tocqueville and Bancroft. Whether American arts, sciences, letters, and ways of life were as "good" as those in Europe was, in Emerson's opinion, not the real question for Americans. His anxiety was directed to this issue: Are Americans bending all their energies, amid their opportunities, to exemplify and make prevail in every manifestation of civilization the best that lies within their competence and their facilities? It was in this sense that mere imitations of Europe by Americans meant to Emerson empty husks of sere harvests, flights from moral responsibilities and intellectual creativeness.

In his address on *The Young American,* after referring to surviving forms of feudalism in contemporary England, Emerson sharpened his point: "It is for Englishmen to consider, not for us; we only say, let us live in America, too thankful for our want of feudal institutions. Our houses and towns are like mosses and lichens, so slight and new; but youth is a fault of which we shall daily mend. This land, too, is as old as the Flood, and wants no ornament or privilege which nature could bestow. Here stars, here woods, here hills, here animals, here men abound, and the vast tendencies concur of a new order. If only the men are employed in conspiring with the designs of the Spirit who led us hither, and is leading us still, we shall quickly enough advance out of all hearing of others' censures, out of all regrets of our own, into a new and more excellent social state than history has recorded." This was for Emerson the mission of civilization in America.

In the age of the democratic upswing, which Bancroft eloquently hailed as progress in civilization, American women, who had always been active in the development of civilization in the United States, began to organize their hitherto dispersed energies, for a threefold purpose: to make their strength more effective in civilization; to bring it to a focus on the great public issues of the time; and to acquire those rights in law and custom which were, as Elizabeth Cady Stanton said, "inalienable to civilization." In the process of organizing, framing programs, educating themselves, and participating in public discussions, leaders in the woman movement discerned the nature, significance, and force of the idea of civilization. And they applied it in all directions to the manifold social problems which they raised in their campaign for civilization and in their discussions of woman's "sphere."

In the midst of a new economic revolution—machine production in a power age—which was rapidly transforming household economy into the factory system, thousands upon thousands of American women understood that an exclusive domestic sphere was no longer possible and decided that their sphere was, by fact, right, and need, identical with the whole social domain. Their opportunities and obligations were widened and in response to the new situation their little groups, formed to consider and act upon issues arising in the social domain, were developed into large groups, local, state, and federated through many sections of the country.

Under the stress of participation in affairs of the whole social domain affected by the industrial revolution, the rights of full citizenship, earlier proclaimed as theory, became for the intellectual leaders of women concrete and burning necessities, imperative for effective action. Needs signified demands and they formulated the demands at Seneca Falls, New York, in 1848, with sympathetic men aiding and abetting, in a "Declaration of Sentiments" largely modeled on the Declaration of Independence proclaimed at Philadelphia in 1776.

Though only a phase of the woman movement, which was indeed as broad as the main stream of civilization, the rights of women asserted at Seneca Falls were specific and were regarded as essential to the full stature of women in society and indispensable to the discharge of their obligations. The privileges for which they called there and in the course of their movement included equal rights in property; elimination of child marriages and prostitution; equality with the husband in the guardianship of children; abolition of discriminations in divorce laws and a liberalization of the matrimonial code; greater economic independence in the changing economy through the removal of exclusions from business and professional opportunities; equal pay for men and women in all common employments; full educational privileges; the right to vote and hold office, that is, to take part in the government of the whole social domain.

Yet prominent as was the discussion of rights in the history of the age, rights always remained, for the philosophers of the woman movement, only one interest among many—fundamental, it is true, but never all-inclusive respecting the purpose of the movement. If the leaders had limited their activities and debates to the matter of rights for women, their path might have been smoother. But holding as they did that rights were instrumental to other purposes and taking the full range of social issues into the scope of their thought and argument, they became involved in the great conflicts of interests which agitated America from one end to the other.

So conceived and so conducted, the woman movement aroused a powerful opposition in three principal quarters. It alarmed unreflective men and women still governed by traditions inherited from the passing age of domestic economy—traditions not innately "evil" but mainly anachronistic. It excited the animadversions of lawyers who combined loyalty to traditions with an inelastic penchant for precedent, fortified by the reactionary doctrines of the British commentator on law, Blackstone. It stirred the emotions of those theologians, Protestant and Catholic, who united in their thought the traditions of the domestic age in economy with belief in the eternal correctness of the role assigned to women in the theological epic of man's fall through woman's sinful action and in the canon law. Three absolutisms the leaders in the woman movement encountered, in short: tradition, established law expounded by men, and theology with its legal corollaries also expounded by men. Armed with the idea of civilization, women faced them resolutely.

Among the forceful personalities in the movement, Lucretia Mott stood out as its early intellectual and moral mentor, although she was active in the task of organization and in her speaking and writing touched nearly every phase of the movement. Through her rearing, training, experience, and associations, she was able to mingle knowledge of the working world with study, meditation, and speculative thought. She was born Lucretia Coffin, in 1793, at Nantucket where women fitted easily, naturally, into the simple economy of the island. Her father, Thomas Coffin, was a captain of a vessel employed in the China trade during her childhood days. While he was away at sea, her mother, like many Nantucket wives, engaged in business on land as a breadwinner for herself and her children to safeguard their future from the hazards of the sea. When the father gave up his seafaring, the family moved first to Boston and then to Philadelphia, and Thomas Coffin became a merchant himself.

At the age of eleven, Lucretia was placed, by the deliberate choice of her parents, founded on their democratic principles, in a public school in Boston. At thirteen, she entered a Friends' boarding school near Poughkeepsie, where she spent almost four years, the last two as a teacher. In 1811, she married James Mott, who had been a fellow pupil and teacher in that school and later had joined her father in his business enterprise at Philadelphia. As they had six children Lucretia was compelled to carry heavy household burdens.

A member of the Society of Friends, Lucretia Mott enjoyed the freedom, common to Quakers, of inquiring and speaking in meetings. Studious, by the bent of her mind, she was also inclined to think on her own account. When a schism occurred in the Society of Friends, she joined the faction led by Elias Hicks as representing more faithfully her Unitarian beliefs, her reformist inclinations, and her conviction that the inner light is the most reliable guide to life. She made the Hicksite motto her own motto: "Truth for Authority; not Authority for Truth." That her intuitive judgments derived by meditation might be informed by knowledge, Lucretia Mott read intensely, if not widely. She developed the habit of reasoning quietly and this became apparent in her sermons delivered to the Friends, in her correspondence with relatives and acquaintances, in her public addresses.

By travel in the United States and England, she stretched

her horizon and acquired more intimacy with public affairs. She was an official delegate to the famous World Anti-Slavery Convention held in London in 1840 and, though excluded from her seat in that assembly after her arrival, for reasons sectarian, traditional, and economic, she visited other cities in Great Britain and often spoke at meetings there. That she might learn something about slavery at first hand and discover for herself the attitudes of slave-owners, she went to talk with them in the South. Moreover, her lecturing and propagandistic labors took her on long trips in the North, giving her direct contacts with people of many sorts and conditions. To equip herself further for the mission she had chosen, she kept in touch with main currents of contemporary thought and opinion.

Believing firmly in the creative spirit and demonstrating it herself, devoted to the ideal and practicing the art of reasoning, conversant with the writings of Thomas Paine on that subject, Lucretia Mott readily added to her intellectual armory the idea of civilization. And after Henry Thomas Buckle's *History of Civilization in England* had appeared, she made a thoughtful review of its major thesis in a public address. The motif of this first systematic treatise on civilization to come out of England was a revolt against authoritarianism in state and church and an advocacy of individualism in every realm of activity. Among Buckle's basic contentions was the proposition that moral truths had been fundamentally the same since ancient times and that "the intellectual principle . . . is quite sufficient to account for the extraordinary progress that, during several centuries, Europe has continued to make."

This conclusion Buckle had not reached lightly, without research and critical thought. In the fourth chapter of his first volume he had painstakingly analyzed the problem which Condorcet had completely ignored—the power of moral forces in civilization. The great dogmas of moral systems, Buckle said, were all announced early in the history of the human race and had undergone little change through the centuries. Furthermore, his contention ran, the most cruel and intolerable deeds in all history had been performed by conscientious persons professing high moral and religious principles. Good and evil actions in history had counterbalanced each other. But the intellectual discoveries of genius calling for no brutalities and oppressions had brought treasures of truth to humanity, are cumulative, and "flow on in a perennial and undying stream."

Anticipating by many years John Morley's criticism of Condorcet for utterly ignoring moral forces in civilization and for his antipathy to religion, Mrs. Mott declared that Buckle's reliance on the progress of knowledge was inadequate and untenable. "The great historian, probably the greatest historian in our day, Buckle," she said at a Friends' meeting in New York in 1866, "has very erroneously, it seems to me, attributed the advancement of the world so far in civilization more to the intellectual development of man than to his spiritual and moral growth and advancement. It seems to me that he mistook the mere sectarian effort of days past (which, he said, died out in a generation and produced no great effect upon the world) for the moral effort at human progress. Let us see what has really been the progress since the great law of love, or right, of regard to man, was proclaimed clearly and extensively by Jesus of Nazareth. . . . The efforts that are made for education, for improvement, morality, and the great numbers in all parts of Christendom, in various parts of the world, enlisted in behalf of improving the condition of society—all go to disprove the idea, which I fear, when put forth by such a historian, would have an undue influence, and warp the judgment of many of his readers, and lead to a lighter estimate of moral effort than really belongs to it. . . . I allude to this, because I think that when a writer becomes popular we are apt to receive his say-so without much criticism or instruction; and I believe that we have intelligence, judgment, and capacity to read and understand. I would not disparge—far be it from me—any intellectual advancement. . . . But, my friends, we are responsible for our reason and its right cultivation."

In her critique of Buckle's theory with her appreciation of the nature of civilization, Mrs. Mott insisted that the ethics of Christianity and the social principle must be planted squarely in the idea of civilization. In her own way she did for the idea what Saint-Simon did for the idea of progress in France. She reasserted the possibility and reality of advance in moral truths and applications as well as in knowledge, and affirmed the primacy of social ethics as even necessary to the civilization of knowledge; that is, as imperative for subduing knowledge, which could serve barbarism equally well, to the social principle progressively developed by the continous effort of men and women.

The particular obligations which were, in her opinion, imposed on women in the contemporary world, Mrs. Mott set forth in her *Discourse on Woman*, published in 1849. She had long felt that women must be brought to fuller consciousness of their role and responsibilities in social development and that men also should become aware of the relationship of women to ethics and the social domain. In that *Discourse*, she urged women to consider their public obligations, declaring that "woman has been but little aware of the high incitements which should stimulate to the cultivation of her noblest powers." She voiced great impatience with women who spent so much of their time at the theater and balls, or poring over "the sickly and sentimental novel and pernicious romance," which, "like stimulating drinks, when long indulged in, enervate the mind, unfitting it for the sober duties of life."

She looked forward to the day "when educated females will not be satisfied with the present objects of their low ambition." The larger objective would both promote individual force and affect man and society. "In the civilization to which we have attained," she said, "if civilized and refined woman would bring all her powers into use, she might engage in pursuits which she now shrinks from as beneath her proper vocation. The energies of men need not then be wholly devoted to the counting-house and common business of life, in order that women in fashionable society may be supported in their daily promenades and nightly visits to the theater and ballroom." They must have stronger and more profitable food than the diet offered in the artificial representations of life.

As better food for thought Mrs. Mott suggested the examples of Elizabeth Fry of England and Dorothea Dix of the United States, who were arousing their nations to the barbarism of their criminology and their treatment of the insane. There was work to be done also in weaning man from his warlike proclivities, his proneness to take the violent way in crises, turning to physical force rather than to the influence "which mind exerts over mind." She urged her auditors and readers in repeated pleas to labor for the substitution of "moral and Christian heroism" for the "heroism displayed in the tented fields." She argued that the rational and ethical attitudes of women could become a revolutionary force in that respect: "As these characteristics come to be appreciated in man, too, his warlike acts, with all the miseries and horrors of the battle-ground, will sink into their merited oblivion, or be remembered only to be condemned. The heroism displayed in the tented fields must yield to the moral and Christian heroism which is shadowed in the signs of our times." Thus she placed a heavy responsibility for civilization upon women at large while she assumed her own full share.

Although Mrs. Mott had taken part in the Seneca Falls convention of 1848 and approved the demand for women's "rights" which had been formulated there, her interests were as broad as the broader movement of thought in her time. She understood and sympathized with women and girls employed in operating machines in mills and factories and endorsed the efforts they were making to improve their conditions by collective action. Her interest in labor conditions was not, however, confined to women alone. "The oppression of the working classes by existing monopolies," she said, "and the lowness of wages often engaged my attention; and I have held many meetings with them [the workers] and heard their appeals with compassion, and a great desire for a radical change in the system which makes the rich richer and the poor poorer. The various associations and communities, tending to greater equality of condition, have had from me a hearty God-speed."

Her world-view brooked no poverty, none of the suffering, none of the crime which often went with poverty. She believed in work, and work in her philosophy was a refinement-ethos. So, exploitation was abhorrent to her, as robbing the human being of self-reliance; and she associated exploitation with freedom of contract. In a letter to her sister she expressed her opinion on this matter: "Let us rather ask *man* to change than nature; so that there shall not be these cruel distinctions: great wealth and abject poverty. I have some hopes that the coöperative trade-unions are going to effect something toward a better state of society, that is, co-partnership in industry."

Before the tribunal of Reason she argued for the abolition of slavery. This plea she carried into the South itself, accompanied by her equally earnest husband. Planters extended hospitality to them and gave evidence of a desire to see a reasonable solution of the slavery problem, she thought. Reason forbade a resort to violence, she believed, and she never joined the party whose methods were bound to lead to the arbitrament of war.

For conventional theology alleged to be necessary to the improvement of mankind or as a system of dogmas opposed to the advancement of women, Mrs. Mott had little tolerance. In writing to friends in Dublin, in 1841, she confessed it: "I am sick of disputes on that subject [theology]. . . . Moreover I think there is so much harm done by teaching the doctrine of human depravity and dependence on vicarious atonement, that I feel constrained to call on all, everywhere, to yield such a mistaken and paralyzing dogma." This statement she elaborated in a later letter to the same correspondents, reading, "Let us venerate the good and the true, while we respect not prejudice and superstition. . . . R. D. Webb thinks I am a humanitarian. I have never given my faith a name."

That Mrs. Mott expected from the progress of civilization a still greater emancipation of the human spirit was revealed in her sermons, as well as in her letters and public addresses. "The true gospel," she preached in 1860, "is not identical with any scheme or theological plan of salvation, however plausibly such a scheme may be drawn from isolated passages of Scripture, ingeniously woven; it is through the intelligence of the age, the progress of civilization, and individual thinking, that the right of judgment has been so far attained, that there is great daring of thought, of belief and expression, and much shortening of the creeds. A great deal that was demoralizing in its tendency has been separated from them. Still, what remains is so tenaciously held as the only touchstone of religious character, that there is a proportionate lessening of the effect of sound morals, and a lowering of the true standards."

But in all her discussions of theology, ever mindful of the needs and progress of civilization, Mrs. Mott was careful to make it clear that she was distinguishing between theology and religion. Invited to join the Free Religious Association which professed an intention to "promote the scientific study of theology," she replied in part as follows: "Doubting the propriety of calling theology a science, I would suggest an amendment in this wise: to encourage the scientific study of the religious nature or element in man—the ever-present Divine inspiration. . . . Let us rather use our time and effort for the promotion of a higher righteousness than is yet demanded by *our* Scribes and Pharisees." Writing to her sister in 1862 she exclaimed: "How easy it is to raise the cry of another Voltaire or Paine 'come to judgment!' But it is not so easy, blessed be our age of free inquiry, skepticism being a religious duty, to frown down investigation into the dogmatic theology of the schools."

During the voyage to London in 1840 she had said to a fellow passenger, Mrs. Elizabeth Cady Stanton, soon to be an influential disciple: "There is a broad distinction between religion and theology. The one is a natural human experience, common to all well-organized minds. The other is a system of speculation about the unseen, and unknowable, which the human mind has no power to grasp or explain; and these speculations vary with every sect, age, and type of civilization. No one knows any more of what lies beyond our sphere of action than thou and I; and we know nothing."

In time, Mrs. Mott hoped, the theological battle would be abandoned and civilization would triumph over absolutist dogmas. "I was wondering the other day," she wrote to a friend in 1866, "what use the increasing number of churches would be put to, as civilization outgrew them." That line of her prophecy was not verified in the years ahead. But despite the objections of theologians to the demands of women for full civil rights, the woman movement gained in strength and momentum as the popular upsurge swept forward to its destiny. Moreover the version of civilization which Mrs. Mott propounded as a substitute for Buckle's, outliving his, remained vital in the twentieth century.

If Lucretia Mott may be called the outstanding philosopher of the woman movement, Elizabeth Cady Stanton may be called its chief lawyer and advocate. Not that Mrs. Stanton was any less universal in her interests and sympathies; indeed she was even more deeply concerned with the laws of marriage and divorce. Nor was she indifferent to the more general speculations attractive to the mind of the older woman. As a matter of fact it was while they were in London together in 1840 that Mrs. Stanton was initiated into complete independence of mind in every direction. She found Lucretia Mott, she said later, like a "being from some larger planet . . . a woman who dared to question the opinions of Popes, Kings, Synods, Parliaments, with the same freedom that she would criticize an editorial in the *London Times*, recognizing no higher authority than the judgment of a pure-minded, educated woman. When I first heard from the lips of Lucretia Mott that I had the same right to think for myself that Luther, Calvin, and John Knox had, and the same right to be guided by my own convictions, and would no doubt live a higher, happier life than if guided by theirs, I felt at once a new-born sense of dignity and freedom; it was like suddenly coming into the rays of the noonday-sun, after wandering with a rushlight in the caves of the earth."

Like the elder woman, Mrs. Stanton was of old American stock. Her father was a distinguished lawyer of Johnston, New York, where she was born—Judge Daniel Cady. Her mother, Margaret Livingston, belonged to the powerful colonial-revolutionary family of that name. While Elizabeth Cady was still very young, the family pastor, Simon Hosack, encouraged her to study Greek, Latin, and mathematics in the local academy, and she did so for several years, taking honors. At the age of fifteen she went to Emma Willard's Academy for Girls and graduated in 1832.

Then a passionate interest was aroused in the law as it affected women. The assumptions of her brothers and their male companions, respecting the superiority of their sex as proved in their larger legal privileges and their knowledge of the law, impelled her to read their law books and to sit in her father's court watching the laws interpreted and applied. What she saw and heard about domestic unhappiness and legal discriminations running against women helped to set the frame of reference for her long labors as a reformer. In 1840 she married a lawyer, journalist, and abolitionist, Henry Stanton.

Inducted into the liberty of Rationalism by Mrs. Mott, Mrs. Stanton entered the struggle against the clergymen who used theology to justify their opposition to the many freedoms for women—matrimonial, parental, economic, political, and educational—which she declared to be essentials of civilization. These freedoms she esteemed as more than mere benefits to women as individuals; she looked upon them also as precious ways and means of raising the physical and moral standards of the whole society. And she would not yield an inch of ground to theological absolutism. But Mrs. Stanton's distinctive work for the woman movement was the employment of her legal talents in editing, writing articles for magazines and newspapers, framing petitions and resolutions, and addressing legislative committees, state and national.

When the question of the Fourteenth Amendment was under consideration in Congress, she took the position that every proposal to limit the suffrage to males was an effort to "turn the wheels of civilization backwards." In asking members of the New York legislature to allow women to vote for members of the coming constitutional convention in 1867, Mrs. Stanton warned them against hostile women: "Remember, the gay and fashionable throng who whisper in the ears of statesmen, judges, lawyers, merchants, 'We have all the rights we want,' are but the mummies of civilization, to be brought back to life only by earthquakes and revolutions."

Mrs. Stanton's interests and activities, however, as her unpublished manuscripts in the Library of Congress show, went far beyond the woman movement, broadly as she envisaged its proper function. Nothing human was foreign to her concerns. Unlike evasive abolitionists, she denounced as outrages the slums of great cities, the long, monotonous, often dangerous and ill-requited labor of industrial workers, the crushing burden of poverty in the North, exclaiming that "the condition of the laboring classes in the North differs little from that of the colored race under the old system of the plantations in the South." She aligned herself with those who insisted that remedies could and should be found and called "healthy discontent . . . the first step of progress." For this resolve she had support in her belief that "the law governing human affairs is change, progress, development in the world of thought as well as action"—the idea of progress in civilization. A popular Lyceum lecturer and speaker in larger assemblies throughout the long years of her public life, she hammered away steadily at complacency with poverty, ignorance, ill-health, and other evils of human life.

With respect to the world-view, civilization, which she espoused, Mrs. Stanton made every good, every value, that she claimed for men and women an imperative of civilization. In 1860 she declared: "There are certain natural rights as inalienable to civilization as are the rights of air and motion to the savage in the wilderness. The natural rights of the civilized man and woman are government, property, the harmonious development of all their powers, and the gratification of desires."

Inevitably women's heresies relative to the eternal perfection of traditional theories and conservative practices stirred emotional opposition couched in ancient, medieval, and modern forms. Though women, of necessity, had to bear the brunt of this opposition, "new men" sometimes shared the burden with the "new women." And among their invincible defenders was the eloquent and vitriolic Wendell Phillips, one of the greatest orators of the ages, consecrated to the social principle in all human relations, and accepting, as he said, "the idea of our civilization, underlying all American life."

Owing to the forthrightness of Phillips' speech and the magnetism of his delivery, audience after audience, riotously trying to silence him when he began an address, was hushed into silence or moved to applaud his sentiments as he gave them voice. He was therefore a powerful recruit for the woman movement which was seeking to universalize in the United States the principles of 1776 and promote the values of civilization; and on many occasions his eloquence was placed at the service of this cause.

In Phillips' outlook on life, women were more than legally underprivileged members of society, though he acknowledged the existence of that undesirable status. They were, he felt, special guardians of the social principle; and he insisted that the public interest no less than their personal good demanded that the opportunities of women to protect, serve, and develop civilization be widened. To the support of this contention he brought up historic experience—the influence of women on the thought and progress of the modern age.

At a women's convention held in New York City in 1856, Phillips gave the grounds of his belief: "This question is a question in civilization. . . . The time has been—and every man who has ever analyzed history knows it—when in France, the mother to Europe of all social ideas; France that has lifted Germany from mysticism, and told England what she means and what she wants; France that has construed England to herself . . . ; when in that very France, at the fountainhead of that eighteenth century of civil progress, it was in the saloons [salons] of woman that man did his thinking, and it was under the brilliant inspiration of her society that that mighty revolution in the knowledge and science of civil affairs was wrought. In this country, too, at this hour, woman does as much to give impulse to public opinion as man does. . . . I welcome this [woman] movement because it shows that we have a great amount of civilization."

Yet Phillips knew that the way to victory for that movement would be long and hard. He told women this in so many words when in 1851, at a convention in Massachusetts, he made an address supporting a set of resolutions calling for the extension of full civic rights to women: "It seems to me to have been proved conclusively, that government commenced in usurpation and oppression; that liberty and civilization, at present, are nothing else than the fragments of right which the scaffold and the stake have wrung from the strong hands of usurpers. . . . Government began in tyranny and force, began in the feudalism of the soldier and bigotry of the priest; and ideas of justice and humanity have been fighting their way, like a thunder-storm, against the organized selfishness of human nature. . . . We know the sneers, the lying frauds of misstatement and misrepresentation, that await us. We have counted all. . . . We only ask an opportunity to argue the question, to set it full before the people, and then leave it to the hearts and intellects of our country, confident that the institutions under which we live, and the education which other reforms have given to both sexes, have created men and women capable of solving a problem even more difficult, and meeting a change even more radical than this."

In Phillips' opinion, women had not only exerted a civilizing influence in society, were not only justified by character in demanding full civic rights; they had the physical and moral courage required for carrying causes to triumph. When in 1835 a Boston mob threatened the life of William Lloyd Garrison and the mayor of the city played a "shuffling and dishonorable part," in the eyes of Phillips, women joined men in organizing meetings of protest. Undaunted by the mayor's warning that it was perilous for women to participate in such public proceedings, they stood their ground, one of them saying to him, "if this is the last bulwark of freedom, we may as well die here as anywhere."

At a meeting held twenty years afterward in memory of that historic affair, Phillips humbly admitted that women had given him a lesson in courage on that occasion. "Let me thank the women who came here twenty years ago, some of whom are here to-day," he said, "for the good they have done me. I thank them for all they have taught me. I had read Greek and Roman and English history; I had by heart the classic eulogies of brave old men and martyrs; I dreamed, in my folly, that I heard the same tone in my youth from the cuckoo lips of Edward Everett;—these women taught me my mistake. They taught me that down in those hearts which loved a principle for itself, asked no man's leave to think or speak, true to their convictions, no matter at what hazard, flowed the red blood of '76, of 1640, of the hemlock-drinker of Athens, and of the martyr-saints of Jerusalem. I thank them for it! My eyes were sealed, so that, although I knew the Adamses and Otises, of 1776, and the Mary Dyers and Ann Hutchinsons of older times, I could not recognize the Adamses and Otises, the Dyers and Hutchinsons, whom I met in the streets of '35. These women opened my eyes, and I thank them and you [turning to Mrs. Southwick and Miss Henrietta Sargent, who sat upon the platform], for that anointing. May our next twenty years prove us all apt scholars of such brave instruction!"

What was this *demos* in movement, this people in the process of civilization? Was it a mere projection of British nationality or "race," striving to duplicate on this continent civilization in Great Britain? Was it merely "European"? Was "the American people" just a fiction of the imagination, a "territorial" democracy as Disraeli called it? Was it to be regarded as a motley aggregation of immigrants from the Old World, ever made more motley by the increasing flood of immigrants flowing westward across the Atlantic? Or did the people of the United States constitute a nation with its own destiny, opportunity, and obligation, but likely to be diverted from its course by the volume and variety of invaders?

These were not all the questions. More were raised. Did a "pure" race, as Count Gobineau and other European "racists" were then maintaining, furnish the one real source of civilization, and a mixture of races lead inevitably to degeneration? In the fifth decade of the century Gobineau flatly declared: "Everything great, noble, and fruitful in the works of man on this earth, in science, art, and civilization, derives from a single starting point; it belongs to one family alone [the Aryan race], the different branches of which have reigned in all the civilized countries of the universe." Was this true?

Out of the debate over this question during the popular upsurge, came a general proposition that the commingling of nationalities, bound together by strong political, economic, and moral ties, worked for the advancement of civilization in the United States.

That thesis had been put forward as early as 1814 by DeWitt Clinton in an address before the Literary and Philosophical Society of New York and published the next year in the North American Review: "We can boast of our descent from a superior stock. I speak not of families or dynasties; I refer to our origin from those nations where civilization, knowledge, and refinement have erected their empire; and where human nature has attained the greatest perfection. Annihilate Holland, Great Britain, Ireland, France, and Germany, and what would become of civilized man? This country, young as it is, would be the great Atlas remaining to support the dignity of the world; and perhaps our mingled descent from various nations may have a benign influence upon genius. . . . The extraordinary characters which the United States have produced may be, in some measure, ascribed to the mixed blood of so many nations flowing in our veins; and it may be confidently predicted that the operation of causes, acting with irresistible effect, will carry in this country all the improvable faculties of human nature to the highest state of perfection." If some political motives could be imputed to Clinton, if his hopes were pitched too high, it was a fact that in the advancement of civilization in the United States the abilities and creative energies of many peoples were being enlisted at a time when there seemed to be abundant elbow room.

Dealing with the same subject in a larger way, a writer in the Atlantic Monthly, in 1858, after the longer experience with the mixed population, asserted that Americans were not just a conglomeration of Europeans, old and new, but were a people stamped with common and peculiar characteristics, induced by life in a new world. The article, unsigned, according to editorial practice, might have been written by James Russell Lowell, although some passages seem to indicate that it was a composite product. In any case the thesis was plain: "The New World is not merely a newly discovered hay-loft and dairy stall for the Old, but is itself a proper household of equal dignity with any."

But how was the allegation to be proved? "Unless there be an American Man, the continent is inevitably but an appendage, a kitchen and laundry for the European parlor." This American man "must likewise be a new man—not merely a migrated European. Western Europe pushed a little farther west does not meet our demand. Why should Europe go three thousand miles off to be Europe still. . . . It would seem like a poverty in Nature, were she unable to vary."

Following the line taken years before by DeWitt Clinton, the author or authors of this article employed the theory of the commingling of peoples to sustain the assertion that Americans were a distinct people in their own right: "Colonel Hamilton Smith makes it quite clear that civilization has found its first centres there where two highways of national movement crossed and dissimilar men looked each other in the face." The United States is such a cross-roads where many peoples meet and the new personality emerges. Besides, Nature is always making variations in types; "ever working and compounding to produce varieties of national genius. Her aim is the same in both cases—to enrich the whole by this electrical and enlivening relation between the parts."

And certain conditions in America especially favor a new type of human being: "We are more in conversation with the heart and pure spiritual fact of humanity, than any other people of equal power and culture. We necessarily deal more with each other on a bond and basis of common persuasion, of open unenacted truth than others. . . . No civilized nation is so little imprisoned in precedents and traditions." There is the fact. "Out of the deeps of destiny, the Man for the Continent, head-craftsman, handcraftsman, already puts his foot to the shore. . . . We give thee joy of new powers, new work, unprecedented futures! . . . We give the world joy of a new and mighty artist to plan, a strong new artisan to quarry and to build in the great architectures of humanity!"

Under what economic policy was this people, this commingling of many nationalities in one political union, to proceed in developing its natural resources and sustaining its expanding life? Was the United States to remain a raw-material province for the industrial nations of the Old World? Or was it to develop a diversified economy conducive to the exfoliation of all the sciences and arts related to a more abundant life? And how was a better distribution of wealth to be effected?

At the moment, the supremacy of agriculture seemed to point to the predominance of provincialism. At the moment also, British classical economics, the ideology of the British manufacturing interests, reigned almost unchallenged over intellectuals in America who theorized on economic policies.

But Henry C. Carey grappled with the issue of economic policy by starting with the proposition that American civilization was not British, but was different in realities and potentials. Rejecting the simple role of provincial subordination for the United States, Carey proposed measures designed to promote a diversified and independent economy—a productive and distributive economy, not a huckstering economy.

The son of Mathew C. Carey, a Catholic refugee from Ireland who had taken a prominent part in the intellectual struggles which accompanied the launching of the American Republic, young Henry Carey received an informal education from his father and, following in his father's footsteps, became a successful publisher first in Baltimore, then in Philadelphia. Early in his thinking about economics, Henry Carey accepted, with some qualifications, the British system of economic theory. It was not until about 1845 that he broke with free trade, while adhering to the general principle of individual initiative and private enterprise. Thereafter he became an irreconcilable opponent of British theory and practice for America and sought to work out, with full reference to the geographical, political, and social characteristics of the United States, a science of political economy adjusted to his idea of civilization in its applications to his own country.

Following the leadership of Adam Smith, the English theorists had abstracted man from civilization and set him up as an economic automaton moved only by the propulsions of the acquisitive instinct. Under the fiction thus created, they formulated certain "iron laws" of society and blended them in a "system of nature" for humanity—all alleged to be as binding as the mechanics of the physical world. Two of the alleged "laws" which Carey especially attacked were the law of rent expounded by Ricardo and the law of population advanced by Malthus, parts of the same scheme of thought.

Ricardo's law of rent declared that, as an increasing population forces a cultivation of poorer and poorer soils, the share accruing to landlords augments, while the shares accruing to labor and capital diminish. To phrase it in Carey's language: "As a necessary consequence of the increasing scarcity of fertile soils, it is held that, with this diminishing return, the land-holder is enabled to take a larger proportion of the proceeds of labor, thus profiting at the cost of the laborer, and by reason of the same causes which tend to the gradual subjugation of the latter to the will of his master." In the terms of formulation this law of nature took for granted the prevailing system of land tenure in general, and British landlordism in particular, thereby assimilating the laws of man to the laws of the physical universe.

According to the second law of British economics, linked with the name of Malthus, population, by a kind of iron necessity, tends to outrun the food supply; the misery of the poor is largely, if not entirely, due to their brute-like fecundity and hence beyond the reach of curative public policies. To state it in Carey's words: "Over-population is held to be a result of a great law of nature, in virtue of which men grow in numbers faster than they can grow the food that is to nourish them; and the poverty, vice, and crime that everywhere exist, are regarded as necessary consequences of this great law, emanating from an all-wise all-powerful, and all-merciful Being. War, famine, and pestilence are regarded as means provided by that Being for restraining population within the limits of subsistence. Charity is regarded as almost a crime, because it tends to promote the growth of population. The landlord excuses himself for taking large rents, on the ground that it is a necessary consequence of the natural tendency of man to increase in numbers with too great rapidity. . . . Capital cannot become more productive, except at the cost of labor; nor can wages rise, except at the cost of capital."

The fundamental assumption of British economists, that man is like a predatory animal driven by acquisitive instincts in the pursuit of material gain and that a "science" can actually be established on that fact, Carey disowned root and branch. He did not deny that economic goods and activities were vital to the existence of society. Far from it, he underscored the importance of these goods and activities for human welfare. Neither did Carey deny the force of economic necessity in human affairs, but he impugned the notion that man is a mere victim of necessity, subject, like falling bodies, to unchangeable laws of nature and his own nature, which consign a large portion of mankind, especially laborers, to irremediable poverty, misery, and deprivation. He looked upon man as an intellectual and moral being, ever at work in and for civilization, advancing through knowledge, the sciences, and the arts to the exercise of an ever-increasing control over the physical and economic universe in the interest of human welfare, partly by means of wise public policies devised and applied. In other words, instead of discussing a robot—the economic man—created by British economists, Carey dealt with historic human beings, real beings, carrying on civilization, with all their powers of creation as manifested in that process.

In the system of British theory, economy was a kind of fixed order or mechanism, treated as if it was the same thing everywhere, ever running in routine under inward propulsions, without the possibility of revolutionary changes. The truth of this proposition Carey questioned. For him economy was a phase of history, changeable, and progressive. On this assumption he virtually applied the method of the historical school which later made devastating inroads on the abstractness, the unreality, of the classical economics so popular in the schools.

In addition to placing economy as development within the process of civilization, Carey employed the comparative method and showed that the economies of nations, in both time and place, varied widely in theory and practice. He studied painstakingly the economies of ancient Greece and Rome and modern England, France, Italy, and Spain; and he examined the changes and effects of public policies pursued by the respective governments. Through comparative studies of civilization he clarified his own mind respecting the essential values of American life and economy, of civilization in the United States, as it existed, as it was becoming, and as it might be given finer form under appropriate policy.

Although references to civilization occurred frequently

in Carey's voluminous writings, indicating its persistent presence in his thought, he deemed it so important as idea that he discussed it in a separate chapter of his volume entitled *The Past, the Present, and the Future*—a title ominous for the theorists of the static order. This chapter he opened by a general statement of his historical thesis: "Civilization has, in all ages and countries, been found where men have accumulated wealth by means of which they have been enabled to subject to cultivation the rich soils of the earth; and it has disappeared as they have been forced to abandon them and fly to the poor soils of the hills for safety. Concentration on the former is essential to the progress of civilization. With each step therein we have diminished machinery of exchange; physical and intellectual. Men exchange more directly with each other the products of their minds and of their hands: and with each step production, material and intellectual, tends to increase."

In this process the diffusion of civilization among the people expands: "With the increase of material product, the proportion of the labourer increases, while that of land diminishes: and with each step, land tends to become more and more divided. With the increase of intellectual product, the machinery for the communication of ideas improves, and the labourer finds increased facility of obtaining knowledge, while the teacher obtains from a small contribution on the part of each of his readers or hearers a largely increased reward. Each step, therefore, in the progress of civilization is marked by a tendency to equality of physical and intellectual condition, and to the general ownership of wealth, whether in land or other machinery of production: or in the possession of books, pictures, statuary, or other things tending to promote intellectual advancement. With the division of land and the diffusion of wealth, the power of the few tends to diminish, while the number of persons interested in the maintenance of peace and in the enforcement of perfect security in the enjoyment of the rights of person and property tends to increase."

With improvement in economic conditions comes improvement in morals: "Moral feeling improves, because of the increased facility of obtaining the necessaries, conveniences, and comforts of life. Improvement and a tendency towards perfect equality of moral feeling are therefore characteristics of civilization. With each step in this progress, jealousy and avarice disappear, and harmony and good feeling, and liberality of thought and action, appear: generosity towards the weak takes the place of oppression: woman becomes the companion of man and ceases to be his slave: children cease to be slaves and come to be companions: parents cease to be tyrants, and children respect and love them: and all, men, women, and children, acquire the habit of self-government. With each step the *necessity* for the use of the machinery of government, public or private, tends to disappear, and with each the *power* of man to govern himself is seen to increase. . . . Civilization is marked by elevation and equality of physical, moral, intellectual, and political condition, and by the tendency towards union and harmony among men and nations. The highest civilization is marked by the most perfect individuality and the greatest tendency to union, whether of men or of nations."

After presenting these general considerations, Carey sketched a history of specific societies from the early days of Attica to his own times, briefly delineating each. England, he thought, led all other European countries in civilization but was still infested with barbarism: "In no part of Europe has the tendency to civilization been so great as in England: yet, if we now examine her condition, the conditions of civilization are complied with in but a very limited degree." After unmasking English landlords and describing their laborers living in mud hovels, he exclaimed: "Here we have the civilization of Rome in the days of Pompey and Caesar: or that of Pomerania, before the changes of the early years of the present century. Where such things are, true civilization has made little progress. Neither can we see much of it in a system that enables great manufacturers to accumulate fortunes of millions of pounds out of the labors of the people who occupy the wretched cellars of Manchester . . . or great coal-proprietors, to fix monopoly prices upon coal mined by naked women and children, to enable them to accumulate fortunes at the expense of poor consumers in London. There is no civilization in the lanes and alleys of Glasgow; nor in its numerous brothels, filled with the daughters of peasants who have been hunted out of their hills. . . . There is no civilization in starving Ireland; none in India. . . ."

Nevertheless Carey offered no perfect satisfaction to the boaster who proclaimed utopia to be already in America:

"In the United States, the conditions of civilization are complied with to an extent far beyond what elsewhere exists, and if they are not fully and completely so the cause is to be found in the fact that they [the United States] cannot control their own actions. So soon as they shall resolve that they *will* do so, they can place themselves at once at the head of all civilization. . . . The whole nation may cultivate rich soils, when it wills that it *shall* be done." By act of will under positive policy, that is, according to Carey's program, by protecting American industry and managing the currency, by developing diversified manufacturing and agriculture, by facilitating immediate exchanges of goods, and by creating the utmost self-sufficiency in economy—the United States could place themselves in the van of civilization.

If this national policy were adopted, then the little schools would become larger and better schools; the fragmentary system of transportation would become a vast network; hamlets would become great towns; land would be more and more divided; men would have large libraries instead of small ones; the farmer would have a daily newspaper instead of his weekly; meetings for the exchange of ideas would become more frequent; women and children would be more and more exempt from the hardships of labor; the cultivation of beauty for living would increase. "Then will the consciousness of power diminish, and the sense of his [man's] duty towards his fellow men increase: and then will he be seen daily more and more exerting himself to aid the afflicted and to help the weak: doing to all, and daily more and more, as he would that others should do unto him."

Such was Carey's general assessment of the possibilities for the advancement of civilization in the United States. In another place, in *The Harmony of Interests,* he paid left-handed compliments to opponents who held a different view concerning the nature and promise of American life. "Much is said of 'the mission' of the people of these United States, and most of it said by persons who appear to limit themselves to the consideration of the *powers* of the nation, and rarely to think of its *duties*. By such men the grandeur of the national position is held to be greatly increased by having expended sixty or eighty millions upon a war with a weak neighbor. . . . By such men, the fitting out of expeditions for the purpose of producing civil war among our neighbors of Cuba, is held to be another evidence of grandeur. Others would have us mix ourselves up with all the revolutionists of Europe; while a fourth and last set sigh at the reflection that our fleets and armies are too small for the magnificence of our position. By some it is supposed that our 'mission' is that of monopolizing the commerce of the world." In his view all this was both uneconomic and uncivilized.

Two systems, he declared, are before the world. One looks to enlarging the proportion of persons and capital engaged in transporting commodities, the other to augmenting the proportion engaged in the production of wealth; one to empire, with expanding armies, navies, and wars, the other to the development of productive potentials at home, abstention from the wars of imperial nations, and advancing human welfare in the United States; one to the centralization of wealth in commercial cities dominated by banker conceptions of economy, the other to concentration on and the diversification of production. "One looks to pauperism, ignorance, depopulation, and barbarism; the other to increasing wealth, comfort, intelligence, combination of action, and civilization. One looks towards universal war; the other towards universal peace. One is the English system; the other we may be proud to call the American system, for it is the only one ever devised the tendency of which is that of *elevating* and *equalizing* the condition of man throughout the world. *Such* is the true *mission* of the people of these United States." And by following this policy and making this demonstration in practice on this continent, Carey argued, the United States would in fact promote civilization throughout the world.

These severe attacks on "the English system" brought equally severe replies from London. The London Times discharged a heavy broadside at Carey's doctrines, applying the phrases "ignorance and imbecility," "folly and iniquity," to persons who held such views. Referring to Carey by name, the Times accused him of laboring "to prove that Free Trade was unsuited to the present condition of his country," but "that, if the Americans would only establish a stringent system of imposts upon foreign manufactures, and persevere in it long enough, they would call into being an industrial power which would enable them in due time to burst upon the world with a Free Trade policy, and overwhelm all creation with their goods. . . . To make the country independent of the foreigner, capable of producing everything for itself, and self-sufficient even if shut off from the rest of the world by a powerful enemy, is a principle of government gravely avowed by persons who on other matters judge and speak with intelligence."

Carey's answer to the Times was given in a pamphlet entitled *Commerce, Christianity, and Civilization versus British Trade,* applying again the idea of civilization to economic policy and condemning the leaders of British policy for permitting the misery of their subjects at home and throughout their vast empire. If the exchange was far from gracious in tone, it at least gave Carey an opportunity to repeat those primary conceptions of American life which controlled his thinking on economic policies.

Nor were all American business men pleased by Henry Carey's theories. If his protectionist doctrines were as satisfactory to American manufacturing interests as free trade doctrines were to Southern planters and to exporting and importing interests, his broad social philosophy was abhorrent to them. Though he was a protectionist, his idea of civilization in the United States did not involve the subordination of agriculture to manufacturing, the transformation of the country into a nation of capitalists and proletarians. On the whole he was inclined to lay greater emphasis on the cultivation of the soil than on manufacturing. Furthermore he was opposed to the concentration of riches and demanded an increasing diffusion of wealth among the whole body of people. He especially objected to the gold standard for the currency, which fastened the economy of the United States to the English system centered in London. He favored a managed currency—"the establishment of that monetary independence which results from maintaining absolute command over the machinery of exchange used within our own borders, leaving to the gold dollar the performance of its duty of arranging for the settlement of balances throughout the world." The gold standard, devised in British interests, he regarded as an instrument used by them in exploiting raw-material nations through international exchange, tying their economies to the policies and fortunes of the British Empire.

As American bankers, often with international connections, took over more and more the financing of American industry and at the same time the business of rationalization for American manufacturers, Carey's idea of civilization in the United States became correspondingly repugnant to ideologues of the academies. As a matter of fact, from their standpoint, it was indeed a menace; by logical extension, revolutionary for practice.

Like-minded with Henry C. Carey in recognizing the relation of economy to the welfare of society, but more revolutionary than he respecting that contradiction to civilization —misery, the social reformers of the democratic era were more extreme in criticisms and proposals. With the uprush of factory towns, the swelling influx of poverty-stricken immigrants, and increasing labor agitations, the problem that had distressed Thomas Paine and Robert Coram fifty years earlier now received more extended consideration from persons higher placed in the social scale: for example, Horace Greeley, Albert Brisbane, and Charles A. Dana.

For a long time the general remedy for misery which many social reformers prescribed was a species of utopian socialism called Associationism; and in numerous self-sufficing colonies, combining agriculture and handicrafts, the prescription was tested. Among the reformers in the era of the popular upsurge who espoused that creed and invoked in support of it a dynamic theory of history, with civilization treated as a phase, socialists of the Fourier type were especially vocal and magisterial. Their doctrines were well represented in the writings of Parke Godwin. Indeed, their whole system was epitomized by Godwin in 1844 in *A Popular View of the Doctrines of Charles Fourier,* a concise exposition based partly on translations from Fourier's works and partly on his own researches. With Fourier he accepted the dynamics of history and civilization as idea and reality but they both regarded civilization as only a transition to the associationist order of perfection.

In the fourth chapter, Godwin dealt with the "General Formula of Social Movement" in which he set forth his theory of historical stages in the development of mankind. "The present form of society," he opened, "not being the first form in which Humanity has existed upon the earth, is not likely to be the last, and it is therefore worth while to inquire into the history of the forms that have preceded it, and to deduce from this, if we can, some probable opinions of the nature of the changes that may follow."

According to the Fourierist scheme, explained by Godwin, four stages had appeared in the development of mankind prior to the rise of civilization, namely, Edenism, Savage-ism, Patriarchalism, and Barbarism, not sharply broken in time-relation but each having its own characteristics. The state of Edenism existed at the dawn of human history in temperate zones where the number of human beings was small and the food supply was abundantly furnished by nature. This was the so-called golden age, or paradise lost, panegyrized in ancient mythology, in the Jewish epic, and by Rousseau and his democratic disciples—so persistent in romantic history.

In the second period, or Savageism, began war, agricul-ture, slavery, organizations for defense and conquest, cruelty to women and children, and the intellectual lethargy that went with war and subjugation. During the third period, Pa-triarchalism, the father became an insolent despot, his wife his slave, his children his servants. Flocks were reared, in-dustries began to develop, fixed attachment to the soil com-menced, and various elements of society were called into existence.

The fourth period, the age of Barbarism, was notable for an extensive growth of agriculture and manufacturing, many manifestations of the higher intellectual faculties, incessant wars by savage hordes, the rise of great military chieftains as founders of states, expansion of societies governed by force and law, the spread of justice, and the growing influ-ence of a fanatical theocracy. In this long history, beginnings of civilization were made, but violence was general. "In the barbarism system the mode of operation is simple, being founded upon violence alone. This fundamental difference is found in all the operations of the two societies; both ar-rive at the same result; but civilization adds cunning to violence. The wily caution of the Tiger in addition to its power. The Lion and the Fox united."

In the age to which Godwin affixed the name of Civiliza-tion, the fifth period, industry, commerce, science, and art made headway, carrying forward work begun in previous periods. "Civilization is the true nurse of Industry. The two or three past centuries, particularly the present one, have wonderfully developed the positive sciences, and given all a rank which they never before held. Agriculture has been improved by a more scientific mode of cultivation, and by the introduction of more perfect implements; manufactures have received an immense extension; new branches have been discovered, and the genius of man has been actively employed in the invention of machinery, which, next to the spontaneous productiveness of the soil, is the greatest source of riches. Experimental chemistry, one of the most important conquests of human intelligence in the material world, has also been called into existence, and is now assuming a high rank as the assistant of industry. . . . Industry . . . struggles against the oppression of the military power, and attains by slow degrees a permanent existence, and an influence in society. Its products become so important to the man of war himself, to enterprise and comfort, that he is forced gradually to respect it."

With the advance of industry came radical shifts in class relations. "The industrial or laboring classes increase in strength and intelligence, until they finally assume a position which enables them to demand and force a concession of their rights. A social transformation then commences, which increases until society completely changes its character, and becomes entirely commercial and industrial in its spirit. . . . The aristocracy of birth has given place to the aristocracy of wealth, and become a mere shadow in those countries where it has lost its possessions. The feudal baron with his dependents, who owe him allegiance, is replaced by the banker or capitalist, who is surrounded indirectly with a train equally dependent and servile. This is particularly the case in France and the United States."

The shifts in class leadership were attended by changes in spirit and manners. "If the pride and power of the baron were in his birth, his titles, and armorial bearings, the pride and the power of the man of our day are in his wealth and financial influence. If the skill of the former shone forth in military exploits, the skill of the latter is displayed in commercial and financial operations. Thus the spirit of society has changed from the military to the purely commercial and industrial. The feuds of powerful families, the exploits of war, glory, honors, no longer occupy the same importance with the heralds of publicity. The balance of trade, the state of exchange, commercial prosperity, and false credit, have taken their place, and become the great objects of public interest. Where commerce has not superseded birth and title, it has made itself their equal in wealth and influence."

Such was his verdict on the civilization in which Godwin found himself in New York City, in 1844. Immense and

given us; in ▓▓▓▓▓▓▓▓ it, and worthy of achieving it!"

At that period in ▓▓▓▓▓lic career, and indeed for a long time after his conversion to the Catholic faith in 1844, Brownson made the idea of civilization a fulcrum of reform. He spoke of civilization as the supremacy of law, as introducing order against barbarism, as involved in the natural and moral order, as identical with Christianity, as characterizing the historic process in general. And he continued to praise American civilization as expressing the greatest development in the human spirit. Only after the Pope, Pius IX, placed "modern civilization" under the ban for Catholics, did Brownson surrender his belief in American civilization and turn upon it the battery of his invective.

While Carey was working out a system of political economy which he thought adapted to the peculiar conditions in the United States, while reformers were importing the utopianism of Fourier, American men and women of letters were likewise considering fundamental questions. What themes were they to choose for literary efforts? Must they come wholly into the European movement of thought or cling to European traditions? Must they be controlled by established forms of expression? In short were they to fit into a European mold or were their temperaments and supreme obligation to be in some measure original and creative in a different environment—in the civilization of the United States?

Given the intrinsic nature and possibilities of this civilization, was it for letters and the arts a mere duplication of Old World civilization in some style? In the very necessity of things, could it be such a civilization? Was there so much fate in it that it could not be diverted back into the channels of history through which civilization in Europe had flowed? Was it identical with that civilization, or could it ever be made so in the economy of destined history?

The men and women of letters who pondered these ques-

through the recognition and adop̶̶̶̶̶̶̶̶̶̶̶ ̶̶̶̶̶̶̶ ̶̶̶̶̶of society as established by Charles Fou̶̶̶̶̶̶̶̶̶ ̶̶̶̶̶ civilization ran through history, as interpreted by Godwin; and civilization, as the existing stage of social development, was to eventuate in something akin to a perfect order. In effect Fourier and Godwin condemned civilization as "bourgeois," as Marx and Engels were soon to do in the *Communist Manifesto*.

Arrayed on the side of the reformers in their attack on misery, until he bowed to papal dogmas, Orestes A. Brownson differed from them in holding that civilization was more than a stage on the way to utopia. Perhaps in no other man of the middle period was the questing spirit that marked the age more vehemently represented. Born in 1803 and brought up in poverty on a Vermont farm, self-educated, especially in philosophic writing, Brownson in his youth joined the Presbyterian church, only to leave it two years later and become a Universalist minister. In a short time the liberal doctrines of Universalism seemed too conservative for him and he withdrew from that communion to engage in teaching, preaching, and writing as a kind of missionary-at-large. During the early period of his career he helped to disseminate the socialistic theories of Robert Dale Owen and Frances Wright, aided in organizing the Workingmen's Party, preached for a time in Unitarian churches, organized a church of his own in a working-class district of Boston, established the Boston Quarterly Review as an organ of Democratic opinion, and made repeated and forceful assaults, in the name of democracy, on organized Christianity, on accumulated riches, and on the cruelties of the penal code.

While he was a young man Brownson displayed an optimistic faith in American and her mission. "We young Americans," he said in 1838, "who have the future glory of our country and of Humanity at heart, who would see our country taking the lead in modern civilization, and becoming as eminent for her literature, art, science, and philosophy, as she is now for her industrial activity and enterprise, must

America: "The American in Europe, if a thinking mind, can only become more American. . . . The thinking American [is] a man who, recognizing the immense advantage of being born to a new world and on a virgin soil, yet does not wish one seed from the past to be lost. He is anxious to gather and carry back with him every plant that will bear a new climate and a new culture. Some will dwindle; others will attain a bloom and stature unknown before. He wishes to gather them clean, free from noxious insects, and to give them a fair trial in his new world. And that he may know the conditions under which he may best place them in that new world, he does not neglect to study them in this."

Then turning upon America the same critical mind, Margaret Fuller asked: "And thou, my Country! wilt thou not be more true? does no greater success await thee? All things have so conspired to teach, to aid! A new world, a new chance, with oceans to wall in the new thought against interference from the old!—treasures of all kinds, gold, silver, corn, marble, to provide for every physical need! A noble, constant, starlike soul, an Italian, led the way to thy shores, and, in the first days, the strong, the pure, those too brave, too sincere, for the life of the Old World, hastened to people them. A generous struggle then shook off what was foreign, and gave the nation a glorious start for a worthy goal. Men rocked the cradle of its hopes, great, firm, disinterested men, who saw, who wrote, as the basis of all that was to be done, a statement of the rights, the *inborn* rights of men, which, if fully interpreted and acted upon, leaves nothing to be desired. . . .

"O Eagle! . . . Thou wert to be the advance-guard of humanity, the herald of all progress; how often hast thou betrayed this high commission! . . .

"How it pleases me here to think of the Abolitionists! I could never endure to be with them at home, they were so tedious, often so narrow, always so rabid and exaggerated in their tone. But, after all, they had a high motive, something eternal in their desire and life; and if it was not the only thing worth thinking of, it was really something worth living and dying for, to free a great nation from such a terrible blot, such a threatening plague. God strengthen them, and make them wise to achieve their purpose!"

Interest in her own country Margaret Fuller had deepened by travel to the Great Lakes region in 1843. It was her desire to see face to face what types of pioneers were building the new settlements and what they were making of the opportunities for a meaningful and happy life. There she encountered, in addition to pioneers from the seaboard, fresh immigrants from Europe, men and women dressed in old world costumes, bringing their arts and crafts to their new homes in the wilderness. That direct observation enlarged the knowledge which she had derived from books and seaboard journeys.

Shortly after she had made this trip, when a volume called *American Facts* was published, she reviewed it in a mood of thought which disclosed the breadth of her view and the nature of her insight. The modest compilation in question could be easily set aside with pleasantry, she commented. But the title had significance, she said, and there was yet to be written, perhaps by "the epic poet or the philosopher," the real book of American facts. "It would be a great book indeed, and one that would require the eye and heart of a great man,— great as a judge, great as a seer,—and great as a prophet,— that should select for us and present in harmonious outline the true American facts. To choose the right point of view supposes command of the field.

"Such a man must be attentive, a quiet observer of the slighter signs of growth. But he must not be one to dwell superstitiously on details, nor one to hasten to conclusions. . . .

"We doubt not the destiny of our country—that she is to accomplish great things for human nature, and be the mother of a nobler race than the world has yet known. But she has been so false to the scheme made out at her nativity, that it is now hard to say which way that destiny points. . . . Only one thing seems clear—that the energy here at work is very great, though the men employed in carrying out its purposes may have generally no more individual ambition to understand those purposes, or cherish noble ones of their own, than the coral insect through whose restless working new continents are upheaved from ocean's breast. . . .

"America is as yet but a European babe; some new ways and motions she has, consequent on a new position; but the soul that may shape her mature life scarce begins to know itself yet. One thing is certain; we live in a large place, no less morally than physically: woe to him who lives meanly here, and knows the exhibitions of selfishness and vanity as the only American facts."

On that perennial issue of the times, so endlessly debated on two continents—the quality and future of American liter-

ature—Margaret Fuller rendered her judgment and in rendering it she also gave her opinion on the conditions favorable to the flowering of literary genius in the United States. That such genius would "rise and work in this hemisphere," she believed, but thought that only the first streaks of the dawn were yet visible. "That day will not rise till the fusion of races among us is more complete. It will not rise till this nation shall attain sufficient moral and intellectual dignity to prize moral and intellectual, no less highly than political, freedom; not till, the physical resources of the country being explored, all its regions studded with towns, broken by the plow, netted together by railways and telegraph lines, talent shall be left at leisure to turn its energies upon the higher department of man's existence. Nor then shall it be seen till from the leisurely and yearning soul of that riper time national ideas shall take birth, ideas craving to be clothed in a thousand fresh and original forms. . . . We cannot have expression, until there is something to be expressed. The symptoms of such a birth may be seen in a longing felt here and there for the sustenance of such ideas. . . . But it needs to go deeper, before we can have poets, needs to penetrate beneath the springs of action, to stir and remake the soil as by the action of fire."

"Another symptom is the need felt by individuals of being even sternly sincere. . . . Truth is the nursing mother of genius. . . . And it is the same with the nation as with the individual man."

If nowhere in her writings, Margaret Fuller articulated all of her observations and meditations about them under the single conception, civilization, it is scarcely to be doubted that she was thinking in terms of civilization. Her numerous letters written while traveling, her causeries, and her columns in the New York Tribune contributed on the invitation of Horace Greeley, reveal the unity of her thought as the unity of the idea of civilization.

To the theme of American civilization as illuminated by the light of Europe's experience, James Fenimore Cooper, affiliated with the landed classes of New York, turned his skill as a writer. Cooper was also prepared by travel and long residence abroad for handling it, and in his novels and letters he frequently discussed it. Far from complacent about the tendency of affairs in the United States, on the contrary often discontented about it, still Cooper broke with the theory of the landed orders that landed property, permanently entailed in owners and their descendants, should rule his country. He also parted company with Guizot's bourgeois theory that capital should govern it. Although extreme in some of his notions of the properties, he thought there was an opportunity in America for a better social order than yet prevailed on either continent and he did not envisage it in urban terms alone.

In his *American Democrat,* Cooper declared: "A government founded on the representation of property, however direct or indirect, is radically vicious." This contention he reiterated in *The Monikins:* "We have had the property-principle carried out thoroughly in our practice, and the result has shown that its chief operation is to render property as intact as possible, and the bones, and sinews, and marrow of all who do not possess it, its slaves." Nor could he approve the cold commercialism and vulgar riches of the rising Whiggery. In a letter written to his wife in 1839, Cooper exclaimed: "God protect the country that has nothing but commercial towns for capitals!" But he did not expect any gains for civilization, at least in the nature of cultural refinements, from a democracy of small farmers and town mechanics.

Cooper believed that a class of large landowners was necessary to civilization and a worthy agency in the civilizing process. It had been argued, he said, that large leasehold estates, carrying in themselves no political power, "defeat the civilization of a country." The argument, he asserted, "is not sustained by fact." Such estates were not contrary to the original policy of the United States; nor were they necessarily bound up, as in Europe, with a royal court or a privileged class. "The real sages of this country," he maintained, "in founding its institutions, no more thought of getting rid of the landlords of the country, than the Church thought of getting rid of its Bishops. The first knew that the gradations of property were an inevitable incident of civilization."

To clinch his case respecting the type of landlordism he advocated, Cooper prefaced Chapter XXVI of *The Redskins* with a quotation ascribed to a Political Essay: "If men desire the rights of property, they must take their consequences: distinction in social classes. Without the rights of property civilization can hardly exist, while the highest class of improvements is probably the result of the very social distinctions that so many decry. The great political problem to be solved is to ascertain if the social distinctions that are

inseparable from civilization can really exist with perfect equality in political rights."

Referring to "the higher civilization that is connected with the tastes and refinements," Cooper wrote: "In Europe they will tell you that a court is necessary to such civilization; but facts contradict the theory. Social classes, no doubt, are; but they can exist independently of courts, as they can, have, do, and ever will in the face of the democracy. Now, connect this class with the landed interest, and see how much your chances for material improvement are increased." Intelligent landlords advance the art of husbandry and introduce profitable innovations. "A body of intelligent, well-educated, liberalized landlords, scattered through New York, would have more effect in advancing the highest interests of the community than all the 'small potato' lawyers and governors you can name in a twelve-month. . . . In a country like this, in which land is so abundant as to render the evils of a general monopoly impossible, a landed gentry is precisely what is most needed for the highest order of civilization, including manners, tastes, and the minor principles, and is the very class which, if reasonably maintained and properly regarded, would do the most good at the least risk of any social class known." Here he was almost Greek in his antipathy to commercialism.

Besides citing contrasts in detail, Cooper, in his *Home as Found*, drew a broad line between Europe and America in a single stroke: "The progress of society in America has been distinguished by several peculiarities that do not so properly belong to the more regular and methodical advances of civilization in other parts of the world. On the one hand the arts of life, like Minerva, who was struck out of the intellectual being of her father at one blow, have started full-grown into existence, as the legitimate inheritance of the colonists, while, on the other, everything tends toward settling down into a medium, as regards quality, a consequence of the community-character of the institutions." Here Cooper was, in effect, certifying to that equalitarian feature of American civilization which irritated defenders of privileged orders and aroused enthusiasm among champions of the American system.

Compared with Cooper, Walt Whitman had slight knowledge of Europe and his acquaintance with American history was not profound; but he was no utterly unlearned bard "singing in the sky." Emory Holloway, one of his biographers, says of Whitman: "He attended lectures, read miscellaneous

magazine articles, Shakespeare, Epictetus, the Hebrew and Hindoo bibles, and Emerson." He knew enough about certain French writings to derive ideas and inspiration from them. But early in his career he asserted that, in substance, spirit, and form, his poetry was American, despite touches of the universal.

In explaining the purpose behind a small volume of his poems printed in 1855, Whitman later wrote: "I dwelt on Birth and Life, clothing my ideas in pictures, days, transactions of my time, to give them positive place, identity—saturating them with the vehemence of pride and audacity of freedom necessary to loosen the mind of still-to-be-form'd America from the folds, the superstitions, and all the long, tenacious and stifling anti-democratic authorities of Asiatic and European past."

In 1872, he indicated that he had thought his way to a very definite picture of the European society against which he set the task of civilization in the United States. The occasion for this rather comprehensive conspectus of his times and his work was the delivery of the commencement poem at Dartmouth College, "As a Strong Bird on Pinions Free." In an article written by Whitman on himself, in the third person, he proclaimed his intention: "He has in mind to chant, in a new volume, of which he gives [in his poem] the first installment, a great composite Democratic nationality."

Here was a vow to sing of democracy—American, not universal democracy. And he ran the gamut of the contrasts between his world and the old world, declaring: "Walt Whitman's form of composition is not attractive at first sight to accustomed readers of verse. He discharges himself quite altogether from the old laws of 'poetry,' considering them and their results unfit for present needs, and especially unfit for the United States, and claims to inaugurate an original modern style, to be followed & expanded by future writers. His theory is that our times exhibit the advent of two especially new creative worlds, or influences, giving a radically changed form to Civilization, namely, the world of science for one, and the world of democratic republicanism for another, and that a third influence, a new poetic world of character and form, adjusted to the new spirit and facts and consistent with democracy and science, is indispensable.

"He says the United States must found their own imagina-

tive literature & poetry, & that nothing merely copied from & following out the feudal world will do. His aim is therefore a profound one & essentially revolutionary. He dismisses without ceremony all the orthodox accoutrements, tropes, verbal haberdashery, 'feet,' and the entire stock in trade of rhyme-talking heroes and heroines and all the love-sick plots of customary poetry, and constructs his verse in a loose and free metre of his own, of an irregular length of lines, apparently lawless at first perusal, although on closer examination a certain regularity appears, like the recurrence of lesser and larger waves on the sea-shore, rolling in without intermission, and fitfully rising and falling.

"In this free metre, and in verses—when you get the hang of them—singularly exhilarating, and that affect one like an atmosphere unusually charged with oxygen, he, by a perpetual series of what might be called *ejaculations*, manages to express himself on about every theme interesting to humanity, or known to the body, passions, experiences, emotions of man or woman, or sought by the intellect and soul, with illustrations drawn largely from our own times and country, & somewhat from every age and country."

Whitman's own explanation of his purpose was confirmed by friends and critics. When Matthew Arnold, referring to Whitman's assertion of literary independence, declared that the American "intellect must inevitably consent to come, in a considerable measure, into the European movement," W. D. O'Connor, a loyal friend and defender of Whitman, replied: "I can't agree that America must come into the European movement, as you say, for, and I am sorry so many Englishmen are blind to it, America has a movement of her own, the source of her life, the secret of her power, and I think, if you will pardon me for saying so, there is far more need and probability of Europe coming into our movement, than we into hers. Democracy, true or false, is the doctrine or principle in which this country has its start, and her movement, in literature as in everything else, must proceed and be sustained from it, and not from anything exterior to it. As well expect that our fauna and flora shall derive from the influences of another zone, as that our letters, or any form of our life, should find its inspiration and sustenance from the central forces of foreign lands."

Long afterward, Bliss Perry brought additional testimony

to show that Whitman's coupling of democracy with civilization was understood and appreciated by at least a few contemporaries in England as well as in America. "Some of the most subtle of the younger English critics," Perry said, "were finding in *Leaves of Grass* a new world of poetry. . . . Here was a band of clever university men, scholars and poets of a new generation, who became convinced of Walt Whitman's claims to be the representative poet of democracy. . . . Some English and Continental admiration of Whitman is no doubt due to the discovery in him of a rudeness and indecorum which were thought indispensable to the rôle of a singer of democracy. But the letters of the more discriminating among Whitman's new readers are ample proof that they went below the surface of boisterous manner, and apprehended something of the deeper drift of Whitman's meaning. Horace E. Scudder, a Boston critic of uncommon poise and sobriety, had sent *Drum-Taps* to W. M. Rossetti in 1866 with the comment that no one had caught so perfectly as Whitman 'the most elusive elements of American civilization.' In Rossetti's ensuing correspondence with O'Connor and with Whitman himself, as shown in the *Rossetti Papers* and elsewhere, there is evidence of sound appreciation of Whitman's prescience as to the vast changes which democracy was working, in England no less than America."

Were the American people, depicted in letters as having their own destiny and creative obligations, actually making progress in civilization in their own way? If so, how? The idea of progress was inherent in the world-view—civilization. These questions were unavoidable, therefore, in the thought about civilization in the United States and writers and orators passed opinions upon them.

On all important aspects of this general subject, the most highly polished orator of the North, Edward Everett, spoke with assurance and no little authority. After his graduation from Harvard, Everett spent five years traveling and studying in Europe. He took his doctor's degree at a German university, at Göttingen. Subsequently he served as professor of Greek literature at Harvard, as a member of the House of Representatives at Washington, governor of his state of Massachusetts for four terms, Senator of the United States, Secretary of State, and minister at the Court of St. James'. His familiarity with the Old World and the New was more than casual or literary.

Americans, Everett steadily maintained, if sometimes with contradictions in emphasis, were making rapid progress in mechanical inventions and in science as applied to manufacturing and agriculture; they were devising and improving the means necessary for the production of wealth required by a civilized people.

To the creation of the practical arts, Edward Everett, on one occasion, attributed the origins of civilization; and to progress in these arts he ascribed the advance in general welfare in the United States. "It is," he said, "these ingenious inventions and useful *arts*,—the product at once and the cause of civilization,—acting upon society and themselves in turn, carried to new degrees of improvement and efficiency by social man, till they have been brought to the state in which we find them . . . it is *these* which form the difference between the savage of the woods and civilized, cultivated, moral, and religious man. It is art which produces and perfects art. . . . The philosophy that denounced accumulation is the philosophy of barbarism."

But Americans had done more, Everett claimed, than adopt and apply the mechanical arts, more than occupy a continent and live on the riches developed by the use of the practical arts: "Merely to fill up the wilderness with a population provided with the ordinary institutions and carrying on the customary pursuits of civilized life, though surely no mean achievement, was not the whole of the work allotted to the United States, and thus far performed with a signal activity, intelligence, and success. The founders of America and their descendants have accomplished more and better things. On the basis of a rapid geographical extension, and with the force of teeming numbers, they have, in the very infancy of their political existence, successfully aimed at higher progress in a generous civilization.

"The mechanical arts have not only been cultivated, but they have been cultivated with unusual aptitude. Agriculture, manufactures, commerce, navigation, whether by sails or steam, and the art of printing in all its forms and in all its applications, have been pursued with surprising skill. Great improvements have been made in all branches of industry, and in the machinery pertaining to them, which have been eagerly adopted in Europe.

"A more adequate provision has been made for popular education, the great basis, humanly speaking, of social improvement, than in almost any other country. . . .

"The Fine Arts have reached a high degree of excellence. . . .

"Our Astronomers, Mathematicians, Naturalists, Chemists, Engineers, Jurists, Publicists, Historians, Poets, Novelists, and Lexicographers have placed themselves on a level with their contemporaries abroad. . . .

"Our constitutions, whether of the United States or of the separate States, exclude all public provision for the maintenance of Religion, but in no part of Christendom is it more generously supported. Sacred Science is pursued as diligently and the pulpit commands as high a degree of respect in the United States, as in those countries where the Church is publicly endowed; while the American Missionary operations have won the admiration of the civilized world.

"Nowhere, I am persuaded, are there more liberal contributions to public-spirited and charitable objects.

"In a word, there is no branch of the mechanical or fine arts, no department of science exact or applied, no form of polite literature, no description of social improvement, in which, due allowance being made for the means and resources at hand, the progress of the United States has not been satisfactory, and in some respects astonishing. . . ."

That progress in the United States transcended mere advance in the practical arts and material welfare, Everett affirmed more than once. "We now have in our possession," he declared in an address at Yale College in 1833, "three instruments of civilization unknown to antiquity, of power separately to work almost any miracle of improvement, and the united force of which is adequate to the achievement of anything not morally and physically impossible. These are, the art of printing, a sort of mechanical magic for the diffusion of knowledge; free representative government, a perpetual regulator and equalizer of human condition, the inequalities of which are the great scourge of society; and, lastly, a pure and spiritual religion, the deep fountain of generous enthusiasm, the mighty spring of bold and lofty designs, the great sanctuary of moral power." Speaking later in 1852, on "Education and Civilization," Everett added a fourth instrument of civilization: public education—which he, as governor of Massachusetts, had zealously labored to advance—public education "as a great system of mental culture, to which, as far as human causes go, we are indebted for the blessings of our civilization."

If to Everett's critics this was smug Whiggery, Democrats could accept a large part of it.

American orators generally agreed also that progress was being made in the wider distribution of wealth among the people. Foreign and domestic critics cited the agreement as proof of intellectual immaturity or "materialistic" obsessions. Reformers railed at it as tending to obscure huge areas of American society blighted by poverty and misery. But the belief was widespread that the standard of living for the masses of the people was higher in the United States than anywhere in the world and was still rising. Even criticism directed against American manners and customs appeared to confirm the contention, for critics were often pointing out or lamenting the fact that servant girls dressed in the modes of their mistresses, and working men were eating meat as often as their employers. Immigration statistics also lent confirmation to the belief. Were not immigrants pouring into the country by the thousands every year, it was asked, and was that not proof that they found a more commodious life in the United States than in the old world?

Nowhere in the popular upsurge was there a more indisputable progress than in the multiplication of schools for the education of the children of the people, all sponsors of the public school system believed. The extension of universal, free, compulsory public education was indeed an outstanding innovation of civilization in the age. And as such it was signalized in addresses and orations.

That indomitable leader in the great educational movement, Henry Barnard, counted educational endeavor a decisive force in the advancement of civilization: "In the right education of early childhood, we must look for a corrective of the evils of society, in our large cities and manufacturing villages, and for the beginning of a better and higher civilization than has yet blessed the world."

Horace Mann also made the cause of public education identical with the cause of civilization in all its aspects. In a public address to friends of education near the close of Andrew Jackson's second administration, Mann assigned to education the vital function of transmitting from generation to generation the precious accumulations of civilization: "To specify the labors which education has yet to perform would be only to pass in review the varied interests of humanity. Its general purpose is to preserve the good and to repudiate the evil which now exist, and to give scope to the sublime law of progression. It is its duty to take the accumulations in knowledge of almost six thousand years, and to transfer that vast treasure to posterity. Suspend its function for but one generation, and the experience and achievements of the past are lost. The race must commence its fortunes anew, and must again spend six thousand years, before it can grope its way upward from barbarism to the present point of civilization."

Americans were doing more than executing projects in the various lines of civilization in the older settlements. They were, orators kept saying, making amazing progress in spreading civilization all over their vast continental domain. In an address before the Phi Beta Kappa Society at Cambridge in 1824, Edward Everett, after pointing out that civilization in the Greek city-states of antiquity penetrated scarcely two hundred miles of hinterland, painted the American contrast in glowing colors. "How different," he exclaimed, "is the picture of the diffusion of the arts and improvements of civilization, from the coast to the interior of America! Population advances westward with a rapidity, which numbers may describe but cannot represent, with any vivacity, to the mind. The wilderness, which one year is impassable, is traversed the next by caravans of industrious emigrants, who go to follow to the setting sun, with the language, the institutions, and the arts of civilized life. It is not the eruption of wild barbarians, come to visit the wrath of God on a degenerate empire. . . . It is the human family led out to possess its broad patrimony. . . . Divisions may spring up, ill blood arise, parties be formed, and interests may seem to clash; but the great bonds of the nation are linked to what is passed. . . . When the Old World afforded no longer any hope, it pleased Heaven to open this last refuge of humanity."

Given this upswing of democracy, this assertion of rights and intellectual and moral power by women, these claims to radical advances in civilization, this optimism about the future—all under the idea of civilization—what attitudes were churches as organizations and the clergy and laymen in churches to take toward democracy, progress, and civilization?

Speaking at Boston in 1824 about the "Demands of the Age on the Ministry," William E. Channing, for example, lauded the progress ascribed to civilization: "It is a consoling and delightful thought, that God, who uses Christianity to advance civilization and knowledge, makes use of this very advancement to bring back Christianity to a purer state, thus binding together, and carrying forward by mutual action, the cause of knowledge and the cause of religion, and strengthening perpetually their blended and blessed influences on human nature."

The state of the contemporary world, Channing thought, as compared with the past, "may be called enlightened and requires an enlightened ministry. . . . We learn now from experience what might have been inferred from the purposes of our Creator, that civilization and refinement are not, as has been sometimes thought, inconsistent with sensibility; that the intellect may grow without exhausting or over-shadowing the heart. . . . A new spirit of improvement is abroad. The imagination can no longer be confined to the acquisitions of past ages, but is kindling the passions by vague but noble ideas of blessings never yet attained." This spirit, in Channing's opinion, was spread widely in the nation, for, in another discourse, he declared: "In this country the mass of the people are distinguished by possessing means of improvement, of self-culture, possessed nowhere else. To incite them to the use of these, is to render them the best service they can receive."

Progress in all the great values promoted by civilization, Channing felt certain, characterized his age. "Human action," he said at Philadelphia in 1841, "is now freer, more unconfined. All goods, advantages, helps are more open to all. . . . The multitude is rising from the dust. Once we heard of the few, now we hear of the many; once of the prerogatives of a part, now of the rights of all. . . . The grand idea of humanity, of the importance of man as man, is spreading silently, but surely. . . . Even the most abject portions of society are visited by some dreams of a better condition for which they were designed. The grand doctrine, that every human being should have the means of self-culture, of progress in knowledge and virtue, of health, comfort, and happiness, of exercising the powers and affections of a man, this is slowly taking its place as the highest social truth. . . . That the great end of government is, to spread a shield over the rights of all—these propositions are growing into axioms, and the spirit of them is coming forth in all the departments of life."

But agreement that organized Christianity could be and should be reconciled to civilization was not unanimous among the clergy and laymen; and a peculiar turn was given to the discussion by a conflict between the Roman Catholic Church and the popular movement in Europe that began to rage furiously, especially after the revolution of 1848. In this conflict the issues of popular sovereignty, liberalism, progress, and civilization were involved, and in time the papacy in Rome officially condemned the new tendencies.

In itself the conflict, connected with the struggle between State and Church in the old world, concerned only the European situation directly; and many native Catholics in America were disinclined to introduce the struggle in the United States. But the congregations of Catholics, already well established and adjusted to American ways and institutions, especially in the conservative regions of Maryland, were now being outnumbered by new throngs of Catholic immigrants accompanied by their old world priests. More and more these immigrants pressed into other regions almost entirely Protestant in religious faith, meeting and displaying antagonisms, social and theological.

Historic differences, which had been acute enough, were sharpened by the militancy of both parties. In the opinion of many Protestants, the immigrants were inveterately alien to everything American. On the other hand, America was alien to many Catholic priests coming suddenly from Europe and finding themselves in a society so unlike the societies in which they had grown up and received their education. To their experiences American life was foreign in essential respects. They had lived in the regions of Europe where the Catholic Church had long been entangled in desperate contests with what it regarded as its mortal foe, Liberalism. Now they discovered that Liberalism had impressive counterparts in the United States—repudiation of privileged orders, separation of Church and State, liberty of conscience and discussion, freedom of the press, secular education, and growing predominance of scientific thought.

In these circumstances the idea of civilization in America, which had previously confronted no organized opposition, was drawn into a contest of well-organized religious and ecclesiastical interests. While Catholic laymen among the immigrants quickly entered in great numbers into the general life of the nation, especially into its economic and political forms, and were on the whole welcomed by Protestant laymen, as the extension of the suffrage to immigrants seemed to show, their spiritual shepherds, accustomed to theological and philosophical disputations, often became engaged in intellectual battles with American Protestants. Sincerely attached to their European heritage, many priests of the Catholic Church made open attacks on the principles which Americans of older stock deemed vital to the existence of the Republic and were assailed by defenders of American theories and practices.

Although it later became fashionable for historians and publicists, who esteemed themselves more enlightened, to speak of "native" resistance to this turn in affairs as "ignorant" and "intolerant," a judicial review of the facts in the case discovers that the merits of the controversy were far from one-sided. It was at bottom, as in parts of Europe, a clash of antithetical world-views. And ample documents in the case demonstrate that neither intolerance nor ignorance was monopolized by either party.

This contest over civilization in the United States—carried on in the name of religion—as it developed during the popular upsurge, can be traced in the bulky volumes of Orestes Brownson, who left the cause of secular reformism in 1844 to become the champion and propagandist of the Catholic faith. In the early period of his new religious course, Brownson vigorously and prolixly defended the idea of civilization, in general and as exemplified in America, against Catholic writers who opposed or deprecated it.

Born and reared in the United States, sympathetic with its laboring classes, and eager to win American converts to his adopted faith, he felt for a long time that the denunciation of modern civilization was not warranted and not good tactics for his fellow-religionists.

Reviewing in 1850 a Catholic writer who had referred to a possible antagonism between spirituality and civilization, Brownson inquired: "How is it possible to regard Catholicity as likely to impede modern civilization, since modern civilization is undeniably the product of the Catholic religion? Indeed, Catholicity is the only thing that can save civilization, and prevent the modern world from lapsing into barbarism and savagism. The author himself holds and proves this. . . . Why, then, does he intimate that it will impede rather than advance our civilization? Simply because he takes the pains neither to think nor to express himself with accuracy. What he means by modern civilization is not modern civilization, but practices and tendencies in modern nations, especially Protestant nations, directly opposed to it, namely the neglect of the higher intellectual culture, worldly-mindedness, selfishness, exclusive cultivation of the physical sciences, and excessive devotion to wealth and mere material prosperity. . . . By what hallucination he should have been led to regard it [Catholicity] for this reason as less friendly than Protestantism to modern civilization is more than we are able to divine."

Dealing generally with religion and the idea of civilization, Brownson regretted that they were so often treated as necessarily antagonistic: "The cause of religion has suffered deeply from the schism between it and civilization, we may say, between it and humanity. The friends of religion seem to be more oppressed with a sense of the weakness and degeneracy of human nature, than encouraged by a sense of its innate greatness and dignity." Modern civilization, he maintained, is in itself an effort to realize Christian teachings in social life. The demand for liberty is an assertion of the free will taught by the church. Effort to ameliorate the condition of the people is an extension of the idea of Christian sympathy and charity. "Your unbeliever, your atheist, whatever his speculative errors, practically follows not seldom the law of Christ, and is a good Christian as a friend, a neighbor, and a citizen." That other phase of modern civilization, democracy, which was making so much trouble for the Church in Europe was, in Brownson's opinion, also an expression of Christian doctrine: "Even democracy, to which the age so strongly tends, is but an earnest effort to realize in society the unity of the race, human brotherhood, and the natural equality of all men, asserted in the Incarnation and Redemption."

In an article published in 1864 bearing a title so objectionable to many European Catholics, "Liberalism and Progress," Brownson again sought a meeting place for religion and civilization, with democracy as a phase of both. "Democracy," he contended, "understood not as a form of government, but as the end of government . . . the common good, the advance in civilization of the people, the poorer and more numerous, as well as the richer and less numerous classes, not of a privileged class or caste, is a good thing, and a tendency towards it is really an evidence of social progress. But this is what the great doctors of the church have always taught, when they have defined the end of government to be the good of the community, the public good, or the common good of all." Liberals have not taken this view of democracy, he argued; have not advocated democracy "for the sake of ameliorating the condition of the people," though they have so pretended; they have used democracy as a means to elevate themselves to power. With the wrath of a prophet, Brownson poured scorn on the "demagogues" of democracy and on greed "masquerading" under the guise of liberalism. But such abuses, he urged, did not warrant the general condemnation of democracy.

Addressing himself to Catholic leaders in the United States and to possible converts, perhaps expressing his Americanism, Brownson also went specifically to the support of American civilization, defective as he deemed it to be: "We are not blind to the faults of our countrymen, whether North or South, East or West, and no man has lashed them more severely than we have. When we speak of American civilization, we speak of the type, the order of civilization the American people have it in charge to realize. We have never pretended, and should be sorry to be thought capable of pretending, that we have as yet fully realized it. In its continuous evolution and realization in law, institutions, manners, customs, habits, &c, consists the life of this world of the American people. We have not yet attained to the end of that life; we have not yet fulfilled our mission, done our work, and harmonized practically religion and civilization. . . . We cannot do it without the Catholic faith and worship, without the Catholic Church and Catholic discipline. But hitherto the church has been presented to us not as the Catholic Church, but as a foreign colony. We need the Catholicity but not the foreignism. . . . The spread of Catholicity associated with the foreign civilization, throughout the country, would destroy the American order of civilization, and reproduce in our new world that of the old world, on which ours is, in our judgment, a decided advance. The American people see this, and hence the little or no progress of the Catholic religion among them." Having thus forcefully stated his opinion, Brownson reiterated the argument that American civilization, despite its faults, had positive merits which represented advances over European ideas and practices and that Catholics would have to reconcile themselves to civilization or be viewed as a foreign body in the society of the United States.

Taking up the vexed question of Catholic schools and education in 1862, Brownson considered that problem in terms of civilization. "The original settlers of the country," he told the faithful of his new persuasion, "were, for the most part, non-Catholic, and but comparatively few of their descendants have been or are Catholics. The very large Catholic population now in the country has not been the growth of the country, but has been chiefly supplied by a foreign and a very recent migration. This is the fact. . . . Catholics from the Old World necessarily bring with them their own civilization, which, whether we speak of France or Italy, Ireland or Germany, is, to say the least, different from ours, and, in some respects, even hostile to it. But this is not all. The civilization they actually bring with them, and which without intending it they seek to continue, is, we being judges, of a lower order than ours."

This assertion of superiority might be due to "our national prejudice and our ignorance of other nations," he said, "but it is nevertheless our firm conviction, from which we cannot be easily driven, that, regarded in relation to its type, the American civilization is the most advanced civilization the world has yet seen, and comes nearer to the realization of the Catholic ideal than any which has been heretofore developed and actualized. We speak not of civilization in the sense of simple *civility,* polish of manners, and personal accomplishments, in which we may not compare favorably with the upper classes of other nations; but of the type or idea we are realizing, our social and political constitution, our arrangements to secure freedom and scope for the development and progress of true manhood. In these respects, American civilization is, we say not the term of human progress, but, in our judgment, the furthest point in advance as yet reached by any age or nation. Those who come here from abroad necessarily bring with them, therefore, a civilization more or less inferior to it, and which, in relation to it, is a civilization of the past. If they educate, then, according to their own civilization, as they must do, they necessarily educate for a civilization behind the times and below that of the country."

Having expressed his mental feelings about the educational controversy, Brownson went into the class aspects of civilization: "The mass of our Catholic population are from the more uncultivated classes of the Old World, with whom it would be ridiculous to pretend that civilization has reached the highest point of development. Whatever respect we may have for the peasantry of Ireland or Germany, how much soever we may honor them for the firmness with which, under the severest trials and temptations, they have held fast to the orthodox faith, we can by no means take them in respect of civilization as the advance-guard of humanity. But the facts themselves, facts which nobody can question, sufficiently prove, at least as to our English-speaking Catholics, that their civilization is of an inferior order. . . . It is not too much to say that the great influx of the Catholic peasantry of different European states into the country, and the conferring on them, almost on their arrival, of political franchises, have done not a little to corrupt our politics and to lower the standard of our civilization. . . . The opposition to us represented by 'Native American,' or 'Know-Nothing' parties or movements, is not opposition to us as orthodox Catholics, nor, in itself considered, to us as foreigners, but simply as representatives of a civilization different from the American, and, in many respects, inferior and opposed to it."

After Brownson had devoted hundreds of pages to expounding and defending the merits of American civilization, notwithstanding its shortcomings, he finally reversed himself and condemned practically all that he had so vigorously asserted in championing American civilization. The occasion for this reversal in Brownson's attitude was the official proclamation of certain policies by the Roman Catholic Church. In 1864 the Pope, Pius IX (Giovanni Maria Mastai-Ferretti, 1792–1878), set forth in *The Syllabus of Errors* a long list of what he defined as the principal errors of the age; and a few years later the doctrine of papal infallibility was officially promulgated.

Much casuistry was employed in explaining the *Syllabus* but no fine-spun discriminations could obscure the plain truth that the Pope had stigmatized as errors separation of Church and State, secular education, freedom of press and speech, and other "liberal" practices, which were incorporated in the American system. There could be no doubt either that, in the eightieth item as the close of the *Syllabus,* Pius IX stigmatized as an error the idea that "the Roman pontiff can and ought to reconcile himself and come to terms with progress, with liberalism, and with modern civilization." The Latin words so translated left no uncertainty as to the fact that it was approval of modern or contemporary civilization that the Pope was setting down as a principal error: *"Romanus Pontifex potest ac debet cum progressu, cum liberalismo et cum recenti civilitate sese reconciliare et componere."*

For a time Brownson seemed confused in his mind as to the course he should follow in view of the papal pronouncements, but at length he decided to yield to their letter and spirit. And given his temperament, he was bound to express his new opinions in the forceful language to which he was accustomed.

In his Quarterly Review for January, 1873, Brownson avowed that he had been in error in trying to present Catholicity to his countrymen in a form "as little repulsive . . . as possible" and announced that he was "not likely to fall into that mistake again." All his previous liberalism he now abandoned: "A *liberal* Catholic I am not, never was, save in appearance for a brief moment, and never can be." He confessed that his respect for his American countrymen had declined: "Methodism is their highest and most cherished form of religion, and Methodism is a compound of sentimentalism and animalism."

Indeed Brownson, notwithstanding the fact that his vocabularly of abuse was enormous, now seemed scarcely able to find words hot enough with which to denounce the things he had formerly praised. Americans, once in the vanguard of civilization, "seem to me to have wonderfully deteriorated during the last third of a century, both intellectually and morally, and with a rapidity unequalled in any other people whose history is known." Their seminaries, houses of refuge for the reform of juvenile offenders, and asylums are "destined to be simply nurseries of error, vice, and crime." Everything in America, except material expansion and growth, "is on the declivity to utter barbarism." To complete his damnation of his native land, Brownson had only to say that it had sunk completely into barbarism.

Democracy might be a good thing where all the people are Catholic and submissive to the law of God as declared and applied by the Pope. "But combined with Protestantism or infidelity in the people," Brownson asserted, "its inevitable tendency is to lower the standard of morality, to enfeeble intellect, to abase character, and to retard civilization, as even our short American experience amply proves." What of the word civilization sowed through his previous pages? "I place little value on what is called material progress, and I regard the boasted progress of modern civilization, in all the respects, as deterioration. . . . Christendom has become heathenized and Protestantism is only carnal Judaism revived. Hence I can have no disposition to concede any thing to it, or sympathy with those who demand an alliance of the church with modern civilization."

For Brownson there was now no compromise. "For myself, I accept the statement of the anticatholic, sectarian, and secular press, that the syllabus condemns all the distinctive features of what is called 'modern civilization'; and draws the line between Catholicity and the world in bondage to Satan, so clearly and distinctly, that there is no mistaking it. It presents the true issue; and those who are not with the pope are against God, and therefore against the rights and interests of men and nations." This left to barbarians the defense of contemporary civilization, if it was to be defended.

Since the idea of civilization was grounded in a theory of history, it was logical that a demand arose, in the popular upsurge, for history-writing in America which would take into account all aspects of American civilization in relation to democracy. Guizot and Buckle were producing works on European, French, and English civilization. What were American historians doing? And how could citizens and statesmen who led in public affairs be properly trained by the study of the right kind of history for the discharge of their functions?

This problem George Bancroft grasped at in his theories of history, democracy, and civilization, but in the volumes of American history which he wrote he made slight efforts to solve it. By 1860 Bancroft had only reached, in his writings, the close of the revolutionary period, and in his treatment of colonial times and the Revolution he had put his principal stress on politics, diplomacy, and wars. He was aware of the need for a more comprehensive history but he did not write it. Nor did he insistently demand that it be written or suggest how it should be written. In execution he fell as far short of the ideal as had Guizot himself.

Ironically, it was a member of the Whig party, so despised by the Democracy for which Bancroft spoke, George Perkins Marsh, who, taking up the demand for the comprehensive history, brought theory closer to practice by indicating those features of American life which ought to be included in such a broad survey. "America," he said, is in origin "new in the history of civilization," and what he actually described as desirable was in reality a history of American civilization written for the people, not for a mere governing élite—written for the commonwealth—although he did not call it a History of American Civilization. The plea and the explication Marsh made in an address entitled "The American Historical School," delivered at Union College in 1847.

The offspring of a family distinguished on both sides for intellectual pursuits, Marsh had received a formal education at Dartmouth College and, like so many men and women of that age, he continued his education throughout his life. He acquired a working knowledge of French, Spanish, Portuguese, Italian, German, and the Scandinavian languages, and became deeply interested in physical geography, especially as modified by human action. To law and scholarship, he added public service in his state, as a member of Congress and as a diplomatic representative of the United States in Europe under Presidents Taylor and Lincoln. His last post, as minister to Italy he held for the closing years of his life, winning Italian admiration as a working scholar whose articles and reviews commanded respect. Dying near Florence in 1882, he was buried at the Protestant cemetery in Rome.

Marsh opened his address at Union College with a differentiation between what may be called metaphysics and earthly history: "The sagest philosophers, under all religious dispensations, have thought the temporal condition and prospects of man a subject, in dignity, importance, and obscurity, inferior only to the greater question of his eternal destiny. Indeed, man's mortal life is perhaps the darker theme; for most wise men, in every age, have held that some ray of Divine illumination has illustrated that more momentous problem, in itself too hard for human solution, while the often-disputed topic of the constant and indefinite progress of our race is elucidated by no revelation, and the hopes and fears of terrestrial man must be determined by the lights which nature has furnished him."

For this undertaking, Marsh thought, mankind has powers of memory, comparison, and reflection; to the revelations of consciousness may be added knowledge of physical laws and practical wisdom, accumulated through the discipline of thousands of years. Since "man is essentially a social being," it follows that the branches of knowledge concerned with his powers, duties, and higher interests are properly called moral sciences. Among these studies, "one of the most important and comprehensive in its applications is the Science (as it is perhaps too ambitiously called) of History, and I propose to ask your attention to a few remarks upon the general character of existing historical literature, the uses of historical knowledge, and the conditions which the peculiar character of our institutions requires in the American historical school."

Marsh was aware of the great advances which had been made in historical scholarship, in the collection of sources, the editing of texts, and the authentication of documents. He referred to progress in such technical matters and expressed his appreciation of its importance and utility for arriving at knowledge of humanity's earthly condition and progress.

But he knew that scholarship and methods were merely instruments of thought, conscious or surreptitious, and he went straight into the problem of the use and interpretation of materials. "History, as too generally written," had been concerned with the crimes, follies, and vices of humanity, with wars, revolutions, conquests. "The conqueror eclipses the renown of the legislator, and the clangor of the trumpet drowns the voice of the arts of peace." Passion and partisanship mar the pages of written history. "But this is not the only error of the modern historical school. History has been written for the ruler, not for the people. . . . It is quite obvious that histories composed upon those principles can be of little real utility to statesmen, who, under any form of government, aim at the greatest good of the whole community, and least of all in a commonwealth where government is recognized as being both for and from the people."

The republican statesman needs to have knowledge of special classes of facts: "the absolute condition of a country at given periods," the actions of public opinion, and "the actual condition of the masses" who do not share in the administration of affairs. Hence the sources usually exploited by historians must be widened to include other records—records relative to the judicial investigations of crime and civil rights, "proceedings of municipal and ecclesiastical corporations, the statistics of the domestic workshop, the course and character of internal traffic, the modes and objects of public and private instruction, the sanitary and economic condition of the people, the position of the learned professions, the correspondence of families and confidential friends, the character and tendency of public amusements, the ephemeral popular literature of different periods, and the private biographies of the humble as well as the great. . . . It will often turn out that the very facts which the historian has scorned to record, as beneath the dignity of his office, do in reality shed more light on the true history of man than the annals of ages of warfare, or the alternate rise and fall of rival dynasties. It is only by a familiar knowledge of the every-day life of a people that we can acquire that sympathy of feeling which is an indispensable condition for the profitable or intelligent study of the history of any nation."

To acquire the mastery of great history, so conceived in its broad sweep, "we must know what have been the fortunes of the mass, their opinions, their characters, their ruling hopes and fears, their arts and industry and commerce; we must see them in their daily occupations in the field, the workshop and the market; witness the solemnities of their temples, the ceremonies of their mourning, and the festivities of their rejoicing; invade the privacy of their firesides and unveil the secrets of their domestic economy; we must live and toil and suffer with them; investigate the moral influences and natural causes, which have conspired to modify their character and control their mode of life; and thus, in short, qualify ourselves to determine both what and why they were." Marsh conceded that "these researches are beset with the greatest difficulty," but "there is no age which promises better to reward the toil of the critical inquirer."

One of the important fruits of these wider and deeper historical inquiries, Marsh thought, would be "the conviction that every homogeneous nation is marked by permanent distinctive traits of moral and intellectual character, and that this character is a necessary element to be considered in determining the appropriate frame and action of its government. National character is formed by the conjoint influence of external circumstances and hereditary opinions. Among the most active of these are climate, natural scenery, habitual modes of life, hostile or amicable foreign relations, free or despotic, colonial or independent government, and, lastly and chiefly, religious belief." From a profound study of these reciprocal and interacting influences might flow guidance for an elevated statesmanship.

Such statesmanship America required: "Our government, instead of resisting, has been smitten by the contagion of a growing trait in the dark side of our national character. We, as a people, are too impatient for present results. Our political husbandry rears no plants save those of annual growth. . . . We have adopted a single form of logical conclusion, *post hoc, ergo propter hoc*. Our present adversity or prosperity is ascribed to contemporaneous or recent political measures, and, like bad grammarians, we uniformly refer all consequences to the nearest antecedent. . . . The trait to which I refer is not one of the original features of American character. . . . The propensity in question is to be ascribed partly to the vacillating policy of a government which too often recognizes as a controlling principle allegiance to a party . . . and partly to our unprecedented and almost portentous growth under the stimulus of free institutions, the impulses of youth, and the excitements of the boundless field of enterprise that lies open before us. . . . We are intoxicated with our success, and giddy with the rapidity of our progress."

While calling for great written history, Marsh did not minimize the importance of constitutional, political, economic, diplomatic, military, and legislative histories. But he maintained that they should be subordinate to the larger theme of general or popular history: "The unique and original character of our political system is eminently favorable to the formation of a true school of popular history." Then, in a single passage, he surveyed the whole course of American history from the founding of the colonies to his present moment, taking in physical geography, natural resources, pioneer and frontier conditions, religion, laws, government, communications, seminaries of learning, the arts and sciences, "the refinements of civilized life"—in brief, American civilization in process. As if answering in advance some later historians, he cited and refuted Volney's declaration that "American society, in its range from the life of the back-woods to that of the city, presents a synopsis of the history of many ages of European progress."

Though acknowledging a certain similarity, Marsh refused to accept that over-simplified parallel. Referring to the creative accomplishments of the Americans who from the beginning had a wilderness to subdue, families to feed, a political society to organize, a nation to found, and a country to defend, he showed the falsity of the parallel: "An origin so remarkable, so new in the history of civilization, could not fail to stamp the institution of which it was the parent with a character as peculiar as the circumstances under which it was formed. Doubtless our social organization has much in common with the European forms, and this is the result partly of a spirit of imitation, and partly of the general law that like causes produce like effects; but no impartial and diligent inquirer can fail to be convinced that the best features of our system, those which give it its efficiency, and constitute its excellence, are not merely improvements or modifications of European institutions, but the spontaneous growth and product of a new combination of the elements of society, under new and eminently favorable conditions. In the comparison of our institutions with those of the old world, we are apt to be misled by a similarity of terms, and, because the poverty of language has compelled us to apply old appellations to new objects, to imagine an identity of character in things which are not even analogous."

A comprehensive study of the American experience and life, in origin "so new in the history of civilization," Marsh held, "ought to distinguish the American historical school, considered as a means of the instruction of a people equal in political rights, and every individual of whom is, potentially at least, a ruler." It would help to overcome the disruptive features of American society while informing statesmen and the people. "The difference of origin and hereditary opinion, the varying local conditions and institutions of different sections of our country, combined with the influence of that policy which indiscriminately admits all comers to an equal participation in every right and every franchise, have hitherto prevented the American people from acquiring a consistent and well-defined predominant character, and this is one of the causes of the vacillation and instability of our public policy. But our free institutions are nevertheless based upon certain traits of character and certain hereditary principles, the maintenance of which is absolutely essential to the permanence of the valuable features of our social and political system. A just comprehension and appreciation of these traits, and an intelligent perception of the relations between them and those institutions which have sprung from them, is attainable only by the study of our history in the spirit and with the aids which I have attempted to describe."

By the study of popular history in America, so comprehended and written, Americans will be the better prepared for the fulfilment of their destiny and the conquest of their opportunity. "A comparison of the spirit of our history with the traits which mark the annals of Europe, will prepare us to appreciate the value of a political system which abridges no right for the value of conferring privileges, imposes no restraints on man's free intellectual or spiritual action, requires no tests, commits no treasonable encroachment on the prerogatives of the Deity, knows no legal difference between the humblest citizen and the highest functionary, the layman and the ecclesiastic, sets up no man as an ideal personification of the state, a human idol, calling on all men to fall down and worship." In other words, by the study of American history in its fulness, assistance may be given to preserving the best features of American life, to shaping national character, and to the framing of public policies calculated to maintain and advance civilization in America.

In the very same year that George P. Marsh made his plea for historical writing appropriate to the characteristics of American civilization, Theodore Parker, a scholar equally learned and perceptive in his way, also cut out the task for the historian in the modern age. Parker's theories of history were expressed in a critical, almost ferocious, review of Prescott's works on Spain and Spanish conquests in America.

Prescott had been hailed by his intellectual coterie as a brilliant scholar, facile writer, and an ornament to the world of letters. Parker, who was versatile in languages, literatures, and philosophies, charged Prescott, as Henry Steele Commager has pointed out in his *Theodore Parker,* with being narrow, aristocratic, superficial, frivolous, and unphilosophic. Striking at "the corpse-cold orthodoxy of Boston," Parker exclaimed: "If a Russian would write a history of France, it would be easy to forgive him if he wrote in the interest of tyrants. But when a man of New England undertakes to write a history, there is less excuse if his book should be wanting in Philosophy and Humanity; less merit if it should not abound therewith." Not content with attacking Prescott's history, while admitting that he was a scholar and an amiable gentleman, Parker even referred to his financial rewards, over which Prescott had haggled with the zeal of a Yankee merchant.

Indeed Parker seemed convinced that Prescott, the son of a wealthy Boston lawyer, besides being trivial in his thinking, scarcely transcended his class—the class that nourished

Edward Everett, who delivered its orations, and Daniel Webster, who delivered its politics and economics. "If the Historian is a weak man," and in Parker's opinion Prescott was, and makes a particular country his special study, he "can but pass thereon with only the general judgment of his class." Prescott does not go behind the aristocratic façade of Spain. He says much of armies, but little or nothing about the life, labor, and institutions of the Spanish people. "In all this History there are no pictures from the lives of the humble. . . . He pays little regard to the progress of society. . . . He has space for frivolous details of court life. . . . The author seems to know nothing of the Philosophy of History, and little, even, of Political Economy. . . . His judgment, the average judgment of a trading town, is readily accepted by the average of men, and is popular with them; but he writes as one with little sympathy for mankind, and seems to think that Spain belonged to Ferdinand and Isabella. . . . He calls womankind 'the sex'; not a very elegant or agreeable title."

Besides disposing of Prescott in this manner, Parker described what in his estimation were the duties properly associated with the office of the historian. The historian "is not a bare chronicler." He is to give us the nation's outer life and to reveal its inner life in the thought and feeling of the people. "He is to inquire what Sentiments and Ideas prevailed in the nation; whence they came, from without the people or within; how they got organized, and with what result. Hence, not merely are the civil and military transactions to be looked after, but the Philosophy which prevails in the nation is to be ascertained and discoursed of; the Literature, Laws, and Religion. The Historian is to describe the industrial condition of the people,—the state of Agriculture, Commerce, and the Arts—both the useful and the beautiful; to inform us of the means of internal communication, of the intercourse with other nations—military, commercial, literary, or religious. He must tell us of the Social State of the people, the relation of the cultivator to the soil, the relation of class to class. . . . The writer of the Nation's life must look at the whole people, not merely at any one class, noble or plebeian, and must give the net result of their entire action; so that at the end of his book we can say: 'This people had such sentiments and ideas, which led to this and the other deeds and institutions which have been attended by such and such results; they added this or that to the general achievement of the Human Race.' "

"In telling what has been," Parker contended, the historian is bound to tell "what ought to be." Lest the nature of what ought to be escape contemporary thought, he outlined his view of it in another place: "We should build up a great state where there is an honorable work for every hand, bread for all mouths, clothing for all backs, culture for every mind, and love and faith in every heart. . . . The noblest monument to Christ, the fairest trophy of religion, is a noble people, where all are well fed and clad, industrious, free, educated, manly, pious, wise, and good." Such was his ideal, but on still another occasion, in a moment of doubting, he declared that America was destined to follow the path of England, arrive at slums and poverty for industrial millions, and establish "the Christian feudalism of gold in Boston as in London." To this wretched end, the thoughtlessness of the American people might finally drive the nation.

In a review of Hildreth's *History of the United States* Parker also gave his specifications for the right kind of history for America: "At the present day, the United States presents one of the most interesting and important political phenomena ever offered in the history of mankind. . . . To be rightly appreciated, American history requires to be written by a democrat. A theocrat would condemn our institutions for lacking an established church with its privileged priesthood; an aristocrat, for the absence of conventional nobility. Military men might sneer at the smallness of the army and navy; and aesthetic men deplore the want of a splendid court, the lack of operatic and other spectacles in the large towns. The democrat looks for the substantial welfare of the people, and studies America with reference to that point."

To what proportion of the American people had the idea of civilization become, by 1860, a comprehensive idea with definite connotations, with clear intimations of a goal toward which the processes of American history were moving, with specific mandates for thought and action? Historical scholarship has not furnished an answer to this question. Nor, in the nature of things, can it provide an answer in mathematical terms. It can only offer certain indices.

Undoubtedly the idea had been widely disseminated and was making a deeper imprint on popular consciousness. For this statement there is positive evidence. Although many of the books, addresses, and articles in which the idea was discussed were directed to small circles, others reached large audiences. Tocqueville's treatise on democracy in America, for instance, attracted the attention of reflective persons in all parts of the country. Clergymen of various denominations who kept abreast of the currents of debate over Church and State must have encountered the idea during the uproar fomented by Orestes Brownson. Powerful persons, women as well as men, whose voices reached multitudes in their efforts to influence public opinion in innumerable directions, had sent this "electric word" broadcast. Other indications that the idea was being diffused more widely and gaining force appeared in the growth of American journalism during the era of the popular upsurge, while public education was increasing literacy among the free native Americans.

In the year 1857, for example, two magazines destined to a long life were established. One was designed to be "a welcome visitor to every household." The other was planned particularly to reach the intellectual élite. One sought the median line in American society; the other, while by no means spurning popularity, aimed to reach the interest of the more highly educated classes in America.

The first of these new magazines was Harper's Weekly and its practical publishers, remembering the appeal of ideas, chose as the subtitle "A Journal of Civilization." Harper's Weekly, they announced in the first issue, "will contain a full and impartial summary of the Political, Social, Religious, Commercial, and Literary News of the day. It will chronicle the leading movements of the age, record the inventions of genius, the discoveries of science, and the creations of art. . . . It will also give due share of attention to the taste, the imagination, and the feelings. Its regular contents will embrace Tales, Incidents of Travel and Adventure, Sketches of Character and Social Life, and Essays on Art and Morals." If the magazine did not exactly fulfil the pledge, it was a sign that exploiting the idea of civilization had become "good journalism."

The second new magazine was the Atlantic Monthly, under the editorship of James Russell Lowell, which enrolled some of the most talented writers of the time. Lowell himself was the spirit of independence incarnate and for him the idea of civilization had the breadth of a world-view. All along he insisted in reply to foreign critics that we have a country, and "not a sutler's camp." In 1866 he expressed to Leslie Stephen in England his objection to Disraeli's remark that America was a "territorial democracy." With unwonted acerbity, he declared: "I know what the land we sprung from, and which we have not disgraced, is worth to freedom and civilization." And in a later reply to the criticisms that had been heaped upon America during the civil war, he told Leslie Stephen brusquely: "We would not rob you of a single one of your venerable institutions—state-church, peerage, pauperage—so long as you like 'em and like to pay for 'em. We really have no use for such things, and you can leave your doors unlocked, so far as we are concerned."

So significant for American destiny, opportunity, and obligation had the idea of civilization become to Lowell, as the tension of the sectional struggle approached and snapped into the violence of war, that he deemed it immediately pertinent to publish in his magazine two long articles on the subject.

The first, unsigned, was called "Barbarism and Civilization." In it the author treated the theme in its historical and varied aspects. The key to origins he could not find: "Who shall define what makes the essential difference between those lowest and these loftiest types? Not color. . . . Not unmixed purity of blood. . . . Not religion. . . . Not climate. . . . We can only say that there is an inexplicable step in progress, which we call civilization; it is the development of mankind into sufficient maturity of strength to keep the peace and organize institutions; it is the arrival of literature and art. . . . We are never weary of proclaiming the enormous gain it has brought to manners, morals, and the intellect."

Yet a fear of civilization, the writer said, seems to exist. "In the midst of our civilization there is a latent distrust of civilization . . . a wide-spread impression that the benefit is purchased by a corresponding physical decay." This contention the author of the article sought to refute by showing that civilized men are best in every walk of life. "The great athletes of the world have been civilized; and the long-lived men have been civilized; and the powerful armies have been civilized; and the average of life, health, size, and strength is highest today among those races were knowledge and wealth and comforts are most widely spread." There is, he admitted, "the most momentous health-problem with which we have to deal—to secure the proper physical advantages of civilization for American women. Without this there can be no lasting progress." A more formidable barrier stands in the way of progress, "a barbarism upon the soil"—slavery—"before which civilization has thus far been compelled to pause." Nevertheless, the article closed on a note of fatih: "The triumph of Civilization over Barbarism is the only Manifest Destiny of America." It was also a prophetic note for January, 1861.

The second article which Lowell published in the Atlantic Monthly, in 1862, also unsigned but written by Emerson, was an extended essay on "American Civilization." Near its close Emerson declared: "Emancipation is the demand of civilization. That is a principle; everything else is intrigue. . . . There can be no safety till this step is taken." That, too, was a prophetic note when it was sounded. And Emerson was able to add a line saying that, after the words had been written, Abraham Lincoln had proposed a plan for the gradual abolishment of slavery. John Quincy Adams' dream, now based on an unshakable confidence in civilization, was coming nearer to realization as "the great horologe of time" ticked off the minutes of that fateful year.

Chapter 6

In the Sectional Struggle

BY THE MIDDLE OF the nineteenth century the idea of
civilization had gained such an empire over the American
mind that leaders in the terrific struggle called sectional,
despite the strong nationalism on both sides of the border,
solemnly invoked civilization as if there were no higher
authority in morals, humanity, and knowledge for justifying their respective positions or proving the rectitude of
their intentions. Whether the struggle was limited to the
slavery issue or extended to economy and politics and history, pleas were made before that court of final jurisdiction. The idea of civilization appeared assertively in briefs
defending slavery and in briefs attacking free labor. No less
vigorously it was used in assailing slavery and in defending
the free labor system. When arguments were made on behalf of the third party to the dispute—the Negroes—thought
of civilization was likewise brought into play. To the aid
of the fourth party—the party which believed that the conflict could be resolved by peaceful processes—the idea of
civilization was also summoned.

At what moment, where, and by whom the sectional conflict was first given the form of a contest over civilization
cannot be determined. Even if all the printed words and all
the manuscripts in archives and private hands were scrutinized this question could not be answered, for the first formulation of the struggle in such terms may have been oral,
unrecorded, lost to history forever. Nor is it yet determined
when, where, and by whom the defense of slavery was first
systematically proclaimed in words. In the probability of
events, however, the defense was not systematized until
strong attacks had been made. Generally the deed justifies
itself unless the word challenges it.

It is likewise indecisive just when the phrases "Northern
civilization" and "Southern civilization" were thrust into
the exchanges of thought that preceded the shock of arms.
But when the diverse interests of North and South reached
a clashing alignment, a division of opinion had certainly

separated "American civilization" in thought and argument into Northern and Southern types.

On the Southern side, no single, inclusive interpretation of the sectional struggle as involving civilization gained universal acceptance, escaped dissents or qualifications. There were, in fact, many Southern views of the conflict. Although some later historians, with their propensity for simplification, tried to reduce the complexities to a single formula, the records in the case warrant no such unequivocal operation. The intelligence and thought of the South were not "solid" before the clash at arms, not even in the fighting years.

However, in the huge bulk of Southern writings on the subject, there was a conception of the conflict with reference to civilization that attained great prominence in the South and served to make the contest acute. This view, which may be called, for convenience, the planting view, centered around the institution of slavery and around slaveowners, especially large slave-owners, imagined as an aristocracy. In this statement of the case, reiterated with varying nuances, certain items were fairly constant: a landed gentry endowed with the qualities of moral responsibility and a high sense of honor; the historical and natural supremacy of whites over Negroes; noblesse oblige with its elegant code of gentility and civility; and physical nature conditioning economy—geography, climate, and soil. Against these fixed items were opposed, in the formulation, the mercantile greed, lack of consideration for free labor, restlessness among industrial workers with its revolutionary import, and the peculiar physical geography of the North.

At the center of Southern civilization, so conceived, were placed the great planting families. But the orators, imaginative writers, and statesmen who devised this pattern never exactly defined the adjective "great." If it included only those planters who owned a thousand slaves or more, it numbered very few; that "aristocracy" was indeed exclusive. If it covered all who held a hundred slaves or more, only 2,292 slave-owners, or two-tenths of one per cent of the white population in families in the South, were admitted to the circle—11,460 persons in all. But whatever the exact number of Southern whites enrolled in the category of "great" slave-owners, they and their families were represented as the full flower of Southern civilization.

According to this image of "a perfect civilization," every planting family lived in a stately house of pillared architecture at the end of a long avenue of trees often festooned with hanging vines, set in a luxuriant grove of magnolias. In appointments of furniture, rugs, and silver, in food and drink, in amenities of entertainment, in loyalties and rectitude—in all that made for charm of living—the planting aristocracy had reached the acme of civilization. The lord of the manor was a cavalier, courteous but quick to avenge an insult to his honor even to the point of dueling. His lady was the embodiment of grace, sparkling with social talents. Every planter's mansion had a library well stocked with the classics and belles lettres in which leisure hours were spent cultivating and refining the mind. In the arrangements of this exclusive society, quality, not pecuniary standards as in the North, prevailed. Worth, not wealth, gave entrance to its magic circle. Within it grew men fit to govern and women skilled in the arts of domestic management and hospitality.

To sustain this superstructure, labor was of course necessary and was taken as a matter of course. John C. Calhoun of South Carolina reminded critics that in every civilized society one portion lives upon the labor of others. And, according to the thesis, the planters were peculiarly fortunate in having at their command the labor of an inferior race, eternally separated from them by the indelible line of color—a black race historically and still practically inferior, beyond all capacity for, or prospects of, equality. Thus the dominant class did not have to soil its hands by manual labor; nor confront the difficult, if not dangerous, business of dealing with hordes of white workers united with it by race and color of skin but set apart from it by indigence and the necessity of selling their labor-power for wages. Again and again, in Southern literature, that predicament of civilization in the North and in Europe was discussed and Southern immunity from labor disputes was extolled as among the essential benefits of slavery.

As befitted such an aristocracy, the master and mistress of the plantation conducted their relations with the laboring orders of persons in the spirit of noblesse oblige. This, too, presented a contrast with the pecuniary spirit of the captain of industry who hired laborers at the lowest possible wages and turned them adrift in sickness, old age, and times of economic depression. "I may say with truth," declared John C. Calhoun, "that in few countries so much is left to the share of the laborer, and so little exacted from him, or where there is more kind attention paid to him in sickness or infirmities of age. Compare his condition with the tenants of the poor houses in the more civilized portions of Europe —look at the sick, and old and infirm slave, on the one hand, in the midst of his family and friends, under the kind superintending care of his master and mistress, and compare it with the forlorn and wretched condition of the pauper in the poor house."

Slavery itself was, in this vision, an aspect of civilization in process. Negroes in Africa dwelt in the darkness, cruelties, and desolation of barbarism. Those who had been transferred to America came under the influences and compulsions of civilization, supported by the benign teachings and practices of Christianity. Thus Negroes, though slaves, were being civilized, raised to a higher level of being. "I appeal to facts," exclaimed Calhoun. "Never before has the black race of central Africa, from the dawn of history to the present day, attained a condition so civilized and improved, not only physically, but morally and intellectually. It came among us in a low, degraded, and savage condition, and in the course of a few generations it has grown up under the fostering care of our institutions, reviled as they have been, to its present comparatively civilized condition. This, with the rapid increase of numbers, is conclusive proof of the general happiness of the race, in spite of all the exaggerated tales to the contrary."

This order of human relations was presumed to be permanent, although the civilizing of the slave might continue indefinitely. It was regarded as indispensable to civilization itself. "In all social systems," explained James Henry Hammond, of South Carolina, "there must be a class to do the mean duties, to perform the drudgery of life. . . . Such a class you must have, or you would not have that other class which leads to progress, refinement, and civilization. . . . We . . . call them slaves. We are old-fashioned at the South yet; it is a word discarded by ears polite; but I will not characterize that class at the North; but you have it; it is there; it is everywhere; it is eternal."

With the very title "Southern" were affiliated elements of physical geography. This type of civilization, so perfect or so nearly perfect, was in the South—a region of mild climate, sunshine, rich foliage, and special crops, all irrevocably fixed by the dictates of physical geography. The boundaries of this South, it is true, were somewhat uncertain as the picture shimmered in the minds of writers and orators. At one moment they seemed to enclose all the slave states from Delaware to Texas, irrespective of internal variations in economy and even in slavery itself. At another moment emphasis was laid on the deep South, or the seaboard regions, or even particular states, such as Virginia, South Carolina, and Louisiana, where the flowering of Southern civilization was considered the most exuberant. But if neither in fact nor in fancy were the geographical limits of Southern civilization precise, the idea of the South as physical section, endowed and bound by physical nature, was persistent and insistent in the planting view of Southern civilization.

By its major premise respecting labor relations the planting view was committed to the idea of an eternally static society, except for slight possible improvements in its amenities. Though slaves were becoming more civilized, their status was permanent. Masters were becoming more humane but their mastery was everlasting. The essentially revolutionary nature of civilization was conveniently overlooked. History had been closed in the South.

The fundamental axioms for the planting view of civilization were presented as early as 1837 by William Harper, eminent jurist and chancellor of the state of South Carolina, in his *Memoir on Slavery*. This document has rightly been called "one of the most important pro-slavery arguments in the history of the controversy." In substance it was a series of propositions deemed primordial, and historicized under an overarching interpretation of civilization, as if that was the supreme jurisdiction in earthly affairs to which Harper could carry the case for slavery.

"The institution of domestic slavery," Harper argued, in summoning history as his witness, "exists over far the greater portion of the inhabited earth. Until within a very few centuries, it may be said to have existed over the whole earth—at least in all those portions of it which had made any advances towards civilization. . . . Professor Dew has shown that the institution of Slavery is a principal cause of civilization. Perhaps nothing can be more evident than that it is the sole cause. . . . Every society which has attained civilization, has advanced to it through this process.

"No scheme of emancipation could be carried into effect . . . without probably throwing a large and fertile portion of the earth's surface out of the pale of civilization—and you have done nothing. . . . *Slavery anticipates the benefits of civilization and retards the evils of civilization.* . . . This inequality, this vice, this misery, this Slavery [of English laborers], is the price of England's civilization. They suffer the lot of humanity. . . . [When England has sunk into an-archical democracy] then in Southern regions, there may be found many republics, triumphing in Grecian arts and civi-lization, and worthy of British descent and Roman institu-tions." While laying down these propositions, Harper de-veloped the familiar argument that slavery lifted Negroes as far as they could go in civilization.

A similar view of Southern civilization was offered by Robert Toombs of Georgia. When he "invaded enemy ter-ritory" in 1856 and delivered in Boston his ringing address to the nation on the crisis at hand, he divided his oration into two parts. In the first he lingered, after the fashion of contemporary politicians, on the constitutional powers and duties of the Federal Government. That was the law of the business. But there was more to it. In the second part Toombs reviewed fundamentals underlying the law and, dealing with the influence of slavery on "the slave and so-ciety," he summarized the planting view of Southern civi-lization.

The white race, Toombs said, is "by nature" superior over the African race. Negroes are incapable of an equal contest with the whites in the course of "progress and civi-lization," and hence it is in the Negroes' interest to be servants, not freemen in the struggle for existence. In Africa they had been mainly in slavery and had not taken a single step in civilization. After emancipation in British Jamaica, they had degenerated. In the free states of the American Union, where they possess only nominal freedom, the brand of inferiority in fact still rests upon them. In the South, they are in a happier condition and receive more of the product of their labor than any unskilled hired workers anywhere in the world.

In pursuing his tactics of weakening Northern opposi-tion, Toombs warned his Boston auditors that the foundations of capitalism were temporary and shaking. In the conflict between capital and labor, he declared, under free competition in new countries where land is cheap, labor can successfully compete with capital, but this condition is exceptional and transitory. Already in the Old World, where land is dear, labor is subject to capital. There on the wall is the handwriting for the North. On the other hand, nowhere in the whole civilized world can be found such contentment and progress as in the South, and no other system would have exhibited a finer civilization—a higher development. If, with the major assumption accepted, logic had power, Toombs enjoyed a triumph.

Two years after Robert Toombs delivered his oration in the stronghold of abolitionism, James P. Holcombe of Virginia gave his neighbors an almost identical version of the conflict. Holcombe was the son of Dr. William James Holcombe who freed his slaves and went to the free soil of Indiana in 1843. After studying at the University of Virginia, the younger James won a reputation as a lawyer, educator, and thinker of large proportions. In an address to citizens of the Old Dominion in 1858, Holcombe gave them his thesis of Southern civilization.

In a eloquent passage he reviewed the spectacle of civilization from ancient times as the story of the Caucasian race. Then he pointed his moral. "Since the dawn of history, the negro race has built no empire, no towered city," has, in sum and substance, made no giant strides in civilization. At bottom the "civilization of the African" differs abysmally from that of the Caucasian; he has the gentler elements of docility, affection, and lightheartedness; but in energy, "a consuming fire to its possessor," he is inferior to the Caucasian.

As if Darwin, whose *Origin of Species* was to appear the next year, had already spoken, Holcombe declared that in the struggle for existence, in competition, an inferior race, with limited means of subsistence, incapable of sustaining competition with a superior, will be destroyed or sink into "hopeless degradation." To submit the Negro to "the unchecked selfishness" of the superior race in free competition would have fatal consequences. It is in personal servitude that the Negro gains "the amelioration of a higher civilization." There were abuses in slavery, Holcombe conceded, but he asked immediately: "Where is the school of civilization from which suffering is banished?" Again, logic seemed victorious.

Another Southern statesman, Alexander H. Stephens of Georgia, warmly attached to the Union as long as Southern "rights" could be preserved within it, who had once spoken on the merits of American civilization, finally came to a defense of the South on grounds of its peculiar civilization. With reference to political forms, he located in the Southern scheme of things "the cause of the Federative principle of Government, against the principle of Empire! The cause of the Grecian type of Civilization against the Asiatic." In 1856 he asked in the House of Representatives: "Are we, Mr. Speaker, to remain a united people? Are we to go on in that high career of achievement in science, in art, and in civilization, which we have so conspicuously entered upon? Or are we to be arrested in our upward course before reaching the half-way point toward ultimate culmination?" There had been advancement in civilization under the Union. It might be continued. But within this general civilization was the peculiar heritage of the South. "In the social and political system of the South the negro is assigned to that subordinate position for which he is fitted by the laws of nature. Our system of civilization is founded in strict conformity to these laws."

After secession had come, in his famous address as Vice-President of the Confederate States of America, delivered on March 21, 1861, Stephens made slavery "the cornerstone" of the Confederacy, and praised the new constitution of that republic founded upon it. It has, he said, "put at rest, *forever,* all the agitating questions relating to our peculiar institution—African slavery as it exists amongst us— the proper *status* of the negro in our form of civilization. This was the immediate cause of the late rupture and present revolution." Jefferson and most of the leading statesmen of earlier time had held the idea that slavery was wrong in principle and that it would "somehow or other" pass away. "These ideas, however, were fundamentally wrong," Stephens declared. "They rested upon the assumption of the equality of races. This was an error. It was a sandy foundation, and the government built upon it fell when the 'storm came and the wind blew.' Our new government is founded upon exactly the opposite idea; its foundations are laid, its corner-stone rests upon the great truth, that the negro is not equal to the white man; that slavery—subordination to the superior race—is his natural and normal condition. (Applause) . . . If we are true to ourselves, true to our cause, true to our destiny, true to our high mission, in presenting to the world the highest type of civilization ever exhibited by man—there will be found in our lexicon no such word as fail."

Such was the planting view of Southern civilization. But loyalty to the historical records in the case cashiers the notion that it was universally accepted, in all details, even by those who approved it in general. For example, a Southern statesman no less eminent than Jefferson Davis, although he related slavery to the process of civilization, was dubious about the permanence of the servile order. He maintained that Negroes seized in Africa were taken from a more degrading slavery than that to which they were subjected in America. "It benefits them," he said, "in removing them from the bigotry and heathen darkness which hangs like a cloud over the interior of Africa, to the enjoyment of the blessings of civilization and Christianity." Here in America, Davis thought, slaves "have advanced in comfort and civilization." And, taking the long future into his vision, he concluded that this slavery "may have for its end the preparation of that race for civil liberty and enjoyment." There he paused.

If it be noted that Davis belonged to Mississippi, and to a newcomer among the planting families, it is pertinent to remember that a dissent from certain features of the planting view was also filed by Robert E. Lee, of Virginia, of whose social standing there could be no question. Lee confessed the belief that there were few "but will acknowledge that slavery as an institution is a moral and political evil," with disadvantages greater to the white race than to the colored. And he hoped that the hard discipline to which slaves were subjected "will prepare them for better things. . . . Their emancipation will come sooner from the mild and melting influence of Christianity than from the storms and contests of fiery controversy."

A second construction of Southern civilization, called here for convenience the agrarian view, centered on agriculture as a way of life rather than on slavery as an institution. It was associated primarily with the economy and fortunes of the whites as if they were firmly united by ties of race; and it varied in its emphasis and intepretation respecting slavery and the status of Negroes. In its broadest range it included farmers and tenants who held no slaves, as well as the slave-owners large and small. Upon agriculture they all depended for their sustenance and by agriculture their modes of life were shaped.

In the agrarian view, the virtues of life and conduct peculiar to a rural economy were glorified, qualities which Jefferson had praised as the hope of the Republic: preoccupation with the production of real wealth, vigor induced by open air labor, contacts with nature, the spirit of liberty nourished by economic independence through direct tillage of the soil, a general equality connected with a similarity of pursuits, frankness of thought and speech, and the ordered community made possible by identity of interests. If the virtues were unequally distributed among planters, yeomen, tenants, and "poor whites," they inhered, according to this doctrine, in the agricultural economy. None was too poor to possess them. Even slaves manifested these qualities in some measure, within limits.

The case for the rural virtues, as fundamentals of civilization, writers and orators reinforced by painting the demerits of Northern life and conduct founded on manufacturing and commerce. In some degree the contrast was cast in the language of contempt, such as members of the landed classes had used for more than two thousand years in speaking of merchants and manufacturers—persons "in trade." Aristotle had placed such persons, of whatever race, among a lower order of human beings. The landed gentry of England had long derided their occupations, methods, and love of money.

Carrying forward this tradition, Southern critics scoffed at Northern civilization, imputing to it many essential vices, such as chicanery, huckstering, schemes of financial intrigue and exploitation, lack of martial fervor, and the dominance of merely pecuniary relations. In the train of those vices, it was repeatedly said, followed poverty-stricken industrial employees, footloose, restless, prone to every form of democratic fantasy or agitation, discontented and turbulent—"the mobs of the great cities," to use Jefferson's words. Civilization based on manufacturing and commerce was, in short, split into two classes, forever antagonistic, and was destined to defeat by the very forces it generated. Only agriculture, to which the South was dedicated, offered the unity and security of civilization.

A third view of Southern civilization—a universal view of master-labor relations—exceeded the planting view and the agrarian view in its scope of details, in its diversity of content, and in its reach of time. Although containing fragments from those views, the third view was unlimited in its sweep. It took in the whole human story, past, present, and future, and, while defending Negro slavery, forecast slavery as the destiny of all laborers, white and black. It differed also in that it proposed to humanize slavery by compelling all property owners to assume a legal responsibility for the care of laboring persons, proportioned to the amount of their respective riches.

This universal view, revolutionary and comprehensive, was formulated by George Fitzhugh of Virginia. Fitzhugh was the son of a doctor, born in Prince William County. After acquiring the rudiments of education, he studied law and specialized in criminal practice. By the process of self-education, usual among Americans of his day, he became acquainted with a large body of social and economic literature and with various theories of society and history then current in Europe and the United States. Unlike many Southern writers on slavery, he traveled extensively in the North and discussed the issues of the hour with leading abolitionists. While he thought most of them were utopian fanatics, he was on friendly terms with them and he sent a copy of his *Sociology for the South; or, the Failure of Free Society* to William Lloyd Garrison, with a personal inscription.

Fitzhugh's fullest treatment of his thesis respecting civilization and slavery appeared in his *Cannibals All! or, Slaves without Masters,* published in 1857. In a single sentence he stated the substance of his argument: "As modern civilization advances, slavery becomes daily more necessary, because its tendency is to accumulate all capital in a few hands, cuts off the masses from the soil, lessens their wages and their chances of employment, and increases the necessity for a means of certain subsistence, which slavery alone can furnish, when a few own all the lands and other capital."

His economic intepretation Fitzhugh expanded in many pages, which may be summarized as follows: the capitalistic system of alleged freedom tore the serfs of Europe from the soil and transformed them into propertyless proletarians; herded them into the slums of cities; paid them less than subsistence wages—a smaller proportion of their product than Negro slaves received in the South; subjected them to long periods of unemployment marked by degradation and suffering; afforded them no security; enabled their masters to evade all responsibility for their welfare; and evoked that dangerous, romantic movement of revolution—socialism—which threatened to pull down civilization.

The socialists, Fitzhugh declared, were absolutely right in their denunciation of laissez-faire capitalism, as reducing workers on the land and in industry to the position of what he called "slaves without masters." In his opinion the liberty vaunted by apologists for capitalism was a delusion and a sham, representing actually a system of workers' slavery in which employers robbed mercilessly, without taking on the burdens of care assumed by the masters of Negro slaves. Leading abolitionists, he said, admitted the existence of this slavery in the North while they denounced slavery in the South.

Moreover, Fitzhugh held, the centralization of power which accompanied the growth of the system he called "slavery without masters" and the practice of free trade that went with it were opposed to the improvement, progress, initiative, and local freedom necessary to the advance of civilization: "After the Romans had conquered Greece, Athens became the school and centre of thought for the civilized world. Men had but one set of ideas, but one set of models to imitate, in the whole range of the fine arts. Inventiveness and originality ceased, and genius was subdued. . . . Men ceased to think for themselves, but looked to the common fountain of thought at Athens; where the teachers of mankind borrowed all their ideas from the past. Improvement and progress ceased, and imitation, chaining the present to the car of the past, soon induced rapid retrogression. Thus, we think, centralization of thought occasioned the decline of civilization. Northern invaders introduced new ideas, broke up centralization, arrested initiation, and begot originality and inventiveness. Thus a start was given to a new and Christian civilization. Now, a centralization occasioned by commerce and fashion threatens the overthrow of our civilization, as arms and conquest overthrew the ancient."

According to this intepretation of history, "advancing civilization" confronted a twofold problem. Millions of white slaves were without masters, and so denied the security which civilization ought to afford. And civilization itself was threatened: on one side by a destructive social revolution; and on the other, by the sterilizing influence of centralization.

That the problem was recognized by other thinkers Fitzhugh demonstrated in citations from their writings. From an article in the British Westminster Review of January 9, 1852, he derived the following evidence: "The last battle of civilization is the severest; the last problem the knottiest to solve. Out of all the multitudinous ingredients and influences of the past; out of the conquest of nature, and the victory of freedom; out of the blending and intermixture of all previous forms of policy and modifications of humanity, has arisen a complex order of society, of which the disorders and anomalies are as complex as its own structure. We are now summoned to the combat, not with material difficulties, nor yet with oppressors nor with priests, but with an imperfect and diseased condition of that social world of which we form a part; with pains and evils appalling in their magnitude, baffling in their subtlety, perplexing in their complication, and demanding far more clear insight and unerring judgment, than even the purity of purpose, or commanding energy of will. This conflict may be said to date from the first French Revolution; and it has been increasing in intensity ever since, till it has reached to a vividness and solemnity of interest, which surpasses and overshadows the attractions of all other topics."

Confirmation for the British presentation of the dilemma inherent in the existence of slaves without masters, Fitzhugh found in an article published by the American abolitionist organ, the National Era, in 1855. The author of the article in question had criticized doctrines proclaimed by Fitzhugh in earlier writings and had expressed a belief that dire poverty could be conquered without recourse to universal slavery. The author, Fitzhugh explained, had adopted "our theory to the fullest extent. He admits the intolerable exploitation and oppression of capital over labor, but looks forward to the day when it will be corrected. He is, like all Abolitionists, agrarian. He holds our doctrines, too, that the serfs were set free to starve, not because liberty was a good or a boon. He further holds, that the poor laborers could not get masters if they wanted them, because the rich can get their labor on better terms. Thus he distinctly shows that Free Society has failed, and why it has failed. We know very well the rich of Western Europe would not willingly take the poor as slaves, but the law should compel them to do so; for that is the only feasible system of agrarianism, the only practicable way of letting in all men to a sufficient, if not equal, enjoyment of terra matre."

However, Fitzhugh continued, the author of the article in the National Era, after acknowledging the nature of the dilemma, merely expressed a hope for reform, without offering a real solution. "We know," said the author in the passage quoted by Fitzhugh, "that the claim laid by capital to the lion's share of profits is itself, under any circumstances, a great obstruction to the progress of the masses; but we believe that even that obstacle will one day be removed— that problem in political science be solved by civilization and Christianity. We believe that the human intellect will never, with the light of the Gospel to guide and inspire its efforts, surrender to the cold and heartless reign of capital over labor."

Then the author dissected Fitzhugh's own solution of the problem and declared the idea, that the enslavement of the poor was possible, to be wholly chimerical: "At any rate, one thing is certain, under the worst form of government, or the best, namely: when Freedom becomes a burden and a curse to the poor, Slavery—that is to say, the enslavement of the mass of laborers, with responsibility on the part of the master for their support—is no longer possible. . . . Who believes that Irish landlords would take the responsibility of supporting the peasantry, on condition of their becoming slaves?" In other words, according to his critic in the National Era, Fitzhugh was himself indulging in fantasies.

Unmoved by the vague prophecy of what civilization and Christianity would or might do, Fitzhugh proposed a plan which seemed practical to him: "Slavery is a form of communism, and as the Abolitionists and Socialists have resolved to adopt a new social system, we recommend it to their consideration. The manner in which the change shall be made from the present form of society to that system of communism which we propose is very simple. Negro slaves are now worth seven hundred dollars a head. As whites work harder, they are worth about a thousand. Make the man who owns a thousand dollars of capital the guardian (the term master is objectionable) of one white pauper of average value; give the man who is worth ten thousand dollars ten paupers, and the millionaire a thousand. This would be an act of simple mercy and justice; for the capitalists now live entirely by the proceeds of poor men's labor. . . . They [laborers under the guardian] would work no harder than they do now, would be under no greater necessity to work, would be relieved of most of the cares of life, and let into the enjoyment of all necessary and valuable rights. What would they lose in liberty and equality? Just nothing. . . . It might be, that their security and exemption from care would render their situation preferable to that of their employers."

Was this form of slavery, which Fitzhugh called communism, likely to come into being? His answer was categorical: "It is falsely said, that revolutions never go backwards. They always go backwards, and generally further back than where they started. The Social Revolution now going on at the North, must someday go backwards. Shall it do so now, ere it has perpetrated an infinitude of mischief, shed oceans of blood, and occasioned endless human misery; or will the Conservatives of the North let it run the length of its leather, inflict all these evils, and then rectify itself by issuing into military despotism? We think that by a kind of alliance, offensive and defensive, with the South, Northern Conservatism may now arrest and turn back the tide of Radicalism and Agrarianism."

In an appeal to reason, however, Fitzhugh felt there was not much comfort: "Socialism, not Abolition, is the real object of Black Republicanism." The Democratic party, purged of its Jeffersonian radicalism, was the best pledge of the new conservative order to come—the communism of universal slavery; beyond that, Fitzhugh hinted darkly, lay an appeal to force.

While Fitzhugh differed from other Southern apologists for slavery in proposing slavery for the North, he differed from them also in attitude toward free trade. He claimed that free trade exploited and enslaved Southern agriculture for the benefit of British and European capitalists, thus retarding, instead of advancing, civilization in that region. He declared that its inevitable tendency was to hold America in subjection to foreign capitalists as a raw-material province of their manufacturing empire, checking the growth of inventions, the arts, and the sciences of civilization in America.

Furthermore, Fitzhugh argued, with citations from British works, free trade was a creed devised by British industrialists, their purpose being to promote the interests of British "exploiters of the poor" at home and the people in the raw-material provinces subject to their economic dominion. Consequently, in his opinion, all American civilization was imperiled by the system of laissez faire in domestic economy and foreign trade. Emancipation from its blighting effects was as necessary, he felt, in foreign commerce as in domestic enterprise, if civilization was to be enriched and its fruits widely distributed among masters, or guardians, and their slaves.

That the doctrine of Harper, Toombs, Stephens, and Fitzhugh, which extolled Southern civilization based on slavery, however stated, was extensively disseminated is discoverable in studies of contemporary newspapers and other documents. The doctrine also found lodgment in Southern imaginative letters. If native fiction did not supply enough glamour, Sir Walter Scott was drafted in the cause. Indeed Mark Twain, who belonged to a Southern family and lived through the civil war, later declared, with his customary license of humor, that Scott actually helped to bring on the war by teaching his Southern readers the "jejune romanticism of an absurd past"—"a sham civilization." This was in line with the sentiments about feudalism which he expressed in *A Connecticut Yankee at King Arthur's Court.*

The world, Mark Twain said, was progressing, but "then comes Sir Walter Scott with his enchantments, and by his single might checks this wave of progress and even turns it back; sets the world in love with dreams and phantoms; with decayed and swinish forms of religion; with decayed and degraded systems of government; with the silliness and emptiness, sham grandeurs, sham gauds, and sham chivalries of a brainless and worthless long-vanished society. He did measureless harm; more real and lasting harm, perhaps, than any other individual that ever wrote.

"Most of the world has now outlived a good part of these harms, though by no means all of them; but in our South they flourish pretty forcefully still. Not so forcefully as half a century ago, perhaps, but still forcefully. There, the genuine and wholesome civilization of the nineteenth century is curiously confused and commingled with the Walter Scott Middle Age sham civilization, and so you have practical common sense, progressive ideas, and progressive works mixed up with the duel, the inflated speech, the jejune romanticism of an absurd past that is dead, and out of charity ought to be buried. But for the Sir Walter Scott disease, the character of the Southerner—or Southron, according to Sir Walter Scott's starchier way of putting it—would be wholly modern, in place of modern and mediaeval mixed, and the South would be fully a generation further on than it is.

"It was Sir Walter that made every gentleman in the South a major, or a general, or a colonel, or a judge before the war; and it was he also that made these gentlemen value these bogus decorations. For it was he that created rank and caste down there, and also reverence for rank and caste, and pride and pleasure in them. Enough is laid on slavery, without fathering upon it these creations and contributions of Sir Walter.

"Sir Walter had so large a hand in making Southern character as it existed before the war, that he is in great measure responsible for the war. It seems a little harsh towards a dead man to say that we never should have had a war but for Sir Walter; and yet something of a plausible argument might, perhaps, be made in support of the wild proposition. The Southerner of the American Revolution owned slaves, so did the Southerner of the American Civil War; but the former resembles the latter as an Englishman resembles a Frenchman. The change of character can be traced rather more easily to Sir Walter's influence than to that of any living thing or person."

When Mrs. T. P. O'Connor undertook to write her record of the times, *My Beloved South*, out of her rich and full memories, she quoted this passage from Mark Twain, picked up the gantlet imperiously, and defended anew the civilization of the South. "In this assertion," she said, Mark Twain could be bolstered up by evidence, "for nowhere in the world was Sir Walter Scott so much loved or so widely read as in the South. . . . There are Southern men,—and my dear father was one,—and there are certainly Southern women, who know every novel and every scene in the novels of all the twenty-seven which Sir Walter has written. Mark Twain said he did measureless harm, more real and lasting harm, than any other individual who ever wrote. But what did he teach? Loyalty and self-sacrifice, a sense of obligation to your kinsfolk, chivalry, tenderness, and protection to women, honour and truth to your neighbour, courage and valour in battle, open-handed hospitality, and a sense of responsibility towards those dependent on you. Isn't that just as good as teaching 'practical common sense, progressive ideas, and progressive works?'

"There is no place where brutality is exhibited with such pride, or where the manners of the lower classes are so detestable, or where there is so much friction to a person of refinement, as New York—our greatest city of 'progressive ideas and progressive works.' And there is not the smallest consolation to an American in the suggestion that the brutality, vulgarity, and bad manners are imported with our bonnets and dresses from various ports, for it is more difficult to endure the insolence of aliens than that of your own people.

"Even Sir Walter Scott, with all his genius, could not impose one dream or vision upon the stony soul of New York. And what would life be worth to some of us without dreams and visions? . . .

"Mark Twain complains of the 'Sir Walter Scott sham civilization,' yet under that 'sham civilization' before the war the South created politicians who were gentlemen of property, distinction, and honour. They did not put their hands into the pockets of the government and withdraw them contaminated with 'graft,' as so many of the politicians of the North have done since the war. Their ideas were not progressive enough for the worship of money; they still believed in honesty, truth, straightforwardness, and, if need be, self-sacrifice and poverty. What statesman was it who said, 'The Southern statesman went for honours and the Northern one for profit'?

"The trusts, that have done such infinite harm in America, did not originate in the South. . . . Southern men had, and still have, great civic pride. . . . As for the 'romanticism of an absurd past that is dead,' who have a better right to a romantic past than we of the South? And Mark Twain is wrong in imagining that for us it can ever die."

From all these views of the sectional struggle in terms of civilization there was a vigorous dissent in general and in particular, in the South as well as in the North. If non-conformity seldom found expression in treatises on Southern civilization, it was nonetheless vocal in the large regions of the South which were occupied entirely, or almost entirely, by white farmers and mechanics who owned few or no slaves. The nature of the sentiments that inspired this dissent flared up during the armed conflict in the slogan of disgruntled Confederate soldiers: "a rich man's war and a poor man's fight." The strength and extent of the sentiments were divulged in heavy desertions from the Confederate armies and in the internal contests that contributed to the downfall of the Confederacy.

While Southern statesmen, orators, professors, editors, and men of letters were creating and disseminating the planting view of civilization, a diametrically opposite view of civilization, generally called Northern, was being developed and broadcast. It was set forth in essays, articles, addresses, and orations. And it was heavily documented by a Southern dissenter from the planting view, Hinton Rowan Helper of North Carolina.

Comparable in influence as an agitator to Thomas Paine of the revolutionary age, Helper also had a hard battle for existence. His father, a petty farmer who owned several slaves, died while Hinton was young and left him to make his own way in the world. By strenuous labor he managed to keep alive, acquire an elementary education, and accumulate enough money for a journey to California. While he was in the West he had an opportunity to see the free labor system in operation. On his return to the South he made a study of national economy and drew up a bill of indictment against slavery which he published in 1857 as *The Impending Crisis*. It was not framed for the benefit of Negroes, whom he despised, but, he believed, for the benefit of the white people of the South whom he now pitied as themselves enslaved to an intolerable system.

According to J. G. de R. Hamilton, a later historian of the South, Helper's *Crisis* made a greater sensation than *Uncle Tom's Cabin;* "it was furiously attacked in the South but few dared to read it and it thus remained without adequate answer." Already collecting their forces for the Armageddon of 1860, Republicans raised funds for printing and distributing 100,000 copies. In the campaign of that year it was the book of books; and after his victory President Lincoln rewarded Helper for his aid by making him consul of the United States in Buenos Aires. Soon afterward Helper's fame vanished into forgetfulness and in 1909 he died a suicide, soured by the "new order" which he had helped to create.

In intention, if not in name, Helper's *Crisis* was an effort to present a balance sheet of civilization for the North and the South. The balance-sheet idea, he explained by a quotation from De Bow, superintendent of the seventh census of the United States, to the effect that statistics "constitute . . . the ledger of a nation, in which, like the merchant in his books, the citizen can read, at one view, all the results of a year or of a period of years, as compared with other periods, and deduce the profit or the loss which has been made, in morals, education, wealth or power." De Bow was a Southern man; and Helper, taking his words at face value, proposed to set up a balance sheet as indisputable as the figures in the merchant's ledger. If he overestimated the exactitude of statistical reasoning, he did not underestimate the power of the statistical tables which crowded page after page of his text in serried array to the conclusion which split asunder the thought and temper of the nation.

The tests which Helper adopted for making the accounting classifications of his ledger, in which North and South were set in opposing columns, were what he, at one point, quoting from a contemporary, called "all the trophies of civilization." To be more concrete, they were the great classes of material goods necessary to commodious living; the signs of intellectual progress in literacy, schools, public libraries, and press; the insignia of moral and spiritual interests afforded by churches and religious activities; and the manifestations of genius in humane letters. Which side had the more? The North or the South?

In a long series of tables, Helper compared "all the trophies of civilization" North and South, under specific heads: agricultural products from wheat and oats to cotton, tobacco, cheese, and beeswax; annual crops per acre; value of farms including implements, machinery, and livestock; wealth, revenue, and expenditure; area and population per square mile; population; exports and imports in tons; manufactured products—capital invested, annual value, and labor employed; miles of canals and railroads; bank capital; militia forces; postoffice operations; public schools, teachers, and pupils; libraries other than private; newspapers and periodicals; illiterate adult whites; value of churches and contributions for Bible, tract, and missionary work. He closed with quotations from Southern testimony against slavery, a comparison of Northern and Southern commercial cities, and a survey of Southern literature. In this trial at the bar of civilization, as Helper conducted it, the South lost on every count. The award for trophies went unreservedly to the North.

The findings of his apparently inexorable tabulation Helper translated into the language of summation and damnation. The South, he said, looked North for "almost every article of utility and adornment, from matches, shoe pegs, and paintings up to cotton mills, steamships, and statuary"; Bibles, books, primers, school books, fashionable apparel, medicines, spectacles, all important elements of physical utility and convenience. In the South "we have no foreign trade, no princely merchants, nor respectable artists." Throughout that section everywhere were obvious "weakness, inertia, and dilapidation." We are "under reproach in the eyes of all civilized and enlightened nations." Southern whites are taught by slave-owners "to look with prejudice and disapprobation upon every new principle of progressive movement." The South is afflicted with literary pauperism; it lacks readers, mental freedom, force, enterprise, mental activity. Yet Southern whites are "vainglorious, self-sufficient, and brutal." Couched in this blazing language, his argument could scarcely fail to inflame multitudes in the North who studied *The Impending Crisis*.

The way was prepared in the North for the reception of Helper's presentment of Southern civilization by a speech which Senator Charles Sumner delivered in 1856, the year before *The Impending Crisis* appeared, pitting the evidences of civilization in his native commonwealth against Southern claims to superiority: "By the intelligence of her [Massachusetts'] population; by the resources of her industry; by her commerce, cleaving every wave; by her manufactures, various as human skill; by her institutions of education, various as human knowledge; by her institutions of benevolence, various as human suffering; by the pages of her scholars and historians; by the voices of her poets and orators,—she is now exerting an influence more subtle and commanding than ever before."

Massachusetts had contributed more than her share of soldiers to the Revolution of 1776; now to the second struggle—"which is not of contending armies, but of contending opinions, on whose issue hangs trembling the advancing civilization of the age,—she contributes, through the manifold and endless intellectual activity of her children, more of that divine spark by which opinions are quickened into life than is contributed by any other State, or by all the slave States together, while her annual productive industry exceeds in value three times the whole vaunted cotton crop of the whole South."

While Sumner saw civilization trembling in the scales, he assured an opposing Senator that there could be no doubt as to the outcome. The Senator "is but mortal man; against him is immortal principle. With finite power, he wrestles with the infinite, and he must fail. Against him are stronger battalions, than any marshalled by mortal arm,—the inborn, ineradicable, invincible sentiments of the human heart; against him is Nature, with all her subtile forces; against him is God."

Four years later, in 1860, after he had recovered from the beating received at the hands of Preston S. Brooks of South Carolina, Sumner delivered an oration blasting slavery along the whole front, and deriding the glorification of Southern society as "the finest product of civilization"— under the title "The Barbarism of Slavery." Step by step he examined the attributes of the slave system—chattel property; parental and family relations; denial of education; punishments meted out to slaves. He sought to make American slavery appear worse than other systems of slavery. From the system, Sumner turned to results, which he tested by standards of civilization.

Like those statesmen of the South who had closed their minds to any compromise between the two sectional systems of economy and life, Sumner gave no quarter. He combed the literatures of two continents for materials on the worst evils or abuses of slavery. Waving aside Southern allegations respecting the humane aspects of the servile relationship, ignoring the contentions of Calhoun and Fitzhugh that all civilization rested upon the exploitation of labor and that chattel bondage was less cruel than any other, Sumner, by citing the most shocking cases of inhumanity under slavery that he could apparently find, brought against it the sweeping charge of "Barbarism"—eternal opposite of civilization.

In so doing he evoked from Senator James Chestnut of South Carolina the cry that on this occasion the abolitionist of Massachusetts had defied "the incarnation of malice, mendacity, and cowardice." On his part Senator Chestnut, an ardent defender of slavery, maintained: "Commerce, civilization, and Christianity go hand in hand and their conjoint efforts receive their chief earthly impulse from this reviled institution." Against the whole Southern theory Sumner launched the full drive of his eloquence.

After a brief exordium, Sumner went straight to the point of conflict: "If I were disposed to shrink from this discussion, the boundless assumptions made by Senators on the other side would not allow me. The whole character of Slavery, as a pretended form of Civilization, is put directly in issue, with a pertinacity and a hardihood which banish all reserve on this side." Then he cited illustrations of the contention that Southern society founded on chattel slavery had superlative merits. "Thus, by various voices, is Slavery defiantly proclaimed a form of Civilization—not seeing that its existence is plainly inconsistent with the first principles of anything that can be called Civilization, except by that figure of speech in classical literature where a thing takes its name from something which it has not, as the dreadful fates were called merciful because they were without mercy."

Slavery, Sumner repeated, is not Civilization but Barbarism. The conflict is not between two civilizations. It is between Civilization and Barbarism: "Between Slavery and Civilization there is essential incompatibility. If you are for the one, you cannot be for the other. . . . As cold is but the absence of heat, and darkness but the absence of light, so is Slavery but the absence of justice and humanity, without which Civilization is impossible. . . . The Barbarism of Slavery appears, *first*, in the *character of Slavery*, and, *secondly*, in the *character of Slave-Masters*." Under these heads, Sumner developed his argument and arraignment.

Anathematizing the Character of Slavery, Sumner pronounced it Barbarism in that it divested man, created in the image of God, of human character and reduced him to the level of a thing, beast, or article of property. "Slavery paints itself again in its complete *abrogation of marriage,* recognized as a sacrament by the Church, and as a contract by the civil power, wherever Civilization prevails. . . . Slavery paints itself again in its complete *abrogation of the parental relation,* provided by God in his benevolence for the nurture and education of the human family, and constituting an essential part of Civilization itself. . . . Slavery paints itself again in *closing the gates of knowledge,* which are also the shining gates of Civilization. . . . Slavery paints itself again *in the appropriation of all the toil* of its victims, excluding them from that property in their own earnings which the Law of Nature allows and Civilization secures. . . . Not from any land of Civilization is this Barbarism derived. It comes from Africa, ancient nurse of monsters. . . . From its home in Africa, where it is sustained by immemorial usage, this Barbarism, thus derived and thus developed, traversed the ocean to American soil. It entered on board that fatal slave ship,

'Built in the eclipse, and rigged with curses dark.'"

Turning from the nature of slavery itself, Sumner took up its "practical results" and compared North and South in terms of the indices of civilization so extensively used by contenders in the sectional struggle: the growth of population, the value of property, manufactures, mining, and the mechanic arts, railroads and canals, the circulation of mail matter through the postoffice, voluntary charity, colleges, professional schools, academies and private schools, public schools, public libraries, the press, and patents. Respecting all these criteria of comparison between Civilization and Barbarism, according to Sumner's figures, the testimony, he declared, was on the side of the former. "At every point is the character of Slavery more and more manifest, rising and dilating into an overshadowing Barbarism, darkening the whole land. . . . Liberty is the first of schoolmasters: nay, more; it is the Baconian philosophy of Civilization, through which the powers and activities of man are enlarged beyond measure or imagination."

The second division of his impeachment Sumner devoted to the influence of slavery upon "Slave-Masters." Summoning American history to his service, he quoted Southern writers as authorities, beginning with the arraignment of the institution by George Mason in the convention that framed the Constitution of the United States: "Slavery discourages arts and manufactures. The poor despise labor, when performed by slaves. They prevent the immigration of whites, who really enrich and strengthen a country. *They produce the most pernicious effect on manners.* EVERY MASTER OF SLAVES IS BORN A PETTY TYRANT. They bring the judgment of Heaven on a country."

To Mason's charge, Sumner added the accusation by Jefferson: "The whole commerce between master and slave is a perpetual exercise of the most boisterous passions, THE MOST UNREMITTING DESPOTISM ON THE ONE PART, and degrading submission on the other. Our children see this, and learn to imitate it. . . . *A man must be a prodigy who can retain his manners and morals undepraved by such circumstances.* . . . With the morals of the people, their industry also is destroyed."

Those articles of prosecution Sumner illustrated by more than fifty pages of items selected as if to demonstrate the barbarizing influence of slavery upon the masters and breeders of slaves: the law of slavery which gives to the owner full control over his property and the right to indulge in his own worst passions; the punishment of slaves, feeding angry tempers; the use of bloodhounds in capturing fleeing victims; the propensity to dueling and other forms of rage; the transference of physical fury into violence of language; the surrender of love of Country to love of Slavery. Ignoring descriptions of the poverty, misery, cruelty, and degradation in the North graphically presented by Southern orators and writers, Sumner transfixed the slave system as Barbarism and nothing else.

Having drawn the conclusion that the sectional struggle then rocking the nation to its foundations was an inescapable conflict between Civilization and Barbarism, Sumner faced the crisis with unwavering faith in the outcome for civilization: "I have spoken for Freedom everywhere, and for Civilization; and as the less is contained in the greater, so are all arts, all sciences, all economies, all refinements, all charities, all delights of life, embodied in this cause. The sacred animosity of Freedom and Slavery can end only with the triumph of Freedom. The same question will be carried soon before that high tribunal, supreme over Senate and Court, where the judges are counted by millions, and the judgment rendered will be the solemn charge of an awakened people, instructing a new President, in the name of Freedom, to see that Civilization receives no detriment."

When, on July 11 of the same year, after Lincoln had been nominated as the Republican candidate, Sumner spoke at the Cooper Institute in New York City in support of Lincoln, he restated his case and called upon the voters to pass judgment: "Would you arrest these terrible corruptions, and the disastrous influence from which they spring, involving nothing less than civilization on this continent, the Republican party tells you how, and in telling you how, vindicates at once its origin and necessity."

Throughout the North, Sumner's address excited a flood of comments in the press. Anti-slavery leaders, even cautious members of the Republican party in search of victory at the polls, greeted it as a masterly presentation of the supreme issue, as establishing in thought the irreconcilable antagonism in the sectional conflict, as projecting from the past the converging lines of irrepressible force.

Judging by the columns of newspapers and the stream of letters that poured in upon Sumner, his interpretation of the struggle as a contest between Civilization and Barbarism struck responsive chords in all parts of the North. Circulated as a pamphlet, used as a text by debaters, it stirred countless citizens beyond the reach of his voice in Washington. Leaders on both sides of the fateful contest were induced to do more thinking about the issue in terms of civilization; and Northern leaders were given assurance of the outcome as a victory of civilization in America. In this relation it was significant that W. H. Herndon, Lincoln's law partner in Illinois, pronounced Sumner's address "most philosophic, logical, and classical" and declared that "We . . . out here . . . are confident of success."

If less strategically placed to make his opinions heard and count in the North, George William Curtis was equally positive about the dynamics of civilization in the sectional conflict. "The logic of history, of civilization, of our national idea, of the universal conscience," he exclaimed in 1859, is "against slavery." Calhoun, he said, "perceived" this "and with the audacity of genius he resolved to stun the country into acquiescence by claiming that slavery was the fundamental law of the land." To Calhoun's "spirit of despotism" were opposed the Constitution as interpreted by William H. Seward and the "passionate eloquence" of the abolitionists.

As to the outcome Curtis had no doubt: "I believe that God did not hide this continent through all time as the spot whereon a nation should be planted upon the only principle that can render a nation as permanent as the race, to suffer the experiment to fail within a century. I believe these truths to be self-evident—that all men are created equal; that they are endowed by their Creator with certain inalienable rights; that among these are life, liberty, and the pursuit of happiness. Do you believe it? If aye, let us go into the battle, and God speed the right."

"The American doctrine of liberty" Curtis analyzed into its elements in 1862 as embracing: "the absolute personal and political freedom of every man: the right, that is to say, of every man to think and speak and act, subject to the equal rights of other men, protected in their exercise by common consent, or law. It declares that men are to be deprived of personal liberty only for crime, and that political liberty is the only sure guarantee of personal freedom. These are the postulates of our civilization. Consequently our normal social condition is a constant enlarging of liberty; and any connivance at the *permanent* restraint of personal, political, or moral freedom, except from essential incompetency, as of youth or insanity, is a disturbance of the divine order in human development." In our system, "public opinion is really the government. . . . Whoever enlightens it lifts people towards peace and prosperity. But there is no method of enlightening it but the freest discussion. Stop the mouth and you stop civilization. Chain down every human right, but leave the right of speech free, and presently it will unchain all the rest." Underlying it all are "virtue, intelligence, and industry." These, Curtis avowed, "are the essential guarantees of civilization."

The Southern argument that the "Caucasian race" had been the civilizing race and that the colored race had made no contributions to civilization, Curtis countered by his version of history; by painting a more complex picture of human progress through the centuries: "Of every variety of race, complexion, capacity, intelligence, and civilization, it is the same human family that streams across the ages, with its daring outposts and pickets, its steady center, its remote wings, its progress like the fluctuating mass of an advancing army, its dim and backward reserves, stretching many a mile from front to rear, over hills and valleys, over plains and rivers; here bivouacking in pastoral repose, there tossed upon the agonizing verge of battle; but one great army still, with one heart beating along the endless line, with one celestial captain, one inspiring, consecrated hope."

The relentless urge that had marked the course of history, Curtis believed, was still operating in America against the forces of social disruption and historical conservatism: "Plant a homogeneous people along the coast of a virgin continent. Let them gradually overspread it to the farther sea, speaking the same language, of virtually the same religious faith, inter-marrying, and cherishing common heroic traditions. Suppose them sweeping from end to end of their vast domain without passports—the physical perils of their increasing extent constantly modified by science, steam, and the telegraph, making Maine and Oregon neighbors—their trade enormous, their prosperity a miracle, their commonwealth of unsurpassed importance in the world, and you may theorize as you will, but you have supposed an imperial nation, which may indeed be a power of evil as of good, but which can no more recede into its original elements and local sources than its own Mississippi, pouring broad and resistless into the Gulf, can turn backward to the petty forest springs and rills whence it flows."

In the midst of the war itself, Orestes Brownson, who had not yet surrendered his personal judgment in political matters, pronounced the civil conflict a struggle between two types of civilization, the one high, the other low, and reproved those among his Catholic brethren who supported the Southern cause. "Their sympathies," he said, "are far closer with the slaveholding South than with the free North, and we need not add that the civilization of the free North is far superior to that represented by the slaveholding South. The civilization of the South is based on slavery as its corner-stone, and slavery is the very essence of barbarism. The distinction between barbarism and civilization is precisely the distinction between slavery and liberty. . . . The war is a struggle for life and death, a struggle between a civilization based on slavery, represented by the South, and a civilization based on constitutional liberty and the rights of men, represented by the free states."

"In this struggle," Brownson further contended, "if, as is the fact, the interest and loyalty of Catholics lead them in large numbers to take sides with the North, their sympathies are very generally with the South. . . . Even, then, where our Catholics aim to be American, it is not American in the sense of the highest, truest, and most advanced Americanism; but in the sense of the lowest, the least advanced, that which is least remote from barbarism, and the furthest removed from that which the church as well as humanity demands, and never ceases to struggle to obtain. We are also borne out in our view by the political history of the country. Politically, the southern leaders have for a long time formed their association with the least intelligent, the least advanced classes in the free states, and these southern leaders are those our Catholic population have followed with the most alacrity. This fact proves, on the one hand, that the South represents the lowest order of civilization in the country, and that Catholics are more easily engaged in supporting it than in supporting the superior civilization represented by the northern states."

Having already given the subject of civilization philosophic consideration, Emerson made a practical application of the idea to the sectional conflict, on January 31, 1862, in Washington, where he delivered an address on the theme of civilization to an audience which included, it was reported, President Lincoln and members of his cabinet. With unequivocal directness, Emerson made the sectional contest a clash between two types of civilization. "We have attempted," he said, "to hold together two states of civilization: a higher state, where labor and the tenure of land and the right of suffrage are democratical; and a lower state, in which the old military tenure of prisoners or slaves, and of power and land in a few hands, makes an oligarchy: we have attempted to hold these two states of society under one law." Now a conflict between the two has arisen. "The times put this question, Why cannot the best civilization be extended over the whole country, since the disorder of the less-civilized portion menaces the existence of the country? . . . Is not civilization heroic also? Is it not for action? Has it not a will?"

And what action is civilization to take? Mere preservation of the Union is not enough. "There does exist, perhaps, a popular will that the Union shall not be broken—that our trade, and therefore our laws, must have the whole breadth of the continent, and from Canada to the Gulf." A compromise might save the Union, but only for a time, for the strife is deep-seated. Emancipation is necessary, for it will alter "the atomic social constitution of the Southern people"; it will, at one stroke, elevate "the poor white of the South and identify his interest with that of the Northern laborer." History will not endure equivocations. "Why should not America be capable of a second stroke for the well-being of the human race, as eighty or ninety years ago she was of the first—of an affirmative step in the interests of human civility, urged on her, too, not by any romance of sentiment, but by her own extreme perils?" Of the outcome there can be no question: "it is the maxim of history that victory always falls at last where it ought to fall; or, there is perpetual march and progress to ideas."

Emerson was not thinking of the mere refinements and elegancies of civilization prized by a cultivated minority. He took the position that "use, labor of each for all, is the health and virtue of all beings, . . . Labor: a man coins himself into his labor; he turns his day, his strength, his thought, his affection into some product which remains as the visible sign of his power; and to protect that, to secure that to him, to secure his past self to his future self, is the object of all government. There is no interest in any country so imperative as that of labor; it covers all, and constitutions and governments exist for that—to protect and insure it to the laborer." It is to the Northern system of labor, land, and suffrage, all "democratical," the Northern "state" of civilization, that the Southern system, Southern civilization, presents an irreducible contrast and will continue to do so until subdued to the former. As to the consummation Emerson had no misgivings: the higher civilization would dominate and history would crown emancipation with victory for the Union.

That the conception of the sectional conflict as a trial in civilization was fixed in the thought of the times is also attested in essays and addresses by persons less well known than Sumner or Curtis or Emerson. For example, while events still hung in the balance, two articles based on this view of the struggle were published in the Continental Monthly, a New York periodical concerned with "Literature and National Policy." The fact that the journal reached no such large audiences as the Atlantic Monthly or Harper's Weekly in no way diminished the pertinence or cogency of its contributions to the discussion of the issue.

The first of these articles, entitled "American Destiny," by

John Stahl Patterson, evidently based on extended study, followed the main line that had become established in Northern thought of civilization. After a general introduction, providing a background of "the earlier stages of modern civilization," Patterson came to the American scene: "There is a manifest difference, however, between the history of our civilization and that of Europe. . . . The people of our nation were not derived directly from a rude and primitive condition as were those of the Old World. The history of our civilization is, in its origin, coördinate with European civilization in the seventeenth century, after modern intellect had been fairly aroused, and the national organizations had been quite fully developed. The chaos and barbarism which the history of European civilization presents, and the play of antagonizing forces through the long periods of centuries . . . does not belong, except as an introduction, to the history of American civilization. Ours is a branch of the European after it had been growing for several hundred years."

In the course of its history on this continent, American civilization, Patterson declared, had made extraordinary progress in commercial, industrial, and political advancement and unification. Out of this "progressive civilization" had arisen an integrated economy and nation. Athwart its path lies slavery, and slavery must go: "If we have not misinterpreted the law of development, slavery, as it exists in this country, is a morbid political condition, a social disease, which stands in the way of the natural course of social evolution. In this law, therefore, is written the doom of slavery. The enlightened world will not permit it to blast the fair field of civilization by its poisonous presence."

Lieutenant Egbert Phelps was the author of the second article in the Continental Monthly and he entitled it "American Civilization." There are two attitudes toward this subject, Phelps began, "the foreign and the native." Foreigners may write about it but they cannot understand it; the historian of American civilization must not only be among us but of us. American life, political and social experience, institutions, individual modes of thought, and national progress are *sui generis,* and are not to be judged by the criteria of other nations. Evils gnaw at this civilization—love of riches, moral disunity, and poverty in literature—but nonetheless it marches. Slavery is on the way to dissolution and the problem of immigration will be solved in the American way, in the American spirit. If to slave-owners and foreigners accustomed to their own types of arrogance, the affirmation was arrogant, it was, in any event, a clear statement of the case.

To Oliver Wendell Holmes the conflict was more than a contest between two sections in the United States. It represented on one side an alliance in spirit between Southern planters and the British aristocracy, which was illustrated in fact by actions of the British government. As such it was also to be a struggle for the emancipation of peoples from all uncivilized governments. The British aristocracy, Holmes wrote in the Atlantic Monthly, in 1863, "with all its dependent followers, cannot help being against us. . . . The people . . . everywhere sympathize with us. . . . We have evidence that this is partially true of the British people. . . . But hard treatment often proves the most useful kind of discipline. One good effect, as far as we are concerned, will be the promotion of our intellectual and moral independence. . . . The American republic was to be emancipated from every Old-World prejudice that might stand in the way of its entire fullness of development according to its own law, which is in many ways different from any precedent furnished by earlier forms of civilization. . . . One American invention, or discovery, has gone far towards paying back all that the new continent owes to the old civilizations. The cradle of artificial *anaesthesia* . . . must be looked for at the side of the Cradle of Liberty."

"Our civilization," Holmes felt, was in advance of all others: "It would hardly be an exaggeration to say that the piano keeps pace with the plough, as our civilization advances. . . . American civilization hates war, as such. It values life, because it honors humanity. It values property, because property is for the comfort and good of all. . . . It wants all the forces of its population to subdue Nature to its services. It demands all the intellect of its children for construction, not for destruction. Its business is to build the world's great temple of concord and justice." But let us not waste our strength on "those misguided governments who mistook their true interest in the prospect of our calamity. . . . No deeper humiliation could be asked of our foreign enemies than the spectacle of our triumph. . . . What all the governments based on smothered pauperism, tolerated ignorance, and organized degradation have to fear is the subterranean fire, which finds its vent in blazing craters, or breaks up all the ancient landmarks in earth shattering convulsions."

After the storm of war broke over the land, Northern leaders in the woman movement postponed for the moment their work for equality of enfranchisement and turned their loyalty and enthusiasm to the support of the Union and the war for its preservation, which they demanded be made a war for the extirpation of slavery. In previous years they had framed their program and placed their hopes of realizing it in the progress of civilization. Now they accepted even violence, after it came, as an instrument of civilization, with assurance that civilization would stand the test.

In this spirit, to concentrate their forces for victory, they called a convention of "the loyal women of the country" which assembled at Cooper Union, in New York City, in the spring of 1863, with Elizabeth Cady Stanton in the chair. After discussing their obligations and pledging their strength to the Union, they drafted a statement of their tenets to be sent to President Lincoln, which Susan B. Anthony read to the Convention for criticism or approval. Its first words constituted a manifesto of their power: "From every free State, we have received the most hearty responses of interest in each onward step of the Government as it approaches the idea of a true Republic. From the letters received, and the numbers assembled here today, we can with confidence address you in the name of the loyal women of the North."

The proposed address as adopted and transmitted to Lincoln read in part as follows: "We come not to criticize or complain. . . . We come to strengthen you with earnest words of sympathy and encouragement. We come to thank you for your proclamation, in which the nineteenth century seems to echo back the Declaration of Seventy-six. Our fathers had a vision of the sublime idea of liberty, equality, and fraternity; but they failed to climb the heights that with anointed eyes they saw. To us, their children, belongs the work to build up the living reality of what they conceived and uttered. . . .

"Born anew to freedom, slave creeds and codes and constitutions must now all pass away. . . .

"It was not enough that we at the North abolished slavery for ourselves, declared freedom of speech and the press, built up churches, colleges, and free schools, studied the science of morals, government, and economy, dignified labor, amassed wealth, whitened the sea with our commerce, and commanded the respect and admiration of the nations of the earth, so long as the South, by the natural proclivities of slavery, was sapping the very foundations of our national life. . . .

"At no time in the annals of the nation has there been a more auspicious moment to retrieve the one false step of the fathers in their concessions to slavery. . . .

" 'The Union as it was'—a compromise between barbarism and civilization—can never be restored. . . .

"Northern power and loyalty can never be measured until the purpose of the war be liberty to man; for a lasting enthusiasm is ever based on a grand idea, and unity of action demands a definite end. . . . If it be true, as it is said, that Northern women lack enthusiasm in this war, the fault rests with those who have confused and confounded its policy. . . . Your Proclamation gives you immortality."

Speaking at this Convention on the nature and tendency of the conflict, Rev. Antoinette Brown Blackwell at one point declared that "the severe discipline of this war is schooling us into a better appreciation of our heritage as a peculiar people," and asked whether the North might expect wholehearted sympathy from any European monarchies. "Cannot they see, also, that two entire opposing civilizations are mustered into the conflict? . . . We are now testing the practical possibilities of democratic theories; and there are those who would a thousand times rather see these shattered into hopeless fragments than any other result which could possibly transpire in the national affairs of all Christendom. . . . Our great national axiom, is *per se,* the eternal foe of all monarchies, aristocracies, oligarchies, of all possible despotism, because it is the fulcrum of a mighty lever which must one day overturn them all, if it be not itself jostled from its resting-place."

The following year Northern women drew up a petition expressing their convictions on vital phases of the struggle and the great human issues involved in the outcome, and circulated it widely to procure a long list of signers. Before this referendum was closed nearly 400,000 signatures had been collected and forwarded to Congress.

In presenting a collection of the petitions to the Senate, Charles Sumner said of the persons who had put their names to it: "They are from all parts of the country and from every condition of life. They are from the seaboard, fanned by the free airs of the ocean, and from the Mississippi and the prairies of the West, fanned by the free airs which fertilize that extensive region. They are from the families of the educated and uneducated, rich and poor, of every profession, business, and calling in life, representing every sentiment, thought, hope, passion, activity, intelligence which inspires, strengthens, and adorns our social system."

In the civil conflict as conducted in terms of thought, a third party had to be taken into account, that is, the Negroes, bond and free, numbering more than four millions. Whether the struggle was treated as a clash between two civilizations or between civilization and barbarism, or between Southern civilization and a system of industrial servitude, this third party was given attention. Slavery might be deemed permanent or an anomaly destined to swift destruction or a slow process of civilization on the way to freedom; but in any case the relation of Negroes to civilization came into discussion and with it a consideration of civilization as a long social process involving that race, in Africa and the United States.

On this issue opinion was also divided. There was extensive, although not universal, agreement in the South on the proposition that slavery had taken Negroes from barbarism in Africa and led them upward along the path of civilization. In connection with this thesis it was generally held that the Negro was a human being and belonged to the same human race as did the whites. But even here dissent was heard. Dr. Josiah C. Nott, a physician who made amateur excursions into ethnology with George R. Gliddon, published in 1854 a large volume, entitled *Types of Mankind*, in which, with prolix illustrations, he sought to establish the counter-thesis that each race of mankind sprang from a distinct source, a fixed type, "permanent throughout all recorded time." In the course of development, he declared, Negroes formed a separate and enduringly inferior order of beings.

But Nott's allegations did not pass undisputed, even in the South. Although George Fitzhugh was a defender of slavery, he pronounced Nott's doctrine contrary to the Scripture, "which teaches that the whole human race is descended from a common parentage," and as encouraging brutal masters to treat Negroes "as wicked beasts, without the pale of humanity." Since ten editions of Nott's treatise were published, however, it must have been accorded a sympathetic reception in some quarters.

Despite Nott's arguments, the belief that slavery was Christianizing and civilizing the Negroes was widely entertained in the South. In this view, a dynamic conception of civilization was upheld. Then where would it lead? In the minds of the optimistically disposed, it led to the conclusion that in the process of time slaves might become fully prepared by religious training and other disciplines to enjoy the privileges of civil rights. By other Southern thinkers, the possibility of this eventuality was denied. The latter contended that the degree of civilization attained by slaves was relatively slight; that unless they were permanently restrained by the authority and superintending care of masters and mistresses their gains in the direction of becoming civilized would dissolve into the natural barbarism of the Africans. At all events there was persistence in the type of Southern opinion which maintained that Negroes could not attain the fulness of civilization; that free Negroes subjected to competition with whites in the North were degraded in the scale of civilized living and, to repeat Fitzhugh, were treated there as "weak, ignorant, and dependent brethren."

In his address on "Civilization against Barbarism," Charles Sumner touched briefly the question respecting the third party in the contest. Although he devoted hours to the subject of slavery, he merely remarked that "this is not the time to enter upon the great question of race, in the various lights of religion, history, and science." And he dismissed it in a swift fashion by saying: "If the African race be inferior, as is alleged, then unquestionably a Christian civilization must lift it from degradation, not by the lash and chain, not by this barbarous pretension of ownership, but by a generous charity, which shall be measured precisely by the extent of authority." To the repeated intimations of Southern orators that the true nature of Northern charity could be tested by the condition of free Negroes in Northern states and cities, Sumner also made no answer. In this manner the problem of the relation of Negroes to civilization was passed upon by the Senator from Massachusetts in presenting his case of civilization against barbarism.

Nevertheless if opponents of slavery and advocates of emancipation were to discuss comprehensively the issue posed as the Negro question, they had to face it realistically within the scope of general history. And as early as 1833 Lydia Maria Child did that in a work entitled *An Appeal in Favor of that Class of Americans Called Africans.* As to scholarship her *Appeal* was in every respect equal, if not superior, to the learning in Sumner's oration. Indeed it is not improbable that Senator Sumner, who esteemed her talents and judgment, drew upon her volume in framing the description of what he called the five features of barbarism inherent in slavery. At all events, in her second chapter Mrs. Child had listed fifteen items in her bill of indictment against slavery—based on extensive researches in the laws and literature of the South— all of which in some form appeared in Sumner's enumerations.

Unlike Charles Sumner, Lydia Maria Child did not have in her youth the advantages of a formal education at Harvard and of travel and study in Europe. Nor was she born into a family of high social standing. Her paternal grandfather was a weaver who had fought at Concord in 1775; her father was a baker. Her only formal education was acquired in elementary schools and one year at a seminary in Massachusetts. Her real education was gained by her own initiative and hard study while she was working as a publicist, editor, and woman of affairs.

Self-educated, a serious student of history, well informed in economics and politics, logical in argumentation, Mrs. Child won a notable place among the leading personalities engaged in the intellectual contest over the sectional antagonism. According to a biographer, her *Appeal* was thrown like "a bomb into the pro-slavery camps, North and South" and was widely read. "Channing, Sumner, Higginson, and other prominent opponents of slavery acknowledged its influence upon them then or later." It was on the basis of recorded facts, as well as personal knowledge, that Whittier wrote of Mrs. Child: "She was wise in counsel; and men like Charles Sumner, Henry Wilson, Salmon P. Chase, and Governor Andrew availed themselves of her sound judgment of men and measures."

Although at points her indictment of slavery burst into flame, despite her effort and general success at sustained calm, Mrs. Child's *Appeal* avoided the vindictiveness and personal abuse, the petty recriminations, which marked so many discussions of the subject. Instead of assailing slave-owners as evil persons, she arraigned the system of slavery. "It would be very absurd," she said, "to imagine that the inhabitants of one State are worse than the inhabitants of another, unless some peculiar circumstances, of universal influence, tend to make them so. Human nature is everywhere the same; but developed differently, by different incitements and temptations. It is the business of wise legislation to discover what influences are most productive of good, and the least conducive to evil. If we were educated at the South, we should no doubt vindicate slavery, and inherit as a birthright all the evils it engrafts upon the character. If they lived on our rocky soil, and under our inclement skies, their shrewdness would sometimes border upon knavery, and their frugality sometimes degenerate into parsimony. . . . *Our* defects are bad enough; but they cannot, like slavery, affect the destiny and rights of millions."

Lifting the controversy above vilification, locating the differences of opinion in different conditions of life, physical and economic, Mrs. Child deplored the current scurrility displayed on both sides: "All this mutual recrimination about horse jockeys, gamblers, tin peddlers, and venders of wooden nutmegs, is quite unworthy of a great nation. Instead of calmly examining this important subject on the plain grounds of justice and humanity, we allow it to degenerate into a mere question of *sectional* pride and vanity. . . . It is the *system*, not the *men*, on which we ought to bestow the full measure of abhorrence. If we were willing to forget ourselves, and could, like true republicans, prefer the common good to all other considerations, there would not be a slave in the United States, at the end of half a century."

While Mrs. Child appealed to sentiments of justice and humanity, she described the political contest among the whites in plain economic terms, in her chapter on "The Influence of Slavery on the Politics of the United States." For this phase of the contest she presented an economic interpretation: "It is sufficiently obvious," she remarked laconically, "that the slave and free States are, and must be, rivals, owing to the inevitable contradiction of their interests. It needed no Machiavel to predict the result. A continual strife has been going on, more or less earnest, according to the nature of the interests it involved. . . . The people of the North have to manage a rocky and reluctant soil; hence commerce and the fisheries early attracted their attention. . . . The Southerners have a genial climate and a fertile soil; but in consequence of the cumbrous machinery of slave labor, which is slow for everything (except exhausting the soil), they have always been less prosperous than the free States. . . . It is certainly very credible that a great proportion of their plantations are deeply mortgaged in New York and Philadelphia."

The old Federalist party represented "the commercial class." The planting class had its politicians. John Taylor, a spokesman of that class, "treats merchants, capitalists, bankers, and all other people not planters as so many robbers, who live by plundering the slave owners, apparently forgetting by what plunder they themselves live." George Washington and his immediate successors had held the conflict of interests within certain bounds, but the class was (in 1833) in danger of bursting its historic limitations.

It was as a person emancipated from many dogmas of the politicians that Mrs. Child approached the race question in relation to civilization and examined the mental and the moral character of Negroes and the prejudices against them. The line of her argument was cast within the scope of general history. She opened it by declaring: "Naturalists are universally agreed concerning 'the identity of the *human* type.'" She cited authorities for the contention that Ethiopia held a high place in ancient times in intellectual and moral development and quoted Herodotus as saying that the Colchians must be a colony of Egypt, because, "like them, they have a black skin and frizzled hair." The sciences, arts, architecture, learning, religions, and laws of the Egyptians had demonstrated the capacity of those people of color to rise far above barbarism and become teachers of the more primitive Greeks. "The wisest of the Grecian philosophers, among whom were Solon, Pythagoras, and Plato, went there [Egypt] for instruction, as our young men now go to England and Germany."

Directing her inquiry to other parts of Africa and the contemporary age, Mrs. Child asserted that "civilization has certainly advanced much farther in the interior of Africa, than it did among the North American tribes" of Indians. Then she confronted the old question: "How is it that the nations of Africa, having proceeded so far in the arts of civilization, have made a full stop, and remained century after century without any obvious improvement?" This inquiry she countered by the question: "How long did the ancient Helvetians, Gauls, and Saxons remain in such a state of barbarism, that what they considered splendor and refinement, would be called poverty and rudeness, by their German, French, and English descendants?" And to what did the European barbarians owe the civilization which they at length attained? Mainly to the art of printing.

If Mrs. Child's argument on the matter of retardation in civilization were compressed into a single sentence, it would read: The Negro belongs to the human race; in the long history of mankind, the nations of the earth have followed an uneven development in reaching stages of civilization; and the fact that any given race is at a given moment on a lower plane than another is no proof of permanent incapacity.

The proposition that the backwardness in civilization exhibited by certain peoples in times and places is due entirely to innate racial characteristics, Mrs. Child met by drawing attention to the special circumstances likely to account for such backwardness. A people may, like the ancient Greeks, fall under the cruel domination of a conquering, barbaric race and be reduced in the scale of the arts and refinements. Again, a people, as in the case of Negroes, may be held back by oppression, cruelty, exploitation, and a denial of opportunities.

This second point Mrs. Child pressed with great emphasis, not sparing in her criticisms the discriminations practiced in the North. She cited cases of individual Negroes who had demonstrated intellectual and moral capacities of a high order, and described virtues manifested by ordinary Negroes, bond and free. "If we are willing to see and believe, we have full opportunity to convince ourselves that the colored population are highly susceptible of cultivation. . . . Try to judge the Negro by the same rules you judge other men; and while you condemn his faults, do not forget his manifold provocations."

In sum and substance, Mrs. Child argued that if Negroes should gain their freedom, if the features of slave legislation which deprived them of their rights and customs belonging to civilization should be abolished, if they should be received into the privileges of liberty, they would become as civilized as the rest of the community. Thus, in 1833, Mrs. Child sought to allay the apprehension, felt in many parts of the country, that general emancipation meant a flood of barbarism from below submerging all civilization.

Other men and women endorsed the idea of civilization but held different views of the sectional conflict before it broke into war. As they were given to understand the course of affairs, the ordeal of fire could be avoided; and, if election returns up to and including the figures of 1860 in reality measured the numerical strength of opinions, those who opposed the arbitrament of arms formed an overwhelming majority of the people.

As to measures and outcomes, however, they disagreed among themselves. One group believed that in the flow of time the civilizing process in its various phases would gradually dissolve slavery. Was it not said that the census reports, not merely the figures used by Helper in his indictment of the South, ran against slavery? Would not the law of diminishing returns make slave labor obsolete with the coming of machines and the cheapening of white labor? Jefferson Davis thought it possible that in the advance of civilization, Negroes, already lifted out of barbarism, might be prepared for civil liberty and the enjoyment of commodious living. Robert E. Lee, who deplored the abuses of slavery, thought that Christianity might overcome it, if zealots would not press for swift and drastic remedies.

A peculiar type of thought, "above and beyond the conflict," was represented in the popular writings of Maria J. McIntosh of Georgia, who after the death of her parents moved to New York and supported herself with her pen. In *Woman in America: Her Work and Her Reward*, Miss McIntosh lamented the quarrels of persons and sects, treated slavery as a phase in the process of civilizing the Negro, discussed the merits and demerits of society in the North and the South, and expressed the hope that through intercourse and exchange the virtues of both could be made to prevail throughout the country. The judgment of history pronounced her theories idyllic but they appealed to that incalculable number of Americans who relied on civilization rather than war to resolve the impending conflict.

"The improvement of the African race among us," she said, "is sufficiently attested. . . . The all-perfect One . . . has made the wrath of man to praise Him, transmuting, with heavenly alchemy, the loathsome selfishness and heartlessness of the slave-trader into the partial civilization and Christianization of the race enslaved, and into the means of promoting the intellectual culture and social refinement of those who were forced into the position of their masters. . . .

"We feel persuaded that even in the South, the listless

repose of the idle will not long continue undisturbed. Changes have already taken place there which betoken the infusion of new elements into the indolent *pococurante* life. These elements are, we believe, the overflowing of the ever-boiling and bubbling caldron of life in New England and Middle States. A happy admixture will this be, if the South will receive strength and activity, and give refinement, without suffering simplicity to be lost in the exchange. . . .

"Will it, in acquiring the virtues of the North, retain its own? Will its members, while adding to their homes the mechanical improvements which minister to comfort, and the treasures of art which at once form and gratify the taste—while thus gaining all that is truly valuable in the most advanced civilization, still wisely refuse to exchange their simple, social habits for the ostentatious display and vulgar pretension which too often mark a sudden increase of wealth? If they do, if maintaining their simplicity of life, they awake to a sense of their responsibility to God and to the world for the improvement and proper use of every talent entrusted to them, if they become '*workers* with God,' seeking wealth,

> Not to hide it in a hedge,
> Nor for a train attendant—
> But for the glorious privilege

of opening to others a nobler life, of elevating to the dignity of man their own dependents, of sending the purifying streams of Christian education through the land—that, each man learning he is the brother of all, the bitter prejudices of sect and party may be discarded, and our country, our whole country, become what God intended it to be, united in one spirit, as well as in one body; if they do all this, then they will have attained to our conception of a true American life.

"And has woman at the South nothing to do in promoting this 'consummation most devoutly to be wished'? It must be mainly her work. . . . Let her make it a law of the social life in which she rules, that nothing so surely degrades a man as idleness and the vices to which it almost inevitably leads. Thus she will proclaim the dignity and worth of labor, and she will find her reward in the new impress made on the yet ductile minds of her children. She has seen them hitherto too often go forth, like bright but wandering stars, into a life containing for them no definite object. In this vast void, she has seen them too often driven hither and thither by their own reckless impulses—But labor will tame these wild impulses—will give to life a decided aim; and, as the strong hand, loosed from the bonds of prejudice, obeys the command of the stout heart, her 'paeans' will be sounded, not for defeat nobly sustained, but for victory won."

Another variant on the theme of avoiding the clash of arms and intrusting the slavery question to civilization was expressed by a writer in the Democratic Review in 1858. That version or interpretation eluded the issue of slavery by resorting to a faith in something inexorable called "nature." After recounting the triumph of the "new and distinguished civilization" inaugurated in America by the Revolution and "the enlightened principles of that new civilization," the author of the unsigned article proposed to eliminate slavery from controversy by abandoning attempts to limit it to "isothermal zones," and by allowing it to go with the course of nature. "In permitting the inhabitants of the new states," this prophet felt, "to settle and to fix their own domestic institutions, the Kansas Act contributes to the maintenance of political equality among the sovereign parts of our confederacy, while, at the same time, it renders the elements of American civilization in strict conformity with those laws established by nature, and destined to endure, when constitutional provisions and legislative restrictions cease to be valid and operative."

Perhaps the most powerful, politically at least, among the thinkers who sought to avoid the arbitrament of war were the historical conservatives. They denied that there were two civilizations and spurned Sumner's formula of civilization against barbarism. Intrinsically, they insisted, there was only one civilization in the United States, an American civilization, in which slavery was an incident, or at any rate, no justification for an armed contest. Whether these conservatives were partisans of political democracy, like writers in The Democratic Review, or old-line Whigs, like Edward Everett and Alexander Hamilton Stephens, they agreed that civilization was an interest which should transcend Southern agrarianism and Northern industrialism, and they used the idea of civilization in their attempts to hold the Union together and preserve a working balance of power.

According to the system of conservative thought and faith,

economic and political differences might disturb the nation but civilization in America would prove stronger than all sectional and sectarian divisions. It offered a guarantee of national unity, provided concern for its values could be elevated above the clamor of fanatics determined to make the slavery issue a question of uncompromising special interests. The cloven hoof of party politics and economic advantage, it is true, often obtruded itself in statements of the conservative case. Yet there was vitality in the sentiment to which men and women of such convictions clung; namely, that forces more primordial than the tension over slavery as mere good or sheer evil, forces more enduring than temporary appearances, existed in American society and would override the disputants in carrying civilization forward.

Insofar as Southern and Northern conservatives, by advocating restraint, postponed the plunge into violence until the North became preponderant in the Union, they helped to make sure, whatever their intentions, the outcome which Emerson and others had forecast as the victory of American civilization—the perpetuity of the Republic and the emancipation of the slaves. If, by merely standing and waiting, conservatives thus served the cause of civilization, they nevertheless suffered a melancholy fate in the judgment of posterity.

Most realistic and in some respects the most foresighted among the views that transcended sectional interpretations of the conflict, was the thesis advanced by a retired New York manufacturer, Thomas Ewbank, in a little pamphlet, *Inorganic Forces Ordained to Supersede Human Slavery*, printed in New York in 1860. Unlike politicians, essayists, and literary experts, Ewbank brought to the subject an engineering mind alert to the social consequences of technology. Prior to the publication of his pamphlet he had shown the bent of his thinking in other works: first in one on water hydraulics, ancient and modern; then in *The World a Workshop*, and *Thoughts on Matter and Force*.

In the opening pages of his pamphlet, Ewbank expressed the opinion that "microscopic views . . . lead the melancholy to mourn," and throughout he maintained the position that it is the broad view which is the correct view and offers the greatest insight and promise. Thus by commitment he was precluded from adopting the outlook of special pleaders and sectarians. With the way for comprehensive thought cleared, he went directly to the main issue: the relation of human slavery to "inorganic forces," that is, to the "progressive" development of science, invention, discovery, and the cheap and expeditious production of wealth by the use of power, all in connection with the advance of civilization.

On the main proposition of labor Ewbank's argument was crystal clear: the progressive forces of production so enumerated particularly differentiate the modern age from antiquity, and regions that have them from regions that must rely principally on the labor of the human body. "Races and nations," Ewbank declared, "are what their agents of labor make them—savages are such because they use no power but their own, while the social, mental, and moral habits improve as other forces are called in. The ancient world arrived at certain stages of progress and then stopped, because the forces in use could carry it no further. Neither the wisdom of Egypt, philosophy of India, ingenuity of Greece, nor the energy of Rome could urge it onward. In this respect the morals of Confucius, the teachings of Pythagoras, and the inspirations of the prophets alike failed." With the power available for the production of wealth so limited at the time, slavery continued to endure, for the time.

The ancient world, the type of society based on slavery, had been superseded by another world, the modern world, with machinery and steam and other motive forces at its command. These agencies, Ewbank perceived, were transforming the economies of all the countries in which they were at work and would pursue their revolutionary course in coming years. As they drove forward in the regions called "the South," he predicted, they would ultimately supplant the ancient and crude system of hand labor in which slavery was such a prominent feature. As a matter of fact, as the industrial returns of each census demonstrated, "inorganic forces" were already making headway there. Small mills were rising in all parts of the South and planters with managerial skill were supplementing or supplanting slave labor by machinery and steam engines. The genie of steam, freed by invention, was descending upon rice fields, cotton crops, and rows of tobacco.

Before these forces, Ewbank felt sure, chattel slavery would fall, inexorably. But he realized that "the world at large is far from being prepared for the change, and may not be for ages; still there are places that seem nearly if not quite ready for it, and of them our country is the most promising. The conflicts of opinion on slavery that have agitated and keep agitating the

Union tend, and are perhaps necessary, to clear the way for it. Here are the inducements, the means, and the men—the science and the skill—to devise the plans, with the best of opportunity to improve and mature them. . . . It [the revolutionary change] has begun with us."

But what about the race question? Ewbank did not shirk it. But he spent little time discussing the innate and eternal superiority or inferiority of races. In his opinion some races, as tested by stages of civilization, were higher than others. There had been "rise and progresses" in civilization. "Could it ever have come," he asked, "had it been dependent upon the lowest?" He answered his query by saying: "The *idea* of progress is peculiar to the Pioneer race. In this matter the world is a Lancastrian school, in which the highest class furnishes instructors and monitors for the lower ones. . . . The mission of the white race is to extend civilization over the earth. . . . It does not follow from this subordination of one race to another, that Nature sanctions our prevailing slave systems. Her code is very different to most of them. . . . It is doubtful if it contains the word 'slave'—certainly not the popular idea and practices connected with it."

In the way of this advance stood the eternal spirit of conservatism, saying that the times are not yet ripe for the change from slave to power labor: "It may be objected that the substitution implies a change for which society in slave states is not prepared and an advance in the arts not attained. Suppose this conceded, is it less a duty to look forward on this subject than on others less important? . . . Wherever slavery is rendered commercially impossible by the superior economy and efficiency of inanimate forces, *there* the ultimate law has begun to prevail."

In the processes of civilization, accelerated by power and machinery, the Negro would assume a place after the extinction of slavery: "There is hope for the Negro. His race is not destined to remain uninformed serfs." In coming times no labor is to be servile: "Labor—free, cheerful, enlightened labor is forever to be the root and spring of human advancement. . . . An increase of labor, or agents of labor will forever be indispensable to progressive civilization." On this proposition Ewbank stood four square to all the winds of doctrine.

Far beyond the approaching end of slavery in the United States, Ewbank looked to the growing use of "inorganic forces" for the increasing emancipation of all mankind.

Critics say "when once we enter upon such a state of things progress must be at an end. Assuredly not. It would be but the commencement of a series of developments that require an eternity to perfect and exhaust. As regards the Day of Science and Discovery, whatever self-love may suggest to the contrary, we only live in the first blush of the morning." Fortifying his argument by an appeal to a theology apparently pantheistic in character, Ewbank declared that we are "coworkers with nature, and therefore with God." In such language, to the sanction of civilization and of nature for his prophecy, he added a kind of divine sanction.

But no such view of civilization in the United States could obtain sway over the minds of impatient partisans and prevail in the nation. It was only after they had tried and endured the ordeal of battle for four years, after they had experienced the harrowing sacrifices of life and property, if ever, that zealots began to wonder whether it would not have been better for humanity in America—white and black—had they, as Ewbank suggested, devised plans and coped with slavery by means other than arms. Then it was too late.

Chapter 7

The Thrust of Individualism and Pessimism

THE GREAT CASE of civilization involved in the sectional struggle, as far as it centered on the institution of chattel slavery, was closed in 1865. As indictment and defense, it had been submitted to the court of public opinion and the verdict had been rendered by arms. That act in the drama of civilization was finished.

Energies which had been concentrated for four years on warfare were now released for civilian pursuits amid opportunities for the most rapid expansion in the history of the Republic. And as the curtain rose on the next historic movement, new acts were heralded in the name of a new doctrine of the perfect good—the doctrine of individualism. As if timed by some intricate precision this doctrine was thrust into the scene where minds contested with minds for supremacy over the way of life, where the idea of civilization was attacked with new weapons and defended in new forms.

On the face of things, individualism seemed to many a mere extension or form of an old idea, that of individuality, proverbial in Western idealism. The doctrine of individual worth, of personal rights, persistent in thought since the age of the Stoics at least and revitalized during the Renaissance, had furnished persuasion for the theory of natural rights so kinetic in the contest between liberty and authority which had opened the modern age. From that source had come inspiration for the Declaration of Independence and for the revolt of men and women against government by "the privileged" in the era of the popular upsurge.

That the individual should not be used for purposes alien to humanity was a creed of seasoned strength. That the individual would manifest a natural excellence if freed from physical servitude and mental bondage to beliefs enforced by Church and State was a creed that had animated the long struggle for liberty of the press, speech, and religious worship —for civil rights in general and particular.

It had promoted the inquiries which helped to emancipate natural science from the tyranny of theological preconceptions. Under its aegis, individuals, once strictly limited by caste or status, were to be liberated to investigate, labor, experiment, and demonstrate their capacities in sciences, arts, letters, and every branch of humanistic interest. Thus the idea of individual freedom had been one of the major forces in American civilization as fact.

But the word *individualism*, though stemming from the same root as individuality, branched off from it fundamentally in accent and content. Individualism was a newcomer in the American vocabulary. Apparently it did not attain a general circulation until near the middle of the nineteenth century. In origins, it seems to have been French or British, not American. The first use of the word cited in the *Oxford English Dictionary* was in 1835, in the translation of Tocqueville's *Démocratie en Amérique* by Henry Reeve. In Tocqueville's treatise the word meant to cut one's self off from one's family, friends, and society—a kind of self-chosen anarchy or outlawry.

The spirit of this arbitrary act of denying one's debts and obligations to family, friends, and society, of declaring one's complete independence from all social relations, entered into the idea of individualism as it was developed, especially in relation to economic activities and vested rights. When it reached a full formulation the idea embraced several very concrete affirmations, such as the following: Society is merely an aggregation of individuals struggling for existence competitively. The qualities or talents of the individual which prepare him or her for that struggle are to be attributed solely to personal merits and efforts; the individual is "self-made." In unrestrained competition, victory goes to the strong, the ambitious, the ingenious, the industrious, the "fittest to survive," and their rewards as victors are proportioned to the contributions of their labors to the total product, as justice requires; they get what they deserve, in short. In the strife among competing individuals, the production of wealth is increased while its distribution runs according to merits. Poverty is due to the indolence, lack of initiative, improvidence, dearth of ambition, the inebriety, or the restlessness of the poor themselves.

This world-view of human beings was reinforced by the rise and spread of Darwinism—the world-view of biological determinism for the activities of all living things, from the lowest to the highest ranges of the vegetable and animal kingdoms. According to that theory the evolution of all life had been and is through the struggle for existence, natural selection, and the survival of the fittest, the victors, in that competition. It is true that the cautious Darwin did not reduce his theory to this single formula, but the ultimate simplifiers did it and popularized it as such. When the apparent force of all nature was joined to the special interests of the men and women who survived and prospered in the prevailing economic regime, the doctrine of individualism seemed invincible to them. The idea of civilization was limited to humanity, but individualism assimilated mankind to the whole order of living things under one iron law.

Terrific momentum was given to the idea of individualism by its utility to the most powerful private interests in the country, now that the planting interests had lost their base in chattel slavery. Capitalists eager to rush forward in the business of making money and owners of property content with their possessions, or desirous of more, snapped up the doctrine as a "scientific" justification for their activities and accumulations. Energetic individuals without property, but bent on acquiring it, also heard the word and pronounced it good. All could resort to it as a shield against government intervention or as warrant for favors asked and received from government according to their personal interests.

If men of the deed and fact were inclined to be inarticulate in terms allegedly philosophic, two classes of intellectuals—lay and academic—became vociferous over the idea of individualism, spun it out, and thrust it into national consciousness with all the force that powerful expression and unremitting propaganda could give to it. Among the lay intellectuals were editors, lawyers, politicians, pamphleteers, and "free literary critics." In this class were enrolled some veteran reformers of the previous age: for example, Charles A. Dana, who forsook the social ideals of his youth, turned cynic, and, while editor of the New York Sun, tried to make individualism the creed of America. But the main body consisted of new recruits: for instance, E. L. Godkin who came full-panoplied from Great Britain and found a place editing The Nation—a constant, facile, and vigorous exponent of individualism all along the line of activities, except when swindlers in municipal, state, and national governments overstepped the proprieties in their kinds of individual enterprise.

The second class of intellectuals from which came energetic support for the idea of individualism consisted of the academic élite now comprising a large army that increased rapidly with the years, as wealth was poured into the treasuries of colleges, universities, and other institutions of learning. By its position, its occupational commitments, and its methods, this élite bore special relations to the formulation and dissemination of ideas, and hence to American civilization in its widest reaches.

As the academic élite approached its full strength in numbers, it represented a larger proportion of the population set aside for scholastic pursuits than had been the case in the Western world since the dissolution of monasteries and convents and the shattering of clerical control over the higher learning. This élite in the United States was presumed to be wholly dedicated to a life of study, teaching, and writing. Its members were preponderantly urban, not agrarian, in modes of living and thinking, and enrolled in the salaried class. They were organized in collegiate bodies and faculties and, according to special studies, into professional associations or gilds, displaying the usual monopolistic propensities of gilds.

The new American élite trained not only apprentices for its own gilds but also men and women by the millions for all other professions and vocations and for leadership in shaping the thought and purposes of the nation. In time the whole educational system down to rural schools came under such directive power as the academic élite could exercise by indoctrination. As the years passed a growing proportion of the men and women active in law, medicine, business, politics, journalism, and public affairs generally, received intellectual discipline and trend of mind from this new, organized, and wide-reaching class of intellectuals. Furthermore, from the chambers of the academic élite came an ever-swelling volume of systematic treatises and monographs on human affairs for the instruction, guidance, and service of the public, especially through the mediation of college graduates in every branch of activity, national, state and local, urban and rural.

In response to the demands of the new universities which were rising throughout the land, and following their own inclinations also, members of the academic élite undertook a more and more minute specialization of inquiry and instruction. Before long, the simplicity and unity of the classical program were corroded and learning crumbled into innumerable fragments. In the humanities, workers in every special "field" of knowledge concentrated on single aspects of civilization, as actuality, often as microscopic as avidity could make them, to the general if not complete neglect of relationships. Thus the intellectual, ethical, and moral unity inherent in the idea of civilization by etymology and long usage was also torn apart; and in the efforts to make separate "systems" of history, politics, economics, anthropology, and other humanistic subjects, the dynamics of the idea of civilization, as a rule, was forgotten.

To this transformation in thought, the presuppositions of the new academic élite contributed powerfully and persistently. Without inquiring how far, if at all, the procedures of the physical sciences were really applicable to studying and generalizing about human affairs, its members usually claimed to be "scientific," that is, "objective," concerned with what is or is alleged to be, not with what ought to be. In method, they professed to be "inductive." Those who specialized in the humanities assumed that they could collect facts about human beings and that from the facts would emerge laws or conclusions, even as to public policies, which would be as valid as chemical formulas and equally free from personal bias. And in their efforts at systematization and generalization they created abstractions: such as economic man, political man, military man, or social man; and they usually treated woman as abstractly as man, if they remembered her existence in society at all. Owing to the nature of their operations, ethics and esthetics practically disappeared from humanistic inquiries and thought or were made branches of abstract studies or were pushed over into departments of speculative philosophy and the fine arts.

By the application of the objective or judicial method to matters in which they could be truly objective, such as the verification of documents, members of the academic élite rendered immense services to the advancement of knowledge about civilization as well as barbarism. But in the selection and organization of their authenticated facts for the purpose of writing and teaching, they were in reality influenced by current assumptions respecting the nature and development of mankind. Their predilections were visible in or between the lines of the essays, chapters, and books which they prepared for the instruction of pupils and the public. And for a long time a popular presupposition among academic writers on human affairs was the idea of individualism, so antithetical in theory and so antagonistic in practice to the idea of civilization.

By members of the two classes—the lay and the academic—the connection between individualism and civilization, as ideas and as facts, was treated in various modes. Some writers stood fast upon the fact of possession and practice, and sought no higher sanction than the description of possessions and practices. Many accepted and defended the unabashed materialism often read into the idea of individualism, especially as it was now fortified by reference to the whole course of nature as interpreted in the name of Charles Darwin and Herbert Spencer; for them nothing approaching a moral justification for individualism seemed necessary.

But some consciences felt the need of an appeal to a tribunal above that of material advantage for approbation of their desires, especially as dissent and criticism poured in upon them. A few, such as J. Laurence Laughlin and John Bates Clark, sought it in an interpretation of Christianity, by correlating their economic principles with Christian teachings. Others in the independent élite and in various branches of the higher learning pleaded the case of individualism at the bar of civilization, in briefs and arguments seemingly as diverse as ingenuity could make them. They even began to identify individualism with civilization.

Before many years had elapsed the formulas put in circulation by the pleaders, insofar as they were at all systematic, clustered around three principal types, with variations and modifications: (1) individualism is the motive force in civilization; (2) civilization is the goal of individualism; (3) individualism is the chief and distinguishing characteristic of American civilization, or indeed substantially if not completely identical with it. No single writer or orator treated the problem in just this order, but in any compilation of their contentions these elements appear. Shifts and turns were made as opposition developed, but these features were fairly constant.

Outside the circle of formal expositors, whose definite and systematic conceptions of civilization are susceptible of classification, were other members of the general and academic élite who used the word civilization lavishly but indiscriminately. Although the latter commentators adhered to the doctrine of individualism as theory or practice, or both, their usage of the word civilization was promiscuous.

Whether employed systematically or carelessly, the idea of individualism was hostile to the social principle in the idea of civilization and it worked as a disintegrating force in many directions—in thought and action, in education and in practical affairs. Its tendency was anarchic despite insistence upon "law and order."

At Yale University, William Graham Sumner elaborated the idea of individualism, as the mainspring in civilization, with particular reference to economics and sociology. The offspring of British parents who had migrated from Lancashire, the home of Manchesterism, of laissez faire, Sumner had been trained for the priesthood in the Protestant Episcopal Church and had been active as a preacher before he was called to his chair at New Haven in 1872. During his studies for the clerical profession, he had acquired an interest in economics and political questions. Indeed in his youth he had been charmed by Harriet Martineau's little synopsis of individualism in her tractate on political economy, and, having taken on the new creed, he applied it with vigor to the problems of the age.

Although he substituted secular dogma for theological dogma and allowed no Christian ethics to interfere with the development and application of his new creed, Sumner did not openly renounce the Christian religion. "I never consciously gave up a religious belief," he said. "It was as if I had put my beliefs into a drawer, and when I opened it there was nothing there at all." With religion out of his way, he did not feel compelled, as did such exponents of individualism as John Bates Clark and J. Laurence Laughlin, to make references to Christian ethics in his treatment of economics and civilization.

Having the ground cleared, Sumner developed the major premise which he had so unreservedly accepted. He followed the logic of his individualism to the very end. He was remarkably consistent. When he spoke of laissez faire, or individualism, he meant just that. He repudiated the partial individualism of the Republicans who were demanding government intervention in the form of high tariffs on manufactures and, in the same breath, nonintervention with their operations in the domestic market. With a wrath more than Jovian, Sumner proscribed that other form of government intervention, imperialism, coupled by Republicans with the protective tariff as a means of enrichment through the conquest of foreign markets.

From start to finish Sumner stood for individualism all around; for no government intervention whatsoever in domestic economy or in foreign commerce. He clung fast to universal free trade. He thoroughly believed in competition and had contempt for American manufacturers who could not take it. The imperialist turn of the war with Spain he execrated in an ironic article entitled "The Conquest of the United States by Spain"—Spain the country that had pursued government intervention in the form of war and monopoly to her own ruin. For self-reliance he had a wholesome respect; for the tyranny of the State he had a wholesome fear; the demagogy, cant, and trickery of politics he heartily disliked. No one in his time defended with more courage and consistency freedom of thought and inquiry.

While Sumner did not feel the need of support from Christian ethics in his advocacy of individualism, he was not content to abide by the facts which the word individualism covered. On the contrary, all the values which he deemed fundamental in the individualistic system he ascribed to, or associated with, civilization, as if that idea gave to his expositions of the creed a higher sanction than the mere facts of individualism. It is true that, like most of his contemporaries, he displayed no precise knowledge of the word civilization, and nowhere indicated fully just what he meant when he used it. Nor was he, though a master logician in dealing with individualism, at all logical in using the idea of civilization. At one point, for example, he represented civilization as built on capital; at another, as offering the emancipation that made capitalism possible; and at a third place, he laid stress upon the interdependence of civilization and capitalism.

Whatever may be said of his logic in this relation, however, there was no doubt about Sumner's repeated recourse to the idea of civilization in his efforts to make individualism invulnerable. As if to say that when one loves civilization one must love capitalism, he declared that "civilization is built on capital; it is all the time using up capital: it cannot be maintained, unless the supply of capital is kept up." Classical civilization rested on human slavery, but "modern civilization is built upon machines and natural agents, brought into play through machines, that is, through capital. Herein lies the true emancipation of man and the true abolition of slavery." Our civilization, he contended, is supported by capital and by modern science.

In another mood, Sumner tried to strengthen his economic doctrine by declaring that civilization was the very fount and source of individualism: "It has been one of the longest and most painful achievements of civilization to open chances for the exertion of individual energy, and to give guarantees that the results of such exertion shall be secure to the one who made it. The progress in that direction within a hundred years has been enormous in proportion to any achievement in the same direction in any earlier period. . . . What men have done, therefore, in the course of civilization is this: they have broken down natural monopolies in the interest of free competitive effort. . . . The reason why an artificial monopoly is so abominable is not only that it interferes to put some men down in order that others may rise at their expense, but that it is a working backward of the state machinery against that whole drift of civilization, which the state machine ought to fall in with and assist by constantly enlarging the fields of individual effort and modifying the play of natural monopolies by intelligent control. . . . Civilization does nothing but open chances. It does nothing to guarantee their advantageous effect. . . . Civilization is in fact one long struggle against the natural monopolies."

In still another mood, Sumner made civilization something else than a source of individualism; he made it a movement toward an end—the end which he deemed good and desirable. That end he visualized as liberty in the possession and use of property, in competition, in security against state interference with the distribution of property "arbitrarily." Centuries of experience confirmed his vista, he said: "The history of modern civilization from the ninth and eleventh centuries . . . down to the present time, reveals the course by which liberty and property have been developed together; but at the same time it reveals that they have grown together only when property has been secure, and the right of property has been strictly maintained, and that nothing has ever been more fatal to liberty than socialistic abuse of property. . . . Liberty is a conquest. It does not lie at the beginning of history and of the struggle of the human race on this earth; it lies at the end of it, and it is one of the richest and finest fruits of civilization. . . . The two great means by which men have won liberty in the course of civilization have been property and knowledge."

Becoming aware apparently that two things could not be the source, cause, or basis of each other, Sumner tried to cut this knot by treating civilization and the type of capitalism he defended as interdependent. There is always, he now argued, the interdependence of wealth and civilization, of civilization and wealth. Property and security of property are essential to civilization, apparently more essential than liberty, for in contests over interference with the distribution of wealth "civilization will win any time at the expense of liberty, if discipline and coercion are necessary to the security of property."

When on one occasion he discussed the nature of civilization, Sumner seemed to regard it as a kind of equilibrium in society brought about by the activities of private interests which public policy could little influence, if at all and, mainly if "not always," to the disadvantage of society. "Organization," he said, "has, of course, been a commanding phenomenon in the development of civilization. . . . In human society, in its lower forms, organization has always produced itself spontaneously and automatically and has, therefore, just suited itself to the case. . . . In civilized society organization is equally spontaneous and automatic. . . . Harmony of action, with the highest possible satisfaction of interests, is the point of equilibrium towards which the organization is always tending. Those men nowadays who can foresee the next steps to be taken to advance on this line are the great generals of the modern industrial army. If the organization is bad, it can waste and impede the effort; if it is good, it can allow the effort to reach its maximum result under the conditions. That is the sum of all that can be said about organization." In what way an organization which springs up spontaneously and automatically may happen to be "bad" or how this spontaneous and automatic organization "produces itself," Sumner did not explain. But he seemed to be sure that organization tending to equilibrium is automatic and spontaneous.

Yet Sumner was equally positive that civilization is artificial —the product of art and effort: "A civilized society exists on an artificial level. . . . The whole environment of a civilized man is artificial. He has cut himself off by his clothes, his house, his fuel, his lights, and so on, from the influence of the natural environment—climate, weather, soil, vegetation—and has made a world for himself on a new plane. . . . Every high civilization is unnatural, inasmuch as it is the product of art and effort. It is, therefore, unstable—ready to fall again to the original level, if the force and intelligence by which it is produced should fail." If organization, spontaneous and automatic, is a commanding feature of civilization and "always tending" toward a point of equilibrium, still it is a product of art and effort, is artificial in character, and through a failure of force and intelligence may fall to "the original level," presumably either to barbarism or primitivism.

Civilization, as artifice and organization, is disciplinary and constraining in nature: "This civilization has cost mankind many inconveniences and it has, in many respects, involved experiences which we do not like. It has subjected us to drill and discipline; the civilized man is disciplined in his feelings, modes of action, the use of his time, his personal relations, and in all his rights and duties. As civilization goes on the necessity grows constantly more imperative that any man who proposes to pass his life in the midst of a civilized society must find a place in its organization and conform to its conditions. At the same time the civilized man, instead of living instinctively, as his ancestors did only a few centuries ago, has become a rationalizing animal." For civilized man there is no liberty "in the sense of unrestrained self-will." In reality "the civilized man is the slave of the industrial organization, of contracts, of the market, of supply and demand—call it what you will, it is, after all, only the weight of existence, and liberty means for us just what it did for the savage; it means that we may maintain existence if we can."

The accusation of reformers that extravagant riches and wretched poverty are the fruits of individualism, Sumner met by making them the necessities of civilization. The very process of civilization, with security for property, results in the great disparity—wealth and poverty: "As we go down in the scale of civilization we find the contrast less and less; as, on the contrary, we go up in civilization, we find the contrast greater. There is every reason to suppose that this distinction will become more and more marked at every stage of advance. . . . It is marvelous to hear the attempts which are made to devise a theory of property as a foundation for the state or for social science. Property gives the theory to all the rest.

The reason why I defend the millions of the millionaire is not that I love the millionaire, but that I love my own wife and children, and that I know no way in which to get the defense of society for my hundreds, except to give my help, as a member of society, to protect his millions."

The greater the wealth possessed by the individual, the greater the liberty: "It may be said, then, that liberty is to be found at the summit of civilization, and that those who have the resources of civilization at their command are the only ones who are free. But the resources of civilization are capital; and so it follows that capitalists are free, or, to avoid ambiguities in the word capitalist, that the rich are free. Popular language, which speaks of the rich as independent, has long carried an affirmation on this point."

Attacks on the disparity of riches and poverty by government action were in effect attacks on civilization, the source and shield of individualism. State intervention with "the economic interests of the people" designed to overcome this disparity was, for Sumner, a reversal of the processes of modern civilization: "If Western Europe and the United States are really to adopt the plan of regulating interests by the management of public functionaries, then they must be prepared to admit that the traditions of civil liberty, and the principles of jurisprudence, which have guided western civilization for a thousand years, are at fault." In short, the course or "drift" of Western civilization has long been toward security for private property, giving individuals a chance to acquire property, guaranteeing them in the possession and enjoyment of it, and breaking down state interference with private interests except to protect life, limb, and property. The state "ought not" to undertake the regulation of these private interests. The state "ought" to aid in enlarging the fields of individual effort. Thus, in Sumner's reasoning, the "drift" of civilization toward freedom for competitive effort seemed precarious and an ethical imperative was introduced to implement the drift—an "ought" for the State.

But in the name of civilization reformers were asserting that society, through the collective agency of government, was morally bound to place at least some floor of social security under the people who suffered from poverty, unemployment, sickness, and other ills. To this demand Sumner referred as the claim "that we ought to see to it that everyone has an existence worthy of a human being." He inquired how the phrase, "an existence worthy of a human being" was to be defined and could discover no definition satisfactory to himself. But if defined, Sumner argued, this idea of minimum security would not be valid unless applied "to the whole human race," and he was opposed to that application. "If I am bound to love my fellow-man," he said, "it is for reasons which apply to Laplanders and Hottentots just as much as to my neighbor across the street." This love must be as wide as all mankind. The theory of minimum security overlooks the fact that millions of people on the globe do not bother their heads about a standard of life, "do not work much and they are quite free from care—very much more so than the average American taxpayer." If made, the effort to provide people with an existence worthy of a human being would merely pauperize them, degrade them, take away the hope of winning such an existence for themselves, and sink them "below any admissible standard of human worth. . . . This noble sentiment is simply a bathos."

That "new social creed," Sumner held, coupled with democracy, was likely to prove perilous to civilization: "We have encouraged ourselves in such demands upon nature or human life that we are ready to declare our civilization a failure because we find that it cannot give us what we have decided that we want." Hence an attempt is made to get "what we want" by resorting to civil organization or the state. The quest is futile, he declared: "No such civil organization has yet been found; we are as far from it as ever. The organization itself has eaten up the substance of mankind. The government of a Roman Emperor, a Czar, a Sultan, or a Napoleon, has been only a raid of hungry sycophants upon the subject mass; the aristocracy of Venice and other city states has been only a plutocratic oligarchy, using the state as a means to selfish ends; democracy has never yet been tried enough to know what it will do, but with Jacobinism, communism, and social democracy lying in wait for it on one side, and plutocracy on the other, its promise is not greater than that of the old forms. It remains to be proved that democracy possesses any stability and that it can guarantee rights."

During a period of thirty-eight years, from 1872 to his death in 1910, Sumner trained thousands of undergraduates at Yale in individualism as if it was an exact science, trying to convince even young Republicans that a protective tariff was no permissible departure from its exactions. He also trained a small army of graduate students who spread over the country as teachers of the science expounded at Yale by the master. By no means all of them—Thorstein Veblen was a notable exception—adopted the system as perfect beyond qualification, but probably not many were as severely critical as this Norwegian farm youth born in Wisconsin. Besides discharging conscientiously his teaching duties, Sumner wrote bulky treatises and popularized his theories far and wide through magazine articles. Few of his academic peers, if any, exerted a more powerful influence, directly and indirectly, on the minds of men especially in high places in education, business, and politics.

A few years after William Graham Sumner began to instruct young students and the public in the creed of individualism, particularly in its economic aspects and in relation to civilization, John William Burgess began expounding his brand of individualism, coalesced with Teutonic imperialism, at Columbia University, but with particular reference to political science. After serving in the Northern army in the sectional war, Burgess had attended Amherst College and completed his formal education in Germany. Called to Columbia, he assumed leadership in forming the Faculty of Political Science, took charge of the training in political science and constitutional law, and soon demonstrated his abilities as a systematic thinker and an impressive teacher. During his long service at Columbia, Burgess helped to educate thousands of young men in the law school and a large body of graduate students who became professors in colleges and universities in all parts of the country. Indeed for many years the overwhelming majority of chairs in political science in leading institutions of higher learning were filled by men who had sat at the feet of Burgess.

Burgess set forth his creed with special force in his *Political Science and Comparative Constitutional Law*, published in 1890. It was particularly in this two-volume work, which exhibited the full range and gravity of his thought on political science, that Burgess laid down his axioms on the proper functions of the state and their relation to civilization. But these he supplemented in detail and with supporting materials in his lectures and in articles written for the academic audience.

Although Burgess did not, as was jestingly said of some German professors, begin his political science with the nebular hypothesis, he started with fundamentals such as geography and peoples. In geographical terms, he said, the ideal state is one whose political boundaries correspond with "natural boundaries" and whose people, homogeneous in race, occupy such a natural geographic unity. With respect to peoples, Burgess declared that each of the great races in history had made its peculiar contributions to civilization and the arts of government. Applying this racial thesis to modern times he promulgated the doctrine that it is the mission of the Teutonic peoples to effect the political civilization of the world.

The Teutonic peoples, Burgess held, were particularly endowed with innate capacity for establishing national states, with a talent for exercising political power justly and moderately, and with ability to effect the "political civilization of the modern world." Having established strong national states at home, combining power with liberty—in economy, laissez faire—the Teutonic nations "must have a colonial policy," and, as "civilized states," undertake the civilization of all backward races. "The civilized states have a claim upon the uncivilized populations, as well as a duty towards them, and that claim is that they shall become civilized; and if they cannot accomplish their own civilization, then they must submit to the powers that can do it for them. . . . The civilized state should, of course, exercise patience and forbearance toward the barbaric populations . . . but it should not be troubled in its conscience about the morality of this policy when it becomes manifestly necessary."

After criticizing the "weak sentimentality abroad in the world concerning this subject," Burgess urged the Teutons to fulfil their mission: "Indifference on the part of Teutonic states to the political civilization of the rest of the world, is, then, not only mistaken policy, but disregard of duty, and mistaken policy because disregard of duty. . . . History and ethnology offer us this elevated ground, and they teach us that the Teutonic nations are the political nations of the modern era; that, in the economy of history, the duty has fallen to them of organizing the world politically; and that if true to their mission, they must follow the line of this duty as one of their chief practical policies." For the fulfilment of this mission, Burgess declared, Germany, Great Britain, and the United States, as Teutonic powers, should unite their forces and move together in a solid phalanx.

When Burgess came to the State as such, he represented it first as a universal abstraction. He proclaimed the "ultimate end . . . the universal human purpose of the state" to be "the perfection of humanity; the civilization of the world; the perfect development of the human reason, and its attainment over individualism; the apotheosis of man. This end is wholly spiritual; and in it mankind, as spirit, triumphs over all fleshly weakness, error, and sin. This is what Hegel meant by his doctrine that morality (*Sittlichkeit*) is the end of the state."

Taking up individual states, four of which he compared in detail—England, France, Germany, and the United States— he defined the immediate purpose of the particular state as "the civilization of the nation." How is it to discharge this obligation? By maintaining law and order within its boundaries, guaranteeing the utmost individual liberty consonant with law and order, abstaining as far as possible from intervention in economic and social activities, and trusting to the individualism so established and guaranteed to carry on the process of civilization. "The primary activity" of the individual state," he said, "must be directed to the creation and perfecting of . . . government and liberty."

To accomplish its immediate purpose, the state must establish and maintain domestic peace. After that comes "the establishment of its system of individual liberty. . . . As the people of the state advance in civilization, the domain of liberty must be widened, and individuals permitted to form private combinations and associations for the accomplishment of purposes which are beyond the powers of the single individual, and which could be otherwise fulfilled only by the power of government." According to this conception, the business of the state is to maintain law and order, uphold individual liberty, charter private corporations or associations for various purposes, aid them, if necessary, in exercising their powers, and hold them to the fulfilment of their public purposes.

The idea that the state itself should promote the general welfare by direct action, as well as maintain order and individual and corporate liberty, Burgess rejected in favor of individualism, despite what he had said about the triumph of reason over individualism in his exposition of the ultimate purpose of the state. It can, for example, he said, do vastly more for education, under certain social conditions, than if it should interfere directly in this domain. By guaranteeing individual and corporate liberty the state indirectly promotes civilization: "the higher the people of the state rise in civilization, the more will the state expand the domain of private rights, and through them accomplish the more spiritual as well as the more material ends of civilization; until, at last, law and liberty will be seen to be harmonious, both in principle and in practice."

In his treatment of private rights under the Constitution of the United States, Burgess dealt with the whole domain of civil liberty, including freedom of press, freedom of speech, freedom of religious worship, and all the historic rights associated with due process of law in civil and criminal matters. But his prime emphasis, especially in his classroom, was upon the rights of property guaranteed to persons and corporations under the fifth and fourteenth amendments of the Constitution. Into the latter amendment he read Herbert Spencer's *Social Statics,* the whole gospel of laissez faire; that is, he read into it categorical prohibitions on the power of state legislatures to enact social or regulatory legislation interfering with individual and corporate property, save in minor respects relative to the police power—public health and safety in a restricted sense.

When all the moralizings, partly borrowed from German philosophers, in which Burgess clothed his appeals to civilization, were put aside and the practical upshot alone considered, his system lay bare in its stark simplicity. Burgess stood for Teutonic imperialism in foreign affairs and extreme individualism in domestic affairs. Imperialism and individualism were to fulfil the law prescribed by Providence, nature, and history—the civilization of nations and the world.

If his thousands of students forgot his dissertations on civilization, they could perhaps remember that government interference with the individualism of private persons and corporations was defiance of God, nature, history, and the Constitution of the United States. So instructed, students of jurisprudence had an ideological equipment for making money in the practice of law; for persuading courts to invalidate what Burgess was constantly calling "socialistic" interference with "private rights"—workmen's compensation, for example.

But Burgess, minimizing the pecuniary aspects of the legal business, looked upon lawyers as offering in the United States the best civilian élite for leadership in the great work of governing and civilizing prescribed in his treatise on political science. The American people, he said, are conscious that "law must rest upon justice and reason," that the Constitution is a more ultimate formulation of justice and reason than are mere legislative acts, and that the judiciary is a better interpreter of these fundamental principles than the legislature. "This consciousness has been awakened and developed by the fact that the political education of the people has been directed by the jurists rather than by the warriors or the priests; and it is the reflex influence of this education that upholds and sustains, in the United States, the aristocracy of the robe. I do not hesitate to call the governmental system of the United States the aristocracy of the robe; and I do not hesitate to pronounce this the truest aristocracy for the purposes of government that the world has yet produced."

Knowing of course that Europe was governed by privileged orders, Burgess realized that the United States was different in this respect, and he proposed to foster in the American Republic an aristocracy of the robe: "I believe that the secret of the peculiarities and the excellencies of the political system of the United States, when compared with those systems founded and developed by priests, warriors, and landlords, is the predominant influence therein of the jurists and the lawyers."

Yet there were hazards in government by lawyers, he admitted. "There is reason to fear that the law is coming to be regarded by the mass of lawyers too much as an industry; and if this be true of them, it will surely follow that it will be so regarded by the mass of the people. It rests with the lawyers and the teachers of law to determine for themselves whether they will divest themselves of their great spiritual power over the consciousness of the people." Loss of this spiritual power will be an inevitable result "if the lawyers separate law from history and jurisprudence, and jurisprudence from ethics."

If lawyers should make their profession an industry, divorce law from ethics and jurisprudence, and lose their spiritual power over the people, the aristocracy of the robe could no longer act as a brake on majorities in the protection of minorities. Then "the courts will be unable to stand between the Constitution and the legislature." In that case, the legislature, in which party passions and personal irresponsibility prevail under universal suffrage, "will have at its mercy those individual rights which we term civil liberty."

Beyond this will lie Caesarism: "The student of political history knows only too well that the despotism of the legislature is more to be dreaded than that of the executive, and that the escape from the former is generally accomplished by the creation of the latter." If compelled to choose between the two forms of despotism, Burgess thus made it clear he would take the despotism of the executive. Since he limited the functions of the state in domestic affairs to the maintenance of order and the protection of private rights and intrusted heavy responsibilities for civilization to individuals and corporations, it followed that, if the aristocracy of the robe should collapse and Caesarism come, the hope of civilization in America, if civilization was not to perish, would be transferred to Caesar. Or to present the case the other way around: since civilization depends on the preservation of its mainspring in the rights of individuals and corporations, it follows that, if such a collapse should occur, for the protection of individualism reliance must be placed on Caesar.

As academicians went into the business of writing history for Americans in what they called the objective, or "scientific," manner copied from the bureaucratic historians of Germany, they incessantly claimed that their thinking and writing were free from the dominance of any general ideas unless it was perchance the idea of "the truth." In selecting historical facts and arranging their statements of facts in sentences, paragraphs, and chapters, they contended that they were relating history as it had actually been; that they were telling the actual truth of it according to the law of "sound" historical writing prescribed by Leopold von Ranke. But their devotion to "the absorbing and relentless pursuit of the objective fact," as one of them stated their aim, did not prevent their using, more or less freely, such words as individualism and civilization—actually preconceived categories through which, to use Hegel's phrase, "impartial historians" see their phenomena. Nor did it prevent their paying tribute to individualism as theory or practice or both, or allowing the idea of individualism to enter into the determination of the kinds of facts to be selected, arranged, and called "history."

Addiction to the use of general ideas and the actual accept-ance of individualism as a controlling value were illustrated in the works of the two most powerful figures in the historical élite. One of them was Woodrow Wilson who afterward be-came President of the United States. The other was Frederick J. Turner whose interpretation of American history possessed for a long time an almost unquestioned empire over profes-sional thought about American history. And both were trained in the historical school of alleged "objectivity" at the Johns Hopkins University.

Woodrow Wilson delighted in writing articles and deliver-ing addresses on a wide variety of topics and in fact employed general ideas in a fashion sometimes more generous than precise. In a five-volume *History of the American People* he interpreted American history to the people in a manner which he deemed appropriate and useful. And in this and other memorials of his time prior to his entrance into politics, he let it be known where he stood in the struggle to make indi-vidualism the dominant note in American theory and practice, although he did not set himself down as an "individualist."

Early in his intellectual life, Wilson accepted the essential elements in the doctrine of economic individualism. While yet a young man at the Johns Hopkins University, he made a special study of the subject under the direction of Richard T. Ely and found it congenial to his spirit. There he also showed, Ely said in his memoir, an "evident displeasure" with a lecture on the labor movement, in which Ely discussed the theme sympathetically if judicially. Fundamentally Wilson was out of harmony with Ely's system of economic thought, which did not conform to the dogma of unqualified individualism then generally prevailing in the academic world. In his own statement of the dogma as applied to politics, made in 1906, he magnified "individual liberty as the object of all law."

To his faith in individualism as practice Wilson clung fer-vently until he entered public life as a candidate for office. In a speech delivered in 1907, he laid the panic of that year upon "the aggressive attitude of legislation toward the rail-roads" and declared that government regulation of railroads would "merely mean taking the power away from the people and putting it into the hands of political discontent." Later in that year he assailed federal regulation of corporations as based on a theory "compounded of confused thinking and im-possible principles of law." About the same time he attacked a proposal to require publicity for the accounts and operations of corporations and ridiculed as socialistic "the rough and ready reasoning of the reformers" who supported it. Turning brusquely on William Jennings Bryan, exponent of "populistic" and "socialistic" doctrines, Wilson called him "foolish and dangerous in his theoretical beliefs," expressed the hope that Bryan might be "knocked into a cocked hat," and refused to sit on a platform with him.

With reference to organized labor, Wilson's individualism was likewise undisguised. In a public letter, issued in January, 1909 he announced: "I am a fierce partizan of the Open Shop and of everything that makes for individual liberty and I should like to contribute anything that might be possible for me to contribute to the clarification of thinking and formation of right purposes in matters of this kind." Lest this notice to the public be insufficient, Wilson renewed the arraignment of trade unions as restraining individual liberty, in an address delivered at Princeton on June 13, 1909.

The following year, when he became a candidate for governor of New Jersey, Wilson began to modify his intransigent individualism; his friends said, as a result of experience, and his critics, as a matter of political expediency. But until that sudden change, Wilson's fidelity to the doctrine had been zealous; and even during his campaign for the presidency, as his speeches afterwards assembled in a volume called *The New Freedom* reveal, the creed of individualism supplied the substructure of his political arguments.

The stock of ideas with which Wilson worked while he was professor and president of Princeton University also embraced the idea of civilization. The word flowed easily, if not copiously, from his pen, and he employed it with increasing frequency after he became President of the United States. But a minute analysis of his published writings discloses no consistency or precision in his usage of the term. As professor and university president he treated it so indiscriminately and rhetorically that it is difficult to grasp his meaning.

Writing on "the Character of Democracy in the United States," for the Atlantic Monthly in 1889, Wilson spoke of civilization in America as "our English civilization" and, in the same article, of "the new civilization of our day," without saying whether he deemed them synonymous or not. Vital changes, he said, were taking place in this new civilization. "The restless forces of European democratic thought and anarchic turbulence" brought to the United States by "alarming masses" of immigrants, combined with printing, steam, and electricity, he declared, "are apt to tell disastrously upon our Saxon habit of government." By the context, it seems, Wilson regarded the disturbing forces as outside, not in, civilization in the United States.

A second illustration of the way in which Wilson treated the idea of civilization is afforded by another article in the Atlantic Monthly, published eight years later, under the heading "The Making of the Nation." After remarking upon the diversity of economic interests in the United States, he wrote: "The country has been transformed within a generation, not by any creations in a new kind, but by stupendous changes in degree. . . . The 'East' is transformed by the vast accumulations of wealth made since the civil war,—transformed from a simple to a complex civilization, more like the Old World than like the New. The 'West' has so magnified its characteristics by sheer growth, every economic interest which its life represents has become so gigantic in its proportions, that it seems to Eastern men, and to its own people also, more than ever a region apart. It is true that the 'West' is not, as a matter of fact, a region at all, but, in Professor Turner's admirable phrase, a stage of development, nowhere set apart and isolated, but spread abroad through all the far interior of the continent. But it is now a stage of development with a difference, as Professor Turner has shown, which makes it practically a new thing in our history."

Once the West was a frontier region, with free lands accessible to settlers. "Now it lies without outlet. The free lands are gone. New communities must make their life sufficient without this easy escape—must study economy, find their fortunes in what lies at hand, intensify effort, increase capital, build up a future out of details." Yet the process of unification is at work. "Many differences will pass away of themselves. 'East' and 'West' will come together by a slow approach, as capital accumulates where now it is only borrowed, as industrial development makes its way westward in a new variety, as life gets its final elaboration and details throughout all the great spaces of the continent, until all the scattered parts of the nation are drawn into real community of interest."

At no point in this survey and discussion did Wilson specify what realities of human relations and experience his word civilization was to cover. But he seemed to imply that, by the accumulation of wealth, the civilization of the East was becoming complex, more like the civilization of the Old World than the New, and that by the accumulation of wealth, along with its accessories, the West would become like the East. If this is a correct interpretation of his thought, he meant that American civilization, in economic terms at least, was capitalistic and growing more like the civilization of the Old World in complexity.

Whatever the meaning to be extracted from such usages, Wilson certainly indicated, at one point in the fifth volume of his *History of the American People*, that he construed American history as including the process of civilization, if not identical with it. When in the preparation of his text he reached the period of the war with Spain and the imperialistic surge which followed it, he wrote as if he thought that the work of American civilization on this continent had been going on through the years and had reached a state of completion, at least in some respects.

About 1898, according to Wilson's treatment of the subject, American history in its continental course had come to a close and the nation had attained a new epoch in its "progress." "It had turned from the developing of its own resources to make conquest of the markets of the world. The great East was the market all the world coveted now, the market for which statesmen as well as merchants must plan and play their game of competition, the market to which diplomacy, and if need be, power must make an open way."

Americans had thus arrived at a parting of the ways. "The spaces of their own continent were occupied and reduced to the uses of civilization; they had no frontiers wherewith 'to satisfy the feet of the young men'; these new frontiers in the Indies and in the Far Pacific came to them as if out of the very necessity of the new career set before them." Apparently, there had been an American civilization on this continent, but now the spaces of the continent had all been subjugated to its uses; and statesmen, merchants, diplomacy, if need be war, "must make an open way" for advance elsewhere—in the Far East.

Yet Wilson's account of the period from the close of the civil war to the end of the nineteenth century did not in fact deal with the reduction of the spaces of the American continent to "the uses of civilization." This volume of his *History* was divided into three chapters covering the period from the death of Lincoln to the age of McKinley. The chapter titles, certainly drafted by his thought, divulged his conception of the history of the American people during the period: Reconstruction, Return to Normal Conditions, The End of the Century. The facts given under those headings were principally political facts—the presidents and the politicians, their policies and actions, legislative and administrative. Thinly dispersed through the chapters, it is true, were occasional references to other affairs—growth of corporations, activities of organized labor, the Centennial Celebration of 1876, and various casual matters outside the domain of politics strictly conceived.

A detailed analysis of this volume purporting to cover the history of the American people during the period shows the author totally indifferent to most of the important matters that might be called phases of civilization, to the uses of which the people were reducing the continent. This analysis also shows that on nearly all the controversial economic and political issues of the period Wilson took the position which had been and was still taken by men who adhered to the idea of individualism as the perfect good. Indeed the whole volume, even in turns of phraseology, is a document in the history of that idea applied to the selection and organization of historical facts. As such it was a contribution to the advancement of individualism as theory and practice in the United States. Yet he had called his treatise *History* and not an interpretation of history.

The only work by a professional historian during the period which was accepted as, if not avowed by its author to be, an interpretation of American history was that of Frederick Jackson Turner, and it revolved around an admixture of civilization and individualism. Born in Wisconsin, on or near the frontier, educated in the State University, later especially trained for writing history at the Johns Hopkins University, Turner combined intimate knowledge of the young middle west with academic discipline. And in the pursuit of his scholarly vocation, he shifted the emphasis in American historiography from the seaboard to the continent as a whole and sought a clue to the distinctive features of history in the United States as a whole.

His supreme generalization Turner presented in an address delivered in Chicago in 1893, entitled "The Frontier in American History." Within a few years his generalization became the most influential single interpretation of American history. Hundreds of disciples, inspired by Turner, diffused it in every section of the continent; and in time Turner was called to Harvard, under the presidency of Charles W. Eliot.

What had Turner said at Chicago? He had declared that the frontier and free land accounted for the characteristics that differentiated the evolution of society in the United States from the evolution of society in the Old World: "The existence of an area of free land, its continuous recession, and the advance of American settlement westward, explain American development." The statement, in its unqualified simplicity, was categorical and sweeping. Apparently Turner believed that if it had not been for the advancing frontier, for the free land on the frontier, if the English colonists had been hemmed in on the Atlantic seaboard, American development would have followed European patterns. If this was his belief, then American civilization, without the advancing frontier, would have duplicated the European process of civilization, at least in its main stream. Indeed Turner in effect said as much: "Limiting our attention to the Atlantic coast, we have the familiar phenomenon of . . . the progress from primitive industrial society, without division of labor, up to manufacturing civilization."

This, however, had not been the main course of American history: "American development has exhibited not merely advance along a single line, but a return to primitive conditions on a continually advancing frontier line, and a new development for that area. American social development has been continually beginning over again on the frontier. This perennial rebirth, this fluidity of American life, this expansion westward with its new opportunities, its continuous touch with the simplicity of primitive society, furnish the forces dominating American character. . . . The frontier is the line of most rapid and effective Americanization. The wilderness masters the colonist. It finds him a European in dress, industries, tools, modes of travel, and thought. It takes him from the railroad car and puts him in the birch canoe. It strips off the garments of civilization and arrays him in the hunting shirt and the moccasin. . . . The advance of the frontier has meant a steady movement away from the influence of Europe, a steady growth of independence on American lines. And to study this advance, the men who grew up under these conditions, and the political, economic, and social results of it, is to study the really American part of our history."

Turner thus conceived American history, including the European part and the American part, in terms of civilization —vaguely it is true, but seriously, as if the idea had profound significance for him. The word appears in various statements contained in the address on the frontier such as the following. In the westward advance, "the frontier is the outer edge of the wave—the meeting point between savagery and civilization. . . . Stand at Cumberland Gap and watch the procession of civilization, marching single file—the buffalo following the trail to the salt springs, the Indian, the fur-trader and hunter, the pioneer farmer—and the frontier has passed by." Through the traders "the disintegrating forces of civilization entered the wilderness." Daniel Boone, advancing into Missouri, "helped to open the way for civilization." In spite of the conflict of interests between the trader and the farmer, "the Indian trade pioneered the way for civilization. The buffalo trail became the Indian trail, and this became the trader's 'trace.' . . . Thus civilization in America has followed the arteries made by geology, pouring an ever richer tide through them, until at last the slender paths of aboriginal intercourse have been broadened and interwoven into the complex mazes of modern commercial lines: the wilderness has been interpenetrated by lines of civilization growing ever more numerous."

However Turner may have defined the idea of civilization for himself, the development of society in the United States, in his mind, was somehow connected with civilization. And a striking if not the primary characteristic of American civilization was, in his view, "individualism" with all its rough and rugged frontier features, including democracy and nationalism: "The most important effect of the frontier has been in the promotion of democracy here and in Europe. As has been indicated, the frontier is productive of individualism. Complex society is precipitated by the wilderness into a kind of primitive organization based on the family. The tendency is anti-social. It produces antipathy to control, and particularly to any direct control. . . . The democracy born of free land, strong in selfishness and individualism, intolerant of administrative experience and education, and pressing individual liberty beyond its proper bounds, has its dangers as well as its benefits. Individualism in America has allowed a laxity in regard to governmental affairs which has rendered possible the spoils system and all the manifest evils that follow from the lack of a highly developed civic spirit. In this connection may be noted also the influence of frontier conditions in permitting lax business honor, inflated paper currency, and wild-cat banking."

Although Turner did not invent the phrase "rugged individualism," he did in effect describe it and identify it with the frontier spirit: "From the conditions of frontier life came intellectual traits of profound importance. . . . To the frontier the American intellect owes its striking characteristics. That coarseness and strength combined with acuteness and inquisitiveness; that practical, inventive turn of mind, quick to find expedients; that masterful grasp of material things, lacking in the artistic but powerful to affect great ends; that restless, nervous energy; that dominant individualism, working for good and for evil, and withal that buoyancy and exuberance which comes with freedom—these are the traits of the frontier, or traits called out elsewhere because of the existence of the frontier. . . . Each frontier did indeed furnish a new field of opportunity, a gate of escape from the bondage of the past; and freshness, and confidence, and scorn of older society, impatience of its restraints and its ideas, and indifference to its lessons, have accompanied the frontier."

By emphasizing individualism, Turner set many historians to thinking that individualism had been the driving force in American civilization. Wittingly or not he fortified the teachings of Sumner in economics and sociology and of Burgess in political science. Accepting the Turner thesis as valid, without critically examining its assumptions or its correspondence to all the relevant facts in the case, hundreds of scholars began to apply it with meticulous care to various sections of the frontier on its westward advance. Portly volumes, documented essays, and learned papers read before professional associations bore witness for many years to its ascendancy as a leading, if not an exclusive, interpretation of American history.

To the disciples of Sumner and Burgess who were indoctrinating their students and the public with the philosophy of individualism, in economics, sociology, and political science, were now added Turner's disciples who were disseminating individualism as a primary force in American history. While Sumner's doctrines were immediately scrutinized by critical contemporaries, including economists, sociologists, and publicists, Turner's assertions long escaped an exacting appraisal. Nearly thirty years passed before scholars began to subject them to severe analysis and compare his dicta with realities of American history. Turner's theory of individualism and civilization either possessed a greater survival power or American historians were less alert than economists.

Another exposition of individualism, qualified in this instance by a reform proposal, was put forward by Henry George. Unlike Sumner, George held no comfortable academic chair; unlike Woodrow Wilson, he had no training in university lore. His native talents were not whetted or dulled by adventures in the higher learning. He was brought up in the school of hard work beyond the campus, saw poverty at first hand, experienced its pangs directly. His incentive to thinking was the search for a solution of the problem which many before him had raised—the contradiction between civilization and misery.

The solution of the problem which George proposed was given to the world in his *Progress and Poverty*, published in 1879, and, in a fuller setting in *The Science of Political Economy*, issued in 1898, after his death. His solution took for granted the principal assumptions and maxims upon which economic individualism rested—such as private property, private enterprise, freedom of contract, and competition—but subject to one large qualification relative to ground-rent.

Like all individualists, George was hostile to socialism, and he was lukewarm if not unfriendly toward trade unions. He believed that wealth and capital, other than land, flowed from individual enterprise and labor; that competition was a necessary spur to economic activity on the part of capital and labor; that all which the individual created belonged to him, in fact would go to him, if the ground-rent paid to landlords was diverted to the uses of society and land thrown open to competitive enterprise. Ground-rent, he maintained, is a product of society in action, not of individual enterprise and labor by landlords. It is therefore, "unearned." If taken from landlords by taxation and dedicated to the support of government, other forms of property and business can be relieved, at least largely, of taxation. At the same time individual capitalists and laborers, by this reform in taxation, will be given free access to land and resources, production will be augmented, and poverty will be abolished. It was mainly in respect of this type of taxation that George's system of pure economics differed from classical individualism. It implied an intensification of the competitive struggle for existence.

Both the problem and the solution proposed in his *Progress and Poverty*, George placed, however, within the framework of civilization. "This association of poverty with progress," he declared, "is the great enigma of our times. It is the central fact from which spring industrial, social, and political difficulties that perplex the world, and with which statesmanship and philanthropy and education grapple in vain. From it come the clouds that overhang the future of the most progressive and self-reliant nations. It is the riddle which the Sphinx of Fate puts to our civilization, and which not to answer is to be destroyed." Land "represents a value created by the whole community," by civilization, and the appropriation of this enormous income by landlords deprives the community of its own wealth and accounts for the distressing poverty that obstructs advance in civilization.

In that section of his *Progress and Poverty* entitled "The Law of Human Progress," George emphasized the social nature of civilization. "Beyond perhaps the veriest rudiments it becomes possible for man to improve only as he lives with his fellows. All these improvements, therefore, we summarize in the term civilization. . . . This is the great fact with which we are concerned: That the differences between the people of communities in different places and at different times, which we call differences of civilization, are not, . . . as Herbert Spencer holds, differences in the units; but that they are differences resulting from the conditions under which these units are brought into the society." Among these varying conditions, George placed divergences in knowledge, beliefs, customs, language, tastes, institutions, and laws. Here he was seeking to demonstrate the strength and ramifications of the social principle, even though he made a gesture toward the fiction that there might have been a man who had brought himself into the world and made some improvements wholly apart from "his fellows."

What is the secret of progress—advancement of civilization? That question George undertook to answer concisely: "Mind is the instrument by which man advances. . . . Mental power is the motor of progress. . . . Association in equality is its force." While the words "mind" and "mental power," standing alone, could be taken as if they referred to something inhering in individual "units," considered in the context of George's whole volume they could only refer to instruments or forces limited by and working in or with the social accumulations at their command—knowledge, beliefs, customs, language, tastes, institutions, laws, and material possessions. At no point in dealing with civilization did he lend countenance to the dogma of "the self-made man" which was in the creed of individualism.

High authority for his conclusion on the simple point of taxing land values, George drew from what he apprehended as the law of civilization and decay: "The truth to which we were led in the politico-economic branch of our inquiry is . . . clearly apparent . . . in the growth and decay of civilizations, and it accords with those deep-seated recognitions of relation and sequence that we denominate moral perceptions. Thus are given to our conclusions the greatest certitude and highest sanction. This truth involves both a menace and a promise. It shows that the evils arising from the unjust and unequal distribution of wealth, which are becoming more and more apparent as modern civilization goes on, are not incidents of progress, but tendencies which must bring progress to a halt; that they will not cure themselves, but, on the contrary, must, unless their cause is removed, grow greater and greater, until they sweep us back into barbarism by the road which every previous civilization has trod."

But, introducing the optimistic note, George went on to assert that if the proper remedy is applied, "the dangers that now threaten must disappear, the forces that now menace will turn to agencies of elevation. Think of the powers now wasted; of the infinite fields of knowledge yet to be explored; of the possibilities of which the wondrous inventions of this century have given us but a hint. With want destroyed; with greed changed to noble passions; with the fraternity that is born of equality taking the place of the jealousy and fear that now array men against each other; with mental power loosed by conditions that give to the humblest comfort and leisure;

and who shall measure the heights to which our civilization may soar? . . . It is the culmination of Christianity—the City of God on earth."

Of all the American economists since the early days of the Republic none, not even Henry C. Carey, treated as comprehensively the interfiliation of economy and civilization as George did in his *Science of Political Economy*. None dwelt more steadfastly and trenchantly on the contradiction between civilization and misery or sought a resolution of the dilemma with a more single-minded devotion. Adverse to the abstractness of classical economists, he did not assume that he could "isolate the economic factors" from the contexture of civilization and derive from them, so isolated in thought, a list of irrefragable axioms, as if they were so isolated in actuality. Instead, he thought of "economic factors" as aspects of civilization.

But he did more. He considered the nature of the modern mind which did the thinking about economics and he repulsed the notion that it was an unconditioned power, independent of the things about which it thought: "The observations and reflections of many succeeding men, garnered and systematized, enable us of the modern civilization to know, and with the eyes of the mind almost to see, things to which the senses untaught by reason are blind." Even the mind that thinks about economics or anything else is caught up with the sifting and accumulation of knowledge that enter into civilization.

Recognizing the fact that economic activities and institutions occur of necessity in civilization, George grasped the twin fact that economics has no meaning outside civilization; and in many pages he explored the idea of civilization—its nature, its origin, and its development—besides recurring repeatedly to civilization in special relations. At the outset he took note that "the word civilization was in common use" and complained that "it is used with vague and varying meanings, which refer to the qualities or results that we attribute to the thing, rather than to the thing itself, the existence or possibility of which we thus assume. Sometimes our expressed or implied test of civilization is in the methods of industry and control of natural forces. Sometimes it is in the extent and diffusion of knowledge. Sometimes in the kindliness of manners and justice and benignity of laws and institutions. Sometimes it may be suspected that we use the word as do the Chinese when they class as barbarians all humanity outside of the 'Central Flowery Kingdom.' And there is point in the satire which tells how men who had lost their way in the wilderness, exclaimed at length when they reached a prison: 'Thank God, we are at last in civilization.' "

Buckle had written two volumes on the history of civilization, "but does not venture to say what civilization is." Guizot had written on civilization, declared its existence and its importance, but had not defined the term. In this confusion, having decided that the idea was vital to his thinking about "the nature of political economy," George attempted a definition himself of the popular but apparently elusive term.

The problem thus posed George attacked directly by way of etymology: "The word civilization comes from the Latin *civis*, a citizen. Its original meaning is, the manner or condition in which men live together as citizens. Now the relations of the citizen to other citizens, which are in their conception peaceable and friendly, involving mutual obligations, mutual rights, and mutual services, spring from the relation of each citizen to the whole of which each is an integral part. That whole, from membership in which proceeds the relationship of citizens to each other, is the body politic, or political community, which we name the state."

But true to the natural-rights world-view of the eighteenth century, already expressed in the writings of Thomas Paine, George held that the relation "suggested in this word civilization" is "deeper, wider, and closer than the relation of the citizen to the state, and prior to it. . . . Civilization is the antecedent and the state the subsequent. The appearance and development of the body politic . . . is the mark of civilization already in existence. Not in itself civilization, it involves and presupposes civilization. . . . The character of the state, the nature of the laws and institutions which it enacts and enforces, indicate the character of the underlying civilization."

In George's theory, civilization not only underlies all states but it is wider than the mere jurisdictions of states and so cuts across those political boundaries: "Whether we consider them in their grand divisions or their minor divisions, the line between what we call civilizations is not the line of separation between bodies politic. The United States and Canada, or the United States and Great Britain, are separate bodies politic, yet their civilization is the same. The making of the Queen of Great Britain Empress of India does not substitute the English civilization for the Indian civilization in Bengal, nor the

Indian civilization for the English civilization in Yorkshire or Kent. Change in allegiance involves changes in citizenship, but in itself involves no change in the civilization. Civilization is evidently a relation which underlies the relations of the body politic."

If George made a slip in logic or history when he defined civilization as the civic relationships of a body politic or political community and immediately declared civilization to be prior to and independent of bodies politic or political communities, there was certitude in his statement that civilization is essentially social in nature and man more than an individual: "He is also a social animal, formed and adapted to live and cooperate with his fellows. It is in this line of social development that the great increase of man's knowledge and powers takes place. . . . The rise of civilization is the growth of this cooperation and the increase of the body of knowledge thus obtained and garnered."

But having treated civilization in this broad sense, George suddenly narrowed it: "It is this body economic, or body industrial, which grows up in the cooperation of men to supply their wants and satisfy their desires, that is the real thing constituting what we call civilization. . . . The body politic or state is really an outgrowth of the body economic." Still, in this restricted sense, the feature of cooperation was an essential item in George's idea of civilization.

Even after he had declared the body economic or industrial to be the real thing constituting civilization, George recurred to his broader view. As if returning to Guizot's distinction between the exterior and the interior aspects of civilization, George wrote: "We measure civilization in various ways, for it has various aspects or sides; various lines along which the general advance implied in the word shows itself—as in knowledge, in power, in wealth, in justice and kindliness. . . . The aspect of civilization most quickly apprehended in common thought is that of a keener sense of justice and a kindlier feeling between man and man. . . . While an increased regard for the rights of others and an increased sympathy with others is not all there is in civilization, it is an expression of its moral side. And as the moral relates to the spiritual, this aspect of civilization is the highest, and does indeed furnish the truest sign of general advance."

Despite his treatment of civilization at one place as if it

were static—the body politic, economic, or industrial in which cooperation occurs—at other points in his discussion of the subject, George made it changeful, dynamic. Man, he contended, is not only a social and cooperative animal; he is "the only progressive animal. Here is the germ of civilization." But he did not think an elaboration of this theme necessary to his *Science of Political Economy.* "To consider the history of civilization, with its slow beginnings, its long periods of quiescence, its sudden flashes forward, its breaks and retrogressions, would carry me further than I can here attempt. Something of that the reader may find in the last grand division of 'Progress and Poverty,' Book X entitled, 'The Law of Human Progress.'" Thus, resembling the classical school of economists in general, George left out of his reckoning the question whether his *Science of Political Economy* might become invalidated by civilization conceived as progress. And, having explored and adopted the idea of civilization, he endorsed the chief features of economic individualism except unearned increment in land.

Even so, and despite his acceptance of individualism and competition, subject to this form of taxation, George antagonized the school of "pure individualism" by placing economic activities firmly in the contexture of civilization—by making economics a phase of civilization. In fact he drove a big wedge into the closed system of economic thought as individualism, whether supported or not by the prestige of an alliance with civilization. He precipitated a terrific debate over the capitalist system of economy. By declaring that the landlord's ground-rent was a product of civilization, in society, and that it should be expropriated for public purposes, he hurled into the forum of discussion the vexing issue as to whether other forms of wealth were not in significant respects the products of civilization and society, also properly subject to expropriation in the public interest.

In his political economy, George separated civilization from the jurisdiction of particular states, or bodies politic, and made it anterior to the state. But in practice he called upon each independent state to abolish poverty, to promote civilization by measures of taxation applicable only within its jurisdiction. While the "laws" of economics applied everywhere, civilization in the United States could be advanced by action taken within the American nation, he believed. So George and his disciples launched a nation-wide agitation to force upon American governments—municipal, state, and federal—the policy of seizing ground-rent by taxation.

In other words, Henry George did more than file an academic dissent from an academic theory. He denied to one intrinsic element of the fully rounded theory relative to capitalist individualism the benefit of a high sanction—civilization. He declared that one great source of private accumulation—ground-rent totaling billions a year in the United States—was a product of civilization in American society and belonged of right to the community. And he helped to restore the social principle to thought about economics from which it had been ousted by extremists of the individualist school, even though he himself espoused for practical purposes nearly all the fundamental principles of individualism.

Not only that. George assailed a main bastion of the capitalist system, not merely by writing a book, but by conducting a campaign of agitation that carried the issue of civilization and individualism into the popular forum where reformers of many kinds were debating all phases of American civilization. If to a few capitalists, notably Tom L. Johnson, George appeared to be an ally, to most of them he was subversive of everything that sustained their system. If to various schools of reform, George's attachment to leading principles of individualism was anathema, his agitation brought grist to their mill. As a consequence, in proposing to qualify unadulterated capitalism, under the formula of civilization, Henry George tightened in many quarters the grip which the idea of civilization had on American minds at the same time that he gave a powerful impetus to the thrust of individualism against civilization.

In spirit the idea of individualism was optimistic whether in its straight and simple type or as qualified by the plan of the single-tax reform proposed by Henry George, and the disruptive force of its thrust into the idea of civilization was the greater on that account. This is not to say that all individualists were confident about the future of their system. They were not. Sumner, like an ancient Hebrew prophet, finding his precepts ignored by dissenters and scouted by reformers, declared that the years ahead would be full of wars and revolutions. His own scheme of individualism, pure and true-blue, which he regarded as rigorously framed and founded on facts, would be disputed, Sumner admitted; indeed was being disputed, by Americans who knew not, or would not abide by, the true faith. As a rule, however, the lay and the academic élite assumed that individualism was good, would endure indefinitely, if not forever, and would march from victory to victory, without running into disastrous storms or into an effective counter-reformation. Optimistic prophecy succeeded optimistic prophecy.

But in many circles prophecies of what individualism would do in advancing civilization were clouded by doubts—which often deepened into pessimism respecting the future of civilization itself. The crudities of individualism in practice shocked hypersensitive dilettantes, intellectually and morally incompetent to grapple with problems in the spirit of their revolutionary ancestors; and they fled in numbers from the scene to Europe, when they had the money, or up the narrow path of complaint at home. The inefficacy of individualism in realizing its promises turned other Americans, with more fortitude but unable to discover a renewed assurance for American civilization, into pessimistic channels.

Letters and essays of the time were poignant with laments about "the low order" of American civilization and its tendencies. After laboring long and zealously in spreading the doctrine of individualism throughout the country, E. L. Godkin, in a way the high priest of the creed, gave up American civilization and exclaimed: "I am not sanguine about the future of democracy. I think we shall have a long period of decline . . . and then a recrudescence under some other form of society. . . . I do not know what the future of our modern civilization is to be. But I stumble where I firmly trod. . . . Things look very black. I think that while money-making will long continue on a great scale, the government will shortly undergo great changes which will be presided over not by men of light and learning, but by capitalists and adroit politicians. . . . I came here fifty years ago with high and fond ideals about America. . . . They are now all shattered, and I apparently have to look elsewhere to keep even moderate hopes about the human race alive."

It remained, however, for Henry Adams and his brother Brooks to cast a black pall of pessimism over the American scene and to historicize their pessimism; that is, to give it what they regarded as an efficient justification in a theory of history buttressed by a selection and ordering of facts. To this gloomy business they came only gradually after they had watched for years the testing of individualism by its fruits.

When Henry Adams published his anonymous novel, *Democracy*, in 1881, he still cherished, despite misgivings, a strong belief in a high destiny for America. In his faith Adams was far more hopeful than his intimate friend, John Hay, who about the same time was writing his anonymous novel, *The Bread-Winners*. Commenting on the theme of Hay's novel, his son, Clarence Leonard Hay, long afterwards said that it was "a defense of the right of an individual to hold property, and a plea for a better protection of that property by law and order. Civilization rests upon law, order and obedience." Fundamentally a spiritual brother of Mark Hanna, John Hay, while demanding law, order, and obedience as the basis of civilization, was agitated by apprehensions concerning the prospects of his own class and faith.

On the other hand, Henry Adams, in his *Democracy*, clung to an optimistic outlook upon the American scene, if, as may be inferred, one of his characters in that novel, Representative Gore, disclosed the author's underlying trust when he said at one place in the story: "I believe in democracy. I accept it. I will faithfully serve and defend it. I believe in it because it appears to me the inevitable consequence of what has gone before it. Democracy asserts the fact that the masses are now raised to a higher intelligence than formerly. All our civilization aims at this mark. We want to do what we can to help it. I myself want to see the result. I grant it is an experiment, but it is the only direction society can take that is worth its taking; the only conception of its duty large enough to satisfy its instincts; the only result that is worth an effort or a risk. Every other step is backward, and I do not want to repeat the past. . . . Let us be true to our time. . . . If our age is to be beaten, let us die in the ranks. If it is to be victorious, let us be first to lead the column. Anyway, let us not be skulkers and grumblers."

But so dark was the pessimism in the circle to which Henry Adams, speaking through Representative Gore, belonged that he scarcely dared to utter such a sentiment publicly. And an esthete who listened to Gore's private affirmation languidly replied to him: "I want to go to Egypt; democracy has shaken my nerves to pieces. Oh, what rest it would be to live in the Great Pyramid and look out forever at the polar star!"

While Henry Adams was still in the mood expressed in his *Democracy*, he wrote a letter to Henry Cabot Lodge on the subject of historical composition, in which he declared that without a definite faith of some kind Lodge would be the victim of other men's thinking. "Unless you can find," he said, "some basis of faith in general principles, some theory of the progress of civilization which is outside and above all temporary questions of policy, you must infallibly think and act under the control of the man or men whose thought, in the times you deal with, coincides most nearly with your prejudices."

Not long afterward, Henry and Brooks Adams, depressed by the course of events, turned intently to studying the "forces" of history, searching for the law or laws governing the rise and tendencies of civilization, the causes responsible for the disasters which had overtaken civilizations in ages past. For many years Henry carried on this search, trying one hypothesis after another; and as a member of the American Historical Association he besought his colleagues to concentrate their abilities on this supreme problem in historical thought.

Henry's equipment for making such inquiries was exceptional as things went among the historical profession. As his father's secretary at the legation in London during the civil war he had gained first-hand experience with great public affairs. Of his own genius for historical work there was no doubt. He demonstrated them as a professor at Harvard and as author of a many-volume *History of the United States*. Possessor of an inherited fortune, he was able to withdraw from the drudgery of teaching, enjoy complete freedom from the strictures of academic endowments and management, and give all his intellectual energies to his quest for the meaning or sense of history.

The first fruits of his historical speculation, Henry laid before the American Historical Association in 1894 in the form of a letter designed to serve as his presidential address. In this communication he told his colleagues that the study of history was serious business and that crises in thought and society lay ahead of them. "Hitherto," he said "our profession has been encouraged, or, at all events, tolerated by governments and society as an amusing or instructive and, at any rate, a safe and harmless branch of inquiry. But what will be the attitude of government or of society toward any conceivable science of history?" Yet the possibility of a science of history, owing to the rate of progress during the previous fifty years, seemed in sight. What shape will it take?

Four probabilities Adams enumerated. If established on lines of its recent development, it would "take its tone from the pessimism of Paris, Berlin, London, and St. Petersburg, unless it brought into sight some new and hitherto unsuspected path for civilization to pursue. If it pointed to a socialistic triumph it would place us in an attitude of hostility toward existing institutions." Would the universities and society tolerate that? A science of history might announce that "the present evils of the world—its huge armaments, its vast accumulations of capital, its advancing materialism, and declining arts" would continue. "Society would shut its eyes and ears." Or this science of history might forecast a reversion to the church, absolute faith in a personal providence and a revealed religion. That would be suicide for science.

Against any such forecasts, Adams declared, one or more prodigious interests would be arrayed: the Church, the State, Property, and Labor. Caught in this maze, Adams was unable to find what he called "some new and hitherto unsuspected path for civilization to pursue" to which he could give his wholehearted allegiance. "Perhaps the crisis will never occur," he said, "and even if it does occur, we shall probably be dead." Yet it might occur, he thought, and "at any time in the next fifty years," that is, between 1894 and 1944, historians might be compelled to answer whether the world moves and in what direction and to make their answers "under the pressure of the most powerful organizations the world has ever known for the suppression of influences hostile to its safety." Perhaps historians should say nothing about it: "Beyond a doubt, silence is best."

Even so Henry Adams did not keep his silence. He borrowed a theory from physics, "the rule of phase," and applied it to history, in a paper finished in 1909. The next year he addressed another letter to the historians in which he applied the theory of the degradation of energy to the possible course of history. But when he got down to practice and faced the deduction of policy from his historical inquiries, he could find no encouragement. Speaking in his *Education* of his Darwinian days, he said: "By rights, he [Henry Adams] should have been also a Marxist, but some narrow trait of the New

England nature seemed to blight socialism, and he tried in vain to make himself a convert."

Indeed the simplifications of Marxism could not be squared with innumerable facts of history commanded by so great a scholar as Henry Adams. To his mind the American version of Marxism represented by a farmer-labor government triumphant in politics seemed preposterous: "Nothing could surpass the nonsensity of trying to run so complex and so concentrated a machine by Southern and Western farmers in grotesque alliance with city day-laborers, as had been tried in 1800 and 1828, and had failed even under simple conditions."

In Henry Adams' interpretation of American history the age of competitive individualism had closed; the age of corporations and trusts, of concentrating capitalism, had arrived, including "the trades-unions and socialistic paternalism which necessarily made their complement." But, under the wider views of universal history dealt with in his essays on that subject, a crisis in thought and economy lay beyond this stage in American development, and Henry could discover no "new and hitherto unsuspected path for civilization to pursue" in America or any other part of the world.

While Henry Adams was becoming pessimistic about the future of civilization in the United States, he was reaching equally gloomy conclusions respecting the academic élite, its methods, its theorizing, and its intellectual performances. Interested in a book which his brother Brooks was writing on civilization, Henry planned to prepare an introduction to it, on the ground that without some memorandum from a historian the volume would not be properly received by the gild. "For," Henry said to Brooks, "without something of the sort, one of two things will happen to you. Either you will be altogether ignored by the old expedient of the 'conspiracy of silence,' or you will be attacked with fury. . . . The teaching profession is, like the church and the bankers, a vested interest. And historians will fall on anyone who threatens their stock in trade quite as virulently as do the bankers on the silver men." It was in fact to prepare the way for the public reception of Brooks' work on civilization, that Henry wrote his address to the American Historical Association in 1894.

Leaving the law for which he had been trained, as Henry had left the academic profession, Brooks Adams also searched for the Ariadne thread to the labyrinth of history, specifically for the law governing the course of civilization. In his studies of American history, he was especially, and not unnaturally, drawn to the character and policies of his grandfather, John Quincy Adams, whom he regarded as the spiritual heir of George Washington; as a noble old Roman who had demanded the dedication of the nation's rich natural resources to the advancement of civilization, who had battled at the last bridge, in vain, against the horde of Jacksonian democrats bent on plundering the public domain from the Alleghenies to the Pacific Ocean. For the Republicans, who after 1865 completed the orgy of plundering, Brooks Adams had equal disrespect.

In 1895 Brooks Adams issued in London his interpretation of Western history under the merciless title *The Law of Civilization and Decay*, a work frankly pessimistic, which anticipated in many ways Oswald Spengler's cyclical theory of history as leading inexorably to the death of civilization. This blast against optimism Brooks Adams supplemented in 1913 by his *Theory of Social Revolutions*, in which, by dwelling on the incapacity of capitalists to govern, he again shook the walls of complacent individualism in theory and practice.

Although the first of these two volumes dealt ostensibly with Europe it had a definite meaning for civilization in the United States: it threw overboard the theory of history by which the idea of optimistic individualism as the primary force in social evolution had been sustained. According to Brooks Adams' interpretation of history, in its actual development the American society to which this conception of individualism had been applied was passing away; centralizing practice under the very theory of individualism was undermining the economic scheme of things which the theory purported to characterize and uphold. Meanwhile the preoccupation with money-making, the growing attention to banking, speculation, usurious tricks, and high financing, during the age which followed the civil war, Adams believed, signified the decay of the virtues that had been primarily responsible for the advance of the nation, especially in the early days of the Republic.

While Brooks Adams could not tolerate the optimism of his contemporaries and prophesied the decay of the system they defended or took for granted, like his brother he could discover no "new and hitherto unsuspected path for civilization to pursue." But unlike his brother, Brooks Adams definitely made up his mind and adopted a particular hypothesis of history which denied the optimism of both civilization and individualism: namely, the cyclical theory—cast in a special form.

It could not be said, however, that Brooks Adams' treatise on civilization was altogether devoid of confusion, although its pessimism was clearcut. His definition of civilization was very abstract. He declared that society oscillates "between barbarism and civilization, or, what amounts to the same thing, . . . movement from a condition of physical dispersion to one of concentration." Nevertheless within the scope of civilization he included all the arts, sciences, and intellectual phases.

In the earlier stages of social development, ran his hypothesis, "the imagination is vivid, and the mental types produced are religious, military, artistic." In those stages the ideal statesman is the warrior who can lead his followers in battle. But, in time, a race reaches "the limit of its martial energy," and must enter upon "the phase of economic competition." Then martial energy declines under the pressure of economic competition; the moneyed man, supplanting the martial man, assumes the power of government; the military man becomes a mere paid official; money lenders form an aristocracy; and "the whole administration of society" falls "into the hands of the economic man."

As consolidation, that is, civilization, proceeds, the arts become sterile. "No poetry can bloom in the arid modern soil, the drama has died, and the patrons of art are no longer even conscious of shame at profaning the most sacred of ideals. The ecstatic dream, which some twelfth-century monk cut into the stones of a sanctuary hallowed by the presence of his God, is reproduced to bedizen a warehouse; or the plan of an abbey, which Saint Hugh may have consecrated, is adapted to a railway station. Decade by decade, for some four hundred years, these phenomena have grown more sharply marked in Europe, and, as consolidation apparently nears its climax, art seems to presage approaching disintegration."

While, in this civilizing process, the martial man, the knight, the saint, and the imaginative artist drop in the scale of authority and talents, woman also sinks in physical and moral energy. In the age of the warrior and the landed aristocrat, women were powerful beings as the lovers of soldiers and the mothers of soldiers. Now, in the age of centralization and pecuniary values, women decay along with their weakling companions obsessed by the pursuit of riches—economic men; women revel in ostentatious display or throw themselves away in worthless competition for place and prestige in capitalistic society—a business for which they have no real qualifications. Once the creators and conservators of life, "the cement of society," women now plunge downward into triviality and sterility and are transformed from constructive into destructive forces in society. Thus men and women, once strong together, degenerate together.

At length under "the law" governing its course, civilization comes to a dead end in disintegration or a reversion to a primitive form. "In this last stage of consolidation, the economic, and, perhaps, the scientific intellect is propagated, while the imagination fades, and the emotional, the martial, and the artistic types of manhood decay. When a social velocity has been attained at which the waste of energetic material is so great that the martial and imaginative stocks fail to reproduce themselves, intensifying competition appears to generate two extreme economic types—the usurer in his most formidable aspect [the finance banker], and the peasant whose nervous system is best adapted to thrive on scanty nutriment. At length a point must be reached when pressure can go no further, and then, perhaps, one of two results may follow: A stationary period may supervene, which may last until ended by war, by exhaustion, or by both combined, as seems to have been the case with the Eastern Empire; or, as in the Western, disintegration may set in, and a reversion may take place to a primitive form of organism." That tragic conclusion, Brooks Adams reiterated in effect, in the Introduction to his *The Degradation of Democratic Dogma*, published in 1919.

Doubtless Henry Adams spoke for the two brothers in an undated letter written apparently about 1895, while the conflict over free silver and gold was at white heat in American politics: "The gold-bugs have resumed their sway, with their nerves a good deal shaken, but their tempers or their sense unimproved. Cleveland and Olney have relapsed into their hog-like attitudes of indifference, and Congress is disorganized, stupid, and childlike as ever. . . . Were we on the edge of a new and last great centralization, or of a first great movement of disintegration? There are facts on both sides; but my conclusion rather is—and this is what satiates my instinct for life—that our so-called civilization has shown its movement, even at the centre, arrested. It has failed to concentrate further. Its next effort may succeed, but it is more likely to be one of disintegration, with Russia for the eccentric on one side and America on the other."

Reduced to elemental terms, the theories of history evolved by the Adams brothers cut in two main directions. They slashed into the optimism that had carried along the happy advocates of individualism as the primary guarantee of civilization. At the same time they announced the bankruptcy of reformers by excluding the possibility of arresting the decay of society and also the possibility of advancing civilization through the adoption of any constructive measures that the wits of human beings could devise. In short their pessimism was almost perfect.

Chapter 8

Counter-Reformation and Asseveration

ASSERTIONS OF INDIVIDUALISM AND PESSIMISM, powerful as they were in form and influence, failed to win undisputed sovereignty over the American spirit. Like the doctrine of slavery as a perfect good, the doctrine of individualism as a perfect good enjoyed its full day in the court of public opinion. It bore the stamp of austere learning and the signatures of high academic authorities. Yet it could not overcome and destroy the idea of civilization as imperatively embodying the social principle.

The continuing contest over world-views was more than a dispute in abstractions and logistics. The course of thought was affected by the course of external events. In the name of individualism, it had been confidently prophesied that the avid pursuit of self-interest by everyone would result, as Adam Smith averred, in the general good, under "the Invisible Hand." But beginning in 1873 one devastating panic after another belied, in the misery, poverty, and unrest attending them, the smooth prediction of endless felicity.

Under the creed of individualism it had also been proclaimed that, if society would confine government to keeping law and order, after turning its natural resources over to private exploitation and protecting industries against foreign competition, individuals would develop the country to the fulness of its potentials while each enjoyed the coveted "independence." In cold fact, corporations, not individuals, built the network of railways, communications, and gigantic industries which created the Great Society of the United States, turned free business men into corporate agents, transformed free industrial workers into attendants on an economic machine, which they could not hope to own as private property, and diminished, instead of enlarging, the independence of the individual operator in the national economy.

According to the theory of individualism the competition of human beings was the natural law of life. In cold fact, great leaders in business enterprise flouted it themselves by forming trusts and combinations in the major industries to restrain its ravages. At the same time industrial workers, instead of being content with a war of each against all, established trade unions on a national scale to mitigate if not stop the war.

Nor did the intellectual bearers of individualism all follow the logic of the creed or in practice effect its realization. "The aristocracy of the robe," to which Burgess looked for leadership in national affairs and for the defense of private rights against popular legislatures and popular unrest, did not proceed exactly as contemplated in the individualist prospectus.

The most powerful members of that aristocracy became retainers of corporations, not of natural persons. They made heroic attempts, successful for a time, to endow corporations with all "the rights of man," of natural persons. In this line of patient endeavor they developed two shining legal devices to break all forms of undesired interference with "free" enterprise: the idea of using the courts to destroy "populist" legislation by appropriate invalidations under specialized interpretations of the Constitution; and the idea of restraining the activities of organized labor through judicial writs of injunction. But, despite their momentary triumphs, with the aid of carefully selected judges, their efforts ended in diminishing, not enhancing, the power and prestige enjoyed by the aristocracy of the robe and the courts of law. Even the *ultima ratio* of that aristocracy—the use of armed forces in disputes of labor and capital—did not bring about supine acquiescence on the part of industrial workers.

At the same time, events also declared futile the concurrent efforts made in the name of individualism to break up trusts, corporations, and combinations into units of human individuals engaged in a biological, tropistic competition, or indeed into petty companies relentlessly at war with one another. Such efforts were immense, continuous, and dogged, but their historical course was marked by an endless chain of failures. For every device which populists could invent, corporate ingenuity was more than equal and from decade to decade the integration of corporate enterprise kept up its march into the unity of national economy.

In the meantime the foreign policy of the Government of the United States, whether conducted by Republicans or Democrats, led to ever-mounting expenditures for martial preparations and to wars—all of which made more and more imperative the creation of gigantic corporate industries, their ever-closer integration into one economic machine, and the adoption of a "war socialism," one and indivisible, sickling individualism over with the pale cast of death.

While in the movement of events the validity of individualism as truth, as an operating philosophy for the American people, met rebuff after rebuff, the idea of civilization was asseverated and applied to the new contests of thought and action arising in the development of the Great Society. Exponents of civilization, who had been temporarily absorbed in the sectional conflict and the abolition of chattel slavery, now put the idea to use in the new conditions of American economy. For example, the ink was scarcely dry on the Thirteenth Amendment abolishing slavery when Elizabeth Cady Stanton united with her renewed demand for the enfranchisement of women a plea for the emancipation of all labor from poverty, ignorance, and disease, and began a long campaign of lectures and speeches across the continent reaffirming the social principle. Definitely allying himself with the labor movement, Wendell Phillips dedicated his talents to the same cause. To such aging leaders were added recruits from the new generations in all sections of the continent.

By the old exponents and the new recruits the idea of civilization was pressed into the discussion of current events and unfolding opportunities. In the correct tradition of the idea, as their forerunners had done they often based it on the theory of great history to which the development of the United States belonged; and they often emphasized, in relation to the changing scenes and possibilities, the social principle, buttressed by a systematic formulation of Christian ethics into a social gospel.

Support for the idea of civilization as embracing the social principle now came also from a new source—from an important body of new learning—anthropology. What had largely been speculation when the idea of civilization was new, when John Quincy Adams discussed this world-view, was now placed on grounds of authentic fact. The study of social origins and evolution in all aspects, from language and tribal mores to industry, arts, and law, discovered social relationships, mutual aid, cooperation, running counter, in time and space, to the formula of individualism as an iron law of nature and life.

The assurance of abstract reasoning in economics, moreover, was subverted by direct observations of contemporary industry, labor, enterprise, and finance. With the multiplication of discoveries and inventions came a realization that the potentials of mass production had outmoded the conceptions of economy based on primitive methods; that, as far at least as physical limitations were concerned, involuntary poverty, servitude to privileged orders, degrading drudgery, and everything associated with the tyranny of an animal-like existence could be mastered and all the American people enter into the work and benefits of civilization.

Representations of the wonderful achievements of mankind throughout the world in the sciences, arts, and technologies, and indices of the victories of civilization yet to be won by progress were assembled at the Centennial Exposition held at Philadelphia in 1876 to celebrate one hundred years of American independence. In connection with this memorial came a concentration of thought on the Republic of the United States as destiny, opportunity, and obligation, under the idea of civilization in its full comprehension of the true, the beautiful, the good, and the useful.

This concentration of thought was fostered and facilitated by the newspapers, linked to the scene by continental telegraph lines, which carried descriptions of the exhibits and reports of events and addresses to cities, villages, hamlets, and farms. Books and pamphlets, often illustrated, dealing with the objects on display and the celebration as a whole or with particular interests exhibited or represented there, were published and widely purchased.

On the most momentous day of the Jubilee, July Fourth, leading officials and the most eminent speakers of the nation delivered addresses at Philadelphia, birthplace of the Declaration of Independence, and in other parts of the nation. They memorialized the century by reviewing the nation's history, its function in universal history, its contributions to humane practices, its present situation, its perils, its potentialities, and the public and private responsibilities of American citizenship.

That the orations on this occasion might be of more than momentary attraction, reach large numbers of Americans, and make an enduring impression on national thought, Frederick Saunders of the Astor Library in New York collected and published a number of them under the title *Our National Centennial Jubilee*.

In his Introduction written for this volume, Saunders represented the hundred years of the Republic as a panorama in civilization. America, he said, is "youngest in the great family of nations" but is "found in the foremost rank of our Christian civilization," thus placing it in a larger historic movement. He admitted, as he proceeded, that America could not "boast of the 'antique glories of the classic arts,'" examples of which had been imported for the Exposition. But America, as a nation, he declared, had "shared liberally with others of maturer growth, in the triumph of modern genius and inventive skill." And in one significant respect America may claim an especial distinction: "the honor of having given to the world the well-attested illustration of the feasibility of popular self-government." The Declaration of Independence had "marked a new era of intellectual revolt against old established institutions and modes of thought. It was natural and fitting, therefore, that America should be the theatre where the great problem of popular liberty and self-government should be solved."

It was natural, and not entirely unfitting, that orators of the day should applaud the advances made by the establishment of independence, the development of popular government, the maintenance of the Republic against disruptive forces, and the elimination of chattel slavery.

Through the outstanding speeches of the Centennial celebration rang the note of confidence—supported by reviews of history—that civilization would win more victories in the United States. The progress of civilization, it was affirmed, would guarantee the growth of representative government in the Republic and the victory of the peaceful arts over the martial arts, tenacious though the martial arts had been in history, and so long glorified. The development of popular institutions in this young nation, though springing from European origins, indicated that it was displaying humane characteristics of its own. Threatened by the assaults of greed and the menaces of aggregated, corrupting wealth, civilization, it was asserted, would overcome those evils and hazards through the preponderance of social and public principles over selfish and private propensities. Thus was repudiated the pessimism of critics, domestic and foreign, who had declared that the Republic of the United States would not survive the Civil War and who were now saying that it would succumb to a plutocracy. While speeches during this Jubilee recognized plutocratic tendencies, they called upon the people to keep watch and ward against them.

Speaking at Indianapolis, B. K. Elliott allied the American institution of self-government to the idea of civilization as a progressive philosophy. "As long as civilization shall advance," he declared, "so long shall a representative government grow in strength and usefulness. . . . The dangers lessen as enlightenment and wisdom prevail. The tendency of civilization is onward. . . . Never since the historic period was civilization so great or knowledge so general as now. . . . We have just reason for high hope. The superstitions which enthralled are fast falling, the bigotry and intolerance which enchained are growing weaker, and the ignorance which darkened and crushed free thought has been conquered."

As if remembering the very etymology of the word civilization, after referring to the downfall of other republics in past history, Elliott declared that the supremacy of the civil arts was a prime guarantee of the American Republic: "The times are vastly changed; men are greatly different. The useful arts engage the attention of men. Great talents are devoted to the sciences. The early republics existed in ages when war was esteemed the noblest and almost the only honorable profession, when warlike exploits only secured power and fame. All this has changed, peaceful pursuits confer high honors, labor is honorable, and the arts and sciences crown with high honor those who have succeeded in them."

It was not representative government in a purely political sense, as something created suddenly by a paper constitution, that was set down to America's credit on the day of the centennial celebration by every speaker. What had been accomplished in this respect represented an advance in a long process of civilization extending through the ages. "The progress of mankind in the ascending path of civilization, enlightenment, and moral and intellectual culture," declared William M. Evarts at Philadelphia, had prepared the people for self-government. Casting aside the simple doctrine of the natural-rights schools to the effect that the privileged orders of Europe had cruelly intervened in a golden age of mankind and prevented its continuation, Evarts assigned them a creative function in the evolution of society, thus upholding a theory of social continuity and development in Europe.

But, Evarts went on, "this Northern Continent of America had been opened and prepared for the transplantation of the full-grown manhood of the highest civilization of the Old World to a place where it could be free from mixture or collision with competing or hostile elements, and separated from the weakness and the burdens which it would leave behind." In the fulness of time, in these circumstances, the people of the United States were made ready in character and wisdom for exercising the sovereign powers of self-government.

Nor did Evarts stop there in his review of social evolution. He did not halt with representative government as the end of creative effort and civilization. The rights which it upheld for individuals were in his opinion not the mere privileges of individuals to be exploited solely for their own interests. His view respecting the objects of government was larger in its civil, political, and social appreciations of human powers, for it included "the happiness, the expansion, the security, the elevation of society, and the redemption of man." In other words, the work of civilization in the United States was to go forward under the unifying and exacting force of the social principle.

Critic of all authoritarianism exercised by privileged orders, Robert G. Ingersoll, speaking at Peoria, Illinois, made the emancipation of mankind from caste rule and slavery the supreme achievement of civilization. "The history of civilization," Ingersoll declared, "is the history of the slow and painful enfranchisement of the human race. In the olden times the family was a monarchy, the father being the monarch. The mother and children were the veriest slaves. The will of the father was the supreme law. He had the power of life and death. It took thousands of years to civilize this father, thousands of years to make the condition of wife and mother and child even tolerable. A few families constituted a tribe; the tribe had a chief; the chief was a tyrant; a few tribes formed a nation; the nation was governed by a king, who was also a tyrant. A strong nation robbed, plundered, and took captive the weaker ones. This was the commencement of human slavery. . . .

"As soon as our ancestors began to get free, they began to enslave others. With an inconsistency that defies explanation, they practised upon others the same outrages that had been perpetrated upon them. As soon as white slavery began to be abolished, black slavery commenced. . . . Fortunes were quickly realized; the avarice and cupidity of Europe were excited; all ideas of justice were discarded; pity fled from the human breast; a few good, brave men recited the horrors of the trade; avarice was deaf; religion refused to hear; the trade went on; the governments of Europe upheld it in the name of commerce—in the name of civilization and of religion. . . .

"Our fathers knew the history of caste. They knew that in the despotisms of the old world it was a disgrace to be useful. They knew that a mechanic was esteemed as hardly the equal of a hound, and far below a blooded horse. They knew that a nobleman held a son of labor in contempt—that he had no rights the royal loafers were bound to respect. The world has changed." It must change more. "We are getting more real solid sense."

Near by, in St. Louis, the Reverend R. A. Holland took democracy—a constituent of our civilization—as his theme on this occasion and asserted that the values inherent in it had been the loftiest values of the centuries. But he did this in no narrow spirit of patriotism. Holland made a clear distinction between the patriotism of the herd and the patriotism of humanity. "There are two kinds of patriotism," he declared, "one of instinct, the other of reason. Patriotism of instinct is attachment to a spot of ground, familiar scenes, inherited customs, a geographical name. It is the love of the fox for his hole, the fowl for her nest. In war [it is] a sort of magic, mobilizing men into instant armies reckless of death; in peace it encourages abuses and invites usurpations by defending every evil that may be done in the sacred name of country. 'My country, right or wrong,' is its confession of faith, and for fetish it worships a flag. Not in this spirit have we assembled to-day to celebrate the hundredth anniversary of our republic, but rather in the spirit of that more rational patriotism which loving truth, right, humanity first, loves country only in so far as these supreme ideas are or may be organized and administered in its policy. For governments are not an end to themselves, but means for achieving an end which is higher, broader, and more enduring. . . .

"When only the few had knowledge and wealth, it was well that the few should govern; but knowledge has now become common, and wealth diffuse. There are no longer in our civilization lord and vassal separated by an impassable gulf. The gulf has been closed by a middle class nobler in intelligence and richer in estate than baronage. The rabble, as it was once called, has by co-operation, risen likewise in consciousness of power and stands before wealth and rank, with bare arms that on provocation might toss them both out of its way. One would have to bind one's eyes with fold on fold of prejudice not to see that the tendency of these changes is towards democracy; that, indeed, by peoples who have graduated from a state of pupilage and know their manhood, no other kind of government will be tolerated long unless in evident transition towards democracy. . . .

"Liberty, equality, fraternity. These ere-while abstractions are household words defined by the heart. Liberty—the right of every man to be himself so far as his self-hood does not trench upon the same right in others; equality—the level on which all men stand before the law, none born to rank or rule, each exercising the authority he obeys, sovereign that he may be subject, and subject that he may be sovereign; and fraternity, which is identity of interest, abolition of caste, every man being as jealous of the rights of every other as his own, and the strongest and wisest willing to bear vexation or hardship that the weak and ignorant may qualify themselves for self-government by the use of rights which, even when least understood, foster self-respect, independence and a lively concern in affairs of state, and thus serve for a moral education.

"The question is not whether democracy be the cheapest form of government, or the shrewdest, or the most facile, or the stoutest against inner or outer foes—in all which qualities superiority may be conceded to despotism; but whether in spite of extravagance, blunders, caprice, it is not the best for man as man, worth its excess of cost in money and toil and sense of danger. . . .

"Nor is it mere . . . spread-eagle rapture to anticipate a democracy as vast as civilization. Be it for good or evil, the peoples will not rest until they have tried the experiment and tried it more than once. The might is theirs and they will exert it; theirs is the right and it will justify the utmost exertion to throw off the yoke of titled accidents; and if progress be the law of humanity, as it is of all things else, might and right must grow with time into graces of unity, peace and concord. Otherwise humanity is a predestined failure, and the ethics of its hope a lie.

"For what else is democracy in the purest notion of it but the religion of politics? It means faith in man and in his destiny; it means that there is more of good than of evil in his nature, and that in the conflict between them the good shall triumph at last; it means the supremacy of conscience over force, and of reason over prejudice and passion; it means that men shall love their neighbors as themselves, and so adopts the golden rule for a civil constitution and charters the brotherhood of the race.

"This, I say, is the ideal of society. Perhaps not to be attained for ages, it will yet be steadily approached by the advance of civilization."

If the overtone of the celebration was praise of past performances, the deficiencies of American society were also specifically recognized, obstacles in the way of progress were discussed, and the horizon of the future was scanned. The smooth and easy optimism of the automatic advance through individualism was definitely decried.

Paying tribute to the representatives of other nations who had shared in the anniversary ceremonies, W. M. Evarts declared that "in sight of the collective evidences of the greatness of their own civilization with which they grace our celebration, we may well confess how much we fall short, how much we have to make up, in the emulative competitions of the times." Americans held their place, he said, "in the great march of humanity." But work remained to be done. "Peace is our duty, peace is our policy. In its arts, its labors, and its victories . . . we find scope for all our energies, rewards for all our ambitions, renown enough for all our love and fame."

But there were more than deficiencies to be cited. There were positive perils to be enumerated and attacked by intellectual and moral energies, as Mercy Warren had warned citizens of the infant Republic. While declaring that "the star of our country's destiny is hope, not memory," General Durbin Ward told his audience at Cincinnati, that, without intellectual vigor and moral force, "wealth and luxury are sources of weakness rather than strength," and that "our unbounded future wealth, and consequent temptations to luxury and dissipation can not but excite the fears of the thoughtful. Shall we live over again the history of old countries?" Will the rich, "as in decaying Rome," enslave the spirit of the people, corrupt their morals by licentious habits, or purchase their suffrage by bribes? "Shall liberty become a form and despotism a fact?" What matters it that fountains and statues adorn the streets, that parks, gardens, and palaces crown the suburbs, that expositions of industry make their displays, that theaters, museums of art, cathedrals, and churches decorate society, if the people are corrupted by power and splendor, if intellectual strength, simplicity of life, and the elemental virtues are subverted by outward signs of material interests and energies?

In drawing this startling picture of a possible future, General Ward must have moved his Cincinnati audience to solemn thought, for it knew that with all his magnetic eloquence he was no mere rhetorician coining polished phrases. It knew that he himself, on many a battlefield in the war for the preservation of the Union, had offered what Lincoln had called at Gettysburg "the last full measure of devotion."

Wherein, then, according to this centennial inventory and appraisal of the nation and its resources, lay the promise of American civilization? In two main forms the answers were cast.

First of all, there was the strength of the national heritage —of the social spirit that had persisted since the establishment of the Republic, notwithstanding the catalogue of violations. Despite blights of selfishness and assaults of private interests, the Republic had been maintained—defended—for a hundred years, through all the terrible trials. This could hardly have been accomplished, Evarts argued, if "public" and "social . . . tendencies and purposes in the whole body of the people," if "the persistent fidelity" of the educated classes and the great men of the country, had not in the long run preponderated over selfish and private tendencies. In this situation both admonition and encouragement were offered to the people.

The second type of answer to the question of the future was the one made by B. K. Elliott at Indianapolis, to which reference has already been made, namely, that the promise lay in the substitution of the useful arts for the destructive arts of war, and in the according of the highest honors to persons who led in the pursuit of peace, not to warriors as of old; to leaders in the creation of wealth, in the arts and sciences, in education and self-government. This transformation had, in a large measure, taken place in the United States. It would be maintained, Elliott believed, in the years ahead.

On the whole the celebration marking the century of independence typified a concentration of thought about civilization in the United States as past history, history in the making, and history to come. From the Jubilee flowed immense stimulation to creative effort.

The orators of the Jubilee passed away but the movement of knowledge and reflective thought continued. Indefatigable researchers and energetic thinkers worked at the discovery of new knowledge which was to furnish materials for new interpretations of fundamental importance for the idea of civilization and its exposition in the century to follow. Dark continents of the mind and experience were explored with greater zeal than ever before in the history of the Republic. The mores and moral manifestations of civilizations, which Condorcet had ignored and Buckle had excluded in their emphasis on the growth of knowledge in civilization, were made the subject of critical analysis and described with fulness of detail and amplitude of historical reach.

Inasmuch as the idea of civilization had been grounded in a theory of history running back to primitive times, it followed that anthropology, one among the many new subjects of inquiry, yielded rich information bearing directly on the nature and forces of civilization. Once data had been taken principally from early writings, the oldest of which belonged, relatively speaking, to the youth rather than the infancy of the human race. Now researchers made direct observations of activities, customs, and ideas among primitive peoples still functioning on primeval lines and peoples functioning on various levels up to the highly complicated societies of the modern age. They studied the remains and artifacts of prehistoric peoples, excavated and collected by archaeologists, the legends of original folkways, and other evidences of social beginnings and social evolution. Out of their long, wide, and patient inquiries, new and authentic knowledge was built up respecting the nature and forms of society in far distant times and in places utterly unknown to recorded history.

These researches helped to broaden thought about history to cover more than politics and wars. They also deepened thought about humanity's long struggle for civilization. They unearthed realities about societies—their sciences and their arts—aeons older than written myths. They tested the theories of biological determinism, the abstractions of economists, and the speculations of closet philosophers by the hard facts discovered in the new inquiries. They restored human beings to society from which they had been wrested under the individualist dogma. They reaffirmed the dynamics of the social principles without which civilization could never have started, continued, developed through the ages, demonstrated efficacy in the contemporary age, or given any certitude to powers even of survival, let alone advancement.

In the establishment of the new knowledge which was to exert a crucial influence on thought about civilization, anthropologists of many nations were leaders. In the list the American, Lewis Henry Morgan, was pre-eminent. The circumstances of his life were propitious for his initiative and participation in this intellectual movement. He was born near Aurora, New York, in 1818, and graduated from Union College in 1840. By the practice of law in Rochester and by advising and investing in a railway company, he acquired the means of independence for the pursuit of his wider interests. They included politics; first as a Whig and later as a Republican, he served several years in the New York legislature. He owned property and thus had direct knowledge of politics and property.

But he was eager to know more about human beings. In his youth he had formed a friendship with Samuel Ely Parker, a pure-blooded Indian, the son of a Seneca chief and an Iroquois who was the daughter of a famous Indian prophet. In the course of time Morgan began a systematic study of Iroquois customs, life, and institutions, defended Indians against avaricious whites, and was adopted into the Hawk clan of the Seneca tribe. Thus admitted to the innermost practices of Indian life, he was able to carry on his inquiries in the most favorable conditions. Later he published technical studies which helped to win for him the title, "Father of American Anthropology."

After recording his experiences with several Indian tribes in America, Morgan studied primitive life in various places by direct observation and by means of records. From his explorations and reflective thought there emerged in 1877, the year following the Centennial celebration, his crowning work, *Ancient Society or Researches in the Line of Human Progress from Savagery, through Barbarism to Civilization*, which was greeted in two worlds as a major contribution to the knowledge and thought of social evolution.

Morgan's *Ancient Society* brought into the theme of universal history the full weight of natural science then disclosing the long record of the physical universe and breaking the tyranny of the Miltonic conception of creation as a single complete act. It gave a new and vast setting for the idea of civilization as a human enterprise. It went beyond Condorcet's brief account of primitive beginnings; beyond Robert Coram's attention to American Indians' customs; beyond John Quincy Adams' recognition of the relation between savagery and civilization; beyond Guizot's hints; beyond Parke Godwin's acknowledgment that modern civilization had its long precursors. Out of his immense personal knowledge and extensive studies Morgan provided a great body of information for those who were concerned with the origins, nature, and course of civilization. Later researches were to modify or correct his statements and views in many respects, but Morgan's leadership in thought about civilization remained indisputable.

Morgan opened his Preface with a comment on the newness and the nature of the new knowledge: "The great antiquity of mankind upon the earth has been conclusively established. It seems singular that the proofs should have been discovered as recently as within the last thirty years, and that the present generation should be the first called upon to recognize so important a fact. . . . The existence of mankind extends backward immeasurably, and loses itself in a vast and profound antiquity. This knowledge changes materially the views which have prevailed respecting the relations of savages to barbarians, and of barbarians to civilized man. . . . The history of the human race is one in source, one in experience, and one in progress. It is both a natural and a proper desire to learn, if possible, how all these ages upon ages of past time have been expended by mankind; how savages, advancing by slow, almost imperceptible, steps, attained the higher condition of barbarians; how barbarians, by similar progressive advancement, finally attained to civilization; and why other tribes and nations have been left behind in the race of progress—some in civilization, some in barbarism, and others in savagery. It is not too much to expect that ultimately these several questions will be answered."

In the course of his studies Morgan came to the conclusion that social evolution had been a continuous and cumulative process. "The principal institutions of mankind originated in savagery, were developed in barbarism, and are maturing in civilization." Inventions and discoveries, registering the growth of human intelligence, likewise stood in serial relations. "The family has passed through successive forms, and created great systems of consanguinity and affinity which have remained to the present time. . . . The idea of property has undergone a similiar growth and development." The third and last stage, civilization, the outcome of accumulated human experience and thought, carried within itself a sifted heritage from the earlier stages, and, according to Morgan, extended from the invention of the phonetic alphabet and the use of writing to the modern time. In short, taking into purview the history of mankind and all major aspects of the civilizing process, Morgan treated stages not as fixed spans of time but as overlapping periods.

The historical evidence upon which the structure of his presentation rested was drawn, in part, from the great sequence of inventions and discoveries stretching along the pathway of human progress; but chiefly from domestic institutions, which express the growth of certain ideas and passions. Inventions and discoveries stand to each other in progressive relations and institutions in unfolding relations. The story has an objective and a subjective side: inventions, discoveries, habits, customs, manners, and other things visible, and accompanying ideas. "The facts indicate the gradual formation and subsequent development of certain ideas, passions, and aspirations. Those which hold the most prominent positions may be generalized as growths of the particular ideas with which they severally stand connected. Apart from inventions and discoveries they are the following: subsistence, government, language, the family, religion, house life and architecture, and property."

Recognizing the dual character of human progress, Morgan arranged the divisions of his work on the principle of idea and external fact. The four great parts dealt with growth of intelligence registered in inventions and discoveries; growth of the idea of government; growth of the idea of the family; and growth of the idea of property. He left out of his treatment of social evolution, save for incidental mention, three great aspects of civilization, namely, the growth of language, the development of religious ideas and institutions, and house architecture. These topics were not excluded because the author deemed them unimportant but, confronting the necessity of limitations, he made his own; and concentrated on inventions and discoveries, government, the family, and property.

To the last of these he ascribed special significance: "Commencing at zero in savagery, the passion for the possession of property, as the representative of accumulated subsistence, has now become dominant over the human mind in civilized races."

In emphasizing property, Morgan may have written as a lawyer for business men and reflected their spirit in part, but his treatment of property differed from that of academic economists who considered civilization in terms of individualism. Their "laws" and axioms took for granted existing forms and distribution of property as then protected by human law, as if such forms and laws partook of the eternal characteristics of physical nature. Morgan, on the other hand, made property a phase of the civilizing process extended over countless centuries, from types of ownership in the early stages of savagery to the complicated types in modern civilization, and sought the connections of property ownership with subsistence, or the struggle for existence. Like Alexander Hamilton, Thomas Jefferson, John Adams, and Daniel Webster, he perceived its intimate bearings on government, society, the process of civilization; and, with its long past in mind, he speculated upon the long future of property and its relations to the democracy professed in the United States.

"Property and office," Morgan declared, "were the foundations upon which aristocracy planted itself. Whether this principle shall live or die has been one of the great problems with which modern society has been engaged through the intervening periods. As a question between equal rights and unequal rights, between equal laws and unequal laws, between the rights of wealth, of rank and of official position, and the power of justice and intelligence, there can be little doubt of the ultimate result. Although several thousand years have passed away without the overthrow of privileged classes, excepting in the United States, their burdensome character upon society has been demonstrated. Since the advent of civilization, the outgrowth of property has been so immense, its forms so diversified, its uses so expanding, and its management so intelligent in the interests of its owners, that it has become, on the part of the people, an unmanageable power. The human mind stands bewildered in the presence of its own creation."

But the forces of civilization seem to be equal to coping

with this problem: "The time will come, nevertheless, when human intelligence will rise to the mastery over property, and define the relations of the state to the property it protects, as well as the obligations and the limits of the rights of its owners. The interests of society are paramount to individual interests, and the two must be brought into just and harmonious relations. A mere property career is not the final destiny of mankind, if progress is to be the law of the future as it has been of the past. The time which has passed away since civilization began is but a fragment of the past duration of man's existence; and but a fragment of the ages yet to come. The dissolution of society bids fair to become the termination of a career of which property is the end and aim; because such a career contains the elements of self-destruction. Democracy in government, brotherhood in society, equality in rights and privileges, and universal education, foreshadow the next higher plane of society to which experience, intelligence, and knowledge are steadily tending. It will be a revival, in a higher form, of the liberty, equality, and fraternity of the ancient gentes."

While giving to civilization a world setting, with an immensity of time-span, and emphasizing its material and institutional phases, Morgan paused on the brink of human beginnings. He did not regard man as a mere animal, governed by tropism—the necessities of nutrition—responding as automatically as an amoeba to stimuli from without. Nor did he look upon man as a creature entirely controlled by abstract ideals, however zealously professed. "Mankind," he declared, "are the only beings who may be said to have gained an absolute control over the production of food; which at the outset they did not possess above other animals. . . . Without obtaining an absolute control over both its variety and amount, they could not have multiplied into populous nations. It is accordingly probable that the great epochs of human progress have been identified, more or less directly, with the enlargement of the sources of subsistence."

But for Morgan this was only one feature of the story: "Among the original germs of thought, which have exercised the most powerful influence upon the human mind, and upon human destiny, are those which relate to government, to the family, to language, to religion, and to property. They had a definite beginning far back in savagery, and a logical progress, but can have no final consummation, because they are still progressing, and must ever continue to progress."

Given the nature of men and women, the need for subsistence, the passions, and relations of the sexes in the family connected with the continuance and care of life, the evolution from savagery through barbarism to civilization seemed to have necessity in it. Yet Morgan, as a cautious historian, found in his review of the past no comprehensive and satisfactory explanation of long evolution and so he took account of features apparently fortuitous. The attainment to civilization, he thought, was in a way inevitable and "yet civilization must be regarded as an accident of circumstances. . . . If mankind had failed to the present hour to cross this barrier [the use of iron], it would have afforded no just cause for surprise. When we recognize the duration of man's existence upon the earth, the wide vicissitudes through which he has passed in savagery and in barbarism, and the progress he was compelled to make, civilization might as naturally have been delayed for several thousand years in the future, as to have occurred when it did in the good providence of God. We are forced to the conclusion that it was the result, as to the time of its achievement, of a series of fortuitous circumstances."

Here Morgan was clearly in an intellectual dilemma—a dilemma as old as philosophic thought—and he closed his final page without attempting to settle it in terms of human ideas and interests alone. "We owe our present condition, with its multiplied means of safety and of happiness, to the struggles, the sufferings, the heroic exertions, and the patient toil of our barbarous, and more remotely, of our savage ancestors." But what, in the nature of things, made necessary or possible this long travail of men and women into civilization ever advancing into the future? Without posing the question exactly in this shape, Morgan gave an opinion in his last sentence: "Their labors, their trials, and their successes were a part of the plan of the Supreme Intelligence to develop a barbarian out of a savage, and a civilized man out of this barbarian."

To the movement of research, observation, knowledge, and reflective thought pertaining to civilization—the movement in which Morgan worked—Lester F. Ward brought multiform experiences of life, indefatigable labors, vast learning, and a mind of many facets. He early grasped the revolutionary import of anthropology for all intellectual activities in the realm of social inquiry and reporting. In his treatment of sociology, this appreciation appeared. He was not satisfied with the simple hypothesis that civilization merely rested on successive bodies of material inventions and institutions more or less visible, all developed automatically in the biological struggle for existence. He tried to understand "the psychic factors" which supplied impulsions in inventing, discovering, and institution-making. With respect to the origins and progress of society, he discerned in the intuition and insight of women a special power which, if fully released, as he thought it should be, would result in a still more rapid advance of civilization. Always at the center of his thinking about humanity was the social principle. He consistently held that, however creative or ingenious an individual mind might be at any stage in history, that mind could apply its ingenuity and creative power only by using the instrumentalities provided by society—ideas, language, institutions, and material acquisitions.

Ward was born in Illinois. His father was a mechanic and his mother the daughter of a clergyman, a woman with intellectual interests and versatility. In Iowa, to which his parents moved, young Ward came to know life and nature on the frontier. But at the age of seventeen he was a laborer in a Pennsylvania factory. Experiences multiplied. After a brief period in an academy he enlisted in the Union army in 1862; retired on account of wounds received in the war, he obtained a position in the Treasury Department at Washington. While in that public service, Ward procured, mainly by study at night, an education at Columbian College in the capital—a training in the arts, the law, and the natural sciences. Soon he was appointed assistant geologist in the Geological Survey and from this post he later moved to that of paleontologist. In these positions he made contributions of a high order to the natural sciences.

From the natural sciences Ward's interests widened out to include the humanistic sciences, especially psychology and sociology. Carrying forward his preparatory studies, he acquired a working knowledge of Greek, Latin, French, German, Russian, Hebrew, and Japanese. Like most naturalists of his time, he accepted the idea of evolution and took the side of science in the strife against theology.

In spare hours away from his scientific work for the Government of the United States, Ward started his study of human society in development and published his results under the significant title *Dynamic Sociology*, in 1883, the year before the academic economist, J. Laurence Laughlin, issued his edition of John Stuart Mill's *Political Economy*, with all the humanity cut out of it. To the end of his life, in 1913, Ward continued to publish books and articles on sociology and cosmic philosophy—after 1906, as a professor in Brown University. Besides being a laborious student, Ward was an ardent controversialist, defending and spreading his world-view on the platform and in the press.

While studying physical and social evolution in the immensity of the ages, Ward gave more and more attention to the primordial mental function which had baffled both Darwin and Morgan. It was the mind, he decided, that marked the great break between the animal kingdom and the human kingdom; it was the mind that gave to humanity its degree of emancipation from sheer necessity and permitted it to escape from subordination to physical nature into creative activities and inventive designing for security, welfare, and progress. This inference growing out of his studies, blended with his warm sympathies for the people from whom he sprang, gave support to Ward's conclusion that the coming years would see purposeful planning occupy a large place in the social sciences; government developed into an agency of the general welfare; and "sociocracy" substituted for individualistic democracy—the commonwealth in short, not a servile order directed by blind force but a free society affording the good life and more happiness for all its members.

It was with precise relevance to his interest in the human spirit working in a social contexture that Ward chose as the title of an influential work, an analysis and a synthesis, published in 1893, *The Psychic Factors of Civilization*. In the analytical parts of his volume, he discussed such subjects as the conative faculty, the origin and function of pleasure and pain, the nature of the soul, the philosophy of desire, the "will" of Schopenhauer, intuitive judgment, female intuition, the psychology of invention, inventive genius, speculative genius, and the intellect. The synthesis of these psychic factors in civilization he effected under six heads: the economy of nature and the economy of mind, meliorism, social consciousness, the social will, the social intellect, and sociocracy. By the title of his volume and by implication, although not by sustained elucidation, Ward really brought the upward course of mankind, above the physical and animal base, under the idea of civilization with its enfolded idea of progress.

On the subject of the origins of civilization Ward dissented from the biological school, especially from the materialistic biologists who declared the mind to be a mere "function of the body." The divergence from physical nature, he repeatedly insisted, lay in the psychic factors of mankind to be distinguished clearly from the animal kingdom. "The development of inventive genius in man," he wrote, "ultimately resulted in the introduction of *art*. It caused the raw materials of nature which had previously constituted his only resources to be discarded and replaced, more and more, and at length almost exclusively, by artificial products. So nearly is this transformation complete in modern civilized countries that the fact is lost sight of even by political economists. That is, they find it so universal that they come to regard it as the natural condition. This leads them into the greatest absurdities." Emancipation from servitude to physical nature through the power of inventiveness belied the whole theory of economic activity as an unconscious, automatic, natural process driven by the blind acquisitive instinct.

The contention that civilization was the outcome of crude physical necessity, often put forward by biologists as the clue to civilization, Ward called thoroughly unsound. In 1893 when he was writing, he admitted, this school "may still be said to be the predominant one." It "is fond of treating civilization as the product of natural forces and of inveighing against everything that any one attempts to do to modify or in any way interfere with those forces, forgetting entirely that civilization in all its essential characteristics is an exclusively artificial product, the product of the inventive genius of man in modifying and altering the course of nature. Every adjustment made at the behest of inventive genius is an interference with the course of natural law. Every object of art is such as nature would never have created. When one looks about and realizes how seldom any other class of objects are ever used by man, some idea may be gained of the intensely artificial character of civilization.

But this is as it should be, for everywhere the artificial is superior to the natural, and what is called progress consists in making everything more and more artificial, i.e., in putting more art into all products, discovering new and added utilities by calling into play still higher flights of inventive genius."

Mingled with artful inventiveness in the making of civilization are will and desire. "With both factors at work the transformation [in the development of society] became rapid and permanent. Nothing equal or at all comparable to it had ever before been accomplished [in the order of pure nature]. It could not await the slow methods of nature in bringing about after millions of generations the anatomical modifications. . . . It worked directly upon the environment radically changing it and rendering structural adaptations unnecessary. This may be why man has really undergone so few of the latter. Structural modifications can only go on under the influence of an environmental pressure in the given direction. But if the moment such a pressure is felt it is immediately relieved by an artificial device, the cause of the change is removed and the tendency to change ceases. This was practically done in the case of man, invention being constantly directed toward the relief of environmental pressure and along the line of free activity in the satisfaction of desire."

What he called "material civilization"—the external creations of desire and the inventive spirit, Ward maintained, "has constituted a true human progress . . . viz., increased happiness. For happiness consists in the continuous satisfaction of the desires as they arise, and its increase results from multiplying the desires that can be thus satisfied. This material civilization accomplishes by improving the quality of everything that man uses in his daily life. . . . It is true that the introduction of the arts, the products of inventive genius, has entailed upon mankind the necessity of labor, and in most ages and countries this has been a severe hardship upon the great mass, but there are extenuating circumstances. . . . It is only by labor that so large a number of human beings can live on the earth. It is the condition of their existence. The choice lies between labor and extinction. . . . If life, such as it is, is a gain, then is the opportunity to labor, i.e., civilization, means to progress. But if it be said that this hardship is due to the unjust distribution of the products of labor, then the answer must be that this is not chargeable to inventive genius but to rapacity, which is a form of the egoistic faculty, and that it presents a problem for the sociologist."

Human development beyond the animal stage, however, as it goes forward under the drives of the mind, Ward said, creates institutions and ethical sentiments which moderate this "rapacity," the tooth and claw struggle of mere animal existence, the competition of animals for survival under the iron laws of physical nature. "All human institutions—religion, government, law, marriage, custom—together with innumerable other modes of regulating social, industrial, and commercial life, are, broadly viewed, only so many ways of meeting and checkmating the principle of competition as it manifests itself in society. And finally, the ethical code and the moral law of enlightened man are nothing else than the means adopted by reason, intelligence, and refined sensibility for suppressing and crushing out the animal nature of man." More than this, combinations of capital and labor now softened the struggles of individuals for the material means of subsistence, although labor was handicapped by lack of cooperation and capital enjoyed the benefits of aid from the civil and military authorities. But the tendency to cooperation, control, and regulation proceeds, against the brutalities of conflicts conducted on the animal level and against the wastes and miseries induced by the continuation of animal methods in society.

Although Ward sometimes treated civilization as if identical with human advancement beyond the animal stage, at one point he distinguished between civilization and social progress and said that they were "not strictly synonymous." Here he defined civilization narrowly as "the product of many men at work with their inventive brains, each seeking to compel the forces of nature to do something for himself." This is a kind of individualism and it results in "a very unequal distribution of the product." Often the inventor himself does not secure a just share of the returns. The major portion "goes not to genius but to the comparatively low quality of cunning or business shrewdness."

Having observed a conflict between civilization so conceived and social progress in a broad sense, Ward stated the dilemma as follows: "This problem fully generalized is that of identifying civilization with progress, of making society at large the beneficiary of the products of art, skill, industry, and labor."

After posing his problem in this form, Ward devoted his own faculty of invention to a consideration of social inventions for the solution of the problem, that is, making the advancement of civilization equivalent to progress in the distribution of its productions. A powerful barrier in the way of this action he found in laissez faire, in "extreme individualism, bordering on practical anarchy in all except the enforcement of existing proprietary rights," blinding the public mind to "the real condition of things," to "the vast theater of woe" in modern society. "The system of political economy that sprang up in France and England at the close of the aristocratic stage in those countries is still taught in the higher institutions of learning. It is highly favorable to the spread of plutocracy, and is pointed to by those who are to profit by that system of government as the invincible scientific foundation upon which it rests. . . . Thus firmly entrenched, it will require a titanic effort on the part of society to dislodge this baseless prejudice, and rescue itself once more from the rapacious jaws of human egoism under the crafty leadership of a developed and instructed rational faculty."

In his appraisal of remedial proposals, Ward criticized arguments in favor of socializing all industrial operations as both inconclusive and a priori in nature, whatever contributions they might make to thought about society. For himself he chose a middle way, pleading for the use of social hypotheses as guides in scientific searches for ways and means of generalizing civilization as social progress. This would put a great strain on popular government, but he thought that democracy, "now the weakest of all forms of government, at least in the control of its own internal elements," was capable of becoming the strongest. Its instruments were to be education, regulation, economic experiments, moving forward to the conquest of the misery that had so far survived the advance of civilization.

To the woman movement in relation to the whole social domain, which had attained such strength during the popular upsurge, the new knowledge in anthropology and sociology brought more illumination and force. Hitherto the sources upon which leaders in that movement had relied for information respecting the role of women in history had been largely limited to works on political, military, legal, and ecclesiastic history written mainly by men for their own purposes. From such documents women had gleaned detached items about historic women which they used to offset man's claims to have made all the history that had been made. That kind of written history had been the matrix in which women's ideas of their function in the past and present were imbedded. But useful to the woman movement as those gleanings from history were, they were not comparable in significance to the new knowledge being placed at their service in the new age.

Now anthropology penetrated the far past, ages beyond the oldest written myths and stories on which historians of politics, wars, laws, and theologies had depended for their information respecting the origins and institutions of society. By its very scope it took into account all the arts and institutions for the maintenance and care of life. It threw new and positive light on the origins and evolution of civilization as well as on secular and ecclesiastical politics and wars. Now sociology, with its stress on psychic factors and its comprehensive concern with all features of society in development, inevitably brought women into extended consideration in connection with the study of all institutions, habits, customs, and other social manifestations enmeshed in the growth of civilization.

Searching for the origins and nature of civilization, anthropology explored the industrial arts which reflected the appearance and growth of civilized minds and furnished a basis of progress in civilization. Indeed in many places the chief materials available to it were surviving artifacts unearthed from ruins and detritus, millennia older than the first written records—belonging to "the dim and dateless past." And in its wide searchings anthropology found women at the very center of civilization in origin and development—as creators and preservers of the arts and of that perennial care for life out of which came reverence for life—the very moral strength of civilization. It was just at this point that anthropology effected one of the greatest revolutions ever made in the history of human intelligence at work—a revolution of vital significance for the role of women in civilization and for man's understanding of it.

Although many anthropologists, perhaps following old

habits, spoke of social origins as the work of primitive "man," as if male beings alone had founded the family and made all the beginnings in the industrial arts and in practices for the care of life, those who wrote with more discriminating exactness specifically described the activities of primitive women in the launching of civilization.

To this realistic school belonged Otis T. Mason who served for many years as curator of ethnology at the Smithsonian Institution and later as curator of anthropology at the National Museum in Washington. On the basis of long and intensive studies Mason came to the conclusion that woman made prime contributions to the arts of civilization, such as spinning, weaving, pottery-making, agriculture; and in her varied activities devoted to the care of life developed moral sentiments—reverence for life—and institutions absolutely necessary to civilization.

This conclusion Mason presented in his *Woman's Share in Primitive Culture* published in 1894. "Civilization," he said in a summary, "is the composite result of progress from the purely natural life of the animal to the purely artificial life of the most enlightened individuals and peoples. This progress has always been made along the lines of satisfying human needs, of gratifying human desires. . . . For the highest ideals in civilization, in humanitarianism, education, and government the way was prepared in savagery by mothers and by female clan groups. . . . Pedagogy and the body politic had their foundations laid there." For the theory that civilization sprang from man's care for his family, clan, and tribe, Mason substituted the reverse: civilization with its arts of peace, care of children, invention of cooking, pottery, weaving, and agriculture—the protection of life—came out of women's function and work.

In his monumental treatise in three volumes called *The Mothers,* published in 1927, Robert Briffault, a British anthropologist, confirmed the revolutionary importance of the discoveries made by such investigators as L. H. Morgan and E. B. Tylor, and the findings of Otis T. Mason. He declared that "when we speak of 'human nature' we generally mean masculine human nature. We are in the habit of regarding the evolution of humanity and of human ideas and sentiments as, in the main, products of the masculine mind." But, he continued, "our knowledge of human origins . . . has undergone a profound transformation within the last fifty years."

One of the revolutionary changes was the discovery of social organizations far older than the patriarchal type described in the Bible and far different in nature. The other was the discovery of the part played in primitive life by women and their influence. In his sections on the division of labor among primitive peoples Briffault described, as Mason had done, the creative work of women in the domestic arts and in the development of sentiments basic to the care of life.

When, a few years after the publication of Briffault's treatise, Alfred N. Whitehead made his inquiry into civilization called *Adventures of Ideas,* he accepted as the greater probability the proposition that it was woman rather than man who first crossed the great divide between animal life and civilization. "Many an ape man," he said, "must have snatched up a stone wherewith to hit somebody, either another man or other animal, on the head, without any reflection upon the course of nature beyond the next few minutes. Also he might notice that some stones are better than others as lethal weapons, and he might even help them out by chipping them. He is then approaching civilization. But he—more probably, she —has crossed the great divide when he puts seeds into a patch of earth and waits for a season."

Given this new perspective on the role of women in history, and the attenuation, if not the disappearance, of old controversies based on ancient misinformation, the way was cleared for sociologists to deal realistically with the evolution and nature of modern societies. It was against this fresh background that some explored and described the relations of women to industry, the family, institutions and practices for the care of life, and government—all features of civilization in the past and in the contemporary age.

Drawing upon the new knowledge and interpretations developed by the anthropologists and sociologists, and supplementing them by independent investigations, Anna Garlin Spencer applied her learning to a study of civilization in the United States and woman's manifold affiliations with that process. She carried forward and enlarged the thought of the woman movement inaugurated by the pioneers of 1848. She broadened the feminist simplifications founded on common law doctrines which gave man dominion over married woman's property and affairs, in the absence of amicable understandings and prenuptial contracts. She sought to clear away the antagonisms created in the relations of men and women by a one-sided emphasis either way, and offered a synthesis of cooperative relationships.

A long life devoted to study, teaching, and lecturing Dr. Spencer crowned by publishing in 1913 a summational work bearing the title, reminiscent of Mason with whose findings she was familiar, *Woman's Share in Social Culture.* Although she used the word culture instead of civilization in the title, she referred to civilization in the text; and her recognition of social dynamics, from the beginning to the end of her volume, showed that she was thinking in terms of civilization.

For the main body of this treatise Dr. Spencer provided a background by sketching a long history of woman's work from primitive times forward. Supporting Mason's thesis, she assigned priority to woman in the arts of continuous productive labor. She maintained that it was woman who first acquired the distinction of "a steady job"; that the work of primitive man was only occasional, if strenuous at times. In the school of the earliest family, of which woman was the center, the discipline of the social principle was developed in forms of mutual aid. Into this association for mutual aid man was led deeper, as the understanding of fatherhood was awakened in him, as he was inducted into large segments of woman's work, as he was domesticated, and, becoming "head of the family," assumed other responsibilities than hunting, fishing, and fighting.

The extreme antithesis presented by some anthropologists as matriarchy against patriarchy, or woman-rule against man-rule, Dr. Spencer declared too simple for the diversity of facts in that case. With reference to the enslavement of woman by man, "the puzzle of the sociologists," she drew attention to striking and numerous exceptions and denied its universality and its unmitigated rigors—in this sustaining, in many respects, the findings of Lewis Henry Morgan. Even in the age of alleged patriarchal supremacy, Dr. Spencer pointed out, woman was by no means wholly bereft of privilege and power: her economic value, her natural weapons of defense, and her self-protecting charms softened for countless women the rigors of custom, even of slavery itself. All through the long ages, called primitive and dark, woman had done civilizing work and exerted continuously, in various conditions, a civilizing influence.

Having presented the social heritage, Dr. Spencer devoted the main part of her treatise to women in the contemporary age. Here she discussed types and work. She brought under review the woman of genius, the spinster, the pathology of woman's labor in the lower ranges of industry, the division of vocations between men and women, the application of the feminine spirit to education, problems of marriage and divorce, the relation of women to religion and the religious observances connected with the great facts of human experience—birth, marriage, child bearing, and death.

One great theme pertinent to the subject remained, namely, Woman and the State. This theme Dr. Spencer developed in a long chapter under that head, displaying in the process knowledge of history, law, theory, and practice. Women had sometimes been rulers in despotic states and heads of families in feudal states, she said. They had been holders of landed estates in times when great property claimed the right to govern. But with the passage of the State from despotism, aristocracy, and property-rule toward democracy, women had temporarily lost their footing in the political arena. In the early stages of democratic tendencies, as society moved toward the universal participation of men in government, women had been overlooked in this relation; great authorities in political science had ignored them in dealing with the "rights of man." And the logic of all this more recent development had been to place women under the perpetual guardianship of men as makers and administrators of law, although the logic had not been universally admitted.

Many circumstances made possible the tendency to subject women to man's "democratic" State. In the eighteenth century, the "family" had been treated as "the social unit." And in the speculations of the time there had been a failure to think of woman as human in the same sense that man is human. Under common law doctrines, applied in the absence of prenuptial and personal agreements, the married woman of the family lost rights of person and property and control over the guardianship of her own children. Under this theory, however mitigated in practice, the subordination of woman to the family, so constituted in law, reduced woman to a political nonentity.

While common men were absorbed in their struggle for political rights and women were overburdened with drudgery, "this exclusion of women from the democratic State was natural." But soon the glaring contrast between the emancipation of the common man and the specific exclusion of all women from the franchise appeared in full force. Moral and intellectual uneasiness resulted, as the State become "consciously responsive to social sentiments." Then the movement for the enfranchisement of women set in, often by granting them a limited franchise for voting in elections where members of school boards were chosen. From such cautious beginnings came the steady extension of the suffrage to women and their increasing emancipation from legal restrictions against their public activities.

This enfranchisement of women came in an age when the narrow theory of the State as largely if not entirely political was being transformed by thought and action, when the State was assuming ever greater responsibilities for social welfare. In this conjuncture of affairs, the woman movement, therefore, had a two-fold significance: it was a part of a general movement toward democracy and an expression of the enlargement in the "social functions of government."

Once the State had adopted the practice of providing for general education, made the care of dependents a public duty, and undertaken numerous obligations respecting social well-being, it needed the direct and varied aid of women, according to Dr. Spencer's thesis. From ancient times women had taught children the arts of domestic life and had ministered to the welfare of family and community. In taking over "women's sphere of social service" the State "must take over women as part of the body politic." Thus, as Dr. Spencer reasoned, in a chapter which conveyed the spirit of her entire volume, "Where Two Walk and Work Together," throughout life and labor in a democratic commonwealth, by fate and opportunity men and women are indissolubly joined.

The influence of new knowledge, offered by anthropology and sociology, upon thought about women in relation to civilization, which had many ramifications, was illustrated by the action of the American Academy of Political and Social Science in May, 1914, when it devoted an entire issue of its *Annals* to the subject of "Women in Public Life." Participants in this symposium in several cases combined principles drawn from anthropology and sociology with the idea of civilization, as they proceeded in their discussions of the themes set for them.

When, for example, George Elliott Howard, head of the department of political science and sociology at the University of Nebraska, author of a great work on matrimonial institutions, surveyed the "Changed Ideals and Status of the Family and the Public Activities of Women," he declared that the quality of American civilization depended upon the family and that the participation of women in public affairs bore a necessary relation to this reality. "There are," he said, "distinct signs of an extraordinary awakening of the social consciousness and the social conscience to the cardinal truth that the family, as already defined, is the basic fact in our national life, and hence the dynamic factor which ultimately, for good or ill, must determine the quality of American civilization. Emphatically, with respect to the ideals of the family, we are at the height of the transition from the old regime to the new. . . . The home is indeed the human soul's most sacred temple. It will not be less sacred when through it flows the swift current of the large social life. For, first and last, do not all human ideals, aims, and strivings center in the triad of personalities, mother, father, and child?"

Thus Howard was reviving in thought about society in development the basic instrument of social strength—the family—while connecting the evolution of the family with the civilization of the modern age. Although Greek political scientists had never overlooked the family in their theories of society and the State, American academicians who dealt with political science, in colleges, had generally neglected the family and concentrated their energies on laws and forms of government, as if the State had nothing to do with the family, or the family with the State. But at last under impacts from anthropology and sociology, and through realistic discussions of woman's role in history, the fundamental relations of Family and State were coming back into American interest in connection with the idea of civilization.

While the idea of woman's creative role in history was gaining recognition and legitimation, it was claimed in many quarters that the attitude of educated women toward marriage, toward the place of man in the family, and toward divorce was disrupting the primary social unit. The claim was examined critically by Howard. "Educated women," he said, "are not shunning marriage or maternity; but they are declining to view matrimony as a profession, as their sole vocation, or to become merely child-bearing animals. Let us not worry about the destiny of college women. It is simply wrong wedlock which they are avoiding. . . . Perhaps in no clearer light is the rising ideal of family life revealed than in woman's fierce revolt against the ancient, man-made standard of the sex relations. She righteously resents commercialized prostitution, the low legal age of consent for girls, the 'conspiracy of silence' regarding venereal disease, and the whole 'double standard of sex-morals' as degrading to her personality. It is in this connection that the new movements for sex education, sex hygiene, and eugenic marriage disclose their chief meaning. Hence they are invariably an accented part of the equal suffrage program."

The question of divorce, so often treated as a mere matter of personal whim, Howard also examined and treated in its social setting: "As civilization advances the more searching is the diagnosis of social disease and the more special or differentiated the remedy. Woman is demanding primarily, not less divorce, but fewer of the bad social conditions which now render the bitter medicine of divorce needful."

When Howard came to the freer and more conscious participation of women in public affairs, he took into account woman's role in early society, as revealed by anthropology, and the broad conception of public affairs afforded by sociology: "The appeal to experience discloses two significant facts which seem to show that for the highest political tasks of the present woman has a special preparation and a peculiar fitness. From the beginnings of society she has been an expert in the very problems and activities with which law and government are now most concerned. While the chief business of man was fighting and hunting, woman was inventing and practicing the arts of peace; attending to the welfare of mother, infant, and child; building the home and ordering the domestic economy. Today state and national legislation deals more and more intimately with these things. They are the real values in civilization.

"Secondly, woman is proving her ability to do a full share of society's political work. Her capacity for organization and her administrative efficiency are being demonstrated in ever new and surprising ways. To her belongs the chief credit for creating the great organized social services. The regenerated American city is peculiarly woman's work. If their present achievements are an earnest of what they can do, it is to be hoped that women may be entrusted with a much larger share in public office. . . ."

While anthropologists and sociologists were building up

their descriptions of the social beginnings and the social development of mankind, demonstrating the persistence of the social principle from primitive times and dissolving the fallacy of individualism as the sole or even the main motive force in civilization, younger economists were chafing under the rigidity of the individualistic theory. Indeed before Sumner and his school got their system completely formulated, a revolt against their dogmas started in many quarters. A sign that this counter-reformation in economics had gained strength as early as 1885 was the creation of the American Economic Association in response to a growing dissatisfaction with orthodox economics.

The protest which eventuated in the establishment of the Association was led by Richard T. Ely, Edmund J. James, Simon Nelson Patten, and other teachers of economics who believed that the abstractions of individualism were unreal and that the idealization of individualism was contrary to the moral code. The preliminary drafts of the platform for the new association, which they first proposed to call, significantly, "Society for the Study of National Economy," published in Ely's *Ground under Our Feet*, bear witness that such was the spirit of their enterprise.

The sources of this intellectual uprising were both critical and constructive. Several leaders in it had received their graduate training in Germany, where the economics of individualism had never gained undisputed sway and all such "plane-surface" systems of economic theory were being subjected to the devastating effects of calm historical analysis. For a number of the dissident economists, Christian ethics, to which they were dedicated by faith, outlawed the theory of "nature red in tooth and claw," and at the same time furnished moral imperatives for a social conception of life and of human responsibilities in society. Into the growth and spread of economic heterodoxy likewise entered the idea of civilization as a summation of values and as covering realities which formed a necessary setting for economic activities. Some of the dissenters, Ely, Commons, and Veblen, for example, related economics to civilization in occasional writings; one, Patten, in a systematic fashion dealt with economics as a phase of civilization.

The methods as well as the ideas of the dissident economists worked for the disintegration of rigid individualism and promoted the study of constructive principles, such as had actuated the reformers of the previous age. Critical inquiries into the evolution of economic activities and economic theories through the ages contributed to a recovery and re-assertion of the idea of civilization. These studies necessarily introduced into the statics of individualist theory the dynamics of change—an essential feature of the idea of civilization. By calling upon the spinners of theory to go out of their cloisters and look at the actual conduct of human beings in all branches of economic enterprise, the insurrectionists invited them, in effect, to check the validity of their abstractions against the concrete performances supposed to be covered by theory. Inevitably this type of realism aided in bringing economics down out of the speculative clouds into the study of civilization as the social process.

Early in the rising tide of revolt against individualism, Simon Patten published, in 1885, his volume on *The Premises of Political Economy,* the very title of which was a challenge to the intellectual foundations of individualism. As Thorstein Veblen soon pointed out with cogent irony, the formulators of individualism as a system had never examined their pre-liminary assumptions, especially those relative to human nature and property. Furthermore they had seemed little to realize, if at all, that their principal conclusions actually flowed out of their unexamined major premises, not inexor-ably from the "facts" brought into play as illustrations of convictions already entertained.

These "inarticulate" major premises, especially as they were exemplified in the writings of John Stuart Mill, Patten probed, and treated with particular reference to American conditions. After examining the assumptions, he dealt with their limitations and then denied the truth of the proposition that laissez faire would automatically develop to the highest possible point the wealth and welfare of American society. From that position Patten went on in his later work to con-nect economics more and more with the idea of civilization as a summation of values capable of guiding economic ac-tivities in the direction of more commodious living and more civilized behavior for the American people.

For this undertaking in path-breaking thought Patten had been prepared by wide varieties of experience in life and in education. Brought up on a rich prairie farm in Illinois, early impressed by the bounties wrung from nature through the application of intelligence to labor, he acquired an optimism about the future of mankind that ran counter to the gloomy outlook of "the dismal science" of economics, as borrowed from England with her poverty-stricken masses of workers in industry and on the estates of great landlords.

After studying for a few years in a local seminary and spending a few months in Northwestern University, young Patten went to the University of Halle. In the Germany of that time he was astonished by the efficiency with which scanty resources were made to yield great returns and by the conservation of natural resources, as vividly contrasted with the wasteful exploitation which he had known in his native land. His imagination was stirred by the work of governments in developing and protecting community interests and his thought was affected by theories of political economy differing fundamentally from the doctrines promulgated in England and the United States. Perhaps not less influential in shaping Patten's conception of economics or economy was his observation of the pleasures derived by the German people from the wise use and consumption of the relatively scanty material goods available to them. It may have been this discovery that led him to develop the theory of thoughtful consumption as a basic feature of economy, so largely neglected by classical economists in their concentration on the factors of production for profits.

Shortly after the publication of his volume on the premises of political economy, Patten was appointed, in 1888, to a chair in the University of Pennsylvania—at Philadelphia, the home of "protectionism," one form of the revolt against laissez faire then supported by powerful interests. That was the city in which Henry C. Carey had spent a long life combating British theories of economy, erected on the assumption of scarcity, and expounding an American doctrine of independence, abundance, and optimism. Carey had been dead less than ten years when Patten arrived in Philadelphia and his economic philosophy was still alive. According to Broadus Mitchell, "the writings of Henry C. Carey and others of the 'Philadelphia school' were at least of equal influence on his [Patten's] thought with his farm background and his observation of German economy."

But in reality Patten's thought was far removed from that of Pennsylvania Republicans who exploited some of Carey's ideas and combined the "state socialism" of protection against foreign competition with the use of the law, the police, and the army to maintain laissez faire for labor at home. His guiding conception was "the public welfare," to be progressively attained by increasing human power over nature, the conservation and wise use of resources, education in the arts of good living, private and public cooperation, and a growing protection of the family and community against ignorance, disease, and poverty. Keenly aware of the possibilities, he interpreted civilization as a development toward "a social commonwealth," in his *Theory of the Social Forces,* issued in 1896, and declared that, "if a progressive evolution continues, other societies will be possible, each of which will differ from its predecessor as radically as the society I describe differs from our present society."

In two major respects, both revolutionary in the light of the times, Patten diverged from the economists of individualism. First, he rejected the theory based on economy as deficit or scarcity—the theory derived from the pre-machine age— and, taking into account applied science and power production, he substituted the theory of abundance, the abundance potential in modern technological civilization. Secondly, while the classical economists reasoned intrinsically in terms of a fixed mechanism essentially changeless, ever running under the motive force of the acquisitive instinct if the State did not interfere except to maintain "law and order," Patten reasoned in terms of civilization as conceived by those who had most fully discussed the potentials of the idea.

Although Patten revealed little interest in the kind of history then taught in the American academies, he studied anthropology and sociology and developed an appreciation of humanity's evolution from primitive times—a historical sense. Philosophically speaking, his writing and teaching were teleological, that is, founded on the conception of design as the true cause or explanation of existence—with civilization as the course of things human in the natural world, progressively unfolding with the aid of creative intelligence. In other words, design, necessity, time, evolution, and the force of creative energies and sentiments were mingled in Patten's directive conception or working hypothesis.

In no single treatise did Patten expound the fulness of his world-view. Early in his career, however, he disclosed the trend of his thinking when he joined his friend E. J. James in urging the formation of an economic association "to combat the widespread view that our economic problems will solve themselves, and that our laws and institutions which at present favor individual instead of collective action can promote the best utilization of our material resources and secure to each individual the highest development of all his faculties." On the constructive side, Patten and James declared, contrary to the capital-land-labor theory of wealth production, that "the state is a positive factor in material production and has legitimate claims to a share of the product. The public interest can be best served by the state's appropriating and applying this share to promote the public ends." Above the special interests of capitalists and laborers as classes, they placed "the general interest of the community."

In a form somewhat special and fragmentary, Patten presented his views in several lectures delivered in 1905 at the New York School of Philanthropy and published in 1907 as *The New Basis of Civilization*. In this work he treated the new basis as laid in resources, heredity, family life, social classes, social consciousness, amusement, and social control. At the outset he made a distinction between old civilizations, such as that of Rome, which were constantly struggling to meet a deficit, and the new civilization "so well situated that thought can be centered on the equitable distribution of a surplus."

In the first type "the civilization must develop its traditions to keep the deficit as small as possible and eventually to overcome it, and in the other to utilize the surplus for the common good, not to undermine energy and productive ability or to create parasitic classes, but to distribute the surplus in ways that will promote general welfare and secure better preparation for the future." All civilizations before the nineteenth century, Patten contended, were based on a deficit or pain economy and were beset by wars and internal disturbances. Modern civilizations, on the other hand, have available the potentials of a surplus economy and they have the means —intellectual, moral, and scientific—for creating and maintaining, through individual and collective action, an economy of abundance and pleasure, an economy of the life good, strong, useful, and beautiful.

In societies controlled by privileged orders, Patten remarked in his lecture on the social classes, "each individual had a status to preserve and an income to guard, and relations to nature were lost in the struggle to keep property. The contest evolved social institutions, which do perpetuate and conserve, but which do not improve man's adjustment to nature. Hence arises the distinction between the social institutions, which save or dispose of the surplus, and the economic institutions, which utilize both the environment and the labor power in it. The former establishes status and the rights of possession and of exploitation; the other increases the mobility of men and goods, promotes industry, and gives each generation renewed power to establish itself in closer relations with nature. . . . The extension of civilization downward does not depend at present so much upon gaining fresh victories over nature, as it does upon the demolishment of the social obstacles which divide men into classes and prevent the universal democracy that unimpeded economic forces would bring about."

But the social obstacles to the extension of civilization, Patten declared, "will never be overcome until an intellectual revolution shall have freed men's minds from the stultifying social traditions that hand down hatreds, and shall have given to thought the freedom that now marks industrial activity."

After treating his subject in detail, with special reference to social work and thus within certain limits, Patten appealed for creative enterprise in a lecture on "The New Civilization": "It is for us to unite the social activities—whose motive forces are charity, religion, philanthropy, revolt, and unrest—into a philosophy that is social and not sectional, in that it gives to them all a reorganized rational body of evidence upon which to proceed. . . . If the social worker would be a social philosopher and the reformer a builder as well as a destroyer, he must know how to use the matter and the spirit that make the philanthropies, the trades unions, the settlements, the institutional churches, and the theatres. Economists groping among the formulae of deficit are surprised and overtaken by the new world, and statesmen are bewildered by the surge of the new democracy of industrial liberty against the barriers of class. But these difficulties only prove that the new civilization will be ready as soon as social work has been made a science and is practised with knowledge and ideals which make clear to the statesman who directs and the workman who produces the treasures in health and happiness and safety of the new time."

In these lectures delivered in 1905 in the School of Philanthropy conducted by the Charity Organization Society of New York City, Patten was at that hour helping to make a revolution in American thought respecting "poor relief." Since the early days of the Republic, philanthropy had been mainly directed to palliating the misery which offered a contradiction to civilization in the minds of critical Americans. But it had long been and was becoming increasingly plain that philanthropy, no matter how generous, was making no real impression on "the vast theater of misery."

In less than thirty years the "theater" was to become so vast that it embraced ten or fifteen million unemployed men and women for whom the economy of deficit could provide no working place. Between 1905, the year of Patten's lectures, and 1929, the year of the great panic, schools of philanthropy in many parts of the country had become Schools of Social Work, concerned with private, community, and public interests, combining increasing technical knowledge with the spirit of Christianity and the Enlightenment, in a national campaign against poverty, in the interest of civilization. Among the thousands of men and women who brought about the development, Patten was a pioneer and loyal worker.

Central to the problem which occupied the attention of economists and to all thought about the future of civilization in the United States was the factory system—not as a figment of economic theory, but as mechanical instrumentalities, organization, management, operations, and consequences. Undoubtedly it symbolized, if as yet in a rough way, that power of "inorganic forces" which Thomas Ewbank had portrayed as offering to mankind an escape from miserable subsistence, or worse, into comparative comfort and a higher civilization through machine production. But in the early stages of the factory system, its crudities and cruelties, its offenses against esthetic taste and moral ideals, had aroused an opposition amounting to great hatred. Even the exponents of individualism, in glossing over or apologizing for its glaring evils, intensified criticism of the system by making it correspond exactly with capitalism already under attack from many quarters.

In the "intellectual climate" of the time swirled derogatory opinions surviving from the previous period as well as new quandaries and pessimism. Still vibrant in many memories was the old Southern prophecy that Northern industrialism, with the factory system and wage workers as its necessary concomitants, would lead inevitably to anarchy and the destruction of the Republic. Still held up before public gaze was the old agrarian picture of rural security and felicity as the one certain guarantee of the Republic, of liberty, and of the good life for the people.

Would the crowds of industrial workers gathered around the mills prove to be, as Jefferson feared, mere "mobs of great cities," sores on the body politic? Was the factory, as many reformers in the era of the popular upsurge had insisted, a blight on civilization to be removed by a return to handicrafts or the organization of self-sufficing colonies of cooperative producers with small workshops close to fields? Was it, as the devotees of handwork charged, the source of the curse which they called "industrial civilization," the enemy of life, liberty, and happiness as well as of creative art? Did the factory system represent, as individualists assumed, aggregations of owners driven by the acquisitive instinct and locked in relentless competition against one another, and aggregations of individual workers fighting one another in ceaseless efforts to climb upward in the social scale? Or did it after all offer reality and progress in the struggle of human beings for civilization?

These were not simply hypothetical questions set by theorists. They had deep lodgment in American minds, as manufacturing industry increased its predominance over agriculture and concern with the fortunes of civilization in the United States intensified. They were among the provocative ideas in popular circulation.

If the use of inorganic forces and inanimate instruments for the production of goods on a vast scale was to find intellectual acceptance as historical necessity and opportunity in civilization, the realities and the potentials of the factory system had to be examined and interpreted with reference to civilization. Granting all the evils that accompanied the rise of this system, did it, on the whole, mean an advance in civilization and offer a reasonable expectation of a movement toward a more ideal goal?

This matter was carefully examined by Carroll D. Wright, student of economics, close observer of actual economic conditions, for twenty years the first United States Commissioner of Labor, and a judicious inquirer often intrusted with the investigation of industrial relations. His conclusions he published in *Some Ethical Phases of the Labor Question*, in 1902.

Unlike many economists and sociologists who had proceeded to aver and affirm without openly revealing their preliminary assumptions, who had left civilization out of account or dealt with it in a gingerly way, Wright confessed his premises and used the idea of civilization in its genuine significance. "The philosophy of history," he said, "will take into account the vital elements of industrial forces in all their grand development as important factors in shaping civilization itself, as well as in shaping the commercial policy of nations in their relations to each other. . . . When we speak of civilization, we have in mind the progress of society toward a more perfect state, as indicated by the growth of a long period of time. We do not simply contemplate specific reforms or especial evils, but the trend of all social influences."

Considered in its full implications, did the factory system really represent an advance in civilization? Wright knew that it would be difficult to persuade the unconvinced. "I am well aware," he said, "that I speak against popular impression, and largely against popular sentiment, when I assert that the factory system in every respect is vastly superior as an element in civilization to the domestic system which preceded it; that the social and moral influences of the present outshine the social and moral influences of the old. . . . Few are ready to adopt the idea that the factory has been of itself and through its own influence an element in civilization or an element in lifting up the social life of any people." But this judgment, Wright insisted, "results from superficial study . . . and also from an inverted vision."

What then is this factory system? Its social function far surpasses the limitations of the capitalist wage system. "The origin of the wage system," Wright explained, "cannot be given a birthday as can the factory system. It is true, however, that the wage system rendered the factory system possible, and they have grown together." But this ligature is not a necessary part of the factory system. The wage system "may give way to some other method for dividing the profits of production; but the factory system, perfected, must, whether under socialistic or whatever political system, remain until disintegration is the rule in society." Thus Wright divorced the factory system in itself from the existing processes of capitalism and appraised it as a new instrument of production that increased wealth and pointed a way to general abundance and better community life.

But grave evils are now associated with this factory system, Wright did not hesitate to admit: "Abuses have existed, great and abominable enough." He did not overlook such frightful conditions as Friedrich Engels had descirbed in his *Condition of the Working Class in England in 1844*, published more than half a century before. But did the factory system in itself create those evils?

In Wright's opinion it did not: "The usual mistake is to consider the factory system as the creator of evils, and not only evils, but of evil-disposed persons. This can hardly be shown to be true, although it is [true] that the system may congregate evils or evil-disposed persons, and thus give the appearance of creating that which already existed." What the factory system actually does is "to bring together a large body of comparatively ignorant persons. It congregates these persons into one community, and hence the results of ignorance and of lower standards of life become clearly apparent because of the concentration. Before the concentration, the ignorance existed precisely the same, but was diffused, and hence not apparent."

In any event, he claimed, things are relative and must be seen in perspective, against the facts of life and labor in the past, not against the idyllic picture—the falsified history—of peace, plenty, and felicity supposed to be the lot of toiling humanity in an imaginary past. Look at that past realistically, as recorded in official documents, Wright pleaded: "None of the systems of labor which existed prior to the present, or factory system, was particularly conducive to a higher civilization. . . . The feudal and slave systems had nothing in them, so far as any progressive elements were concerned, from which society could draw the forces necessary to growth. On the contrary, while modern civilization owes much to the feudal system, and slavery was in its origin a great step in civilization, these systems reflected the most depressing influences, and were in great measure the allies of retrogression."

But "there is a class of writers who are very fond of drawing comparisons between conditions under the factory system and those which existed prior to its establishment." In this connection Wright again turned to the record: "History teaches the reverse; for it shows . . . that prior to the establishment of the factory the working classes of England lived in hovels and mud huts that would not be tolerated even in the worst coal-mining districts of this country or in England today. The factory graduated all these people from the mud hut. But what was this old system? Degrading, crime-breeding, and productive of intemperance in the worst form as compared with the factory today."

Using British parliamentary reports and other documents opening up pauperism and domestic industry, Wright painted a vivid picture of tragic labor in the old order: "Under the domestic system of industry grew up that pauper class in England, which was a disgrace to civilization. It was fed by the agricultural districts more than by those devoted to manufactures. It continued to grow until one-fourth of the annual budget was for the support of paupers. The evil became fixed upon the social life as one of its permanent phases."

Given this heritage of slavery, feudalism, pauperism, ignorance, and intemperance—the evils now concentrated in industrial cities and displayed to the gaze of even superficial observers—how does the factory system advance civilization, in the long view of history? It strengthens the social bond, awakens and fortifies the spirit of association: "The principle of the factory is that each laborer, working separately, is controlled by some associating principle which directs his producing powers to effect a common result, which it is the object of all collectively to attain. Factories are, therefore, the legitimate outgrowth of the universal tendency to association which is inherent in our nature, and by the development of which every advance in human improvement and human happiness has been gained." In its way the factory exerts a civilizing influence upon people hitherto isolated in ignorance and poverty. It "means education, enlightenment, and an intellectual development utterly impossible without it—I mean to a class of people who could not reach these things in any other way. It is an element in social life. By its educational influences it is constantly lifting people from a lower to a higher grade." Here again Wright was taking the historical view.

In other respects also the factory is preparing working people for a higher position in society. It "brings mental friction, contact which could not exist under the old system." And as a matter of fact, "better morals, better sanitary conditions, better health, better wages—these are the practical results of the factory system as compared with that which preceded it; and the results of all these have been a keener intelligence. Under the domestic system there existed no common centres of thought and action." Nor is it true, Wright declared, that the factory has a "dwarfing influence upon skill" and degrades skill "to common labor." The opposite is the truth, for this diversified machine process gives skill innumerable opportunities to demonstrate its power.

It is the factory system, with its division of labor, under the associative or collective principle of adjustment, that makes possible the immense production of wealth in modern society. It is by no means perfected. Its full potentials are not yet fully appreciated. It will be improved in the future. "The growth of industrial ethics" will shorten and mitigate the effects of "periods of depression." Other evils will be overcome. "With true men at the head of industrial enterprises, with a political economy which shall recognize the power of moral forces in the accumulation and distribution of wealth, modern productive industry will be . . . the most powerful element in civilization." Already the factory system "has changed the conditions of masses of people. It has become an active element in the processes of civilization and has changed the character of legislation and national policy everywhere."

Such was the new industrial system as it appeared to Carroll D. Wright, when the socializing principle was injected into thought about it, when it was considered not as a perfected scheme of production but as a potential itself in evolution, when it was treated in historical perspective as a phase of civilization. By its very nature, Wright's verdict traversed all wholesale criticisms of the system—those asserted by apologists for the planting system, by the agrarians, and by idealists of every school. It was opposed to that idea of individualism under which science and machinery were often regarded primarily as mere objects of exploitation by self-made individuals. Above all, Wright maintained, this industrial system was dynamic—not a perfected, unchanging system—and would be brought more and more into line with the requirements of civilization as the ethical principles of common good were increasingly applied to its development and management.

Wider in range than the question of the factory system as such and yet entangled in its nature and fortunes was the issue of control. It was raised, in connection with the growth of corporate dominance over industry in general, by the inconsistencies which events effected in competitive economy, by the accumulations of great private riches through the astute exercise of financial power, and by the political and propaganda methods employed in such operations. On the exploration and discussion of this problem Henry Demarest Lloyd, among many others, expended his time and energies. In the process he impugned the doctrine of individualism; he invoked the social principle in the name of the commonwealth; and he promoted a counter-reformation against individualism by developing and applying the idea of civilization. Whatever may be the final judgment of critical scholarship on Lloyd's utterances respecting the merits or demerits of particular industrial leaders, his activities and his writings gave compulsion to the interest in civilization.

The offspring of a pioneer family, son of a strict Calvinist father, and a graduate of Columbia College trained for the law, Lloyd began his public work in the spirit of his American heritage. Early in his public career he threw himself into reform projects in New York City and led in the struggle which brought about the temporary dethronement of Tammany Hall. Leaving such practical politics, Lloyd entered journalism in Chicago as a financial and editorial writer on the Chicago Tribune. While in college he had delivered an oration against monopolies. In his new position he studied trusts, railways, and "high finance" meticulously.

At the moment the alleged machinations of the Standard Oil Company were under investigation and discussion, and Lloyd gave days and nights to the study of the legislative reports and judicial decisions involving that Company. In 1881 he condensed his materials and opinions in his "Story of a Great Monopoly," which was published in the Atlantic Monthly then under the direction of a sympathetic editor, William D. Howells. Long before Veblen, Lloyd studied the methods of business enterprise and, on the basis of legislative and judicial investigations, showed the discrepancy between the smooth theory of the classical economists respecting the utility of all business activities and the adventitious practices —monopolies, speculation, rebate-granting, and other devices —by which a few persons enriched themselves within the scheme of production.

Five years after the publication of his article on the Standard Oil Company, Lloyd retired from the Tribune and gave the rest of his life to exposing the acquisitive spirit and methods of great industrialists, upholding the rights of consumers and laborers, and proclaiming the primacy of commonwealth over extreme individualism. Although he had no sympathy with anarchy as a philosophy or a movement, he braved the wrath of persons in high places by declaring that the anarchists accused in the Haymarket riot case had been unjustly convicted and he joined in the demand for a commutation of two death sentences pronounced by the court. Familiar with the backgrounds of the Pullman strike in 1894, he defended the leader, Eugene V. Debs, against his detractors. That same year he published a voluminous survey of the Standard Oil Company in which he rendered his judgment and reasoning under the title, *Wealth against Commonwealth.* While traveling in England and New Zealand, Lloyd's interest in cooperation, industrial co-partnership, and labor legislation was enhanced. He aided John Mitchel and Clarence Darrow in championing the miners during the coal strike of 1902 and supported them so laboriously as to impair his health. The following year, while he was working for the municipal ownership of street railways in Chicago, death closed his career.

Although he cast off his father's grim Calvinism, Lloyd remained religious in sensibilities to the end of his life. Near its close he worked out for himself a philosophy that fused Christian ethics with economic cooperation. This philosophy he incorporated in a series of essays and papers entitled *Man, the Social Creator,* published after his death under the editorship of Jane Addams and Ann Withington.

Despite some confusions and contradictions at various points, this work, which did not receive Lloyd's final revision, revealed his profound faith in common humanity, struggling for existence through the ages, climbing higher and higher through civilization, drawing together in sympathetic union, growing more and more conscious of its powers and mission, and approaching its triumph in the commonwealth, equipped with science and obedient to the ethical teachings of Christ. For this world-view he offered factual support: slavery was abolished; "the unresting spirit of Redemption" then put forward the claim of the people to citizenship; citizenship won; "the citizen must have the Commonwealth. Beyond the Commonwealth lies unending a line of ascent. The persistence of the Golden Rule in its progress toward supreme jurisdiction can now be regarded as a verified scientific fact in the political history of the race. But the political is but one department of social; industrial is also social. The law of the one must be the law of the other."

Civilization Lloyd defined tersely at one place in his *Wealth against Commonwealth*, as "the process of making men citizens in their relations to each other, by exacting of each that he gives to all that which he receives from all." It is a process involving cooperative efforts, loyalties, a sense of responsibility, "the record of the progressive embodiment of ideals in institutions for the life together—sexual, social, and spiritual." Hitherto "our civilization has followed the self-interest of the individual to learn that it was only one of the complex forces of self-interest." But this over-balance is to be corrected. "To just the extent to which civilization prevails, society will be held as inviolable as the individual. . . . The line of conflict between individual and social is a progressive one of the discovery of point after point in which the two are identical. Society thus passes from conflict to harmony, and so on to another conflict. Civilization is the unceasing accretion of these social solutions. We fight out to an equilibrium, as in the abolition of human slavery; then upon this new level thus built up we enter upon the struggle for a new equilibrium, as now in the labor movement."

Modern economic activities, Lloyd maintained, are preconditioned by civilization; especially all their cooperative aspects are expressions of the civilizing process. For example, "the spectacle of the million or more employés of the railroads of this country dispatching trains, maintaining tracks, collecting fares and freights, and turning over hundreds of millions of net profits to the owners, not one in a thousand of whom would know how to do the simplest of these things for himself, is possible only where civilization has reached a high average of morals and culture. . . . The same rising genius of democracy which discovered that mankind did not cooperate in the State to provide a few with palaces and king's-evil, is disclosing that men do not cooperate in trade for any other purpose than to mobilize the labor of all for the benefit of all, and that the only true guidance comes from those who are led, and the only valid titles from those who create."

But the great money-makers are concerned merely with adding to their wealth, not with promoting civilization: "Of gods, friends, learnings, of the uncomprehended civilization they overrun, they ask but one question: How much? What is a good time to sell? What is a good time to buy? The Church and the Capitol, incarnating the sacrifices and triumphs of a procession of martyrs and patriots since the dawn of freedom, are good enough for a money-changer's shop for them, and a market and shambles. Their heathen eyes see in the law and its consecrated officers nothing but an intelligence-office and hired men to help them burglarize the treasures accumulated for thousands of years at the altars of liberty and justice, that they may burn their marbles for the lime of commerce. . . . A fury of rule or ruin has always in the history of human affairs been a characteristic of the 'strong men' whose fate it is to be in at the death of an expiring principle. . . . To a dying era some man is always born to enfranchise it by revealing it to itself."

Indeed, Lloyd believed, it was the manipulators of finance capitalism, so eulogized by many defenders of individualism, not industrial workers, who threatened the destruction of civilization: "If our civilization is destroyed, as Macaulay predicted, it will not be by his barbarians from below. Our barbarians come from above. Our great money-makers have sprung in one generation into seats of power kings do not know. . . . Without restraints of culture, experience, the pride, or even the inherited caution of class or rank, these men, intoxicated, think they are the wave instead of the float. . . . To them science is but a never-ending répertoire of investments stored up by nature for the syndicates, government but a fountain of franchises, the nations but customers in squads. . . . They claim a power without control, exercised through forms which make it secret, anonymous, and perpetual. . . . They are gluttons of luxury and power, rough, unsocialized, believing that mankind must be kept terrorized. Powers of pity die out of them, because they work through agents and die in their agents, because what they do is not for themselves."

The power of strong men dedicated to accumulating riches, as a matter of fact, impinges adversely on all aspects of civilization, Lloyd declared: "Art, literature, culture, religion, in America, are already beginning [1894] to feel the restrictive pressure which results from the domination of a selfish, self-indulgent, luxurious, and anti-social power. This power, mastering the markets of a civilization which gives its main energies to markets, passes without difficulty to the mastery of all other activities. When churches, political campaigns, the expounding of the law, maintenance of schools and colleges, and family life all depend on money, they must become servile to the money power. Song, picture, sermon, decrees of court, and the union of hearts must pass constantly under stronger control of those who give their lives to trade and encourage everybody else to trade, confident that the issue of it all will be that they will hold as property, in exclusive possession, to be doled out on their own terms, the matter by which alone man can live, either materially or spiritually."

Now in these circumstances, Lloyd observed, Americans are wondering what will be the fate of their civilization. "The breakdown of all other civilizations has been a slow decay. It took the Northerners hundreds of years to march to the Tiber. They grew their way through the old society as the tree planting itself on a grave is found to have sent its roots along every fibre and muscle of the dead. Our world is not the simple thing theirs was, of little groups sufficient to themselves, if need be. New York would begin to die tomorrow if it were not for Illinois and Dakota. We cannot afford a revolution in the hearts by whose union locomotives run, mills grind, factories make. Practical men are speculating today on the possibility that our civilization may some afternoon be flashed away by the tick of a telegraph. All these cooperations may be scattered by a word of hate too many, and we left, with no one who knows how to make a plough or a match, a civilization cut off as by the Roman curse from food and fire. Less sensitive civilizations have burst asunder."

Nevertheless Lloyd believed that civilization would advance, overcoming the perils, by effecting great political and economic changes: "We are to apply the cooperative methods of the post-office and the public school to many other common toils, to all toils in which private sovereignty has become through monopoly a despotism over the public, and to all in which the association of the people and the organization of processes have been so far developed that the profit-hunting Captain of Industry may be replaced by the public-serving Captain of Industry. But we are to have much more. We are to have a private life of a new beauty, of which these are to be merely the mechanical exhibitions on the side of politics. . . . We are to be commoners, travelers to Altruria. We are to become fathers, mothers, for the spirit of the father and mother is not in us while we can say of any child it is not ours and leave it in the grime. We are to become men, women, for to all about reinforcing us we shall insure full growth and thus insure it to ourselves." Civilization will advance in America. And it will widen beyond our borders "into the reciprocal service of all men."

Support for the affirmation of the social principle in civilization, as against the system of thought which made the individual historically prior to society and practically the chief source of civilization, also came from a man whom many Americans had long supposed to be merely eager for money and power. This man was Andrew Carnegie. After accumulating a fortune in industry, exhibiting managerial skill and no little hardness of head in doing it, Carnegie, unlike nearly all other great captains of industry, spent time thinking about his world and his own experiences in it.

Using the realm of industry as his laboratory of research and supplementing knowledge derived from this source by the study of books, Carnegie became interested in civilization, decided that it rested upon wealth, and arrived at the deduction that the accumulation of riches in his time depended largely on the growth of society; that many accumulators were parasites; that the primary end of economy was production for the commonwealth. His opinions Carnegie set forth in magazine articles and books that diverged from the theories of his brethren in the game of making money and the professors of individualism in the schools. He was especially emphatic in his *Gospel of Wealth* written while business men in general were fighting against the adoption of the income tax by the Federal Government. He did more than express opinions. He illustrated them by dedicating substantially all of his immense fortune to causes which, he believed, represented the advancement of civilization.

Contrary to William Graham Sumner's dictum that envy and jealousy inspired criticism of current tendencies in the acquisition of wealth, Carnegie demonstrated that knowledge and experience might lead a man of great wealth to make a thorough-going attack on the individualism of his times. Certainly Carnegie had no ground for envying the rich or wanting to "divide the wealth" in his own interest. In fact he was more inclined to feel sorry for the rich than to envy them. "Millionaires who laugh," he said, "are rare. . . . The most miserable of men, as old age approaches, are those who have made money-making their god; like flies bound to the wheel, these unfortunates fondly believed they were really driving it, only to find when tired and craving rest that it is impossible for them to get off, and they are lost—plenty to retire upon but nothing to retire to, and so they end as they began, striving to add to their useless hoards, passing into nothingness, leaving their money behind for heirs to quarrel over, only because they cannot take it with them—a melancholy end much less enviable than that of their poorer fellows. Wealth confers no fame, although it may buy titles where such prevail. Nor are the memories of millionaires as a class fondly cherished."

In Carnegie's matured view of wealth in relation to civilization and society, four propositions stood out in bold relief. "Wealth," he declared, "is undoubtedly a great factor in civilized life—a very great factor indeed, since civilization itself rests upon it as its foundation. . . . When there was no wealth there was no civilization; none was possible. All was necessarily savage or barbaric." In the next place, private property marked a stage in the evolution of humanity: "Many things hitherto held in common became private property, and at last, out of the savings of men (capital), durable things were built and civilization dawned." In the process creative individuals also enacted an important role: "the great administrator" in manufacturing, merchandising, transportation, and banking, and the inventor make contributions to the production of wealth and deserve special rewards. So far the doctrine of individualism was not seriously fractured by Carnegie's inferences and reasoning.

But Carnegie went further into the complicated processes of economy and matters of public policy. Of the great administrator in creative business, he said: "In the interest of the community . . . he should not be disturbed while gathering honey, provided that it be destined largely for the general hive, under a just system of taxation, when he passes away." Yet even creative individuals, as well as manipulators of finance, work in society, depend upon its strength and growth for a great part, if not all, of their accumulations.

In support of his declaration that wealth is primarily the product of society and that individuals, even of the creative type, are heavily indebted to the community for their fortunes, Carnegie described the main avenues to the acquisition of riches. "The greatest increase of any single department in wealth," he said, "arises from increased value of land." What is the mainspring of this increased value? "The greatest growth of wealth from any one source in our times comes from the increased value of real estate upon which little or no labor is bestowed, the increase of population raising values." One man owns a farm distant from a city, labors on it, and remains to the end a simple farmer in comfortable circumstances. His brother owns a farm near a growing city, its value rises; he becomes a millionaire. "Now who or what made this difference in wealth? Not labor, not skill. No, nor superior ability, sagacity, nor enterprise, nor greater public service. The *community* created the millionaire's wealth."

Many of Carnegie's colleagues in the business world were doubtless willing to agree that so far he had reason on his side, even if they questioned his wisdom in advertising the facts. But, what was worse to them, he went beyond Henry George and land values: "Now let us trace the acquisition of wealth by the active business man who has some personal part, and often not a small one, in creating it." Did a business man acquire wealth by investing in railways while they were rapidly expanding? "It cannot be denied that the chief creators of his wealth were the increasing communities along the railroads, which gave the traffic that lifted these lines into dividend-payers upon a capital far beyond the actual cost." Did a man, united with partners, go into the coal and iron business in Pittsburgh in the early days and grow rich? "Much of the wealth of the concern came from these minerals, which were once the public property of the community, and were easily acquired . . . upon trifling royalties. Their venture was made profitable by the demand for their products, iron and steel, from the expanding population engaged in settling a new continent."

Did a man go into the meat-packing business in Chicago and build up a big fortune? "Here, as before, it was the magnitude of the business based solely upon the wants of the population, that swelled the yearly profits and produced prodigious fortunes." What of the business man who embarked upon copper mining? "The amount of copper and silver required by the teeming population of the country and of other lands kept prices high, and hence his enormous profits mined from land for which only a trifle was paid to the general government not so long ago. He did not create his wealth; he only dug it out of the mines as the demands of the people gave value to the previously worthless stones." What of the speculator in stocks who rose to wealth on a tide of prosperity? "It was an era of rising values, and he soon acquired wealth without increasing values, for speculation is a parasite of business feeding upon values, creating none." Inventors and great administrators in various branches of business do make important creative contributions to the production of wealth and deserve special consideration; but even they are dependent, "in great part," upon the community for all they do and accumulate.

Besides attacking the classical doctrine that accumulated riches are the reward of individual saving and production, Carnegie derided the idea that contemporary agitation against the capitalistic system was a mere outcome of enemy and evil. "The unequal distribution of wealth," he declared, "lies at the root of the present Socialistic activity. This is no surprise to the writer. It was bound to force itself to the front, because, exhibiting extremes unknown before, it has become one of the crying evils of our day." Yet he dismissed, as useless, discussion of the problem stated in the exclusive terms of individualism against socialism. "Whether the Communists' ideal is to be finally reached upon earth, after man is so changed that self-interest, which is now the mainspring of human action, will give place to heavenly-neighbor interest cannot be known. The future has not been revealed. He who says yes, and he who says no, are equally foolhardy. Neither knows, therefore neither should presume to consider, much less to legislate in their day for a future they can know nothing of."

On the constructive side, Carnegie offered no comprehensive program but instead a number of expedients designed to ease the tension over "the unequal distribution of wealth." They included taxation of incomes and inheritances, some forms of public ownership, cooperation, and new attitudes on the part of employers and workers. Taking up the labor question, he held "one point to be clear, viz. that the next step toward improved labor conditions is through the stage of share-holding in the industrial world, the workman becoming joint owner in the profits of his labor." With approval, he quoted from John Stuart Mill a passage in support of co-partnership as the most desirable form of association in industry; that is, ownership by the workers of the specific capital with which they carry on their operations and the exercise of self-government under managers of their own choice. This rejection of universal state ownership and the substitution of private group ownership, "uniting the workman and the capitalist in one and the same person," offered, in Carnegie's opinion, "the highly satisfactory and final solution."

Asseveration also took the form of a systematic social gospel. Committed by faith to Christ's teachings, Christian socialists made this body of ethics frankly supreme over private economic interests; and they worked out imperatives of civilized conduct in the ownership, organization, and management of economic instrumentalities. Relatively few in numbers, they nonetheless reached multitudes of people in all parts of the country and impressed their world-view indelibly upon thought about the social responsibilities of citizens and "what the classes owe to each other." Commenting on Charles H. Hopkins' *Rise of the Social Gospel in American Protestantism*, published in 1940, Charles A. Ellwood, sociologist, declared that "no movement has been more significant in the development of American civilization than the rise of the so-called social gospel." If this evaluation attributed too much weight to it, certainly leaders in that movement, especially the Christian socialists, strenuously combated the dogma of individualism and the current tendency to harmonize existing accumulations of wealth and pomp with a "righteous civilization." Constructively, they proposed a socialist commonwealth inspired by a love of humanity inculcated by the Christian spirit.

Deriving their dogmas from the Christian teachings respecting human brotherhood and the moral responsibility laid upon members of the brotherhood for mutual aid and welfare, these new disciples put their stress upon "social redemption"—upon the realization on earth of the kingdom of heaven by cooperative action. They disagreed among themselves over programs of immediate action, over the extremes to which measures of amelioration should be carried, but in their minds and hearts the contradiction between great poverty and civilization, so long connected with the discussion of civilization, assumed a poignancy as deep as religious sentiments.

Committed to a social interpretation of their faith, they were bound to controvert the doctrine that individuals and social classes owe each other little, or "nothing" as William Graham Sumner put it; they were impelled to point out with the severity of ancient seers the fallacy of the assumption that American civilization had almost, if not entirely, accomplished perfection. So obligated they naturally came into collision with that form of economic individualism which claimed the cosmic sanction of biological determinism wearing the guise of Darwinism.

In the Christian social movement to which many clergymen consecrated themselves, George D. Herron long exerted a notable influence, particularly in the middle west. By birth, education, and early professional life he belonged to the region. He was born in Indiana. For a brief period he studied in the preparatory department of Ripon College in Wisconsin. From 1879 to 1882 he worked at the printer's trade. Casting off the craftsman's role, he entered the ministry and soon evolved his religious faith into a gospel of social action.

As early as 1891 Herron sounded the note of the new dispensation in an address to Congregational ministers assembled in Minneapolis, by taking as his theme "The Message of Jesus to Men of Wealth," a plea for "the application of Christian ethics to business." Soon afterward he became professor of applied Christianity at Grinnell College in Iowa and there he sought to "translate Christianity into social, political, and economic terms." The work of local teaching he supplemented by long lecture tours to expound his doctrines to audiences in various parts of the country, including the Ohio Valley. By the spoken and printed word he reached thousands of clergymen, college students, business men, and laymen generally, stirring up controversies while making converts to his philosophy. Before the end of the century Herron had become a prominent figure in a stormy period marked by the panic of 1893, the Pullman strike of 1894, and the imperialist outburst of 1898.

In 1894 Herron published *The Christian Society*, a collection of five addresses which, by their titles, disclosed the burden of his thought: The Scientific Ground of a Christian Sociology, The Christian Constitution of Society, The Gospel of Jesus to the Poor, The Message of Jesus to Men of Wealth, and The Political Economy of the Lord's Prayer. Proclaiming the supremacy of the spirit over matter, minimizing the formalities of theology and ceremony, Herron declared the necessity of bringing the outward and visible signs of civilization into conformity with the teachings of Christ. The mission of the Church was to apply the touch-stone of Christ's teaching to every phase of life and society, to all earthly things and activities; to summon into being a civilization in harmony with divine purpose.

Speaking of the suffering in the business depression of the time, Herron made the treatment of its distresses a test of American civilization: "The social strain of this winter of 1893 and 1894 is the beginning of the first real test of the worth of our American civilization, which must be known by its fruits. Whether swiftly or slowly, the strain will in-tensify until it proves to be either the formative or consum-ing trial of our government. It may seem unwise and revolu-tionary so to prophesy. But danger comes to a people through warnings unheeded rather than warnings spoken. . . . This social strain, this winter of unemployment and want, is without excuse to a righteous reason. There is no war; no pestilence; no failure of harvests. There is abun-dance in our land for the people. Yet this richest nation of the world, in the midst of a material prosperity so marvelous as to become the object of political worship, suddenly finds a vast population face to face with famine, dependent upon some quality of public philanthropy."

Where lay the cause of this crisis in American society? Herron scorned as futile any discussion of tariffs, coinage, and party changes, and attributed national troubles to the centralization of wealth, the control of industry by the cun-ning and the strong, the moral irresponsibility of those "who indirectly rule the lives and economies of the people." Back of it all lay "the irresponsible egotism produced by a false science of society," the science that made individualism the driving force of civilization. "This false science has given us the hardest masters and the most helpless slavery. . . . Sociology has not yet become a science. It has bewildered our social troubles with an anarchy of figures, but has found no ground for human relations; it has given us no construc-tive knowledge of social order. The observation of existing phenomena apart from moral facts and forces, a reverence for statistics and an aversion to principles, has been the fatuity of all attempts to create a science of sociology. . . . Its work only begins with the observance of existing phe-nomena. It must give society knowledge of how to create phenomena that shall be just. . . . Sociology can become a science only by becoming a science of redemption. . . . Sociology must be a science of justice to be a science of society."

The outstanding protagonist of "the false science" of sociology, Herron named and denounced—William Graham Sumner who was teaching, as science, at Yale University, the formula of individualism in its baldest Darwinian terms as the mainspring of civilization. "The heart of all our social disputes," said Herron, "is what Mulford calls 'the crude assertion of an enlightened self-interest as the law of human activity.' This assertion is the essence of the gospel which Professor Sumner proclaims from his chair in a great Christian university. Social classes, he decides, owe each other nothing; benevolence is simply barter, and 'the yearning after equality the offspring of envy and covetousness.' This is a gospel which would have caused the proclaimer to be mobbed in the streets of Athens in the days of Pericles; a gospel which would have astounded Moses, and seemed ancient and barbarous to Abraham. The supremacy of the law of self-interest is the conclusion of Herbert Spencer's materialistic philosophy; and of the wretched pessimism of Hartmann and Schopenhauer. It is the principle upon which Cain slew his brother. . . . It is the principle upon which crime is committed. . . . It is the principle upon which railroads are bonded and bankrupted for private ends. . . . It is the principle upon which a Chicago financier proceeds, with no more moral justification than the highwayman's robbery of an express train, to 'corner' the pork market, and thus force from the hungry mouths of toiling families a million and a half of dollars into his private treasury—a deed for which the giving of some thousands to found city missions and institutions will be no atonement in the reckoning of the God who judges the world in righteousness and not by the ethics of the stock exchange."

The materialist conception of civilization Herron condemned unqualifiedly: "What we call civilization is infinitely short of the goal of progress. It bruises the divine life in man, even when you have said all you can in civilization's behalf. Polished manners, systematic theologies, fashionable clothes, the sciences of the universities, electric street cars, towering temples of trade, are not life; in fact they are not civilization. . . . They obscure our vision of God and his world, fastening our faith to things rather than righteousness; to values stamped on paper and anarchies of commercial architecture. God will keep bringing man's civilizations to naught till we have a civilization that is the order of his providence. . . . The natural development of our civilization will not unfold the solution of our industrial problems. When we watch the mammoth enginery of this modern civilization through the assurances of a partisan press, or the mercenary declamation of the politicians . . . the movements of its great wheels seem wonderfully safe and perfect; but when we, in our sober, honest, thoughtful moments, view it through the sympathies and purposes of the divine Man of Sorrows, we see torn, bleeding, mangled, sorrowing, famishing multitudes beneath the wheels of its remorseless enginery; we see that greed and not love is the power that moves our civilization; we see politics, commerce, and the social club moving on the economic assumption that selfishness is the only considerable social force, and assuming that civilization can advance only through the equal balancing of warring, selfish interests."

Civilization so visualized offers nothing good to humanity. "A civilization based on self-interest, and securing itself through competition, has no power within itself to secure justice. We speak to pitiless forces when we appeal to its processes to right the wrongs and inequalities of society. The world is not to be saved by civilization. It is civilization that needs saving. A civilization basing itself upon self-interest has a more dangerous foundation than dynamite. . . . It is atheistic because it treats God and his righteousness as external to itself. . . . It is a civilization which Bishop Huntington declares 'leads by a sure course to barbarism.' It is a civilization under whose procession John Stuart Mill affirms the very idea of 'justice, or any proportionality between success and merit, or between success and exertion,' to be 'so chimerical as to be relegated to the region of romance.' The end to which the civilization of the present tends is material, and not moral; it tends to the enslavement of society and the smothering of its highest life. Civilization is the flower of the dominant classes; it is an effect more than a cause; its forces originate in character; its activities are the expression of the people's being."

Hope for a true civilization lay in inner righteousness socially applied: "No civilization can be made righteous, or can make itself righteous, by any restraints or regulations external to itself. . . . There is no power in abstract truth, either economic, ethical, or theological, to cure our social ills. . . . Ethical truth taught to an unspiritualized race, or generation, or civilization, is a childish waste of time and strength. . . . We cannot look to the state to solve our social woes and grant our social hopes." Civilization and the State as now constituted represent merely unregenerate people.

Only by the redemption of the people through Christianity can the just civilization come into being. "A righteous civilization can have no other source than the inward righteousness of those who originate and control its forces. . . . There is no ethics apart from religion. . . . There is no ethical truth other than the expression of the will of God. . . . The people must be righteous before the state can be righteous. . . . The state cannot, by any possible process, make the rich man unselfish, or the poor man thrifty. The state cannot establish justice and righteousness on the earth; but justice and righteousness must establish the state. Except the state be born again, it cannot see the kingdom of God."

In this predicament, according to Herron's analysis, Americans had a choice between Christ and Cain: "God's solvent of the social problem of our day is the cross. And the cross is more than an historic event. It is the law by which God acts, and expects men to act. It is the creed of God which will never be revised. It is the principle upon which creation and history proceed. It was the assertion intensified which God has been making through all history, of self-sacrifice as the law of human development and achievement. Self-sacrifice is the law which God asserts in Christ over against the law of self-interest which Satan asserts in Cain. The trial in progress is Christ *versus* Cain. The decision to which the times are hastening is, Shall Christ or Cain reign in our American civilization? And well may the heavens await our decision in silent and awful wonder; for we are deciding the destiny of the earth."

If the generalities of the social gospel, whether independent or blended with socialism, were to be more than abstractions, they had to be applied to concrete problems of society, Christian Socialists averred. The need for this practical operation was early felt by the Reverend W. D. P. Bliss, who had been active in founding the Christian Socialist Society in 1889. As if in the tradition of the great French encyclopedists, Bliss broke the large schemes of "social re-

demption" down into specific issues of reform and, with the
cooperation of many experts, prepared a compendium which
dealt with nearly all aspects of civilization—*The Encyclopedia of Social Reform,* a volume of 1439 pages, first published in 1897, containing articles ranging from "Abandoned
farms" to "Zone-tariff system."

Freer than those compendium-makers who professed
"complete objectivity" or seemed to assume that they had
reached that goal with more or less finesse, Bliss laid bare
in his Preface his scheme of reference, his fundamental purpose. "The encyclopedia," he said, "is for general workers
and students in social reform." Its nature—the subjects
chosen for treatment—indicated the richness and diversity
of thought about society then current among such Americans. In its scope it comprised nearly every phase of social
theory and practice on which the critical and creative energies of reformers were at the time concentrated. The extensive acceptance and use made of the *Encyclopedia* supported the presumption that optimistic reliance on strict
individualism as the mainspring of civilization was being
traversed even in the age of its formulated ascendency.

While exposing, with a frankness not customary among
encyclopedists, his controlling intellectual interest, Bliss
strove for accuracy in the hundreds of articles included
within the ample folds of his volume. "Reliability" he placed
first among the requisites of an encyclopedia. This requi-
site, he explained, had been sought by "having every article
either written or revised by some specialist on each particular subject. In the case of all proposed reforms the
statement of the reform has been written, or at least revised,
by a believer in the reform; but, together with this, or by
reference to an article on the opposing side, a statement of
the opposing view will be found. . . . The encyclopedia . . .
has been prepared by specialists for those who are not specialists. . . . This work is a pioneer of its kind. Its aim has
been to give on all the broad range of reform the experience
of the past, the facts of the present, the proposals for the
future." Thus plans of creative reform were united with
history and description.

Limitations on the enterprise were admitted, however, by
the Editor in stating his purpose: "The subject is so vast,
and may be made so inclusive, that almost any subject might
be included here; but this encyclopedia aims to distinguish

sharply between subjects that belong mainly to the individual and those that belong mainly to society. A few subjects, such as religion, science, &c., that concern both the individual and society, are treated only in their social aspects." There was, for instance, no article on Christianity as such; but more than thirty pages were devoted to Christ and social reform, Christianity and social reform, Christian socialism, the Christian Social Union, the church and social reform, the church and the working men, the Church Social Union, and the Church temperance society, among others. To these were added articles on Methodism and social reform, the Roman Catholic church and social reform, the Presbyterian church and social reform, and other denominations in the same relation. Supplementary articles on special phases of the religious interest, such as usury and institutional churches, illustrated Christian theory and practice in long processes of history. Although science and technology did not appear under separate headings, manifestations of their applications were treated in appropriate places.

While Bliss procured the services of many experts for his enterprise, such as A. T. Hadley, who did not share his opinions on the mandates and urgency of the social gospel, he made a point of giving space to the reformers who had entered the lists against the creed of individualism, for example, Edward Bellamy, Helen Blackburn, Emily Blackwell, John R. Commons, E. W. Bemis, and Carroll D. Wright. Moreover he included brief biographies of social reformers as well as representatives of other schools.

However considered with reference to the merits of particular articles, the *Encyclopedia* provided ammunition for critical and constructive leaders in the movement that was drawing public attention away from individualism as the promise of American life and directing it to the idea of commonwealth as that promise. In so doing, perhaps more than incidentally, it contributed to the rise and growth of institutional economics which also helped to undermine the sway of the classical doctrine in the academies. Although it contained no special article on civilization as such it was a voluminous document in the written history of civilization.

In the later phase of the Christian social movement, which was asseverating the social principle against the disintegrating encroachments of individualism, spirited leadership was taken by Walter Rauschenbusch, a son of German immigrants who had fled to America from the reaction against the revolution of 1848. He was prepared for the Baptist ministry in the University at Rochester, New York, his birthplace, and by higher studies in Germany. When his formal education had been completed, he put aside an opportunity to occupy a comfortable pastorate and deliberately chose to labor among the poor of New York City, serving especially German immigrants who poured into the metropolis.

During the great blizzard of 1888, in ministering to sick and wretched members of his congregation, Rauschenbusch was stricken by influenza and suffered a physical shock from which he never fully recovered. The great business depression that followed the panic of 1893 sickened his sensitive spirit. "One could hear human virtue cracking and crushing all around," he exclaimed. It was while living and preaching in a desolate quarter of the great city that Rauschenbusch became acquainted with the writings of Henry George, Tolstoi, Mazzini, Marx, Ruskin, and Bellamy, and began to wonder how the misery he saw on every hand could be remedied by the application of Christian teachings. Unable at length to carry the physical burden of his labors in the metropolis, he accepted a call to a professorship in the Rochester Theological Seminary and there began a career of lecturing and writing in which he sought to bring the kingdom of heaven closer to earth.

During the short-lived but ominous financial crash of 1907, Rauschenbusch published his *Christianity and the Social Crisis*. In this work he focussed his historical learning and humane sympathies on what was for him the master issue of his time. "Western civilization," he wrote, "is passing through a social revolution unparalleled in history for scope and power. Its coming was inevitable. The religious, political, and intellectual revolutions of the past five centuries, which together created the modern world, necessarily had to culminate in an economic and social revolution such as is now upon us. . . . The social revolution has been slow in reaching this country. . . . The vastness and the free sweep of our concentrated wealth on the one side, the independence, intelligence, moral vigor, and political power of the common people on the other side, promise a long-drawn grapple of contesting forces which may well make the heart of every American patriot sink within him. It is realized that religion can play, and must play, a momentous part in this irrepressible conflict. . . . The relation between Christianity and the social crisis is one of the most pressing questions for all intelligent men who realize the power of religion, and most of all for the religious leaders of the people who give direction to the forces of religion."

The first dire effects of the industrial revolution in European countries, Rauschenbusch maintained, had been greatly mitigated by labor organizations, state intervention, and awakened social conscience, and chiefly, by fear of the social democracy. But no such mitigation had as yet come about in the United States: "Our machinery is speeded faster; our capital centralizes faster; we use up human life more recklessly; we are less hampered by custom and prejudice. If we are once headed toward a social catastrophe, we shall get there ahead of schedule time." In American life lies a serious contradiction: "We cannot join economic inequality with political equality. As Oliver Cromwell wrote to Parliament 'If there be any one that makes many poor to make a few rich, that suits not a Commonwealth.'"

Out of the intimate knowledge he had gained as pastor of a poverty-stricken congregation, Rauschenbusch described what he deemed appalling evils in America—misery, garish wealth, self-centered individualism, cold and merciless resistance to every effort in the direction of reform. In making his list of evils he did not omit the effort of New York merchants to defeat a bill in the legislature which provided that they must furnish seats for women clerks and allow them to sit down behind counters when not serving customers. The inequities of the common law doctrines which prevented immediate compensation to working people mangled in machine industries—doctrines then brilliantly defended by powerful minds—drew from Rauschenbusch protests of pathos and scorn.

Having presented the gospel of Christian mercy, love, and justice and the contrast of industrial individualism in America, Rauschenbusch warned his country of breakers ahead: "The continents are strewn with the ruins of dead nations and civilizations. History laughs at the optimistic illusion that 'nothing can stand in the way of human progress.' It would be safer to say that progress is for a time only, and then succumbs to the inevitable decay. One by one the ancient peoples rose to wealth and civilization, extended their sway as far as geographical conditions would permit, and then began to decay within and crumble away without. . . . What guarantee have we, then, that our modern civilization with its pomp will not be 'one with Nineveh and Tyre'? The most important question which humanity ought to address to its historical scholars is this: 'Why did these others die, and what can we do to escape their fate?' . . . There is no inherent cause why a great group of nations, such as that which is now united in Western civilization, should not live on in perpetual youth, overcoming by a series of rejuvenations every social evil as it arises, and using every attainment as a stepping-stone to a still higher culture of individual and social life. It has never yet been done. Can it be done in a civilization in which Christianity is the salt of the earth, the socal preservative?"

Could it be done? That was the question for Rauschenbusch. "Nations do not die by wealth, but by injustice. . . . Progress slackens when a single class appropriates the social results of the common labor, fortifies its evil rights by unfair laws, throttles the masses by political centralization and suppression, and consumes in luxury what it has taken in covetousness. Then there is a gradual loss of productive energy, and increasing bitterness and distrust, a waning sense of duty and devotion to country, a paralysis of the moral springs of noble action. Men no longer love the Commonwealth, because it does not stand for the commonwealth. Force has to supply the cohesive power which love fails to furnish. Exploitation creates poverty, and poverty is followed by physical degeneration. Education, art, wealth, and culture may continue to advance and may even ripen to their mellowest perfection when the worm of death is already at the heart of the nation. Internal convulsions or external catastrophes will finally reveal the state of decay. . . . The cry of 'Crisis! crisis!' has become a weariness. Every age and every year are critical and fraught with destiny. Yet in the widest survey of history Western civilization is now at a decisive point in its development."

In this decisive hour, Rauschenbusch cried, there must be a moral revival! "In the last resort the only hope is in the moral forces which can be summoned to the rescue. If there are statesmen, prophets, and apostles who set truth and justice above selfish advancement; if their call finds a response in the great body of the people; if a new tide of religious faith and moral enthusiasm creates new standards of duty and a new capacity for self-sacrifice; if the strong learn to direct their love of power to the uplifting of the people and see the highest self-assertion in self-sacrifice— then the intrenchments of vested wrong will melt away; the stifled energy of the people will leap forward; the atrophied members of the social body will be filled with a fresh flow of blood; and a regenerate nation will look with the eyes of youth across the fields of the future. . . . If at this juncture we can rally sufficient religious faith and moral strength to snap the bonds of evil and turn the present unparalleled economic and intellectual resources of humanity to the harmonious development of a true social life, the generations yet unborn will mark this as that great day of the Lord for which the ages waited, and count us blessed for sharing in the apostolate that proclaimed it."

In terms more concrete Rauschenbusch found his specific answer in the selfless sacrifice of Christian communism, which, he declared, had long been the ideal of Christianity. "Ask any moral teacher who is scouting communism and glorifying individualism, what social institutions to-day are most important for the moral education of mankind and most beneficent in their influence on human happiness, and he will probably reply promptly, 'The home, the school, and the church.' But these three are communistic institutions. . . . Each member of the family has some private property, clothes, letters, pictures, toys, but the rooms and the furniture in the main are common to all, and if one member needs the private property of another, there is ready sharing. . . . The housewife is the manager of a successful communistic colony, and it is perhaps not accidental that our women, who move thus within a fraternal organization, are the chief stays of our Christianity. Similarly our schools are supported on a purely communistic basis; those who have no children or whose children are grown up are nevertheless taxed for the education of the children of the community. . . . Our churches, too, are voluntary communisms which all share and others are warmly invited to share."

Referring to the multiplying functions of government undertaken in the name of the general welfare, Rauschenbusch declared: "It can fairly be maintained, too, that the State, another great moral agent, is communistic in its very nature." How far this communistic trend was to go, he left "to the common sense of the future." As for himself he believed that only by a resort to more or less communism, inspired by love and justice, not by class hatred, could civilization be preserved and promoted; could Christianity come into its noblest and triumphant expression.

It was not only clergymen who were stirred by the gospel of social redemption. By sermons in cities and towns its apostles influenced thousands of laymen. By lectures in colleges and universities they kindled the enthusiasm of young men and women. The diffusion of their teaching penetrated the studies of scholars concerned with the humanities, at least those scholars who had not built a wall of "objectivity" between themselves and the world of realities or subjected their ethical impulses to the economic or biological determinism so intensively cultivated in scientific circles. At the risk of being called sentimental by their brethren who boasted of their science or their hard heads, several scholars recognized the force of the social gospel and introduced Christian ethics into their systems of thought. A few, at the risk of academic security, publicly proclaimed this gospel, in the age of militant industrialism, as a faithful interpretation of Christianity.

In the thought and aspirations of Vida Scudder of the Wellesley College faculty, learning in literature and learning in Christian idealism, Catholic and Protestant, were intermingled and gave force to her leadership in the Christian socialist movement. Early in her teaching career she began to inculcate, in lectures, essays, pamphlets, and books, the ethical commands contained in great pieces of literature from the letters of St. Catherine of Siena to the writings of John Ruskin. Her matured tenets she propounded in 1917 in *The Church and the Hour*. In this volume she sought "to draw out the social significance of the Gospels, to define Christian duty in terms of industrial justice for an industrial age." The task had been too long neglected, despite the work of the pioneers. Now it must be faced without flinching: "Concrete and stinging must be the application of Christian ideals made by the Church to modern civilization and modern Christian lives."

Signs of such action seemed visible to her: "The Federal Council of the Churches of Christ in America expresses again the deepening conviction that the scope of the gospel and the program of the churches must include the creation on earth of a Christian civilization, organized upon the ethical teachings and controlled by the Spirit of Jesus Christ." Besides, the general convention of the Protestant Episcopal Church, in 1913, had delivered an "outspoken repudiation of *laissez faire.*"

But these were only beginnings, Miss Scudder said—signs within the Church that it was becoming conscious of its obligations to society. She kept hammering at its failures to act upon that consciousness in more vital ways. The Church is not appealing to the working classes, she declared. It does not boldly lift the curtain on "the social causes of poverty." Divided, hesitant, and backward, the Church "has apparently no contribution to make, as an official body, either toward the healing of the nations or toward the healing of social disorders. . . . Religion has consoled the bereaved, it has strengthened the dying, it has established vast works of philanthropy; for any statesmanlike attempt to evolve justice between nations or classes by the application of the law of Christ, men have looked to it in vain." The "accredited type of piety" in the United States has been "suave-mannered, pleasant voiced; endangering nothing in particular, an ornament to the Sunday pews; devoted to good causes in proportion to their remoteness, intent on promoting safe philanthropies and foreign missions, but, so far as home affairs are concerned, ignorant alike of the ardors of the mystic and the heroisms of the reformer."

The creation of "a Christian civilization," Miss Scudder contended, meant grappling with the central problems of the modern world: the abolition of war among nations, overcoming "the dangerous commercial rivalries of the nations"; establishing equality and justice among capitalists, employers, and workers; the shifting of industry from off "its basis of profits upon that of human welfare"; lifting women to a position of freedom and equality; removing the handicap of poverty from submerged millions; uplifting the backward races of the earth, but not by force; the extension of democracy; the development of efficiency and honesty in democracy. These objectives, she asserted, "are within the power of human effort when sustained and scientifically organized, and henceforth they are to be ever before the churches. They call for faith and consecrated endeavor on an unprecedented scale."

On the answer of the churches to such questions, she stated

emphatically, depends "the salvation of civilized life. . . . Realities become masked with the advance of civilization. Many masks have fallen now. . . . The social order is seen stark naked; it is not a lovely sight." In a hideous glare "it is possible to see Mars and Mammon, twin supporters of the old Capitalistic order, rushing to their own destruction. . . . If civilization, with its science, its culture, its thousand graces of heart and mind, is not to be abandoned to the powers of evil, the revolutionary principle of love must be accepted as the practical basis for all human relations, industrial and national. But, for the Christian, what a tremendous IF!"

The movement of events, new knowledge, and thought relative to civilization burst into the realm of imaginative letters. It found expression in the literature of description and analysis concerned with personal character and class relations. It gave color and form to the literature of constructive searching for ways and means of bringing into fuller realization the potentials of greater civilization in America.

Having early arrived at quandaries and convictions respecting the course of American civilization and the numerous divergencies between American principles and practices, William Dean Howells employed various media of literature, including fiction, in conveying his sentiments and opinions to his large reading public. In special ways Howells was well endowed for interpreting American affairs. He was born and bred in the equalitarian society of Ohio before the civil war—a society of farms, villages, and small towns. In his veins flowed Welsh, German, English, and Irish blood—the blood of farmers and artisans. His father, a Quaker turned Swedenborgian, was a poor printer and journalist enlisted in the anti-slavery cause. In his father's shop the boy learned the printer's trade and in a nook in his humble home he educated himself in languages and letters, all the while living the simple life of a simple community.

Having won the attention of Lincoln by a biography of him which he wrote for the campaign of 1860, when working at journalism in Columbus, Howells was rewarded by a consulate in Venice. There he began an acquaintance with the Old World, which was later enlarged by extended journeys. After serving for a season on The Nation under Godkin, he formed a connection with The Atlantic Monthly, which brought him into long and close association with prominent writers of the New England school. Perhaps even more intimate and influential was his life-long friendship with Mark Twain, also an American from the middle west, who in his youth had likewise imbibed the spirit of an equalitarian society and in his later years shared many of Howells' deep resentments over the turns taken in American affairs.

According to some literary critics, Howells' social sympathies were tepid and unrealistic—pale flickers of a European culture useful to his literary career. But his writings as a whole, including his correspondence, do not sustain this judgment. He knew many American reformers personally and was acquainted with reformist literature. He never substituted a class feeling for the fraternalism derived from the plain Ohio community in which his formative years had been spent. A biographer of Lincoln and a public servant under The Emancipator, Howells belonged to the generation that took seriously the solemnity of the Gettysburg Address.

It is true that hundreds of his letters, written to men and women with whom he had business relations or casual social connections, displayed conformity to the canons of conventional intercourse. Yet other letters, especially his correspondence with Mark Twain, who seemed closest to his deepest and most constant self, revealed his central interests and his driving hopes and fears. It is in these writings that Howells' governing scheme of thought and aspiration is to be discerned. But the expression of his fundamental convictions was not confined to private correspondence. It appeared in innumerable slight sketches written for the popular magazines as well as in his novels.

Howells did not tear passion to tatters or wear signs of his formative sympathies on his sleeve. In the business of making a living with his pen, the way to which he seemed destined by youthful propensities and the nature of his mind, he often indulged in the trivialities required by editors and audiences; but he never, even to the very end, lost his interest in popular movements or ceased to look with concern upon the social struggles.

One example illustrates the contention. Though the tempest of popular agitation was foreign to his spirit, he petitioned Governor Richard Oglesby to commute to imprisonment the death penalty pronounced on the Chicago anarchists and in 1887 wrote a letter to the New York Tribune explaining his position with reference to that celebrated case. In this action he faced a fanatical and infuriated press and public, enduring even the shock of the misleading headline which the Tribune placed above his communication. In the letter he betrayed in two simple sentences more insight into the event than all his angry critics combined: "The justice or injustice of their sentence was not before the highest tribunal of our law, and unhappily could not be got there. That question must remain for history, which judges the judgment of courts, to deal with; and I, for one, cannot doubt what the decision of history will be."

That he was not merely concerned with entertaining and amusing readers, Howells avowed to Edward Everett Hale in 1888: "The most I can do is perhaps to set a few people to thinking: for as yet I haven't got to *doing* anything, myself. But at present it seems to me that our competitive civilization is in a state of warfare and a game of chance, in which each man fights and bets against fearful odds." Again, in the same year, he disclosed to Henry James a spirit that was far from complacent: "I'm not in a very good humor with 'America' myself. It seems to be the most grotesquely illogical thing under the sun; and I suppose that I love it less because it won't let me love it more. I should hardly like to trust pen and ink with all the audacity of my social ideas; but after fifty years of optimistic content with 'civilization' and its ability to come out all right in the end, I now abhor it, and feel that it is coming out all wrong in the end, unless it bases itself anew on a real equality. Meantime, I wear a furlined overcoat, and live in all the luxury my money can buy." Unlike Henry James and Edith Wharton, he did not desert his native land and renounce his citizenship. He kept on working at home.

In his inmost psyche Howells fretted over the incongruity between the ideals proclaimed at the foundation of the Republic and the performances of the élite which instructed and governed the country in his own age. When Mark Twain burst out in fury against American indifference to the overthrow of a monarch and the establishment of a republic in Brazil in 1889, Howells gave a reason for that indifference to his indignant friend: "I have just heated myself up with your righteous wrath about our indifference to the Brazilian Republic. But it seems to me that you ignore the real reason for it which is that there is no longer an American Republic, but an aristocracy-loving oligarchy in place of it. Why should our Money-bags rejoice in the explosion of a Wind-bag? They know that at the bottom of the hole where their souls ought to be that if such an event finally means anything it means their ruin next; and so they *don't* rejoice; and as they mostly inspire the people's voice, the press, the press is dumb."

After he had won a place in American letters, as a novelist and an editor, Howells, in 1891, moved to New York where he continued to wrestle with subjects rooted in the tough conflicts attending the industrialization of American economy. He had lived in that metropolis only three years when he published *A Traveler from Altruria*, an excursion into the nature of American civilization as opposed to an ideal civilization in an imaginary commonwealth, Altruria.

This analysis of contemporary society took the form of a debate among spokesmen of various professions and interests, projected against a background of conditions likewise presumed to be representative. And the dream of a better life was expressed through the medium of a visitor from a strange realm who, by inquiries of his own, answers to questions put to him by others, and finally by a long speech, pointed out the discrepancy between the ideal and the real; between the noble doctrine of liberty, equality, fraternity, and the pursuit of happiness, as the American way of life, and the actualities of behavior in the American society as he observed them in 1894.

In the characters of *A Traveler from Altruria* the class aspects of American society were delineated. A lawyer, who in a moment of hesitation thought that the law had some relation to justice, stood fast in general for things as they were. Not too upset by the conflict between Christian teachings and the practices of his parishioners, a parson doubted whether human nature was equal to establishing the Kingdom of Heaven on earth. A professor from the academy recited the phrases of Ricardo, Malthus, and Sumner—overpopulation, the improvidence of the poor, supply and demand, and the follies of expecting anything better. A manufacturer, who had smashed a trade union by a lockout, stuck by his guns without whitewashing his own crowd.

Speaking for finance capitalism, with a sense of humor, of proportion, a banker conceded the drift away from competition in business toward monopoly and displayed an amused willingness to consider speculations concerning the future of the drift, while flicking ashes from his cigar. A poor farming family in New England voiced the inchoate laments of rising populism. From industrial workers arose rough shouts of protest. A society woman, whose logic seemed deficient, fluttered around with charities and culture but managed to reach conclusions deemed "sound" by her set.

On the edges of the scene hovered a novelist, an author of pleasing books for American women who found time for reading while their men were too busy or too tired to read; in the interstices of conversation, the novelist managed to insert, occasionally with some confusion, maxims gratifying to his patrons. Experienced in his way with human nature, a physician seemed to tolerate all the talk with a certain degree of detachment and to suspect that many things might happen to the professor's best of all possible worlds.

In the course of conversations and discussions, "our civilization," on which the story turned, was submitted to historical and practical examination. The transformation in American life since the establishment of the Republic was sketched by the banker in an answer to his own question: "What should you say was our ideal of greatness?" In the early days the great politician, publicist, and statesman had represented our ideal. As the country grew older, "the literary fellows" had shared the honors that were going around. The civil war had brought the soldier to the front for a time. Then came the era of material prosperity: "I don't think there is any doubt but the millionaire is now the American ideal. . . . It is the man with the most money who now takes the prize in our national cakewalk." Yet, of course, things were moving into the future and the banker could contemplate the possibility of a new order in American development, without showing a sign of apoplexy.

The doctor, who had once engaged in charity practice and did not think that unemployment was a mere consequence of improvidence, agreed with the banker that many things could happen. Just what would happen he was not sure. The country might go forward into a stage of social democracy, such as the Altrurians had reached. Again, it might revert to some old order in which the master would possess the man. Again, nothing might happen: "We may hitch and jog along indefinitely as we are doing now." Such was his answer to the lawyer's question: "What should you say was the logic of events among us for the last ten or twenty years?" Accustomed to dealing with flesh and blood, rather than logic, the physician merely retorted: "There's nothing so capricious as the logic of events." The country might go forward into socialism, turn back to a kind of slavery, or simply "hitch and jog along indefinitely" as at present.

Though Howells was an adept in fiction, *A Traveler from Altruria* was not a full-length novel with an abstruse plot. It was barely a novel at all, just enough of a narrative to convey an interpretation and projection of American history amid the tangle and jangle of conversations revolving around the idea of civilization. The past, its theories and practices, was reviewed firmly, if in snatches, sketches, and fragments. "Our civilization" at the stage reached in 1894, was limned against the background of history, was compared with civilization in the ideal commonwealth of Altruria as described by the visitor from that realm. In due time, the transformation of America was to come about by evolution, by the democratic process of the ballot, as the capitalistic system in its inexorable drive toward concentration entered into its maturity.

If any doubts about the interpretative intent of the social drama were raised for the readers by the persiflage and casual arguments at the beginning of this story, they were resolved for them by the long address of the Altrurian near the end. The brusque fashion in which farmers and industrial workers snatched the lead from the middle-class guests of the summer hotel where the scene was laid, as well as caustic passages in the Altrurian's discourse, brought to light Howells' opinion of the process by which the transition from "our civilization" of that age to the new civilization in America might be effected.

While Howells was still at Boston, before he had confessed his social philosophy in *A Traveler from Altruria*, a newspaper man in western Massachusetts, Edward Bellamy, had been moved by the same incongruities between professions and practices which had caught and fixed Howells' interest. Spurred by curiosity as to the future and by his social sympathies, Bellamy wrote *Looking Backward*, published in 1888—an equally simple and likewise didactic story but composed on different lines. Bellamy made mankind victorious through science, machinery, and technology over poverty and degradation and at last possessing the securities and prospects long forecast by the idea of civilization. The argument of this story he amplified and supplemented in another novel, *Equality*.

By its very time-span, as well as by its structure, *Looking Backward* rested on a theory of history; and the upshot was a projection of the civilizing process, facilitated by the new technology, into a highly advanced social order at the end of the twentieth century. Bellamy did not, therefore, create his utopia out of sheer dreaming. The ideal society which he placed in that distant time was not to descend upon the earth from the clouds. "The elements which were to develop" the commonwealth of the year 2000 "were already in ferment" in 1887, he said; and every feature of that new society was an idealization or extension of some fine and humane characteristic of American civilization at the stage to which it had evolved by 1887.

In short, Bellamy united and universalized fragments of an ideal civilization in the process of becoming in 1887, and foreshadowed inventions and institutions still more ingenious and beneficent, many of which were indeed created before Bellamy's generation passed away. A careful study of his *Looking Backward,* his other books, and his articles in The New Nation, established to spread his ideas, justifies the assertion that he was thinking under the appeal of civilization, implicitly and explicitly.

In the first chapter of *Looking Backward*, Bellamy pictured current strikes, disorders, unrest, and demands of industrial workers, described the alarms which accompanied the manifestations of discontent, and epitomized discussions of the situation carried on among the élite of Boston at the time he was writing his book. The sanguine among the participants in the conversations "argued very forcibly that it was in the very nature of things impossible that the new hopes of the workingmen could be satisfied, simply because the world had not the wherewithal to satisfy them. . . . It was not the capitalists whom the laboring men were contending with, these maintained, but the iron-bound environment of humanity, and it was merely a question of the thickness of their skulls when they would discover the fact and make up their minds to endure what they could not cure." That was the optimistic view of things in Boston in 1887.

"The less sanguine" among the disputants "admitted all this. Of course the workingmen's aspirations were impossible of fulfilment for natural reasons, but there were grounds to fear that they would not discover this fact until they had made a sad mess of society. . . . Some of these desponding observers went so far as to predict an impending social cataclysm. Humanity, they argued, having climbed to the top round of the ladder of civilization, was about to take a header into chaos, after which it would doubtless pick itself up. . . . Human history, like all great movements, was cyclical, and returned to the point of beginning. The idea of indefinite progress in a right line was a chimera of the imagination, with no analogue in nature. . . . Tending upward and sunward from the aphelion of barbarism, the race attained the perehelion of civilization only to plunge downward once more to its nether goal in the regions of chaos."

It was in part to offset this pessimism, to demonstrate the possibility and probability of a straight-line development in civilization to higher and higher levels, and to put on record his sympathies with striving humanity that Bellamy composed and published *Looking Backward*. He had already indicated his interest in popular causes by an acute portrayal of agrarian unrest—by writing his novel *The Duke of Stockbridge,* a story of Shays' rebellion of 1786. Now in his systematic utopia he proclaimed a way of emancipation for all humanity. Not only did *Looking Backward* stir Americans; it was translated into many tongues and kindled in lands beyond the seas visions of better days to come.

Bellamy's epic dream served as a torch from which were lighted the aspirations of multitudes in the United States. In houses of the rich, in tenements of the cities, on lonely farms, it was read, reread, and discussed by millions of men and women. The enthusiasm of youth was quickened by its glowing hopes, and many young citizens destined to play active parts in national affairs got from its pages their first insight into America's latent economic and social powers.

The seed sown by Bellamy fell on fertile soil. Farmers, suffering from the effects of prolonged depressions, were drawing together under the banner of populism. Labor organizations, battling to improve the standing and lot of industrial workers through collective bargaining, were growing more conscious of the total economy and the need of a social philosophy. Members of the clergy and their parishioners, inspired by the social gospel of Christianity, were wrestling with the disparity between their ideals and the reality of the people's struggle for a mere existence. Intellectuals, alarmed by current tendencies, were searching for clues to the "course of civilization"—sign-posts to the way of action—and many of them were prepared to accept Bellamy's interpretation of American history as leading to an ideal order of society.

Excited to further activity by the amazing success of *Looking Backward,* Bellamy flung down the gage to E. L. Godkin's *Nation,* mouthpiece of unregenerate laissez faire, by founding a magazine of his own, *The New Nation.* While his novel rolled from the presses in edition after edition, Bellamy discussed in his journal current events with reference to the goal he had set for civilization. He periodically reported advances of his cause in all parts of the country, such as the growth of cooperation and municipal ownership of public utilities and the nation-wide struggle against "predatory wealth." With news and comments he carried essays, original or borrowed, on the historical backgrounds, which integrated his anticipations with the long process of civilization in the past, thereby recognizing the fact that his argument needed a firmer support than imagination or the logic of science or American principles could alone supply.

For example, in an article by Edward W. Searing of New York entitled "The Reign of the Huckster," the revolution in economy since the establishment of American independence was reviewed. "Priestly and kingly government being abolished, the founders supposed the republic would, of course, be governed for and by the people. It would have been nearly a perfect government theoretically if industrial conditions had continued as before, but the nineteenth century was at hand, bringing with it new forces, new agencies, new factors of society, new conditions of life, which have changed, or shortly will result in changing, the mass of the nation from independent workers with individual capital to wage workers without capital. . . . In the eighteenth century nearly the entire cost of producing went into the hands of the laborers producing it, if it was free labor. Now, the same articles being produced in the great factory, by complex machinery and enormous capital, the greater part of the cost goes to the machine, the capitalist, and the trader." For personal relations in economy, monetary relations have been substituted. Between the producers of various goods, the huckster, bent upon pecuniary gains, has intervened, and throughout society the seeking of money becomes a dominant force, transforming, re-creating all features of American life in the image of gain.

"We find the huckster's reign alike in church and state," Searing said, "in the teachings of our public schools, in the ethics of professional life, in the inspiration of our literature, and in the heads and hearts of a large part of the intelligent portion of the people, who have come to believe more in the protection of property than in the protection of man—in property rights than in human rights. . . . That the government of this republic, in spite of its glorious history and constitution, has passed into the control of the huckster, is shown by the Senate gradually filling up with millionaires, unknown except as plutocrats; by the application of the money standard to every function of society; and by the giving of the highest offices to the men who spend the most money in elections. . . . Now every writer employed on the editorial staff of the daily newspaper can but speak and write according to the policy of the paper. . . . The reign of the huckster extends even into our schools, teaching not humanity, but selfishness; not hunger and thirst after righteousness, after nobility, honor, greatness, but to seek money. Our schools do not teach the desire for the noblest, truest life, that the highest and only happiness is in love, friendship, duty. In learning A.B.C., children are taught that the only object of learning is its help to heap up gold."

But Searing protested in the name of civilization, saying, in America, "time, the father of empires," united a rich endowment in natural resources with "modern civilization." The purpose was not to heap up mountains of gold. "It was to develop man into a higher, nobler human being. . . . Our fathers established a republic which eliminated the reign of the priest and the king from the commonwealth. . . . The powers that have organized but enslaved in the past—the church and the army—having been so completely separated from government, Americans have been educated to believe that the republic secures freedom, equality, and just opportunity to all. . . . Civilization demands the highest and the most complete organization of industry attainable. We want industry as scientific, as orderly, as effective as war. We need all the advantages and economies which result from concentrated action, disciplined organization, and regulated economic and scientific production as we now see carried on by the great captains of industry in organizing trusts, pools, and monopolies. The interests of civilization may therefore require that, as in war, the result of these economies be developed as a social function for the use of the people, instead of for the benefit of a class to exploit the wealth of the community.

"The priest, soldier, and plutocrat in different stages of progress have in turn succeeded each other in government, and . . . the growth of social and moral feeling is now checked and blighted by the government of the huckster. . . . Plutocracy cannot be abolished except by social growth, and by attaining a higher and truer conception of the social function of capital. The huckster's government cannot be overturned by violence. It can only be changed by peaceful means, by developing political government, which allows the reign of the huckster, into an industrial commonwealth. If a higher social integration demands a government industrial organization as effective as war organization, this demand can only be attained when public opinion compels a public office to be administered as a public trust, and the enforcement of a civil service that secures continuity of employment, promotion, and retirement, with a pension in old age. Are not these demands reasonable, moderate, on a line of progress and growth, and of such a nature as will insure efficient and economic production? A cursory analysis of history seems to show a certainty of progressive change of this kind based upon the development of civilization, and the active wants, material, intellectual, and social, of mankind."

In another article which Bellamy reprinted, "The Wage System of Labor" was examined by John Clark Ridpath, the historian who had recently published his four-volume *Cyclopedia of Universal History*. In his survey, Ridpath presented a construct of history with civilization culminating in the reign of cooperation. In an early period of human development, he said, slavery was a form of labor, especially in low-lying level countries where staple crops were produced. "It is an incident of the agricultural stage in the evolution of the civilized life. . . . When the agricultural stage begins to give place to an epoch of manufactures and commerce, then wage-hire takes the place of slavery. We are now in the age of competitive manufacture and speculative commerce. Concomitant with this we have the wage-system of industry. . . . With this change has come also a change in name. Men have flattered themselves by naming the wage-system free labor. Our own country has fondly imagined that by substituting the purchase of labor for the purchase of men emancipation has come; that thus has been attained the freedom of the laborer as well as of the capital that buys his industry."

But civilization goes forward in time. "Without doubt there is good ground for preferring wage-hire to human bondage; but this by no means implies that the wage-system is the final form which civilization will invent. . . . As a matter of fact the increasing enlightenment of the age has brought a knowledge of the injustice, hardships, cruelty, and universal unhappiness springing out of the wage-hire system. There is an agitation reaching down to the sea-bed of humanity and, if we mistake not, the purchase and sale of human labor as a commodity of the market can not much longer continue. The reason of this is that labor is not, as men say, a commodity. . . . Labor is a part of the laborer. It is himself in action. It is impossible to conceive it as separated from him. To buy labor is to buy a part of the laborer; that is, a part of a man—not all of him, but a part." Buying and selling labor as a commodity is akin to slavery—to buying and selling human beings.

From classical economics Ridpath appealed to history, to the developing consciousness of mankind: "These ideas, which can be here no more than merely stated in words, are acting as a ferment in the thought and hope of our age. They are as yet not consciously, but unconsciously entertained. They are entering the consciousness of the people. They will presently become spoken and written thought, and will then take form in that great change which is to mark the end of the wage-system of industry and bring in the system of co-operation. Co-operation shall supervene in the place of that cruel system which has bartered and sold the labor of human beings as though it were an objective material product. No problem of today is more important than that of the safe and easy transference of society from the wage-system of industry to the system of peaceable and universal co-operation." The forces of history are aligned in this direction: "The wage-system of industry is about at an end. Civilization has reached a stage which will no longer tolerate the purchase and sale of human labor. The law of evolution is working here as elsewhere."

As the counter-reformation against individualism rampant proceeded, accumulating force and extending ever more widely in American society, stirring reflective thought from sea to sea, it was paralleled by organizations and actions in harmony with its various mandates. Thousands of committees, societies, and groups sprang up to promote one or more phases of civilization in the United States by concerted activities—community, local, state, and national.

In a way, a synthesis of the new undertakings and affirmations was effected at Chicago by an informal association of men and women for whom the Hull House was a center of conferences, open discussions, and planning. In that immense city were brutal illustrations of individualism in full swing: on the one side, huge fortunes and ostentation built upon avid enterprises in railways, industries, and real estate speculation; on the other, square miles of slums unfit for human habitation and industrial strife bitter and violent. In one of the slums, where immigrants of many nationalities herded, in a jungle of the underprivileged, the Hull House had been opened by Janes Addams and Ellen Gates Starr in 1889, as a stronghold of sympathy and aid for humanity.

The Hull House furnished a forum for the free discussion of all the issues then surging up in American civilization but so conveniently neglected in many closed circles and largely manhandled in the press. It was in a broad sense an educational institution designed, as Jane Addams said, to build for immigrants and natives, "a bridge between European and American experiences in such a wise as to give them both more meaning and a sense of relation." It also provided conference chambers for devising, scrutinizing, and testing new forms of social legislation for the state of Illinois, then backward in this respect and torn by industrial warfare. So constituted as a social laboratory it became a place of instruction for thousands of young men and women from all parts of the United States who were later to apply the new learning as teachers, journalists, social workers, business men, and clergymen in far-scattered places. Although its influence cannot be measured, the guess may be hazarded that no other single institution of the period did as much to counteract the dogma of individualism and restore the social principle to thought about civilization.

The spirit of the whole Hull House was imparted in the

speeches and writings of Jane Addams, its head. Among the guiding principles of the institution she placed "a profound conviction that . . . those 'best results of civilization' upon which depend the finer and freer aspects of living must be incorporated into our common life and have free mobility through all elements of society if we would have our democracy endure." In her opinion the "resources of civilization" were veritable bonds of society, though they had been unappreciated too long. "Because we are no longer stirred," she said in respect of one problem, "to remove fetters, to prevent cruelty, to lead the humblest to the banquet of civilization, we have allowed ourselves to become indifferent to the gravest situation in our American life." She was especially perturbed by the tendency of civilization to separate privileged persons from the toil and moil of laboring humanity and believed that the separation must be ended by planning and social action.

Among the members of "the Hull House group of Illinois social service leaders," as Harvey Wish called it in the American Historical Review for July, 1941, were significant figures in American history. Besides Jane Addams and Ellen Gates Starr, it included Florence Kelley, Julia C. Lathrop, Mrs. Joseph Bowen, and Alzina P. Stevens—with whom were associated in the social service program Clarence Darrow, Graham Taylor, Albion W. Small, Edward Bemis, Henry D. Lloyd, Nicholas Vachel Lindsay, and Edgar Lee Masters.

Some of the women from Hull House, notably Florence Kelley and Julia C. Lathrop, later transferred their activities to the East and led in the development of "national welfare services at Washington as pioneers of a greater Federal responsibility for dependent social groups—the embryo of contemporary legislation on social security." By writing, speaking, and making demonstrations in practice, members of the Hull House circle, wherever they were, helped to arouse the nation to a consciousness of "the resources of civilization," and at the same time impressed upon it the necessity of mobilizing the resources in action against the theory and applications of crass individualism, "if we would have our democracy endure."

Leaders of the Hull House group had the confidence, cooperation, and support of John P. Altgeld, one of the best loved and most hated men of the age, who, while governor of Illinois, aided in translating many of their proposals into law and administration. Indeed their agitations had nourished the public sentiment that elected him to office and sustained his public policies. Nearly everything in his program was in their program: the demand for "essential statistical information on industrial conditions in Chicago," extension of child-labor legislation from mines to factories, extermination of sweat shops in cities, introduction of factory inspection, arbitration in labor disputes, regulation of public utilities, abolition of the exploitation of convict labor by private contractors, enlargement and improvement of state welfare institutions, lifting the state university to a high position as a center of learning in the public service, and advancement of popular education in every department.

To the realization of this program Altgeld consecrated his energies to the full. Again and again in his public addresses, he explained that his great concern was not with material signs of power but with the inner resources of civilization, and their outward manifestations in customs, institutions, and instruments—with the advancement of civilization.

In an address delivered in 1893 at the laying of the cornerstone of the Academy of Sciences in Chicago, Altgeld adverted to the railroad, factories, warehouses, office buildings, energy and enterprise of the city, but warned his listeners that "its glory will fade unless it builds on more than material foundations. The generations to come will care nothing for our warehouses, our buildings or our railroads; but they will ask what has Chicago done for humanity; where has it made man wiser, nobler or stronger; what new thought, or principle, or truth has it given to the world?" Rome had material splendors, agencies of material power; but they are covered with the dust of time. What the world remembers is the age "when poetry flourished, when jurisprudence was studied, when art was cultivated, and literature was patronized. . . . We, of Chicago, must learn from the past that gold cast upon the waters will return no part bread, but sinks forever out of sight, while ideas given to the world go on for generations, and every new principle coaxed out of Nature's secrets will assist mankind in the onward struggle." The Academy of Sciences is to be devoted "to science, devoted to analysis, investigation, to discovery; a temple in which the youth of the land may be instructed in all those branches of knowledge which lie at the basis of modern civilization."

On unveiling, in the Memorial Hall of the National Capitol,

the statue of General James Shields—Irish-born immigrant, soldier in the Mexican war, warrior for the Union in the late civil conflict, classical scholar commanding modern tongues, urbane in manner, witty in discourse—Governor Altgeld discussed the hero as historic ideal and symbol and led up to the hero in relation to civilization. At one stage "nearly all the heroes were warriors," he said. Then, "as civilization moved a league onward," founders of states were celebrated. "And then, when civilization had again moved a step forward . . . when it was discovered that there is nothing fixed or stationary in all the universe; that change and consequent growth or dissolution are perpetual; . . . that those laws apply not only to the heavens and to the entire physical creation, but to all social, religious, economic, and political existence; when it was noticed that the tendency of the strong to devour the weak was inherent and eternal; that grasping selfishness is but a manifestation of universal law; that government, instead of being the protector of the poor and the weak, is in constant danger of being used as an instrument by the cunning and designing to despoil the ignorant and the unwary; when it was found that it required constant vigilance to prevent the very best institutions from becoming productive of great wrong, and that problems constantly arise that are difficult of solution, and vitally affect the happiness of men, then the world created another class of heroes. It began to honor the men who devoted their lives to the solution of these problems. . . . It built statues to the men who, whether in office or out of office, helped to light the way for humanity."

Chapter 9

Nature and Incidence of Foreign Criticisms

CIVILIZATION IN THE United States, as the preceding pages show in detail, was subjected all along, from the foundation of the Republic, to the analysis of native critics who tried it by the standards inherent in the idea and by the potentials of remedial and constructive action required in the execution of its mandates. In animus and intent this criticism was based upon acceptance of the fact that American civilization had branched off from civilization in Europe, had its own destiny, opportunity, and obligations; and upon the conviction that Americans who worked in it were bound by their responsibilities to carry it forward on this continent with all the agencies of critical and creative power which they possessed. That type of criticism was indeed essential to creativeness.

But all along its course American civilization was under attack from another quarter—from foreign critics, strongly intrenched in European points of view, who condemned it in detail or in general according to the tests of their predilections, values, and purposes. Criticisms coming from that source were wholly different in animus and intention from the spirit which had inspired domestic critics since 1776. They were directed by interests, passions, and resentments as deep as the conflicts within and among the European nations from which the immigrants who had founded and developed America had fled in search of freedom and security. Moreover, they were often deliberately designed to aid parties and causes in Europe or to bend American policy and powers to the uses of European nations locked in death grapples for dominion. In any event, apart from mere captious faultfinding, criticisms from European sources, including British sources, taken collectively, ran to the very roots of life in the Old World and the New.

Although in various ways foreign criticisms of the United States merely returned in full or overflowing measure the steady, often savage attacks made by American writers and orators on British and European institutions, policies, and societies, there was a difference in the methods and the effects or incidence of the two operations. American critics of Europe seldom went there to carry on propaganda. Europe had no huge settlements of American immigrants to whom agitators could appeal for aid and financial support, with disturbing consequences. Nor were American agitators respecting the nations of Europe designed to pull those countries into any game of general power-politics. Thus Americans who assailed Europe could not easily implement their words; their criticisms of British and continental peoples were largely academic and could be lightly thrown off by those to whom they were directed. On the other hand, foreign critics of American civilization had innumerable instruments in the United States for giving force to their verbal attacks and undercover machinations.

The prolonged censure of American civilization by foreign critics acted as an aggressive, divisive force, introducing intellectual disorder and embittering factional and racial disputes in the United States. It gave support to alien agents engaged in promoting the designs of alien governments and other alien interests in the United States. It slashed into the idea of civilization and into the unifying forces and potentials of civilization as actuality. Often it diverted American talents and affections from concentration on tasks clearly within the scope of American capacities and opportunities, clearly delimited by the necessities of American life. It diverted them to romantic enthusiasm for designs remote and obscure, or to an equally romantic pessimism respecting the future of civilization in the United States.

Above all, foreign criticism directed against American civilization in its various aspects aided in fomenting tempers and moods in the United States inimical to laborious and fruitful studies of American history and genius. At the same time it intensified the grip of domestic chauvinists and special interests upon popular imagination. It lent them protective coloration in their resistance to native criticism designed to bring the realities and practices of American life into closer harmony with the ideals of civilization. In no small measure it distracted American energies from examining with critical and informed care just what resources, material and spiritual, the United States actually had and just what such talents as

America possessed could do with these resources in the way of development and creative extension.

In the tempers and moods fostered by foreign criticisms and by American weakness displayed in reactions to the impacts, multitudes of young men and women were brought to such a plight that they derided the whole American scene. Some fled from it and tried to make themselves at home in Paris, London, Berlin, Munich, Vienna, or Moscow. Others remained at home and, taking up without social analysis criticisms from Europe, assailed American civilization in the same or similar terms. Their disgust with their Republic seemed to reach an ultimate in the verdict voiced by the clamant journalist, Dorothy Thompson, at Canton, New York, on June 14, 1937: "The world envies our technical and scientific achievements, but no country in the world envies or admires the kind of society we have. That is the shameful fact about us." (*What They Said in 1937*, p. 195)

Some foreign critics left to inference the simple fact that they were selecting details of American life for disapprobation and making judgments upon it from European points of view. Others, with complete frankness, let it be known exactly from what angle of vision they surveyed the United States and pronounced their sentences in particular and general. For example, Alexander Mackay, whose estimates were recorded in his *Western World*, published in 1850, openly displayed his animus: "England has her fixed position in the family of nations, and at the head of civilization—a position which she has long occupied, and from which it will be some time ere she is driven. We care not, therefore, what the foreigner says or thinks of us. He may look or express contempt as he walks our streets, or frequents our public places. His praise cannot exalt, nor can his contempt debase us, as a people." From this firm, if not immovable base, Mackay inspected civilization in the United States: "Other nations boast of what they are or have been, but the true citizen of the United States exalts his head to the skies in the contemplation of what the grandeur of his country is *going* to be."

French visitors and commentators were no less certain of their position at the head of civilization. Michel Chevalier, an economist who spent two years in the United States, with similar national pride, in 1836 placed Americans in a lower category: "It is because France is the heart of the world; the affairs of France interest all; the cause which she espouses is not that of a selfish ambition, but that of civilization. When France speaks, she is listened to, because she speaks not her own feelings merely, but those of the human race. When she acts, her example is followed, because she does what all desire to do." Victor Hugo likewise felt so well satisfied with France that he blandly urged Americans to emulate her example: "French civilization is so above and apart from that of all other peoples, that my countrymen need not shrink from encouraging people like those of the United States in their ambition to imitate the glories of France." Long afterward André Siegfried in his critique of the United States revealed a comparable partisanship: French civilization leads all the others and by its standards American civilization must be placed far down in the scale, if in the scale at all.

Many foreign critics, it is true, more or less attenuated their animus and some wrote as if they were applying pure or absolute standards of judgment to the United States—standards unrelated to the plain biases of any nation, race, class, or earthly interest. But of course none of the foreign critics who discussed American civilization was, or could be, in fact, a disembodied spirit, timeless and placeless, dissociated from experiences in specific human societies, and entirely emancipated from the affections, sentiments, and directives acquired or developed in those experiences.

In getting their perspectives on civilization in America, they stood somewhere in time and with reference to the intimate and necessary ties of their social status, country, and associates. British observers, for example, came from Great Britain. They occupied social positions more or less definite in that country; that is, they were military men such as Captain Basil Hall, the naval officer of high Tory connections; or members of the middle class, such as Fanny Trollope, Richard Cobden, and Harriet Martineau; or connoisseurs with aristocratic tastes, such as Matthew Arnold.

French visitors and critics also had their earthly attachments and established valuations before they set foot on American shores. Tocqueville, for example, belonged to the French aristocracy which had recently suffered disasters in the great revolution and still confronted the rising tide of democracy in Europe. Although he possessed a cool temper and a hard head for concrete facts and general practices, Tocqueville appraised American people and affairs with a mind already well formed and he carried persistently in that mind a fixed interest in the probable course of democracy in France, as it might be foreshadowed in the American experience of which he wrote with such balance of thought and precision of statement.

That civilization in the United States was defective in having no established leisure class capable of giving it a high tone was among the most frequent forms of censure. Early in the nineteenth century Captain Basil Hall, the son of a Scotch geologist who had married the daughter of Sir John Hunter, made a great point of America's having no class of this character, secure but not too rich, accustomed to refinements of living and setting a steady example to the lower orders of society. The lack of this class made a strong impression upon Captain Hall who enlarged at great length upon the deficiency in his book of travels in America, published in 1829. For a long time the topic continued to be a subject of surprised and pained comment.

Arguing for the utility of such a class, Captain Hall declared that it should be firmly grounded in society, competent in the art of spending money "with grace and distinction—the highest of arts, more difficult than the art of making it—the art of spending it like a gentleman." Members of the class, according to such criticisms, would be free from vulgarizing operations connected with making a living and accumulating wealth by their own effort. They would be impregnable in their status; they would disburse gratuities to those beneath them with courtly finesse; they would live with dignity and restraint; they would bestow favors with elegance; they would overawe, instruct, and civilize the stolid or turbulent masses, set before them models of good manners, remind them of their inferiority by presenting to them examples of superiority. Thus the vulgarity of American manners and morals could be improved and gratitude, awe, and respect generated even among the poorest and most obtuse strata of the population.

Just how this leisure class was to be sustained in America or was to acquire the arts of elegance, Captain Hall did not state. But he observed with dismay the attacks then being made on the estates of the manorial lords in the Hudson River Valley and regarded the proposed dissolution of their large holdings as subversive to civilization. Yet there seemed to be no way out of the impasse for, as Captain Hall remarked, the property law of America ran against primogeniture and concentration, in the direction of diffusion: "The property of the parent . . . is generally divided equally amongst the children. This division, as may be supposed, seldom gives to each sufficient means to enable him to live independently of business; and consequently, the same course of money-making habits which belonged to the parents necessarily descends to the son. Or, supposing there be only one who succeeds to the fortune, in what way is he to spend it? Where, when, and with whom? How is he to find companionship? How expect sympathy from the great mass of all the people he mixes amongst, whose habits and tastes lie in totally different directions?"

In this fashion Captain Hall picked out and characterized as a dangerous defect in America the diffusion of property—a social policy which great Americans among the founders of the Republic had deliberately adopted. In the very midst of the revolutionary war, Jefferson had led in Virginia the struggle for the destruction of primogeniture, the breakup of large estates, the annihilation of the economic mainstay for seasoned families among the "gentry." Soon the wider diffusion of property became a fixed principle of American law, generally accepted as a basis of republican government. Perhaps more than any other economic feature of American society, it represented to its champions the fundamental distinction between the popular order in the United States and the order of privilege in Europe. So Captain Hall had, in this particular criticism, chosen as an object of reproach the "defect" which leveling Americans looked upon as a principal virtue of their civilization.

The second primary feature of American civilization strongly disapproved by foreign critics was the general spirit of equality which prevented the formation of a permanent and docile serving class, such as European feudalism had disciplined through the centuries. This deficiency made life for the middle class in the United States more irksome than it was for the corresponding class in Europe, able to profit from that phase of the feudal heritage. The fluidity of social lines in the new world, the "impertinence of the lower orders," and the necessity of performing menial tasks on their own behalf made it difficult for the American middle class to develop in peace and comfort civilization on European lines.

Oppressed by this hard practice of equality, Sir Lepel

Griffin expatiated upon it at length in his book, *The Great Republic,* published in 1884. Men of the professional and salaried classes, so well served in England, he complained, enjoyed no such luxury in America; living was expensive and vexatious for them in the United States.

As Matthew Arnold remarked in commenting on Sir Lepel's curtain lecture, "A man of this sort has in England everything in his favour; a society appears organized expressly for his advantage. . . . It is in England that an income of from three or four to fourteen or fifteen hundred pounds does so much for its possessor, enables him to live, with so many of the conveniences of far richer people. For his benefit, his benefit above all, clubs are organized, and hansom cabs ply; service is abundant, porters stand waiting at the railway stations." In America such men must ride in tram cars, shine their own boots, carry their own luggage, and fend for themselves amid the hustling, jostling throngs of common people.

Owing to the general spirit of equality and the abundance of openings for other employment, regular servants lacked the deference appropriate to a properly ordered society, critics said, and this, too, put a drag on the arts and refinements of life, especially among the middle class. Not only that, members of families who rendered domestic service did not correctly assume the duties of the office. "At a place called the Little Falls, where we stopped to dine," exclaimed Captain Hall, "a pretty young woman, apparently the daughter of the master of the house, also served us at dinner. When her immediate attendance was not required, she sat down in the window with her work, *exactly as if she had been one of the party*. There was nothing, however, in the least degree forward or impudent in this; on the contrary, it was done quietly and respectfully, though with perfect ease, and without the least consciousness of its being contrary to European manners."

The third striking characteristic of what was called civilization in the United States—the utilitarian nature of American intellectual interests—appeared almost constantly in the inventory of critics who considered the American scene from European points of view. Without indulging in severe strictures, Tocqueville noted that American intelligence was intensely practical in tendency. Other commentators, more emotional than he in their recording, carped at practical thinking and contended that in America intelligence, if not inherently devoid of great qualities, worked at a low level, on useful projects; that the United States had produced no philosophical or theological systems claiming to solve the riddle of the universe: had produced no Kant, no Hegel, no Schopenhauer, no Schelling, no Darwin, no Spencer, no Plato.

To the fourth category into which fell special assessments of the United States belonged the oft-repeated complaint that women dominated intellectual and social life in America to the detriment of the country. Herbert Spencer, who had made the status of women a test of civilization, declared in his *Principles of Sociology* that they had reached an extreme position in America, "in which a lady wanting a seat stares at a gentleman occupying one until he surrenders it, and then takes it without thanking him." The German student of social psychology, Richard Müller-Freienfels, wrote in his *Mysteries of the Soul* that in America, "women . . . are so dominant that some Europeans have spoken of gynocracy. Even the young girl behaves with an independence which is startling to the European, and seems to him 'unfeminine'; and conversely, he often detects feminine traits in the American man. In both cases he is mistaken; the sexes have not interchanged their roles; it is only that the differences are not so extreme. . . . While with us the relation of adults to children (like that of the husband to the wife) is from the sociological point of view very like that of master and servant, in America youth enjoys much more extensive rights. The result may often be regarded by the European as lack of respect, disobedience, and libertinism, but it is not so regarded in America, since the adult does not ask for respect and subordination."

A fierce debate was raised over this subject when Albert Einstein, after finishing a lecture tour in the United States, was reported to have said, before embarking for his home, in Germany at the time, that America suffered from "intellectual poverty" and was under the sway of women. Subsequently he denied that he had been correctly quoted. But springing into the fray, Ramsay Traquar declared that the opinions attributed to Einstein conformed to the facts in the case. American society, Traquar asserted in 1923 in an article in the Atlantic Monthly, is thoroughly feminized, its men are soft, boys ought to be trained by men for intellectual activity, and from the ranks of men "must come the scientists, the artists, the poets and the thinkers who alone can gain for the country an honored name."

In the fifth type of criticism launched against the United States, its civilization was declared to be soulless, unlike the soulful, spiritual, and free civilizations of Europe. This form of condemnation was so extensively reiterated, in special and general presentments, that it needs only a single illustration here. The whole case framed in these terms was stated by Müller-Freienfels in his chapter on "the Americanization of the Soul" in his treatise on *The Mysteries of the Soul*.

The American, in the eyes of this author, presumably had some vestige of a soul but it was rudimentary and earthy. "The American has no perception of the incommensurable." In his mechanical society, the human soul is rationalized and this means "the prevalence of practical thinking, of the concentration of the intellect on the practical, useful, and efficient, and the obverse of this attitude is the repression and suppression of all that is merely agreeable, emotional, and irrational in the personality. . . . Man himself is becoming mechanized, is considered solely with regard to his performances. . . . Taylorism and Fordism are the systematic accomplishment of this mechanization of the human being. . . . In no other country are the individuals reduced to such a dead level as in the United States. . . . If you . . . express your own ideas, you will be in danger of becoming a social outcast."

To imaginative letters and the arts, foreign critics applied their standards with equally disparaging results. From the day when Sydney Smith exclaimed "Who reads an American book?" through all the subsequent years, visiting critics complained that in letters and the arts, save possibly architecture, Americans could not equal Europeans achievements or in fact do any work of truly fine quality. In 1888 Matthew Arnold decided that "in literature they [Americans] have as yet produced little that is important. . . . The Western States are at this moment being nourished and formed, we hear, on the novels of a native author called [E. P.] Roe, instead of those of Scott and Dickens. . . . I asked a German portrait-painter, whom I found painting and prospering in America, how he liked the country. 'How *can* an artist like it?' was his answer."

Although later critics conceded that here and there in the United States something worthy of their notice, even their praise, had been done in letters and the arts, their judgments in general were either negative or so qualified as to represent American achievements in these branches of civilization as commonplace, lacking in the signs of sustained power. A collective summation of their views in respect of letters and arts amounted to this: as Americans have been unable to reach the higher levels of reflective thought and soulfulness, so they have been unable to rise above the commonplace, the average, in letters and the arts to the high realms occupied by European writers and artists.

As in the case of criticisms directed against particular phases of American civilization, so appraisals of it as a whole, here called general for convenience, frequently assumed the tone of hauteur, if not sweeping condemnation. In a volume bearing the title *Civilization in the United States*, published in 1888, the British apostle of "sweetness and light," Matthew Arnold, while conceding certain virtues to America, dismissed the country as "uninteresting." He admitted that "the United States had constituted themselves in a modern age; that their institutions conformed well with the form and pressure of those circumstances and conditions which a modern age presents. Quite apart from all question how much of the merit for this may be due to the wisdom and virtue of the American people, and how much to their good fortune, it is undeniable that their institutions do work well and happily." Reports of corruption in America, he thought, had been exaggerated. Like most travelers in America from the eighteenth century onward, Arnold noted that "the people of the United States were a community singularly free from the distinction of classes, singularly homogeneous; that the division between rich and poor was consequently less profound than in countries where the distinction of classes accentuates that division."

For the practical intelligence of America, Arnold expressed a condescending esteem. Given the modern conditions in which they worked, and being "in a healthy case," the Americans displayed good sense. "The community there uses its understanding with the soundness of health; it in general, as to its own political and social concerns, sees clear, and thinks straight. Comparing the United States to ourselves, I said that while they are in this healthy and natural condition, we, on the contrary, are so little homogeneous, we are living with a system of classes so intense, with institutions and a society so little modern, so unnaturally complicated, that the whole action of our minds is hampered and falsened by it; we are in consequence wanting in lucidity; we do not see clear or think straight, and the Americans here have much the advantage of us." The great weakness of America did not lie in a want of wisdom and virtue with respect to the essential concerns of a modern society in the modern age.

Nor did Arnold join those of his countrymen who had given much attention to the lack of trained and dutiful servants for leisured and middle-class families. This might be unfortunate for such families but it was not a conclusive point against American civilization, he thought. He observed that America did not produce the finest of hot-house peaches or Marie Louise pears. He noted that the humbler people of America did have many luxuries and conveniences of which similar orders in Europe were deprived.

But such facts, he contended, were not conclusive either on the point of civilization. The question of material well-being for the people he waved aside as irrelevant to his main proposition: "Of course, if happiness and civilization consists in being plentifully supplied with the comforts and conveniences of life, the question presents little difficulty. But I believe neither that happiness consists, merely or mainly, in being plentifully supplied with the comforts and conveniences of life, nor that civilization consists in being so supplied." With this gesture, Arnold disposed of those who, in their estimations of American civilization, treated it in terms of commodious living.

Other types of enterprise generally included under the head of civilization, Arnold also made extraneous to his concern: "Partial and material achievement is always being put forward as civilization. We hear a nation called highly civilized by reason of its industry, commerce, and wealth, or by reason of its liberty or equality, or by reason of its numerous churches, schools, libraries, and newspapers. But there is something in human nature, some instinct of growth, some law of perfection, which rebels against this narrow account of the matter." Here Arnold approached his crowning reason for discountenancing American civilization. Unquestionably, great emphasis had been laid on American industry, wealth, liberty, equality, churches, schools, libraries, and newspapers, as evidences of civilization, though by no means the whole, of civilization. But whatever merits those possessions might have, they did not form, according to Arnold's conception, the essence of civilization.

With the way thus opened by eliminations, Arnold came to his supreme edict on what he called American civilization: It is *uninteresting*. If on first thought this finding seems trivial, an examination of the material, social, and artistic content which he gave to the word "uninteresting" reveals that Arnold was making an interpretation of all Western history; that he was referring to every constituent which divided the modern age from the middle ages and antiquity, especially to the chasm which separated American history from the history of Europe. He was belittling the merits of everything that had been claimed for American civilization by its promoters and defenders from Jefferson and Everett to the men and women who were affirming it at the very time Arnold visited the United States. In its materiality his world-view was that entertained by European privileged orders. He was, in fact, quarreling with history in the Old World and frowning upon history in the New World. Nothing less than this was involved in his dismissal of civilization in the United States as uninteresting.

What makes a civilization *interesting?* Arnold had strong opinions on the subject: "Now, the great sources of the *interesting* are distinction and beauty; that which is elevated, and that which is beautiful. Let us take the beautiful first, and consider how far it is present in American civilization. Evidently, this is that civilization's weak side. There is little to nourish and delight the sense of beauty there. In the long-settled States east of the Alleghanies the landscape in general is not interesting, the climate harsh and in extremes. The Americans are restless, eager to better themselves and to make fortunes; the inhabitant does not strike his roots lovingly down into the soil, as in rural England. In the valley of the Connecticut you will find farm after farm which the Yankee settler has abandoned in order to go West, leaving the farm to some new Irish immigrant. The charm of beauty which comes from ancientness and permanence of rural life the country could not yet have in a high degree, but it has it in an even less degree than might be expected. . . . If we in England were without the cathedrals, parish churches, and castles of the catholic and feudal age, and without the houses of the Elizabethan age, but had only the towns and buildings which the rise of our middle class has created in the modern age, we should be much in the same case as the Americans. We should be living with much the same absence of training for the sense of beauty through the eye, from the aspect of outward things. The American cities have hardly anything to please a trained or a natural sense for beauty."

From speaking of beauty manifest in visible signs, Arnold passed to beauty manifest in human relations considered, in effect, as class relations. Here, too, American civilization was found wanting. In discussing this theme, Arnold took as his point of departure Amiel's statement that "the human heart is, as it were, haunted by confused reminiscences of an age of gold; or, rather, by aspirations toward a harmony of things which every day reality denies to us." This mystic yearning, Arnold explained, Amiel had translated in terms of class characteristics: "He says that the splendor of high life is an attempt by the rich and cultivated classes to realize this idea, and is 'a form of poetry.' "

Poetry in the style of the privileged orders awakens poetry in the lower orders: "The interest which this attempt awakens in the classes which are not rich or cultivated, their inde-structible interest in the pageant and fairy tale, as to them it apears, of the life in castles and palaces, the life of the great, bears witness in a like imaginative strain in them also, a strain tending after the elevated and the beautiful. In short, what Goethe describes as '*was uns alle bändigt, das Gemeine*—that which holds us all in bondage, the common and ignoble,' is, notwithstanding its admitted prevalence, contrary to a deep-seated instinct in human nature, and repelled by it."

Stripped of all rhetorical polish, this was what Jefferson meant when he said that the privileged orders in Europe applied the wealth wrung from the people to live "in splen-dor and idleness, to fascinate the eyes of the people, and excite in them an humble adoration and submission, as to an order of superior beings"—the very thing against which American civilization, such as it was, constituted a revolt and an irreparable divergence.

Americans had achieved some beauty in architecture, in a small way, Arnold acknowledged: but "of the really beautiful in the other arts, and in literature, very little has been pro-duced there as yet. . . . The American artists live chiefly in Europe; all Americans of cultivation and wealth visit Europe more and more constantly."

The implication was clear. The Europe which he had in mind, the Europe which Americans visited in search of beauty, was the Europe of the middle ages, not the Manchesters of England, the Lilles of France, or the Essens of Germany. It was the Europe of the old privileged orders, with which, for weal or woe, history in the Old World, and above all in the New World, had dealt so inconsiderately during the past three hundred years. Unless that regime could be revived exactly as it had been, unless it could be duplicated in the United States, there was little or no hope for civilization as Arnold understood it. European history was irreversible and American history evidently could not be made what it had never been.

After beauty, in Arnold's idea of civilization as interesting, came distinction. "As to distinction, and the interest which human nature seeks from enjoying the effect made upon it by what is elevated, the case is very much the same. There is very little to create such an effect, very much to thwart it. . . . If there be a discipline in which Americans are wanting, it is the discipline of awe and respect. . . . The Americans have produced plenty of men strong, shrewd, upright, able, effective; very few who are highly distinguished." Hamilton and Washington had been distinguished, "but these men belong to the pre-American age." There was Lincoln, called the typical American. "Now Lincoln is shrewd, sagacious, humorous, honest, courageous, firm; he is a man with qualities deserving the most sincere esteem and praise, but he has not distinction." In the matter of distinction, no qualifications could be admitted. "In truth, everything is against distinction in America, and against the sense of elevation to be gained through admiring and respecting it. The glorification of 'the average man,' who is quite a religion with statesmen and publicists there, is against it. The addiction to 'the funny man,' who is a national misfortune there, is against it. Above all, the newspapers are against it."

Thus stated, the case for civilization in America was hopeless or almost hopeless. "In America, he who craves for the *interesting* in civilization, he who requires from what surrounds him satisfaction for his sense of beauty, his sense of elevation, will feel the sky over his head to be of brass and iron. The human problem, then, is as yet solved in the United States most imperfectly; a great void exists in civilization over there; a want of what is elevated and beautiful, of what is interesting. The want is grave. . . . The want is graver because it is so little recognized by the mass of Americans; nay, so loudly denied by them." If a number of leading spirits in the United States would acknowledge the fault, admit that Americans were crude as beginners in civilization, and would rise above the crudities, Arnold would be more lenient with the country. But Americans were boastful; they took pride in the equality, liberty, industry, democracy, hustle and bustle; they insisted that they had a civilization expressed in such terms; and of common-sense criticism directed against "all this hollow stuff there is in America next to none."

More heavily documented and more detailed than Matthew Arnold's sketch was the general critique of the United States written by André Siegfried in a treatise given to the English-speaking world in 1927. Siegfried, who belonged to a prominent Alsatian family, had traveled widely in America, once as secretary-general to the mission of the French government sent over for the purpose of propaganda, among other things, when the Allies were seeking to increase American aid during the first world war. After a tour including almost every state in the Union, in 1925, he commented and preached on his experiences in a volume which bore the simple title in its French edition *Les États-Unis d'Amérique,* but was published in English as *America Comes of Age.* Crowded with statistics, with statements purporting to be factual, and with swift personal judgments, the work was hailed in certain American circles as a triumph of genius. So great was the general furor over Siegfried's manifesto on America that it was translated into German—but without the preface written by Albrecht Mendelssohn Bartholdy at the publisher's request, which pointed out the animus of the whole work.

Not content with picturing a bridgeless abyss between American civilization and that of Europe, especially of France, Siegfried made a great divide between ingenious European immigrants and Negroes in the United States on the one side and dull, materialistic, puritanical Anglo-Saxons on the other. "Without generalizing," he remarked, "one may say that when you notice a sparkling eye or a nimble mind it is often in an Italian, a Jew, or a Russian. Like uncut jewels, they had come from Europe with their traditions of brilliant civilizations, which they were asked to abandon at one fell swoop. Many, especially among the intellectuals, deliberately refused. The American-Italian who writes English with a Mediterranean flourish, the American Jew with his centuries of accumulated knowledge, and even the Negro, whose music and dancing have added to the artistic patrimony of the whole human race, have all contributed to American civilization; and when they enroll themselves in the movement they insist that they should be received just as they are and with all the honours of war."

Here, however, Siegfried was doubtless referring to recent immigrants or specially "brilliant" persons, for in another passage, dealing with the third generation of immigrant families, he said that "the immigrants and their sons have lost the rich heritage of magnificent civilizations, and the amputation has been clean and merciless." Then he revealed the locus of his affections: "As the immigrants are usually of the lower classes, one might say that they had little to lose." In other words, being of the lower classes, such immigrants merged easily with the older Americans who had no heritage of "magnificent civilizations."

Impressed by the power of public opinion derived from leveling tendencies, Siegfried underscored the difference between civilization in the United States and civilization in countries blessed with privileged orders. "In older nations where the civilization is more subtle," he remarked, "the currents of public opinion break down or wear themselves out against established institutions that have grown up like fortifications throughout the centuries. The family and the clan are both impregnable to outside influences, and so are certain universities where independence of thought is encouraged. The same applies to such bodies as the army, the church, the law, and also to certain groups of intellectuals who are indifferent to public opinion. In the United States, such barriers exist only where assimilation has not taken place. The Roman Catholic Church, for example, keeps aloof. . . . It acts as a brake to some extent, but all the other institutions—the universities, the Protestant churches, the business world, and society—seem to be ready to swell the tide of popular opinion and to work for the common goal."

Siegfried's critique was in fact a reprobation of basic features long and generally associated with civilization in American expositions of the idea. American civilization, in his view, was mainly concerned with "materialism," with the production and wide distribution of goods, with commodious living for as many persons and families as possible. Active in it was an almost universal desire among the American people to share in abundance the pleasures of good living that had once been almost monopolized in Europe by kings, nobles, cardinals, bishops, archbishops, and members of the higher clergy generally.

"In America," Siegfried declared, "the dominant force that is threatening to carry everything before it, Protestant, Catholic, and Jew, is the obsession for tangible and material accomplishments." American civilization is lacking in the fixed institutions of Europe which serve as barriers against this interest and protect the finer values marking "more subtle civilization." Ingrained in the American spirit is a flair for general equality, despite economic divisions, an absence of deference to rank and position, a passion for free and easy intercourse across class lines. This propensity seems almost invincible in its drive against the subtleties, graces, and appreciations common to civilizations resting on army, clan, great families, church, and other intrenched institutions. All sciences, arts, philosophies, and practices in America are directed toward a single goal of uniformity, and the high-grade personalities of precious individuals are subjected to vulgar disdain.

Feeling that these features were irrevocably imbedded in American civilization, Siegfried devoted his concluding chapter to painting in hard strokes the irreducible contrast between American civilization and European civilization. "Having first cleared away all hampering traditions and political obstacles, the American people are now creating an entirely original social structure which bears only a superficial resemblance to the European. . . . The old European civilization did not really cross the Atlantic. . . . To the American, Europe is a land of paupers, and Asia a continent of starving wretches. Luxury in every-day consumption and the extension to the many of living conditions previously reserved for the few—these are new phenomena in the history of mankind." Toward this single end the United States marshals everything, even idealism and religion: "It is a materialistic society, organized to produce things rather than people, with output set up as a god. . . . If the aim of society is to produce the greatest amount of comfort and luxury for the greatest number of people, then the United States of America is in a fair way to succeed."

So pictured, the United States presented an affront to

"certain conceptions of mankind which we in Europe consider the very basis of civilization. . . . This change in the center of gravity in the life of the individual marks an absolute revolution in the ideas on which society in Western Europe has been built up." It sacrifices "individual refinement and art. . . . Even the humblest European sees in art an aristocratic symbol of his own personality, and modern America has no national art and does not even feel the need of one. . . . Big profits overshadow liberty in all its forms, and the exercise of intelligence is encouraged only if it fits in with this common aim."

Given the general commitment to this point of view and this practice, the individual in the United States becomes a puppet in a machine as compared with the free individual in Europe: "In the light of the American contrast we see that material pursuits have not entirely absorbed the soul of Europe, and that it can still appreciate free and disinterested thought and spiritual joys which can often be obtained by renouncing comforts and fortune. . . . From this unusual aspect we perceive certain traits that are common to the psychology of both Europe and the Orient. So the discussion broadens until it becomes a dialogue, as it were, between Ford and Gandhi."

Despite his numerous references to Europe as a whole, Siegfried finally made it patent that after all he was really comparing American civilization with the civilization of France. Americans were more like the terrible Germans or the British or the Swiss. "When Americans come to France and see us persisting in our individualism and preferring liberty to discipline, they are almost shocked; for they are really more at home in countries like Switzerland and Germany, where rules are rigidly enforced. . . . When with their charming simplicity these friends of France praise her, they seldom touch on what she herself considers the essence of her civilization. Those who understand and love the soul of France are rare exceptions. . . . In Paris we have many of these uprooted spirits, who are more French than the natives and would realize themselves exiles if ever they were to return to their own country. . . . France's best points escape the hasty observations of the passing tourist, for the refinements of her civilization do not lie in telephones or trains, and so escape the notice of simple folk who are over-anxious about creature comforts."

Caring little or not at all about the preciosities of the French "soul," a central interest of Siegfried, another French publicist, Lucien Romier, turned to the United States to study the force of mass production, labor organization, and mass consciousness. Romier was too realistic merely to pine for any older order now that Europe was shot through and through with the popular revolts that grew out of the first world war. He was a student of history and finance-capitalism, and, holding the opinion that old-world capitalism and its shadow, old-fashioned socialism, were moribund, he wished to investigate at first hand new-world capitalism and the attitude of Americans toward their economic system. He was apparently casting around for traces of a nascent system with more élan to be adopted in Europe, and in his search for vitality he wished to know more about the United States. After a sojourn in America for a brief season, he published in 1927 his *Qui sera Maître, Europe ou Amérique?* which Matthew Josephson translated the following year under the title, *Who Will be Master, Europe or America?*

More sophisticated than most foreign observers since Tocqueville and remarkably frank about his own predilections, Romier began his report on the United States by saying: "All of us, whether great or small, whether we live splendidly in a great city or humbly in some village, are accustomed to reasoning about the universe by relating it all to our immediate lives. We all tend to place ourselves squarely in the center of things, in order to understand, appraise, use, and dominate them, as if we could be at will now master of all, and now impassive spectator. . . . In the realm of pure ideas, as in that of practical affairs, we should be guilty of the sheerest stupidity if we pretended to ignore those insuperable limitations which reflect eternally the ambitions and the prejudices of particular egoisms." Yet, while making no profession of unearthly detachment, Romier granted that one mind could be richer than another in its interest and knowledge; and that when any frame of thought is adopted for a specific operation, such as his, a multitude of relevant facts come into consideration as necessary to an appropriate intellectual procedure.

Breaking with the plan generally followed by foreign observers of American life, Romier spent no time poignantly recalling the refinements of certain classes in Europe or railing at the standardization, equality, and "vulgarity" among the people in the United States. He started his discussion with a section on "The Phenomena of Mass Civilization." Here he gave attention to a trend common to the Western world: "Human societies in their evolution are becoming aware more and more of the preponderance of the masses. The older societies were hierarchies. Present day societies are moving away from the established forms toward a type in which the inequalities of social levels disappear, all men being considered as cogwheels in a vast machine which cannot function without each and every one of its parts; there remains thus only an organic interdependence of mutual service. This is what is meant by the saying that all people are becoming 'equal.' "

Instead of accepting time-encrusted types of capitalist and communist analyses, Romier went in the direction of a fascist simplification, while always keeping in mind the nature and influences of economic interests and activities. In speaking of the masses, he did not refer to great crowds or mobs of undifferentiated men and women as if they existed apart from their occupations, interests, customs, and morals. His interpretation was more penetrating. He treated the masses rather as blocs in society, as aggregations of interests and occupations, such as banking, coal mining, oil production, or railroading, all linked together, sometimes in a certain degree of harmony and sometimes in open competition with one another. These economic or occupational blocs, ever changing in time with changing methods and instruments, were acquiring new propensities which were disrupting their inherited traditions, manners, morals, and values. They operated in society and in civilization conceived in its largest sense as including men and women, the family, sex relations, the arts, and sciences, the whole composite of values.

In the United States Romier found the idea of a mass civilization so generally upheld and so abounding in applications that he was amazed by "the originality of America." He tried to understand the psychic and economic source of the business. America's distinctive vitality sprang from its practical interests, he decided: "The American civilization, more than any other, has steered clear of theoretical systems, of preconceived frames, of too purely rational guiding principles, and shaped itself under the influence of concrete facts as they arose one by one. . . . The American civilization . . . shines

much better in the sphere of action than in that of reflection.
. . . And in truth is not the very awkwardness of the American in expressing himself a sign of originality and of independence? If he were more like us, we should understand him more easily."

This originality Romier did not ascribe, however, to the virtues or follies of Americans. "If they have come to build their civilization along lines that scarcely resemble at all, and even oppose, at times, the European model, it is not through ignorance or misunderstanding or hostility. It is the outcome of completely different conditions, needs, problems."

And what did Romier give in detail as the original traits of mass civilization in America? Summarized in a small compass from many of Romier's pages, they are: uniformity and disaccord extending everywhere over a vast space; novel as well as traditional forms of human activity carried on at amazing speed and on a colossal scale; colorless and rather meaningless politics (1927) rather indifferently regarded by the people; emancipation from the classical mold set by the privileged orders of Europe; general interest in economic activities; supremacy of economic over politics; wide liberty for economic and social activities; diversity of races in a certain unity called American; facilities for men and women seeking to attain position in society; flexibility for mass, as well as individual, movements; opposition to old forms of intolerance by people who have fled from persecutions and misfortunes in Europe; equality and fluidity of the population movement amid the absence of rigid class layers; hostility to abstract theories as the source of bigotry; appreciation of the material comforts and conveniences, such as were enjoyed by the privileged classes in Europe; constant quest for such comforts and conveniences as necessary to human dignity; youth, élan, liberal-mindedness about matters viewed dogmatically in Europe; passion for efficiency; sense of vast space and herculean effort in contradistinction to the fragmentation and more limited efforts of Europe; zeal for social well-being as against European individualism; generosity expressed in charities and benefactions and in sympathy and succor offered to fellow men; leadership in realizing a new conception of human dignity; libraries, universities, institutions, and organizations shaped and conducted with the object of sustaining and promoting the civilization so conceived and evaluated.

For special comment Romier singled out what he called the "humanity" of America. He did not minimize hard and brutal features of American life or the lack of "excess courtesies and refinements," but he was impressed by evidences of the humane spirit in the United States. "Youth, *élan*, the genius for enterprise—they are the attributes which chance has brought, or products of a great effort; they do not form the basis for an ideal. If America possessed only these qualities, her penetration throughout the world would after all have been slight. But she does seem to us authentic, and leader of the world, through the new conceptions of human dignity which she has carried out."

In intellectual and esthetic daring America might be far down in the scale; her energies might be concentrated on objects of utility and convenience in living; but America had exalted, amid the vulgarity and equality of social living, "new conceptions of human dignity." It might be due to "chance" or to deliberate effort, but care for the worth of the human being, for the equality of human beings, had found expression in America, despite the devotion to ends branded as "materialistic" by many critics.

Yet, after giving his long list of American qualities which seemed to be virtues, Romier wheeled right around and pronounced judgments on the United States that might well have been his secret judgments on France from a fascist standpoint. Having dwelt long upon American qualities, he then joined Müller-Freienfels and other soulful mystics in discounting America by a merely quantitative measurement: "In truth, to understand America we must always bear this fact in mind: that the social structure of the United States does not compose a unified historical nation, nor a body politic: it is a community of purely economic origin. The social tie exists only through the economic one; in other words, through the interaction and interdependence of collective groups, or of individuals, equally embraced within the cycle of work and profit. Hence the obligation to 'make money,' which is the very basis of American morals. . . . It is scarcely astonishing, then, if all social relations organize themselves almost solely for the pursuit of gain. . . . The duty to 'make money' and to be efficient in a material sense, accepted as the gospel, reacts upon customs, and changing them little by little, transforms morality too. Here we touch the Achilles' heel of the American colossus. . . . The principle of getting rich and getting-rich-quick establishes the whole scale of values and affects even the daily speech and imagination of the average American. . . . It is for such reasons that America represents completely that type of civilization which M. Paul Valéry called the *quantity* civilization."

With this quantity civilization in America Romier coupled poverty of intelligence and spirit: "Despite the great innovations and the original methods which America has brought to the social domain, she remains passive so far as the arts and the purely intellectual pursuits are concerned. To be sure there are artists, writers, scientists, and 'groups of serious thinkers.' . . . But as far as the whole mass of Americans is concerned intellectual activities seem to have little force or penetration. This mass even when found in the schools or universities seems to be insensitive to what we call 'personal creativeness' and 'higher culture.' . . . Already American literature and criticism are on the road to being 'standardized': and the standard is not established at the level of great and original art, but at the considerably lower level of common preference, the 'public taste.' " For this sad state of affairs in the United States education offered no hope: "The problem is not to be solved by sending people to school, as one may see from the state of American education." If scientists and philosophers will not assume the higher leadership, "then some slave to the crowd, some low journalist or venal politician, avid of popularity and profit, will answer instead."

Romier in effect warned American business men against their own masses: "This [American] aristocracy of business seems fully capable, if conditions remain as they are, of maintaining and still advancing the prosperity of the United States. But unless it is ready to go to great lengths of self-sacrifice, it may prove unequal to saving the framework of American civilization in the event of an economic emergency that threatens the prosperity of the mass—a terrible and blind mass, which will be found, perhaps, in that awful hour, to have utterly lost the stabilizing and sustaining force of moral and family traditions."

For Romier, the phrase "family traditions" contained special admonitions for Americans. With the insight displayed by many other foreign critics, especially from the continent of Europe, he recognized the role of women in making or breaking the fortunes of any cause, indeed of any society. A hundred years before, Tocqueville had grasped its significance. Now Romier told his readers in France that no kind of new order could be established there unless women were first subdued to its ideology.

"Man may invent and advance a civilization," Romier declared, "he may supply the mechanism for it: but he cannot, alone, give it lasting life. It is woman who must provide the stability and the durable qualities of a people. The American woman will decide the future of the United States as a nation! . . . Every great fortune must some day or other be defended by warriors. Now it is woman who makes warriors —not, of course, the woman who 'consumes' all and whom advertisements flatter and shops fawn upon, but the woman who is also a 'producer,' the woman of veritable force, dear to the hearts of traditional moralists." Fascists, confirmed or incipient, informed and shrewd in gaining ends, knew full well that women could defeat their designs and must be won over if their campaigns for conquest were to succeed.

Although few foreign critics who considered the full area of American civilization failed to find one or more aspects worthy of commendation, Sigmund Freud condemned it all by calling the very discovery of America a terrible mistake. He had visited the United States and was acquainted with many American disciples who had flocked to his clinics in Vienna to hear the true word of psychoanalysis, and he had contacts with Americans practicing his specialty at home. Thus he possessed some knowledge of Americans and American affairs. He also wrote a volume on *Civilization and Its Discontents* which showed that the idea of civilization was a part of his consciousness. It would seem, therefore, that more than an empty and momentary passion led Freud to pronounce the United States a total failure, and worse.

Desirous of discovering the grounds of Freud's discontent with America, Max Eastman visited him at Vienna in 1926. As they sat together in Freud's house, Eastman put to the distinguished professor of psychoanalysis the direct question:

"What makes you hate America so?"

"I don't hate America, I regret it!" replied Freud. "With pouts and wry faces and gestures like a man fighting clouds or doing the Australian crawl," according to Eastman's report, Freud continued: "I regret that Columbus ever discovered it! America is a bad experiment conducted by Providence. At least I think it must have been Providence. I at least would hate to be held responsible for it."

Not yet satisfied, Eastman pressed his inquiry further. With one eye on a picture in Freud's studio—"The Night Mare" —showing a "horrid monster with a semi-evil laugh or leer squatting upon a sleeping maiden's naked breast"— Eastman asked: "In what way bad?" To this Freud made answer: "Oh, the prudery, the hypocrisy, the national lack of independence! There is no independent thinking in America, is there? . . . I'll tell you what I want you to do. I want you to go home and write a book on America and I'll tell you what to call it. *Missgeburt*—what is that word in English?"

Eastman ventured one quick and literal translation: "Abortion?" Finding Freud not pleased with that, he suggested another: "Monster?" To this Freud replied: "Well, that will do. You write about this monstrous thing that America turned out to be. The word is *miscarriage*, 'The Miscarriage of American Civilization,'—that shall be the title of your book. You will find out the cause and tell the truth about the whole awful catastrophe."

Whatever the explanation of this severe judgment—whether a vanity injured by American skepticism respecting some of his alleged discoveries or by insufficient cordiality in American scientific circles—it certainly was all-inclusive and pitiless.

Some light is thrown upon the source of the malediction, however, by the fact that, in his *Civilization and Its Discontents,* Freud declared that "our so-called civilization is itself to blame for a great part of our misery, and we should be happier if we were to give it up and go back to primitive conditions."

The disintegrating force of debate engendered by criticisms directed against American civilization after the close of the sectional conflict in 1865 was increased by an ecclesiastical challenge and by the continuance of the sectarian controversy that had broken out during the popular upsurge. The challenge was the *Syllabus of Errors* issued by Pope Pius IX in 1864, the year before the fate of the federal Republic was decided at Appomattox. The official title of this historic document was *The Syllabus of the principal errors of our time, which are stigmatized in consistorial allocutions, encyclicals, and other apostolic letters of our Most Holy Father, Pope*

Pius IX." The *Syllabus* was not sent forth as a body of "faith and morals" absolutely binding upon all Catholics everywhere in all their thinking and acting. It was rather a statement of principles formulated for their guidance, particularly with reference to conflicts between Church and State then exploding in various parts of Europe. But by its general terms it was applicable to the United States or at least was so adjudged in many American circles, Protestant, Catholic, and secular.

In unequivocal language Pius IX stigmatized as an error the doctrine that "every man is free to embrace and profess the religion he shall believe to be true, guided by the light of reason"; and likewise the principle that "men may in any religion find the way of eternal salvation, and obtain eternal salvation." From these errors the Pope moved to Protestantism and branded as an error the proposition that "Protestantism is nothing more than another form of the same true Christian religion, in which it is possible to be equally pleasing to God as in the Catholic Church."

Taking up the relations of Church and State, the Pope proscribed a long list of "errors" under this head. He stigmatized as errors the following doctrines: that "it is allowable to refuse obedience to legitimate princes; nay, more, to rise in insurrection against them"; that "the Church ought to be separated from the State, and the State from the Church"; that "the ecclesiastical power must not exercise its authority without the permission and assent of the civil government"; that "the civil power, even when exercised by an unbelieving sovereign, possesses an indirect and native power over religious affairs"; that "in the case of conflicting laws between the two powers, the civil law ought to prevail"; and that "the civil authority may interfere in matters relating to religion, morality, and spiritual government."

Respecting the subject of education, Pius IX was equally positive. He listed as an error the idea that "the most approved theory of civil society requires that popular schools open to the children of all classes, and, generally, all public institutes for instruction in letters and philosophy, and for conducting the education of the young, should be freed from all ecclesiastical authority, government, and interference, and should be completely subject to the civil and political power, in conformity with the will of rulers and the prevalent opinions of the age." Emphasis in public education on natural and earthly things was likewise put under the ban. The

Syllabus branded as an error the proposition that "this system of instructing youth, which consists in separating it from the Catholic faith and from the power of the Church, and in teaching exclusively, or at least primarily, the knowledge of natural things and the earthly ends of social life alone, may be approved by Catholics."

As if to guard against any possible misunderstanding of the broad purpose underlying the *Syllabus of Errors*, the Pope declared it to be an error that "the Roman Pontiff can and ought to reconcile himself and come to terms with progress, with liberalism, and with modern civilization."

Six years after the issuance of the *Syllabus*, the Vatican Council, in solemn convocation, officially recognized the doctrine of papal infallibility and prescribed rules for the government of the Church. The Church now proclaimed that all the faithful of Christ must believe that the Holy Apostolic see and the Roman Pontiff possess the primacy over the whole world. It declared that the clergy and laity, both individually and collectively, were bound to submit "not only in matters which belong to faith and morals, but also in those that appertain to the discipline and government of the Church throughout the world" to the primacy of the Roman Pontiff. It asserted the right of the Pope to communicate with clergy and laity throughout the world and rejected the idea that this communication could be lawfully impeded. Lest doubts arise respecting such matters, the enunciation declared that when the Pope, speaking *ex cathedra*, lays down a doctrine of "faith or morals" he speaks infallibly. "If any one—which God avert—presume to contradict this our definition, let him be anathema."

The reception accorded by Catholics in the United States to these papal pronouncements, immediately and later, varied with some reference to their training, predilections, knowledge of American society, and ability for statesmanship. No American Catholic, apparently, attempted the formation of a clerical party on the model of certain European parties, for the purpose of entering the political arena, suppressing the "errors" listed in the *Syllabus*, and establishing in law or practice the positive doctrines implied in the list of negatives. But the issues involved in the *Syllabus* were widely discussed in periodicals published by various Catholic groups, in some cases temperately and cautiously and in others with vehemence.

That famous American convert to Catholicism, Orestes A. Brownson, who made nearly as much trouble for his new brethren as he made for Protestants, finally bowed to the *Syllabus* without reservations. He had previously praised American civilization voluminously and steadfastly. Now he condemned it with equal vigor, root and branch. "Protestantism of every form," he declared, "has not, and never can have any right where Catholicity is triumphant. . . . Heresy and infidelity have not, and never had, and never can have any right, being as they undeniably are, contrary to the law of God."

A Catholic clergyman in New York City, Thomas Scott Preston, also a convert, several years later won the reputation of being "rather more Catholic than the Pope," by demanding complete obedience to the papal program. Speaking in 1888 of Leo X, the successor of Pius IX, Preston declared: "Every word that Leo speaks from his high chair is the voice of the Holy Ghost and must be obeyed. To every Catholic heart comes no thought but obedience. It is said that politics is not within the province of the church, and that the church has only jurisdiction in matters of faith. You say, 'I will receive my faith from the Pontiff, but I will not receive my politics from him.' This assertion is disloyal and untruthful. . . . You must not think as you choose; you must think as Catholics. The man who says, 'I will take my faith from Peter, but I will not take my politics from Peter,' is not a true Catholic. The Church teaches that the supreme Pontiff must be obeyed, because he is the vicar of the Lord. Christ speaks through him." More force was given to Preston's belligerency by reason of the fact that he had been influential in obtaining a year before, the excommunication of Father Edward McGlynn who had accepted the single-tax theory as a solution of the problem of poverty which so grievously oppressed him as a pastor among the wretched poor of New York City.

While in general distinguished Catholic leaders in the United States refused to treat the *Syllabus of Errors* and other papal pronouncements as commanding them to declare intellectual warfare on American civilization all along the line, many Protestants and secularists insisted that it really meant just such an irreconcilable conflict. Having so resolved they took up the gage and on their own motion, or in disputes with Catholics inclined to controversy, they produced a storm in the United States over liberalism, progress, and civilization.

For science and secularism John W. Draper long served as a learned and trenchant champion. In his young manhood he had come, with his widowed mother and her other children, to the United States from England, his native country, and had embarked here on a career in natural science. With the aid of money earned by a talented sister, an artist, he studied chemistry, physics, and medicine in the University of Pennsylvania, from which he was graduated in 1836. Two years later he became professor of chemistry in New York University and subsequently head of the medical school in that institution. In connection with his profession Draper made important discoveries in chemistry and electricity and wrote technical works well received by scientists.

But Draper was more than a laboratory expert. He early perceived the relevance of freedom for work in pure and applied science to the wide authoritarianism over the human mind claimed by theologians in various domains of secular inquiry and thinking. In 1863 he published a *History of the Intellectual Development of Europe* in which he described the long struggle for the emancipation of science from a priori absolutism of every kind. It was quickly translated into all the leading languages of Europe and, coming just at that moment, helped to fan into stronger flame the conflict between Church and State in the Old World. Incited to additional labors in the intellectual field, he added fuel to the blaze by publishing in 1874 a *History of the Conflict between Religion and Science,* in which he dealt specifically with the *Syllabus of Errors* and other documents that had recently emanated from Rome. This volume was translated into Japanese, as well as the chief European tongues, and like his *Intellectual Development* was put on the Index Expurgatorius of the Roman Catholic Church.

From its point of view that Church was justified in banning Draper's book from its list of authorized literature, for the author had devoted three chapters to treating the Roman Church as the mortal enemy of science, free inquiry, liberty of thought, and improvements in the condition of the people. In one of these chapters, "Latin Christianity in Relation to Modern Civilization," described the Church as having been for centuries a foe of human progress, as a defender of ignorance and superstition, and as tyrannical in its assertions of power. In another chapter, "Science in Relation to Modern Civilization," he reversed the tables and praised science. It had freed the human mind from bigotry, he said, and substituted exact knowledge of the physical universe for theological errors. It had furnished instruments for augmenting the production of wealth, for improving the health of the people, spreading popular education, and promoting civilization in innumerable ways.

Having drawn the two pictures in black and white, with little shading, Draper discussed "The Impending Crisis." The *Syllabus of Errors,* the doctrine of papal infallibility, and other papal enunciations he called "arrogant assumptions." They subordinate reason to faith and condemn modern civilization in such terms that "an impassable and hourly-widening gulf intervenes between Catholicism and the spirit of the age." They "mean a revolt against modern civilization, an intention of destroying it, no matter at what social cost. To submit to them without resistance, men must be slaves indeed!" Will they submit? "As to the issue of the coming conflict, can anyone doubt?" Draper was certain of the outcome in his own mind and closed with a note of defiance chosen from the Bible: "As for Truth it endureth and is always strong; it liveth and conquereth for evermore."

To Protestant clergymen inclined to controversy, the propositions incorporated in the *Syllabus of Errors,* whether considered as a whole or by particulars, were also notices of an impending struggle to the finish. This interpretation was made by the Reverend Josiah Strong, a representative of the Congregational Home Missionary Society and later head of the Protestant Evangelical Alliance. In a volume entitled *Our Country,* published in 1891 as an enlarged version of an earlier pamphlet, Strong placed "Romanism" among the enemies of our country, cited articles and passages from Catholic publications criticizing American principles of liberty in politics, government, education, speech, and press, and gave examples of such criticism in his text.

For instance from an essay in the Catholic World, Strong selected the following paragraph: "The supremacy asserted for the Church in matters of education implies the additional and cognate function of the censorship of ideas, and the right to examine and approve or disapprove all books, publications, writings and utterances intended for public instruction, enlightenment, or entertainment, and the supervision of places of amusement. This is the principle upon which the Church has acted in handing over to the civil authorities for punishment criminals in the world of ideas." Indeed it called for no great cleverness or research on the part of such Protestant militants as Strong to discover in journals and books by Catholic writers many pronouncements that could be interpreted as arraying the Church in a holy war against American civilization.

In his description of the contest between the principles of "Romanism" and the principles of the American democratic Republic, Strong arranged his items under heads: the sovereignty of the Pope is opposed to the sovereignty of the people; the highest allegiance of Roman Catholics in the United States is to the commands of the Pope as against the constitution and laws of the land; "the alien Romanist" in seeking citizenship swears obedience to the Pope and does not renounce all allegiance to "any foreign prince, potentate, state, or sovereignty as required by our laws"; Romanism teaches religious intolerance instead of religious liberty; Rome demands censorship of ideas and of the press, instead of freedom of press and speech; against the American principle of the separation of Church and State, Rome presents the doctrine that Church and State are to be united; and, finally, Rome is hostile to our system of public schools. "Manifestly," Strong concluded, "there is an irreconcilable difference between papal principles and the fundamental principles of our free institutions." Through the parochial schools, Roman Catholics seek the isolation and protection of their youth "against the broadening and Americanizing influences of our civilization."

Weighted with citations and incisively written, Strong's book created a national sensation. It ran through many editions and sold 150,000 copies within a short time. The agitations started by his book Strong augmented by taking to the platform, and making long journeys up and down the country, delivering lectures, speeches, and sermons in a similar vein.

In the course of their attacks on the doctrines enumerated by implication as truths in the *Syllabus of Errors,* American critics represented its data as offering straight contradictions to the principles and progress of civilization in the United States. Their objections could easily be put into the form of simple propositions. Federal and state constitutional laws proclaim the principle that Church and State are to be forever separated. This doctrine the Pope condemns as an error. The sovereignty of the people over all internal affairs of the United States is an indefeasible rule of American government. Under an explicit interpretation of the *Syllabus,* this is an error. According to American law and practice every person is free to embrace any religion he pleases or none at all. The *Syllabus* makes this doctrine of religious liberty an error. American Protestants regard their forms of religion as representing true Christianity. In so doing they are all in error.

American law and practice provide free public education, secular in character and under the direction of persons emancipated from ecclesiastical control, and this education is primarily, if not exclusively, in knowledge of natural things and the earthly ends of social life. The law an practice of American public education the *Syllabus* stigmatizes as errors. America stands for progress, liberalism, and modern civilization. It is an error to maintain that the Roman pontiff can and should reconcile himself to them. The ineradicable opposition thus offered to fundamental principles of civilization in the United States, as cherished by the overwhelming majority of the people, is disruptive to the peace, unity, and good order of American society wherever and whenever pressed to conclusion of the logic inherent in the *Syllabus of Errors.* Such was the Protestant and secular case against "Romanism."

Herein lay the potentials of a civil conflict in the name of religion. Eminent Catholic leaders were quick to see the dangers and evils of such a contest, and the most discerning among them avoided interpretations and applications of papal pronouncements which might lead to an open breach in the nation. But, wherever the responsibility lay for keeping up the controversy, discussions of the issues arising from antagonism in fundamental principles continued to disturb the course of thought about civilization in the United States, in ways both open and disguised. Though generous concessions were made on both sides, a complete and unreserved reconciliation was not attained.

The difficulties of a perfect reconciliation were illustrated in an essay by the Reverend Francis X. Talbot, of the Jesuit Order, contributed to the symposium on *America Now,* published under the editorship of Harold Stearns in 1938. Far from condemning the American constitutional system, which embraced many errors listed in the *Syllabus,* Dr. Talbot represented Catholics as endorsing it: "The Catholic holds the theory, proved in practice, that the better Catholic he is, the better American he must be. Within the past few years, he has been inclined to believe that the Catholics are the largest bloc in the dwindling number of Americans who hold fast to the Constitutional and traditional Americanism that made the country what it was before 1914. And if he indulges in a bit of prophecy, he might submit the proposition that, when the inevitable crisis is reached in the United States some few years hence, he and his fellow-Catholics will be the strongest force upholding democracy, the American institutions, the Constitution and, in the world sphere, Western Civilization."

But only conditionally could the Catholic accept the American system of government—that is, in the absence of a better or Catholic government: "The American Catholic, enthusiastically affirming that the American constitutional system of government is the best non-Catholic form yet devised, claiming, furthermore, that the American Declaration of Independence and Constitution were derived from Catholic sources, can declare in utter good faith that a government erected on the Leonine principles would be a more perfect instrument." Even so, the Catholic is committed to traditional democracy: "Now a virile, vigilant, and clear-eyed American citizenry must defend our traditional American democracy from these northern, middle, and lower European influences"—communism, nazism, and fascism. "That is the Catholic view. . . . But American Catholics are not supported in their contentions by official Protestantism and Judaism."

On the subject of civilization in general and in detail, Dr. Talbot was somewhat less than precise. At one point in his essay, he ventured the prophecy that in the coming crisis Catholics would be "the strongest force" in upholding "in the world sphere, Western civilization." He did not explain the term or say whether he meant "modern civilization," but his meaning might have been illustrated by the support extensively given at the moment by American Catholics to Spanish, German, and Italian fascists in their war on the Spanish republic.

At any rate, in discussing civilization in the United States, Dr. Talbot did not outlaw it wholesale, but, in speaking of American Catholics in relation to it, he said: "They have a persuasion that American civilization needs their ideas, dreadfully, and that this civilization can only be saved by the infiltration of the Catholic theory of human and divine relations."

Far from conceding that the principle of universal toleration reigned in the United States, Dr. Talbot declared that Catholics encountered obstacles in making converts "principally because of the American heritage of bigotry and the agnostic mentality that now exists."

In another passage Dr. Talbot seemed to put the Catholic society and American civilization in opposition, in certain details and in general: "American civilization and the Catholic church are in open conflict on practically every phase of sex." Again, in general: "I suggest that the Catholic and Catholicism are adversely affected by the current civilization in the United States. The disabilities are not to be attributed to popular persecution or to constitutional limitations. They well from the American society itself which, dropping to lower levels, draws Catholic society with it. Being materialistic, naturalistic, agnostic, turning rapidly to neo-paganism, it creates an environment that tends to stifle the Catholic spirituality and supernaturalism. Being capitalistic, idolizing wealth, it distorts the Catholic doctrine of poverty of spirit and social justice. Being rationalistic and liberalistic, it weakens the Catholic insistence on authority and absolute truth." In the name of Catholicism, Dr. Talbot repudiated capitalism, which certainly had been and still was in 1938 a phase of the American economic system: "Capitalism is not Catholic. It is a development of the Protestant Reformation."

When Dr. Talbot's declarations involving civilization were placed in juxtaposition, his interpretation of the term might not have been obvious to all his readers. Catholics, he said, would be the strongest force in upholding Western civilization in the world sphere; that seemed to be a kind of reconciliation with civilization as lately introduced. Catholics were good Americans, but American civilization—a term nowhere clearly elucidated by Dr. Talbot—seemed to be in a bad way, to need Catholic ideas; it could only be saved by Catholic theory. There was something to be saved in American civilization, it seemed, but what that was remained obscure in Dr. Talbot's exposition. When he came to details, he condemned several features of American civilization: it was materialistic, naturalistic, rationalistic, and liberalistic. Its government was "the best non-Catholic government ever devised," but a government "erected on Leonine principles" would be better. Thus seventy-four years after the *Syllabus of Errors* was issued, the conflict between primary Catholic dogmas and American civilization was by no means wholly resolved in theory or in practice.

The effect produced in America by foreign criticisms focussed on single aspects of American civilization, or on all of it, could not, of course, be measured with any precision; nor could it be separated entirely from the synchronous development of criticisms made by Americans themselves. But the mood or temper, associated with the fusion of foreign criticisms and domestic reactions, was in part bewilderment, in part discouragement, in part defeatism and pessimism. Among pure idealists lacking in discrimination it was in some measure due to longing for an intellectual and moral escape into flights of utopian fantasy. Since utopia was not in the United States, it must be somewhere else—in some other place or some other time.

For this intellectual confusion writers of American history and academic literary criticism were no doubt heavily responsible. Historians had failed to take the advice of Marsh, Bancroft, and Andrew D. White; they had written no great and comprehensive histories of civilization or even of ideas in America for the instruction of the people and their intellectual, moral, and political leaders. They had made beginnings at this task in special fields with limited monographs; but in the main, as far as general works were concerned, they had written and rewritten political and military history. Academic critics of letters and arts, often utterly uninformed by historical knowledge respecting their own craft or overspecialized into indifference about the social contexture in which letters and arts function, usually contented themselves with furnishing to youth the dry husks of philology scholasticized, formal analyses of style, typologies of character, and biographical details. In fine, teachers had failed to prepare rising generations for discriminative and constructive thinking and for coming crises in national destiny and in the apparently rock-founded establishments of Europe.

Why, however, aside from the teachers, did so many American critics fall in readily with criticisms of the United States from foreign standpoints, especially, indeed above all, the feudal? Critics during the democratic upsurge, often mainly self-trained, such as Emerson, Margaret Fuller, Parker, and Lowell, had placed themselves squarely on the revolutionary heritage of America, had grounded their critiques in the long history from which the United States had emerged, and had not been daunted by capitalist ideology. Nor did leaders in the asseveration try to cut themselves loose from the roots of American economy and life and imagine themselves able to remodel American thought and practice in any of the purely European class images. Yet in the early years of the twentieth century a host of Americans wrote books, essays, articles, and reviews by the thousands which represented America, contrasted with Europe, as historyless, promiseless, and soulless, without revealing openly, or apparently understanding, the frames of reference within which fell their dissents, laments, and assertions. Whatever the explanation, the fact remained.

In this complicated situation, with foreign criticisms and domestic criticisms based on foreign points of view flowing together in a torrential stream, native writers, enamored of foreign animadversions, turned fiercely on almost everything American.

By the middle of the third decade of the twentieth century, the uproar, the distempers, and the perturbations of the so-called intellectuals attained the force of a hurricane. If their writings provided any criteria for judgment, there was in America no common ground, no idea or set of ideas, no canon of conviction, hope, or aspiration around which the people could rally.

In the essays on special aspects of American civilization published in the symposium on *Civilization in the United States* in 1922, certain fundamental strictures passed upon American life by foreign critics were accepted as valid, reinforced, and re-echoed for the instruction of Americans, especially on the Eastern seaboard but with repercussions in the hinterland. In his chapter on "Intellectual Life in America," the editor, Harold Stearns, taking his cue from European metaphysicians, declared that Americans showed "an attitude of contempt for mere intellectual values"; that American intelligence was just utilitarian and devoid of the high qualities characterizing intelligence in Europe. He also agreed that poverty of intellectual life in America was largely due to feminine influences, and asserted that the intellectual life of American women "turns out on examination not to be intellectual life at all, but sociological activities. . . . What women usually understand by the intellectual life is the application of modern scientific methods to an enlarged and subtler course in domestic science." The growth of pragmatism, which he defined as a kind of handmaiden to the art of "getting on," Stearns assured his readers, had been made possible "precisely because the intellectual atmosphere has been surcharged with this feminized utilitarianism."

Scarcely less severe was the judgment passed on American letters by Van Wyck Brooks in the Stearns symposium. According to the Brooks of that day and mood, American literature lacked integrity—the first principles of power; the creative will in America was a sickly plant; and it was like expecting figs from thistles to hope that any great literature could come out of American utilitarianism. The "traditional drag . . . in the direction of the practical, which has been the law of our civilization, would alone," Brooks asserted, "explain why our literature and art have never been more than half-hearted. . . . It is certain that as long as the American writer shares what James Bryce calls the 'mass fatalism' of the American people, our literature will remain the sterile, supine, inferior phenomenon which, on the whole, it is."

If American letters were in a shocking state in 1922, music was no better. "We squander millions every year upon an art that we cannot produce," Deems Taylor wrote for the symposium. "The American composer . . . lacks taste. . . . The curse of bathos is upon us." Taylor was especially grieved by America's inability to create grand opera. Without showing the slightest recognition of the fact that opera was in spirit and substance a political and decorative institution for a society feudal in interest and therefore out of keeping with American civilization, he kept on clinging to the hope that this feat could be accomplished sometime.

On the whole, George Jean Nathan thought, the American theater was "not much above the Midway Plaisance." A similar doom was pronounced by Walter Pach on American art as represented by painting: the artist has to seek desperately for a living in the United States owing to the lack of "an active demand from the people" such as holds good in other civilizations; and, besides, "Puritan morality and Quaker drabness" have turned Americans away from the satisfactions of the senses, the pleasures of the arts.

Indeed if the composite laments of the Stearns symposium were taken at face value, American civilization was devoid of power, quality, imagination, creative force, and, above all, any promise that could rally the faith and enthusiasm of youth. The symposium was, it is true, not without hope; indeed a constructive purpose was avowed; but it left hanging in midair the question why anybody should expect something to come out of nothing or at least next to nothing—great history to come out of no history.

In numerous ways the Stearns volume symbolized the attitude of defeat, surrender, and resentment prevailing extensively among American intellectuals between the close of the nineteenth century and the end of the third decade of the twentieth century. The justice of this statement is confirmed in some respects by the revelations called *Opinions of Oliver Allston* published by Van Wyck Brooks in 1941, nearly twenty years after the appearance of that symposium. In his confessions Brooks described with singular clarity and frankness many shades of the temper which had shaped the thought of imaginative letters and literary criticism during the preceding forty years. In his pages was disclosed the manner in which many critics, shocked by the crudities, cruelties, and cant of applied individualism, swung from utopian expectations into pessimism, and then from pessimism into idealizations of violence that were equally utopian—two moods equally incompatible with the idea of civilization in the United States; at variance with the creative energies of sustained and patient power by which civilization is promoted and defended.

While the agitations stirred up by criticisms of American society from foreign points of view were in full current, the idea of civilization in the United States came into collision with two other ideas bidding for acceptance, both foreign in center of interest even when expounded by Americans: the idea of Marxian communism and the idea of internationalism here described as "general" to differentiate it from the communist type of internationalism. In expositions of the two ideas it was claimed that each represented a universal reality in the process of becoming: a world communism or a world, or at least a Western civilization, in which American civilization was being and was fated to be merged.

Marxism connoted a world proletariat ultimately subduing divisive nationalisms to a "cosmopolitan" order. General internationalism assumed the existence of things called "the indivisible world of all mankind" and "the international mind," and treated the becoming world-order as a union of peoples not merely proletarians. Both schools of ideology, with varying degrees of passion, upbraided national sentiments and affections, lashed out at primary allegiance to America as a form of intolerable "nationalism," and in extreme cases proposed the surrender of national sovereignty to some super-sovereignty.

As against American society, propagandists of Marxian and general internationalism alike disputed its right to an independent course and execrated concentration on the advancement and protection of civilization in the United States by continental action. Marxists called openly or covertly for a revolution in this country and for American aid to communists waging war anywhere in the world. General internationalists demanded American intervention in the conflicts among nations, in the alleged interests of peace, and American participation in every war among nations which, in their opinion, menaced "world order." Thus in formulation and application, the idea of Marxian communism and the idea of general internationalism presented to the idea of civilization in the United States the most thoroughgoing opposition which it had ever met in the long course of its development.

The basic doctrines of Marxism were proclaimed in the *Communist Manifesto* of 1848. This document treated the histories of all nations as one history, reduced that single history to the history of class conflicts, derided civilization as bourgeois, and announced the coming world merger, or union, of proletarians, triumphant over the middle class.

Following a preamble, the *Manifesto* declared that "the history of all society, up to the present time, has been the history of class struggles." This assertion was so sweeping that by its very terms it appeared to cover the history of all the arts, sciences, religions, and literatures of all countries in all ages. Indeed Marx said elsewhere: "The production of ideas, representations, consciousness, is, primarily, directly interwoven into the material activity and the material intercourse of human beings, is the language of actual life. Representation, thought, the intellectual intercourse of human beings, arise as the direct outcome of their material behaviour. The same is true of mental production, as displayed in the language of the politics, the laws, the morality, the religion, the metaphysics, etc., of a people. Human beings are the producers of their representations, ideas, etc.; but the actual working human beings are determined by a specific evolution of their productive powers and of the appropriate method of intercourse in its furthest ramifications. . . . What individuals are depends upon the material conditions of production."

Although the *Communist Manifesto* made "the history of all society up to the present time the history of class struggles," as if there had been no other kind of history, it described in a synoptic fashion the rise and spread of industry and commerce, as if there had been something in history besides class conflicts; and it brought the whole process of industrial and commercial expansion under the conception of "civilization." In a compact form, it declared: "The bourgeoisie, by the rapid improvement of all instruments of production, by the immensely facilitated means of communication, draws all, even the most barbarian, nations into civilization [*Zivilisation*]. . . . It compels all nations on pain of extinction, to adopt the bourgeois mode of production; it compels them to introduce so-called civilization [*Zivilisation*] into their midst, that is, to become bourgeois themselves. In a word, it creates a world after its own image." Hence the *Manifesto* expounded in almost interchangeable terms the idea of a world process as constructed by classical economists and later adopted by the advocates of general internationalism and world unity.

In other passages the *Manifesto* laid emphasis on the process of denationalization. "The bourgeoisie has through its exploitation of the world-market given a cosmopolitan character to production and consumption in every country. To the great chagrin of Reactionists, it has drawn from under the feet of industry the national ground on which it stood. . . . In place of the old wants, satisfied by the productions of the country, we find new wants, requiring for their satisfaction the products of the most distant lands and climes. In place of the old local and national self-sufficiency and seclusion, we have intercourse in every direction, universal interdependence of nations."

This denationalization, it read, is not limited to matters of material production: "As in material, so also in the productions of intelligence and sentiments [*in der geistigen Produktion*]. . . . National one-sidedness and narrow-mindedness become more and more impossible, and from numerous national and local literatures arises [or "is formed," *bildet sich*] a world literature." Given the language of the original text—*die geistige Produktion* and *die geistigen Erzeugnisse* —it would seem that the *Communist Manifesto* enclosed all sciences, arts, letters, and other manifestations of the human mind and spirit within the scope of the denationalizing, universalizing process which blends the various peoples of the earth into the unbroken unity of internationalism.

Spreading over the world with an inexorable force that levels down local and national heritages, the process of bourgeois civilization, the *Manifesto* asserted, overruns agriculture and rural life: "The bourgeoisie has subjected the country to the rule of the towns. It has created enormous cities, has greatly increased the urban population as compared with the rural, and has thus rescued a considerable part of the population from the idiocy of rural life [*dem Idiotismus des Landlebens*]." Here, in two lines, Marx exhibited the pure urbanism of his interest and thinking. Neither he nor Friedrich Engels had any intimate, first-hand knowledge of rural ways of life; both spent their lives in industrial cities; both despised, with ill-concealed hatred, the peasant as well as the farmer, the landed gentleman, and agriculture itself. Although Marx admitted that the business of agriculture is complicated in nature and unwieldly "in all its parts," he had contempt for it as practiced: "Agriculture is besides given over to the most stupid class of human society and is, as at present conducted, the business most deadening to the human intellect and spirit [*das geisttötendeste Geschäft*]."

According to the *Manifesto*, it is the urban and industrial proletariat as such that is to overthrow the urban bourgeoisie and usher in the world order and true internationalism: "Subjection to capital" in England, France, America, and Germany, wherever it prevails, has stripped the proletarian "of every trace of national character. . . . The workingmen have no country. We cannot take from them what they do not possess. . . . National differences and antagonisms between peoples are daily dwindling more and more, owing to the development of the bourgeoisie, to freedom of commerce, to the world-market, to uniformity in the mode of production and in the conditions of life corresponding thereto. The supremacy of the proletariat will cause them to vanish still faster. United action, of the leading civilized countries at least, is one of the first conditions for the emancipation of the proletariat." Bereft of national character, having no property stake in his country, the proletarian, it would appear, belongs to no race, to no place, to no heritage of local culture, to no particular civilization.

This is not to say that nations were unrecognized by the *Manifesto*. On the contrary, it declared: "Since the proletariat must first of all acquire political supremacy, must rise to be the leading class of the nation, must constitute itself the nation, it is, so far, itself national, though not in the bourgeois sense of the word." But national differences "between peoples" are vanishing and it is the special mission of communists to facilitate the denationalizing process: "In the national struggles of the proletarians of the different countries, they point out and bring to the front the common interests of the entire proletariat independently of all nationality. In the various stages of development through which the struggle of the proletariat against the bourgeoisie has to pass, they always [*stets*] and everywhere represent the interests of the movement as a whole." Thus, while the proletariat of each country will constitute itself the nation and be "so far, itself national," it will become denationalized, international. In this spirit and in history so conceived, "the proletarians have nothing to lose but their chains. They have a world to win. Proletarians of all countries, unite!"

In efforts to prove the inevitability of the world revolution, Marx brought into play the dogmas of classical economics on industrialization, free trade among nations, and the internationalizing operations of capitalism. In this connection he took into particular reckoning the significance of free trade in relation to growing internationalism and approved it. "We accept," he declared in 1847, "everything that has been said of the advantages of Free Trade. The powers of production will increase, the tax imposed upon the country by protective duties will disappear, all commodities will be sold at a cheaper price."

But, under the law of capitalist production, he maintained, wages will fall and labor will receive no corresponding benefits from free trade. "Is that to say that we are against Free Trade? No, we are for Free Trade, because by Free Trade all economical laws, with their most astounding contradictions, will act upon a larger scale, upon a greater extent of territory, upon the territory of the whole earth; and because, from the uniting of all these contradictions into a single group, where they stand face to face, will result the struggle which will itself eventuate in the emancipation of the proletarians." Having adopted the prime doctrine of capitalistic economists respecting the universalization of trade, Marx thus turned it against them, prophesying the growth of a revolutionary internationalism among the denationalized proletarians, in the widening of free trade.

From start to finish, communist internationalism repudiated, as enduring values, to be preserved at all costs, the principal tenets of the Enlightenment incorporated in the idea of civilization: freedom of press, liberty of conscience, personal rights, democracy, the settlement of social conflicts by rational processes. Civilization Marx regarded as a mere "outgrowth of your bourgeois production and bourgeois property," as if all the humane ideas and sentiments accumulated in the evolution of society for thousands of years were simply the mechanical or biological products of production methods.

The liberties of mankind proclaimed in declarations of rights were to Marx not values good in themselves, but means to the end of a civil war spread throughout the earth, preliminary to the seizure of power. Freedom of press, freedom of speech, the right of assembly, and toleration were mere devices to be used by proletarians for their purposes in waging their war, for the conquest of power—dictatorial power. Whether the condition of proletarians would be better or worse under the coming order of things Marx did not even deign to discuss with any fulness of detail. Indeed he brushed aside, as futile, plans for developing a more enlightened and humane social order on the morning after communists had won the civil war, had obtained power throughout the world.

By its very origin and nature as an interpretation of history, the Marxian invention called dialectical materialism clashed with the idea of civilization, as Prussianism clashed with the French Revolution and afterward with the conquering Napoleon. It was developed by a German steeped in the Prussian learning dominant at the University of Berlin during his time, and rested on the alleged solution of the riddle of the universe to which Hegel had finally come in his search for the rationale of history. It had close kinship with the mentality of the old Prussian drill sergeant and the new authoritarianism at which German philosophers had arrived in a hunt for an ultimate support for the liberty proclaimed by the French Enlightenment and for a way out of the tragedy precipitated by the dictatorship of Napoleon.

The collision between the two interpretations of history— civilization and Marxian materialism—was as cleancut as the antagonism between the Enlightenment and Prussianism. The idea of civilization was grounded in an interpretation of history as a continuous process involving ethics no less than necessity; and as a struggle within human personalities no less than within and between classes—a struggle pointed toward a higher objective for humanity, enlisting all the powers of men and women for progressive, civilizing purposes, yet with no final act for the drama of history, thus giving room for endless creativeness individual and social. Dialectical materialism, on the other hand, represented history as all deterministic; like Hegel's system, fate without ethics. Marx took the mechanical god which Hegel had created and turned to the service of the Prussian State, and transformed this god into a materialist god operating on the same plan in making history—thesis, antithesis, and synthesis—in the service of the urban proletariat.

The immense medley of events, personalities, ideas, and interests in time-movement, which is in history, Marx arbitrarily arranged in periods under conflicting fronts called thesis and antithesis, resolved by a third process called synthesis. But to serve their purposes Marx and Engels broke away from their own logic, which demanded that the dialectical process go on forever. To have pursued their logic to the end would have subjected their triumphant proletarian front to a new revolutionary antithesis, destined to overthrow it in another synthesis. So to make their drama come out to suit them, Marx and Engels declared that the dialectical process would terminate in the triumph of their proletarian heroes; that history of the old kind which they had used for their purposes, by a revolutionary spring into freedom (*der Sprung in die Freiheit*), would be closed.

Any qualifications on the simple doctrine of utopian freedom by revolution which Marx made in his numerous writings and miscellaneous utterances, such as the intimation that in Great Britain and the United States the revolution might be effected without violence, merely served to bring into relief the centrality of his doctrine. "The Communists disdain," he said, in the *Manifesto*, "to conceal their views and aims. They openly declare that their ends can be attained only by the forcible overthrow of all historic existing [*bisherige*] social conditions." He added, it is true, that the proletarians "have a world to win," but what the world would look like after all existing social conditions, "bourgeois civilization," had been overthrown, Marx did not deem worthy of extended consideration. Sufficient unto the day was the deed—the act of physical force.

But when his colleague Friedrich Engels and his later disciple Lenin dealt with the prospects of the day after the deed, they could only promise that there would be a spring into freedom; that the State would "wither away"; that man would be "lord over Nature, his own master, free." This however was apocalyptic utopianism, not simon-pure Marxism. Benedetto Croce had documentary support when he declared that Marx produced "a teleological materialistic historicalism without a breath of humanity or liberty: Marx was nearer than one imagines to Prussianism and to its cult of brutal force. . . . Communism is constrained, even against the intentions of its authors, to enter upon the beaten track which every absolutism, every despotism, every tyranny has always entered upon."

The repudiation of American civilization was direct and explicit in the creed of Marxian communism as developed in the United States. A large proportion of the propagandists who advocated it on this continent were themselves of foreign origins, immediate or recent—men and women reared in the civilizations of Europe from the Channel to the Siberian steppes. Before they had reached American shores they were what they had become in the times and places of their birth and rearing. On arriving, most of them knew little or nothing about American society or its history. And after their arrival, few among them, if their writings are to be used as criteria of judgment, took the trouble to acquaint themselves with the history and nature of the country to which they had migrated.

Indeed to their purposes that process of education was unnecessary, for, in their world-view, American society was merely another capitalist society and the economic man in the United States was the same as the economic man in every capitalist society in the Old World. To be sure they were often amazed and disgruntled by the refusal of the American working classes to act as the proletariat was supposed to act everywhere but, in such cases, they were inclined to attribute the refusal to a peculiar kind of American obtuseness—difficult to explain under their own dogmas.

The utterly alien nature of Marxism was illustrated by the fact that neither foreign born nor native Marxists produced any significant contributions to thought in relation to American history or economy. Attempts of communists to rewrite American history and to make "good comrades" out of Jefferson and Lincoln, besides betraying an unfamiliarity with relevant facts in the case, usually fell into the category of elementary declamations. Indeed they seemed to be so obsessed by the abstractions of their creed that they could not apply the realism in the Marxian analysis of *die geistige Produktion* and *die geistigen Erzeugnisse* to the material realities of American history and life, and effect any kind of illuminating reticulation. With sheer force substituted for the process of enlightenment, moreover, the reconciliation of Marxism with the idea of civilization in the United States was practically impossible.

Before the first quarter of the twentieth century came to a close, general internationalism was also worked into an elaborate scheme of thought in the United States. It rested, tacitly or openly, on two assumptions: (1) that the unity, not the diversity, of mankind is primordial, is desirable, is possible, is inexorable; (2) that there is such a thing as Western civilization or world civilization irrespective of historic and actual variations among peoples and their social arrangements. In support of the foregoing assumptions, in endeavors to give them the appearance of facts, necessity, and imperatives, general internationalists drew upon economics and international law.

As program, general internationalism in its full formulation demanded four courses of action: the leveling of barriers, economic and political, among nations and perhaps ultimately among subject peoples; the substitution of an international association or State for existing independent States; the merging of nations and races in a world society; and the creation of a world citizenship.

Besides offering their creed as an intellectual mandate, general internationalists clothed it in a form of morality, esteemed superior and absolute. Practically everything that general internationalists accounted an interference with their progress, and thus evil in their eyes, they covered with the single word "nationalism."

In its assumptions and program, general internationalism, therefore, clashed with the idea of civilization in the United States. Basic to that idea was the belief that American civilization was founded in the modern age by certain types of immigrants, had a unique history, was stamped by national characteristics differentiating it ineradicably from European civilizations as well as Oriental civilizations, and had a destiny and obligations of its own to fulfil. To general internationalists all such national theories and sentiments were mere chauvinism or worse. They represented the inhumanity of man to man.

According to their dogmas this concernment with the United States was an insufferable affront to their superior morality—to be overborne by agitation and by various devices of political manipulation in domestic and foreign affairs. As they were accustomed to phrase the charge, nationalism is the offspring of tribal barbarism, represents a primitive kind of human loyalty or a vulgar type of "religion," and is, besides, outmoded by economic developments. Persons who clung steadfastly to or confessed supreme interest in American civilization were stigmatized as the spiritual descendants of Cain who murdered Abel and then asked: "Am I my brother's keeper?" Indeed general internationalists seemed scarcely able to express their feelings adequately in the English lanas they contemplated anything so "nationalistic" as the idea of civilization in the United States.

If the very idea of nationalism was a disease in the diagnosis of internationalists, national sovereignty—especially the sovereignty of the American people in their continental domain—was a plague. It is true that by no means all internationalists completely discarded that national feature of sovereignty. But, since nationalism stood in the way of realizing the perfect world order, it followed logically that the sovereign State must be abrogated and the American people subjected to a higher sovereignty somehow constituted out of all humanity (except, perhaps, Negroes and subject races) with little or no reference to separate national histories and national stereotypes. To be sure, internationalists met difficulty in discovering any other great nations—British, German, French, Italian, Russian, or Japanese—which had renounced or were prepared to renounce their sovereignty in the interest of the world order; but such lapses in the perfection of things did not soften the charges against Americans who clung to their nationalism, so "barbaric" in origin and so outworn in the "modern" age of universal economy.

To aspersions on nationalism and national sovereignty, general internationalists usually joined declamations against American policies designed to diversify American economy, protect it against the competition of nations with low living standards, and guarantee to it a high degree of internal security. While sometimes conceding to this economy a history differing from others in certain respects and a measure of self-sufficiency, they asserted that it really depended on a world order for essentials of its very existence. Constantly referring to the machine, technology, industrialization, they declared that American economy was in fact assimilated to other economies, absorbed in a world economy. By resorting to a materialism just as bald as that of the *Communist Manifesto*, they made the "machine men" of the world akin, if not exactly alike, in spirit, and thus intellectually and morally prepared to usher in the unity of mankind when "nationalists" could be suppressed and extirpated.

Under the internationalist formula, the people of the United States could not preserve their liberties, could not protect and promote their civilization as the founders of the Republic and succeeding generations had visualized the task and privilege of the nation. According to that formula, the undertaking was physically and morally impossible as well as chauvinistic or barbarian in inspiration; the American people were absolutely dependent on foreign trade for their standard of living, measured in material terms. By no domestic action could they protect or raise their standard of living, lift the nation into abundance. For maintaining the current standard or escaping from the suffocation of the alleged "overproduction" there was just one device—a world order with free trade throughout the earth.

As economic Manchesterism had proposed one system of commerce for the world, as Marxism had proposed liberty for the proletariat in universal revolution, so now general internationalism proclaimed Americans powerless to carry higher the process of civilization in the United States by their domestic efforts. It offered them one hope only, even of survival—submergence of their energies in the promotion and defense of world civilization, or at least "Western civilization." If Americans could not by peaceful methods accomplish this end, they could attain it by war—war being just and righteous if waged under the banner of general internationalism. It was as if the general internationalists had amended the communist slogan to read: "Americans, unite with other peoples of the earth. You have nothing to lose but your chains."

A well-rounded statement of general internationalism, in terms of supra-national civilization, was published by Louis Finkelstein under the title of "American Ideals and the Survival of Western Civilization," in the Contemporary Jewish Record of June, 1941. It is true that Dr. Finkelstein seemed to limit his view to "the West," while other exponents of such internationalism often took in a wider territory and history. But his exposition of the doctrine, especially as regards the responsibilities of the United States in the matter, was clear and cogent.

The key to his thesis and his program for the United States was offered in Dr. Finkelstein's first sentence: "America has a significance for civilization today vastly transcending its political power and its economic resources. The federal union is more than an efficient technique of government. It is a brilliant spiritual achievement and already has exerted a profound influence over the western world. It has demonstrated that the concept of human brotherhood and equality can be applied to a people of diverse origins and conflicting interests. . . . The commandment, 'Thou shalt love thy neighbor as thyself,' is applied not only across political boundaries but also between diverse political units. . . . Federalism and the doctrine of human equality from which it derives have prevented the United States from becoming an imperialistic nation."

While the United States was making its demonstration in brotherhood and equality, according to Dr. Finkelstein's argument, the world was drawing together. "Modern science and invention have reduced all mankind to a social unit. The new worlds opened up by explorers and colonists are being drawn from the periphery of human conflict into its vortex. Whether we desire it or not, a world society is in the making."

But it is not necessarily bound to be an ideal society, from Dr. Finkelstein's point of view. It may be evil or it may be good. "It may take the form of a restored Roman empire, pagan in religion, dictatorial in government and ruthless in policy, with its capital in Berlin and the earth as its domain. Or, advancing beyond ancient Rome, we may develop an association of free and independent nations, striving together for the common good and the progress of civilization."

To these two choices Dr. Finkelstein saw the United States limited, whatever independence and uniqueness had hitherto been attributed to its civilization: "Mankind thus faces the alternative of uniting on the basis of a common brotherhood or being united on the basis of a common enslavement. There is no third possibility. Brought within easy approach of one another, all men must either be friends or enemies. The age of distinct human societies, indifferent to the fact of one another, has passed forever. Civilization, adopting the principle of universal human brotherhood, will conquer ruthlessness, or ruthlessness will destroy civilization."

While insisting that the United States was caught between the two alternatives—merging its sovereignty and independence in a world brotherhood or accepting the dominion of Berlin—Dr. Finkelstein felt moved to record a default in American civilization: "We have yet to develop the same trust and confidence in those of different territorial origins. The enemies of America are well aware of this infirmity of our minds and are prepared to use it for the destruction of our liberty." But for this domestic shortcoming there is also a remedy: cooperation among Catholics, Protestants, and Jews, to eliminate antagonisms, assure unity on fundamental values, and "deal with the chronic diseases of society."

Internationalist proposals for the merger of American civilization in Western or world civilization originated not only with individuals and private associations. By 1941 advocacy had reached such a point that the legislature of North Carolina could pass a resolution demanding the surrender of American political independence and the formation of a world union, the House voting unanimously and the Senate forty-five to five in its favor. The resolution was entitled "The Declaration of the Federation of the World." It called upon the Senators and Representatives of North Carolina in the Congress of the United States to introduce and secure the passage of a resolution by the national legislature "committing the United States to the acceptance of the principle of The Federation of the World" and requesting the President to summon an International Convention to "formulate a Constitution for The Federation of the World" to be submitted to "each nation" for its ratification.

The North Carolina resolution embodied the whole creed of general internationalism and declared the conflict between totalitarianism and democracy to be "irrepressible and decisive." It asserted that "just as feudalism served its purpose in human history and was superseded by nationalism, so has nationalism reached its apogee in this generation and yielded its hegemony in the body politic to internationalism. . . . Mankind must pool its resources of defense if civilization is to endure." World federation is the one hope for humanity. "It regards as sacrosanct man's personality, his rights as an individual and as a citizen and his rôle as a partner with all other men in the common enterprise of building a civilization for the benefit of mankind. . . . It releases the full energies, intelligence and assets of society for creative, ameliorative and redemptive work on behalf of humanity. . . . It apprehends the entire human race as one family, human beings everywhere as brothers, and all nations as component parts of an indivisible community. There is no alternative to the federation of all nations except endless war."

Having surrendered the idea of an American civilization as grounded in the properties of American nationality and as distinct from the civilizations of Europe and the Orient in vital respects, the North Carolina legislature declared its "profound and irrevocable conviction" that "there exists an international community, encompassing the entire world, which has no government," and that "all human beings are citizens of this world community, which requires laws and not treaties for its government." Then, as if contemplating, if not urging the United States to enter the war then raging in Europe, the legislature averred that "it is morally incumbent upon all free peoples, before this war proceeds further," to write in a definitive treaty of peace the terms of the world federation, "in order that those who are called to give their lives and fortunes for the triumph of democracy may have positive knowledge of the incorruptible utility of their sacrifice, and in order that this conflict may not be fought to found a new world order at the conclusion of hostilities but to defend the existence of one already established by The Federation of the World."

Yet, as if mindful of realities inhering in an American civilization, the North Carolina legislature declared that "federation vitalizes all nations by endowing them with security and freedom to develop their respective cultures without menace of foreign domination." How nations and national cultures—the indefeasible sources of the nationalism decried as historically obsolete—could be developed in "freedom" and "security" without continuing the old evil, the legislature did not attempt to explain. It contented itself with proposing to renounce the independence of the United States Government, asserting the rights of all mankind, and proclaiming the brotherhood of all human beings, "in order to preserve civilization and enable mankind to live in peace and be free." In effect the North Carolina manifesto called upon all human beings, not merely proletarians, to abolish the sovereignty of existing governments and unite as "free men' under "The Federation of the World." Presumably the phrase "all mankind" included Negroes and other colored races of the Western hemisphere, Asia, and Africa, many of them, at the moment, subject to the national sovereignties coming under the head of "the democracies." If so, the North Carolina legislature made its internationalism truly universal.

In three ways the impacts of criticism from foreign points of view were intensified by special activities in the United States. The first was the academic transformation and condensation of political economy into an abstraction called "economics" supposed to be universal in application. The second was propaganda made possible by "peace" organizations and by enormous grants of money from Foundations. The third was the agitation carried on by the promoters of special interests among the various nationality elements in the United States and by the agents of foreign governments in power or in exile—all manipulated to affect opinions and policies relative to the course of American civilization.

The transformation of political economy into mere economics was effected shortly after the idea of individualism approached the climax of its influence over thought about society. It was in part the result of a provincial propensity for borrowing and in part the scholastic urge for pure theorizing. "Economics" had become a vogue in England after Alfred Marshall founded his new "school" at Cambridge; and for economists of that generation the act of borrowing was apparently easier than the act of independent thinking. Besides, the exclusion of "politics" from the consideration of economic activities made "thinking" about those activities simpler, for it eliminated all impinging and penetrating realities which might interfere with the pleasant, arm-chair operation of deducing "economic laws" from undisturbed major premises. In any event before the nineteenth century came to a close the old subject of political economy, which had at least recognized the existence of nations and governments, had been almost completely abandoned in favor of a subject known and taught in American universities as "economics."

Having thrown politics out of their reckoning, a large army of academicians belabored "economics" and its subsidiary fictions such as the economic man, land, capital, rent, interest, and labor, treated as if they had no historical or social settings. The *homo economicus* of the economists was supposed to be a universal man, torn out of the contexture of history, European, American, African, or Asiatic, out of the contexture of civilizations as realities in time and place. A capitalist was supposed to be a capitalist, acting automatically under the impulse of his interest, whether in England, the United States, Siam, or Senegambia. Labor was labor, whether American, British, German, Russian, Chinese, or Hindu. Land was land, without reference to the tenures under which it was held. From this conceptual realm of economics were excluded women, save perhaps as factory "hands" equivalent to male "hands," families, national traditions and aspirations, and historical heritages. It is true that distinctions among countries were sometimes noted more or less in passing but they were treated as incidental or transitory and not allowed to mar the perfect picture of the economic fictions. All these theoretical constructs of land, capital, and labor fitted into the world image of both communism and general internationalism.

By substituting "economics" for "economy" the new scholastics further simplified their subject and separated it still more sharply from the concrete aspects of concrete civilizations. The older word economy, borrowed from the Greeks, as used in the English language at least from the sixteenth century onward, had meant the science and art of managing a household in all its relations, material, financial, and human, with the widest connotations of physical things, moral attributes, training, and social qualities. Even the word economics, in as late as eighteenth century usage, retained the ethical and social spirit of "economy." In 1770 Langhorne said: "Economics, so far as they regard only inanimate things, serve only the low purposes of gain; but where they regard human beings they rise higher."

But when the term "economics" became almost universally accepted by the academicians, it was taken to mean "the science relating to the production and distribution of material things" or things and services exchangeable for material goods. In this form the very idea of economics served the ends alike of Marxism and general internationalism. Economic conditions, promoters of these ideas could say, are becoming the same all over the earth's surface and the proletarians or the whole people, as the case may be, are being made ready by this course of affairs for "free" trade, for "free and equal" access to raw materials, for the world society in which the nations are to be merged by unification or federation.

The development of economics, as limited to the production and distribution of material wealth, also facilitated thinking about civilization as mere progress in the invention of machines, thus depriving it of national, societal, and ethical features. The identification had been made as early as the second quarter of the nineteenth century. Capitalists, who profited largely from machines, were easily inclined, not unnaturally, to hail each invention as another triumph in civilization. Their journalistic and literary abettors aided in making this a popular idea. Even educators fell into the practice. Caught up in the new enthusiasm, orators increasingly adopted the custom of celebrating anniversaries with praises of inventions and scientific discoveries.

This identification of mechanization with civilization also supplied grist for the Marxian and general internationalist mills. Are not all peoples, white, yellow, and black, making inventions and scientific discoveries? Is not the use of machines spreading throughout the earth and proving that all peoples are alike? Are not all civilizations thus becoming so similar or so uniform in nature that their amalgamation must be regarded as the next logical and inexorable step in the history of mankind?

For the idea of civilization in the United States the dropping of the adjective "political" from thought about economy was perhaps more devastating than the creation of the economic man or the fulsome praise of machines. Had economists treated economy in its original sense and in its political and social setting, they would, of necessity, have been compelled to take into account concrete nations and governments, their histories, and their particular policies domestic and foreign. In so doing they would have been also forced to reckon with many aspects of civilization dissociated from purely material ends, and yet expressed in the politics and policies of nations as actualities. By barring government, national policies, and the social contexture of economic transactions from their thought, writings, and teachings, American economists helped to take all sense out of the idea of civilization in the United States, as Marxists and general internationalists did. If they had sought this result deliberately in the interest of these two causes, their work would have been scarcely less destructive to the idea of American civilization in its civil, political, and social meaning.

The simplification of political economy—a unity—into disparate fictions was particularly helpful to the promotion of general internationalism among the middle class in America to which that world image appealed. The simplifications made by academic economists had no taint of the revolutionary proletariat. War might be needed to realize the dream of the world order but not the kind of war represented by the revolutionary violence of the working classes in the United States or anywhere.

General internationalism as a system cast in theoretical terms would have attracted the interest of abstractionists among academicians by the sheer force of its simplicity. But to intellectual and moral appeals were added practical considerations. During the opening years of the twentieth century, millions of dollars were made available to scholars in colleges and universities all over the country for research and teaching under the head of internationalism. Indeed collegiate and university instruction in diplomacy, foreign relations, and war was nearly all transformed, with the aid of munificent grants of money, into an open and avowed propaganda for general internationalism. In this manner many minds were prepared for the depreciation or suppression of thought about civilization in the United States and the substitution of thought about Western or world civilization as the major responsibility and concern of the American people.

While the abstractions of economics were useful for every type of internationalist propaganda, they were particularly serviceable to those internationalists who indulged in the pleasing, imposing, and safe business of planning world orders for the American people to put into effect by their support, with arms if necessary. Such abstractions could be readily combined with the illusions of *Geo-politik* borrowed from the Germans and the fictions of Geo-technics manufactured at home. With maps depicting continental land masses, islands, and seas, with charts exhibiting the distribution of natural resources, with tables giving the statistics of population, and with columns of figures representing kinds and amounts of raw materials and finished products, world planners could work out new patterns showing just how peoples and things were to be arranged to bring prosperity, the four freedoms, security, and peace to everybody, everywhere—peace to be maintained under policing if necessary.

Equipped with the whole battery of abstractions, world planners could spare themselves the pain of thought about numerous races, nationalities, subject peoples, religions, customs, habits, prejudices, superstitions, history, governments, protectorates, colonies, imperial domains, political parties, vested interests, time-encrusted historical heritages, age-long attachments, hatred, and wars, and all the degrees of civilization in existence from the Andaman Islands to Manhattan Island. By ignoring such hard, intractable, inconvenient facts, they could speak with authority to Americans trained in the schools to think in abstractions. And they could enlist thousands of men, women, and children in phalanxes to fix up a warring world by means of American energies, treasure, and blood, at the same time that they added to national bewilderment by pouring odium on other Americans who questioned the validity, utility, and advantage of such expeditions.

When, in the midst of this turmoil over general internationalism, its advocates recognized that "an effective international law must rest upon a supranational class," Professor Quincy Wright, one of its most brilliant sponsors, advanced a suggestion, printed in the American Historical Review for April, 1942, page 559: "Might not the fourth estate of intellectuals, the press, and the radio commentator eventually provide such a class?"

Criticism of American civilization from European points of view was made the more feasible and destructive by reason of the fact that the American population embraced millions of foreign-born residents and citizens representing in their ancestry all European nationalities. Thousands of aliens were frankly transients solely interested in accumulating enough money to return home and live there in greater comfort than would be possible otherwise. The overwhelming majority of immigrants no doubt sought to mingle their life and work with life and work of the permanent residents and to accept American civilization, such as it was, without much equivocation; and a larger proportion would have done this if the attitude of native Americans had been more considerate and helpful.

But in connection with several nationalities settled in the United States, promoters of special interests in industry, journalism, politics, and other types of activity took advantage of the peculiar situation. To such professional promotors of divisive forces it became a matter of pecuniary advantage and personal prestige to prevent the complete admixture of the respective nationalities in America, to keep alive their separate presses, schools, customs, and predilections as against the tendency of American civilization to uniformity. The longer the antagonisms to this absorptive process could be maintained among foreign nationalities in the United States, the more drastic the criticism that could be directed against American society, the greater the pecuniary returns, power, or prestige accruing to the promoters who fostered separatism.

More or less closely associated with promoters of special interests among nationalities represented in the American population were thousands of refugees who had fled from the oppressions, conflicts, and wars of Europe, not to make permanent homes for themselves in the United States, not to merge themselves into American civilization, but to use America and American resources with a view to recovering old power, or gaining new power in one or more European countries. These temporary armies of occupation were enlarged by the secret and open agents or propagandists sent to the United States by foreign governments either to stir up fright and frenzy in American society or to divert American energies, intellectual and moral, from concentration on the promotion and defense of civilization in the United States to the support of one or more contending powers engaged in the controversies and wars of Europe. Often foreign agents operated under the guise of Marxian or of general internationalism; but whatever their mechanism of justification their agitations meant in actual effect the same end: aiding one or more foreign governments in the pursuit of their avowed interests.

Although the consequences to flow from all the criticism directed against civilization in the United States and all the divisive forces in American society were hidden in the future, many facts in the situation were indubitable. Never before in the history of the world had the population of any country included so many people of other national origins bound by affections and agitations to the interests of foreign powers or been subjected to such impacts tending to disunity and dissolution. No other contemporary society was beset by stresses and strains so sustained by powerful alien interests. Not even civilization in the last days of the Roman Empire offered an appropriate or usable analogy.

Chapter 10

World Mission under Arms

UNTIL NEAR THE END of the nineteenth century few if any persons in the United States ever dreamed that any responsible official high in public life would call upon them to use the armed power of the country for the purpose of imposing civilization on other peoples in distant parts of the earth or underwriting civilization throughout the world. It is true that military and naval forces had often been sent on war missions to various places far away and that imperial expansion had been advocated on grounds of practical interests. It is true also that echoes of the European formula for spreading civilization had long reverberated in the United States. Napoleon on his way to Egypt incited his soldiers by a glamorous proclamation that their conquests would bring immeasurable results to civilization. In France and Great Britain men of letters had defended imperial victories in all quarters under the claim that backward peoples overcome by arms were being given the blessings of French or British civilization as the case might be; and politicians in Paris and London had taken up the refrain. But Americans had been little inclined to think of their civilization as a commodity to be distributed throughout the world by armed might.

From the establishment of the Republic, to be sure, sympathies had been freely expressed for popular uprisings against despotic governments in Europe. Distinguished Americans had frequently given voice to the hope or belief that American demonstrations in self-government would encourage the growth of republican or democratic institutions in Europe and Asia. Yet such sympathies and hopes had not been backed up by using the arms of the United States to spread American civilization in Europe, Asia, Africa, Latin America, and the islands of the seas.

But by 1898 Albert J. Beveridge could bring Boston men to their feet by employing the idea of civilization in justification of imperial expansion by arms. "American factories," Beveridge declared, "are making more than the American

477

people can use; American soil is producing more than they can consume. Fate has written our policy for us; the trade of the world must and shall be ours. And we will get it as our mother [England] has told us how. We will establish trading posts throughout the world as distributing-points for American products. We will cover the ocean with our merchant marine. We will build a navy to the measure of our greatness. Great colonies governing themselves, flying our flag and trading with us, will grow about our posts of trade. Our institutions will follow our flag on the wings of our commerce. And American law, American order, American civilization, and the American flag will plant themselves on shores hitherto bloody and benighted, but by those agencies of God henceforth to be made beautiful and bright." A more rhetorical combination of explosive ideas could scarcely have been concocted, even in Boston: great riches, great sea power, American law and order, the American flag, American civilization, and the comprehensive sweep—all agencies of God.

Although President McKinley betrayed uncertainty at first as to the purposes or uses of the war against Spain, he came finally to the civilizing view of American imperialism. Before the war, in his message of December 1897, he had said: "Forcible annexation . . . cannot be thought of; that, by our code of morality, would be criminal aggression." During the war, as James Ford Rhodes remarked, McKinley declared, with "a shrewd trading instinct": "While we are conducting war and until its conclusion we must keep all we get; when the war is over we must keep what we want." Later, in 1899, McKinley explained his policy of annexation to his Methodist brethren in the language of civilization: "I didn't want the Philippines and when they came to us as a gift from the gods, I did not know what to do with them." Then he sought counsel from Democrats and Republicans, but got little help. As if baffled in search of earthly wisdom, he went down on his knees and "prayed Almighty God for light and guidance more than one night." Late one night a kind of revelation came to him; it would be "cowardly and dishonorable" to give them back to Spain; they could not be turned over to "our commercial rivals in the Orient"; they could not be intrusted with self-government; "there was nothing left for us to do but to take them all, and to educate the Filipinos, and uplift and civilize and Christianize them, and by God's grace do the very best we could by them as our fellowmen for whom Christ also died."

For this imperialist crusade in the name of civilization propagandists had been striving to prepare the American people during the years that immediately preceded the outbreak of the Spanish war. On the practical side, old sentiments of manifest destiny still lingering, blended with pride in the successful use of warships in subduing pirates and other disturbers of order who interfered with American trade, probably made many Americans accessible to the appeal for a more general undertaking abroad. But to the propagandists of great crusades such practical considerations did not seem to be sufficient unto the new occasion. Judged by their writings, they felt that a more universal, more ethical sanction was necessary to inspire popular confidence in their cause. And they seized upon the idea of civilization which they frequently suffused with theology.

Two types of intellectual endeavor appeared in the literature designed to make attractive and popular the appeal to civilization in the imperialist undertaking. One was general and moral. The other was technical and moral. Suggestions of both appeared in the relevant literary currents between 1880 and 1900. Nowhere was the first more forcefully illustrated than in the writings of Josiah Strong, militant Congregational clergyman; or the second more diffusely illustrated than in the works of the militant naval officer, Alfred Thayer Mahan.

Josiah Strong was a passionate worker for the Congregational Home Missionary Society who branched out from concern with domestic evangelizing to an unlimited concern with a world mission. In 1891 Strong presented his larger thesis, that Americans, in conjunction with the English, had an obligation to civilize the rest of the earth, in a volume entitled *Our Country*, the elaboration of a pamphlet written several years before for the Home Missionary Society. This volume immediately produced a big tempest. It was translated into European and Oriental languages and, according to Strong's biographer, "created a sensation. . . . It made Strong a national figure, brought him repeated requests for lectures and speeches, and was the occasion of his appointment as secretary of the American Evangelical Alliance. . . . Passionate in his prophetic zeal, he was statesmanlike in his ingenious devising of practical methods of action." In the course of his many journeys, Strong visited England where he met a hearty reception for which the way had been paved by an immense circulation of his writings.

In his volume, Strong described what he termed the evils in American society. The nation had immense natural resources and industrial skills which could feed and enrich a billion people but its very foundations were shaky: a multitude of foreign immigrants largely congested in cities, "Romanism" defying American doctrines of liberty, the lack of religious teaching in the public schools, Mormonism, intemperance, socialism, aggregated wealth and the worship of Mammon, disproportionate growth of cities and their corruption, and the approaching exhaustion of cheap public lands.

In realistic language, Strong recounted the rise of industries, the development of an immense urban proletariat, the stubborn nature of social conflicts carried on under materialistic slogans on both sides, the concentration of wealth and control under corporate leadership, and the demoralizing effects of panics and depressions. "This," he said, "is modern and republican feudalism. These American barons and lords of labor have probably more power and less responsibility than many an olden feudal lord. They close the factory or the mine, and thousands of workmen are forced into unwilling idleness. . . . We have developed a despotism vastly more oppressive and more exasperating than that against which the thirteen colonies rebelled." To this state of affairs, Strong maintained, socialism is a kind of natural answer but also an answer in terms of similar greed and hence a road to the ruin of American civilization.

In this situation Strong felt the need of a great remedial program and he gave it the form of a union between Protestantism and Anglo-American imperialism. "Every race," he explained, "which has deeply impressed itself on the human family has been the representative of some great idea—one or more—which has given direction to the nation's life and form to its civilization. . . . The Anglo-Saxon is the representative of two great ideas. . . . One of them is that of civil liberty. . . . The other great idea of which the Anglo-Saxon is the exponent is that of a pure *spiritual* Christianity." The Teutonic branch of the race in Germany is Protestant, but it is militarist, its state churches are formalist in religion, and all the German missionary societies combined, "in the number of workers and amount of contributions," do not equal "the smallest of the three great English missionary societies." Consequently "it is chiefly to the English and American peoples that we must look for the evangelization of the World."

Positive that he had the secret of history and God's Providence, Strong shared it with the people: "Does it not look as if God were not only preparing in our Anglo-Saxon civilization the die with which to stamp the peoples of the earth, but as if he were massing behind that die the mighty power with which to press it? My confidence that this race is eventually to give its civilization to mankind is not based on mere numbers—China forbid! I look forward to what the world has never yet seen united in the same race; viz., the greatest numbers, *and* the highest civilization. . . . America is to have the great preponderance of numbers and of wealth, and by the logic of events will follow the sceptre of controlling influence. This will be but the consummation of a movement as old as civilization. . . . Arts, sciences, and empire had traveled westward. . . . It surely needs no prophet's eye to see that the civilization of the *United States* is to be the civilization of America, and that the future of the continent is ours. . . . We are to have not only the larger proportion of the Anglo-Saxon race, but we may reasonably expect to develop the highest type of Anglo-Saxon civilization."

The hour of action approaches: "The time is coming when the pressure of population on the means of subsistence will be felt here as it is now felt in Europe and Asia. Then will the world enter upon a new stage of its history—*the final competition of races, for which the Anglo-Saxon is being schooled.* . . . The mighty *centrifugal* tendency, inherent in this stock and strengthened in the United States, will assert itself. Then this race of unequaled energy, with all the majesty of numbers and the might of wealth behind it—the representative, let us hope, of the largest liberty, the purest Christianity, the highest civilization—having developed peculiarly aggressive traits, calculated to impress its institutions upon mankind, will spread itself over the earth. If I read not amiss, this powerful race will move down upon Mexico, down upon Central and South America, out upon the islands of the sea, over upon Africa and beyond. And can anyone doubt that the result of this competition of races will be the 'survival of the fittest'?"

As this coalition of numbers, riches, and aggression rolls

over the earth, what of the inferiors? Strong discovered an answer in the writings of Horace Bushnell, another Congregational theologian: "Nothing can save the inferior race but a ready and pliant assimilation." He also claimed support from Darwin: "At the present day civilized nations are everywhere supplanting barbarous nations, excepting where the climate opposes a deadly barrier; and they succeed mainly, though not exclusively, through their arts, which are the products of the intellect." Extinction, rather than assimilation, seems to be the coming fate of inferiors.

With his sense for realism, however, Strong asserted that "the pioneer wave of our civilization carries with it more scum than salt. Where there is one missionary, there are hundreds of miners or traders or adventurers ready to debauch the native. Whether the extinction of inferior races before the advancing Anglo-Saxon seems to the reader sad or otherwise, it certainly appears probable. . . . While on this continent God is training the Anglo-Saxon race for its mission, a complemental work has been in progress in the great world beyond. God has two hands. Not only is he preparing in our civilization the die with which to stamp the nations, but, by what Southey called 'the timing of Providence,' he is preparing mankind to receive our impress."

In the keeping of Americans, under God, lay the fortunes of mankind, not yet settled, but trembling in the balance, despite all the assurances of Strong's faith in the Anglo-Saxon's mission. "How far his civilization will be materialistic and atheistic, and how long it will take thoroughly to Christianize and sweeten it, how rapidly he will hasten the coming of the kingdom wherein dwelleth righteousness, or how many ages he may retard it, is still uncertain; but *is now being swiftly determined*." That the kingdom would come was scarcely to be doubted. Americans, it seemed to Strong, had the power to hasten or retard its coming. "Notwithstanding the great perils which threaten it, I cannot think our civilization will perish; but I believe it is fully in the hands of the Christians of the United States, during the next ten or fifteen years, to hasten or retard the coming of Christ's kingdom in the world by hundreds, and perhaps thousands, of years. We of this generation and nation occupy the Gibraltar of the ages which commands the world's future." In the geographic and temporal latitude of his apocalyptic vision, Strong surpassed the exuberance even of Rudyard Kipling.

While Strong's conception of American civilization militant was seeping into the minds of the tens of thousands who read his works or heard his impassioned speeches, an American naval officer, Alfred Thayer Mahan, was preaching a similar gospel in naval circles, to politicians, and among the readers of his books and numerous articles on Sea Power. Mahan was not exactly an Anglo-Saxon. His father, Dennis Hart Mahan, was an offspring of Irish parents baptized in the Roman Catholic Church, but his mother was of Protestant American stock and his biographer, C. C. Taylor, could say that Alfred Thayer Mahan was "one-half Irish and one-quarter English, the remaining quarter coming of French-American stock." At all events the systematist of American imperialism was a member of the Protestant Episcopal Church and he thought that in his personality he recognized "the predominance which the English strain has usually asserted for itself over others." Whether his analysis of himself was or was not correct, Mahan developed a profound admiration for English sea power and world-wide imperialism, as well as for the English people.

If Mahan thought he was avoiding the evangelicism of Strong, he was not entirely successful for, with a cold materialism of commercial interest and sheer military force, he mingled tender respect for God's providence and a reliance upon Christ's teachings. Like Strong, he often appealed to God and civilization in vindication of his doctrines; but, unlike Strong, perhaps owing to his obsession with English imperial power, he took little interest in American civilization as such. God, presumably, presided over the fortunes of all mankind, but "the world's history and the welfare of mankind . . . are bound up, so far as we can see, in the security and strength of that civilization which is identified with Europe and its offshoots in America." When he spoke of "our civilization," Mahan generally indicated that he meant Western civilization. It was as an "offshoot of European civilization" that, in his opinion, America should "take her share of the travail of Europe" and "assume an inevitable task, an appointed lot, in the work of upholding the common interests of civilization."

Mahan's scheme of thought respecting American imperialism was a compound of several other ideas with that of civilization. Educated in naval affairs at Annapolis, he apparently had meager acquaintance with the learning of the humanities. As tested by his voluminous writings, he had slight knowledge of any history, except naval wars, and only a second-hand knowledge of them. At all events in numerous passages he proclaimed the doctrine of self-interest in naked terms. "Self-interest," he said, "is not only a legitimate, but a fundamental cause for national policy; one which needs no cloak of hypocrisy. . . . It is vain to expect nations to act consistently from any other motive than that of interest. That, under the name of Realism, is the frankly avowed policy of German statecraft." In the pursuit of self-interest, Mahan reiterated, the United States should build a huge navy, secure naval bases in various parts of the world, and promote commerce by the engines of power; that is, follow exactly in the course pursued by the imperialist nations of Europe. "Acquisition by war," he maintained, "is a legitimate international transaction."

In consonance with his advocacy of a world crusade, Mahan took slight or no interest in the improvement of social conditions in the United States as a phase of civilization. Social legislation he deplored if for no other reason than it diminished the tax revenues available for war and preparations for war. True to his philosophy of war as a masculine function, he vigorously opposed woman suffrage and the whole woman movement. With all the self-satisfaction of Emperor William II and, later, the official exponents of German National Socialism, Mahan assigned women entirely to "that indoor sphere which we call the family," as if millions of them were not battling for their very existence in the industries of the United States. "Christianity—which is the cornerstone of European civilization—while inculcating equality, emphasizes differentiations and denies identity of function. . . . You cannot stop with the vote. . . . There is no drawing the line here other than that of sex. Remove that barrier as is proposed and you reverse what has heretofore been fundamental in our society."

Although he was associated with American imperialists and therefore presumably concerned first and foremost with American commercial interests, Mahan spoke frequently in terms of British interests and the good and happiness of the whole world, to be promoted by imperialism and war: "If force is necessary, force must be used for the benefit of the community, of the commonwealth of the world. . . . If the plea of the world's welfare seems suspiciously like a cloak for national self-interest, let the latter be accepted frankly as the adequate motive which it assuredly is. Let us not shrink from pitting a broad self-interest against the narrow self-interest to which some opponents of imperialism would restrict us." In spreading the benefits of civilization, he thought, the British Empire and the American Empire had obligations to increase "the world sum of happiness."

When other writers, however, criticized his doctrine of self-interest and war in the pursuit of self-interest, Mahan shifted his ground to a theory of morals and declared that "the inciting causes of war in our day are moral." In this setting, good and bad were opposed; the wars which Mahan approved were righteous Christian wars.

For such judgments he leaned upon quotations from the Bible and in the new role he became the advance agent of Christianity as well as power and prosperity: "To right what is amiss, to convert, to improve, to develop, is of the very essence of the Christian ideal. Without man's responsive effort, God himself is not powerless but deprived of the instrument through which he wills to work." When force becomes necessary, it should be used "for the benefit of the community, of the commonwealth of the world."

Flattered into ecstasy by the attentions he received from British imperialists, the German Kaiser, and the militarists in Japan, well paid for the articles he contributed to British magazines expounding his world imperialist creed, Mahan went beyond the strictly American imperialism of Beveridge and McKinley. If his vague, confused, and often contradictory pronouncements were to be taken at face value, he seemed to be a world crusader, more British than American in his susceptibilities but still a universal dreamer bent on driving the United States into a world-spanning imperialist mission in the name of Christ and civilization.

Speaking of future international conflicts, he summed up in a single sentence the theme-song which rang like a quavering threnody through his speculations: "In this same pregnant strife the United States doubtless will be led, by undeniable interests and aroused national sympathies, to play a part, to cast aside the policy of isolation which befitted her infancy, and to recognize that, whereas once to avoid European entanglements was essential to the development of her individuality, now to take her share in the travail of Europe is but to assume an inevitable task, an appointed lot, in the work of upholding the common interests of civilization."

In its platform of 1900 the Republican party supported President McKinley's final idea of the imperialist adventure as a civilizing mission. Referring with the customary pride to its "record," the party declared: "While the American people, sustained by this Republican legislation, have been achieving these splendid triumphs in their business and commerce, they have conducted, and in victory concluded, a war for liberty and human rights. No thought of National aggrandizement tarnished the higher purpose with which American standards were unfurled. It was a war unsought and patiently resisted, but when it came the American Government was ready. . . . To ten millions of the human race there was given 'a new birth of freedom,' and to the American people a new and noble responsibility. . . . Our authority could not be less than our responsibility, and wherever sovereign rights were extended it became the high duty of the Government to maintain its authority, to put down armed insurrection and to confer the blessings of liberty and civilization upon all the rescued peoples."

More men from the Navy, like Mahan, praised their branch of the armed service for its aid in the world-civilizing crusade. George Washington Littlehales, a graduate of the Naval Academy in 1883, writing on "The Navy as a Motor in Geographical and Commercial Progress," in 1899, declared: "The spirit of honorable adventure which prompts voyages of exploration and the persistent striving against the obstacles of nature which results in the acquisition of fresh information and the discovery of new lands have placed the naval service of the United States among the forceful agencies of the nineteenth century in extending the confines of knowledge to a wider horizon and in opening avenues through which the industries of the people have poured millions of treasures into the nation's lap, and coordinated it with the missions of the Christian Church in bringing the people of distant lands within the generous folds of western civilization." Here was imperialism in a nutshell: honorable adventure, extension of knowledge, millions of treasures, the Christian Church, and civilization.

A third of a century later, a naval ensign, E. E. Marshall, won a prize at the Academy with an essay on "Our

Navy in Peace," in which he stated that "the Navy is constantly striving to aid China in her progress towards a better civilization, and has always endeavored to protect China from exploitation by greedy foreign powers, even as it protects Central and South American states from similar colonization. . . . To withdraw American interests would seriously handicap the countries involved, since they owe much of their economic, social and political development to the work of Americans."

To the idea of a world crusade for the promotion of civilization in far places, the War Department gave its homage. During the administration of President Coolidge, it reviewed its contributions to this process since 1898. In a report on the work of the Army, the Department exulted: "In other lands—the Philippines, Hawaii, Cuba, Porto Rico, and Panama—the Army has given impetus to the forces of civilization. It has built public utilities, stamped out disease, educated the children, promoted the spiritual welfare."

The Secretary of War, John W. Weeks, was even more extensive in his claims: "The Philippines, Hawaii, Cuba, Porto Rico, and Panama—all have histories of achievement —history in which the progressive forces of civilization have struggled against reaction and decadence. That civilized forces are triumphant is due primarily to the intelligent administration and constructive talents of the American Army. Building up public utilities, eradicating terrible diseases, educating the children, attending even to the spiritual needs, creating the institutions of self-government and protecting these institutions from aggression—in all these has the Army left its seal upon our possessions and protectorates and proven itself once more the Pioneer of the American Pioneers."

It could not be said with truth, however, that the crusade for civilizing backward peoples, while increasing commerce, proved to be in the minds of all the American people, especially Democrats, a complete success. If they seemed to commend it in the presidential elections of 1900, 1904, and 1908, nevertheless a powerful opposition existed and was also obvious all along. The prosperity forecast when the adventure was launched was not exactly realized in fact. In many circles, the burdens entailed by the enterprise were considered useless and irksome. Nor were all Americans satisfied and silent concerning the military treatment of the

Filipinos and other peoples deemed backward by the civilizers.

Indeed an agitation for withdrawal from the Philippines started off soon after the victory over Spain. By 1916 disillusionment with that imperialist adventure was widespread. Before he became President of the United States, Woodrow Wilson had written of the adventure as if it had been a necessary phase of American civilization but after he became President of the United States, he signed, in 1916, a bill granting larger autonomy to the Philippines and greeted it as a step toward independence for the Islands. This accorded with general public opinion.

The year following the passage of the bill granting larger autonomy to the Philippines as a step toward independence, President Wilson led his nation into the war then raging in Europe and initiated "The Great Crusade," as it was styled by Preston W. Slosson, a historian of the conflict. In explaining and justifying this course, the President, while placing the blame on the German government for starting the war, at first declared that it was to become a "war for democracy," to make the world safe for democracy, to liberate oppressed peoples in Europe, and a "war to end war." At the moment French and British exponents of war aims were designating it a "war for civilization." But President Wilson did not make that formula his chief instrument of moral justification until after the war had ended. It was when he faced the task of inducing the American people to support the League of Nations, as devised in the covenant to the peace treaty framed at Versailles, that he repeatedly and urgently invoked the spell of civilization over their minds and emotions.

In this new line of argument, President Wilson did not discard democracy but he seemed to exalt civilization above it, based plea after plea upon the supreme value of civilization, and called upon his countrymen to join him in underwriting and advancing civilization throughout the earth.

On the negative side, the immediate obligation was to prevent a return of such threats to civilization as the German government had recently made. After condemning the autocratic system of Germany, he declared: "There must not be men anywhere in any private place who can plot the mastery of civilization."

On the positive side, Wilson contended that the United States was the only country whose leadership was steadying the world in the civilizing process and asserted: "If we do not give it, we may look forward, my fellow citizens, to something like a generation of doubt and of disorder which it will be impossible to pass through without the wreckage of a very considerable part of our slowly constructed civilization."

And what did Wilson mean by "our civilization"? At the moment in any case he meant "world civilization"; for in maintaining that the prosperity of the United States depended on foreign commerce, he spoke of civilization as having arrived at a world unity: "We have managed in the process of civilization, my fellow citizens, to make a world that cannot be taken to pieces. The pieces are dovetailed and intimately fitted with one another, and unless you assemble them as you do the intimate parts of a great machine, civilization will not work."

Indeed the very purpose of the League of Nations covenant, Wilson avowed, was to underwrite and advance civilization throughout the world: "America alone cannot underwrite civilization. All the great free peoples of the world must underwrite it, and only the free peoples of the world can join the League of Nations. The membership is open only to self-governing nations. Germany is for the present excluded, because she must prove that she is self-governing; she must prove that she has changed the processes of her constitution and the purposes of her policy; but when she has proved these things she can become one of the partners in guaranteeing that civilization shall not suffer again the intolerable thing she attempted. It is not only a union of free peoples to guarantee civilization; it is something more than that. It is a League of Nations to advance civilization by substituting something that will make the improvement of civilization possible. I call you to witness, my fellow citizens, that our present civilization is not satisfactory. It is an industrial civilization, and at the heart of it is an antagonism between those who labor with their hands and those who direct labor."

And what did Wilson think that the word civilization meant? A great task of mankind, he declared, is to provide that "the handsome passions, the handsome sentiments, the handsome purposes, shall always have a dominating and working majority, so that they will always be able to out-vote the baser passions, to defeat all the cupidities and mean-nesses and criminalities of the world. That is the program of civilization. The basis of the program of civilization, I want to say with all the emphasis that I am capable of, is Christian and not pagan, and in the presence of this inevitable partner-ship with the rest of the world, these gentlemen [opponents of the League of Nations] say, 'We will not sign the articles of co-partnership.' . . . The underlying thought of what I have tried to say to you tonight is the organization of the world for order and peace. . . . My fellow citizens, the pledge that speaks to us from these graves [of American soldiers] is demanded of us. We must see to it that these boys did not die in vain. We must fulfill the great mission upon which they crossed the sea."

Yet President Wilson in speaking of civilization did not neglect practical matters any more than President McKin-ley had done. Taking up the old imperialist argument that American industries must have foreign outlets for surpluses of goods or perish, Wilson offered a remedy for the disease in the underwriting of world civilization: "So long as the world is not reassured its industries will not begin again; . . . unless its industries begin again there will be nothing to pay for anything with, . . . unless its industries begin again there will be no market for the goods of America, and . . . we shall have to rest content with our domestic markets at the very time when we have enlarged our enterprises in order to make peaceful conquest of the world. The very processes of war have driven our industries to a point of expansion where they will be chilled and ruined if they do not presently get a foreign outlet. Therefore, on the lowest basis, you have got to guarantee and underwrite civilization or you have ruined the United States. But I do not like to talk about that side of it. I believe in my heart that there is hardly a man in America, if you really get back of his super-ficial thoughts, who is not man enough to be willing to make the sacrifices to underwrite civilization. It is only sacrifice that tells."

If world civilization was all of one piece and America had to underwrite it on grounds of morals and self-interest, yet, Wilson averred, America had special virtues which fitted it for the world mission of leading and guiding civilization: "In almost every other country there is some class that dominates, or some governmental authority that determines the course of politics, or some ancient system of land laws that limits the freedom of tenure, or some ancient custom which ties a man into a particular groove in the land in which he lives. There is none of that in America. . . . We do not have to get the approval of a class as to our behavior. . . . America does not march, as so many other peoples march, looking back over its shoulder. It marches with its eyes not only forward, but with its eyes lifted to the great distances of history, to the great events which are slowly culminating, in the Providence of God, in the lifting of civilization to new levels and new achievements. That is what makes us Americans."

Finally, Wilson declared, only by embarking on the mission of underwriting civilization everywhere could the dangerous issues of industrial relations be successfully met: "You cannot compose these differences [between capital and labor] in the midst of war, and you cannot advance civilization unless you have a peace of which you make the peaceful and healing use for bringing these elements of civilization together into a common partnership, in which every man will have the same interest in the work of his community that those have who direct the work of the community. We have got to have leisure and freedom of mind to settle these things." Evidently Wilson thought that America could not have peace in which to advance civilization and compose the differences of capital and labor by domestic action; for he said: "We must have peaceful means; we must have discussion—we must have frank discussion, we must have friendly discussion—and those are the very things that are offered to us among the nations of the world by the Covenant of the League of Nations."

On such grounds, notwithstanding differences between civilization in America and in the Old World, America must, President Wilson pleaded, concentrate her forces on underwriting a world civilization. "When the world learns, as it will learn, that America has put her whole force into the common harness of civilization," he exclaimed, "then it will know that the wheels are going to turn, the loads are going to be drawn, and that men are going to begin to ascend those difficult heights of hope which have sometimes seemed so inaccessible. I am glad for one to have lived to see this day. I have lived to see a day in which, after saturating myself most of my life in the history and traditions of America, I seem suddenly to see the culmination of American hope and history—all the orators seeing their dreams realized, if their spirits are looking on; all the men who spoke the noblest sentiments of America heartened with the sight of a great Nation responding to and acting upon those dreams, and saying, 'At last, the world knows America as the savior of the world!' "

After Mussolini and Hitler had declared an open and avowed ideological war on civilization, a large number of public officials and writers in the United States engaged in a defense of civilization—in speeches, books, editorials, essays, magazine articles, pamphlets, leaflets, advertisements, and manifestos. As the conflict of ideas verged in the direction of an armed conflict and finally exploded in a European war, public officials and writers who held that the United States should take an active part in the war again appropriated the idea of civilization as providing a high moral guarantee that their policy was well founded. This they did with such reiteration and profusion that a full record of their uses of the word civilization would require a work no less voluminous than an encyclopedia. But the general purport of their utterances under the head of civilization may be indicated by a few citations.

When the United States became involved in the "shooting war" subsequent to the passage of the Lend-Lease Act in 1941, President Roosevelt and Premier Churchill met "somewhere in the Atlantic Ocean" to take counsel on winning the war. They held conferences, considered common measures of war against Hitler and his associates, discussed the nature of the conflict, and drew up in the name of the United States and Great Britain a declaration of principles relative to the war, which was immediately known as "the Atlantic Charter."

Respecting the nature of the combat in ideas and arms, they agreed that the actions of Germany and her allies were menaces to "world civilization" against which the United States and Great Britain must take steps to assure their safety. To use the language of their official announcement: "The President and the Premier . . . have considered the dangers to world civilization arising from the policies of military domination by conquest upon which the Hitlerite government of Germany and other governments associated therewith have embarked, and have made clear the steps which their countries are respectively taking for their safety in the face of these dangers."

On August 21, 1941, President Roosevelt laid before Congress a brief message pertaining to his conferences with Premier Churchill, an official statement respecting their exchanges and transactions, and their declaration of principles in full. Although the official statement, incorporated in the presidential message, referred to the aggressions of the Axis powers as dangers to "world civilization," President Roosevelt, in giving force to his argument, seemed to narrow the range of the joint interpretation of the conflict by saying that "the declaration of principles at this time presents a goal which is worth while for our type of civilization to seek."

After the United States became completely engaged in the war everywhere, President Roosevelt confronted the task of finding a word or brief phrase, purporting to describe it, that would bind all the people to it, warm their hearts in support of it, and command their unqualified intellectual consent. In the spring of 1942 he remarked to representatives of the press that he was searching for the right word or phrase. At a conference of Latin-American ambassadors and ministers, on April 14, he discussed his quandary openly. Sensitive to the cultural difficulties in developing harmony in the Western hemisphere, the President seemed to be struggling for a formula that would not rest too heavily on the idea of civilization. And yet that idea kept coming back to the center of his consciousness as if it had an irresistible fascination for him or was the point of gravity to which the eccentricities of his thought constantly returned.

"I want a name for the war," he said to the diplomats. "I haven't had any very good suggestions. Most of them are too long.

"My own thought is that perhaps there is one word that we could use for this war, the word 'survival,' The Survival War. That is, it comes pretty close to being the survival of our civilization, the survival of democracy, the survival of a hemisphere—the newest hemisphere of them all—which has developed in its own ways.

"On the surface these ways may be a bit different, but down at the bottom there is the same kind of civilization that has come from a love of liberty and the willingness to pioneer. So I think that survival is what our problem is, survival of what we have all lived for for a great many generations.

"I think in all of the republics we have, relatively speaking, quite an ancient civilization—reckoned since we have had independence, and even for a good many years before that. . . .

"And when it comes to cleaning up the mess at the end of this war, after the Axis is defeated, we will have again an Hemispheric Council around here to see what we are going to do all over the world, because we will have a very great voice in preventing, in the future, an attack on our American civilization.

"I haven't prepared any speech. These are just some thoughts that come to me every day—day and night.

"We are going places. We will get somewhere. And we are going to have a couple of years, perhaps three years, before we can make sure that our type of civilization is going to survive. . . ."

By the autumn of 1942 President Roosevelt seemed convinced that it was not "our type of civilization" or "American civilization" or "Western civilization" that would triumph in the war, but "world civilization." Speaking over the radio to the youth of the world on September 3, he said: "Today the embattled youth of Russia and China are realizing a new individual dignity, casting off the last links of the ancient chains of imperial despotism which had bound them so long. This is a development of historic importance. It means that the old term, 'Western civilization,' no longer applies. World events and the common needs of all humanity are joining the culture of Asia with the culture of Europe and of the Americas to form, for the first time, a real world civilization."

Whether speaking officially for the Administration or not, the Secretary of the Navy, Colonel Frank Knox, long an ardent pleader for aggressive imperialism in the Far East, expounded, in an address to the American Bar Association on October 1, 1941, his war policy, making references to "our civilization" and "the advancement of civilization." The United States and Great Britain, he declared, should unite, crush the Axis aggressors, police the seven seas, and keep the sea lanes open throughout the world in the future. The task he imposed on the two powers, Secretary Knox made an obligation to civilization: "Freedom of the seas, the keeping of the highways of the seas clear of pirates, is as essentially a duty of civilization as it is a part of the function of any organized society to take strong measures against bandits on its highways."

According to opinions held in the official world it was not only "world civilization," "our type of civilization," and "the advancement of civilization" that were at stake in the war and the peace to follow. An appeal to "human civilization" was made by the Vice President, Henry A. Wallace, in outlining a program designed to guarantee freedom and prosperity to everybody, everywhere in the world, at the end of the war—a plea published in the Atlantic Monthly for January, 1942. Such a program, he argued, was not really separate from measures necessary to win the war: "Planning for the future peace must of necessity be a part of our all-out war program."

In the course of his allocution, Vice President Wallace made an attack on "the isolationists" in the United States. They were, in his opinion, largely responsible for the collapse of the world after the first world war and were likely to interfere with the Administration's plans for making "freedom of speech and expression, freedom of worship, freedom from want, and freedom from fear" prevail for everybody, everywhere. Ordinarily, he said, there would be no ground for objecting to a renewal of isolationist politics after the war. "But," he insisted, "the really serious aspect of the matter is that the whole future not only of this country but of human civilization itself may depend on the ability and willingness of the American people to take the broad view." Hence, by implication, "isolationist" or other tactics likely to extinguish "the broad view" were not to be tolerated, at least not as freely as they had been in the past.

"The broad view," upon which the future of "human civilization" and the United States, presumably sharing in human civilization, might depend, Vice President Wallace extended to cover a number of policies and measures to be adopted and executed after the war. "The people of all Europe should feel that there are available, in the United States, in Latin America, and in the British dominions, tremendous quantities of raw materials which can be used for food, clothing, and shelter within a short time after the war comes to an end. . . . Both strategy and humanity will be served if we take every opportunity to let the people of the occupied countries know that we intend to stand behind them in their efforts to get back on their feet." Raw-material countries from which the United States and Great Britain are buying heavily for war purposes must be assured that their business will not collapse after war purchases stop. "There would be no better use to which this country's gold could be put than in making such purchases" beyond the time of war needs.

The industrialization of backward countries, Vice President Wallace maintained, must be promoted to raise their level of living: "Certain minimum standards of food, clothing, and shelter ought to be established, and arrangements ought to be made to guarantee that no one should fall below those standards." This world program would cost money no doubt, but "We in the democracies . . . can afford to invest whatever amount it takes to win the peace. . . . Probably the English-speaking peoples of the world will have to take the lead in underwriting world prosperity for a generation to come." While aware that "many persons in the United States are deeply disturbed over the heavy government borrowing" and shifts in our economy made necessary by the war, the Vice President saw "hopeful signs for the future," despite such alarms—if the tactics of isolationists could be avoided and the people of the United States would take "the broad view" on which the future of "human civilization" may depend.

The writings and documents on the war of ideologies and arms, which private citizens and organizations began to produce in an increasing flood after the rise of Mussolini and Hitler to power, contained appeals to the idea of civilization, in justification of American intervention in Europe, still more profuse and various than in official pronouncements. In the abundance of possible citations three principal versions appeared: (1) Mussolini and Hitler have declared a war, ideological and military, on civilization; against this attack, civilization in the United States cannot be defended by the United States alone; it must join in the general war for civilization. (2) Western civilization is in mortal peril; American civilization is a part of Western civilization; for the sake of Western civilization as well as for its own safety, the United States must participate in the war of arms. (3) World civilization is in danger of destruction by the Axis powers; civilization is indivisible; civilization in the United States cannot proceed alone; it must dedicate its blood and wealth to save and promote civilization everywhere in the world; or perish with world civilization. The spirit of all these protestations was well voiced in 1942 by a teacher of American youth, previously at Harvard, then at the Massachusetts Institute of Technology, George de Santillana, in the avowal that "it is easier to plan a world than to plan a nation."

A variant on these exhortations was provided by Henry R. Luce, in a condensed polemic, *The American Century,* published early in 1941, first as an article in his magazine Life and then as an advertisement in great metropolitan newspapers, and finally as a booklet. The son of American missionaries, born in China and always interested in that country, Luce mingled a prophet's wrath with a prophet's faith. Like other advocates of American participation in the war who had once warmly assailed American civilization— Dorothy Thompson, for example—Luce belittled the achievements and aspirations of Americans at home and their preoccupation with domestic affairs. But he offered them salvation and vast profits in a crusade to spread the principal features of American civilization throughout the world.

Like Beveridge, Strong, Mahan, and other advocates of a militant world mission, Luce summoned to his aid the genie of civilization. "We are," he declared, "the inheritors of all the great principles of Western civilization—above all Justice, the love of Truth, the ideal of Charity." Given this heritage of principles, it was his opinion that we had failed in trying to apply them in the United States and could only succeed in our bounden duty if we dedicated our energies to putting them into effect all over the world.

It was unquestionably America's mission, Luce asserted, to make them prevail throughout the earth: "The other day Herbert Hoover said that America was fast becoming the sanctuary of the ideals of civilization. For the moment it may be enough to be the sanctuary of these ideals. But not for long. It now becomes our time to be the powerhouse from which the ideals spread throughout the world and do their mysterious work of lifting the life of mankind from the level of the beasts to what the Psalmist called a little lower than the angels." Other nations may survive without the spirit of world crusading but America cannot "truly endure" unless it embarks upon such a high course.

In previous centuries "this continent teemed with manifold projects and magnificent purposes." But "above them all and weaving them all together into the most exciting flag of all the world and of all history was the triumphant purpose of freedom. It is in this spirit that all of us are called, each to his own measure of capacity, and each in the widest horizon of his vision, to create the first American century." —the subjugation of the earth to the ideals of civilization.

Whereas former imperialist crusaders for the spreading of American civilization had acclaimed America as rising in economic strength and political power, as having rounded out the continent and subdued it to the uses of civilization, to use Woodrow Wilson's phrase, Luce portrayed this nation as simply bewildered and half defeated. "We Americans are unhappy. We are not happy about America. . . . We are nervous—or gloomy—or apathetic. As we look at the rest of the world we are confused." In comparison, the British people, amid the horrors of war, "are profoundly calm." Far from being triumphant, the American people have failed to solve the problems of the time. The government debt is immense. A huge bureaucracy has been created. Young people are looking to the government as the source of life. The party in power has for years "been most sympathetic to all manner of socialist doctrines and collectivist trends."

And what of triumphant democracy all caparisoned to transform the world? "The fact is that Franklin Roosevelt failed to make American democracy work successfully on a narrow, materialistic, and nationalistic basis. And under Franklin Roosevelt we ourselves have failed to make democracy work successfully." At home, government, finances, democracy, the spirit of the people, all are in a sad plight, for Americans have been too much absorbed in their own affairs. Their only chance to make democracy work is "in terms of a vital international economy and in terms of an international moral order."

What was to be the nature of the new crusade for civilization? The plain old imperialists had promised to do good on a limited scale to them that sat in darkness; but Luce took the position that America should send its engineers, scientists, doctors, road builders, teachers, educators, and even "movie men" everywhere "throughout the world," providing leadership to all mankind in creating the right kind of civilization. America must feed the hungry everywhere: "We must undertake now to be the Good Samaritan of the entire world. It is the manifest duty of this country to undertake to feed all the people of the world who as a result of this worldwide collapse of civilization are hungry and destitute—all of them, that is, whom we can from time to time reach consistently with a very tough attitude toward all hostile governments." Americans should produce all they can and send it, with "a humanitarian Army of Americans," to "every man, woman and child on this earth who is really hungry."

In terms of doing good to suffering peoples, Luce outdid the old imperialists in the universality of his distributive charity. He outdid them also in terms of economics by promising more stupendous advantages to the practical interests that had been associated with imperialism of the old style. Americans were to make the "system of free economic enterprise" prevail universally in the twentieth century. This "free economic enterprise," as generally understood in the United States in 1941, meant individualistic, capitalistic, competitive enterprise, if it meant anything—just the kind of enterprise which plain, unvarnished imperialists had proposed to carry on everywhere in the world under the protection and force of the United States Government. They too had spoken of "America as a world power" and they had meant by freedom for commercial promotion just what Luce seemed to mean when he asserted "the right to go with our ships and our ocean-going airplanes where we wish, when we wish and as we wish," and presented "the vision of America as the dynamic leader of world trade."

Before the audience to which free enterprise appealed, Luce dangled prizes of profits in world trade more enormous than any which the shortsighted imperialists of other years had ever conjured up in their wildest fantasies. "Let us rise to its tremendous possibilities. Our thinking of world trade today is on ridiculously small terms. For example, we think of Asia as being worth only a few hundred millions a year to us. Actually, in the decades to come Asia will be worth to us exactly zero—or else it will be worth to us four, five, ten billions of dollars a year. And the latter are the terms we must think in, or else confess a pitiful impotence." For more than three hundred years the "fabulous riches" to be won in the Far East had been displayed by writers and orators through a shimmering sheen of romance before the dazzled eyes of merchants in Western civilization. It remained for Luce to offer American traders prospects of gain so glittering as to make Marco Polo's lures look like Stygian murk.

In dealing with the politics of his economics, Luce with ferocity derided "the moral and practical bankruptcy of any and all forms of isolationism" and called upon the Republican party to work out a program for "America's initiative and activity as a world power." In 1933, amid the crisis into which the country had plunged, President Franklin D. Roosevelt had turned his back, for a time, on the theory that prosperity could be won only through the manipulation of international finance and commerce; he had sought to lift the country out of the slough by resorting to domestic measures. For this procedure, the President was harshly upbraided by Henry Luce in the declaration that, during the pursuit of this domestic policy, President Roosevelt "was more of an isolationist than Herbert Hoover or Calvin Coolidge." In a sense that was true. But Luce soon found comfort in what he believed to be a change in Roosevelt who at last seemed, in his opinion, to be exhibiting the qualities of a world leader. To the President in this role, Luce tendered power and immortality if he would lead Americans, as "inheritors of all the great principles of Western Civilization" on a crusade to feed and uplift the earth's multitudes, to spread "free enterprise" everywhere, and to make the twentieth century "the American century."

Emancipated from the accountancy of trade, escaping into the empyrean of the National Capital, a band of poets even rose above the color and immensity of Luce's luxuriance in hymns to the grand services that American song could render to the cause and victory of civilization in war. Under the general direction of Archibald MacLeish, head of the Congressional Library, who had once written *Land of the Free*, and under the immediate management of Joseph

Auslander, author of "Hell in Harness" and "Letters to Women" among other things, poets resolved, as Auslander and Kenton Kilmer reported in The Saturday Review of Literature for April 25, 1942, "to build, in the National Library in Washington a visible Citadel, an Ivory Tower of poetry."

"The poet's quiet tower," the two rhapsodists explained, "with its glass floor over the caverns of Hell, its skylight turned toward Heaven, and its doors and windows toward the four corners of the earth, is not the cloister of a withdrawn and impartial observer, but the core of the tumult. Here is the very symbol of civilization, the focal point of enemy attack, for the inspired paper-hanger and the divine manufacturer of cheap imitations of cheap gadgets are directing their wrath against the human free-will that finds its culmination in artistic originality. Poetry, with the sister arts, marks civilization from savagery, as the ability to think and to express thought marks man from the beast."

The right kind of poetry, they declared, "will do more to put a drive behind the shoulders and into the diaphragm of the soldier with a bayonet than any amount of hollow-sounding martial music or jingoistic ballads about hitting Hitler, mussing up Mussolini, and slapping the Jap. Let the mind of man feed upon its proper food, truth, goodness, and beauty, and man is serene and unconquerable."

Chapter 11

Convergence

DESPITE DIVERSIONS to war uses under powerful impulses of the State, distractions, criticisms, and intrusions, from whatever source domestic or foreign, the idea of civilization in the United States gained in strength as providing certitude for civil, political, and social action on this continent. So firmly was it fixed in American consciousness—the American spirit —that it could not be rooted out by efforts to destroy its individuality and to merge it in the constructs of a proposed internationalism or in conceptions of Western or world civilization.

Indeed, more and more, reflective minds in every domain of intellectual, ethical, and esthetic interest converged upon the idea as originally affirmed and continuously validated in the history of the Republic. Often called upon by orators to remember the fate that befell old Rome through wars, invasions, and the ambitions of politicians, Americans, amid the tensions and distractions of a warring age, seemed to draw instinctively to the idea as a symbol of unification, a guarantee of security, a directive for constructive programs, with special zeal after the convulsions that followed the crash of 1929. Thinkers working in particular fields at problems raised in such recurring upheavals—political, economic, educational, scientific, and philosophic—moved together, as if under the compulsion of an irresistible force, upon the idea of civilization as affording a common basis for confidence in the nation's future. And this centripetal tendency was reflected in every medium of expression and in all forms of constructive action on a national scale.

Out of this American spirit rose antagonism to the imperialist project for spreading American civilization, as soon as it was officially announced. Nothing Republican leaders in the crusade did by way of counteraction was effective enough to crush the revolt. In their campaign of 1900 the party officially proclaimed its intention "to put down the armed insurrection" in the Philippines and to "confer the blessings of liberty and civilization on all rescued peoples." To blanket protests, the

502

Republican National Committee drafted and circulated a vituperative pamphlet entitled "Anti-imperialism is Old Copperheadism." But Democrats, refusing to be intimidated, in their platform of that year, characterized the war as a war "of 'criminal aggression' against the Filipinos" and spurned the apocalyptic vision by declaring: "We are not willing to surrender our civilization, or convert the Republic into an empire."

Opposition to the "civilizing" process in the Philippines had the support of distinguished men and women, including many Republicans as well as Democrats, who held that the new policy departed ominously from the letter and spirit of American civilization. Members of Congress, clergymen, and eminent representatives of American letters insisted that it was inimical to American civilization and charged its sponsors with launching the Republic on a course leading to frightful calamities, if not destruction, in times to come.

Shortly after the McKinley administration had decided upon the annexation of the Philippines, Senator George Gray, a member of the American Peace Commission then conducting final negotiations with the representatives of Spain in Paris, cabled to John Hay, the Secretary of State, a protest against that action. In moral revolt, he delivered a blast against the decision as a reversal of historic American policy and a violation of pledges shameful to "the advanced civilization we claim."

"Even conceding all benefits claimed for annexation," Gray said, "we thereby abandon the infinitely greater benefit to accrue from acting the part of a great, powerful, and Christian nation; we exchange the moral grandeur and strength to be gained by keeping our word to nations of the world and by exhibiting a magnanimity and moderation in the hour of victory that becomes the advanced civilization we claim, for doubtful material advantages and shameful stepping down from high moral position boastfully assumed."

The declaration of war on Spain had been accompanied by a solemn renunciation of territorial ambitions, Gray reminded the State Department. And he cried out: "Let us simply keep our word!" In his very instructions to the Commission, President McKinley had expressed noble intentions. "Above all," Gray protested, "let us not make a mockery of the injunction contained in those instructions, where, after stating that we took up arms only in obedience to the dictates of humanity and in the fulfilment of high public and moral obligations, and that we had no design of aggrandizement and no ambition of conquest, the President among other things eloquently says: 'It is my earnest wish that the United States in making peace should follow the same high rule of conduct which guided it in facing war.'"

Likewise irreconcilable was George F. Hoar, veteran Republican Senator from Massachusetts. He opposed imperialism as a violation of the Constitution of the United States in that it involved governing subjugated peoples without their consent. He took up the arguments put forward to justify the conquest of the Filipinos, and declared them on a par with the doctrines of Lord North, George III, and all the Tories, English and American, against whom the American Revolution had been fought.

Most of all, Hoar deplored the shift of interest to foreign adventures, the leaving of "our own country, to stand on foreign ground," and the scoffing at "the warnings of our fathers and of the Farewell Address of Washington." Foreseeing terrible consequences for the ages ahead, Hoar exclaimed: "The question the American people are now considering . . . is not a question of a day or a year, or of an administration, or of a century. It is to affect and largely determine the whole future of the country. We can recover from a mistake in regard to other matters which have interested or divided the people, however important or serious. Tariffs and currency and revenue laws, even foreign wars, all these, as Thomas Jefferson said, 'are billows that will pass under the ship.' But if the Republic is to violate the law of its being, if it is to be converted into an empire, not only is the direction of the voyage to be changed, but the chart and compass are to be thrown away."

Senator Hoar's protest was quoted and enlarged upon in a pamphlet on *American Imperialism* written by George D. Herron who was then laboring for what he regarded as the Christianization of American civilization itself. In imperialism he found one more justification for saying that this civilization in its purely material aspects, unregenerated by the law of Christian service, was the apotheosis of greed. "Pray," he exclaimed in 1899, "where can we turn to find the gospel more brutally misunderstood than in the pulpit—the pulpit that proposes to send 'the blessings of our Christianity and of our civilization' to the peoples across the seas? Shall we send to them the blessed condition of the thousands who spend their lives in mines for two hundred dollars a year? Shall we send to them the blessings of the men and women who toil in the 900 sweat-shops of this city of Chicago? Shall we send to them the blessings of civilization which enables private corporations to openly and insolently govern seventy millions of people for private profit? May God deliver the islanders of the sea from our civilization! . . . There was no need of this conflict, even after we had taken possession of the Philippines."

The war of imperialism in the Philippines and imperialism itself, Herron contended, set at naught official pledges made at the opening of the Spanish war, stained the honor of the nation before the world, stirred the Protestant pulpits to "hideous and blood-thirsty" sermons, and betrayed the historic ideals of America. "Surely," he exclaimed, "there must be left in this nation, in the great common heart and life of this people, enough of the spirit of the Pilgrims, who crossed the seas in order that they might be free to live their own lives; enough of the spirit of the Huguenots, who laid down their lives rather than live under lies; enough of the spirit of the New England fathers, who gathered in those mass meetings which Mr. Lecky calls 'riots and mobs'; enough of the spirit of Jefferson and Phillips and Sumner and Lincoln; enough for our inheritance of liberty, of moral honesty, of spiritual reserve, to declare to our government that this massacre of men and women struggling for liberty shall come to an end."

How had this violation of the principles of civilization in the name of civilization come about? Herron gave this answer: "If we had been decent with the envoys of this people [Filipinos], if we had given them some satisfactory word, if we had even told them what we intended to do, the conflict would have been avoided. But the conflict came because the administration of this nation is the bureau of plutocratic interests, and dared not show its hand to the public. There is one sole purpose behind imperialism and expansion, and that sole purpose is commercial speculation. Having destroyed the purchasing power of the people here in America—the power of the people to buy what they produce—the large corporations now seek markets abroad; they seek contract-slavery; they seek an inferior labor market; they not only seek to take possession of weaker nations for markets, but to establish an order of things which shall send the sons of this nation, at the people's expense, to protect them in their exploitation. No friend of labor or of liberty will for one moment do anything but protest against American Imperialism."

If in substance and form Herron's attack on imperialism represented the views of a mere fraction among the Protestant clergy, Bishop John Lancaster Spalding doubtless spoke for a large portion of the Catholic hierarchy when he condemned it in language scarcely less forthright. Spalding's brethren were, it is true, dismayed at the thought of an American invasion of the Catholic stronghold in the Philippines. But whatever weight the religious question had in Spalding's mind, he deprecated the adventure in imperialism as throwing overboard the principles of American civilization.

Born, reared, and mainly educated in the Republic of the United States, Spalding knew well the old American ideals now flouted by imperialists. He was a descendant of Thomas Spalding who had settled in Maryland in the middle of the seventeenth century. Kentucky was his own birthplace. After studying at St. Mary's College and Mount St. Mary's Seminary, both in the middle west, he attended the American College at Rome and the American College at Louvain. Shortly after his return home, he was consecrated Bishop of Peoria, Illinois, and associated himself with humane public efforts to improve the conditions of living among the people of the United States.

In 1899, while the campaign for spreading American civilization through imperialist adventures was being pressed in the country, Bishop Spalding delivered an eloquent address at Peoria on "Opportunity," in which he expounded American principles of civilization and branded imperialism as a lapse into the evil ways of European nations. He warned his audience against over-weening vanity: "There is still enough evil in the world to save us from self-complacency, from the foolish and vulgar habit of self-laudation." There is, however, he said, inspiration for youth in our heritage and more noble work to be done at home: "The triumphs of the Nineteenth century have been sufficiently real and great to inspire confidence and courage in the young who are preparing to take their place in the Twentieth as strong and faithful workers in every righteous cause.

"Here in America, above all, the new age approaches offering opportunity. Here only a beginning has been made; we have but felled the forest, and drained the marsh, and bridged the river and built the road; but cleared the wildwood and made wholesome the atmosphere for a more fortunate race, whom occasion shall invite to greater thoughts and more god-like deeds. We stand in the front rank of those who face life, dowered with all the instruments of power which the labors of the strongest and wisest in all time and place have provided. We might have been born savages or slaves, in a land of cannibals or tyrants; but we enter life welcomed by all that gives worth and joy, courage and security to man. There is inspiration in the air of America. Here all is fresh and young, here progress is less difficult, here there is hope and confidence, here there is eagerness to know and to do."

And toward what high ends did America strive? "The outcome of civilization, if we continue to make progress, must be that to each and every one work shall be given to do, which while it provides the necessaries and comforts of life, will cheer, strengthen, console, purify, and enlighten; and when this day comes the Nineteenth century shall appear to have been but little better than the Ninth; for a society in which millions are condemned to dehumanizing work or starve is barbarous. The century that is now drawing to an end has been so filled with wonders, with progress in science and wealth, with discoveries and inventions, that it seems to illuminate the pages of history with a blaze of glory. But it is not all light. The failure is as serious as the success is great. The individual has not risen as his knowledge has widened and his environment improved. . . . The material is good but in so far as it is a means to spiritual good." In the spiritual good Bishop Spalding included the values to which the material implements of civilization could be dedicated.

But here in this century of opportunity, in which so much progress has been made in civilization, in which the light is brilliant, the Bishop went on, "greed has led to a world-wide struggle as cruel as that of nature, in which only the strongest or the most cunning and conscienceless survive. Our society makes criminals, and our penal institutions harden them in wrong-doing. The people are taxed to support vast armies and to supply them with more and more expensive and effective instruments of murder; and wars are waged not to liberate and uplift weaker races, but to rob and oppress them; and these crimes are committed in the name of religion and civilization. The great powers of Europe look on with stolid indifference while helpless populations are massacred; and America, which has always meant good-will to men and opportunity for all,

seems to be drifting away from what Americans have loved
and lived for into the evil company of these Old-World nations,
drunken with lust for conquest and lust for gold. . . . The
power of sustained thought, of persevering labor for high
and unselfish ends, the spirit of sacrifice and devotion, faith
and hope, the love of liberty and independence are, it is to be
feared, diminishing." In this fashion, as Bishop Spalding interpreted events, America was forsaking the ideals of its
civilization and rushing into the scramble of the European
powers for empire, foreign trade, material advantage.

The mental feeling of Bishop Spalding on the "civilizing"
crusade was shared by that outstanding leader in the business
world, Andrew Carnegie. So vigorously did Carnegie object
to the imperialist program for spreading American civilization
by arms that John Hay declared the great ironmaster to be
out of his mind. Whether Hay or Carnegie was out of his
mind remained to be decided by history yet to come, but
Carnegie's opinions were at least lucidly expressed: "Moral
force, education, civilization, are not the backbone of Imperialism; these are the moral forces which make for the
higher civilization, for Americanism. The foundation for
Imperialism is brutal physical strength, fighting men with
material forces, war-ships and artillery." In the Philippines
and the tropics generally, "the intruding race cannot be
grown," and "where we cannot grow our race we cannot give
civilization to the other. We can only retard, not hasten,
their development. India has been subject to British rule for
nearly two hundred years, and yet not one piece of artillery
can yet be intrusted to native troops. The people have still to
be held down as in the beginning. . . . We challenge the Imperialist to give one instance to the contrary in all Britain's
possessions."

Imperialism, Carnegie believed, could not "give civilization"
to conquered and subject races. He was equally convinced that
it would mean abandoning the ideals and practices long
deemed solemn obligations of the Republic. "In order to make
herself an imperial power she must do as imperial powers do—
she must create a navy equal to the navy of any other power.
She must have hundreds of thousands of regular troops to
cooperate with the navy." The horoscope of immense trade
and prosperity for the American people cast by imperialists
in glowing terms he called a sheer delusion. The adventure
would merely entangle the United States in the endless wars

of European imperial powers. So Americans, Carnegie held, confronted a crucial choice: "Two questions are submitted to the decision of the American people: first, Shall we remain as we are, solid, compact, impregnable, republican, American? or second, Shall we creep under the protection, and become, as Bishop Potter says, the 'cat's paw' of Great Britain, in order that we may grasp the phantom of Imperialism."

Caustic as Carnegie's declaration against the imperialist crusade was in style and content, it was mild in comparison with the curse pronounced on it by William Graham Sumner in 1898 in an article entitled "The Conquest of the United States by Spain." This excoriating document was an argument that the United States, though proclaimed "victorious" in the war, was in fact being conquered by the very imperialism which had led to the degradation of Spain, was forgetting everything that had made America decent and honorable among the nations of the earth, was blindly plunging out on an adventure beset by wars and leading to decadence. From page to page Sumner raised vital questions and replied to them in staccato answers.

How had the Spanish war originated? "It was a move of partisan tactics in the strife of parties at Washington." What did imperialism mean for the United States? Efforts to silence critical opinions by the beating of war drums; "the same vanity and self-conceit of which Spain now presents an example"; the triumph of militarism under which military men "learn to despise constitutions, to sneer at parliaments, and to look with contempt on civilians"; the militarism "which forbids the people to give attention to the problems of their own welfare and to give their strength to the education and comfort of their children"; ever-mounting expenditures for war purposes and ever-increasing burdens of debts and taxes: "war debt, taxation, diplomacy, a grand governmental system, pomp, glory, a big army and navy, lavish expenditures, political jobbery"; the adoption in the United States of the pretensions to a civilizing mission like those of the British, French, Germans, Russians, Mohammedans, and Spaniards; and all justified under the inflated and specious rhetoric of America's moral obligations, as a great power, to humanity.

In the hurricane of "vituperation and cant," Sumner declared, objectors to imperialism are being howled down; press and pulpit are surrendering; "the university also, which ought to be the last citadel of truth, is succumbing." The minds of the people are being diverted from their own interests to a lust for glory and power: "The thirst for glory is an epidemic which robs a people of their judgment, seduces their vanity, cheats them of their interests, and corrupts their consciences." In plans for the imperialist government of other races, the first condition of the American Union was being transgressed, namely, "that all the states members of it should be on the same plane of civilization and political development." Nearly every phase of American life was adversely affected, Sumner maintained: "It seems as if this new policy was destined to thrust a sword into every joint in our historical and philosophical system." And in the future, with this background of imperialist policy, "our politicians will have no trouble to find a war ready for us the next time that they come around to the point where they think that it is time for us to have another."

In three pages of closely-knit statements, Sumner reviewed the history of America and the "possibility which was within our reach if we had been wise enough to grasp and hold it." Long ago Americans had gone into the wildnerness with the arts, sciences, and letters which "civilization had produced." Throughout their career they had labored to escape the "follies and errors" connected with manors, barons, ranks, prelates, idlers, paupers, armies, debts, pomp, ribbons, orders, decorations, titles, diplomatic intrigues; and to realize on this continent their dreams of freedom. "It is by virtue of this conception of a commonwealth that the United States has stood for something unique and grand in the history of mankind and that its people have been happy. It is by virtue of these ideals that we have been 'isolated.' . . . Yet there are people who are boasting of their patriotism, because they say that we have taken our place among the nations of the earth by virtue of this war."

Others might turn to such vainglory, but Sumner stood fast on America's historic policy that was now being spurned by politicians, preachers, professors, and intellectuals at large. "My patriotism," he concluded, "is of the kind which is outraged by the notion that the United States never was a great nation until in a petty three months' campaign it knocked to pieces a poor, decrepit, bankrupt old state like Spain. To hold such an opinion as that is to put shame and scorn on all that our ancestors tried to build up here, and to go over to the standards of which Spain is a representative."

Three years after Sumner had flayed American imperialism as a perversion of American civilization, Mark Twain paid his respects to it with vitriolic irony in a letter directed "To the Person Sitting in Darkness." The Philippine war was still going on and the great powers of the world had just stamped out, by united action, a revolt of Chinese patriots against foreign interventionists engaged in dividing and dominating their country. Taking the two adventures in imperialism as one piece, Mark Twain drove into the middle of the civilizing business by asking three mocking questions: "Shall we go on conferring our Civilization upon the peoples that sit in darkness, or shall we give those poor things a rest? Shall we bang right ahead in our old-time, loud, pious way, and commit the new century to the game; or shall we sober up and sit down and think it over first? Would it not be prudent to get our Civilization tools together, and see how much stock is left on hand in the way of Glass Beads and Theology, and Maxim Guns and Hymn Books, and Trade Gin and Torches of Progress and Enlightenment (patent, adjustable ones, good to fire villages with, upon occasion), and balance the books, and arrive at the profit and loss, so that we may intelligently decide whether to continue the business or sell out the property and start a new Civilization Scheme on the Proceeds?"

From one standpoint, Mark Twain said, the business of spreading civilization by force might seem profitable, but there were troubles in the offing: peoples sitting in darkness were not all accepting thankfully the blessings of civilization. "Extending the Blessings of Civilization to our Brother who Sits in Darkness has been a good trade and has paid well, on the whole; and there is money in it yet, if carefully worked—but not enough, in my judgment, to make any considerable risk advisable. . . . The Blessings-of-Civilization Trust, wisely and cautiously administered, is a Daisy. There is more money in it, more territory, more sovereignty, and other kinds of emolument, than there is in any other game that is played. But Christendom has been playing it badly of late years, and must certainly suffer by it, in my opinion. She has been so eager to get every stake that appeared on the green cloth, that the People who Sit in Darkness have noticed it—they have noticed it and have begun to show alarm. They have become suspicious of the Blessings of Civilization. More—they have begun to examine them."

Great Britain, Germany, Russia, and the United States,

Twain observed, had been so careless with the use of weapons and other strong-arm methods in the Orient that people sitting in darkness were nursing "dangerous thoughts" about the blessings of civilization handed out to them. Orientals were really wondering: "Is there no salvation for us but to adopt Civilization and lift ourselves down to its level?" Filipinos were muttering subversive opinions. "The truth is, the Person Sitting in Darkness *is* saying things like that; and for the sake of the Business we must persuade him to look at the Philippine matter in another and healthier way. We must arrange his opinions for him."

In a manner much gentler than that of Sumner and Mark Twain, but equally resolute, Charles Eliot Norton spoke up against the imperialist course, and pronounced it a reversion toward barbarism, not a forward movement in civilization. "America," he said in a public address during the summer of 1898, "has been compelled against the will of all her wisest and best to enter into a path of darkness and peril. Against their will she has been forced to turn back from the way of civilization to the way of barbarism, to renounce for the time her own ideals." To a friend he wrote shortly afterward: "The old America of our hopes and our dreams has come to an end, and a new America is entering on the false course which has been tried so often and which has often led to calamity. This war will in the long run result in far more evil to the United States than to Spain. We shall nominally win, but at the cost of what infinite loss!"

Yet in time the Philippine insurrection was suppressed and public discussion of the new mission designed to spread American civilization by arms seemed to die away. To all appearances the policy of the Republican party had triumphed. But the commercial advantages pledged by the crusaders were by no means realized, the costs of the adventure exceeded expectations, public interest shifted, as if relentlessly, to domestic affairs, and the big push for enlarging the colonial empire subsided.

At length in 1934 a promise to redeem the pledges made by the Democrats in 1900 was written into an Act of Congress opening the way for Philippine independence at the end of a term of years—an Act signed by a Democratic President, Franklin D. Roosevelt. Although the essentials of the foreign policy integral to the imperial adventure in the Far East were continued in full force by the State Department, belief in the power of imperialism to bring prosperity to American industries declined swiftly in the United States. And the formula of spreading commerce and American civilization among backward peoples ceased to evoke tumult and shouting in the forum or the market place—for a time.

The proposal to use the power of the United States in underwriting civilization through a permanent connection with the great powers in the League of Nations, after the first world war of the twentieth century, suffered a reverse even swifter than that encountered by the program for extending American civilization by arms in the Far East. Indeed it did not enjoy the appearance of a single popular approval at the polls.

In the rejection of the second civilizing crusade for America it was now the role of Republicans to lead, as it had been the part of Democrats to assail the former crusade sponsored by Republicans. And it was the lot of each party to accuse the other of "playing politics." In November, 1918, before the armistice had been declared on the battlefront in Europe, the voters, though urged by President Wilson to elect a Democratic Congress to support his policies, returned Republicans to power in both houses.

During the debate over the League of Nations Covenant incorporated in the Versailles Treaty, the idea of civilization became a rallying point for contestants on both sides. In his speaking campaign across the country earnestly seeking popular backing, President Wilson represented the underwriting of civilization as the moral obligation of the United States to the world and necessary to American interest and security. On the other hand, Republican orators, with matching fervor, controverted Wilson's arguments by insisting that the drastic terms of the Versailles Treaty profaned all such noble aspirations, the very principles of civilization to which he had appealed.

In the heat of the political controversy, parties to the dispute ran into extremes. Among some Republicans, goaded on by Henry Cabot Lodge, long a vociferous advocate of imperialism, was developed a form of assertive "isolationism" so extravagant that it almost denied to the United States all moral responsibility in international relations. Among the Democrats, idealists passed lightly over the strike of European governments for power in the new League and pleaded the cause of "internationalism" in a language of intransigence and sentimentality scarcely, if any, less inordinate. Thus the debate degenerated into a fog-battle over two abstractions, "isolationism" and "internationalism," and in the nature of things became an exhibition in logomachy. Amid the clamor the voice of moderation was stifled.

At the end of wearisome wrangling no compromise was effected. President Wilson turned a cold shoulder on modifications in the Peace Treaty which were proposed by Senators in the name of American interests. If he had approved them the United States might have become a member of the League of Nations, with limited obligations; but he would not have it that way. Rebuffed by the President, Republican leadership in the Senate defeated his whole program. Wherever the responsibility for the final breakdown lay—and its locus was not easy to find—the United States definitely rejected his plan for an American underwriting of civilization throughout the world.

Whether American affiliation with the League of Nations would have altered in any substantial respect the course of European or Asiatic struggles and wars became a matter of dispute which in the nature of things could never be settled out of knowledge. Likewise indeterminate was the question whether the blame for the outcome was to be placed on the conduct of European and Asiatic governments and nations, on politicians in Washington, or on the American people at large. Only two prime facts seemed knowable. The first was that this crusade for underwriting civilization everywhere through the League of Nations had ended in a débâcle comparable to that which had overtaken the imperialistic crusade for spreading American civilization by arms. The other was that, after the close of the second armed crusade, American thought and practice began to display signs of a strong reaction against intervention in European and Asiatic affairs; and a stiff resolve to underwrite civilization in the United States by domestic measures directed against disruptive forces from all quarters, external and internal.

Expressing in many respects this revulsion and this determination to protect American civilization against European and Oriental invasions, immigration legislation, especially the Acts of 1921 and 1924, stood out in public discussions and in law as positive testimony to renewed concentration on the reinforcement of civilization in the United States. For more than a hundred years certain European governments by law or policy had sought to escape their problems of pauperism, unemployment, and degradation by encouraging the dumping of their people on the United States, while often deliberately seeking to prevent their assimilation and to draw upon their earnings here to help sustain economies at home. And soon after the first world war came to an end, millions were eager to rush to America. In 1920 more than 800,000 immigrants poured into the United States and, as Roy L. Garis said in his *Immigration Restriction*, "it was evident that fully two millions would be willing and able to come each year for several years."

By a series of Acts and amendments of Acts, beginning in 1917, in which the Act of 1924 was fundamental, Congress raised insurmountable barriers to the threatened flood of immigrants. In general this legislation made a drastic reduction in the number of European immigrants to be admitted each year, finally to 150,000 annually, and based the quota to be allotted to each European country on the proportion which its nationals already in the United States bore to the total population of continental United States, with a few exceptions. As to practical effect, the legislation meant not only a radical reduction in the number of immigrants admitted annually but also the limitation of such immigration almost entirely to peoples from northern and western Europe. Besides, the Act of 1924 explicitly forbade the admission of Japanese immigrants and thus made the blockade on Japan as tight as the blockade on other Oriental countries.

The nature of the intentions and reasoning behind the bill of 1924 became plain as soon as its provisions were announced to the public. The steep reduction of European immigration indicated an adamant decision to ease the strains on the assimilative processes of American civilization. The discrimination among nationalities revealed a conviction, right or wrong, that some of the nationalties represented "types" or "stages" of civilization contrary and inimical to the civilization of the United States. On the basis of the arguments and materials presented to committees of Congress, in the House and the Senate, and in public discussions of the bill, the law might well have been entitled "An Act to Protect 'Our Civilization.'"

On this point there was little doubt as to Japanese immigrants. The votes of Japanese in the United States were negligible in congressional elections. Few Americans, save spokesmen of Protestant missionary organizations, were prepared to intervene on behalf of these Orientals. But their friends and advocates of restriction alike could and did speak frankly of the issue in terms of differences in civilization.

In supporting the Japanese exclusion section of the bill before the Senate committee on immigration, V. S. McClatchy maintained that there was a fundamental opposition between civilization in Japan and civilization in the United States. For his authority he quoted Theodore Roosevelt as follows: "In the present state of the world's progress it is highly inadvisable that peoples in wholly different states of civilization, or of wholly different types of civilization, even although both equally high, shall be thrown into intimate contact. This is especially undesirable when there is a difference in both race and standard of living. In California the question became acute in connection with the admission of the Japanese."

At a committee hearing on the bill, Gilbert Bowles, interpreting the spirit of Protestant missions in Japan, admitted that the issue of civilization was pertinent to the debate; but he approved the principle that Japan had "endeavored to incorporate into her body politic all the best ideas and ideals of western civilization." At first, he said, Japan had been inclined to adopt Western things wholesale, but "from the beginning of the present century the attitude of the Japanese had been certainly one of fair and unbiased criticism of whatever is best in western civilization." In short, in Bowles' opinion, Japanese immigrants should not be excluded on grounds of diversity of civilization.

In the discussions of the discriminative as well as the exclusive provisions of the immigration bill, in Congress and outside, the idea of civilization was treated by advocates and opponents as relevant if not indispensable to a correct judgment on the proposal. Attempts were made by a few statisticians to attribute a larger proportion of the crime, insanity, disease, pauperism, and other evils in American society to various nationality groups from southern and eastern Europe already in the United States, than their relative numbers warranted. Out of such representations, which, to say the least, were highly dubious if not utterly unscientific, came a war of words over the alleged superiority or inferiority of various races and civilizations; and in this controversy opponents of the measure, in Congress and outside, ascribed to sponsors of the bill a belief that the nationality groups to be discriminated against were inferior in civilization.

Attacking the discriminatory lines of the proposed law, Senator Walsh asked: "What are the nationalities whose coming to America is chiefly curtailed by this arbitrary resort to the 1890 census?" They were, he said, as if to shame opposing Senators, peoples who ranked high in civilization: "The Greeks, to whom civilization owes so much in the fields of literature, science, art, and government. The Italians, who from the day of early Roman history have contributed immensely to civilization along the lines of government, literature, art, music, and navigation, including the gift of the discoverer of America. The liberty-loving Poles, whose sacrifices and struggles for freedom have arrested the imagination of mankind. . . . The Jews, who contributed to the world literature, religion, standards of righteous conduct that cannot be overvalued."

Senator Walsh granted that the thought of classifying any nationality as inferior or superior was not universally entertained by Senators on the other side: "I am aware, Mr. President, that many of the advocates of the bill deny any contention of inferiority of certain races." But he insisted that "the popular and pseudoscientific propaganda of the bill is not so scrupulous."

Speaking on the bill in April, 1924, Senator Underwood agreed with its sponsors that a restriction of immigration had been made necessary by changes in American economy and that the fortunes of civilization were involved in the proposed legislation; but he objected to basing its provisions so distinctly on differences in nationalities. Up to the year 1880, he argued, there had been no necessity for a restriction of immigration: "We had a great empire in the West which was unsettled and which needed the acquaintance of the plow and the advance of civilization. The immigration which was coming from Europe at that time came unassisted; it came to find homes; it paid its own way. . . . The restrictions on immigration then practically related merely to character and to health."

These conditions had passed away and limitations were now imperative, Senator Underwood acknowledged; yet he was against the discriminative lines drawn by the bill, and declared that "the real issue involved is the standard of American life and American living. . . . Where that standard is most difficult to be maintained is in the field of labor. The fight in all the civilized world from the beginning of civilization has been at the bread line, where the human being fought for his daily bread."

Having laid down that postulate, Senator Underwood called for legislation framed in its logic. The bill as proposed, he claimed, was based on other and indefensible grounds—the exclusion of immigrants, "not because they endanger American civilization, not because they endanger labor at the bread line, but, forsooth, because we have become so nice that we do not wish to associate with people coming from particular foreign countries."

Advocates of the bill before congressional committees and in Congress insisted all along, however, that this interpretation of their purposes was incorrect. They repeatedly asserted that the issue was not whether any foreign civilizations were inferior or superior but whether they were so different in nature as to make immigrants coming from them less readily assimilable then immigrants from other regions. This position was illustrated by the argument of Elon H. Hooker before the Senate committee on immigration: "It is important to stress the point that I am not considering any question of superiority or inferiority of one race over another. The point which we must squarely set before us is the differences between races and civilizations. . . . Honorable James J. Davis, Secretary of Labor, has said: 'More foreigners have passed through Ellis Island within a few months than were in the hosts of Huns and Vandals who utterly destroyed the boasted civilization of the Roman Empire. The historians and scientists tell me that all the great civilizations of the past have fallen, not through hostile invasion, but through the peaceful penetration of alien peoples, usually entering their gates as workers or slaves.'"

On the floor of the lower house, Representative C. F. Lea of California conceded all that could be urged on behalf of the excellence or even superiority of European civilizations and still he called for the selective curtailment of immigration. "The exclusion of aliens is not a reflection upon them. Fancy if you will, a superior alien people coming to our shores, peacefully penetrating this Republic and finally supplanting our institutions and our civilization by their own. . . . Concede we knew in advance that the admission of such aliens would result in the supplanting of our civilization by a better civilization, would that justify us in failing to resist it? This is our land, our Nation, and our Government. Whether or not it be the best of all governments is not the question. . . . It is 'ours' and that calls us to its service and defense. No others will answer that call."

On a similar explanation of the bill Representative Knud Wefald of Minnesota took his stand: "The question is our own to solve in the manner we see fit to solve it. The glory of no European country lies within the borders of the United States. We do not intend to close the door because we were here first but because it is our door. We are now under a reaction of the effects of the World War; we are sick and tired of Europe and all its works; we want to develop our character along our own lines. We have heard so much sneer about the superiority of the great nations of Europe that we now want to close the door more tightly while we take stock of ourselves. We do not wish to advise Europe on any question, but should we wish to do so we would remind her that there is plenty of room in many other places. South America, Australia, Canada, and Africa still have untold acres to put under cultivation, and in Europe many people claim a foundation has been laid for a new civilization better than ours. If that is the case we say, go to Russia with her limitless natural resources and grow up with the new civilization. We ask no favors of anybody; we only wish to be allowed to mind our own affairs for a while."

Although advocates of the bill disavowed all intention of representing American civilization as superior to others, the charge that they did in fact hold such an opinion was made repeatedly until the end of the debate. And no doubt resentments against the measure based on this charge strengthened the force of the opopsition. For example, in a vigorous protest against the bill, the Sons of Italy brought up the issue by declaring: "Peoples of all the nations sought to be legislated against have made positive and valuable contributions to civilization and to America."

But advocates of the bill were unyielding in their resolve. A powerful regiment was marshaled against them. They persisted in their course. The State Department objected publicly to the section providing for the explicit exclusion of Japanese immigrants. Twenty of the twenty-two Democratic members from New York in the House of Representatives joined in condemning the bill as "particularly objectionable because it discriminates against certain nationalities already going to make up a great part of our population and fans the flames of radical, religious, and national hatreds and brands forever elements already here as of an inferior stock." Promoters of special interests lobbied against the bill. Memorials of dissent from various nationality groups and organizations poured in upon members of Congress. Representatives of industrial enterprises made strong pleas for the continued admission of laborers in large bodies, meaning "cheap laborers." The specter of "the foreign vote" was raised and advocates of the bill were threatened with defeat in coming elections.

Nevertheless the bill was passed by an overwhelming majority in both houses of Congress. Warnings delivered in the names of "the foreign vote" could not offset the stanch support given to the proposal by organized labor, representing in part large numbers of recent immigrants and headed by a distinguished immigrant, Samuel Gompers, then near the end of his long and active life as a labor leader. Pleas made for the oppressed of all lands were unavailing. And the party responsible for the new Act was triumphant at the polls in the autumn. Evidently the Act represented a potent national resolve.

Whatever status might be assigned to American civilization in the scale of inferiority or superiority, however interpreted, it was to be protected against intrusions which the Act outlawed as disruptive. In celebrations of victory after the passage of the Act, leaders among proponents of the measure declared that lines of force projected in the early days of the Republic, deflected for more than a hundred years, were now returned to the original direction as sound practice. The founders of the Republic, it was claimed, had opposed the immigration of nationalities steeped in absolutist traditions and inexperienced in the arts of self-government; for a century the nation had disregarded their admonitions; but at last the new Immigration Act had restored and given permanence to their policy.

The concentration of interest on the idea of civilization in America and the principles long accepted as imperatives under it reached a new climax in the convulsions that followed the financial crash of 1929. As shocks succeeded one another without a pause, it was realized by everybody capable of observation or feeling that the nation had entered a crisis in economy; and, by reflective persons, that a crisis in thought equally grave was agitating the nation, inviting, if not forcing, a reconsideration of its intellectual and spiritual resources, its destiny, its opportunity, and its obligations.

In themselves the outward and visible signs of the crash brought all current doctrines and theories of history under critical review as searches proceeded for ways out of the calamities of the time. This much even Bourbons who had forgotten nothing and could learn nothing confessed, as they crowded around President Roosevelt in the spring of 1933 and pledged their sacred honor in support of his efforts to steer the Government of the United States through the storm.

Leaders in high places of power had relied upon individualism—called "rugged"—to carry civilization from height to height, and in 1928 had buoyantly spoken of soon putting an end to poverty. But now millions of people were unemployed, families were breaking apart, vagrants were swarming in the city streets and along the rural highways, banks were exploding, and poor wretches were digging into garbage cans for food. Individualism, if good, did not seem to be a perfect good, an unquestionable guarantee of civilization.

Leaders in high places had long promulgated in simple optimism the fiction that the automatic multiplication of mechanical contrivances was synonymous with civilization and would assure the endless and unbroken progress of civilization. But in the scene to be observed and felt by all were machines without number—idle. Power to invent and build more undoubtedly existed. Yet the wonderful machines were not setting themselves in motion, and the power to create more machines was not expanding the production of wealth.

Leaders in high places had boasted of science and the scientific methods as pledges of progress in civilization. Yet they likewise appeared to be afflicted with paralysis, unable to furnish guidance for the revival and expansion of production. Indeed science and scientific methods were mere a-moral instruments of mankind, to be used either for civilization or for barbarism, as their possessors might or could decide; they were powerless in themselves to indicate any choices in the calamity that had settled over the nation. For the moment, like men, the instruments were palsied.

In the days of facile romanticism it had been claimed by prominent instructors of the nation that imperialism, money-lending, and diplomatic huckstering would provide outlets for "over-production," keep American industries humming, and enlarge domestic felicity. These devices had been tried amid shouts and tumults. Now they too were judged by their fruits.

During the bewilderment of the crisis, new prophets arose and proclaimed formulas imported from Europe to be the magic potions that would make everything right—communism from Russia, fascism from Italy, national socialism from Germany. The prophets apparently assumed the history and temper of the American people—intellectual, moral, and spiritual—to be so similar to the history and temper of the Russians, Italians, or Germans that a reproduction of one of their systems was possible in the United States and would resolve the American dilemma. The state of those European nations, however, was not such in fact as to inspire an overnight transformation of America in any of the images offered as a correct vision.

That the crisis in economy, as it immediately concerned the United States, was national in extent, certainly nothing less, was demonstrated by a form of creative thought and action devised to cope with it, known as national planning. Given the nature of the great society in the United States, the universal allegiance pledged to the Republic one and indivisible, the extensive uniformity of culture, and the integration of industries into a national economy, the planning movement reflected, as if by necessity, a national consciousness wide, deep, aroused, and intense. And this too was significant for the times and the future.

It was the vogue, no doubt, among some Americans to belittle this planning movement or to take it seriously and decry it as introducing a revolutionary device into American practices. Such resistance did not stay its course. In fact the United States itself had begun in a plan and the whole history of constitution-making, legislation, and large-scale industrial development in the United States had been a history of planning and, in vital respects, of administrative achievements in the execution of plans.

After 1929, the planning movement, as a voluminous literature proved, was promoted by organizations national in compass, including the United States Chamber of Commerce, the American Federation of Labor, and the Federal Council of Churches of Christ. It was fostered by influential leaders in industry, such as Daniel Willard, Gerard Swope, and Owen D. Young. With some fluctuations in interest, it gained increasing momentum among the people, and among the commanding figures in the political, economic, and intellectual life of the nation.

By 1942 the planning movement had gained such strength and had ramified in so many directions that it took 110 pages in George B. Galloway's book on *Postwar Planning in the United States* to list and describe with utmost brevity the agencies and organizations, public and private, which were carrying on activities in this field of interest; and thirty pages were required to give the bare titles of books, articles, and other pieces of literature bearing upon the subject of planning.

The investigations supported by these agencies and organizations covered nearly every aspect of civilization in the United States: economy in all its branches, government, administration, arts, sciences, letters, jurisprudence, education, medicine, public health, housing, standards of living, recreation, institutions of human care, relations of the sexes and the generations, indeed every interest coming under the head of general welfare. Their proposals, tentative and matured, taken collectively, called for and represented deliberate and informed efforts to surmount obstacles in the way of economic recovery and effect an expanding production and distribution of wealth, material and immaterial. The movement itself signified a determination to substitute design for chance, enlightened choice for blind luck, clarified social purposes for shortsighted trust in the automatic beneficence of individualistic propensities.

In connection with the crisis in economy and thought and with the proposals, policies, and activities that appeared in attempts to resolve it, fundamental questions were posed in all parts of the country—questions reflecting a common consciousness of American conditions, problems, and possible solutions, a national consciousness. What is the crisis in its inmost nature? Under what theory of history can the most satisfactory explanation of its origins and course be obtained? To what most worthy objects is it actually a peril? To what summation of values possessing the highest validity and utmost compulsion can minds turn for direction in framing policies calculated to overcome the crisis, for giving credence to such policies in the national consciousness and spirit? What unifying principle and faith can supply the optimism and ethical dynamics necessary to carry such policies into effect? To what sources can the nation look for assurance that forces of destiny itself are enlisted on the side of progress in eliminating the violent stresses and strains of the crisis?

It was in these circumstances that the convergence of national consciousness on the idea of civilization was intensified, in public and private life; that a quest began for answers to such fundamental questions—questions inescapable to reflective thought and revealed by the anxieties of contemporary minds. Evidences of that convergence stood out in official papers, essays, books, articles, editorials, news comments, and public addresses—expressions of the American spirit in innumerable varieties. Few Americans, from the President of the United States to the plainest citizen, seemed able to speak of the crisis and its tensions, in thoughtfulness and with full awareness of their gravity, without relying upon an interpretation of civilization for support and vindication.

As President of the United States and endowed with immeasurable power, Franklin D. Roosevelt was compelled to deal with the crisis—with the conflicts of ideas and interests which disquieted every reflective person in the country. And when in the inquiries of his own spirit he plumbed for fundamentals—for convictions concerning the nature of things, inspiration in formulating policies, and ethical validations of work proposed and done—he seemed unable to find, under God, any ultimate beyond civilization.

In the early days of his first administration, when President Roosevelt gave an opinion on the intrinsic nature of the crisis, he described it as a dislocation in "our civilization," due to a departure from our ideals. "A year ago," he said in 1933, "things were going wrong with our civilization. We might as well admit it. We know at least the ideals of the men and women who settled America. . . . In the latter years, conditions had greatly changed—perhaps we had not forgotten the older ideals, but at least we were disregarding most of them."

To what end were the policies of his administration directed? In a radio broadcast to the nation in 1933 on "What we have been doing and what we are planning," President Roosevelt defined his objective: "We are working toward a definite goal, which is to prevent the return of conditions which came very close to destroying what we call modern civilization. . . . Our policies are wholly within the purposes for which our American Constitutional Government was established one hundred and fifty years ago. I know that the people of this country will understand this and will also understand the spirit in which we are undertaking this policy."

During the autumn of 1933, while relief for the unemployed and the impoverished was a pressing issue, the President discussed it over the radio and declared that remedial measures must rest upon "the fundamental basis of our American civilization." At the time a small number of Americans, he said, had assumed that the Government should take over all relief work and that the people should not be expected to subscribe to local relief or charity. This was, in his opinion, founded on a misconception of our civilization: "The overwhelming majority of the American people understand clearly" that individuals, communities, and the states must cooperate in providing relief to the limit of their resources, and then the Federal Government must stand ready to help in case such efforts combined are not sufficient.

Speaking to the country on the problem of unemployment, in a national broadcast on November 14, 1937, President Roosevelt brought that issue before the tribunal of "our civilization." He said: "I am confident that this nation of ours has the genius to reorder its affairs, and possesses the physical resources to make it possible for everyone, young or old, to enjoy the opportunity to work and earn. . . . The inherent right to work is one of the elemental privileges of a free people. Continued failure to achieve that right and privilege by anyone who wants to work and needs work is a challenge to our civilization and to our security." Thus the President declared, in effect, that this nation possesses the intellectual, spiritual, and material resources for meeting the threat so indubitably presented by continued and widespread unemployment, for making "our civilization" prevail over the crisis in the United States through reconstruction in domestic affairs.

In a public address delivered on the fiftieth anniversary honoring the Statue of Liberty, President Roosevelt paid tribute to the immigrants who had built America and expressed his belief that civilization will continue to advance in America, and "by our own example perhaps" in other parts of the world. "For over three centuries," he said in amplification of his statement, " a steady stream of men, women, and children followed the beacon of liberty which this light symbolizes. They brought to us strength and moral fibre developed in a civilization centuries old but fired anew by the dream of a better life in America. They brought to one new country the cultures of a hundred old ones. . . . Even in times as troubled and uncertain as these, I still hold to the faith that a better civilization than any we have known is in store for America and by our example, perhaps, for the world. Here destiny seems to have taken a long look. Into this continental reservoir there has been poured untold and untapped wealth of human resources. Out of that reservoir, out of the melting pot, the rich promise which the New World held out to those who came to it from many lands is finding fulfillment."

Then the President reviewed the system of privileged orders and political absolutism from which America had offered an escape, against which it stood out in vivid contrast: "Four hundred years ago, in Europe as well as Asia, there was little hope of liberty for the average man of courage and good will. The ambitions of a ruling class and the times alike conspired against liberty of conscience, liberty of speech, liberty of the person, liberty of economic opportunity. Wars, dynastic and religious, had exhausted both the substance and the tolerance of the Old World. There was neither economic nor political liberty—nor any hope for either. Then came one of the great ironies of history. Rulers needed to find gold to pay their armies and increase their power over the common men. The seamen they sent to find that gold found instead the way of escape for the common man from those rulers. What they found over the western horizon was not the silk and jewels of Cathay but mankind's second chance—a chance to create a new world after he had almost spoiled an old one. And the Almighty seems purposefully to have withheld that second chance until the time when men would most need and appreciate liberty, the time when men would be enlightened enough to establish it on foundations sound enough to maintain it."

Renominated in 1936 by his party for the great office he held, President Roosevelt, in his second speech of acceptance, again fitted the policies and program of the hour into the requirements of civilization: "The brave and clear platform adopted by this Convention, to which I heartily subscribe, sets forth that Government in a modern civilization has certain inescapable obligations to its citizens, among which are protection of the family and the home, the establishment of a democracy of opportunity, and aid to those overtaken by disaster. . . . We do not see faith, hope and charity as unattainable ideals, but we use them as stout supports of a Nation fighting the fight for freedom in a modern civilization. . . . There is a mysterious cycle in human events. To some generations much is given. Of other generations much is expected. This generation of Americans has a rendezvous with destiny."

President Roosevelt's expressed concern with the civil convulsion and the state of the country came to its zenith in his inaugural address of January 20, 1937, shortly before he became immersed in the issues of war. In writing that famous document, the President seemed to summon all the force of his spirit in an effort to bring the creative energies of the nation, working with its magnificent endowment of natural resources, to victory over the obvious ills that cursed a third of the nation, mocking the will and skill of civilization. Driving straight at the tragedy of the Western world—the conflict between the ideal and the real, he exclaimed: "We are beginning to wipe out the line that divides the practical from the ideal; and in so doing we are fashioning an instrument of unimagined power for the establishment of a morally better world."

Referring in his second paragraph to the opening of his first administration, he recalled an earlier covenant: "Instinctively we recognized a deeper need—the need to find through government the instrument of our united purpose to solve for the individual the ever-rising problems of a complex civilization. Repeated attempts at their solution without the aid of government had left us baffled and bewildered. For, without that aid, we had been unable to create those moral controls over the services of science which are necessary to make science a useful servant instead of a ruthless master of mankind. To do this we knew that we must find practical controls over blind economic forces and blindly selfish men."

In the President's mind rose an image of America and work to be done: "I see a great nation, upon a great continent, blessed with a great wealth of natural resources. Its hundred and thirty million people are at peace among themselves; they are making their country a good neighbor among the nations. . . . But here is the challenge to our democracy: In this nation I see tens of millions of its citizens—a substantial part of its whole population—who at this very moment are denied the greater part of what the very lowest standards of today call the necessities of life. . . . I see one-third of a nation ill-housed, ill-clad, ill-nourished. It is not in despair that I paint you that picture. I paint it for you in hope—because the Nation, seeing and understanding the injustice in it, proposes to paint it out."

President Roosevelt vowed that the work so dramatically described would be undertaken: "Today we reconsecrate our country to long-cherished ideals in a suddenly changed civilization. In every land there are always at work forces that drive men apart and forces that draw men together. In our personal ambitions we are individualists. But in our seeking for economic and political progress as a nation, we all go up, or else we all go down, as one people. . . . Out of the confusion of many voices rises an understanding of dominant public need. Then political leadership can voice common ideals, and aid in their realization."

When Henry A. Wallace, Secretary of Agriculture in the Roosevelt cabinet, confronted the task of giving the domestic crisis a historical and social setting, in writing his volume entitled *New Frontiers,* in 1934—one of the leading documents on the New Deal—he also impressed into his service the idea of civilization. He treated civilization as a rythmic process from rise to decline and declared that the problem in the United States was to break the rhythm and keep civilization advancing, without resorting to communism or fascism. The theory of the short-term economic cycle, to which economists had given so much attention, Wallace recognized as meriting consideration; but that cyclical theory, in his opinion, was not broad enough or realistic enough to furnish the total framework for the contemporary crisis. Taking account of fluctuations in human affairs and seeking an explanation in a more comprehensive theory, he first made use of European conceptions of civilization as moving in cycles.

Under the head "Smoothing Out the Cycles" Wallace said "The longest cycles of which we have historic record are those dealing with civilization itself. Judging from the past, we may say that a civilization ordinarily is born, expresses itself, and sinks into darkness in 1500 or 2000 years. Petrie the Egyptologist and Spengler the German philosopher, in analyzing the cycles of civilizations, assume that, culturally speaking, the United States is part of the European civilization which found its birth about the year 1000."

Without stopping to inquire whether Flinders Petrie the Egyptologist or Spengler the mathematician knew anything about American history worthy of notice, or universal history for that matter, or whether such ideas of historical repetitions had any valid application to America, Wallace presented a version of the Spenglerian fiction as if useful to his exploration of the situation in the United States: "During the first 800 or 900 years civilizations customarily express themselves in religious architecture, sculpturing, painting, music, and philosophy. The somewhat vague idealism of philosophy leads to the more concrete investigations of science, and science brings about the more definite control of nature. This produces wealth. Wealth eventually saps the vitality of the earlier cultural ideas, and the bonds of political unity. After five hundred years of wealth there comes an increasing tendency for people to say, 'What's the use?' Then a barbarous and more virile people, formerly under the domination of the center of civilization and formerly respecting it, overthrow the old center. A period of unrest ensues. The different races are fused. New ideas begin to take form and serve eventually as the seeds of the next culture."

Indices to an explanation of the downward turn in the Roman cycle of civilization Wallace discovered in certain economic tendencies analogous to those present in recent American history: "Toward the close of the Græco-Roman civilization, from the time of Cæsar onward, it is interesting to read of the increasing drift of people into the cities as wealth increased. Here they formed guilds or trade unions. Many efforts were made, often with the help of the government, to fix wages and prices. Life in the cities became more attractive than on the Italian farms. The city population wanted cheap bread. So the Italian wheat farmer was sacrificed for the benefit of the wheat farmer of Northern Africa. A permanently unemployed class developed in the cities. They felt that the government owed them free bread and entertainment at the circuses. When the funds did not exist to take care of unemployment either by public building or by bread and circuses, it was always possible to draft the unemployed into the army. This served simultaneously to take care of the unemployment problem, and to replenish national funds by a drive for plunder against a neighboring region."

In the next paragraph Wallace made his application: "There is sufficient likeness between the Græco-Roman civilization and our own to make us consider to what extent we are in a period somewhat similar to that of Augustus Cæsar [the reformer, warrior, and dictator deified in death]. To what extent are we cutting the firm base out from under us? We have abused our soil. . . . To what extent are we making it possible for the cities to suck the life blood of the countryside? To what extent are we allowing certain sections of our population to use the centralizing power of government to set prices and wages in a way which will distort the balance between farm and city? . . . In studying the cycles of civilizations, it is interesting to trace changing attitudes toward money and banks. Early in the civilization, while the agricultural element is still dominant, prices are low. . . . The pressure of the increasing burden of debt over the centuries seems to be on the side of continually rising prices with intermediate recessions of from twenty to fifty years duration. The battle between debtors and creditors as they try to influence the money mechanism in line with their prejudices is almost as significant as the battle between farmers and city people. . . . A truly enduring civilization will discover how to meet both problems and thus achieve a stable civilization."

Wallace did not accept Spengler's fatalistic view of "the inevitable decline." Instead, in line with systematic expositions of the idea of civilization in the United States, he recognized the potentialities of the creative spirit, the obligation to stimulate its exercise, and the possibility of concentrating intellectual and moral resources on the advancement of civilization in this country. "With modern machinery, modern science, and the insight obtainable in our modern universities, there is no necessary compulsion for this civilization to follow the rhythms of the past. Nevertheless, attitudes taken by our city people, both in industry and labor, have been such during the past twenty years as seriously to alarm the more thoughtful farm leadership. Some are beginning to wonder if there may not be some force in human nature itself which causes a civilization to go through certain successive stages, and finally after control over Nature has created wealth, to enter into the period of decline. Did Roman leaders in the time of the Cæsars speculate on the causes of the decline of the ancient Egyptian and Persian civilizations? Probably not—and to that extent we may have a decided and determining advantage over the Romans. We have the opportunity to profit by their mistakes and prevent convulsive upset."

Indeed the major portion of Wallace's volume was devoted to a review of the domestic measures that had been recently adopted by the National Government for coping with the crisis in American economy and to a consideration of the prospects for an upward swing in the course of American civilization. These measures, he felt sure, would counteract dangerous tendencies in American agriculture and industry, for which he had found analogies in the history of ancient Rome. Moreover he declared that new frontiers for the expansion of American civilization were being opened by scientific and institutional inventions. For practical purposes, therefore, the Secretary of Agriculture rejected the deterministic philosophy of Spengler and, by a circuitous route, arrived at the idea of civilization as it had been developed in the history of American thought since the end of the eighteenth century.

That widely advertised member of President Roosevelt's official family, Rexford Guy Tugwell, before his admission to the circle, during his first period of service and during his time of banishment, used the idea of civilization as having the quality of a moral directive and as rendering constitutional service to systematic thought in economics. A graduate of the University of Pennsylvania who had come under the influence of Simon Patten—an early critic of classical economics, especially the doctrines of individualism and scarcity—Tugwell employed Patten's social philosophy in analytical inquiries, and carried it forward in the form of concentration on planned measures for realizing the values of civilization.

In his volume *The Industrial Discipline,* published in 1933, Tugwell sketched the current crisis in terms of that contrariety between civilization and misery which had been so often discussed, since the days of Robert Coram, in works dealing with the idea of civilization in the United States. Speaking specifically, at the moment, of economic considerations, Tugwell declared: "Theories and traditions will again be weighed in the balance against the economic insecurity with which civilization has now joined battle. . . . Men and women do not ask much from this world in which they find themselves —not more, at least, than ought to be guaranteed them by our resources and achievements. They ask security—security of access to the goods of simple living, security of employment, security in ill health and old age, security of maintenance and training for their dependents, security in the exercise of technical tasks which involve progress in the ancient struggle to escape labor." Unemployment, he continued, seems to us "a very bad thing"—and "we are apt to measure our civilization in its terms."

In the presence of this menace to "our civilization," Tugwell maintained, routine thinking under old assumptions must give way to creative thinking in the spirit of reason applied to the clash of interests and the possibilities of constructive actions against jeopardies to civilization. "Any social theorist now must talk and write . . . against time and against the opposing pressures of stubborn privilege on the one side and dark destructive intention on the other, which threaten to obliterate civilization between them. It is difficult to be calm and analytical in these circumstances; a sense of panic must sometimes obtrude itself upon the most detached discussion. The reason seems sometimes a feeble instrument among these much more powerful ones; their sinister acceptability to the human mind cannot be denied, and yet there is no escape from the effort. There is a kind of duty among civilized beings now not to desert reason but to press its claims insistently."

While employing the idea of civilization as an instrument of validation in the search for large policies, to be adopted by leaders in government and industry, Tugwell also applied it as exigent in such minute matters as the intensive training of individuals for their work in society. "The continuance of our kind of civilization," he said, "depends upon the steady graduation into industry of individuals equipped not only with the ordinary outfit of health and intelligence but also with special training for particular jobs."

Although, after the war broke out in Europe in 1939, critical thinking about civilization in the United States became unfashionable in many quarters, Tugwell adhered without remorse to his original position. He had continually dwelt upon the role of critical and constructive intelligence in the protection and advancement of civilization. He had repeatedly denounced indifference to the convulsive forces that were beating against civilization in this country. And when the European war flared up in 1939, he refused to join his many friends in apologizing for the strictures they had once passed upon evils in American society, as they turned to proposals for intervention in that war.

"The intellectual history of the period since September 1939 when outright hostilities were resumed in Europe," he wrote in the magazine Common Sense, in October, 1941, "has been enlivened if not enriched by certain loud affirmations of guilt. The *mea culpas* have resounded throughout the land. Sackcloth has been used; ashes have filled the air. Men of my age: Mumford, MacLeish, Millis, Lerner, Counts, Niebuhr, have been treading on each others' heels as they hurried to recant. I have felt the wind of their reversal but no impulse to follow: indeed I have felt a slight embarrassment for them rather than for myself. For I have been unrepentant. I feel now as I have always felt that American institutions are far less than perfect although on the whole they seem to me better than any others. Above all, Americans seem to me capable of progress; but I cannot now, any more than I ever could, see how progress is possible without critical assessment and even resentment at injustice.

"One of the most valuable privileges we possess," Tugwell affirmed, "is the right to say what we think is wrong with our institutions and how we think they may be improved. And why should we feel shameful to have exercised that privilege? Perhaps that shame ought to be reserved for not having done it more effectively. If we had, our country might have been better prepared to meet the crisis which is now upon us. Was it wrong of me, for instance, in all the years when I was a teacher to insist that my students' minds should be open to facts and possibilities, especially damaging ones, and that they should develop ingenuity in projecting betterments? I do not believe it. What was the alternative? The alternative was to have got up some phoney myth—such as racial superiority or identity with a determined history— and to have attempted the shaping of fanatical loyalties. . . . To cast some American professor in the role of Goebbels is an outlandish suggestion, perhaps, but that is what some of our contemporaries, in the heat of sudden patriotism, now suggest."

In drawing a chart for troubled years, national and international, called *New Directions in the New World*, published in 1940, Adolf A. Berle, Jr., long a member of the Roosevelt administration, used the idea of civilization as giving meaning to history and setting a goal for public policies in America. In distant times, he said, "the almost implacable idealism" of Christianity had conquered the barbarism that accompanied the collapse of the Roman empire; but by the eighteenth century that idealism, seized upon by privileged orders, had become weak, and tyranny had been exalted. "By the eighteenth century, prelate and noble, captain and clerk, accepted the positions they had attained, without feeling the obligations that were imposed. The result was tyranny, justified merely by material advantages."

In this state of things burst the great revolution in France and America—"a revolution toward individualism, emphasizing the free soul: the right to worship, to hold property, to give consent to the form of government. Of this revolution the United States is the oldest, and today the greatest remaining, monument. . . . The civilization of the United States included everyone in its religion, its politics, and its economic life, reconquering the theory of universality without conquering the free soul in the process."

But against that achievement in civilization, Berle reminded his readers, had come a new revolt—a revolt which took account of the unemployment and misery that civilization had not mastered and at the same time threatened humanity with a new slavery, especially in Italy, Germany, and Russia, thus raising difficult issues even in the United States. Here in America, however, are great resources and traditions which import a new triumph for civilization in the spirit of the Revolution that was accomplished amid the clashes of interests and personalities at the close of the eighteenth century: "We have the men, the materials, the technique to give the country a civilization more superb than any yet known, a strength beyond parallel in history; and to give to every individual powers and duties larger in scope than have ever been offered to any people in the world. Beside this possibility, the pale dreams of a dictatorship are ridiculous; for the liberated talent of millions, coördinated by a common will to make a common civilization, infinitely transcends both the vision and the power of any single man or of any oligarchic group."

Resistance to the dogma that America must rely upon some world mission at arms to spread civilization or to underwrite it in order to keep its own economy running at high tempo was proclaimed in 1938 by another participant in the Roosevelt administration, Jerome Frank, while he was chairman of the Securities and Exchange Commission. In a volume bearing the emphatic title *Save America First*, he presented with learning and force the doctrine that the primary and necessary concern of the Republic of the United States is with the maintenance and advancement of civilization in the United States.

In fact Frank framed the whole case for the idea of civilization in America as destiny, opportunity, and responsibility. He insisted that the United States is not Europe or Russia; that capitalism in this country is not bound to take the course of capitalism in Great Britain; that America has a whole continent of diversified resources to develop; that extensive foreign trade is not necessary to the attainment and protection of high living standards in the United States; and that American democracy can save itself by implementing the spirit of cooperation, by applying the social arts to the ideals and business of advancing civilization on this continent.

After analyzing the problem so formulated and discussing the ways and means appropriate to meeting it, Frank drew his inferences for American civilization. "We have before us," he said, "a magnificent opportunity, through wise statesmanship, to make in America a unique civilization—an economic-political democracy every citizen of which will have a full life. . . . The modifications of our traditions which will be necessary to reach our goal need not, it would seem, involve the dangers of a civil war.

"If we use creative intelligence, the European-made solutions, 'isms' and vocabularies can be ignored—because the problem about which those solutions center need not be our problem. The abstract words which symbolize the European reactions to that problem can become irrelevant and anachronistic for us. Our problem is far easier to solve than that which confronts Europe—but it will not be easier to solve if we try to deal with it in European terms. To insist that only through borrowed European programs can current American problems be solved is to aid in provoking a comic tragedy. . . .

"We are like men fighting over crusts, when around the corner is a banquet for everyone. . . . We need no longer go on living in a half-sick world, but we still have the habits of invalidism. European thought patterns and word patterns keep us blind and deaf. . . .

"We need to fix our full attention on the basic American problem today: how to make actual the vast increase in production which can be made possible by the maximum use of power and mass production in an integrated, well-supplied continent, and thus to provide for our people the enjoyment of an ever-increasing quantity of consumer goods, with adequate leisure and education. We must have that increased production of goods which modern science and our natural resources render entirely feasible, and we must see that they are distributed among our citizens."

The reiteration of the predicate that the protection and advancement of American civilization is the imperative interest of the nation continued after the United States became involved in the second world war in 1941. This affirmation was made in many official statements; for example, with special clarity and brevity in a report of the National Resources Planning Board issued in January, 1942, which was transmitted to Congress with a covering letter by President Roosevelt. The Board, he explained, "is correlating plans and programs under consideration in many Federal, State, and private organizations for post-war full employment, security, and building America."

Looking ahead to the major task of the nation in the post-war years, the Board declared: "We can, if we will, maintain business prosperity. We can sustain a continuing demand for goods. We can keep industry going at high levels. We can maintain substantially full employment. We can achieve a society in which everyone capable of and willing to work can find an opportunity to earn a living, to make his contribution, to play his part as a citizen of a progressive, democratic country."

With its analysis and recommendations, the Board coupled a nine-point declaration of personal rights, which harmonized in every respect with the conception of civilization in the United States as it had been developed in the previous decades, and gave a bill of specifications for "an advancing civilization":

1—The right to work, usefully and creatively, through the productive years.

2—The right to fair pay, adequate to command the necessities and amenities of life in exchange for work, ideas, thrift and other socially valuable service.

3—The right to adequate food, clothing, shelter and medical care.

4—The right to security, with freedom from fear of old age, want, dependency, sickness, unemployment and accident.

5—The right to live in a system of free enterprise, free from compulsory labor, irresponsible private power, arbitrary public authority and unregulated monopolies.

6—The right to come and go, to speak or to be silent, free from the spyings of secret political police.

7—The right to equality before the law, with equal access to justice in fact.

8—The right to education, for work, for citizenship and for personal growth and happiness.

9—The right to rest, recreation, and adventure; the opportunity to enjoy life and take part in an advancing civilization.

Outside the official world, the convergence of interest on civilization in America, either in the avowed form of planning or in less closely organized thought about the deficiencies, tasks, and potentials of the nation was reflected in writings so abundant as to defy full compilation and classification. This convergence was evident in the writings and statements of journalists, business men, lawyers, and engineers. It appeared in works on political science, sociology, and education. Philosophers who made their speculations functional to life in America in this age also indicated, as if by sheer necessity, that they had come under the influence of the world-view, civilization.

Impressed by the need for constructive efforts to make American economy work efficiently, George Soule sought to think his way all around the subject and in 1932 published the results of his adventure in ideas and interests in *A Planned Society*. As a specialist in economics and labor relations, Soule had had a long experience in journalism in New York City and Washington. He had served as an investigator of the great steel strike in 1919, as adviser to the Secretary of the Interior on reclamation and rural development in the South, and as chairman of the National Bureau of Economic Research.

In the first chapter of *A Planned Society* Soule recalled the complacent belief in the automatic progress of civilization so general on the eve of the first world war. "Before 1914," he said, "there had been a naïve faith in millennialism. Science and invention were preparing the way for the fulfillment of civilization. New wonders seemed daily to enlarge the powers and satisfactions of mankind. Injustices and confusions existed, but there was belief that they would shortly be surmounted. . . . The war shocked us by its revelation of the survival and diabolical power of forces which the late Victorian had jauntily assumed were buried with the old centuries. But at the same time it intensified the drive for social change."

While that long war was going on, a strong opposition arose, among the foes of Germany, to "the anachronistic forces of destruction" personalized in that country, and reasoned efforts were devoted to planning measures for the purpose of preventing a recurrence of such a disaster to civilization and assuring a better future. "We could," Soule commented, "proceed to organize a new civilization, fit for the maturity of the human race. International peace and justice, making possible disarmament, could be established by some League of Nations. As for economic organization, you could choose among a number of well-defined and neatly cohesive schemes of reform or revolution. The socialists had one program, the syndicates another, the guild socialists a third, the consumers' cooperatives a fourth. The Catholic intellectuals, opposing the 'servile state,' offered their program of 'distributivism.'

"Almost all sensitive and active minds were engaged in one public cause or another, whether it was feminism and votes for women, the enlargement of the labor movement, the political program of the British Labor Party, the Plumb plan for the railroads in the United States, or nationalization of the mines. We read, and debated about, H. G. Wells, Bernard Shaw, Sidney Webb, G. D. H. Cole, Georges Sorel, or G. K Chesterton and Hilaire Belloc."

Thus, it seemed to Soule, the world stage was set for the planning of a world civilization, at any rate the kind of civilization projected by British writers. But, according to his interpretation of recent history, Americans refused to join in the play. Having discovered the shams of the Allies' war myth, they averted their eyes from the world drama, looked homeward, and decided that their civilization had values of its own and tasks to be executed on this continent. "The United States revolting inchoately against the whole liberal mythology of the War, returned to the dogma of isolation. Americans had been brought up on the belief that their country embodied a new hope, a civilization different from that of Europe, and superior to it. We had turned aside to engage in a European struggle and had got nothing out of it— not even the ideals and the new world for which we had been told we were unselfishly fighting. The groups which all along had denied these international ideals gained supremacy."

But in fact at this stage in the American history, many intellectuals, artists, and poets fled to Europe for satisfaction or dropped into the mood of the pessimism that makes the worst of everything. They found nothing to merit their affections or elicit their efforts in American civilization. For a moment in the confusion, Henry L. Mencken, in the role of an intellectual mentor to the nation, then offered his philosophy. During his brief regime, Soule said, "the key to the world was a facile popularization of the Nietzschean theory. Persons were divided into two classes—superior persons and inferior persons. The chief delusion of history was that the inferior persons were of any account whatever except as vulgar nuisances. They could do nothing for themselves and nothing should be done for them. The only duty of the superior person was to himself. . . . Nevertheless, Mr. Mencken was running up a blind alley. The inferior cannot be banished, and the society of which both they and the superior are parts may sorely limit the freedom of the superior to pursue their superiority."

The chaotic state of things in America just after the economic breakdown of 1929 Soule discussed under the head of "An Unmanaged Civilization." For the time being all kinds of American citizens appeared to be confused and helpless "in relation to the total complex of society. Each of us snatches partial and temporary satisfactions, but the aimless drift of civilization entire thwarts each of us, some more seriously, some less." A contradiction in ideas occurs— a dilemma of liberalism. "Liberalism is a customary name for the opinions of many who are critical of civilization. Strangely enough, that civilization itself which the liberals criticize, particularly as embodied in the great democracies of the United States, France, and England, is theoretically based on a liberal philosophy. This indicates an unsolved problem at the heart of liberalism. . . . The concept of freedom as an absolute and universal attribute will not withstand the most elementary analysis. . . . The mistake of liberalism arose from concentration on its negative aspect—

of trying to free the individual from being forced into ways of behaving that were unsuited to a new intellectual and physical environment. Today more than ever we need synthesis, coordination, rational control. We need these things socially because we need them individually."

After ranging widely in his thought, historically and geographically, under his conception of civilization, Soule, near the conclusion of his volume, reached the point of action. Then he came concretely to the United States. Now he did not offer, as his objective, specific measures for advancing civilization universally, but proposed the substitution of a managed for a hit-and-miss civilization within the jurisdiction and power of this country. He acknowledged the fact that the United States was in the world of nations and that a certain amount of world planning was necessary to a realization of America's purposes in their fulness at home.

"But," he quickly added, "world planning is inconceivable without national planning as a basis. . . . When national economic policies are dictated by private and partial interests as at present, when nations pursue simultaneously inconsistent aims—such as selling without buying, investing without accepting payment in goods—no adjustment of any sort is possible. . . . It is absurd to say that we can do nothing at home. . . . We do not have to wait for others to act, or for a world organization to arise."

The force of specialized thought about planning in terms of civilization was augmented by general tendencies of interest in the realm of industry and commerce. Supplementing his extensive experience as a manufacturer and business man in Philadelphia by long study and meditation relative to the influence and responsibilities of industrial procedures in modern society, Samuel Fels came to the conclusion that those procedures turned upon the nature and idea of civilization. Through the argument of his volume *This Changing World*, published in 1933, ran this theme. Acquainted with the writings of Henry George, he had, presumably, read George's illuminating pages on the idea and the characteristics of civilization. At all events he showed familiarity with the essential elements covered by the idea of civilization, applied their implications to business enterprise, and pondered on ways and means of making a general advance by conscious and deliberate efforts.

In underlining the social principle as against the dogma

of individualism conceived as the war of each against all, Fels made use of Kropotkin's *Mutual Aid*. He had known Kropotkin personally and had studied his writings. He had also known at first hand what Carroll D. Wright had pointed out long before, namely, the associational character of the factory system. Combining the results of his own experiences as a manufacturer, his larger observations, and his reading, Fels decided that mutual aid is "far more important than the law of mutual contest. . . . Man, owing to his higher intelligence and knowledge, may mitigate the harshness of the struggle for life between man and man. We are finding ways to meet human needs without some of the old tooth-and-claw accompaniments, and experience has shown that whenever the cause is removed, these accompaniments also drop away. Competition is still an expression of our characters, but the driving force of the absolute necessity of competition is relaxing."

To the social principle Fels affixed a second connotation of the idea of civilization: namely, creative intelligence as a dynamic force in the civilizing process. Habit, tradition, and superstition, he declared, have in all times held a wide sway; but "during each generation a few unusual and talented individuals have been inclined to break away from the established standards of thought and action. It is with these few that we associate the forward movements in humanity's struggle with the conditions of life. They tended to increase in number as certain tribes or peoples made advances toward what we now call civilization; and there gradually grew up a respectable minority, which still comprised but a very small fraction of the communities to which they belonged, who welcomed innovation instead of combating it."

While recognizing creative intelligence as a force in civilization and appreciating the fact that it had hitherto been evinced by relatively few men and women, Fels insisted that it had not been confined to an "upper class" of any kind and was now manifesting itself among broader masses of people. "We are coming within the shadow of the time," he said, "when the many rather than the few will arrive at conclusions based not chiefly on the past but on the living present; when a fresh approach to life will give human initiative its opportunity, and human reason its full quota of responsibility for all conclusions."

From this assumption it was but a step to the thought

of the civilizing process as a mass movement—a conception bracketed with the idea of civilization since its systematic formulation. Fels took the step by affirming the dynamic character of civilization everywhere. "No civilization," he declared, "can hold its position unless it continues to go forward. To be lasting, it must have within itself elements which represent the aspirations of the large masses of men and women of the time. The weakness of past civilizations has been that they have too often expressed the aspirations of a minority whose leisure was gained by the enslavement of others—either menials or subject races or both. The civilization of the Occident differs from those of previous epochs in its wide employment of machinery and power, which promises to eliminate drudgery. Even our present improvements presage the coming of the time when the millions will have the leisure genuinely to participate in the advantages civilization affords."

The temper and practices of the new age, Fels reasoned, facilitate broadening the range of civilization in its course: "The civilizations of yesterday represented advances made by the few for the few; and the subjects to which they gave consideration were limited in number by want of knowledge and by the absence of any general disposition to search for wider solutions. In contrast, with education becoming universal, with the spirit of brotherhood steadily, if hesitatingly, enlarging its bounds, our Western civilization (though but in its primary stage) can, if we will, take shape as the civilization of a whole people, with the whole life as its frontier."

The ever-widening production and distribution of goods, tangible and intangible, increasing the mass character of civilization, Fels construed as marking a transition from a deficit to a surplus economy. In support of this contention he cited Simon Patten's *The New Basis of Civilization* and quoted from it the following passage: "Those who predict tomorrow's economic states from a study of the states of Rome or Venice overlook the difference between a society struggling to meet a deficit and one so well satisfied that thought can be centered on the equitable distribution of a surplus."

A wider distribution of tangible and intangible goods had been promoted, in Fels' opinion, by modern business methods but the methods needed drastic improvement if they were to attain the goal of general abundance. "Modern merchandising," he said, "in its half-thwarted capacity to minister to a greater volume of physical needs than were ever served before in the world's history, creates an atmosphere in which the other good things of life, artistic, social, spiritual, can be enjoyed more widely, an atmosphere in which an all-round civilization has a greater opportunity to grow and flourish. Modern manufacture sends obsolescent machinery and methods to the scrap-heap, when better ones for their purposes are found; and thus gives a broad hint how to re-place and evolve ideas. Thomas A. Edison has said: 'Problems in human engineering will in the future receive the same genius that the last century gave to engineering in more material forms.'"

But the full potentials of civilization equipped with marvelous instruments for advance are as yet unlocked. Too many people are still entangled in customary ways of thinking unfitted to the opportunities of the new age, and are inclined to contentment with narrow and meager living: "As a whole, humankind has never availed itself of the broad gift of freedom, either of mind or body. We have neither appreciated the opportunity to achieve it, nor the boon that its practice can confer on us. Nothwithstanding this absence of practical experience with the results of constructive free-dom, there has been a widespread belief in the right of human beings to be free. This is the more surprising when we recollect that less than a century ago, large numbers of people believed in the actual necessity of slavery and de-fended it as a divine institution. In its modern forms, also slavery seems doomed, but these forms fade away more slowly."

Thought of our destiny, our opportunities, and our re-sponsibilities, however, is deepening and expanding. It is spreading among multitudes hitherto passive or unawak-ened. Knowledge of undeveloped potentials in our civiliza-tion stirs a restless wondering: "Our awareness that, amid all successes, we have not yet mastered the business of living itself sharpens our discontent. We are especially conscious of this when an economic depression . . . challenges the competence of the whole set-up of our industrial civilization; but the question is there, only a little beneath the surface, in what we call good times; and in our individual encounters with success and failure."

What must be done to unlock these potentials of industry and advance civilization more rapidly? The mind must be liberated from the maxims of economy derived from an age of agricultural scarcity: "We have been caught in trying to negotiate one of the greatest industrial changes in history without modifying overmuch the social habits, legal forms or economic apparatus that were devised long ago for an agricultural civilization. Nature is just as prodigal as before; man was never so well equipped with skill, energy and knowledge to make use of the largesse of nature; but we find ourselves too poor to buy what others produce because they are too poor to buy what we turn out—though the longing of humans to buy and consume is nowhere in sight of limit."

Given a greater liberation of the mind, what would be the nature of the problem in terms of action? "The issue of human progress hangs not alone on whether human genius will unlock further and further secrets of the natural universe," Fels said, "but on whether we can organize our mastery over them. . . . In last analysis, we are learning that we must be *civilized* together. Any real program offered by a community, whether in the moralities or in the arts, in government or industry, which points to better ways of living together, adds momentum to the other influences which make up the more visible advance which we call civilization. . . . If we are to live together in ways commensurate with the growth of our civilization we must rebuild half our cities. They are as truly survivals as the layered debris which archaeologists dig up along the Nile and the Tigris. Broad planning on a large scale is called for. . . . We are moving steadily in the direction of collective effort, with an ever increasing readiness to try out new ways."

Although in the terminology of the Marxian lexicon, Fels was a "capitalist," he was unorthodox enough to declare that, in the search for ways and means of advancing civilization in the United States, something might be learned from the upheaval in Russia. "What seemed to many of our generation," he said, "as one of the greatest recessive steps was the Russian Revolution, which apparently cut a broad swath through civilization as we had come to regard it. As time passes, we are beginning to sense that this revolution contained much of affirmative good at the same time that it tore up by the roots a jungle of wrongs. I have little doubt that much the same thing could be said of many of what were regarded as steps backward in the past. Had the chroniclers of those days been so fortunate as to have the same experience, knowledge and understanding as men of today, then a different history would have been handed down."

Without presuming to pass final judgment on the Russian experiment, Fels dwelt upon the spirit necessary to advance civilization in the United States: "We cannot rest in an easy confidence that by a process of drift the liberated minds are going to carry the day. Our great mechanistic advances may overpower and flatten us. . . . As a whole our western civilization is no stronger or more eager than the men and women who compose it. . . . Our civilization may be stalled in narrow ruts of life and work. We must shake loose from those ruts if we would either get the thrill of existence or share in the drama of a developing and adventurous civilization." This meant in effect displaying what Matthew Arnold called a high achievement of human intelligence—the ability to turn in upon one's self, to take stock of one's major premises, and to do creative work.

Convergence on the idea of civilization in the United States, as fact and as argument, and supported by more historical documentation than Fels supplied, was also the theme of A. J. Snyder's volume *America's Purpose* which came from the press in 1937. Like Fels the manufacturer, Snyder lived in Philadelphia, but he was a lawyer, trained in the University of Pennsylvania, bringing another variety of experience to bear on the subject. He was born in that city in 1892, the son of Monroe B. Snyder who was long head of the mathematics department in the Central High School and as an independent investigator received recognition from the Royal Astronomical Society and the American Philosophical Society. Continuing his work at law after serving as an officer in the first world war, young Snyder also taught the law of property for several years as professor in the Temple Law School.

Out of his studies of American legal, economic, and literary history, including the writings of Edward Bellamy, Snyder became interested in the relation of law to civilization. After the financial crash of 1929 he was profoundly disturbed by distresses of the widespread calamity. He began intensive searches to discover the nature of the America philosophy, if there was one, and then sought to apply its principles to the resolution of the economic impasse. After publishing his *America's Purpose,* he started work on a second volume, *A Basis for Civilization,* an inquiry into the application of American principles to international relations—a study not yet completed.

Making the idea of civilization a focal point in his *America's Purpose,* Snyder surveyed the major tenets of humanism that had been central to the idea since the establishment of the Republic. He then examined what he regarded as the main hindrances to the realization of the nation's ideal purposes and concluded with the statement that the drive of the times was toward "greater unity" of effort in a national resolve to overpower the obstacles.

The supreme feat of human thought in all history, according to Snyder's thesis, "was the discovery of the natural law of human equality. This principle, although it is only intangible thought, marked the beginning of civilization." From the Old World this principle was brought to the New: "The struggle for equality was carried over to a new battlefield, a new continent, America. . . . Here a condition of natural equality provided an opportunity for man to apply the knowledge he had gained through civilization, without heeding the precedents which, in the civilized world everywhere, dragged upon the coat-tails of his progress." The nation built upon this continent "was not to be an aimless collection of humanity, but a new kind of nation; a nation with a purpose to realize human rights. The purpose was clearly and concisely stated in the Declaration of Independence: 'That to secure these rights, governments are instituted among men.' "

This doctrine the founders of the Republic had promulgated as a positive guide to policy, not as a mere statement of fact, Snyder said: "It was not the intent of those who adopted the Declaration of Independence to misrepresent conditions among mankind. They were not voicing a philosophy based upon things as they were, but which 'by right, ought to be.' This evolutionary view of our American philosophy was clearly explained by Lincoln when he said, 'They meant to set up a standard maxim for free society, which should be familiar to all, and revered by all constantly looked to, constantly labored for, and even though never perfectly attained, constantly approximated, and thereby constantly spreading and deepening its influence and augmenting the happiness and value of life to all people of all colors everywhere.' "

The principle as enunciated was more than an abstract theory. From the early years of settlement on American shores realities in the everyday life of the new society conformed to it. "Books and pamphlets were not necessary to teach the colonists the true relationship of man to nature. The rugged features of nature itself were always vivid reminders of the source of all men and all things. They saw and understood more clearly than did those who were surrounded by the gilted courts and stone monasteries of Europe, from which emanated the philosophy of inequality, feigned superiority and 'divine right of kings.' They knew that king and serf were made of the same clay; that rich and poor alike were dependent upon the same earth. To these hardy pioneers, nature alone was the sovereign whose decrees must be respected. The natural elements were the powers and forces with which they were compelled to reckon. The trees, rocks, soil and sand were the money with which they banked. Fundamentals of nature were valuable knowledge, all else superficial. No theory was more strongly implanted in the colonial mind than that nature and nature's God had built into the universe basic principles, which neither man nor his institutions could alter; that attempts by man to contravene these natural laws by his own ordinances were void."

Under Snyder's formula this equality was in society, not prior to and independent of it, and was subject from the beginning to the social principle. "Man's ability to survive the struggle for existence was not due to his individual fitness. The strongest man could never have withstood this test. United with other men he accomplished what he could not have accomplished alone. It was mankind as society, and not man as an individual, that survived. . . . The champions of inequality argue that the combination of mankind in society does not alter the law of beasts that the strongest individual is still entitled to 'all he can get.' The advocates of equality say the purpose of society is to equalize the rights of all according to the principle of the brotherhood of man. The one argues the basis of government is the 'divine right' of the mighty to rule the weak; the other believes in self-government, and states that the true source of government is the consent of the governed. . . . The one insists upon acceptance of his doctrines by force; the other appeals to reason."

If there is to be advancement in civilization on the lines thus laid down, Snyder contended, then the distribution of wealth, indispensable to life, must be freed from the trammels of sheer might and fixed privilege and subdued to the needs of civilization. "The first basis for distribution was might, rather than right. The stronger forced the weaker to accord him a greater share, even though his efforts contributed the least to the result. . . . In time, the element of might yielded to a question of right based upon the amount of labor contributed. This basis was the result of the theory that labor gave the basic right of property. Carried into economics, it created the theory that all value is created by human labor. This doctrine, however, ignores the contribution of nature, of the store of natural resources which is the equal endowment of all.

"Throughout all the economic systems in vogue up to the time of our Revolution, the same fallacy was the basis for distribution. None made any provision for the right of society, as trustee for all, despite the fact that all the materials, and much of the forces, were drawn from the earth and nature, which is the common property of all mankind."

Reaffirming a maxim which had been reiterated times without number, Snyder declared the wretchedness of poverty to be an intolerable barbarity against which civilization had struggled, was bound to struggle, and must struggle till poverty is abolished. In opening up this theme he cited Thomas Paine's *Agrarian Justice* and quoted the following passage from that famous tract: "Whether that state which is proudly, perhaps erroneously, called civilization, has most promoted or most injured the general happiness of men, is a question that may be strongly contested. On one side the spectator is dazzled by splendid appearances; on the other, he is shocked by extremes of wretchedness; both of which it erected. The most affluent and the most miserable of the human race are to be found in the countries that are called civilized."

An effort to resolve this fundamental problem of civilization, Snyder asserted, made it necessary to explore the nature, forms, and uses of property. "In the different stages of civilization, the ownership of property has been determined in different ways." New conditions, new powers, especially the victories of science and mechanics, render imperative a consideration of changes in property appropriate to and effective for the advancement of civilization to the height of economic security for all. "We have witnessed the erection of a great productive machine capable of providing an abundant supply.

We have achieved the first essential of our economic democracy, a productive system able to satisfy the needs of every American. But we have seen production stifled, and stopped, just as it was about to accomplish its purpose. Poverty and want still stalk in our land, but through no lack in the bounty of nature, or in our ability to produce. We must seek the flaws in other parts of our economic structure, the systems of distribution and property ownership. . . . Life itself was diverted from the 'pursuit of happiness' to the quest for property. This institution, which could have served a useful purpose in sustaining and adding to the enjoyment of life, had been distorted into an instrument of power. This had led philosophers to question, 'whether that state that is proudly, perhaps erroneously, called civilization, has most promoted or most injured the general happiness of man.' "

What constitutes the major intellectual drag on readjustments of property rights which are required for the advance of civilization against the wretchedness of poverty? Snyder found the explanation in a continuance of feudal conceptions in American thought and law respecting the nature, ownership, use, and responsibilities of property. "The history of civilization has been a constant struggle between the laws of nature and the feeble ordinances of man. The history of our nation has been a similar struggle between the sound philosophy expressed in the Declaration of Independence, and the doctrines written into the Constitution in order to compromise all the interests and inequalities that were represented in its making. Every crisis of this nation has witnessed one or more changes in the Constitution. . . . The effect of amendment has been to make the Constitution conform more nearly with the philosophy of the Declaration of Independence. True friends of the Constitution should work for the ultimate achievement of this ideal. . . . Unfortunately, we have not succeeded in abolishing feudalism as completely as we did slavery. It is still present in our American economic and legal systems. . . . Certainly no one can contend that feudalism is an American institution, yet, in upholding 'existing institutions,' we are overlooking the fact that many of them are of feudal origin."

The barrier to the progress of civilization imposed by traditional theories and laws of property surviving from the fuedal order must be broken by modifications in the rights of property. Direction for such modifications is provided by principles already accepted in the United States and by plain facts of economy: "The earth in its natural state was capable of supporting all its inhabitants throughout their lives. The intervention of civilization should have increased the security of all. Society, as trustee of the common rights of the individual, is the rightful owner of all of nature, its substance and its natural forces, and also of the vast accumulation of knowledge and improvement remaining from the efforts of past society. This great heritage, which according to American principles is the equal endowment of all, is a sufficient social fund, if used by society for the benefit of all its members equally, to provide security against all the contingencies of life. That which is needed is not a new social order, but perfection of the social order that lived in the minds of our forefathers, the fulfilment of their ideal of social democracy. We need only to complete the evolution of our institutions to achieve this goal."

Such projection of new policy does not mean, however, the abolition of all private property. It does call for the elimination of abuses; and, since property is a social product, society has the right, as well as the obligation, to make the changes necessary for the removal of obsolete impediments. "Many wise philosophers have charged to the abuses of private property much of the world's misery, and all of its poverty. Supported by our feudal laws, these abuses now threaten to destroy the institution of private property itself. Only by disclaiming the abuses, can society save the institution, and preserve its usefulness. The institution of property depends for its existence upon society. Since society is called upon to protect private property, it has the right to decide what shall be private property, and what shall not."

In the struggle precipitated as civilization progresses, "the problem confronting America is whether those who control the economic forces will dominate society, or whether society as a whole will dominate its own economic affairs." On the one side "Americans are told they must accept depression, poverty, and defeat, as necessary conditions, as part of the 'normal cycle' of existence. Placated by empty promises of 'prosperity,' and equally empty claims of 'recovery,' they exchange their right to an abundance for a crumb of 'relief.' Their appetite for happiness has been so long denied, that it is easily sickened by a few charitable sweets. The sterner stuff from which Americans were made has become too thin. The Continental European philosophy of 'contentment amid poverty' threatens to replace the American 'right to the pursuit of Happiness.' Vague hopes for future rewards are accepted in exchange for the fundamental belief in a kindly Creator of an abundant nature here on earth." On the other side are arrayed the converging forces of American civilization which march against this negative, this resisting philosophy of acquiescence in defeat and poverty.

Here, according to Snyder's brief for civilization, the issue is joined and the question of method moves to the front of the stage. Will it be the method of revolution? From history come hints of probability: "So long as civilization binds itself too firmly to the past, its natural advance can continue only after it has torn itself away by revolution." In support of this proposition Snyder quoted James Wilson, a distinguished leader in the first American revolution: "Society ought to be preserved in peace; most unquestionably. But is this all? Ought it not to be improved as well as protected? Look at individuals from infancy to youth, from youth to manhood. Such is the order of Providence with regard to society. It is in a progressive state, moving towards perfection!"

Taking up the argument himself, Snyder delivered his own opinion: "It is not necessary that all revolutions be accomplished by violence and bloodshed. . . . Violence occurs only when progress has been too long impeded, hence calamity results." Moreover, he rejoiced, the nature of American political institutions facilitates progress without resort to violence, and violence is indeed contrary to the genius of American institutions under which the appeal is to reason.

In the crux thus presented by progress and resistance, Snyder pleaded for recourse to the first principles of the Republic, to its philosophy: "When the laws of a nation fail to meet its problems, it must turn to its philosophy. If a nation is without an underlying purpose it must fail. If it has a philosophy, and it is false, the nation will fail. But if a nation possesses a philosophy, founded on the very principles of nature, if its citizens understand the intent and meaning of that philosophy, and if the nation turns to those principles in time and renews its determination, it will pass victoriously through every crisis, and by each effort make a bold advance toward the accomplishment of its purpose."

Accepting wholeheartedly the American principles of social and political policy such as Samuel Fels and Albert Snyder had treated as imprescriptible, an electrical engineer, Carl Dreher, withdrew from the practice of his profession to concentrate his energies on seeking ways and means of raising American economy out of the slough in which it had floundered after the crash of 1929. "Our task," he decided, "is to make a civilization above the animal level by freeing the machine and by freeing men from the machine." Like Fels, he had taken part in industrial enterprise. Like Snyder, he had studied American history, especially the economic history. Weaving experiences and researches together, he prepared a body of propositions and plans, supported by revelant data, for actualizing the wealth-creating possibilities of science and technology—within the frame of a democratic society. This work he published in 1942 under the grim but commanding title *The Coming Showdown*—the approaching hour of decision for the people of the United States.

Out of his inquiries Dreher drew three sovereign statements which he deemed inescapable. The first was that under the law of its own development the capitalistic system as previously operated could not release the full power of science and technology for the production of wealth; could not produce and distribute efficiently enough wealth to give full employment to labor and relax the dangerous internal tensions threatening American society with disruption. The second was that only positive and carefully planned measures, adequately implemented by national resolve, could effect this end. The third was that there were two types of such planned operations between which the American people could choose: (1) fascist collectivism with war and imperialism as necessary to its very life; and (2) democratic collectivism with human welfare as its goal. Dreher's choice was democratic collectivism.

The proposition with respect to the fated limitations of American capitalism, Dreher based on findings derived from a study of its past performance. They may be tersely stated as follows. Under this type of capitalism, the United States had never attained a high degree of prosperity except in connection with brief and intermittent periods of wars, land booms, and speculative frenzies. The free and easy exploitation of natural resources had come to an end. Capitalism had not been, and is not, able to pay wages sufficiently high to provide a buying-power for the people that will absorb the ever-swelling output potential in science and technology.

Competition and the urge for self-preservation and advantage had driven industries into ever-greater aggregations. A growing belief among the people, that unemployment and misery in the presence of potential plenty is an intolerable anomaly, has made them unwilling to endure quietly the deprivations necessary to the cycles of capitalism. In these circumstances government has been compelled to enter the economic field, undertake the stimulation of production, and influence the distribution of wealth.

The political measures under the New Deal, Dreher noted, had taken two forms: (1) heavy borrowings of money to finance consumer buying-power through huge expenditures for public activities; and (2) the curtailment of production in various lines, especially agriculture. The first device had plain limitations in the capacity of the government to borrow money and pile up debts. The second diminished the volume of real wealth upon which all the debts ultimately must rest for security. Neither singly nor combined could such devices bring into full use the powers of technology and universalize high standards of life for the people. For capitalism they were constricting, not liberating, measures in the long run, and there was a time limit to their efficacy as palliatives.

If, however, the people of the United States insisted on preserving the historic capitalism under which things had been brought to such a plight, Dreher concluded, there was only one possible political measure that would unloosen the full possibilities of technology and employ on some level all workers: that was unrestricted military expenditures, as in Germany for example after 1933. But inevitably this meant piling higher and higher the mountain of debt—a process bound to end sometime in a social explosion unless success in conquering and robbing neighbors, in Hitler's style, permitted an indefinite postponement.

Being in essence destructive, war, however, laid waste the wealth on which it subsisted and could scarcely be regarded as endless, as providing a permanent liberation of productive forces. Even though just, as Dreher declared the struggle of the United States against the Axis powers to be, war did not and could not open the way for the full application of technology to the promotion of general welfare; nor did the economics practiced under the New Deal offer a solution of the problem to the American people or, by his hypothesis, to any other people.

Having made his analysis and prognosis, Dreher outlined a program designed to take the restraints off the productive powers of technology and usher in full production and employment for the general welfare in a time of peace, should it ever return. He proposed to nationalize the great key industries already highly centralized and, by positive actions, set them to pouring out wealth in the form of capital and consumer goods under carefully drawn plans of procedure and administration—wealth to be distributed in accordance with equally well-planned wage scales. In addition, Dreher proposed to augment existing productive powers by huge grants of money to scientific research for the purpose of making new discoveries in physics, chemistry, and biology—the invention of inventions. While sketching the general outlines for procedure and management in respect of key industries, he left room for large areas of individual enterprise and adapted his projects to principles of popular government.

Although Dreher felt certain that a planned collectivism of some kind was coming, was actually under way, he did not profess to know that the democratic form would ultimately prevail as against the fascist brand. As he studied speeches in Congress on the labor question, he discerned what he thought to be frank fascist proclivities in certain quarters. He was moved to record that during such a debate, "Rankin of Mississippi argued that 50 cents an hour was plenty for airplane workers, on the ground that his fortunate rural constituents were lucky to get 10 cents, whereupon Hobbs of Alabama interrupted to tell the House, with some pride, that in his district the farm wage was nearer 5 cents an hour. Soon the discussion took on overtones of vigilantism and incitement to extra-Congressional violence. Cox of Georgia shouted 'Treason!' in the House day after day, and urged Congress to outlaw all strikes in defense industries. 'How much longer must the coddling of this vermin be tolerated?' he demanded. 'How much longer must it go on before Congress or somebody rises up to do something about it?' Representative Rich proposed to put the leaders of the Vultee strike in concentration camps."

Refusing to accept an American fascism as "inevitable," yet confessing incertitude respecting the outcome of the crisis, Dreher was sure that the whole case for which he pleaded at the bar of public opinion was a case for civilization. "Our task," he averred in his concluding chapter, "is to make a civilization above the animal level by freeing the machine and by freeing men from the machine. It must be done, or such beginnings of civilization as we have attained will go to smash. It is the only foreseeable method of keeping technology pointed toward the goal of human welfare while defending ourselves by technology against those who have abandoned that vision. It will require all the strength and understanding we can muster up. If the effort is beyond us we shall go the way of the others, and our fate will be deserved. But it is a goal worthy of America."

Inside the academic world, as well as among laymen, the crisis in American economy and thought evoked a consciousness of the need for concerted efforts on a national scale. Charles E. Merriam, of the University of Chicago, who had received and deserved the title of "dean of the political scientists," brought this need to the front persistently in books, articles, and lectures. An assiduous student of government, and active participant in public affairs, pledged by conviction to the American system of constitutionalism, Merriam could speak with authority and competence. And in various sections of his volume *The New Democracy and the New Despotism* (1939), he associated his plea for policies designed to vanquish the crisis with the idea of civilization and ways and means of advancing it in the United States.

As to the basic issue, Merriam took his stand squarely on the proposition "that the gains of civilization are essentially mass gains and should be distributed throughout the community as rapidly as possible." He acknowledged the existence of the counter contention: "There are those who insist that the gains of civilization are essentially the creation of a few men who are the real foundation of the nation or society in which they live, and that others contribute only in a minor and subordinate way." He also recognized the existence of "those who demand the public protection, heritage, and advantages of the nation and are not willing to subordinate their private claims to it." But he barred out their demands as indefensible on grounds of fact and incompatible with democracy as theory and practice.

In listing the assumptions of democracy, on which rested his plea for giving the widest possible distribution to "the gains of civilization," Merriam included nearly all the fundamentals that had been brought into the idea of civilization by systematic thinkers since its formulation: "The essential dignity of man, the importance of protecting and cultivating his personality on a fraternal rather than a differential principle. . . . Confidence in a constant drive toward the perfectibility of mankind. The assumption that the gains of commonwealths are essentially mass gains and should be diffused as promptly as possible throughout the community. . . . The desirability of popular decision in the last analysis on basic questions of social direction policy, and of recognized procedures for the expression of such decisions and their validation in policy. Confidence in the possibility of conscious social change accomplished through the process of consent rather than by the methods of violence."

On the ethical validity of these principles, Merriam grounded his proposed policies: "The mechanical contrivances of democracy must give assurance that the gains of civilization shall be equitably distributed, including here the material goods and the non-material values as well. The means of effecting this result are subordinate to the ends in view. . . . It is the special task of the system of democracy to scrutinize the gains of civilization and their diffusion, and to set up the ways and means within the limits of intelligence by which these gains may be translated into terms of democratic living. . . . It cannot be too strongly stated that one of the primary methods of validating the assumption that the gains of civilization are essentially mass gains and should be distributed throughout the community as rapidly as possible is the *deliberate, continuing, systematic analysis of civilization's gains in a commonwealth, the mode and range of their distribution, the enlargement of national income and the consequent adjustment of mass gains to total gains*. The underlying principle is more important than the particular mechanisms or methods adopted."

These controlling propositions, Merriam held, lead necessarily to some kind of national planning, firm but not too rigid, designed to effect more rapidly the distribution of "civilization's gains." Mere "economic planning" he criticized as insufficient to accomplish the ends posited. "National 'production,'" he said, "is not merely, as many seem to suppose, the building of factories in which goods are made, but the production of a civilization out of which comes the skill to invent the machinery of the factory, and the skills to operate it after it is set up. A planned technology or a planned education might be more important than a planned 'economy.'" Indeed, having recognized immaterial values as vital to and accompanying civilization, Merriam was compelled to differentiate them, if only for convenience, from the material values represented by economic goods, and to take account of them in connection with planning as a means of effecting a wider distribution of "civilization's gains."

Scholars especially concerned with the contexture of society in development agreed with experts in forms and functions of government that an hour for great decisions on public policies had arrived. Many professional sociologists, when they sought to apprehend the dynamics of American society, discovered lines of social forces converging on associational efforts, public and private, to promote civilization in the United States. The idea of civilization they often found convenient in its generality as an instrument of interpretation, as corresponding in the highest degree to many of the very processes they were studying and describing. Their constructive proposals also came readily under that idea and called for concerted actions at various levels of community and national life.

This type of social inquiry and reflective thought was so common and so intricate that no selection for purposes of illustration can adequately indicate its strength and character. But its nature was brought to light in the scholarly work of Howard Odum, at the University of North Carolina, founded on extensive and intensive researches into the structure and dynamics of American society. His analytical investigations, carried on with the aid of colleagues at the University and with the support of grants from Foundations, covered regions, counties, towns, villages, families, individuals, farms, and industries. With the study of physical geography and resources this group united the study of human geography and resources. The findings were recorded in statistical tables, on maps, in types of graphic presentation, and in other forms of description wide in scope and yet almost microscopic in minutiae. In organizing the materials, interpreting them, and offering constructive proposals, Odum drew upon an immense body of social and historical theories and axioms.

Certain paramount conclusions reached in the course of his numerous investigations, Odum incorporated in his *American Social Problems* published in 1939. In the opening pages he struck into the center of thought about civilization in the

United States as a persistent force, and as requiring for advancement more creative action in an age of crisis: "If we begin our treatise by saying that there is being enacted today the most momentous drama of survival-struggle that has yet tested the enduring qualities of American civilization, this is one way of emphasizing vividly and forcefully the importance of understanding American problems and of sensing the need for mastery of the physical, technical, and societal forces that sweep down upon us in the changing times of today and tomorrow. It is also one way of saying that the American people, both in their own right and as leaders in modern civilization, are face to face with extraordinary opportunities. . . . If we continue by pointing out the fact that it is possible to catalogue a long and distinguished list of authorities who agree that the present is a time of crisis and dilemma in which civilization itself is at stake and in which democratic institutions are endangered, this is one way of saying that we approach the study of our American problems through a background and setting of a world peculiarly conscious of tension and struggle."

If American civilization is to survive and to advance, Odum argued, specific formulations of the problems to be attacked are a prerequisite. The problems he grouped into four main categories as follows: "The first is the problem of developing, conserving, and adapting the people and their resources to the living geography of the American continent. This is a basic Americanism of work and planning. A second problem is that of conserving liberty and freedom within the framework of American civilization. This is also a basic Americanism. A third problem is the struggle of universal culture seeking to achieve enduring civilization in harmony with both technology and natural heritage. The fourth problem, then, is essentially one of progress in the attainment of these ends in relation to the world outlook of the present and in particular the titanic struggle between the democratic process and certain of the European trends toward totalitarianism."

Since intolerance, desperation, and revolt are stirring in the land, successful action on these problems calls for the exercise of intellectual and moral qualities more complex than qualities appropriate to the order and simpler stages of American development: "Ideology is not enough; . . . action is not enough; audacity is not enough. Everywhere this picture [in America] reflects deficiencies in the hard, long processes of intellectual effort and technical skill. There must be colossal preliminary work preparatory to the new social reconstruction. There must be capacity for purposeful control from without the tides of emotion and action; there must be measured ways of determining margins of capacity in each stage of democratic control; there must be scientific selection of elements left and elements right; there must be measures for the conservation of what has been gained in the nation's whole experience, and in particular for conserving the recent gains; there must be ample preparation for next steps when first steps have failed. And there must be checks and controls for the impatience and immaturity of intellectual and common man alike."

Coming to the consideration of forces likely to be potent in advancing civilization, Odum first raised questions respecting the nature of pertinent dynamics: "What is it that will speedily bring America to full motivation and capacity for such united action as will provide for the new mastery? What is it that will impel the nation's leaders to design and follow such new and adequate steps as will bring this next act of its drama to happy ending? Is it crisis and disaster? Or concerted will and purpose? Or science and knowledge and technology? Or is it all of these and something more, intangible and powerful, which can inspire the bridging, by social technology and purpose, of that sheer chasm of contrast between the old and the new?"

In offering his own answers to questions so perplexing, Odum avoided oversimplification and yet was positive in statement. He expressed confidence that numerous routines, individual and group, essential to the process of civilization, would go on amid the very necessities of living. That individual manifestations of the humane spirit, also indispensable to the process, would continue, he was likewise certain. But to these, he insisted, must be added, after clarification of purposes, social planning—national, state, regional, community, and group—equipped with all the agencies of civilization available to the people of the United States.

It was not only individual thinkers and investigators who requisitioned the idea of civilization for their explorations, and arrived at the conclusion that a concentration of talents and efforts was necessary to realizing various values inalienable to civilization in the United States. This tendency was also explicit and implicit in reports of scholars working collectively. In fact the most comprehensive single document dealing with American society in development produced in the twenty years following the first world war, *Recent Social Trends in the United States* (1933), bore the impress of group convergence in thought about civilization in America.

The survey on which the great document rested was initiated at the request of Herbert Hoover, President of the United States, in 1929, and was directed by the Research Committee on Social Trends, composed of well-known scholars: Wesley C. Mitchell, economist; Charles E. Merriam, political scientist; Shelby M. Harrison, specialist in social work; Alice Hamilton, professor of industrial medicine at Harvard University; Howard W. Odum, sociologist; and William F. Ogburn, sociologist. They divided the great survey into several "fields." For conducting the minute inquiries in each of the fields, they chose experts representing the excellence of scientific learning and experience. In their labors, the Committee and its assistants made drafts upon departments of government, upon public and private institutions, upon hundreds of individuals working in all branches of activity and knowledge. Without exaggeration it could be said that representations of the best in American wisdom, understanding, and knowledge were summoned to the aid of the Committee in its monumental undertaking.

The two huge volumes, which contained the findings of the Committee itself and summations of findings by others in the several divisions, bore the title *Recent Social Trends*, but they might have been called, with equal propriety, *A Survey of Recent American Civilization*. Indeed for a reprint of the Commission's findings issued in 1934 by its publisher with its authority, for use in the schools, the title *American Civilization Today* was chosen and may be taken as official and correct.

That the overarching conception provided by the idea of civilization was definitely in the thought of the directors was also disclosed by the Committee in explaining the nature of the work and conclusions: "The problems before the nation as they are affected by social change fall into three great groups. One group is the natural environment of earth and air, heat and cold, fauna and flora. This changes very slowly; it is man's physical heritage. Another group is our biological inheritance—those things which determine the color of our eyes, the width of our cheek bones, our facial characteristics apart from environmental influences. And this also changes slowly. A third is the cultural environment called civilization, our social heritage, in which change is going forward rapidly."

This statement, supplemented by other declarations, showed that the Committee was positively operating under a unitary conception of the whole task. "It may be said," explained the Committee, "that the primary value of this report is to be found in the effort to interrelate the disjointed factors and elements in the social life of America, in the attempt to view the situation as a whole rather than as a cluster of parts. The various inquiries which have been conducted by the Committee are subordinated to the main purpose of getting a central view of the American problem as revealed by social trends. . . . The meaning of the present study of social change is to be found not merely in the analysis of the separate trends, many of which have been examined before, but in their interrelation—in the effort to look at America as a whole, as a national union the parts of which too often are isolated, not only in scientific studies but in everyday affairs. The Committee's procedure, then, has been to look at recent social trends in the United States as interrelated, to scrutinize the functioning of the social organization as a joint activity. . . . A nation advances not only by dynamic power, but by and through the maintenance of some degree of equilibrium among the moving forces."

The divisions into which the survey was separated were divisions into aspects of civilization in America as the titles and subject matter of the several chapters show: population, use of natural wealth, influences of invention and discovery, agencies of communication, trends in economic organization, shifting occupational patterns, education, changing social attitudes and interests, rise of metropolitan communities, rural life, status of racial and ethnic groups, vitality of the American people, the family and its functions, activities of women outside the home, childhood and youth, labor groups in the social struggle, the people as consumers, recreation, the arts in social life, changes in religious organization, health and medical practice, crime and punishment, privately supported social work, public welfare activities, growth of governmental functions, taxation and public finance, public administration, law and legal institutions, government and society. While some significant phases of American civilization were neglected, such as trends in ethical, esthetic, and religious *thought,* the Committee's report was in fact a remarkable contribution to written history of American civilization and to systematic thought about its nature and development.

The Committee's findings did not take the form of mere descriptions of plane-surface conditions. The Committee recognized the truth that realistic descriptions relative to human affairs must take account of movement in processes as well as the surface of the fleeting moment called "stage" or "status quo." So its findings presented "the cultural environment called civilization" as dynamic, as rapidly changing, and as displaying "startling inequality in the rates of change, uneven advances in inventions, institutions, attitudes and ideals, dangerous tensions and torsions in our social arrangements."

Although scrupulous in the collection, verification, and statement of facts, the Committee transcended the neutrality of descriptions. It made use of the facts in the creative spirit and with reference to an ideal posited end. It assumed the obligation of "analyzing and appraising our problems as those of a single society based upon the assumption of the common welfare as the goal of common effort." Having faced this obligation in the domain of ethics, the Committee then made the pertinent inquiry: "What are the prerequisites of a successful, long-time constructive integration of social effort?"

"Indispensable" among the prerequisites, the Committee placed the following: "Willingness and determination to undertake important integral changes in the reorganization of social life, including the economic and the political orders, rather than the pursuance of a policy of drift. Recognition of the role which science must play in such a reorganization of life. Continuing recognition of the intimate relationships between changing scientific techniques, varying social interests and institutions, modes of social education and action and broad social purposes. Specific ways and means of procedure for continuing research and for the formulation of concrete policies as well as for the successful administration of the lines of action indicated." To the creative ethical impulse, specific recognition was given: "The clarification of human values and their reformulation in order to give expression to them in terms of today's life and opportunities is a major task of social thinking."

In short, the Committee on Recent Social Trends treated "the cultural environment called civilization" as possessing a unity, as changing rapidly, but marked by uneven development in its several phases. To measure degrees of progress in various lines, it set up an ethical ideal, "the common welfare as the common goal." In considering the possibilities of progress toward that goal it deprecated reliance on "a policy of drift"—on faith in the automatic beneficence of individualism. Then it called for a clarification and reformulation of human values and for "a successful, long-time constructive integration of social effort" in overcoming obstacles and tensions in the way of progress toward the ideal of common welfare. Thus the report of the Committee from beginning to end reinforced the idea of civilization in the United States and illustrated in an extraordinary manner the convergence of American thought on the advancement of civilization by concerted efforts.

While President Hoover's Research Committee on Social Trends was surveying major aspects of American civilization, another committee, sponsored by the American Historical Association, was investigating the problem and nature of "the social sciences" in the American system of education. This organization, known as the Commission on the Social Studies, was composed of scholars representing the various branches of the subject, such as history, politics, economics, sociology, and education. It, too, was assisted by expert counselors in cognate divisions of learning.

After long preparations, with the aid of generous grants of money from the Commonwealth Fund and the Carnegie Corporation, the Commission began its work in January, 1929, prosecuted its investigations until 1934, and issued numerous special and general reports. In mapping its course, the Commission found it necessary to define its field of interest and its objectives broadly, as a guide to particular inquiries; and it closed its labors with a final volume of *Conclusions and Recommendations*.

The first of its documents, entitled *A Charter for the Social Sciences in the Schools*, unanimously approved by the Commission in May, 1931, was the result of common counsel at many conferences. Created to examine and report on education for life and citizenship in the United States, the Commission deemed it mandatory to consider the characteristics of the nation which civic education is designed to serve.

It asked, in effect, what is the nature of the American society in which the schools operate, the great interests of which they are intended to promote? "The people of this country," it declared in the *Charter*, "are engaged in no mere political experiment, as often imagined, but are attempting to build a civilization in a new natural setting, along original lines, with science and machinery as their great instrumentalities of work."

Indebtedness to Europe was duly acknowledged but the divergence of American history from European history was accepted as fact. "Though an offspring of European civilization, America has never imported a large part of the Old World heritage and is constructing a social order of many ingredients that are distinctly unique in emphasis at least. We cannot import civilization wholesale from Europe. To be sure, pictures may be bought, musicians brought over at handsome figures, castles may be carried across the sea and transformed into mansions for plutocrats, and ideas transferred, but civilization is no borrowed plumage, no plaster decoration that can be stuck on any kind of solid structure."

The American heritage, the Commission knew full well, was not identical with the European heritage, in 1931. The future, in which any program of American education was to be carried out, the Commission believed, would also be different: "Having rounded out the Continent, the American people have turned in upon themselves and are taking time to wonder about the next great tasks ahead. While a few critics go abroad for inspiration, while the wise search for ideas wherever they may be found, the great body of thinkers still agree with Emerson that we must stand fast where we are and work out our destiny along lines already marked out—build a civilization with characteristics sincerely our own, in harmony with historic ideals and yet incorporating novel practices adapted to changing needs. As in all other civilizations four aspects will always be in the foreground—political, economic, ethical, and esthetic."

At a later place, the *Charter* indicated some of the differences between civilization in the United States and in the Old World. It stated that American society "has no decorative classes established by law, giving grace and elegance at the top to offset poverty and ignorance at the bottom. The cultivated classes of Europe, according to Amiel, represent 'aspirations toward a harmony of things which everyday reality denies to us and of which art alone gives us a glimpse.' The American masses, by contrast, are striving toward a certain harmony in reality that can be vouchsafed to the humblest willing to pay the price of a quest for it. Therein lies the substance of the American ideal so often scorned by European writers given to comparing the superiority of privileged orders with the commonness of democracy. Those who do not like this American ideal may flee from it; all others must work under the limitations of its influence."

Into the idea of civilization thus expounded, the Commission brought the element of progress required by its etymology and historical usage: "Underlying all these national ideals is a belief that the lot of mankind can be continuously improved by research, invention, and taking thought. This is the philosophy of progress and if rightly conceived is one of the noblest conceptions yet created by the human mind. The environment and conduct of men and women can be modified by effort in the light of higher values and better ends. Human relations, constitutions, economic arrangements, and political practices are not immutably fixed. If there is anything which history demonstrates, it is this generalization. All legislation, all community action, all individual effort are founded on the assumption that evils can be corrected, problems solved, the ills of life minimized, and its blessings multiplied by rational methods, intelligently applied. Essentially by this faith is American civilization justified."

If "in this development of ideas," the Commission went on to say, "emphasis has been laid on material means, the pressure behind it has come mainly from ethical impulses—the desire to see a more even distribution of the benefits of civilization. Assailed as sentimental and humanitarian by some practical men of affairs and by one professed school of humanists, it nevertheless stands on its own merits and is to be defended on good humanist grounds. Civilized people have reached such a stage in moral evolution that they cannot sit comfortably in the midst of plenty while starvation and misery do devastating work a stone's throw away. Whether this is the fruit of religion, philosophy, or revolt, or all three, it is an emergent reality in every modern society that makes pretensions to civilization. Social science cannot ignore ethical considerations; otherwise it would become a branch of inert scholasticism without direction or motive force."

Having recognized the force of aspiration for progress toward social perfection as enclosed in the idea of civilization, the Commission turned to that other form of aspiration inseparable from the first, namely, for individual perfection. "If ethical considerations recommend a wide distribution of the benefits of civilization, they likewise enjoin a simplicity and sincerity of living which inevitably runs counter to the habits of luxury and extravagance so widely praised in the United States as indispensable to the good life. . . . It is the business of social ethics to criticize and expose the perils inherent in animal materialism and to bring into active influence standards of moderate and sincere living."

Firmly among the interior aspects of civilization, the Commission also placed the powers and aspirations of esthetics: "If in the course of American development, emphasis has been laid on the material aspects of culture, this does not mean that all American life is to be subdued to the exigencies of utility without reference to esthetics. It simply means that art and beauty, if they are genuine, must work their way through the medium which society in the United States provides. Even in their higher forms they have seldom been wholly separated from practical uses, for such separation carries sterility with it; and in America they must inevitably be nourished in relation to the major interests of this civilization. . . . Nor is this so alien to American experience as some critics would have us believe. From the beginning of our history, the poorest among us have desired to mingle with their work and recreation some elements of symmetry and beauty. In spite of the heavy handicaps imposed upon a pioneering people engaged in subduing a continent, the esthetic interest has been both latent and potential in American life. . . . Social science in the schools, therefore, must bring forward the esthetic interest, illustrate it by notable examples in letters and the arts, indicate its uses and potentialities, inculcate respect for it, and show how through individual and community action it can be more richly and effectively embodied in the visible and outward signs of American life and in the tastes and graces of the home."

Although the Commission on the Social Studies unanimously agreed in 1931 that American civilization had features distinguishing it fundamentally from European civilization, it also approved, with four dissenters, in 1934, *Conclusions and Recommendations* which presented a contradiction in one fundamental respect. In the latter document the Commission declared that "the civilization of the United States has always been a part of European, or 'Western,' civilization. . . . Moreover, the swift development of technology, industry, transportation, and communication in modern times is obviously merging Western civilization into a new world civilization."

In saying that American civilization was a "part" of Western civilization, did the Commission mean an interchangeable or identical part? Did it mean that in the "new world civilization" each of the "parts" would slough off its history—the characteristics which differentiated it from, and often threw it into sharp conflicts with, other civilizations—would surrender its very historical and practical individuality? On these points the Commission's final document was silent.

Yet on the very page of its *Conclusions and Recommendations* on which appeared the submergence of American civilization in European and then world civilization, the Commission reaffirmed, in substance, the declaration contained in the *Charter for the Social Sciences:* "The American nation is an entity with distinctive aspects, traditions, and usages—geographical, economic, political, social, and cultural —of perduring vigor and strength, which must be taken into account if social science instruction is to be something more than abstract, if it is to be properly concrete, realistic and serviceable." When the Commission spoke concretely and realistically, it spoke of civilization in the United States as having its own history and constituent attributes. In its recommendations for educational actions, it advocated a concentration of talents, individual and collective, on serving the advancement of civilization in the United States.

Concerned with the largest manifestations of the human spirit, philosophers grounded in American traditions also converged on civilization in the United States, its problems, and its advancement.

Thinking of American civilization in broad terms, Irwin Edman, teacher of philosophy at Columbia University, a writer on that and other related subjects, at home on the two continents, predicted in 1940 an accentuation, rather than a diminution or obliteration, of America's purposes in her continental domain, no matter how the war in Europe might end. This interpretation of current events he published under the title "Look Homeward, America!" in Harper's Magazine for December of that year.

The accentuation, at least in significant part, would be due, in Edman's opinion, to changes in Europe over which Americans would have no permanent control: "Among the things that would have seemed incredible as late as ten years ago is the vanishing of Europe as a combination Nirvana and happy hunting ground for educated or semi-educated Americans. Certainly if the Nazis win (and even if they do not), the peculiar part Europe has played in the lives and imaginations of the more literate Americans is permanently ended. For Europe as Nirvana is over. Europe once meant liberation, it once meant escape. It provided at once a moral holiday and a spiritual tonic. The angles and crudities of the workaday American world, all business and all Philistinism, were left behind. One went abroad to live in the past and in a present steeped in a past. It was an excursion into a cultural paradise."

Through the long course of American history, many intellectuals, artists, members of the "cultivated classes," had looked to Europe for inspiration and standards, had been interested in life there rather than in promoting civilization at home. Even persons who had tried to proclaim American independence in intellectual and esthetic matters early in the nineteenth century had at the same time, Edman pointed out, "turned eastward, Emerson to Carlyle and to the Germans, Longfellow to Dante and the Italian past, Hawthorne to Italy and Greece. A multitude of lesser Americans followed them in their spiritual pilgrimages and, when they could afford to, turned their spiritual longings into physical visits." In the twentieth century, after the first world war, Americans continued to look to Europe for their utopias or at least for the fundamental directions of life—to England, France, or Vienna, or to Sweden as the home of the middle way. But the collapse of Europe into conflict and war altered the European scene for Americans, made it physically and spiritually less easy of access, "made it clear to even the most sentimental idealizing American that Europe was no longer a museum or a spiritual haven."

It was true that in the earlier days, Edman said, the Americans who fled in distress from their native land to Europe were usually fitful and trivial abroad as they had been at home. Henry James, "the most gifted of the refugees from American life," confessed that his flight had been largely in vain. He was not at home in the United States or anywhere else; "he was a spectator, not a dramatist; a collector of bric-a-brac, not an artist." But after the crashes that followed the first world war in Europe, even the most romantic escapists from America could see that the Europe of their fantasies no longer stood intact and that flights in the old style were no longer possible. By remaining at home they had to be sterile or associate themselves more or less with those Americans who had been all along primarily concerned with civilization in the United States.

Despite the disruptive influences at work in the United States, many Americans, Edman claimed, "had begun to examine the materials of American culture in terms both of their own patrimony and their own present. . . . It hardly needed the catastrophe of a world war to make Americans, especially writers and artists, aware, with delight and with hope, of colors and intimations of the civilization they were living in and which, as a nation, they were creating. . . . Americans had already begun to discover that they had a past, a short one, but crowded with interest, even by the most fastidious standards of art and thought. . . . Americans found that they did not have to go to the châteaux of the Loire or the Renaissance palaces of Italy to have something for the imagination to feed upon."

Yet, sharing the opinion of those Americans who since 1776 had insisted that their nation's main business was the making of a civilization on this continent, Edman understood that the United States had much to learn from Europe: "It would be absurd to turn one's back on that European tradition of which America is, in the largest perspective, a variation and extension. Isolationism, autarchy in the arts, is as absurd and unworkable in art as it is in the realm of economics and politics. . . . But it is also true that the arts have always flourished in their own soil and out of their own roots. In each instance they have been nourished by the sun that lighted other soils and by the winds that blew from a 'world elsewhere.' But they have always grown where they grew in their own way and in their own climate. . . . There is, moreover, at this dubious moment in Europe's destiny, a special reason, not unconnected with the nature of democratic life, why Americans should look homeward. There is, oddly enough, a political condition for the fine arts which both passionate democrats and passionate artists and connoisseurs forget. That is the condition of freedom, of spontaneous choice. Artists in uniform are not artists at all."

In advising Americans to look homeward, then, "to the civilization they were living in and which, as a nation, they were creating," Edman was merely describing an actual situation: the old avenues of flight to Europe had been altered, if not entirely closed; in spite of their often angry assertion of a will to escape, Americans could not cease to be what they were, that is, Americans; they could not become that which they were not. Edman also suggested to them, graciously in accord with his wont, that, if to them American civilization was thin, even contemptible, as many were accustomed to say, some of the thinness and shoddy was in their own minds, behind their own eyes, in their own lack of power and imagination. In other words, while fleeing from the banality of American life, as they called it in effect, they were really fleeing from their own banality and impotence in America— to be banal and impotent in Europe, as a rule. They were, in substance, making American civilization the scapegoat for their own lack of interest and powers.

By looking homeward, Edman reminded them, they could see "a great people of many stocks, enriched of late by the sad accidents of European destiny, by the best of European minds and creative art. Here are stories crying to be told, pictures to be painted, feelings to be transmuted into the 'potable gold' of poetry. Here are audiences too, larger, more eager, and more discriminating than they have ever been. Here is a future, possibly the only future for culture or creation in the Western world. Americans may still go to Europe after the war, as they go to the ruins of Rome at Baalbek, or of Greece at Epidaurus and Delphi, beautiful cemeteries of the spirit of man. But for the future of their own imagination and thinking, for the possible survival of art and thought at all, Americans will have to look to their own land and lives for incitement and materials. It would be arrogant to believe that the will to create or widening audiences or maturing talents will produce, of themselves, anything comparable in stature to the great monuments of European genius of the past two thousand years. It would be shocking not to be shocked that a long tradition of genius may be coming to an end. But the spirit bloweth where it listeth; to-day the conditions for creation are ours, and our works will at least not be poorer because they are honestly and natively our own."

Intrinsically Edman's views, sentiments, and convictions were correlative with a special type of philosophy that had been developed in the United States during recent years as a modification of a heritage received from Great Britain. The new American philosophy was variously known as Pragmatism, Relativism, or Instrumentalism. None of these names described it exactly or even gave intimations of its fulness. Each name was inadequate and insofar misleading. But one or another could be, and was, used for convenience in distinguishing the American philosophy from all systems of absolutism.

Narrowly scanned in one of its many aspects, namely, its challenge to abstract propositions, the new American philosophy was practical and critical. Its exponents asked of each philosophic proposition asserted as truth, of every worldview declared to be perfect, complete, unconditioned, the following questions: Is this formula, in respect of human life, an empty abstraction? If not, if it has concrete applications to human affairs, what does it signify in terms of humane attitudes and conduct and in terms of the agencies used to implement them in individual and social actions? In short, will it work? In working, has it redounded or will it redound to the good of the individual and the good of society, that is, promote the decencies and virtues of individual and social living? To what noble ends or purposes is it relative?

The American philosophy also challenged the basic assumptions necessary to all systems of absolutism however constituted. In efforts to reconcile absolute schemes of thought with patent contradictions of human experience, exponents of such systems had created a fiction called realism or idealism. To state it in philosophic language, they regarded "the world of sense which is revealed to us empirically in time and space as being merely the phenomenal form of a non-sensuous existence which constitutes the real underlying actuality." Furthermore, many absolutists presumed to dictate, on the authority of some inelastic dogma, the only correct rules for thinking about and conducting human affairs, individual and social. They claimed, in effect, that they could describe and "explain" the ultimate design of the universe, or at least that this operation could be performed by some mind and that concentration on the operation was the true business of philosophy.

Such claims "pragmatic" philosophers in the United States declared to be empty pretensions, contrary to reason and experience—achievements beyond human capacity and within the competence only of omnipotence and omniscience. They did more: they declared that the pursuit of such absolutism only led up blind alleys to futility—to ultimate problems of understanding beyond the reach of finite minds. They insisted that concentration on that type of speculation warped the mind by turning it away from its primary obligation of making explorations in thinking which would help human beings to live with merit, courage, and dignity. They made a salient point of the fact that moral commands deduced from absolutist postulates had been used to bolster up powerful interests of State, Church, Army, and Economy in Europe and were in this respect perilous to democracy in the United States.

With the American philosophy stated as criticism of absolutist philosophy, the line of controversy was firmly drawn and there could be no compromise. Hence the American philosophy invited and received condemnation, sometimes the curses, of opponents foreign and domestic. It was called childish, the fruit of ignorance, the product of shallow brains, even a work of the devil. An almost perfect example of foreign contempt for the American philosophy was provided in 1942 in *The Destiny of Western Man* by W. T. Stace, a former British civil servant engaged at Princeton University in teaching American youth. In this volume Stace, after rejecting theological absolutism and substituting a compulsion akin to it, dealt extensively with the idea of civilization and, in the course of his argument, with the pragmatism of James and Dewey.

There was no evidence in Stace's work that he had paid any particular attention to the idea of civilization in its origins, its etymology, or its meanings in historical usage anywhere. Nor did his knowledge of pragmatism seem to be exhaustive. But the state of his learning on these points did not prevent his discoursing on both.

One phase of Dewey's thought Stace characterized as "dull and stupid" and another as "grossly superficial." To cap his climax, Stace gave a fanciful picture of Professor Dewey at a

banquet "inappropriately" propounding "his solemn revelation that eating is nothing but an instrument of living," as if
"the pleasures of the civilized palate," as if the amenities of
table manners, were beneath Dewey's consideration. The
theory of knowledge which Stace ascribed to James and
Dewey he sought to discredit by calling it "practically indistin-
guishable" from Nietzsche's theory of knowledge deduced
from Schopenhauer's primacy of the will.

Having made this exhibition of his understanding, Stace
confessed: "It is above all things surprising that this philosophy should have been brought to birth and should flourish in
the land which is *par excellence* the home of democracy,"
therewith exhibiting at the same time his knowledge of democracy in the United States. But neither his understanding of
democracy nor his surprise nor his erudition estopped him
from dismissing the American philosophy as stupid, superficial, and contemptible.

If the formulators of the American synthesis were childish,
ignorant, shallow, stupid, and evil, as critics charged, they
were not entirely unlettered in the doctrines of absolutism in
its various forms. Nor were they wholly unfamiliar with the
personalities, animus, or circumstances pertaining to the
origins of absolutism. They had some knowledge, at least, of
those doctrines, personalities, and circumstances. They were
also more or less acquainted with the European literature of
criticism which had exposed the nature and force of numerous
conflicting absolutisms and had classified them one and all as
figments created by human imagination, if not conceit,
whether tested by their internal logic, by their epistemology,
by their influences as revealed in British and Continental
societies, or in the personal character and conduct of their
originators and promoters.

In view of the tone and temper displayed by his critics, it
was not strange that William James, in a jovial mood, once
exclaimed: "Damn the Absolute!" Not less forcibly the resistance offered by the American philosophy to criticisms
made in the name of some Absolutism was voiced by Max
Eastman, whose philosophic studies in the United States and
Europe certainly gave him qualifications for dealing with it.
Referring specifically to Thomas Mann's suggestion that
"what we are really fighting for in the war against Hitler is
'The Absolute,'" Eastman declared: "To me one of the chief
virtues of American culture is the total absence up to this date

of any important intrusions from 'The Absolute.' One of our chief virtues is that when we hear people say things like that we feel inclined to laugh. Laughter actually plays among us somewhat the role played in Germany by the same 'Absolute.' It enables us to carry on through the painful complications of the relative, the imperfect—in short the real facts—with buoyancy and courage. Our culture took its start from matter-of-fact knowledge and pioneer humor instead of mythical belief and solemn rituals of consolation. That is what makes it a new and exciting creation. I sincerely hope we are not going to be 'enriched' by Europeans to the point of muddling our constructive labors on our own distinct task and adventure . . . in these days when we must harbor Europe's great men as well as smile at their condescension."

But the critical aspects of the American philosophy and its resistance to all forms of "The Absolute" were merely features of its constitution. They alone did not represent the fulness of its content or the substance of its meaning for life. Every philosophy, like every other body of thought, ancient or modern, European or American, as a French scholar has said, is to be comprehended not merely by an exploration of its internal structure, but rather by constant reference to the personalities and circumstances intimately connected with its own origin and development.

On its positive side the American philosophy was a body of practical ethics concerned with promoting the good life for individuals in society. Among the personalities associated with its origin and growth, in one phase or another, were William James, John Dewey, Lester F. Ward, Edward A. Ross, Charles H. Cooley, and Charles A. Ellwood. They were all ethical teachers who accepted the humane postulates of American democracy and participated in many movements designed to apply these principles. From their lives, experiences, sympathies, and interests American philosophy derived substantial meaning and connotations. The contexture of ideas and interests with which they were intimately connected, from which their work also drew the fulness of its significance, comprised the programs and aspirations of American democracy during the closing decades of the nineteenth century and the opening decades of the twentieth.

Their synthesis, as Moses J. Aronson stated the case in the Journal of Social Philosophy for October, 1940, "bears the impress of the American soil and reflects the characteristics of a frontier-nurtured athletic mentality grappling with the perplexities engendered by the rising tide of industrialism swirling against the background of a rural economy. A spontaneous native growth, the ferment of ideas which accompanied the turn of the century was responsive to deep national needs, and represents the first self-conscious formulation of an American philosophy of life. Into this system of thought there entered, to be sure, a number of European ingredients. These foreign components, however, were taken up and fused into an autochthonous unity." The synthesis was "engendered within the matrix of an expanding civilization." Moreover, "original in spirit and distinctive in content," it was "a national philosophy" which "guides the path of American civilization."

The inner nature of this American philosophy Aronson explained succinctly in his review. Trained in philosophy at home and abroad, he had qualifications for analysis, comparisons, distinctions, and characterizations. The American philosophy, as he summed it up, conceives our universe "to be a changing, a growing, an expanding, an energetic universe. Fluid and evolving, nature is interpreted as being the external manifestation not of a static geometrical formula, but rather of a vital force which strives unceasingly toward an infinitely distant and undefined goal. . . . American philosophy postulates the reality of an open and dynamic universe. A fluid universe is not a place to rest in, nor does it encourage the esthetic delight of passive contemplation. A world in constant process of unfolding stimulates the active imagination and invites the exercise of muscular intelligence. . . .

"Under the sway of an evolutionary philosophy, the human mind assumes the status of a vital organ, and is endowed with a survival value in the struggle for existence. . . . Thought serves a function in the human economy, and justifies itself by the efficacy with which it enables mankind to prosper in a world replete with danger and surprise. To the extent that scholars become imbued with the instrumentalist theory of knowledge they forego the inquiry into origins as well as the quest for ontological definitions [the science of being or existence], and concentrate their energies upon the formulations of purposes which may best serve to enhance human existence."

Far from being unethical, devoid of positive moral values as points of reference for theory and practice, American philosophy, Aronson maintained, is "permeated through and through with a fervent idealism. This idealism, however, is secular rather than sacred, humanistic rather than supernatural. Predicating salvation not so much on grace as on works, our humanistic idealism takes the form of an ethical meliorism. Imbued with an optimistic faith in progress, the ethical idealism characteristic of the past half century recognizes the reality of evil and struggles to eradicate it. Formulating ideals and implementing their execution, a humanistic philosophy unleashes the creative intelligence in the service of ethical causes."

Inseparable from this philosophy, constantly associated with it, is the idea of "social control." The methods of natural science are by analogy brought into the service of advancing civilization. "Analogous to the engineer who with the help of his formulæ molds physical nature into an ideally conceived shape, the social scientist with his accurate, albeit less mathematical, knowledge may be enabled to guide the currents of civilization into rational directions and to impress upon the various aspects of culture an ideal pattern. Given the imponderable characteristics of the materials he is obliged to manipulate, the sociologist's formulæ are bound to be more vulnerable to error than those of the engineer, but they remain instruments of rational control all the same—instruments which like the presumably best scientific tools have to be sharpened continuously, have to be improved upon perpetually. The concept of social control raises to a new level of rationality the inveterate drive toward adjustment in a changing world. Freed from the vagaries of Utopian aberrations, grounded in the data of experience, the notion of social control is bound up with the activistic idealism of the modern era, and furnishes the rationale of disciplined reform."

Had Aronson been inclined he might have reversed the tables on the absolutists, who denounced the American philosophy as "materialist" and devoid of ethics. He might have turned to his account the treatment of this subject by a European philosopher, Albert Schweitzer in his *Civilization and Ethics*. A doctor of theology, a doctor of philosophy, and a doctor of medicine from the University of Strassburg, Schweitzer could and did speak with authority on the absolutist systems of European philosophies. By careful analysis, he showed that in Kant's theory of the universe, for example, "ethics is deprived of its object," paralyzed and made meaningless. Applying the same method to Hegel, Schweitzer concluded: "Hegel bows himself in courageous awe [to fate] as being the Very Truth. His world-view is supra-ethical mysticism. The ethical is to him but a phase in the development of the spiritual. Civilization he comprehends not as something ethical, but only as something spiritual," that is, reflecting mechanically a hypothetical "realism" or idea underlying all things. It was to this kind of mechanistic "spirit" that the American philosophy was opposed from start to finish.

All the principal points in Aronson's summary were abundantly illustrated in the writings of John Dewey. One of the leading characteristics of Dewey's thinking lay in the fact that he clearly understood the intimate interlocking of all philosophies with stages or types of civilization. "Philosophy," he said in his *Philosophy and Civilization*, "like politics, literature, and the plastic arts, is itself a phenomenon of human culture. Its connection with social history, with civilization, is intrinsic. . . . Philosophers are parts of history, caught in its movement; creators perhaps in some measure of its future, but also assuredly creatures of its past. . . . Open your histories of philosophy, and you will find written throughout them the same periods of time and the same geographical distributions which provide the intellectual scheme of histories of politics, industry, or the fine arts. . . . It follows that there is no specifiable difference between philosophy and its role in the history of civilization. Discover and define its right characteristic and unique function in civilization, and you have defined philosophy itself." But Dewey did not make philosophy a mere reflection of historical events in movement. He said distinctly: "In forming patterns to be conformed to in future thought and action, it is additive and transforming in its role in the history of civilization."

If philosophers are human beings in history and civilization, in times and places, if they are not disembodied spirits devoid of sentiments, interests, and propensities connected with their times and places, then in their efforts to create a philosophy based on "pure reason" or "pure intellect" they are deluding themselves, Dewey contended. "Bacon, Descartes, Kant each thought with fervor that he was founding philosophy anew because he was placing it securely upon an exclusive intellectual basis, exclusive, that is, of everything but intellect. The movement of time has revealed the illusion; it exhibits as the work of philosophy the old and ever new undertaking of adjusting the body of traditions that constitute the actual mind of man to scientific tendencies and political aspirations which are novel and incompatible with received authorities." On such grounds Dewey was charged with being "anti-rational" or "anti-intellectual," but in fact he was applying reason, intelligence, and knowledge in an effort to ascertain the actual nature of philosophy and its function in society.

Considering this problem with reference to the United States, Dewey illuminated it: "The presence or absence of native born philosophies is a severe test of the depth of unconscious tradition and rooted institutions among any people, and of the productive forces of their culture. For the sake of brevity, I may be allowed to take our own case of civilization in the United States. Philosophy, we have been saying, is the conversion of such culture as exists into consciousness, into an imagination which is logically coherent and is not incompatible with what is factually known. But this conversion itself is a further movement of civilization; it is not something performed upon the body of habits and tendencies from without, that is, miraculously. If American civilization does not eventuate in an imaginative formulation of itself, if it merely rearranges the figures already named and placed—in playing an inherited European game—that fact is itself the measure of the culture we have achieved. . . . Any philosophy which is a sincere outgrowth and expression of our own civilization is better than none, provided it speaks the authentic idiom of an enduring and dominating corporate existence."

In his various writings on ethics, esthetics, education, science, industry, labor, and the social implications of philosophy, Dewey declared and described his belief in the humane values of the good life in itself, and in relation to the specific ideas, institutions, and practices of American democracy. But he assumed no omniscient role. He was content to stand upon his belief in these values as established and tested by experience, without claiming that they are absolutely true, right, and good always and everywhere under the sanction of some absolute authority above human experience. "Adherence to any body of doctrines and dogmas based on specific authority," he declared, "signifies distrust in the power of experience to provide, in its ongoing movement, the needed principles of belief and action."

In letter and spirit the American philosophy thus briefly outlined corresponded in many essentials to the idea of civilization as systematically developed in the United States. But it was not completely coterminous with that idea. It had never been brought fully into line with a consistent theory of history. Nor had the American philosophy ever been given systematic and unified expression. Although members of the American philosophic school wrote on various aspects of civilization, such as economy, morals, esthetics, and social ethics, none among them fused all these phases under a single type of philosophic coherence.

There were other grounds of distinction. Unlike the American idea of civilization, the American philosophy was drawn into an acrimonious and continuous struggle with absolutism over a fundamental theory of knowledge, and in this way became so ensnared in sensationalist empiricism and biological Darwinism that its constructive nature was obscured in the dust of battle.

The intellectual problem arising from this contest can be stated as follows: Empiricists, with whose views pragmatism was generally associated rightly or wrongly, had asserted with varying degrees of emphasis that there were no truths except those derived from sensations, desires, customs, facts of social life.

This claim, idealists protested, really meant that the human spirit was tightly bound to material elements and mere sensations; that there was no reason or idea above the facts; that there was no independent organizing and creative power in the human mind. If so, they went on to argue, mere conservatism or the dictates of bare facts reign in human affairs; there is no source from which can come inspiration, instruction, and heroic efforts designed to impose order on disorder, to realize potentials known to exist, to bring more ideal human conditions into actual being. From the idealist point of view it was, in short, a case of idea against facts, imagination against things seen or felt, conquering reason against the tough substance of unyielding habituation.

This knot the idealists of absolutism cut by four declarations: the human mind has an independent power of thinking; reason or grand idea lies behind the facts of experience—the appearances of things; in history, reason or idea has been and is being realized on earth; and reason or idea supplies power and justification for efforts to make liberty, human worthiness, and general welfare prevail. For practices not in accord with supreme reason or idea, it is the task of humanity to substitute good practices—a categorical imperative; and in the fulfilment of its task, humanity is aided by a progressive realization of the supreme reason in the history of the world. Humanity works—so ran the plea—with, not against, the main stream of history.

Caught in the clash between empiricism and absolutism, the idea of civilization yielded to neither. It countered the conservative and deadening influences of empirical servitude to habits, customs, and things experienced, by three specific assertions: progress in human affairs is as much a fact as the perpetuation of customs and habits; human intelligence is creative as well as routine in nature; and a study of development in history—creative intelligence at work—yields truths as indefeasible as those derived from a study of habitual experience.

Without a resort to an absolute reason above human experience, in connection with the idea of civilization was evolved the contention that the progressive realization of reason and good is *in* history, though not the sum of history. Carefully avoiding efforts to "explain" the whole universe, exponents of the idea of civilization in the United States eschewed the mechanical limits of materialism and the mechanical logic of absolutism. For the idea of civilization it was sufficient that ideals and illustrations of the true, the good, the beautiful, the social, the useful had existed in human experience from the beginning of recorded time—sufficient for inspiration and guidance in conquering the forces of disorder and opposition and bringing the real closer to the ideal.

So the idea of civilization in the United States, strengthened in numerous relations by the American philosophy, escaped some of its limitations connected with empiricism. The idea of civilization was, moreover, integrated with a theory of history and it offered to the reflective spirit such a degree of unity and coherence that it became an ultimate construct of values for countless Americans.

At the risk of tiresome reiteration, it may again be said: This idea of civilization, in a composite formulation, embraces a conception of history as a struggle of human beings in the world for individual and social perfection—for the good, the true, the beautiful—against ignorance, disease, the harshness of physical nature, the forces of barbarism in individuals and in society. It assigns to history in the United States, so conceived, unique features in origins, substance, and development.

Inherent in the idea is the social principle. That is to say: the civilization of men and women occurs in society, and all the agencies used in the process—language, ideas, knowledge, institutions, property, and inventions—are social products, not the products of individuals working in a vacuum. Inherent in the idea also is respect for life, for human worth, for the utmost liberty compatible with the social principle, for equality of rights and opportunities, for the dignity and utility of labor, for the rule of universal participation in the work and benefits of society. In this process arts, sciences, letters, machines, and devices are to be regarded as manifestations and instruments, not guarantees of civilization. The only guarantee is to be found in humane character, talents, and purposes, supported by appropriate institutions and directed in individual and associational efforts to the advancement of civilization.

This idea of civilization combats the pessimism that proclaims the world to be the necessary home of misery and ineptitude; that views all things in the worst possible light. To all pessimism as negation, resignation, or nihilism, it opposes a world-view as optimistic as the need and the will to live, expressed in the endless becoming and persistence of life —life ever engaged in a struggle for a decent and wholesome existence against the forces of barbarism and pessimism wrestling for the possession of the human spirit.

From the idea of civilization as systematically developed in the United States are excluded, as imaginary and unserviceable transcendencies, all forms of total determinism—whether that of a divine drama supposed to justify to man the ways of God otherwise inexplicable; or that of a secular philosophy which interprets history as the inexorable realization of a super-mundane idea with human beings serving as pawns; or that of a so-called materialism presumed to account for all manifestations of the human spirit in terms of "matter." The idea does not pretend to "explain" the universe, to give the whole truth of history, to supplant the consolations of religion, or to pronounce anathemas upon dissenters. It offers, instead, a construct, or view of life, summational and relative

—universal in scope but applicable to times, places, and circumstances—from which inspiration and guidance may be derived in the search for individual and social perfection.

As to ultimates, while rejecting a total determinism, the idea of civilization predicates a partial determinism, such as an irreversible and irrevocable historical heritage, and a partially open and dynamic world in which creative intelligence can and does work; in which character can and does realize ethical values; in which virtue can and does make effective choices; in which individual and collective efforts, now and in the future, can make the good, the true, and the beautiful prevail more widely, advancing civilization, amid divagations, defeats, and storms, toward its distant, ever-enlarging vision.

Despite the mutability of things human, there is one invariable in the history of men and women. This is war. And inasmuch as the efficiency of war in spreading death and destruction depends upon some degree of civilization, it follows that, subject to the law of thermo-dynamics, if there be one, the future of civilization in the United States has at least this much assurance.

Bibliography

Adams, Brooks: *The Law of Civilization and Decay* (1896); *Theory of Social Revolutions* (1913); *The Degradation of the Democratic Dogma* (1919) includes letters by Henry Adams to the historians. Macmillan.

Adams, Henry: *Democracy*, a novel (1881); *The Education of Henry Adams*. Houghton Mifflin, 1918.

Adams, John: *Defence of the Constitutions of the United States*, (1787); *Discourses on Davila*.

Adams, John Quincy: *Progress of Society . . . to Civilization*, Baltimore Sun, December 3, 1840. See Brooks Adams, *The Degradation of Democratic Dogma*, introductory chapters.

Addams, Jane: *Twenty Years at Hull-House* (1912); *The Second Twenty Years at Hull-House* (1930). Macmillan.

Altgeld, John P.: *Live Questions*. Published by the author, Chicago, 1899. See Harvey Wish, "Altgeld and the Progressive Tradition." Am. Hist. Rev., July, 1941.

Anthony, Susan B.: with reference to *Resolution* of Loyal Women sent to Lincoln, see *History of Woman Suffrage*, Vol. II, pages 66ff.

Arnold, Matthew: *Civilization in the United States*. First edition, 1888.

Aronson, Moses: "Roscoe Pound and the Resurgence of Juristic Idealism." Journal of Social Philosophy, October, 1940.

Auslander, Joseph, and Kilmer, Kenton: "Citadel: Poetry in the National Library." Saturday Review of Literature, April 25, 1942.

Bancroft, George: *Literary and Historical Miscellanies*. Harper, 1855.

Barlow, Joel: *Political Writings*, containing "Advice to the Privileged Orders of Europe," etc. New York, 1796. *Letter to his fellow citizens of the United States*. Paris, 1799. *The Columbiad*. 2 vols. Philadelphia, 1809.

Barnes, Harry Elmer: *The History of Western Civilization*, with the collaboration of Henry Ward. 2 vols. Harcourt, Brace, 1935.

Beard, Charles A. (editor): *Whither Mankind* (1928); *Toward Civilization* (1930). Longmans, Green. *America Faces the Future*, Houghton Mifflin, 1932. *The Idea of National Interest*, with the collaboration of George Smith. Macmillan, 1934.

Bellamy, Edward: *Looking Backward*. First edition, 1888.

Berle, Adolf, Jr.: *New Directions in the New World*. Harper, 1940.

Beveridge, Albert Jeremiah. See Claude Bowers: *Beveridge and the Progressive Era*. Houghton Mifflin, 1932.

Blackwell, Antoinette Brown. *Speech* at convention of the Loyal Women of the Country, in *History of Woman Suffrage*, Vol. II, pages 69ff.

Bliss, W. D. P. (editor): *The Encyclopedia of Social Reform*. 1897.

Boodin, John Elof: *The Social Mind*. Macmillan, 1939.

Brooks, J. G.: *As Others See Us*. Macmillan, 1910.

Brownson, Henry F.: *The Works of Orestes A. Brownson*. Detroit, 1888.

Buckle, Thomas Henry: *History of Civilization in England*. Vol. I, 1857; Vol. II, 1861.

Burgess, J. W.: *Political Science and Comparative Constitutional Law*. Ginn and Company, 1890.

Bury, J. B.: *The Idea of Progress*. Macmillan, 1921.

Calhoun, John C.: *Works*. 1851-55.

Carey, Henry C.: *The Past, the Present, and the Future* (London, 1856); *The Harmony of Interests* (New York, 1856); *Commerce, Christianity, and Civilization versus British Free Trade*. Letters in reply to the London Times. Philadelphia, 1876.

Carnegie, Andrew: *The Gospel of Wealth*. Collection of essays forming a volume in complete works edited by Burton J. Hendrick. Doubleday, Doran, 1933.

Channing, William E.: *Works*, 6 vols. First complete edition, Boston, 1841. *The Perfect Life in Twelve Discourses*, edited from his manuscripts by W. H. Channing. Boston, 1873.

Child, Lydia Maria: *An Appeal in behalf of that class of Americans Called Africans*. Boston, 1833.

Civilization, The Drift of. 50th Anniversary Number of the St. Louis Post-Dispatch. Simon and Schuster, 1929.

Clinton, DeWitt: *Discourse*. North American Review, 1815.

Commission on the Social Studies: *A Charter for the Social Sciences*. Scribner's, 1932. *Conclusions and Recommendations*. Scribner's, 1934.

Condorcet: *Esquisse d'un tableau historique des progrès de l'esprit humain*. France, 1795. Translated and published in Baltimore, 1802, as *An Essay on the Progress of the Human Spirit*.

Cooper, James Fenimore: *The Monikins; American Democrat; The Redskins; Home As Found*. See *Fenimore Cooper, Critic of His Times* by Robert E. Spiller. Minton, Balch, 1931.

Coram, Robert: *Political Inquiries, to Which Is Added a Plan for the General Establishment of Schools throughout the United States.* Wilmington, Delaware, 1791. See *Liberalism and American Education in the Eighteenth Century* by Allen O. Hansen. Macmillan, 1926.

Curtis, George William: *Orations and Addresses.* Vol. I. Harper and Brothers, 1894.

Curtius, Ernst Robert: *The Civilization of France.* Translated from the German by Olive Wyon. Macmillan, 1932.

Denison, J. H.: *Emotion as the Basis of Civilization.* Scribner's, 1928.

Dewey, John: *Philosophy and Civilization.* Minton, Balch, 1931.

Dorn, Walter: *Competition for Empire,* 1740-1763. See chapter on "Age of the Enlightenment." Harper, 1940.

Dorsey, George A.: *Man's Own Show: Civilization.* Harper, 1931.

Draper, John W.: *History of the Intellectual Development of Europe* (1863); *History of the Conflict between Religion and Science.* D. Appleton, 1874.

Dreher, Carl: *The Coming Showdown.* Little, Brown, 1942.

Eastman, Max: "A Significant Memory of Freud." The New Republic, May, 1941. *Heroes I have Known.* Simon and Schuster, 1942.

Edman, Irwin: "Look Homeward, America!" Harper's Magazine, December, 1940.

Elias, Norbert: *Über den Prozess der Zivilisation.* Basel, 1939. Vol. I, Soziogenetische und psychogenetische Untersuchungen.

Ely, Richard T.: *The Ground under Our Feet.* Macmillan, 1938.

Emerson, Ralph Waldo: *Works.* Riverside edition. Houghton Mifflin, 1889.

Engels, Friedrich. See Karl Marx.

Everett, Edward: *Orations and Speeches.* 4 vols. Little, Brown, 1883.

Ewbank, Thomas: *Inorganic Forces ordained to supersede Human Slavery.* N. Y., 1860. A pamphlet.

Febvre, Lucien: *Civilisation—le Mot et l'Idée.* La Renaissance du livre, 78, Boulevard Saint-Michel, Paris, 1930.

Fels, Samuel S.: *This Changing World.* Houghton Mifflin, 1933.

Ferguson, Adam: *An Essay on the History of Civil Society.* Edinburgh, 1767.

Finkelstein, Louis: "American Ideals and the Survival of Western Civilization." Contemporary Jewish Record, June, 1941.

Fitzhugh, George: *Sociology of the South; or, The Failure*

of Free Society (1854); *Cannibals All! or, Slaves without Masters* (1857).

Fosdick, Harry Emerson: "On Being Civilized to Death." The Church Monthly, February, 1936 See also *Living under Tension.* Harper, 1941.

Fosdick, Raymond: *The Old Savage in the New Civilization.* Doubleday, Doran, 1928.

Fourier, Charles. See Parke Godwin.

Frank, Jerome: *Save America First.* Harper, 1938.

Fuller, Margaret: *Writings.* (Ed. by Wade Mason.) Viking, 1941.

Furnas, C. C., and S. M.: *Man, Bread & Destiny.* Reynal and Hitchcock, 1937.

George, Henry: *Progress and Poverty* (1879); *The Science of Political Economy* (1898). Doubleday & McClure.

Godwin, Parke: "Constructive and Pacific Democracy." Magazine, The Present, Vol. I, December, 1843. *A Popular View of the Doctrines of Charles Fourier* (1844).

Gray, George: Telegram to John Hay printed in G. F. Hoar, *Autobiography of Seventy Years*, Vol. II, pp. 313-315.

Grimké, Thomas Smith: Oration—Fourth of July, 1809. Charleston.

Guizot, François Pierre: Translations in many editions of his French works on *Civilization in Europe*; and *Civilization in France.*

Hammond, James H.: *Selections from the Letters and Speeches of the Hon. J. H. Hammond*, 1866.

Harper, William: *Memoir on Slavery.* 1837.

Hay, John: *The Bread-Winners.* 1883.

Hedger, George A. (Editor): *An Introduction to Western Civilization.* Doubleday, 1933.

Hegel, G. W. F.: *The Philosophy of History.* Translation by J. Sibree. Colonial Press, New York, 1920. See also Herbert Marcuse, *Reason and Revolution.* Oxford University Press, 1941.

Helper, Hilton Rowan: *The Impending Crisis.* 1857.

Herron, George D.: *The Christian Society.* Fleming H. Revell, 1894. *American Imperialism.* Social Forum, I. 1899.

Hoar, George F.: *Autobiography of Seventy Years.* Scribner's, 1903.

Holcombe, James P.: *An Address* delivered before the Seventh Annual Meeting of the Virginia State Agricultural Society, 1858.

Hopkins, Charles H.: *The Rise of the Social Gospel in American Protestantism.* Yale Press, 1941.

Howard, G. W.: "Changed Ideals and Status of the Family and the Public Activities of Women." Annals of the American Academy of Political and Social Science, May, 1914.

Howells, W. D.: *A traveler from Altruria*. Harper, 1900. See also *Life in Letters of W. D. Howells*, Mildred Howells, Editor. 2 vols. Doubleday, Doran, 1928.

Immigration Acts. See Garis, *Immigration Restriction*. Macmillan, 1927. See also *Congressional Record* and *Hearings* of Committees on the bill of 1924.

Jameson, J. F.: *The American Revolution Considered as a Social Movement*. Princeton University Press, 1926.

Jefferson, Thomas: *The Writings of Thomas Jefferson*. Memorial edition, Washington, D. C., 1907. 20 vols. Includes correspondence with John Adams.

Johnson, Charles S. (Editor): *The Negro in American Civilization*. Holt, 1930.

Knox, Frank, Secretary of the Navy: *Address*. New York Times, October 2, 1941.

Lehmann, W. C.: *Adam Ferguson and the Beginnings of Modern Sociology*. Columbia Univ. Press, 1930.

Littlehales, G. W.: *The Navy as a Motor in Geographical and Commercial Progress*. Bulletin of the American Geographical Society, 1899.

Lloyd, Henry Demarest: *Wealth against Commonwealth*. Harper, 1894. *Man, the Social Creator*, Jane Addams and Ann Withington, Editors. Doubleday, Page, 1906.

Lochore, R. A.: *History of the Idea of Civilization in France* (1830-1870). No. VII in Studien zur abendländischen Geistes- und Gesellschaftsgeschichte, translated by Hermann Platz. Ludwig Rohrscheid Verlag, Bonn, 1935.

Lowell, James Russell: *Barbarism and Civilization*; and *American Civilization*, the Atlantic Monthly, 1861, 1862. Vol. I of his *Letters* contains his letter to Leslie Stephen.

Luce, H. A.: *The American Century*. Farrar & Rinehart, 1931.

McElroy, Robert: *Jefferson Davis, the Unreal and the Real*. Harper, 1937.

McIntosh, Maria J.: *Woman in America: Her Work and Her Reward*. Appleton, 1850.

McKinley, William. See C. S. Olcott, *The Life of William McKinley*. Houghton Mifflin, 1916. See also J. F. Rhodes, *The McKinley-Roosevelt Administration*. Macmillan, 1923.

Mahan, Alfred Thayer. See C. C. Taylor, *Life of Admiral Mahan*. Doran, 1920. For analysis of his numerous writings see C. A. Beard, *The Idea of National Interest*. Macmillan, 1934.

Mann, Mary (Editor): *Life and Works of Horace Mann*. 5 vols. Cambridge, Mass., 1867.

Mann, Thomas: *Friedrich und die grosse Koalition*. 1915. A copy in the Yale Library.

Marsh, George Perkins: *The American Historical School*. 1847. Pamphlet in the Yale Library.

Marshall, E. E.: *Our Navy in Peace*. Proceedings of the U. S. Naval Institute, February, 1932.

Marx, Karl: *Marx-Engels Historische Kritische Gesamtausgabe*. 11 vols. Berlin, 1929-1931. See also O. Rühle, *Karl Marx*. Viking Press, 1929. See also *The Communist Manifesto*.

Mason, O. T.: *Woman's Share in Primitive Culture*. Anthropological Series edited by Frederick Starr. Appleton, 1894.

Merriam, Charles E.: *The New Democracy and the New Despotism*. McGraw-Hill, 1939.

Moras, J.: *Ursprung und Entwicklung des Begriffs Zivilisation im Frankreich* (1756-1830). In Hamburger Studien zu Volkstum und Kultur der Romanen.

Morgan, Lewis Henry: *Ancient Society or Researches in the Lines of Human Progress from Savagery through Barbarism to Civilization*. Holt, 1877.

Morley, John: *Critical Miscellanies*. Vol. II for essay on Condorcet. Macmillan, London, 1886.

Mott, Lucretia. See *Life and Letters of James and Lucretia Mott* edited by Anna D. Hallowell. Houghton Mifflin, 1884. See also *History of Woman Suffrage*. 3 vols.

Müller-Freienfels, Richard: *Mysteries of the Soul*. Knopf, 1929.

Nef, J. U.: *The United States and Civilization*. University of Chicago Press, 1942.

North Carolina Joint Resolution Providing for a Declaration of the Federation of the World, 1941. Reprinted in International Conciliation, June, 1941.

Norton, Charles Eliot. See Bernard Smith, *The Democratic Spirit*, for extracts from the writings by Norton. Knopf, 1941.

Nott, Josiah C.: *Types of Mankind*. 1854.

O'Connor, Mrs. T. P.: *My Beloved South*. Putnam, 1913.

Odum, Howard W.: *American Social Problems*. Holt, 1939.

Otto, Max: "Philosophy in a Time of Crisis." Journal of Social Philosophy, July, 1941.

Our Common Cause—Civilization. Proceedings of International Congress of Women, Chicago, July 16-22, 1933. National Council of Women of the United States, New York.

Paine, Thomas: *Rights of Man; Agrarian Justice; Age of Reason*.

Parker, Theodore: *Works*. Boston, 1907-1913. See also H. S. Commager, *Theodore Parker*. Little, Brown, 1936. For comments on Prescott and Hildreth, see Massachusetts Quarterly Review, 1847, 1849, 1850.

Pater, Alan F., and Landau, Milton: *What They Said in 1937*. The Paebar Co., N. Y., 1938.

Patten, Simon N.: *The Premises of Political Economy*

(1885); *The Theory of Social Forces* (1902). Huebsch. *The New Basis of Civilization*. Macmillan, 1921.

Patterson, John Stahl: "American Destiny." Continental Monthly, 1863.

Perry, Bliss: *Walt Whitman: His Life and Work*. Houghton Mifflin, 1906.

Phelps, Egbert: "American Civilization." Continental Monthly, 1864.

Phillips, Wendell: *Speeches, Lectures, and Letters*. Boston, 1863. See also *History of Woman Suffrage*. 3 vols.

Pierson, George W.: *Tocqueville and Beaumont in America*. Oxford University Press, 1938.

Prentice, Ezra Parmalee: *Hunger and History*. Harper, 1939.

Rauschenbusch, Walter: *Christianity and the Social Crisis*. Macmillan, 1916.

Recent Social Trends. 2 vols. McGraw-Hill, 1933.

Ridpath, John Clark: "The Wage System of Labor." The New Nation, April, 1892.

Romier, Lucien: *Who Will Be Master: Europe or America?* A translation from the French by Matthew Josephson. The Macaulay Co., 1928. Lee Furman, Inc., Successors.

Roosevelt, Franklin Delano: *Public Papers and Addresses*, in nine volumes. Random House (Volumes covering years 1932-1936); Macmillan (Volumes covering years 1937-1940). *Address* on Pan-American Day, in New York Times, April 15, 1942.

Rush, Benjamin. See A. O. Hansen, *Liberalism and American Education*. Macmillan, 1926.

Saunders, Frederick (Editor): *Our National Centennial Jubilee*. N. Y., 1876.

Schapiro, J. S.: *Condorcet and the Rise of Liberalism*. Harcourt, Brace, 1934.

Schweitzer, Albert: *The Philosophy of Civilization*. 2 Parts. Part I, *The Decay and Restoration of Civilization*; Part II, *Civilization and Ethics*. Macmillan, 1923, 1932.

Scudder, Vida: *The Church and the Hour*, Reflections of a Socialist Churchwoman. Dutton, 1917.

Searing, Edward W.: "The Reign of the Huckster." The New Nation, January, 1892.

Shaw, Charles G. (Editor): *Trends of Civilization and Culture*. American Book Co., 1932.

Siegfried, André: *America Comes of Age*. Translated from the French by H. H. Hemming and Doris Hemming. Harcourt, Brace, 1927.

Snyder, Alfred J.: *America's Purpose*. The Declaration Press, Philadelphia, 1937.

Soule, George: *A Planned Society*. Macmillan, 1932.

Spalding, John Lancaster: "Opportunity." In *Modern Eloquence* edited by T. B. Reed, Vol. IX, pp. 1076-97. N. Y., 1900.

Spence, Anna Garlin: *Woman's Share in Social Culture.* Lippincott, 1913.

Spengler, Oswald: *The Decline of the West.* 2 vols. Translated from the German by Charles Francis Atkinson. Knopf, 1926.

Stace, W. T.: *The Destiny of Western Man.* Reynal and Hitchcock, 1942.

Stanton, Elizabeth Cady. See *History of Woman Suffrage.* 3 vols.

Stanwood, E.: *A History of the Presidency.* Vol. II contains the Republican and the Democratic party platforms of 1900. Houghton Mifflin, 1916.

Stearns, Harold E. (Editor): *Civilization in the United States.* Harcourt, Brace, 1922. *America Now.* Scribner's, 1938.

Stephens, Alexander H.: See Henry Cleveland, *Alexander H. Stephens in Public and Private.* Philadelphia, 1866.

Stoddard, Lothrop: *The Revolt against Civilization.* Scribner's, 1922.

Strong, Josiah: *Our Country: Its Possible Future and Its Present Crisis.* Baker & Taylor, N. Y., 1891.

Sumner, Charles: *Complete Works.* Lothrop, Lee, 1900.

Sumner, William Graham: *Earth-Hunger and Other Essays* (1914); *War and Other Essays* (1911). Yale Press.

Tocqueville, Alexis de: *Democracy in America.* Gilman edition, Century Company, 1898.

Toombs, Robert. For his Boston *Address* of 1856 see A. H. Stephens, *The War between the States.* Vol. I, Appendix G. 1868.

Tugwell, Rexford: *The Industrial Discipline and the Governmental Arts.* Columbia University Press, 1933.

Turner, F. J.: *The Frontier in American History.* Holt, 1920.

Twain, Mark: *Letters.* Edition edited by Albert Bigelow Paine, 1917. *Writings.* Harper.

Veblen, Thorstein: *The Place of Science in Modern Civilization.* Huebsch, 1919.

Wallace, Henry A.: *New Frontiers.* Reynal and Hitchcock, 1934. "Foundations of the Peace," the Atlantic Monthly, Jan., 1942.

Wallis, W. D.: *Culture and Progress.* McGraw-Hill, 1930.

Ward, Lester F.: *Dynamic Sociology* (1883): *The Psychic Factors of Civilization* (1893). Ginn & Co.

Ware, Caroline F. (Editor): *The Cultural Approach to History.* Selection from papers read at annual meeting of the

American Historical Association. Columbia University Press, 1940.

Warren, Mercy: *History of the Rise, Progress and Termination of the American Revolution*. 3 vols. 1805.

Weeks, John W.: *The Work of the War Department of the United States*. Government Printing Office, Washington, D. C., 1924.

White, Andrew D.: "The Field of Historical Study," in *Modern Eloquence*, Vol. IX, pp. 1177-98. 1900.

Whitman. See Bliss Perry, *Walt Whitman: His Life and Work*. Revised edition, Houghton Mifflin, 1906.

Wilson, Woodrow: *History of the American People*. Harper, 1918. See Baker and Dodd, *Public Papers of Woodrow Wilson*. Harper, 1925. See also R. S. Baker, *Woodrow Wilson—Life and Letters* (1927-1939), 8 vols. Doubleday, 1927-1939.

Wish, Harvey: "Altgeld and the Progressive Tradition," The American Historical Review, July, 1941.

Wright, Carroll D.: *Some Ethical Phases of the Labor Question*. American Unitarian Association, Boston, 1902.

Index

Index

Absolutism, doctrine of, 573 f., 579 f.

Abundance, economic theory of, 370 f.

Adams, Brooks, comment on natural resources policy of John Quincy Adams, 144 f.; concept of civilization, 28; pessimism of, 331

Adams, Henry, idea of civilization in his *Democracy*, 328 f.; in his theory of history-writing, 329; in his letter to the American Historical Association, 329 f.; and Marxism, 331; pessimism of, 328 ff.; relation to Brooks Adams, 331.

Adams, John, concept of civilization, 95, 108 ff.

Adams, John Quincy, concept of civilization, 140 ff.

Addams, Jane, on function of Hull House in diffusing civilization, 415 ff.

Agrarian view of Southern civilization, 253 f.

Altgeld, John P., as an American reformer, 416 f.; on civilization, 417 f.

Agriculture. *See* land

Allen, Florence E., war as foe of civilization, 38

American civilization. *See* Civilization, American

American Economic Association, creation of, 368

American Historical Association, Commission on Social Studies, work of, 563 ff.

American Revolution influence on Western world-views, 83 f.

Anthony, Katherine, contributor to *Civilization in the United States*, 31

Anthony, Susan B., in woman movement, 277 f.

Anthropology, study of, broad-

ens idea of civilization, 347 ff.

Aquinas, T h o m a s, Christian philosophy of, 14

Arnold, Matthew, criticism of American civilization, 427, 428 ff.; culture defined, 62

Aronson, Moses J., nature of American philosophy, 574 ff.

Art, American, foreign criticism of, 455

Aryan race, theory of, 191 f.

Ash, John, includes *civilization* in dictionary, 63 f.

Associationism, doctrine of, 202

Atlantic Charter, promulgation of, 492

Atlantic Monthly, The, early articles on civilization, 242 f.

Bach, Richard F., contributor to *Toward Civilization*, 34

Badeau, l'Abbe, early use of word *civilization*, 65, 67

Bancroft, George, identifies democracy w i t h civilization, 161 ff.

Barbarism, conflict with civilization, 23 f.; Fourier's doctrine of, 202 f.; Emerson's tests of, 174 f.

Barlow, Joel, concept of civilization, 96, 127 ff.

Barnard, Henry, function of education, 223 f.

Barnes, Harry Elmer, historical concept of civilization, 40 ff.

Beard, Charles A., co-editor of symposium *Whither Mankind: A Panorama of Modern Civilization*, 32 ff.; editor of symposium *Toward Civilization*, 34 f.

Beaumont, studies of American democracy and civilization, 155 ff.

Bellamy, Edward, literary work of, influence on American

595

civilization, 408 ff.

Berle, Adolf A., Jr., idea of civilization, 533 f.

Beveridge, Albert J., imperialism justified by spreading civilization, 477 f.

Blackstone, William, criticism of, by Robert Coram, 120 ff.

Blackwell, Antoinette Brown, conflict between American civilizations, 278

Bliss, W. D. P., social reform of, 394 ff.

Boodin, John Elof, philosophic concept of civilization, 43 f.

Boulanger, M., first use of word civilization, 65, 67

Bowles, Gilbert, on discrimination in Japanese immigration, 516

Bowen, Mrs. Joseph, in social service, 416

Briffault, Robert, woman's influence on civilization, 361 f.

Brooks, Van Wyck, contributor to Civilization in the United States, 31; criticism of American letters, 455

Brownson, Orestes A., class aspects of civilization, 230 f.; conceives American civilization as deterioration, 232 f.; conflict between Roman Catholic Church and American civilization, 227 ff.; criticism of American civilization, 446; social doctrines of, 207 f.; sponsors Northern civilization, 272 f.

Buckle, Henry Thomas, adds to confusion as to origins of the word civilization, 69; knowledge and moral forces in civilization, 181 f.

Burgess, John William, individualism with Teutonic imperialism, 305 ff.

Burke, Edmund, champions civilization, 81

Bury, J. B., loose translation of word civilization, 69 ff.

Calhoun, John C., champion of

Southern civilization, 264 f.; opposition to Smithson's endowment for national institution, 147

Campbell, Thomas D., contributor to Toward Civilization, 34.

Carey, Henry C., concept of civilization, 196 ff.; criticism of Guizot's concept of civilization, 89; promotes diversified and independent economy, 194 ff.

Carnegie, Andrew, views of civilization and social reform, 385 ff.; opposition to imperialism, 508 f.

Capitalism, 283, 299 ff., 372, 375 ff., 386, 457 ff., 471, 499, 551 ff. See Wages System

Capitalists. See Capitalism

Centennial Exposition at Philadelphia, emphasis on progress of civilization, 339

Chafee, Zechariah, contributor to Civilization in the United States, 31

Channing, William E., the ministry and civilization, 225

Charter for the Social Sciences in the Schools, 563 ff.

Charter for the Social Studies, Commission on Social Studies in the Schools, 47

Chase, Stuart, contributor to Whither Mankind: A Panorama of Modern Civilization, 32

Chevalier, Michel, criticism of American civilization, 421 f.

Child, Lydia Maria, indictment against slavery, 281 ff.

Christian social movement, rise of, 389 ff.

Christianity, communism, ideal of, 400 f.; concept of civilization, 46 f.; individualism identified with, 297; influence of, on medieval thought, 14 f.; social movement, rise of, 388 ff.; world-view of, diversities in, 17. See also Protestantism, Religion, Roman

Catholic Church, Jews

Church, 15 ff., 91, 227 ff., 389 ff., 443 ff. See Religion and State

Churchill, Winston, and Atlantic Charter, 492

Civilization, idea of, advanced by commingling of nationalities, 191 ff.; American, accentuation of, 567 ff.; American, conflict with general internationalism, 456 ff.; American, conflict with Marxian communism, 456 ff.; American, early Republic conceptions of, 148 ff.; American, equality factor in, 150 f.; American, geographic factor in, 150; American, imperialism contrary to, 502 f.; American, influence of philosophy upon, 578 ff.; American, Negro in, 35 f.; American, Northern, 263 ff.; American, opportunity a factor in, 151 f.; American, Southern, 245 ff.; as artificial, 301 f.; as organization, 301 f.; as world-view, 263; balance sheet of, for North and South, 263 ff.; broadened by anthropology, 347 ff.; built on capital, 299 f.; Christian concept of, 46 f.; classification of usage, 19 f.; complexity of, 28 f.; conflict with barbarism, 23 f.; courses in, college, 50 ff.; culture and, 55 ff.; culture as, 48 ff.; definitions, 43, 46, 48, 53, 55, 57, 58 f., 66 ff., 87 ff., 95, 97, 100, 105, 109 ff., 112, 147 ff., 170 ff., 320 ff., 333, 358 f., 489, 528, 580 ff.; democracy as phase of, 158; early uses of word civilization, 64 ff.; economics as phase of, 368 ff.; economic concept of, 42 f.; economic factors as aspect of, 321 f.; etymology of word, 66 f.; eugenics necessary for continuance of, 29; gain in revolutionary France, 84 f.; government, representative, as instrument of, 222; Gui-

zot's concept of bourgeois individualism with, 85 ff.; historical concept of, 39 ff.; individualism identified with, 297 ff.; in political discourse, 52; in sectional struggle, 245 ff.; Jefferson's concept as historical, 95 ff.; machine age, 34 f.; man's handiwork, 26 f.; Mark Twain's analysis of, 52 ff.; origin of, 63 ff.; philosophic concept of, 43 ff.; popularized by Thomas Paine, 101 f.; poverty impediment to, 30; psychic factors of, 354 ff.; psychological forces as impediment to, 29 f.; related to theory of history by Condorcet, 80 f.; social gospel and, 392 ff.; sociological approach to, 354 ff.; ultimates of, 582; war and, 53 f., 582; war as foe of, 38; war for, designated by Wilson, 488; woman's influence on, 365 ff.; woman's share in primitive society, 360 ff.

Clark, John Bates, individualism and Christianity, 297

Clinton, DeWitt, commingling of nationalities advances civilization, 192 f.

College, courses in "orientation," 50 ff.

Columbiad, The, Barlow, praise of civilization in America, 133 ff.

Columnists, on civilization, 55 f.

Communism, Christian, 400 f.; Marxian conflict with American civilization, 456 ff.

Communist Manifesto, 457 ff.

Conclusions and Recommendations, Commission on Social Studies, 563, 567

Condorcet, concept of civilization, 76 ff.; relation to idea of civilization, 72 ff.

Considérant, Victor, concept of civilization, 90

Control, industrial, economics of, 379 ff.

Cooley, Charles H., contribution to American philosophy, 574

Cooper, James Fenimore, writings of, 215 f.

Coram, Robert, concept of civilization, 95, 117 ff.

Criticism, domestic, 452 ff.; foreign, nature and incidence of, 419 ff.

Culture, civilization and, 55 ff.; civilization as, 49 ff.; etymology of, 61 f.

Curtis, George William, sponsors idea of Northern civilization, 270 ff.

Curtius, Ernest Robert, concept of civilization and culture, 59

Cyclical theory of history, 332 f.

Dana, Charles A., sponsor of individualism, 294

Darwin, Charles, influence on individualism, 293 f., 297

Davis, Harvey H., contributor to *Toward Civilization*, 34; on teaching of civilization, 51

Davis, Jefferson, slavery as civilizing institution, 253

Dawes, Rufus, concept of civilization, 36

"Declaration of Sentiment," asserts rights of women, 178 f.

de Forest, Lee, contributor to *Toward Civilization*, 34

Democracy, 154 ff., 161 ff., 175 ff., 191, 328 f., 334, 352, 407, 488, 500, 545 ff.; Emerson's attitude toward, 175 ff.; phase of civilization, 157 f.; progressive philosophy of civilization, 341; war for, Wilson engages nation in, 488

Denison, J. H., concept of civilization, 29 f.

Dewey, John, on civilization and philosophy, 574, 577 ff.; contributor to *Whither Mankind: A Panorama of Modern Civilization*, 32

Divorce, educated woman's attitude toward, 366 f.

Dodds, Harold W., concept of civilization, 51

Dorsey, George A., concept of civilization, 26 ff.; contributor to *Whither Mankind: A Panorama of Modern Civilization*, 32

Draper, John W., champion for science and secularism, 447 f.

Dreher, Carl, on planned economy, 552 ff.

Eastman, Max, interview with Freud, 442 f.; against absolutism in philosophy, 573

Economic man, 470 ff.

Economics, as phase of civilization, 368 ff.; concept of civilization, 42 f.; counter-revolution in, 367 ff.; independent economy for America, 193 ff.; transformation of political economy into, 470 ff.

Economy, crisis in, 1929, 520 ff.

Edenism, Fourier's doctrine of, 202 f.

Edman, Irwin, accentuation of American civilization, 567 ff.

Education, academic élite, influence as a class on individualism, 295 ff.; Catholic schools, 230; need for equal, 114 f., 122 ff., 132, 137, 146; public, banned by Pope Pius IX, 444; public, instrument of civilization, 222 ff.

Educators, concepts of civilization, 39 ff.

Elias, Norbert, conflict between civilization and culture, 60 f.; research on history of civilization, 64 f.

Elliot, B. K., self-government a progressive philosophy in civilization, 341

Ellis, Havelock, contributor to *Whither Mankind: A Panorama of Modern Civilization*, 32

Ellwood, Charles A., contribution to American philosophy, 574

Ely, Richard T., leader of counter-revolution in economics, 368

Emancipation, a p p r o v e d by woman movement, 277 ff.; demand for, in name of civilization, 243 f.

Emerson, Ralph Waldo, analysis of idea of civilization, 170 ff.; conflict b e t w e e n Northern and Southern civilizations, 273 ff.; demand for emancipation, 244

Encyclopedia of Social Reform, edited by W. D. P. Bliss, 395 ff.

Enlightenment, The, and concept of civilization, 68 f.; world-view of, 15 f., 17 f.

Equality, discovery of, beginning of civilization, 546; factor in American civilization, 150; spirit of, in America, subject of foreign criticism, 424 f.

Evarts, William M., self-government in accord with social principle, 341 f.

Everett, Edward, belief in progress in America, 220 ff., 224 f.

Evolution, social, a continuous and cumulative process, 349 f.

Ewbank, Thomas, civilization t r a n s c e n d i n g sectionalism 288 ff.

Factory system, and civilization, 374 ff.

Family, 27, 179, 350, 360 ff., 365 ff., 424, 434, 441

Febvre, Lucien, research on history of civilization, 63 f.

Federation of the World, Declaration of, passed by North Carolina, 468 ff.

Fels, Samuel, and planned economy, 540 ff.

Feminist m o v e m e n t. See Woman movement

Financial crash of 1929, 520 ff.

Finkelstein, Louis, statement of g e n e r a l internationalism, 467 ff.

Fitzhugh, G e o r g e, universal view of civilization, 255 ff.;

upholds human status of Negro, 279 f.

Flanders, Ralph E., contributor to Toward Civilization, 34

Foreign criticism, nature and incidence of, 419 ff.

Fosdick, Harry Emerson, concept of civilization, 22 f.

Fosdick, Raymond B., concept of civilization, 23 ff.

Fourier, Charles, concept of civilization, 90 ff.; social doctrines of, 202 ff.

Frank, Jerome, maintenance of American civilization, 534 f.

Free trade, exploitation of South by, 259; Marxian concept of, 460 f.; opposed by Carey, 194 f.; opposed by Fitzhugh, 259 f.

French Revolution, relation to Western world-views, 81 ff.

Freud, Sigmund, criticism of American civilization, 442 ff.

Frontier, 156 f., 313 f., 315 ff.

Frontier life, individualism of, 318.

Fuller, Margaret, writings of, 209 ff.

Galloway, George B., Postwar Planning in the United States, 523

Garis, Roy L., advocates immigration restriction, 515

Geographical factor, in American civilization, 150

Geo-politik, German, 474

George, Henry, on civilization, reform, and individualism, 319 ff.

Geo-technics, 474

Gilbreth, Lillian, contributor to Toward Civilization, 34

Gildersleeve, Virginia, questions understanding of civilization, 62

Gobineau, Count, states Aryan racial hypothesis, 191

Godkin, E. L., pessimism of, 327; sponsor of individualism, 294

Godwin, Parke, concept of civilization, 90 f., 202 ff.

Goethe, a c c l a i m s American freedom, 135 f.

Gold standard, o p p o s e d by Carey, 201

Gompers, Samuel, opposes restriction of immigration, 520

Government. *See* State

Gray, George, opposition to imperialism, 503 f.

Griffin, Sir Lepel, criticism of American civilization, 424 f.

Grimké, Thomas Smith, concept of civilization in America, 136 ff.

Ground-rent, reform proposed by George, 319 ff.

Guaranteeism, Godwin's doctrine of, 205 f.

Guizot, Francois, belief in progress, 155; civilization with bourgeois individualism as upshot, 85 ff.

Hall, Basil, criticism of American civilization, 422 ff., 425 f.

Hamilton, Alice, member of Research Committee on Social Trends, 560

Hamilton, Walton, contributor to *Civilization in the United States,* 31

Hammond, James Henry, slavery essential to civilization, 248

Harper, William, axioms for planting view of civilization, 249 f.

Harper's Weekly, publication of, "a journal of civilization," 242

Harrison, Shelby, member of Research Committee on Social Trends, 560

Harvard University, courses offered in civilization, 50

Hedger, George A., concept of civilization, 48 f.

Hegel, Georg Wilhelm Friedrich, extols America as land of future, 136 f.

Helper, Hinton Rowan, balance-sheet of civilization for North and South, 263 ff.

Herron, George D., Protestant opposition to imperialism, 504 f.; social gospel of, 390 ff.

Hill, Frank E., co-editor of symposium *Whither Mankind: A Panorama of Modern Civilization,* 32 ff.

Hirschfield, C. F., contributor to *Toward Civilization,* 34

Historians, American, portrayal of American civilization, 233 ff.

History, American, individualism in writing of, 311 ff.; concept of civilization in, 39 ff.; cyclical theory, adopted by Brooks Adams, 332 f.; idea of civilization, 580; science of, possibilities for, 329 f.

Hitler, Adolf, declares ideological war on civilization, 492, 496; or will-to-power philosophy, 13

Hoar, George F., opposition to imperialism, 504

Holcombe, James P., planting view of civilization, 251 f.

Holland, R. A., democracy loftiest value of centuries, 343 ff.

Holmes, Oliver Wendell, conflict between Northern and Southern civilizations, 276 f.

Hooker, Elon H., on discrimination in immigration, 518

Hoover, Herbert, appoints Research Committee on Social Trends, 560

Howard, George Elliot, woman's influence on civilization, 365 ff.

Howe, Frederic C., contributor to *Civilization in the United States,* 31

Howells, William Dean, literary work of, influence on American civilization, 408 ff.

Hugo, Victor, c r i t i c i s m of American civilization, 422

Hull House, 415

Hunger, impediment to civilization, 30

Hutchins, Robert M., concept of civilization, 51

Immigrants, factor in American civilization, 150; Japanese, restriction of, 515 f.; legislation restricting, to protect American civilization, 514 ff.; transient, critics of American civilization, 475; types of, needed in America, 116 f.

Imperialism, American, in name of civilization, 477 ff.; reaction to, 487 f.; Teutonic individualism with, 305 ff., Teutonic, sponsored by Burgess, 308

Improvement, defined by Guizot, 89; need for, sponsored by John Quincy Adams, 145 f.; spirit of, needed in American society, 137 f.

Indians, state of civilization among, reported by Jefferson, 99 f.

Individualism, counter-reformation against, 415 ff.; decline of, 336 ff.; doctrine of, 292 ff.; economic and sociological, of Sumner, 298 ff.; identified with Christianity, 297; identified with civilization, 297 ff.; political, of Burgess, 305 ff.

Industrial control, economics of, 379 ff.

Ingersoll, Robert G., emancipation of human race accomplished by civilization, 342 f.

Intelligence, American, practical nature of, subject of foreign criticism, 425 f.

Internationalism, general, conflict with American civilization, 456 ff.; Marxian, 456 ff.

Invention, product and cause of civilization, 221

James, Edmund J., leader of counter-revolution in economics, 368, 371 f.

James, William, contribution to American philosophy, 574

Japanese immigration, restriction of, 515 f.

Jefferson, Thomas, civilizing influence of slavery, 100 f.; concept of civilization, 95 ff.; Indian policies of, 100 f.; indictment of slavery, 269; intimate of Condorcet, 73

Jews, 22

Johnson, Charles S., editor of The Negro in American Civilization, 35

Johnson, Samuel, rejects civilization for dictionary, 63

Journalism, A m e r i c a n, and spread of idea of civilization, 242 ff. See Columnists

Kelley, Florence, in social service group, 416

Kimball, Dexter S., contributor to Toward Civilization, 34

Klein, Julius, contributor to Whither Mankind: A Panorama of Modern Civilization, 32

Knight, Frank H., concept of civilization, 51

Knowledge, diffusion of, a sign of civilization, 173. S e e Buckle and Lucretia Mott

Knox, Frank, war policy refers to "our civilization," 494 f.

Kolb, G. F., concept of culture, 60

Labor, domestic system compared with factory system, 375 ff.; factory system, economic problems of, 374 ff.; influence of Christianity on, 14; wage-system, survey of, 413 ff.; women workers, 184

Labor sponsored by woman movement, 338

Land, 65, 107 ff., 120 ff., 144 ff., 194 ff., 217 ff., 246 ff., 274, 316 ff., 370, 386 f., 529 ff. See George, Henry

Lardner, Ring, contributor to Civilization in the United States, 31

Lathrop, Julia C., in social service group, 416

Laughlin, J. Laurence, individualism identified with Christianity, 297

Lea, C. F., advocates restriction of immigration, 518

League of Nations, rejection of, as underwriting civilization, 513 ff.; urged by Wilson in name of civilization, 488 ff.

Lee, Robert E., slavery as moral evil, 253

Leisure class, lack of, in America, subject of foreign criticism, 423 ff.

Liberalism, American, opposed by Roman Catholic Church, 225 ff.

Lippmann, Walter, concept of civilization, 55

Literature, American, criticism of, 455; development of a distinctive, 207 ff.; foreign criticism of, 427 f.; influence on American civilization, 403 ff.

Littlehales, George Washington, imperialism in name of civilization, 486

Lloyd, Henry Demarest, economy of industrial control, 380 ff.

Lowell, James Russell, concept of A m e r i c a n civilization, 243 f.; editor of "Atlantic Monthly," 242 ff.

Lovett, Robert Morss, contributor to Civilization in the United States, 31

Lowie, Robert H., contributor to Civilization in the United States, 31

Luce, Henry R., and spread of American civilization, 497 ff.

Ludwig, Emil, contributor to Whither Mankind: A Panorama of Modern Civilization, 32

Mackey, Alexander, criticism of American civilization, 421

Mahan, Alfred Thayer, imperialism, in name of civilization, 479, 483 ff.

Mann, Horace, on function of

education, 223 f.

Mann, Thomas, conflict between civilization and culture, 59 f.

Marriage, educated woman's attitude toward, 366 f.

Marsh, George Perkins, plea for historical presentation peculiar to American civilization, 233 ff.

Marshall, E. E., imperialism in name of civilization, 486 f.

Martin, Everett Dean, contributor to Whither Mankind: A Panorama of Modern Civilization, 32

Marxian c o m m u n i s m , and American civilization, 456 ff.

Mason, George, indictment of slavery, 269

Mason, Otis T., woman's contributions to civilization, 361 f.

McBain, Howard Lee, contributor to Whither Mankind: A Panorama of Modern Civilization, 32

McClatchy, V. S., supports Japanese exclusion, 516

McIntosh, Maria J., mediation between North and South, 285 ff.

McKinley, William, imperialism in name of civilization, 478 f.

Mechanical arts, product and cause of civilization, 221

Mencken, H. L., contributor to Civilization in the United States, 31

Merriam, Charles E., member of Research Committee on Social Trends, 560; on civilization and planning, 555 ff.

Michelet, concept of civilization, 90

Middle ages, degradation of, so-called, 14

Mill, John Stuart, comment on de Tocqueville's study, 160

Millikan, Robert A., contributor to Toward Civilization, 34

Mitchell, Wesley C., member of Research Committee on Social Trends, 560

Moore, George Foot, concept of

civilization, 30

Morals, improved with economic conditions, 197 f. *See* Knowledge

Morgan, Lewis Henry, anthropological studies promote interest in civilization, 348 ff.

Morley, John, criticism of Condorcet's *Sketch*, 78 f.

Moras, J., research on history of civilization, 64

Mott, Lucretia, conception of civilization, 180 f.; leader in woman movement, 180 f.

Müller-Freienfels, Richard, criticism of American women, 426 f.; criticism of soullessness of American civilization, 427

Mumford, Lewis, contributor to *Civilization in the United States*, 31; contributor to *Whither Mankind: A Panorama of Modern Civilization*, 32

Music, American, criticism of, 455

Mussolini, Benito, declares ideological war on civilization, 492, 496 f.

Nathan, George Jean, criticism of American theater, 455

Nationalities, commingling of, civilization a d v a n c e d by, 191 ff.

National Council of Women of the United States, congress to canvass subject of civilization, 36 ff.

National Resources Planning Board, protection and advancement of American civilization, 536 ff.

National states, rise of, create diversities in Christian worldview, 17

Nationalism, 457 ff.

Natural resources, development of, for advancement of civilization, 144 ff.

Nef, John U., historical concept of civilization, 41 f., 51

Negroes, status in civilization, 35 f., 247 f., 279 ff.

New Deal, civilization and, 54 f.; political measures of, 553

New Nation, The, founded by Edward Bellamy, 411

Nietzsche, Friedrich, 13

North Carolina, passes resolution entitled "The Declaration of the Federation of the World," 468 ff.

Northern civilization, conception of, 263 ff.

Norton, Charles Eliot, opposition to imperialism, 512

Nott, Josiah C., questions humanity of Negro, 279 f.

O'Connor, Mrs. T. P., influence of Sir Walter Scott on South, 261 ff.

O'Connor, W. D. O., defends Whitman's literary independence, 219

Odum, Howard W., member of Research Committee on Social Trends, 648; structure and dynamics of American society, 560 ff.

Ogburn, William F., member of Research Committee on Social Trends, 560

Orientation courses, in civilization, 49 ff.

Otto, Max, philosophic concept of civilization, 44 ff.

Pach, Walter, criticism of American art, 455

Paine, Thomas, concept of civilization, 95 f., 101 ff.; intimate of Condorcet, 73; publicist of idea of civilization, 101 f.

Parker, Theodore, criticism of Prescott's historical work, 239 f.; prescribes duties for American historians, 239 ff.

Parsons, Elsie Clews, contributor to *Civilization in the United States*, 31

Patten, Simon Nelson, leader of counter-revolution in economics, 368, 369 ff.

Patterson, John Stahl, conflict between Northern and Southern civilizations, 274 f.

Peale, Norman, concept of civilization, 22

Perry, Bliss, defends Whitman's literary independence, 219 f.

Pessimism, world-view of, 12 f.; views of Henry and Brooks Adams, 327 ff.; opposite of idea of American civilization, 581

Phelps, Egbert, conflict between Northern and Southern civilizations, 275

Philanthropy, concept of civilization, 23 ff.; private, for advancement of civilization, 385 f.; revolution of thought in, 373 f.

Philippine independence, insured by Act of Congress, 512 f.

Phillips, Lena Madesin, concept of civilization, 37

Phillips, Wendell, on civilization and the relation of women to it, 189 ff.; sponsors labor movement, 338

Philosophy, conflicts of American, 578 ff.; Christian, of Thomas Aquinas, 14 f.; concept of civilization, 43 ff.; criticism of American, 572 ff.; idea of American civilization, 567 ff.; nature of American, 574 ff.

Pius IX, Pope, condemns liberalism of age in The Syllabus of Errors, 231, 443 ff.

Planning movement, 522 f.

Planting view of Southern civilization, 246 ff.

Political economy, transformation into economics, 470 ff.

Political discourse, use of term civilization in, 51

Political parties, civilization and, 54 f.

Population, Malthusian law of, attacked by Carey, 195

Poverty, 105 ff., 119 ff., 184,

188, 207, 254, 338, 377 ff., 391 ff., 406, 415, 521, 527, 531 f., 548 ff.

Prentice, Ezra Parmalee, concept of civilization, 30

Prescott, William Hickling, work criticized by Parker, 239 f.

Preston, Thomas Scott, Roman Catholic acceptance of Syllabus of Errors, 446

Primitive. See Anthropology and Indians

Princeton University, courses offered in civilization, 51

Printing, instrument of civilization, 222

Progress, belief in American, 220 f.; conditions for, auspicious in America, 149; Jefferson's concept of, 98 f.; idea of, formulated by Condorcet, 75 ff., 79

Property, acquisition of, phase of civilizing process, 351; Coram's inquiry as to the origin and nature of, 120 f.

Property rights, influence on civilization, 216 f.

Propagandists, foreign, critics of American civilization, 476

Protectionism, economic doctrine of Carey, 194 ff.

Protestantism, world-view of, 15

Psychic factors of civilization, 353 ff.

Psychological forces, impediment to civilization, 29 f.

Pupin, Michael, contributor to Toward Civilization, 34

Ranke, Leopold von, criticism of Bancroft, 169

Rauschenbusch, Walter, social gospel of, 397 ff.

Recent Social Trends in the United States, study of American society in development, 560 ff.

Redfield, Robert, concept of civilization, 51

Reform, social, of Christian Socialists, 394 ff. See Poverty

Refugees, critics of American

civilization, 474 f.

Relief, unemployment, a governmental responsibility, 525

Religion, concept of civilization, 21 ff.; contest over civilization in United States, 226 ff.; instrument of civilization, 222; ministry and civilization, 224; progress makes new demands of, 224 f. *See also* Christianity, Protestantism, Roman Catholic Church.

Renovation, spirit of, needed in American society, 137 f.

Rent, Ricardo's law of, attacked by Carey, 194 f.

Republican party, sponsors McKinley imperialism, 486

Republicanism. *See* Democracy *and* Civilization

Research Committee on Social Trends, appointed by Herbert Hoover, 560

Ridpath, John Clark, wage-system of labor, survey of, 413 ff.

Robinson, Geroid T., contributor to *Civilization in the United States*, 31

Robinson, James Harvey, contributor to *Whither Mankind: A Panorama of Modern Civilization*, 32

Roman Catholic Church, criticism of American civilization, 445 ff.; opposes liberalism, 226 ff.; schools of, 230. *See also* Brownson, Spalding, *and* Talbot

Romier, Lucien, criticism of American civilization, 437 ff.

Roosevelt, Franklin D., concept of civilization, 54 f.; and Atlantic Charter, 492; insures Philippine independence, 512 f.; planning program of government, 524 ff.; seeks name for war, 493 f.; "world civilization" to triumph in war, 494

Ross, Edward A., contribution to American philosophy, 574

Rush, Benjamin, concept of civilization, 115 ff.

Russell, Bertrand, contributor to *Whither Mankind: A Panorama of Modern Civilization*, 32

Saint-Simon, concept of civilization, 90 ff.

Santillana, George de, 497

Saunders, Frederick, American contribution to civilization, 340

Schapiro, J. Salwyn, *Condorcet and the Rise of Liberalism*, 72 f.

Schopenhauer, Arthur, exponent of negative world-view, 12 f.

Schweitzer, Albert, absolutist systems of European philosophies, 576 f.; confused ideas of civilization and culture, 58 f.

Schweitzer, Arthur, exponent of philosophy of human perfection, 15 f.

Scott, Sir Walter, influence on Southern civilization, 260 ff.

Scudder, Horace E., appreciation of Whitman, 220

Scudder, Vida, social gospel of, 401 ff.

Searing, Edward W., revolution in economy renewed by, 411 ff.

Servile class, lack of, in America, subject of foreign criticism, 424 f.

Shaw, Charles G., editor of symposium *Trends of Civilization*, 47 f.

Shih, Hu, contributor to *Whither Mankind: A Panorama of Modern Civilization*, 32

Siegfried, André, criticism of American civilization, 422, 433 ff.

Slave-masters, influence of slavery upon, 268 f.

Slavery, abolition by civil war foreseen by John Quincy Adams, 148; abolition and woman movement, 184 f.; as civilizing institution, 252 f.; indictment against, 280 ff.; influence of Christianity on, 14;

issue of civilization in, 245 ff.; Jefferson's attitude toward, 100 f.; viewed as barbarism, 266 f.

Smith, Adam, intimate of Condorcets, 72

Smith, Sidney, criticism of American literature, 427

Snyder, A. J., idea of civilization, 545 ff.

Social gospel, rise of, influence on A m e r i c a n civilization, 389 ff.

Social principle, conditions auspicious for, in America, 148 f.; influence of, needed in American society, 138; inherent in idea of civilization, 581; women special guardians of, 189

Social reformers, work of, 202 ff.

Social Studies in the Schools, Commission on, American Historical Society, A Charter for the Social Studies, 47

Sociology, psychic factors of civilization, 354 ff.

Soule, George, advocates a planned society, 537 ff.; contributor to Civilization in the United States, 31

Soullessness of American civilization, subject of foreign criticism, 427

Southern civilization, agrarian view of, 253 f.; conception of, 246 ff.; planting views of, 246 ff.; universal view of, 255

Spalding, John Lancaster, Catholic opposition to imperialism, 506 ff.

Specialization, 295 f., 470 ff.

Spencer, Anna Garlin, woman's influence on civilization, 362 ff.

Spencer, Herbert, criticism of American women, 426; influence on individualism, 297

Spengler, Oswald, confused ideas of civilization and culture, 56 ff.

Sperry, Elmer E., contributor to

Toward Civilization, 34

Spingarn, J. E., contributor to Civilization in the United States, 31

Stace, W. T., concept of civilization, 46; criticism of American philosophy, 572 ff.

Stanton, Elizabeth Cady, demand for emancipation of labor, 338; leader in woman's movement, 178, 186 ff.

State, 89, 91, 103 ff., 117, 128 ff., 136, 166 f., 222, 231, 303 ff., 306 ff., 364 f., 372, 384, 388, 400, 417, 443 ff., 522 ff., 545 f.

Starr, Ellen Gates, co-founder of Hull House group of social service leaders, 415 ff.

Stearns, Harold E., editor of symposium Civilization in the United States, 31; 454 ff.

Stephens, Alexander H., planting view of civilization, 252 f.

Stevens, Alzina, P., in social service, 416

Stevens Institute of Technology, courses offered in civilization, 51

Stoddard, Lothrop, concept of civilization, 27 ff.

Strong, Josiah, attacks Roman Catholic doctrine, 448 ff.; imperialism, in name of civilization, 479 ff.

Sumner, Charles, champions Northern civilization, 265 ff.; status of Negro in civilization, 280 f.

Sumner, William Graham, concept of civilization, 88 f.; individualism as mainspring in civilization, 298 ff.; opposition to imperialism, 509 ff.

Swope, Gerard, advocates planning movement, 522 f.

Syllabus of Errors, criticism of civilization, 231, 443 ff.

Talbot, Francis X., Roman Catholic reconciliation with American civilization, 450 ff.

Taylor, Deems, contributor to

Civilization in the United States, 31; criticism of American music, 455

Teutonic peoples, political supremacy of, 305 ff.

Theater, American, criticism of, 455

Theology, rights of women and, 185

"Thirty intellectuals," concepts of civilization in symposium, *Civilization in the United States,* 31 f.

Thompson, Dorothy, concept of civilization, 55; criticism of American society, 421

Time factor, in American civilization, 149 f.

Tocqueville, Alexis de, practicality of American intelligence, 425 f.; studies of American democracy and civilization, 154 ff.

Toombs, Robert, planting view of civilization, 250 f.

Traquar, Ramsey, criticism of American women, 426

Tugwell, Rexford Guy, idea of civilization, 531 ff.

Turner, Frederick Jackson, individualism and civilization in American history, 315 ff. *See* Frontier

Twain, Mark, analysis of civilization, 52 ff.; characterizes the Southern gentleman, 260 f.; opposition to imperialism, 511 ff.

Underwood, Senator, on discrimination in immigration, 517 f.

Unemployment, problem of, a responsibility of civilization, 525.

Union, need for, in America, 137 ff.

Universal view of Southern civilization, 255

University of Chicago, courses offered in civilization, 51; fiftieth anniversary, 21

van Doren, Carl, contributor to *Whither Mankind: A Panorama of Modern Civilization,* 32

Van Kleeck, Mary, status of Negro in American civilization, 35 f.

Van Loon, H. W., contributor to *Civilization in the United States,* 31; contributor to *Whither Mankind: A Panorama of Modern Civilization,* 32

Veblen, Thorstein, economic concept of civilization, 42 f.

Voltaire, historical thinking impressionistic, 69 f.

Vorhees, Stephen, contributor to *Toward Civilization,* 34

Wages, system, 376 ff., 388, 413 ff. *See* Capitalism

Walker, Ralph T., contributor to *Toward Civilization,* 34

Wallace, Henry A., appeals to "human civilization," 495; attacks isolationists, 495 f.; idea of civilization, 528 ff.

Wallace, L. W., contributor to *Toward Civilization,* 34

Walsh, Senator, on discrimination in immigration, 517

War, civilization and, 53 f.; foe of civilization, 38; invariable in human history, 582

War Department, imperialism in name of civilization, 487

Ware, Catherine F., editor of symposium, *The Cultural Approach to History,* 49

Ward, Durbin, questions future of American civilization, 345 f.

Ward, Lester F., contribution to American philosophy, 574; sociological approach to civilization, 353 ff.

Warren, Mercy, concept of civilization, 95, 113 ff.

Wealth, in civilized life, Carnegie's view of, 385 ff.; justification of, in civilization, 302 f.

Webb, Sidney and Beatrice, contributors to *Whither Mankind: A Panorama of Modern Civilization,* 32

Weeks, John W., imperialism in name of civilization, 487

Wefald, Knud, advocates restriction of immigration, 519

White, Andrew D., calls on historians to write history of civilization, 40

Whitehead, Alfred N., woman's influence on civilization, 362

Whitman, Walt, poet of American civilization, 217 ff.

Wickenden, William E., contributor to *Toward Civilization*, 34

Willard, Daniel, advocates planning movement, 522

Wilson, Woodrow, grants larger autonomy to Philippines, 488; individualism in American history, 311 ff.; urges League of Nations in name of civilization, 488 ff.

Winslow, C.-E. A., contributor to *Whither Mankind: A Panorama of Modern Civilization,* 32

Women, American, subject of foreign critics, 426; attitude toward rights of, 73 f., 159; educated, attitude toward marriage, and divorce, 214; enfranchisement of, 364 f.; influence upon early civilization, 361 ff.; place of, in the state, 173 f.; rights of, asserted in "Declaration of Sentiments," 178 f.

Woman movement, "Declaration of Sentiment," 178 f.; during War between the States, 277 ff.; influence of anthropology upon, 359 ff.; Mott, Lucretia, work of, 180 ff.; opposition to, 179; Stanton, Elizabeth Cady, work of, 186 ff.

World-views, changes in, influence of, 18; Christian, diversities in, 17; Christian, impressed during middle ages, 14 f.; classification of, 12 f.; civilization, idea of, 18; definition of, 11 f.; early American republic, 94 ff.; Enlightenment, diversity in, 17 f.; historical influence of, 13; individualism, doctrine of, 292 ff.

Wright, Carroll D., factory system, place in civilization, 375 ff.

Wright, Quincy, creation of a supranational class, 474

Wright, Roy V., contributor to *Toward Civilization,* 34

Young, Owen D., advocates planning movement, 522